D0205305

THE CAMBRIDGE COMPANION TO
THE GREEK AND ROMAN NOVEL

The Greek and Roman novels of Petronius, Apuleius, Longus, Heliodorus and others have been cherished for millennia, but never more so than now. *The Cambridge Companion to the Greek and Roman Novel* contains nineteen original essays by an international cast of experts in the field. The emphasis is upon the critical interpretation of the texts within historical settings, both in antiquity and in the later generations that have been and continue to be inspired by them. All the central issues of current scholarship are addressed: sexuality, cultural identity, class, religion, politics, narrative, style, readership and much more. Four sections cover cultural context of the novels, their contents, literary form and their reception in classical antiquity and beyond. Each chapter includes guidance on further reading. This collection will be essential for scholars and students, as well as for others who want an up-to-date, accessible introduction into this exhilarating material.

A complete list of books in the series is at the back of the book.

THE CAMBRIDGE
COMPANION TO

THE GREEK AND
ROMAN NOVEL

EDITED BY

TIM WHITMARSH

CAMBRIDGE
UNIVERSITY PRESS

PA
3040
·C36
2008

CAMBRIDGE UNIVERSITY PRESS
Cambridge, New York, Melbourne, Madrid, Cape Town, Singapore, São Paulo, Delhi

Cambridge University Press
The Edinburgh Building, Cambridge CB2 8RU, UK

Published in the United States of America by Cambridge University Press, New York

www.cambridge.org
Information on this title: www.cambridge.org/9780521684880

© Cambridge University Press 2008

This publication is in copyright. Subject to statutory exception
and to the provisions of relevant collective licensing agreements,
no reproduction of any part may take place without
the written permission of Cambridge University Press.

First published 2008

Printed in the United Kingdom at the University Press, Cambridge

A catalogue record for this publication is available from the British Library

ISBN   978-0-521-86590-6 hardback
ISBN   978-0-521-68488-0 paperback

Cambridge University Press has no responsibility for the persistence or
accuracy of URLs for external or third-party internet websites referred to
in this publication, and does not guarantee that any content on such
websites is, or will remain, accurate or appropriate.

CONTENTS

University ....
Carnegie Mellon University
Pittsburgh, PA 15213-3890

CONTENTS

NOTES ON CONTRIBUTORS

SHADI BARTSCH is the Ann L. and Lawrence B. Buttenwieser Professor of Classics at the University of Chicago. Her first book was *Decoding the Ancient Novel: the Reader and the Role of Description in Heliodorus and Achilles Tatius* (1989). Since then she has published widely, notably on early imperial culture (*Actors in the Audience: Theatricality and Doublespeak from Nero to Hadrian* (1994)) and the Roman poet Lucan (*Ideology in Cold Blood: a Reading of Lucan's* Civil War (1997)). Her most recent book is *The Mirror of the Self: Sexuality, Self-knowledge, and the Gaze in the Early Roman Empire* (2006).

EWEN BOWIE was until his retirement in 2007 the E. P. Warren Praelector in Classics at Corpus Christi College and Professor of Classical Languages and Literature at the University of Oxford. He has published extensively, for almost forty years, on the novels and the literary culture of Roman Greece. He is preparing a commentary on Longus' *Daphnis and Chloe*.

JOAN B. BURTON is Professor and Chair of Classical Studies at Trinity University, San Antonio. She has published *Theocritus's Urban Mimes: Mobility, Gender, and Patronage* (1995) and *A Byzantine Novel*: Drosilla and Charikles, *a Bilingual Edition* (2004), as well as articles and book chapters on Hellenistic and Byzantine literature and culture.

CATHERINE CONNORS is Associate Professor in the Department of Classics at the University of Washington, Seattle, and is the author of *Petronius the Poet: Verse and Literary Tradition in the* Satyricon (1998). She has also published articles on the ancient novel and its reception, and on Roman epic, comedy and satire. Her current research focuses on representations of nature and geography in literary texts.

MASSIMO FUSILLO is Professor of Literary Criticism and Comparative Literature at the University of L'Aquila. His interests range from ancient narrative to the modern reception of classical literatures. He has written on the Greek novel (especially *Il romanzo greco: polifonia ed eros* (1989; French translation 1991)) and on the reception of Greek myth (*La Grecia secondo Pasolini: Mito e cinema* (1996); *Il dio ibrido: Dioniso e le Baccanti nel Novecento* (2006)).

SIMON GOLDHILL is Professor of Greek at Cambridge University. He has written widely on all aspects of Greek literature, including *Foucault's Virginity: Ancient Erotic Fiction and the History of Sexuality* (1995), and is particularly interested in the relation between literature, cultural history and literary theory.

STEPHEN HARRISON is Fellow and Tutor in Classics at Corpus Christi College, Oxford, and Professor of Classical Languages and Literature in the University of Oxford. He has written widely on the Roman novels; he is editor of *Oxford Readings in the Roman Novel* (1999), and author of *Apuleius: a Latin Sophist* (2000).

RICHARD HUNTER is Regius Professor of Greek at the University of Cambridge and a Fellow of Trinity College. His research interests include ancient literary criticism, the Greek and Latin novel, and Hellenistic poetry and its reception in Rome. His most recent books are *Plato's Symposium* (2004), (with Marco Fantuzzi) *Tradition and Innovation in Hellenistic Poetry* (2004), and *The Shadow of Callimachus* (2006).

LAWRENCE KIM is Assistant Professor of Classics at the University of Texas at Austin. His research focuses on imperial Greek literature as well as ancient literary criticism, and he is currently completing a book on the reading of Homer in the second sophistic.

JASON KÖNIG is Senior Lecturer in Greek at the University of St Andrews. His publications include *Athletics and Literature in the Roman Empire* (2005), *Ordering Knowledge in the Roman Empire* (2007, jointly edited with Tim Whitmarsh), and a wide range of articles on the Greek literature and culture of the Roman world. He is currently working on a book on representations of consumption and the symposium in Greco-Roman and Christian fiction in the first to fifth centuries CE.

ANDREW LAIRD is Reader in Classical Literature at the University of Warwick. He has published widely on Roman and renaissance Latin poetry, the ancient novel and classical and contemporary literary theory, including the philosophy of fiction. He is author of *Powers of Expression, Expressions of Power: Speech Presentation and Latin Literature* (1999), and he has edited *Ancient Literary Criticism* (2006) and (with Ahuvia Kahane) *A Companion to the Prologue of Apuleius'* Metamorphoses (2001). His most recent book, *The Epic of America: an Introduction to Rafael Landívar and the Rusticatio Mexicana* (2006) draws attention to the rich tradition of writing in Latin from colonial Spanish America.

HELEN MORALES is Senior Lecturer in Classics at the University of Cambridge, and a Fellow of Newnham College. A specialist in the ancient novel and in gender politics, she is co-editor of *Intratextuality: Greek and Roman textual relations* (2000) and author of *Vision and narrative in Achilles Tatius*, Leucippe and Clitophon (2004) and *Classical mythology: A very short introduction* (2007). She is also co-editor of the literary journal *Ramus*.

JOHN MORGAN is Professor of Classics at the University of Wales Swansea, and has published widely in the area of ancient fiction. His edition and commentary of *Daphnis and Chloe* was published by Aris and Phillips in 2004. He was also responsible for the translation of Heliodorus in B. P. Reardon's *Collected Ancient Greek Novels* (1989). He is currently working on books on Longus and Heliodorus.

MICHAEL REEVE held (from 1984 to 2006) the Kennedy chair of Latin at Cambridge, where he is now a Director of Research in the Faculty of Classics. He has published editions of *Daphnis and Chloe* (1982), Cicero's speech *Pro Quinctio*, and Vegetius' *Epitoma rei militaris*, and articles on the transmission of Latin and Greek authors. He is currently editing Geoffrey of Monmouth and studying the transmission of Pliny's *Natural History*.

JAMES ROMM is the James H. Ottaway Jr Professor of Classics at Bard College in Annandale, New York. He specialises in ancient geography and ethnography, in particular the areas where these fields overlap with fiction and historiography. He is currently editing Arrian's *Anabasis* for the Landmark Series of Ancient Historians.

GERALD SANDY is Professor Emeritus of Classics at the University of British Columbia. His research has focused on various aspects, including reception, of the ancient Greek and Latin novels: his publications have ranged broadly, from *Heliodorus* (1982) to an edited collection *The Classical Heritage in France* (2002). More recently he has published on late antiquity, the renaissance reception of Apuleius, and Philippo Beroaldo.

SUSAN STEPHENS is Professor of Classics at Stanford University. She has written widely on Hellenistic and Greco-Roman literature, culture and papyri. With Jack Winkler she edited *Ancient Greek Novels: the Fragments* (1995); more recent publications include *Seeing Double: Intercultural Poetics in Ptolemaic Alexandria* (2003). She is currently completing a project on Callimachus and (with Phiroze Vasunia) editing a collection on classics and national cultures.

TIM WHITMARSH is E. P. Warren Praelector in Classics at Corpus Christi and Lecturer in Greek Language and Literature at the University of Oxford; until 2007 he was Professor of Ancient Literatures at the University of Exeter. He has published widely on the Greek literature of the Roman period, including *Greek Literature and the Roman Empire: the Politics of Imitation* (2001) and *The Second Sophistic* (2005). He is currently finishing a book on narrative and identity in the Greek novel; future plans include work on links between Greco-Roman and near-Eastern narrative.

FROMA ZEITLIN is Charles Ewing Professor in the Department of Classics at Princeton University; she also teaches in Jewish Studies and Comparative Literature. She has written extensively on Greek and Roman culture for over forty years, including important publications on Petronius (1971) and more recently on the Greek novel. Other publications include the co-edited volumes *Before Sexuality?*

Structures of Erotic Experience in the Ancient Greek World (1990) and *Nothing to do with Dionysus? Athenian Drama in its Social Context* (1990) and a collection of her essays *Playing the Other: Gender and Society in Classical Greek Literature* (1996). She is currently engaged in a project called *Vision, Figuration and Image from Theater to Romance* (forthcoming).

ACKNOWLEDGEMENTS

The editor would like to thank the contributors warmly; also Bracht Branham, Dan Selden and Niall Slater. Stephen Harrison has been helpful well beyond the call of duty; Francesca Stavrakopoulou has also offered invaluable advice on matters Semitic. Michael Sharp at the Press has been both supportive and indulgent throughout the gestation of the project.

ABBREVIATIONS

A&A	*Antike und Abendland*
A&R	*Atene e Roma*
AAntHung	*Acta Antiqua Academiae Scientiarum Hungaricae*
AJPh	*American Journal of Philology*
AN	*Ancient Narrative*
AncSoc	*Ancient Society*
Annales (ESC)	*Annales: Economies, sociétés, civilisations*
ANRW	*Aufstieg und Niedergang der römischen Welt* (Berlin, 1972–)
ASNP	*Annali della Scuola normale superiore di Pisa, Classe di lettere e filosofia*
BAGB	*Bulletin de l'Association Guillaume Budé*
BICS	*Bulletin of the Institute of Classical Studies*
BMC	*Catalogue of books printed in the XVth century now in the British Museum* (London, 1907–63)
BMGS	*Byzantine and Modern Greek Studies*
BollClass	*Bollettino dei classici*
CErc	*Cronache ercolanesi*
CJ	*Classical Journal*
ClAnt	*Classical Antiquity*
CPh	*Classical Philology*
CQ	*Classical Quarterly*
CRAI	*Comptes rendus de l'Académie des inscriptions et belles-lettres*
DBI	*Dizionario biografico degli italiani* (Rome, 1960–)
DOP	*Dumbarton Oaks Papers*
FGrH	*Die Fragmente der griechischen Historiker*, ed. F. Jacoby *et al.*, 1st edn (Berlin, 1923–)
GIF	*Giornale italiano di filologia*
GRBS	*Greek, Roman and Byzantine Studies*

HSCPh	*Harvard Studies in Classical Philology*
HumLov	*Humanistica Lovaniensia*
ICS	*Illinois Classical Studies*
IG²	*Inscriptiones Graecae*, 2nd edn (Berlin, 1924–)
IGR	*Inscriptiones Graecae ad res Romanas pertinentes*, ed. R. Cagnat (Rome, 1964)
IJCT	*International Journal of the Classical Tradition*
ISTC	*Incunabula Short-title Catalogue*, 2nd edn, available at http://www.bl.uk/catalogues/istc/index.html
JHS	*Journal of Hellenic Studies*
JÖByz	*Jahrbuch der Österreichischen Byzantinistik*
JRS	*Journal of Roman Studies*
JWI	*Journal of the Warburg and Courtauld Institutes*
LCM	*Liverpool Classical Monthly*
MAMA	*Monumenta Asiae minoris antiquae* (Manchester and London, 1928–)
MD	*Materiali e discussioni per l'analisi dei testi classici*
MH	*Museum Helveticum*
P&P	*Past and Present*
P. Fay.	*Fayum Towns and their Papyri*, ed. B. P. Grenfell *et al.* (London, 1900)
P. Mich.	*Michigan Papyri* (Ann Arbor, 1931–)
P. Oxy.	*The Oxyrhynchus Papyri* (London, 1898–)
Pap. Mil. Vogl.	*Papiri della R. Università di Milano* ed. A. Vogliano *et al.* (Milan, 1937–)
PCPhS	*Proceedings of the Cambridge Philological Society*
PIR²	*Prosopographia imperii Romani*, 2nd edn (Berlin, 1933–99)
PMGF	*Poetarum melicorum graecorum fragmenta*, vol. 1: Alcman, Stesichorus, Ibycus, ed. M. Davies (Oxford, 1991)
PP	*La parola del passato*
PSN	*The Petronian Society Newsletter*
RE	*Paulys Realencyclopädie der classischen Altertumswissenschaft*, 1st edn (Munich, 1903–78)
REA	*Revue des études anciennes*
REG	*Revue des études grecques*
REL	*Revue des études latines*
RhM	*Rheinisches Museum für Philologie*
RHR	*Revue de l'histoire des religions*
RHT	*Revue d'histoire des textes*

RPh	Revue de philologie, de littérature et d'histoire anciennes
RSBN	Rivista di studi bizantini e neoellenici
RSC	Rivista di studi classici
SCO	Studi classici e orientali
SEG	Supplementum epigraphicum Graecum (Leiden, 1923–71; Amsterdam, 1979–)
SEJG	Sacris erudiri
SemRom	Seminari Romani di cultura greca
SIFC	Studi italiani di filologia classica
SVF	Stoicorum veterum fragmenta, ed. H. von Arnim (Leipzig, 1923–4)
Syll³	Sylloge inscriptionum graecarum, ed. W. Dittenberger, 3rd edn (Leipzig, 1915–24)
TAM	Tituli Asiae minoris (Vienna, 1901–)
TAPhA	Transactions of the American Philological Association
WJA	Würzburger Jahrbücher für die Altertumswissenschaft
WS	Wiener Studien
YClS	Yale Classical Studies
ZPE	Zeitschrift für Papyrologie und Epigraphik

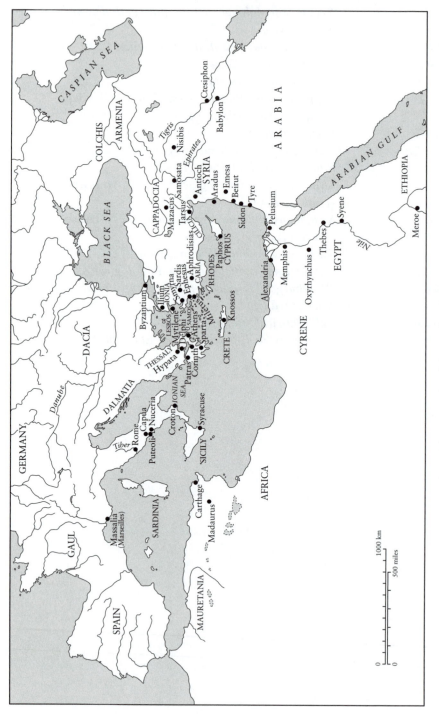

Map. The geography of the Greek and Roman novel

I

TIM WHITMARSH

Introduction

Denounced through the nineteenth and much of the twentieth century for its triviality, smuttiness, and pastiche (to say nothing of intimations of 'oriental' influence), the Greco-Roman novel began to find in the late years of the last century a much more enthusiastic audience. Perhaps better than any other ancient form, the novel embodies the spirit of (post-)modernity; of a prosaic world, politically and ethically complex beyond compare yet questing after simple truths, pluralist yet hierarchical, riven by global homogenisation. Art, literature, music, dance and film have all drawn inspiration from these texts.[1] The worlds of scholarship and teaching have been similarly energised: across the world university programmes, conferences, organisations, websites and publications testify to the vitality of novel studies.

The *Cambridge Companion to the Greek and Roman Novel* offers eighteen new essays by internationally distinguished experts in the field of Greek and Roman narrative fiction. It seeks to provide students, scholars and the interested public with a sophisticated yet accessible point of entry into these beguiling texts. It is not designed as a general survey: although it is aimed at readers new to the novels as well as those with more familiarity, the *Companion* has no text-by-text discussions, and indeed no single agenda.[2] Rather it consists of a series of state-of-the art provocations, interlocking in overall design but written from a range of intellectual positions. Taken together, these essays represent both the culmination of the latest thinking on the novel and a stimulus to future exploration.

The volume is divided into four sections: 'Context', 'The world of the novel', 'Form' and 'Reception'. The book thus begins with the cultural background from which the novels emerged, progressing through content to literary analysis, before concluding with what readers (ancient, mediaeval, renaissance and modern) have made of them. Although structural divisions

[1] See Fusillo, this volume.
[2] For introductory works on the ancient novel, see the 'Further reading' appendix to Bowie, this volume.

like this are useful, however, all these fields are ultimately interconnected by myriad pathways; it is the aim of this introduction to encapsulate all these into a single whole.

What is the 'Greek and Roman novel'?

I begin with a short answer to this question. For the purposes of this volume, 'the novel' means, primarily, seven texts from the period of the Roman empire: in Latin, Petronius' (fragmentary) *Satyrica* and Apuleius' *Metamorphoses*; in Greek, Chariton's *Callirhoe*, Xenophon's *Anthia and Habrocomes*, Achilles Tatius' *Leucippe and Clitophon*, Longus' *Daphnis and Chloe* and Heliodorus' *Charicleia and Theagenes*. Attention is also given to the impressive range of Greek texts preserved either in summary or (showing up in ever-increasing numbers) in fragments.[3] Still within range, but at greater distance, are related works such as Lucian's *True stories*, the two known Greek versions of the *Ass* story (which also underlies Apuleius' *Metamorphoses*),[4] the *Alexander Romance* (a fictionalised version of the conquests of Alexander the Great, which achieved extraordinary popularity: eighty versions survive from antiquity and the middle ages, in twenty-four languages including Pahlavi, Arabic, Armenian and Bulgarian), and the *History of Apollonius, King of Tyre*. All of these works are written or achieve canonical form in the period of the Roman empire, and mostly from the first three centuries. Readers unfamiliar with the content and chronology of these texts may at this point choose to consult the 'Index of Greek and Roman novelists'.

The novel, on the definition adopted in this volume, is very much a product of imperial times. There were, of course, earlier works of inventive prose narrative: the fabulous travel accounts of Antiphanes of Berge (c. 400 BCE), Euhemerus of Messene (c. 300 BCE) and Iambulus (c. 100 BCE);[5] the romanticised Persian and Indian histories of Ctesias (c. 400 BCE), and their numerous Hellenistic acolytes (now mostly lost);[6] Xenophon's *Education of Cyrus* (c. 350 BCE), an important intertext for Chariton in particular;[7] the inventive rewritings of the Trojan War by Hegesianax (under the pseudonym 'Cephalion of Gergitha') and Dionysius 'the leather arm' (second century BCE);[8] and the collections of local myth by Parthenius (first century BCE) and

---

3 Stephens and Winkler (1995); see further *P. Oxy.* 4760–2.
4 For the new *Ass* see *P. Oxy.* 4762.
5 See in general Holzberg (2003b); Winiarczyk (2002) provides more context, together with specific discussion of Euhemerus.
6 For Ctesias as a forerunner of the novelists, see esp. Holzberg (1992).
7 Perry (1967) 169–74.
8 For Dionysius Scytobrachion see Rusten (1992).

Conon (first century BCE – first CE).[9] Among the latter might well belong the notorious but now lost *Milesian affairs* of Aristides, alluded to by Apuleius as a precursor at the outset of his *Metamorphoses* ('Milesian discourse', 1.1).[10]

The novels discussed in this volume, however, represent something different from their Hellenistic precursors: they use wholly invented characters (that is to say, not mythical or historical); they are consistently (if not identically) erotic, with a particular emphasis upon romantic love (or parodies of it) despite obstacles and separations. This, however, raises a new question: can we speak meaningfully of the novel as a single literary form? The concept of genre as a tool for reading and writing is considered in Goldhill's chapter in this volume, but it will be worth our while to pause and consider an issue that is arguably more fundamental to a collected volume like this: does it make sense to bundle together all these diverse texts, written in Latin and Greek, spanning some three centuries?

As is often noted, antiquity not only avoided literary-critical discussion of the novel,[11] but even (apparently) lacked any distinctive name for it: words such as the Latin *argumentum* and the Greek *plasma* simply mean 'made-up story', the Latin *fabula* means 'story', and the Greek *drama* means 'action'. The English word 'novel' is only a label of convenience, which does not correspond directly to any ancient generic concept (the same goes for 'romance', sometimes used of the Greek texts). Nor are formal criteria any help. Poetic genres are often indicated by metre (hexameter for epic, iambic trimeters for tragic speech, and so forth), but these obviously do not apply to prose. Finally, there is no performance context to decide genre: whereas, for example, classical Athenian tragedies and comedies were performed during the relevant phase of the festival of the Great Dionysia, novels would have been read (whether in isolation or collectively) in different environments that were wholly unrelated to their content.

On these grounds, it has been claimed that there was no concept of the novel as a genre at all in antiquity: the novel is, we are told, 'a container of styles rather than itself a homogeneous and distinctive style'.[12] There are, however, problems with this formulation. That novels are radically intertextual – that is to say, that they (or most of them) rework literary motifs from

---

9 On whom see, respectively, Lightfoot (1999), Brown (2002). For a general account of Hellenistic prose fiction see Whitmarsh (forthcoming).

10 On these see Harrison (1998c).

11 The only explicit discussion is in Macrobius' commentary on Cicero's *Dream of Scipio* (1.2.8, end of fourth century CE), and even that is very brief. Julian's comment on 'fictions . . . narrated in earlier authors in the guise of history' (*Epistles* 89b 301b Bidez) is often cited in connection with the novel, but in fact Julian is unlikely to have thought of writers of the imperial period as 'earlier' (Whitmarsh (2005a) 607–8).

12 Nimis (1994), at 398.

an astonishing range of sources – does not itself mean that they necessarily lack any distinctive style of their own. After all, tragedy makes liberal use of epic, lyric and rhetorical forms, but no one would argue that it lacks its own qualities. There are, in fact, good reasons to take the novels upon which this collection focuses as a distinctive genre – so long as we use the concept flexibly.[13] Let us turn now to consider how we might capture this idea of the Greco-Roman novel.

Novels and ideals

Critics often argue for the unity of the genre using the concept of the 'ideal' novel: the five major Greek texts all focus upon the enduring love of a young heterosexual couple through a series of tribulations; they are united in conclusion, apparently to live happily ever after.[14] They are all set in the distant past (or at least a historically indeterminate setting that might be the past). Against this backdrop, the 'non-ideal' texts can be read as deliberate perversions of the norm. Of the five Greek texts, Achilles Tatius' *Leucippe and Clitophon*, with its recurrent emphasis upon earthier motives and hints of a darker aftermath to the text, looks like a subversion, even a parody, of the protocols of ideal romance.[15] The various novels preserved in fragments and summary offer further examples: Lollianus' *Phoenician Affairs*, with its scenes of human sacrifice and (perhaps) gay plot; *Iolaus*, with its bawdy take on mystery-cult; Iamblichus' *Babylonian Affairs*, with its entirely non-Greek setting and its grotesque elements (such as ghostly goats and man-eating dogs).

The Roman novels too have been held to presuppose – and subvert – the generic norm of the ideal romance. Since a classic article by Heinze (1899), Petronius' *Satyrica* has often been read as wittily undermining the romantic ideology of the Greek version, substituting rapacious male pederasts (i.e. boy-lovers) for heterosexual *naïfs*, lust for love, and quotidian, contemporary 'realism' for sepia-tinged classicism. Current hypotheses over the dating of the novels raise a problem with this thesis: if Chariton's *Callirhoe* is the earliest Greek novel at c. 50 CE, then Petronius – assuming our author is the Neronian courtier – can hardly have been responding to a major literary vogue (he committed suicide in 66 CE). Ultimately, however, there are just too many uncertainties around the dating of both texts to allow for any real conclusion either way.

---

13 Literary-theoretical discussions of genre are numerous: for guidance, see Goldhill, this volume.
14 See e.g. Holzberg (1995) 43–60.   15 Parody: Durham (1938); Chew (2000).

Apuleius' *Metamorphoses* is at first sight a different kind of work: quite explicitly a take on a Greek original ('a Greekish story', *fabulam Graecanicam*, 1.1), but on the *Ass* story rather than the ideal romance. *Ass* narratives seem to have circulated in a number of Greek forms. The ninth-century bishop Photius records that he has read two, one that he takes to be the original, and another that he ascribes to Lucian (the prodigious satirist of the second century CE).[16] The latter survives, although scholars do not all follow Photius in treating it as the work of Lucian himself. Fortuitously, a further papyrus fragment has turned up, apparently from a different version of the same narrative, describing a sex scene between a woman and an ass.[17] Apuleius' version, then, is a sophisticated version, packed with literary flamboyance and blended with a Platonising account of conversion to the cult of Isis, of a scurrilous tale that circulated around the Greek world in multiple forms.

Even so, there are grounds for thinking that Apuleius – who was very aware of the Greek intellectual currents that washed around him[18] – was reacting to the dominant Greek narrative form of his day, *viz.* the heterosexual novel. Specifically, the famous inset tale of Cupid and Psyche that dominates the central part of the text (books 4–6), and which is (so far as we know) unparalleled in Greek versions, looks very much like a gesture towards the ideals of sublime, heterosexual love. This tale, moreover, is narrated to a young woman whose story that, told from a different angle, might very well have been a kind of romance.[19] This Charite (whose name might even recall the novelist Chariton) has been kidnapped by bandits on her wedding night, attempts escape, is recaptured and threatened with a grim death, before being finally rescued by her disguised fiancé Tlepolemus. This 'novel', however, has a grim aftermath: Tlepolemus is brutally murdered, and Charite kills herself on his tomb – but not before her husband's murderer has tried it on with her. Apuleius' assault upon ideals of romantic love seems even more starkly brutal than Petronius'.

The works discussed in this volume, then, revolve around the matrimonial ideals fostered in the Roman empire, even if the shapes of their orbits are very different. Such ideals of mutual affection and support (with overarching control, it almost goes without saying, ceded to the male) are expressed in a range of works by Seneca, Musonius Rufus, Plutarch and others, and

16 *Library* codex 129.
17 *P. Oxy.* 4762. This narrative is externally narrated, whereas that of 'Lucius' seems, to judge from Photius' summary, to have been a first-person account. The papyrus also seems to mix verse and prose.
18 Sandy (1997); Harrison (2000).
19 Lalanne (2002). For the Greek-novelistic tone of the whole bandit episode see Mackay (1963).

have been memorably discussed by Michel Foucault in the third volume of his *History of Sexuality* (see Morales in this volume). Foucault (following the lead of Paul Veyne) detects a series of shifts during the Hellenistic and Roman periods, away from pederasty (boy-love) towards heterosexual marriage, away from civic virtues towards the more ostensibly private ideals of self-reflection and the 'care of the self'.[20] The 'ideal' novels are thus read as an expression of the social, indeed sacramental, importance of marriage among the traditional Greco-Roman aristocracy. These, frustrated (so the argument goes) at their newly limited opportunities for political advancement, focused their energies instead upon preserving the traditional, aristocratic structures of the family (the very structures that radical Christians would seek to destroy through the ascetic denial of sexuality). Meanwhile the 'less-than-ideal' novels (to coin a phrase) can be read as riffs around the same theme, subverting rather than promoting these same ideals.

We should pause, however, to nuance the concept of the ideal novel. Like all ideals, it does not exist in practice: even the most philosophically high-minded novels are idiosyncratic, sophisticated, playful and ethically complex. For example, the earliest novel, Chariton's *Callirhoe*, turns upon the story of a woman who loves her husband; after he has jealously kicked her into a coma and she has been abducted by pirates, she is forced to marry a second husband for the sake of her unborn child (for which she earns comparisons with the arch-bigamist Helen of Troy, 2.6.1, 5.2.8, 5.5.9). Hardly an 'ideal' love story, then, on any criterion. Nor is the demotion of boy-love quite as uniform as is sometimes suggested.[21] In a well-known discussion, Simon Goldhill accuses Foucault and his followers of 'virginity' – that is, intellectual naivety – in reading the novels as straightforwardly moral narratives.[22] What is ultimately significant, however, is not whether the novels are serious or playful, a question that has been running (under various guises) for years,[23] and which no doubt deserves more than a box-check answer. The more important lesson of these debates is that each novel needs to be taken on its own terms, as an individual creation. What makes the notion of the 'ideal' novel problematic is the implication that some of the novels are straightforward, unreflective expressions of ideology.

These issues bring us back to the question of what we should expect from a genre. Genres are not templates, recipes, or checklists, but loose

---

20 Foucault (1986); cf. Veyne (1978). See further Konstan (1994); Swain (1996) 101–31; Cooper (1996) 20–44.
21 See e.g. Effe (1987). Broadly sympathetic pederasts appear in Petronius, Xenophon and Achilles; Iamblichus' *Babylonian Affairs* possibly even featured a lesbian relationship, between Berenice and Mesopotamia (see Morales, this volume).
22 Goldhill (1995).   23 See esp. Anderson (1982); Winkler (1982); Dowden (1996).

affiliations of ideas: they rest on 'family resemblances', in Stephen Heath's (Wittgensteinian) formulation, rather than phylogenetic properties.[24] Most people's intuitive idea of a cowboy movie might involve a pistol duel, but the absence of such a scene would not disqualify a particular movie from the genre. Similarly, a number of the Greco-Roman novels feature abduction by pirates and shipwrecks, but that does not make those without such episodes any less novelistic. In fact, arguably, quite the opposite is true: it is when a text subverts or frustrates our expectations that the idea of a generic 'law' is most forceful. When, for example, Longus' Daphnis is kidnapped by sea-faring robbers, generically attuned readers expect them to initiate a narrative of travel and pursuit, rather than (as actually happens) having their boat capsized by marauding cows before they have left the harbour (Long. 1.30.2).

Love and learning

The novels discussed in this volume also share a chronological range between the first and the third centuries CE (although Heliodorus may be fourth).[25] In addition to its distinctive sexual ethics (discussed above), this period is also characterised by a preoccupation with Greek culture, particularly embodied in the prose literature of classical Athens. Across the empire, the elites immersed themselves in Thucydides, Plato, Xenophon and Demosthenes, absorbing not only their subject-matter but also their dialect and style. To be educated meant to be conversant with the Greek classics, and (particularly from the second century onwards) to be able to write and perform in the 'Attic' form of Greek peculiar to Athens of half a millennium or so earlier.[26] The Greek past does not simply offer an excuse for escapism: as Connors shows in her chapter, it is better imagined as a set of imaginative resources through which to explore, allegorically, political issues in the present.

The novels are located squarely within this culture of education, or (to use the Greek term) *paideia*.[27] They are highly sophisticated works, as contributors to this volume emphasise, in terms of style (Laird), narrative strategy (Whitmarsh, Bartsch) and allusions to earlier literature (or 'intertextuality': Morgan, Harrison). The Greek novels of the second century and later (Achilles, Longus, Heliodorus) are composed in the Attic dialect, often ostentatiously brandishing linguistic features (such as the optative mood) that

24 Heath (2004) 168.   25 For dates see the 'Index of Greek and Roman novelists'.
26 Bowie (1970); Swain (1996); Schmitz (1997); Whitmarsh (2001a), (2005b); Goldhill (2001a); Borg (2004).
27 This has been a cornerstone of novel studies since Rohde (1914), the first edition of which was published in 1876.

had disappeared from normal usage. The Latin novelists are virtuosi of the same stature; Apuleius in particular has an astonishing facility with rhythm, word-play and literary reminiscence, setting him right in line with the Greek sophists of his day.[28] Although (as we have seen) not explicitly recognised by contemporary intellectuals, the novel is (as Bowie shows in this volume) deeply enmeshed with the literary currents of its day. These formal aspects are not merely stylistic; as well as enriching the literary texture, they also clearly position the texts socioculturally, as products of and for the elite. Nor was the training of the elite confined to mental activity: bodily fitness was crucial as well, and this concern is also expressed in the novels (see König's chapter).

Paideia is also a theme within the very narrative of the novels. Characters in the Greek novel (particularly in Chariton) are routinely said to be 'educated'.[29] Longus' *Daphnis and Chloe* is centrally about education, in that it focuses upon the upbringing of two young children. Although the particular kind of education they seek is erotic, literary culture is never far away: the sculpted prose, suffused with Sapphic and Theocritean resonance, combined with the rural setting (the uneducated were commonly derided as 'rustics'), convert this apparently simple tale of rustic naivety into a complex allegory testing the reader's own *paideia*.[30] Longus does not, however, allow his educated readers to repose comfortably: the one figure actually described as 'educated' is Gnathon (4.17.3), a voracious pederast who attempts (and comically fails) to seduce and then rape Daphnis.

The most satirical account of Greek *paideia* comes in a Latin novel, Petronius' *Satyrica*. This narrative is entirely presented through the eyes of a pretentious Greek, Encolpius, a 'mythomaniac' who overlays his sordid story with inappropriately highbrow reminiscences of classical texts.[31] In the most famous (and unfragmented) part of the text, Encolpius sneers at the ignorance of the Roman freedman Trimalchio, whose banquet epitomises tasteless vulgarity (26–78).[32] Another character, Eumolpus, is a teacher of philosophy who seduces the boy under his tutelage, to the point where the boy becomes more ardent than he: the whole episode is a gleeful reworking of Plato's *Symposium*, where Alcibiades lusts after Socrates rather than

---

28 As Laird in particular highlights in this volume; see also Sandy and Harrison.
29 Char. 1.12.6, 1.12.9, 2.1.5, 2.4.1, 2.5.11, 3.2.6, 4.7.6, 5.5.1, 5.9.8, 8.5.10 (Dionysius), 6.5.8, 7.5.6 (Callirhoe), 7.2.5 (Chaereas), 8.3.10 (Demetrius); Xen. Eph. 1.1.3; Ach. Tat. 1.8.4; Long. 1.8.1; Hld. 2.33.5.
30 Hunter (1983), e.g. 59; Zeitlin (1990); Whitmarsh (2001a) 100–3.
31 The phrase 'mythomaniac' is Conte's (1994).
32 The name 'Trimalchio' seems to invite derivation from the Semitic root *MLK* (Hebrew מלך) denoting royal rule.

the reverse.[33] For all that Petronius mercilessly attacks the venality and corruption of contemporary Rome (there is more than a whiff of Nero about Trimalchio), he also targets the hypocritical Greeks who affect an air of moral superiority.

The status of the novels

The reasons behind this widespread emphasis upon Greek learning have been widely debated, and are beyond our present scope.[34] It will be important to us, however, to underline that this was an empire-wide phenomenon, and not simply limited to mainland Greece. There were certainly those inhabitants of the old Greek centres, particularly Athens, who saw themselves as defending their cultural purity against the hordes of barbarian outsides.[35] There were, however, also those from further afield like the Gaul Favorinus and the Syrian Lucian (both second-century CE) who saw Greek education as an opportunity to transform themselves from locals to cultural citizens of the empire: for such figures, 'Greek' signified power, status and respect, not just ethnic affiliation.[36]

It is, in this connection, particularly significant that the settings of the novels tend to avoid mainland Greece, apparently systematically (as Susan Stephens emphasises in this volume). The picture painted of Athens in particular is notably gloomy.[37] Chariton's *Callirhoe* is set on Syracuse in the aftermath of the failed Athenian invasion of 415–413; Callirhoe herself is the daughter of the victorious general Hermocrates (a figure familiar from the fourth, sixth and seventh books of Thucydides' *Histories*). This anti-Athenian feeling percolates even to the pirate Theron, who gives the Piraeus a wide berth because he despises the 'inquisitiveness' of the Athenians (1.11.6). In Heliodorus' *Charicleia and Theagenes*, meanwhile, Athens is the setting for Cnemon's inset story of treachery, tragedy and illicit passion, which serves as a counterpoint to the main tale that we read (which is set entirely in Africa).[38] The one exception is the *Ass* tale (both the Greek and the Latin version), but even this is set in Thessaly, in the semi-civilised north, where a veneer of Hellenism hides a world of magic and weird ritual.

This avoidance of cultural centres reflects the provenance of the novelists themselves, who tend to hail (as Stephens again notes) from the frontiers of the empire. The earliest Greek authors hailed from Asia Minor: Chariton

---

33 *Sat.* 87; Plato, *Symposium* 219b–c; Dimundo (1983).
34 See the works cited in n. 26 above.
35 An excellent example is Agathion (second century CE), at Philostratus, *Lives of the Sophists* 552–4. See Whitmarsh (2001a) 105–8.
36 Whitmarsh (2001a) 116–29.　　　37 Oudot (1992).　　　38 Hld. 1.9–17; Morgan (1989a).

of Aphrodisias (the Carian city favoured by the Julio-Claudian dynasty, and plausibly the origin of the *Ninus* romance too),[39] and Xenophon of Ephesus. Petronius may have been a Neronian courtier, but Apuleius was from Madaurus in north Africa. Achilles Tatius, according to the Byzantine encyclopaedia known as the *Suda* and the manuscript tradition, was from Egyptian Alexandria (if this is not simply an extrapolation from the wide-eyed description of the city that opens book 5). Iamblichus, author of the fragmentary *Babylonian Affairs*, was apparently a Syrian for whom Greek was his third language after Babylonian and (presumably) Syriac.[40] Lucian (the author of the *True Histories*, and perhaps *Lucius or the Ass*) was also a native Syrian, from Commagene. Another Syrian was Heliodorus, who hailed from Emesa (modern Homs); he signs off by declaring himself a 'Phoenician, from the race of the sun' (10.41.4). The last phrase alludes to the local Semitic cult of Elahagabal (famously embraced by the Severan dynasty at the behest of the empress Julia Domna, another Emesene): the name is composed of two parts, the first of which (the Canaanite El, i.e. Aramaic *elāhā* ~ Hebrew *'ēl*, Arabic *ilāh-* / *Allāhu*) was Hellenised into Helios ('sun').[41] For the novelists, as for many other contemporary figures, Greek *paideia* is the common stock of civilised humanity, and not limited to those few who happened to hail from Greece itself.

Were the novels written with a female readership – now more educated than ever before – in mind? It has sometimes been speculated that the ideals of symmetrical marriage, pursued by determined, active, intelligent young women like Chariton's Callirhoe and Heliodorus' Charicleia, would have appealed to precisely this female readership.[42] Antonius Diogenes' *Wonders beyond Thule*, indeed, is (fictitiously) constructed as an account of the author's travels addressed to his sister Isidora.[43] This is, however, no concrete evidence either way; and, as Morales' chapter shows,[44] the representation of women can also titillate male readers. Moreover, it is questionable how many women were educated up to the standards envisaged by the novelists. Still, it is worth keeping an open mind on the matter: audiences are not uniform, nor has any writer ever imagined them to be.

---

39 For the importance of the Ninus and Semiramis story to Aphrodisias, see Yildirim (2004).
40 See the scholion to Photius cited at Habrich (1960) 2, and translated at Stephens and Winkler (1995) 181. On the problems raised by this testimony see Stephens and Winkler (1995) 181–2, and further Millar (1993) 489–92.
41 Nothing is known of Longus or Antonius Diogenes.
42 Egger (1988), (1994a–b); cf. Johne (2003) 156–64; fuller bibliography in Hunter's chapter below.
43 Photius, *Library* codex 166, 111a = Stephens and Winkler (1995) 127.
44 Cf. Morales (2004).

For all the close association between *paideia*, sophistication and social elitism, it is however important also to keep in mind the strong links between the novel and a more populist story culture. Critics are no longer as keen to assert the 'origins' of the novel as they once were (literary forms, after all, do not evolve like biological species),[45] but the novels themselves seem to invite a link back to the world of oral story-telling. This theme is strong in Chariton, Xenophon, Apuleius, Achilles, Longus and Heliodorus, all of which contain long sections of oral narrative (as Richard Hunter notes in this volume). Xenophon's *Anthia and Habrocomes* and Longus' *Daphnis and Chloe* conclude with the dedication in temples of accounts of their adventures, which suggests that the story we are reading has become part of the mythhistory of the local community. We know, thanks principally to collections of stories by Parthenius, Conon and Antonius Liberalis, of a number of erotic tales tied to locales (for example: Caunus and Byblis, Myrrha, Stratonice and Antiochus).[46] The latter do not share the same systematic narrative structure of the standard Greek novel (e.g. the 'happy ending'), but it is nevertheless within this tradition that Xenophon and Longus seem to locate their narratives.

It is even possible that some novels were performed for popular consumption. Xenophon's *Anthia and Habrocomes*, it has been argued, bears the hallmarks of an oral narrative.[47] The same may be true also of the Greek *Ass* story, which shares the same simple, paratactic narrative (although there are also some signs of ambition at the level of vocabulary and allusion).[48] Versions of the other Greek novels may have been performed as popular mimes.[49] It does not follow from this, however, that the novels were an ancient equivalent of modern pulp fiction: beyond the examples we have just discussed, the novels anticipated an educated readership deeply familiar with the literary classics (see Morgan's and Harrison's chapters), and indeed the papyri on which fragments survive suggest expensive, high-status productions (see Hunter's chapter).[50]

---

45 Originary hypotheses in Rohde (1914) (Hellenistic travel narratives and erotic poetry); Lavagnini (1922) (local mythology); Kerényi (1927) (mystery texts); Barns (1956) (Egyptian literature); Giangrande (1962) (prose paraphrase); Anderson (1984) (Egyptian and near-eastern literature); West (2003) (women's tales). Against the 'evolutionary' approach see Perry (1967), esp. 14–15.
46 Surveyed at Whitmarsh (forthcoming); see also Lightfoot (1999) 433–6.
47 O'Sullivan (1995). Xenophon has also been suspected of having been epitomised, since Bürger (1892).
48 Discussed by Van Thiel (1971).
49 See Lucian, *On the Dance* 2, 54; *The False Critic* 25, with Hägg and Utas (2003) 49–50; also Mignogna (1996).
50 See further Stephens (1994); also Bowie (1994a).

Some critics have claimed that the novels anticipate a different kind of expertise, that of esoteric religion. All the novels are overseen by divine providence (what scholars sometimes call a *Götterapparat*); some, most notably Apuleius' *Metamorphoses*, actually contain scenes of initiation or conversion.[51] Since Karl Kerényi (1927; also 1971) suggested that the novels grew out of the sacred narratives of Isis cult, some scholars have sought to identify them more closely with religion, to the extent that Reinhold Merkelbach has claimed that (apart from Chariton's *Callirhoe*) they 'actually are mystery texts'.[52] This claim has been widely derided,[53] but the problem actually lies in its ambiguous phrasing: what does it actually *mean* to call a novel a 'mystery text'? Is it envisaged that the text would have been used as part of a liturgy? Or that it was written for initiates? Or that initiates would detect signals that others would not? In a later book focusing narrowly on Longus' *Daphnis and Chloe*, Merkelbach argues more specifically that this novel is designed to be read on two levels, the deeper of which reflects the eternal truths of Dionysiac cult.[54] Now, while few would accept even this, to the extent that Merkelbach wants a *systematic and comprehensive* religious undertow, there is a sense in which he is indubitably right, as Froma Zeitlin observes in this volume. Narrative and initiation share many features: both are fundamentally providentialist, promising ultimate revelation and interpretative 'closure' in compensation for the confusion and chaos of the present. The novels, moreover, were composed by and for people whose daily lives were saturated with religiosity: the ancient world lacked any real concept of a secular literature.

The novel and its readers

The overlap between religious and narrative sensibilities explains the attractiveness of the novel as a paradigm for communicating real theology. Prose narrative was already common in the Semitic near East before it was in Greece, as testified by the *Aḥiqar* tradition (the oldest, Aramaic version of which dates to the fifth century BCE) and the 'Jewish novels', among the apocrypha of the Hebrew Bible (e.g. *Esther, Judith, Daniel*).[55] The fascinating *Joseph and Aseneth*, telling the biblical story of Joseph's marriage to a young Egyptian maiden (*Genesis* 41:45, cf. 26:20), fuses this tradition with the Greek novel to produce a powerful mix of eroticism and Judaic theology:

51 See also the fragmentary *Iolaus*: Stephens and Winkler (1995) 358–74.
52 Merkelbach (1962) ch. 7; this position also underlies Petri (1963).
53 Most enthusiastically by Turcan (1963); Geyer (1977); Stark (1989). See also Beck (2003).
54 Merkelbach (1988), esp. 138–9.
55 For the phrase 'Jewish novel' see Wills (1995), (2002). See also Barns (1956) on Egyptian fiction.

Aseneth is beautiful like a goddess (4.2), struck with amazement on seeing Joseph (6.1) and with grief when they are separated after their initial meeting (8.8), and so on.[56] The dating of this text is difficult to determine precisely; the most recent estimate is that it belongs in the third or fourth century CE, and is overlain with Christian motifs.[57]

The relationship between Christianity and the novel is complex. There are ancient traditions recording that Achilles Tatius and Heliodorus wrote their works in their youth, later becoming Christian bishops.[58] Although it was long assumed that these are later fabrications, recent scholarship has reopened the matter by pointing to thematic and lexical parallels between the Greek texts (even the earliest, *Callirhoe*) and the Christian gospels.[59] It has also been argued that the novelists' recurrent interest in cannibalism (scenes are found in Petronius, Achilles Tatius and the fragmentary Lollianus) may have been sparked by the Christian eucharist.[60] Readers may judge for themselves whether such convergences result from the direct impact of Christianity, a more diffuse form of cultural osmosis, or mere coincidence. We are on safer ground, however, with the impact of the Greek novel on Christian literature: the authors of martyr acts, the apocryphal acts of the apostles and the Clementine *Recognitions* borrowed directly and frequently from the novel to structure their accounts of suffering and endurance in the service of the Christian god.[61] Most surprisingly, perhaps, St Augustine read Apuleius' *Metamorphoses* (*Civ.* 18.18).

Islam too embraced the novel: the poem *Vāmiq u 'Adhrā* composed by the eleventh-century Persian poet 'Unṣurī is clearly based upon the Greek *Metiochus and Parthenope*, which survives only in fragments, but enough to show the overlap.[62] It is possible that 'Unṣurī based his poem on an Arabic text, translated like so many other originally Greek works in the 'House of wisdom' of al-Ma'mūn at Baghdad.[63] If so, this consolidates the extraordinary status of the novel as the only 'literary' (i.e. non-scientific) form to pass from Greek into Arabic. The other example of an Arabised ancient novel is the *Alexander Romance* (echoes of which even appear in the Qur'ān).[64]

Much of the late classical and mediaeval reception of the novel remains shrouded in mystery. We simply do not know how *Metiochus and Parthenope* made its way to Iran, as we do not know whether anyone read Longus

---

56 For novelistic motifs see further Philonenko (1968) 43–8; West (1974).
57 Kraemer (1998) 225–42.
58 *Suda*, under *Achilles Statius* (*sic*) = Ach. Tat. T V in Vilborg (1955); Socrates, *History of the Church* 5.22 = Hld. T I in Colonna (1938) (cf. also T III).
59 Ramelli (2001).   60 Bowersock (1994) 125–36.   61 See the survey at Pervo (2003).
62 Hägg and Utas (2003).   63 Hägg and Utas (2003) 195–6.
64 Stoneman (2003), with literature.

during this period (see Hunter's chapter). Firm ground hoves into view in the Byzantine period, when (as Burton discusses) the Greek novel inspires a new wave of Greek poets, keen to exploit their classical past but also to mark their distance (particularly as Christians) from it. Thereafter, the Greco-Roman novel has been in constant dialogue with European and American arts and literature (as chapters by Reeve, Sandy, Harrison and Fusillo show).

The reception of ancient texts is not simply an interesting epilogue to the real business of reading them in their ancient contexts. The final section of this volume dramatises the important point that the meaning of an ancient work shifts over time and space, and indeed from individual to individual: Augustine's Apuleius is not Poggio's, Lytton's Petronius is not Fellini's. Ancient texts can sometimes speak to us with what seems like an alarming directness: this is certainly the case with the novel, which (as we have seen) has struck a resonant chord with modernity. The theme that overarches the contextual, interpretative and reception-based parts of this volume, however, is that the process of meaning-making is ever ongoing.[65]

65 This volume uses *Metamorphoses* as the title of Apuleius' novel, and *Satyrica* for Petronius'. See further the 'Index of Greek and Roman novelists'. Greek names are given in their more familiar, Latinised forms, except for the post-antique period.

PART I

Contexts

2

EWEN BOWIE

Literary milieux

'Am I always to be a listener? Am I never to get my own back?' With these words the Latin poet Juvenal in the early second century CE opened the first of his *Satires*, purporting to give his readers a reason for his taking up writing. He goes on to give 'reasons' for his choice of satire. These can be only some of the factors we might want to see as contributing to an explanation for his writing what he did, but his opening offers us a good way into the issues relevant to why, in the literary world of the high Roman empire, somebody might choose to write poetry or prose at all, and into the factors that might have influenced a would-be writer either to choose an unusual genre or even to develop one that could be seen as in all or many respects new. Some of these factors are different in the Greek and the Latin worlds, and the greater part of the following exploration of the place of novels in the literature of the Roman empire will focus on the setting of the Greek novels within Greek literary production and consumption.

My discussion of the Greek novels will attempt to set each of four surviving 'ideal' novels in the context of the Greek literature that had recently been written.[1] For each period I shall ask what sort of literature was already prevalent when a choice to write a novel was made; what features in that literature might have encouraged or contributed to the novelist's project; and in assessing the subsequent period will ask whether there are any traces of the novel impinging on literature in other genres. This procedure will involve the heuristic device of artificial periodisation – roughly, 31 BCE–50 CE; 50–160 CE; 160–220 CE; 220–70 CE – which should not be taken to imply that these divisions are important for anything other than this investigation. It will also require careful distinction between features that might be claimed as specifically 'novelistic' – in the sense 'characteristic of the five ideal novels' – and others which may be generally associable with other

---

1 Xenophon's *Anthia and Habrocomes* will only be mentioned *en passant*. His date remains controversial, his work's closeness to that of Chariton undoubted, and many of the questions and answers sparked by Chariton would apply to Xenophon too.

sorts of erotic writing, for example types of short story, *novelle/Novellen*, including *Milesian Tales*.

First, however, the general issue of consumption must be addressed. Wherever in the Roman empire Greek was the language of the educated elite, the 'cultivated men' (*pepaideumenoi*), the vast majority of the texts read were poetry and prose of the classical period. This was not least because such texts were studied and used at all levels of education,[2] from the learning of the alphabet to training by a rhetor or sophist in the skills of forensic, political and epideictic rhetoric: they thus became both the texts that were widely known and the texts of which knowledge had to be displayed in order to establish a claim to culture (*paideia*), the defining characteristic of the 'cultivated person', *pepaideumenos*. Quotations in authors with substantial surviving *oeuvres* – for example, Dio of Prusa, Plutarch, Aelius Aristides, Lucian and Philostratus – and the distribution of papyri found in the rubbish dumps of (admittedly bookish) Oxyrhynchus suggest a broadly similar range of reading in the years from 50 to 250 CE. Only occasionally does any of these authors earlier than Philostratus mention a Greek writer of the imperial period, and even more rarely offer any citation from one. Correspondingly only a very low proportion of papyri have yielded texts of imperial Greek writers.

The message to anyone who contemplated embarking upon a literary work was mixed. On the one hand those literary works that were read often enjoyed great authority; on the other hand the authority accorded to works from the archaic and classical past was much greater than could be expected by a work composed more recently, and even if a new work succeeded in achieving distribution by *samizdat* and by the book trade it was very unlikely ever to join the canon of those cited with reverence, far less those used in the educational system.[3] At the same time it is clear that to be known as a writer had a cachet that could give an individual worthwhile leverage among those who were attempting to join, or to rise within, the constantly competitive society of Greco-Roman civic elites. In picking out participants in his *Sympotic Questions* as 'the philosopher', 'the rhetor' or 'the poet' Plutarch was recognising a claim to status that was significant however ephemeral their productions might turn out to be. One of our most telling documents is from a slightly later generation. A text inscribed in Aphrodisias preserves two decisions taken to honour C. Iulius Longianus, one by the Council and People of Halicarnassus, the other (taken on the 27 March 127 CE) by the

---

2 T. Morgan (1998); Cribiore (1996), (2001). For visual evidence of the prestige of learning cf. Zanker (1995).
3 Note, however, that the crash-course in elevated reading suggested by Dio of Prusa, *Oration* 18, does at least allow some attention to more recent writers.

synod of Dionysiac artists. This synod decree identifies Longianus as a tragic poet and resolves to honour him with an 'a painted likeness' – presumably a painting – in whichever part of his native city he preferred; the Halicarnassians gave him citizenship and resolved to honour him with bronze statues, one to be set up next to that of 'old Herodotus'. Longianus was commended for 'diverse displays (*epideixeis*) of every sort of poetry' which entertained the old and improved the young: hence it was also decided that his books should be lodged in the libraries so that the young might learn from them as from the classics.[4]

About the same time an aspiring poet from Side, known to us only by his Roman *cognomen* (part of his nomenclature) Marcellus, succeeded in bringing his voluminous medical poem in hexameters, loftily entitled *Chironides* (*Daughters of Chiron*), to the attention of the emperor Hadrian, with the outcome (as an epigram presumably composed by Marcellus himself claims) that its forty-book text was lodged in official libraries in Rome by Hadrian and then by Pius.[5] No later than 128/9 CE an Athenian decree honoured Q. Pompeius Capito of Pergamum with a statue in the theatre of Dionysus and Athenian citizenship 'on account of his poetic virtuosity, demonstrated in impromptu performances in every rhythm and metre'.[6] Similarly, at some date in the second century, Rhodiapolis in Lycia honoured its poet Heraclitus as the 'Homer of medical poetry' with statues in its theatre – a gilded statue of Heraclitus himself and a statue of 'Education' or 'Culture' (*Paideia*).[7] Heraclitus was also honoured at Athens by the Epicureans and by the Areopagus – presumably also by the erection of statues.

An aspiring writer, then, might dream of recognition. However it may not be accidental that all the above honours were conferred for the production of poetry. Some writers of prose did indeed achieve great prestige and significant honours, above all sophists: but in this last case it was for their epideictic performances before live audiences and for their contribution to teaching that they seem to have been honoured.[8] As far as can be seen it is also true of philosophers that they were accorded the title 'philosopher'

---

4 *MAMA* 8.418 (a) and (b), re-edited Roueché (1993), no. 88, 223–7. See further Bowie (1989b) 202.
5 *Palatine Anthology* 7.158, cf. Bowie (1990) 66–7.
6 *IG*² II/III 3800 (= *IG*² III 769). Athenaeus, *Sophists at dinner* 8.350C cites an epic poet (*epopoios*) Capito who dedicated 'Commentaries' (*hupomnēmata*) to a Philopappus – the item that Athenaeus reports from the fourth book of these 'Commentaries' is a *bon mot* of the Hellenistic citharist Stratonicus. He might well be the same as this Q. Pompeius Capito, and his dedicatee could then be the Antiochus Philopappus known from Plutarch and from his monument on the Hill of the Muses in Athens, *PIR*² I 151.
7 *TAM* II 910 = *IGR* III 733, cf. Robert (1980) 14 and the temple of Asclepius dedicated by Heraclitus: *TAM* II 906 = *IGR* III 732.
8 For a comprehensive analysis of the inscriptions in which sophists and rhetors figure see now Puech (2002).

without reference to specific written works.[9] Public honour of a historian as such is rare,[10] though it was manifestly for historical research at some level concerning the claims to kinship between his own city Aegeae and Argos that the sophist Publius Anteius Antiochus was honoured by Argos,[11] and predictably the historian of an emperor's military achievements might expect imperial recognition.

In what follows one further qualification applies. The short account of a love-affair that ended disastrously can be found in Greek literature of almost any generation, beginning with the classical period.[12] It is tempting but perhaps mistaken to register these as elements in the Greek literature of my various artificial periods that might be seen as important for illuminating the place of the novels. Such stories are indeed introduced as sub-plots in many novels, often to offer a stark contrast with the main narrative. But they can turn up in almost any literary genre, and they differ crucially from the narratives of the novels in lacking a happy ending (to say nothing of a teenage, mutually attracted couple). I have decided therefore neither to flag their presence in writers of any of these periods nor to adduce that presence as an explanation of a novelist's choice of theme. Thus I am not inclined to see the stories of Zarinaea and Stryangaeus in Nicolaus of Damascus (*FGrH* 90 F 5) or of Radine and Leontichus,[13] both anecdotes of ill-fated lovers who kill themselves,[14] as important for the context of Chariton's writing, nor Plutarch's similar stories of Cammas and Sinatus in his work *On the Virtues of Women*[15] and of Epona and Sabinus in the *Tale of Desire*[16] as important for the context of that of Achilles Tatius. The same applies to the ghost story of the ill-fated love of Machatus and the deceased Philinnion that opens the surviving text of *On Things Miraculous* by a freedman of Hadrian, Phlegon of Tralles, apparently written early in the 140s CE:[17] in itself it does not seem to me to have great importance for the context in which Achilles Tatius or

9 E.g. the statue base honouring Arrian as 'philosopher' *SEG* xxx 159, cf. Stadter (1980) 189 n. 5 and 198 n. 89.

10 The statue honouring Dexippus as a rhetor and historian was erected by his children, *IG*² II/III 3800 = Puech (2002) 220 no. 95, line 5.

11 Cf. Puech (2002) 68–74 no. 10.   12 Cf. Trenkner (1958).

13 A version of the Radine story is quoted from Stesichorus (= *PMGF* 278) by Strabo 8.3.20; the name of the cousin who fell in love with her, Leontichus, appears only in Pausanias 8.5.13.

14 For discussion and further bibliography see Pignataro and Di Giglio in Stramaglia (2000) 299–304 and 263–6.

15 See 20, 257e–258c with Stadter (1965) 103–6: for further bibliography see Romani in Stramaglia (2000) 97–103.

16 See 24, 770c–25, 771c: for further bibliography see Romani in Stramaglia (2000) 147–54.

17 Text in *FGrH* 257; Giannini (1966); further bibliography see Stramaglia in Stramaglia (2000) 167–84.

Iamblichus wrote. Nor, finally, does the Milesian tale of Pseudo-Aeschines *Letter* 10, probably composed in the later second century CE,[18] help our understanding of Longus.

31 BCE–50 CE

What, then, might have been the calculations of a citizen of Aphrodisias in the 40s or 50s CE, Chariton the secretary of a rhetor Athenagoras, when he decided to embark upon an eight-book work of romantic prose fiction, thereby either following some writer of the recent past who had developed this genre or, as I judge more likely on the evidence currently available, actually 'inventing' a new genre?[19]

In the 40s and 50s the Roman province Asia may have begun to respond culturally to the two generations of peace and economic prosperity that had passed since Actium ended the Roman civil wars in 31 CE. But the figure whom Philostratus picked out as the first sophist after Aeschines to merit a biography, (Tiberius?) Claudius Nicetes of Smyrna, may only have been at the very beginning of his career, and Scopelianus of Clazomenae not even that. The most recent works to have made their mark in Greek literature had been produced by Greeks of Asia Minor who seem to have spent some time in Rome – perhaps most of his life, in the case of Dionysius from Halicarnassus, author both of a historical work, *Roman Antiquities*, and of several rhetorical monographs, including one evaluating the classical Attic orators; and significant parts of their lives in the case of Strabo from Pontic Amaseia, author of a *History* (now lost) and of a historically sensitive *Geography*, and of Nicolaus of Damascus, whose historical writing included an account of the reign of Augustus. A naturalised Athenian, Gaius Julius Nicanor, had composed poetry in Augustus' reign that earned him the flattering soubriquet 'new Homer' on several honorific statue-bases,[20] but not a line of his poetry survives, and we cannot tell if it made any impact in the Roman province Asia even though its city Hierapolis seem to be his origin.

The works we still have may be seen to some degree as responding to the new situation: from Dionysius a version of Roman history that often tried to assimilate Rome to a Greek city,[21] and an attempt to offer elite Greeks and Hellenophone Romans a rhetoric that might appeal to Roman taste and at the same time highlight the contribution to sound rhetorical technique

18 For discussion and bibliography see Mignogna in Stramaglia (2000) 85–96.
19 For the dating of Chariton, both absolute and relative to other novelists, see Bowie (2002), where I argue that the Ninus novel was composed slightly later than Chariton's *Callirhoe*.
20 *IG*² II/III 3786–9; cf. *PIR*² I 440.   21 See Gabba (1996).

of classical Athens[22] (about the same time Caecilius of Caleacte initiated a genre later to be expanded by Plutarch, comparison of a great Greek orator – Demosthenes – and a great Roman orator – Cicero); from Strabo a geography that expounded to elite Greeks the vast Roman empire within which they all had to operate and in which some of them would try to move their careers onto an international level;[23] from Nicolaus a work explaining the rise and rule of the man now most powerful in the Greek world, Augustus. Traces of other historical work – for example by the philosopher Athenodorus of Tarsus[24] – remind us how much has been lost, and it must be allowed that if we had a complete set of Greek works produced in the period 31 BCE to 54 CE we might well discern a different pattern.[25]

Literature composed principally for entertainment, however, might be thought to have been thinner on the ground. Greek epigrams indeed flourished, but some, such as most surviving poems of Crinagoras, were calculated to maintain good relations with Rome and the Julio-Claudian household.[26] A lighter touch is evident in some other epigrammatists, for example Argentarius, and by the reign of Nero satirical epigram had made a splash with the poetry of Nicarchus and Lucilius.[27] But another type of epigram is of especial relevance to the novel. Erotic epigram, well established since the third century BCE, attracted an especially elegant exponent who seems to belong around 40–60 CE and whose activity is suggested by one epigram to have been near but not in the city of Ephesus, Rufinus.[28] It is vexing that we cannot date Rufinus more precisely: did his handling of the commonplaces of love give a cue to Chariton in nearby Aphrodisias, or was the influence the reverse, or even mutual? It is certainly tempting to think that the production in the same area of western Asia Minor of a slim volume of (heterosexual) erotic epigrams and of a work of prose fiction centred on the adventures of a teenage (heterosexual) couple was not wholly accidental.

---

22 See Hidber (1996).   23 See Clarke (1999).   24 *FGrH* 746.

25 This brief examination excludes from its category 'Greek literature' the many technical works on grammar, metre and other sorts of scholarship that can be assigned to this period, more or less technical philosophical work such as the work of Thrasyllus on the Platonic corpus, and the voluminous output of the Hellenising Jew Philo of Alexandria.

26 The classic study remains Cichorius (1922). For commentary see Gow and Page (1968).

27 For texts and commentary of Argentarius and Nicarchus see Gow and Page (1968); for assessment of these and of Lucilius see Nisbet (2004). Lucilius' place in his contemporary world was the subject of a masterly essay by Louis Robert (1968).

28 For the date Cameron (1982). For a not always sympathetic commentary, Page (1978). For the proximity to Ephesus see Rufinus I Page = *Palatine Anthology* 5.9, though Page's belief that the location of Rufinus' home as Samos is confirmed by Rufinus 17 Page = *Palatine Anthology* 5.44 is rightly questioned by Robert (1982). See now Höschele (2006); Floridi (2007).

50–160 CE

Between the composition by Chariton of his *Callirhoe* (which I have argued to be in the 50s CE)[29] and by Achilles Tatius, probably from Alexandria, of his *Leucippe and Clitophon* (perhaps written nearer 120 than 150 CE) the landscape of contemporary Greek literature changed radically. The sophist and (after what he himself claimed as a conversion) philosopher Dio of Prusa (c. 40 –?115 CE) had not only circulated speeches purporting to have been delivered to Greek cities concerning their politics and to the Roman emperor (supposedly Trajan) concerning the characteristics of a good king. He had also composed essays addressing philosophical and literary-critical issues on a relatively vulgarising, unprofessional level, and he had composed two 'What if . . .' works exploiting literary fictionality in different ways. One was a long speech, probably first delivered at Troy, in which he argued that Homer had misrepresented the outcome of the Trojan War – it had in fact been a victory for the Trojans. This may be a version chosen for its commendability to the contemporary descendants of Aeneas ruling from Rome, as well as to citizens of the Roman colony of Alexandria Troas, but the engine which keeps the speech in motion is the enjoyment of speaker and audience in clever reversals of the Homeric story argued on the basis of the text of Homer's *Iliad* itself. The second of Dio's excursions into entertaining prose fiction is a narrative of his shipwreck on the east coast of Euboea and his encounter there with the family of a virtuous hunter. His family's virtues are opposed to the corrupt practices in the city on the margins of whose territory he, his cousin and their families live by hunting. Several features locate this *Euboean Oration* (7) of Dio not very far from the Greek novels: themes of travel, the protagonist's encounter with a culture different from that of the Greco-Roman *polis* (also found in the *Borysthenite Oration* 36) and a love-interest, albeit here involving minor characters – the hunter's son falls in love with, and marries, his cousin's daughter (very much the girl next door).[30]

Another philosopher, Plutarch of Chaeronea, also showed great skill and interest in using absorbing narrative to construct tense situations, lively dialogue and sympathetic characters. The overall objective of his parallel *Lives* may have been education and not mere entertainment,[31] but his 'heroes' are often found in cliff-hanging situations comparable to those in novels (e.g. Marius hiding in the marshes, *Marius* 37–38), and love-affairs play an important part in several *Lives* (notably the *Antonius*) albeit they never provide their dominant framework, nor are they teen romances. Adventure and

29 Bowie (2002).   30 Dio of Prusa, *Oration* 7.67–80.   31 Cf. e.g. Duff (1999).

sexual passion also surface from time to time in his *Essays*, but in some cases, for example that in his work *On the Virtues of Women*, with unhappy consequences (see the *caveat* above p. 20). Another of these essays, the *Tale of Desire*, has a decidedly novelistic plot: in the city of Thespiae, which alone had a major cult of Eros, a wealthy widow kidnaps and carries off to her home a handsome young man for whom she lusts. Interlocutors propose different reactions, but she is allowed to keep him.

We cannot judge whether Chariton was read more in mainland Greece, in the province Asia and in Rome itself than Dio or Plutarch (as he certainly seems to have been in Egypt, where he is attested by papyri from the Greek city of Oxyrhynchus as Dio is not), but both these philosophers acquired a high reputation for the production of edifying literature, and that their varied *oeuvre* included themes and modes of writing contiguous with those of Chariton and Xenophon may well have encouraged some 'cultivated men' (*pepaideumenoi*) to be readier to extend their reading to novels. It is a corollary, of course, that these other writers' awareness of the success of *Callirhoe* and the like may have encouraged them to include amatory subjects.

In general there is rather more evidence of writing on erotic themes between the reigns of Nero (54–68 CE) and Pius (138–61 CE). Philostratus reports a work he describes as *Araspas in Love with Pantheia*, a reworking of a tale of faithful love immortalised by Xenophon in his *Cyropaideia*: some attributed this to the sophist Dionysius of Miletus, but Philostratus judges it alien to his style and pronounces his enemy Celer, perhaps the imperial secretary Caninius Celer, to have been its author.[32] Whether a declamation or a properly novelistic book-text (on whatever scale) it attests romantic themes enticing a writer at the highest social level. A book of homoerotic epigrams by Strato of Sardis can plausibly be dated to the reign of that emperor most sympathetic to its subject-matter, Hadrian.[33] Finally Antoninus Liberalis' collection of forty-one *Metamorphoses*, many of them brought about by amatory misadventures, seems to belong in this period.

Alongside such works, which accommodated *erōtica* somewhere on their canvas, there were indeed many more in the century from 54 CE to 161 CE that addressed subjects less hospitable to *erōs*. In this context a mere list must suffice, but it will show their range and number. In moral philosophy

---

32 Philostratus, *Lives of the Sophists* 524. Stramaglia (2000) suggests that the title given by Philostratus counts against the view of Perry (1967) 168–9 and Bowie (1994a) 445 that this could have been a novel: but is the phrase 'Araspas the lover of Panthea' actually a title? We may note how Philostratus rewrites the title of Pollux's *Onomasticon* ('Word-book') as simply 'Words', *Lives of the Sophists* 592.
33 See Cameron (1982); Bowie (1990) 56–7.

Musonius Rufus and Arrian's version of the lectures of Epictetus; in more technical philosophy Favorinus; in historiography with a global sweep Arrian of Nicomedia (most famously his *Anabasis of Alexander*), Claudius Charax of Pergamum, Amyntianus, Appian of Alexandria;[34] in geography and astronomy Ptolemy; in physiognomonics Bryson and the sophist Polemo of Laodicea; in literary criticism the work *On the Sublime* attributed to a Longinus. As to poetry, we know of epics and tragedies, some by sophists, all almost entirely lost, and some lyric poems that survive by Hadrian's freedman Publius Aelius Mesomedes.[35]

Finally we should take note of some often loosely structured collections that catered either to the appetite for bizarre or unusual stories or simply for scientific (or pseudo-scientific), literary or linguistic knowledge. Between Pliny's *Natural History* in Latin from the 60s and 70s CE and the Praenestine Claudius Aelianus' *Miscellaneous History* in Greek from the 220s CE no straightforward examples survive, unless we admit the *On long-lived people and things miraculous* by another freedman of Hadrian, Phlegon of Tralles, apparently written early in the 140s CE.[36] But such material was exploited by Plutarch in several essays and adapted to more elegant presentation in dialogue form in his afore-mentioned *Sympotic Questions* (written between 99 and 116 CE) and was similarly dressed up by Aulus Gellius in his (largely) Latin *Attic Nights*. Less artistic presentation of similar material seems to have characterised the *Memoirs* of the Epidaurian lady Pamphile[37] and the *Varied History* and *Memoirs* of sophist and philosopher Favorinus of Arelate.

This is how we moderns might see the world of letters in which Achilles Tatius chose to follow Chariton, Xenophon, the author of *Metiochus and Parthenope*, and doubtless other early 'ideal' novelists unknown to us, and to write his eight-book *Leucippe and Clitophon*. Achilles Tatius and his local bookseller might well have known a quite different selection of recently published Greek literature and consequently have formed a different perspective. It must be admitted that nothing in what we know prepares us for what recent scholarship has brought out in *Leucippe and Clitophon* – sophisticated handling of erotic and other commonplaces, occasional play with the game of fiction and persistent inversion of Platonic dialogue.[38] Apparently writing

---

34 Note, however, his careful telling of the story of Stratonicea's infatuation with Antiochus, *On Syria* 308–28, already narrated in Plutarch, *Demetrius* 38 and later in Lucian, *On the Syrian Goddess* 17–18, cf. Lightfoot (2003) *ad loc.* and Romani in Stramaglia (2000) 271–81.

35 For the Greek poetry of this period see Bowie (1989) and (1990). On Mesomedes see Whitmarsh (2004). That Mesomedes was not insensitive to the possibilities of erotic writing is clear from his poem on a sponge (no. 9 Heitsch).

36 Text in *FGrH* 257; Giannini (1966).   37 Cf. Photius, *Library* codex 175.

38 Most (1989); Bartsch (1989); Goldhill (1995); Morales (2004); also forthcoming work by Ian Repath.

in a much more active Greek literary world than that of Chariton, Achilles very probably turned down a wider range of literary opportunities than his predecessor, and may have done so because in Roman Egypt, at least, he saw that the novel had come to stay. Not that he put all his eggs in one basket. He is one of only two of our novelists to whom ancient evidence (in each case the *Suda*) ascribes other works:[39] a work entitled *Etymologies*, a *Miscellaneous History* and a work *On the Sphere* which might possibly be identical with a surviving commentary on Aratus ascribed to an Achilles.[40] These works (if correctly assigned to Achilles Tatius) suggest a mind with several strands of interest – scientific and philological – and make it easier to understand why *Leucippe and Clitophon* so often presents to its readers 'scientific' digressions whose contributions to the narrative are *prima facie* unsatisfying. But it is also relevant to their interpretation how much 'Miscellaneous history' was being written, as we have seen, in diverse literary forms. So too the discussion of the respective advantages of homoerotic and heterosexual sexual activity (2.35–8) might have particular appeal for readers in times that witnessed or recalled Hadrian's infatuation with Antinous. Achilles' extensive scene-setting in Egypt and his glittering *ecphrasis* (description) of Alexandria can also be seen to fit respectively into a widespread Hellenic interest in things and creatures Egyptian, going back to Hecataeus and Herodotus and tapped in a long speech (*Oration* 36) composed c. 147–9 CE by the sophist Aelius Aristides, and into one of the basic tasks assigned young men during their rhetorical training, the 'praise of a city'.

It might be argued tentatively, then, both that Achilles Tatius' novel shows some responses to the literary tendencies of the decades since Chariton, and (less confidently) that the non-novelistic literature of that period might have been different had it not been for the diffusion of Chariton's novel.

160–220 CE

What of our next novel, Iamblichus' *Babylonian Affairs*? Its author's claim to have predicted the successful outcome of Rome's war against Parthia (161–5 CE), reinforced by his story that he had been tutored by a captive in the earlier Parthian war of Trajan (114–17 CE) not only gives us an unusually secure date (surely shortly after 165 CE) but also shows that its author was quick to exploit an interest in the world Rome claimed to have conquered (just as Lucian, *On how to write History* 2, assures us that many historians jumped onto the bandwagon of writing up the war itself). In

---

39 The other is Xenophon, to whom the *Suda* (under 'Xenophon of Ephesus'), perhaps conflating two different writers, gives a work *On the city of Ephesus*.
40 For the problem see Stramaglia (2000) 10–11.

other respects too the *Babylonian Affairs* seem to move closer to history and mythography. Iamblichus' narrative ran to at least sixteen books,[41] so its bulk alone might have helped its ambiguous title to lead a reader or purchaser to expect a historical rather than novelistic work. The names of some of its chief characters – Euphrates, Tigris and Mesopotamia[42] – might also induce a reader brought up on poetic *Origins* and on local prose historiography (which seems to have flourished in the second century CE)[43] to see the *Babylonian Affairs* as an exploration of mythical traditions about the Euphrates valley – and indeed the writer claimed to draw his material from indigenous sources.[44] The work seems also (to judge from Photius' summary) to have had a higher proportion of bizarre and even miraculous events than the three preceding ideal novels; but that this component is unlikely to be a function of the time of writing (though we might note Lucian's near contemporary use of such material in his *Lovers of Lies*) is clear from a comparable mixture in Antonius Diogenes' *Wonders beyond Thule*, written at least two generations earlier.[45]

The delayed entry of Lucian to this plot should not be taken as a low evaluation of his importance. Of all Greek authors of the first and second centuries CE he shows most signs of writing in a literary environment where prose fiction was a significant player. Fictionality of various sorts and on differing scales can be found in almost all parts of Lucian's *oeuvre* – produced between the 150s and early 180s CE, although few works can be precisely dated. Many pieces need owe little to the now established genre of extended prose fiction: for example, the *Dialogues of the Gods* are miniature transpositions from epic, the *Dialogues of Courtesans* from New Comedy and from the *bons mots* of the Hellenistic iambic poet Machon; the fictionality of the *Nigrinus* reworks that of Platonic dialogue, that of the *Dream* owes much to Plato's *Apology*. But *Toxaris*, with its parallel Greek and Scythian tales of friendship, and the tall stories in his *Lovers of Lies* share the novels' exploitation of exotic locations. Moreover, as has been recently argued, *Toxaris* offers its readers a coded commentary on the novels so that

41 So Photius, *Library* codex 94: the *Suda* entry, more probably corrupt, gives thirty-nine books.
42 Photius, *Library* codex 94, 75a40–3 etc.
43 See cursorily Bowie (1970) 19–22. The dates of some authors (e.g. Telephus of Pergamum) remain uncertain, as does the identity of the author of *On the City of Ephesus*, perhaps (see n. 39) confused by the *Suda* with Xenophon of Ephesus. See also Strubbe (1984–6).
44 Cf. the *scholion* in manuscript A (Venice, Bibl. Naz. Marciana, gr. 450) on Photius, *Library* codex 94, printed at Habrich (1960) 2 and translated at Stephens and Winkler (1995) 181, which seems, like Photius' summary, to have been written by somebody with access to a full text of Iamblichus.
45 For a dating of Antonius Diogenes in or around the 90s CE see Stramaglia (1999), Bowie (2002). A case for an even earlier date, c. 60 CE, is made in Bowie (2007).

it becomes not merely comic fantasy, moralistic rhetoric or something inde-finable in between, but also a practical exposition of the theory of reading and writing fiction.[46] Other aspects of the reading and writing of fiction are explored in Lucian's *True Story*, and even if the most important targets of his parody are the classical authors Homer, Ctesias and Herodotus, with some admixture of the Hellenistic Iambulus, Photius may have been right to assert a degree of dependence on Antonius Diogenes' *Wonders beyond Thule*.[47] More imponderably, the narrator in Lucian's *On the Syrian Goddess* expounds to Greek readers an exotic cult of the sort that sometimes catches novelists' eyes in a tone and voice that is less plausibly interpreted as that of a real, pious pilgrim than that of a fictive quasi-Herodotean narrator and ironic parodist.[48]

That Lucian should have read and reacted to the ideal novels and expected his own readers to appreciate his engagement with their codes of fiction is all the more intelligible if, as seems likely, he was also the author of a version of the *Ass* story. There seem to have been at least three Greek versions of the story that Apuleius took up and ran with in his Latin *Metamorphoses*: a work in some thirty pages (fifty-six chapters) transmitted with other works of Lucian in Byzantine manuscripts in which the narrating 'I' claims to be Lucius of Patrae; a work summarised by Photius (*Library* codex 129) which he supposed to be written *by* a Lucius of Patrae; and a prosimetric version different in at least some details, a papyrus fragment of which has recently been published.[49] The Greek of the first of these is of a lower register than found elsewhere in the Lucianic corpus, and on present evidence it seems most likely (as argued by Perry) that the version summarised by Photius is to be credited to Lucian. If that is so, or indeed if any one of the versions is by Lucian, then we find him both reacting in some writing, above all the *Toxaris*, to prose fiction which includes the ideal novels, and deciding to make a contribution of his own to those other strands of prose fiction which may in different ways be represented by Antonius Diogenes and by the papyrus fragments of the Iolaus story and of Lollianus' *Phoenician Affairs*.

Lucian is not the only late second-century Greek writer who shows some interaction with the novels. The decades between Iamblichus and Longus – it is uncertain how many these were, but one guess would put Longus between 190 and 220 CE – are ones from which fewer works have survived than from the previous half-century,[50] but one of the four, Pausanias' *Tour of Greece*, can be claimed to have influenced Longus and perhaps to show novelistic

---

46 Ní Mheallaigh (2005) 115.   47 *Contra* Morgan (1985).
48 On the problem cf. Lightfoot (2003) 161–221.   49 *P. Oxy.* 4762; cf. below, p. 37.
50 Again I omit declamations and technical works (e.g. Hermogenes, *On ideas* of c. 184 CE, or the lexica of Phrynichus and the *Word-book* of Pollux, also chiefly works of the 180s).

influence and another, Philostratus' *Heroicus*, to have been influenced by the novels.[51] A fifth work, the collection of letters purporting to be by the Attic orator Aeschines, might also belong in this period, and likewise has a novelistic feature.

Pausanias' composition of his work in fact seems to straddle the point at which Iamblichus is likely to have been writing (c. 165–70 CE) with book 1 of the *Tour of Greece* composed perhaps as early as the early 160s CE, and book 10 as late as the late 170s.[52] An interest in local origins, noted above as a feature shared by Iamblichus and regional Greek historians, is also of course prominent in Pausanias. Moreover at least two of these prompt him to tell a brief erotic tale in explanation of a religious custom – the story of Comaetho and Melanippus (7.19.1–5) – or of a toponym – that told shortly after, of Callirhoe and Coresus (7.21.1–5).[53] Like the stories told by Nicolaus and Strabo (see above with nn. 13–14) these end with the death of one or both lovers. But Pausanias rounds off that of Comaetho and Melanippus with a vehement insistence on the power of Eros: while stating that the annual sacrifice of a boy and a girl to Artemis Laphria ordered by Delphi was pitiable, Pausanias insists that he does not see the sacrifice of the furtive lovers Comaetho and Melanippus themselves as a disaster:

> as for those young men and maidens who because of Melanippus and Comaetho died in honour of the goddess, although they had done nothing, their fate and that of their families was most pitiable. But I reckon that of Melanippus and Comaitho outside disaster, for the only thing that for a human being is of equal value to life is for someone who has fallen in love to attain its object. (7.19.5)

This uncompromising claim for the value of attaining the object of desire (*erōs*) sets Pausanias apart from earlier writers in whom similar *Novellen* have been noted.[54] It may also be relevant that only in book 7 of Pausanias, on Achaea, do we find such erotic *Novellen*, together with a brief reference to the tomb of Radine and Leontichus (whose story was told in full, but without naming its hero, by Strabo 8.3.10, see above with n. 14) at 7.5.13:

---

51 The other two works are Aristides' *Sacred Tales* and Athenaeus' *Sophists at Dinner*. I take Aristides' preoccupation with his salvation and his readiness to seek and accept divine advice, not least through dreams, to be features that his *Sacred Tales* share with the general *mentalité* of his age rather than their showing any link with the use of broadly similar motifs by novelists. Although we have particular testimony to an interest in dream-interpretation in the later second and early third century both in the *How to interpret Dreams* of Artemidorus and in their important place in the first historical work of Cassius Dio, sadly lost, on the rise to power of Septimius Severus, this is an on-going preoccupation throughout the ancient world and there is little to suggest particular cross-fertilisation with the novels.

52 See Bowie (2001a).

53 For discussion and further bibliography see Stramaglia (2000) 129–133 and 81–4.

54 Cf. above p. 20 with nn. 12–17.

some have suspected that for his account of Achaea Pausanias has drawn on a source with greater interest in *erotica* than those used for other books,[55] but the extent of Pausanias' mechanical dependence on his sources now seems to be less than that judged by older scholarship. Wherever he got the stories, his asseveration about desire reveals a 'cultivated man' (*pepaideumenos*) responsive to the values esteemed in the ideal novels, and perhaps one who had recently been reading one or more such books.

As for Athenaeus' *Sophists at Dinner*, probably written c. 193 CE,[56] the absence of any direct reference to Greek novels is more likely to be due to the absence of any recondite material these might have yielded on things and texts sympotic or metasympotic than to their generic unpretentiousness or recent composition: after all, Athenaeus cited the Hadrianic poet Pancrates – though Pancrates could be seen as an exception, being as he was from Naucratis, and admittedly composing some species of a higher genre, epic.[57] But Athenaeus does cite at least one striking *Novelle*, the story of Zariadres and Odatis, which shares more features with the ideal romances than do most *Novellen*.[58] Zariadres and Odatis are not only of high birth (he a king, she a princess) and outstanding beauty; after falling in love not by meeting but by dreaming of each other Zariadres abducts Odatis just when, at a specially convened symposium (from which Zariadres is of course absent) her father has told her to marry whomever she chooses. It seems that the couple lived happily ever after, and so renowned was their *erōs* in Asia that it figured in public and private painting and parents named their daughters Odatis. Athenaeus introduces the story, which he found in the Alexander-historian Chares of Mytilene, to support the claim that sometimes people fall in love with a person they know only by reputation. To some extent, perhaps, his choice of this excerpt reflects his awareness of contemporary interest in loveplots with happy endings, but since his source is a historian of the late fourth century BCE that argument cannot be pressed.

The strongest case can be made for Philostratus' *On Heroes* (*Heroicus*) a work whose bearing upon the development of Greek prose fiction and on religious ideas of the period has justly begun to attract much recent attention.[59] Of course it offers a very different brand of fiction from that of the

---

55 Already Kalkmann (1886) 132–3. For 7.19.1–5 Reinach (1925) 138 suggested the *Achaean History* of the Hellenistic poet Rhianus of Bene. For further bibliography see Dorati in Stramaglia (2000) 132.

56 As argued by Zecchini (1989).

57 For the poem of Pancrates see Bowie (1990) and (2001b).

58 Athenaeus, *Sophists at Dinner* 13.375 = Chares of Mytilene *FGrH* 125 F 5; for other uses of Chares by Athenaeus cf. esp. 12.538a–539b = F2, on the mass cross-cultural wedding at Susa, and Zecchini (1989) 60–8.

59 Editions: de Lannoy (1977); Maclean and Aitken (2001); Rossi (1997); Beschorner (1999); Grossardt (2006). Discussions: Bowie (1970) 30, (1994); Aitken and Maclean (2004).

ideal novels. It is a dialogue between a vintner in the Thracian Cherson-nese and a Phoenician sailor delayed by winds (neither is named); although slightly longer than *Daphnis and Chloe*, it is not divided into books; its psy-chological progression is not to do with desire (*erōs*) but with belief – the vintner's belief in the continued if ghostly existence of the heroes who fell in the Trojan War, to which he ultimately converts the Phoenician. Over-all, then, it is a work more reminiscent of Dio's *Euboean oration* than of the novels. But within it is a panel that strongly recalls them. The love of Achilles and Helen on the White Island[60] started not when they saw each other (since Helen was in Egypt while Achilles fought at Troy) but on the basis of what they heard about each other's beauty. Philostratus' account picks up the novelistic theme of passion between the most handsome youth and the most beautiful young woman and resolves the doubts that must have struck some readers of ideal novels about what happened after the end: *did* the couple live happily ever after (as claimed in Xenophon 5.15 and Longus 4.39.1)? What happened when they grew old? Since Achilles and Helen are divinised or divine they, at least, never grow old, but perpetually sing of their mutual desire (*erōs*).[61]

So three authors of the period 170–220 CE, Pausanias, Athenaeus and Philostratus arguably make some of their choices in a way they would not have done in a world without novels. What of the choice made by the nov-elist Longus? On the one hand (as I have argued for Achilles Tatius and Iamblichus) his decision to compose a novel might reflect a sense that the genre was well established. On the other hand his decision to fuse an 'ideal' novel and Theocritean pastoral poetry (with a dash of Hellenistic pastoral epigram) could be argued with equal plausibility to reflect a sense that the genre was tired and needed to take a new direction, or that it was so vigorous that even drastic modification could be applied without endangering its sur-vival. In either case the direction in which he decided to go can only in part be explained by the Greek literary climate of his time. Rural scenarios are also chosen by Aelian for his *Rustic Epistles* but a precise date for these is want-ing – around the 220s or 230s CE would fit what we know from Philostratus of Aelian's career – as it is for Longus, so it is unclear which writer made the first move (and even less clear is the relative chronology of Alciphron and Aelian). The exploitation of Theocritus is not matched by any other evidence that he was especially in fashion in this period (and the commen-tary activity of Munatius of Tralles seems to be rather earlier). The interest in religion and local cults (in Longus' case ostentatiously rural, not urban cults) is indeed comparable to what we find in Pausanias and Philostratus'

60 Philostratus, *On Heroes* 54. 61 Ibid. 54.12.

Heroicus, but it is also well documented in earlier imperial Greek literature, notably in Plutarch's presentation of Delphi in the late first and early second centuries.[62] All in all, it is very difficult to pin down elements in Longus that can be confidently explained as reactions to contemporary literary trends.

220–270 CE

The artificiality of my periodisation (in this case guided by a supposed date for Longus) becomes even more blatant for this last section. On the one hand the year 220 CE bisects the important literary career of Philostratus. On the other, the place of a single work, Heliodorus' *Charicleia and Theagenes*, remains to be assessed, yet on its date there is as yet no consensus, and one view would put it a century later than 270 CE. Three different stories will be offered in the awareness that only one (if that) can be true.

(a) Heliodorus of Emesa (as the end of *Charicleia and Theagenes* claims its author to be) may be writing about the same time as Philostratus composed his later works, the 220s and 230s CE. His Ethiopian council of Gymnosophists and details of his description of the phoenix[63] seem to draw upon Philostratus' eight-book work on Apollonius of Tyana, and his magisterial plot-creator and internal narrator Calasiris may also owe something to Philostratus' Apollonius. The hymn to Thetis sung by the Thessalian religious delegation to Delphi rings out like a clever upstaging of a closely similar hymn to Achilles in Philostratus' work of c. 214 CE, *On Heroes*.[64] In some details, then, Heliodorus seems to react to the *oeuvre* of a major literary figure of the period 200–40 CE. His presentation of religion also shares the seriousness of Philostratus' Apollonius, and although his plot is built around the mutual attraction of two young people, Charicleia and Theagenes, their relationship is soon moved onto a spiritual plane, and in *Charicleia and Theagenes* physical sexuality characterises 'bad' minor characters, such as the promiscuous young Thisbe and the older women Demaenete and Arsace, or the men who

---

62 Such interests probably also figured in Arrian's history of his own part of western Asia Minor, his *Bithyni(a)ca*, which mentioned his priesthood of Demeter and Kore, Photius, *Library* codex 93, 73a37 = *FGrH* 156 T 4 (a).

63 The academy of Gymnosophists in Philostratus, *Apollonius* 6.6 seems to be taken over by Heliodorus (2.31.1 etc) for Ethiopian Gymnosophists who speak Greek (9.25.3) and act as a council for king Hydaspes (10.2.1 etc). The phoenix's attribution to India *or* Ethiopia (6.3.3) may reflect its claim for India at Philostratus, *Apollonius* 3.49 (an alternative tradition already known to Lucian, *Peregrinus* 28) combined with its allocation to Ethiopia at Achilles Tatius 3.25 and Alexander of Aphrodisias, *On Fate* 28, p. 199.17 Bruns = *SVF* III p. 165 no. 658. The apotropaic qualities of the magical stone called *pantarbē* (8.9–11) may also be based on the *Apollonius* 3.46.

64 Bowie (1989a).

lust after Charicleia. There can be little doubt that Heliodorus knows some earlier novels, since he repeatedly plays with and upstages their conventions; and direct knowledge of Achilles Tatius and of Longus' *Daphnis and Chloe* has been claimed.[65] But among the many ways in which he reworks the novelistic tradition is a shift towards a more spiritual texture – something that might be seen as showing the influence of the *Apollonius*, if *Charicleia and Theagenes* does indeed belong around 240 CE.

(b) An alternative chronology has set the writing of *Charicleia and Theagenes* around 270–5 CE.[66] Our knowledge of literary activity in that period is sketchier than for the earlier third century, but nothing that we know can be construed as a text to which Heliodorus seems to be responding. Sophistic rhetoric of course continued to be a dominant cultural form, but nothing we know of Nicagoras (himself proud to be a descendant of Plutarch and Sextus of Chaeronea)[67] or read in Menander Rhetor differs from earlier recipes in a way that might be used to explain features of Heliodorus' unusual style. Nor is there any obvious point of contact with the (largely lost) histories of the Athenian P. Herennius Dexippus.[68] Much more neo-Platonic writing was available to be read by the later third century, some of it from Heliodorus' own part of the Greek world, for example, the work of Iamblichus. That would indeed chime with the neo-Platonic ideas that have been observed in Heliodorus, but is not strictly a *literary* influence, and it is anyway clear that neo-Platonic thought was already being disseminated by the 230s and 240s CE.

(c) An influential body of scholarly opinion now sets *Charicleia and Theagenes* in the later fourth century, based partly on the argument that Heliodorus' account of the siege of Syene (9.3–8) draws significantly from Julian's account of the siege of Nisibis in his *First* and *Third Orations* (of c. 353 CE).[69] As in the case of the later third-century dating, it is hard to see to what in contemporary Greek literature Heliodorus might be reacting, though our knowledge of this Greek literary scene is rather better. Neither Julian's own speeches, even if one or two suggested details for the siege of Syene, nor his intense and satirical *Caesars* or *Beard-hater* seem likely stimuli, unless in the limited sense that they might have encouraged Heliodorus to take Hellenic paganism seriously and totally to ignore Christianity. That too might have been the consequence if Heliodorus had spent time reading speeches or letters of Libanius, but despite the huge volume of Libanius'

---

65 Achilles Tatius: Szepessy (1978); Longus: Bowie (1995).
66 Rohde (1914) 496–7, arguing from the emperor Aurelian's promotion of the cult of Sol/Helios.
67 *Syll.*³ 845, Puech (2002) no. 180, 357–360.   68 *FGrH* 100, cf. Millar (1969).
69 Good statements of the arguments in Bowersock (1994); Morgan (2003a) 418–19.

surviving works nothing, so far as I know, has been spotted that might be linked to anything in *Charicleia and Theagenes*. Not surprisingly, perhaps, the writing that stands closest to that of Heliodorus is Christian, whether the discourses of Cappadocian fathers on the merits of virtue and chastity, martyr acts with tortures and burnings, or saints' lives like the influential Athanasian life of St Antony. It is possible, but in my view unlikely, that such texts made an impression on Heliodorus, but if so he has muffled their impact. His response to Homer, Herodotus and to Attic drama (both tragedy and comedy) is much clearer than any reaction to such contemporary writing.

Moreover some writers from the Greek-speaking world were now choosing Latin as their medium – Claudian and Ammianus Marcellinus – and it seems that the Latin west was a more lively literary forum: among the works it generated were two with novelistic links, the occasionally fraudulent, always mischievous *Augustan History* and a Latin translation of Philostratus' *Apollonius*. It would be entertaining to suppose, with Bowersock, that the former drew inspiration for its description of the triumph of Aurelian in 274 CE from Heliodorus' account of Blemmyes and Seres in Hydaspes' army when he defeated the Persians (9.17) and of Blemmyes, Seres and Auxumitae among the embassies to the victor (10.26–7), with a giraffe among their gifts (10.27). But neither the giraffe nor these exotic nations are unique to the texts in question.[70]

Whichever of the dates proves correct, then, it seems that Heliodorus' work made no impact on other Greek writing that we can now discern. Only if Heliodorus was writing shortly after Philostratus' *Apollonius* can we claim some reaction to contemporary Greek literature (which is not in itself, of course, an argument in favour of this date). Moreover it is the reaction to a single work of a single author. If such a Heliodorus was also writing shortly after the publication of the contemporary history of Herodian or the massive (eighty-book) Roman history of Cassius Dio, he either did not read these works or had almost no use in his novel for what he read.[71]

It has been possible to suggest some respects in which Greek novels show affinity with some other Greek writing of their time or an awareness of the tastes that that writing implies. That such affinities are clearest for writers of the period c. 120–240 CE, Achilles Tatius, Iamblichus, Longus and (perhaps) Heliodorus, the period from which a much higher volume of Greek literature survives, should be a ground for caution. I have suggested that Chariton was partly responding to a world in which Greek literary activity was more

70 Bowersock (1994) 149–60.
71 A single exception might be his account of Phoenician dancing 'Assyrian style' at 4.17.1 which is strikingly similar to Herodian's unsympathetic account of Elagabalus' performances when sacrificing, 5.38, cf. again 5.5.9, 6.1, 7.4, 7.6.

constricted: but perhaps the constriction is simply in our own knowledge. Equally if Heliodorus *were* writing c. 270 or c. 370 a fuller understanding of Greek pagan literature of the time *might* allow us to see affinities that currently elude us.

As to influence on other writing, the case is strongest for the impact of novels upon Lucian and Philostratus. The former has enjoyed a high reputation, albeit not principally for his narrative fictions, since the renaissance, and the latter's high standing in the renaissance is now beginning to be regained. If by dreadful misfortune the single manuscript containing Chariton and Xenophon had perished it is perhaps comforting to think that the presence of the novel in the literature of the second sophistic would not have been charted only by the works of Achilles Tatius, Longus and Heliodorus, but also by Lucian, Pausanias and Philostratus.

Latin novels

The trajectory of Latin literature and its relation to the writing and reading of Latin novels is very different from what we have seen in the Greek world. In the first century BCE Romans writing in Latin had produced a vast quantity of literature, much of it of very high quality, spread across the established Greek genres – in prose, oratory, historiography and epistolography; in verse, epic, tragedy, didactic, pastoral and lyric – and even creating new genres, as satire certainly was, and both love elegy and the verse epistle arguably were. Both as students and as adult readers of Latin literature Romans of the two succeeding centuries knew and admired a body of literature whose writers had almost all become classics in their own lifetime. Much of the Latin literature of the first and second centuries CE is a reaction to this corpus of classics: for an aspiring writer there were many genres whose rules and boundaries he could attempt to tweak, and for readers there were few tastes not catered for. Most significantly, perhaps, the world of quasi-historical fiction inhabited by Metiochus and Parthenope and by the characters of Chariton and Xenophon was much exploited in hexameter poetry, leaving less scope or demand for the creation of such a world by prose. Admittedly the majority of hexameter epic still handled traditional subjects from Greek mythology, but alongside this there was a genre of historical epic, created by Ennius early in the development of Latin literature in the second century BCE, and exploited by at least two first-century CE poets, Lucan and Silius Italicus.

Against this background it is perhaps not surprising that not simply were only two works of prose fiction in some way related to Greek novels composed but, as far as we can tell, they stood close to just one end of the

Greek spectrum, the picaresque narrative represented for us by fragments of Lollianus, the Iolaus-story and our Greek versions of the *Ass*-story. The two are Petronius' *Satyrica* and the *Metamorphoses* or *Golden Ass* of Apuleius: the inset tale of *Cupid and Psyche* in Apuleius' *Metamorphoses* is the nearest Latin fiction gets to the Greek ideal romance. Both works are hard to evaluate: they are not similar enough to each other to be seen as representatives of one and the same tradition – nor does Apuleius signal Petronius' *Satyrica* as a forebear – and the absence of any other surviving literary production by Petronius and the fact that Apuleius' *Metamorphoses* are in many ways different from his other writings make it hazardous even to conjecture what the two authors' reasons for composing these works might have been.

Their historical and cultural contexts are certainly diverse. Petronius is almost certainly the arbiter of elegance known from Tacitus' account of Nero's reign, a man who was forced to commit suicide at Cumae in the year 66 CE.[72] The previous decade had seen an efflorescence of Latin writing, some at least a response to the artistic tastes of the new and (for a time) young emperor Nero. Alongside Seneca, whose later writings are Neronian – both verse tragedies and prose philosophical treatises and letters – the hexameters of Persius, Lucan and Calpurnius Siculus covered satire, epic and pastoral respectively. The elder Pliny alone was prolific in prose. Why Petronius wrote at all, then, may be partly explained by the over-heated climate of scribbling among the Neronian elite in Rome; and why he chose to write the *Satyrica* may be explained (again partly) by the fact that many established genres were already bespoke. What drew him to the extraordinary prosimetric novel of which less than one-fifth survives hangs on the unresolved question of whether it is a masterpiece of generic bricolage or whether he was drawing on some Greek original.[73]

In either case some elements parody Greek literature – the south Italian wanderings of Encolpius and Giton are ultimately Odyssean, their homosexual affair seems to parody the idealised heterosexual teen-couple of the very recently invented and perhaps (by the early 60s) fashionable Greek novels. Other elements equally clearly exploit knowledge of Latin literature: the prosimetric form has an antecedent in Varro's satires, the comic banquet and legacy-hunters in Latin verse satire, and the poetic sequence of the *Sack of Troy* pokes fun at the *senarii* (iambic verses) of Senecan tragedy just as the *Civil War* does at some contemporary poem on that subject, most probably Lucan's. Alongside parody of literature in Greek and Latin goes biting

---

72 Tacitus, *Annals* 16.18–19, cf. *PIR*² P 294.
73 For the latter view, cf. e.g. Jensson (2004); for the former e.g. Bowie (2007).

satire – in *Dinner at Trimalchio's* satire of the ambitions and fractured culture of freedmen and of others much lower in society than Petronius and
most presumed readers, and, throughout, satire of the demeaning effects of
the interplay of the human pursuit of sex, money and power. Little of this
can be explained as a response to the state of Roman society and Latin literature in the first decade of Nero's reign: if anything is to explain why the
inventive brilliance of a Latin writer was catalysed in this way at that particular time it is surely the emergence of novelistic forms in the Greek world,
whether Petronius evolved parody of the ideal novel himself or whether he
encountered it already embedded in a Greek picaresque narrative.

Greek literature also makes a more important contribution to the explanation of Apuleius' writing the *Metamorphoses* than the development of Latin
literature. In the century following the composition of the *Satyrica* we know
of no Latin writer whom it provoked to novelistic writing of any sort. Traditional Roman prose genres of oratory, historiography and epistolography
continued to attract writers and readers, and to established poetic genres of
lyric and of mythological and historical epic Martial added books of satirical
epigram – most written under Domitian – while Juvenal's rhetoric, spanning
the reigns of Trajan and Hadrian, ratched up satirical hexameters to a new
level of intensity. To judge from surviving works and our few testimonia
the reigns of Pius (138–61 CE) and Marcus (161–80 CE) saw contraction or
lassitude: historiography is represented by epigonic epitomes – Florus and
Granius Licinianus – though there will have been Latin, as there were Greek,
historians of Verus' Parthian Wars, and indeed one such was contemplated
by Fronto, whose *Letters* are among the few major survivals from the principate of Pius.

Among these survivals must be counted the earlier works of the Latin
sophist Platonic philosopher Apuleius. If we accept the view that the *Metamorphoses* belongs late in his career, perhaps around 180 CE, it can be seen
as the work of a writer who had already played with several established
genres – epideictic and court rhetoric, Latin versions of Greek philosophical treatises, some technical and miscellanistic writing – and had turned to
the adaptation of another Greek genre at least partly to display his literary range and virtuosity, making this choice in a literary ambience where,
epideictic rhetoric apart, there was little literature of the imagination, perhaps no longer even mythological epic. Whatever the precise identity of
the Greek *Ass*-story Apuleius used,[74] he produced a very Roman work
of Latin literature whose blending of Latin literary traditions (such as the

---

74 See Mason (1978), (1999): the problem has been further complicated by the publication of
a prosimetric fragment of a Greek *ass*-story that is not from the Lucianic *Ass* and seems not
to fit the *Metamorphoses* summarised by Photius, *P. Oxy* 4762. Cf. above, p. 28.

Aeneid and Roman Comedy)[75] with Greek (the *Ass*-narrative and versions of Milesian tales) gives the same impression of a much-Romanised Greece as the nearly contemporary *Attic Nights* of Aulus Gellius. With *Attic Nights* the *Metamorphoses* also share a privileging of interesting detail and atmospheric incident over order and structure and a keenness to revive archaic Latin usage (admittedly the culmination of a development discernible since Hadrian).

In some ways, then, the *Metamorphoses* responds to the state of Latin literature in its time. But like the *Satyrica* it is a response that could hardly have been predicted, and the work seems to have been similarly unchallenged by emulators or successors.[76] Moreover it is likewise hard to discern any impact on what we know of the course of Latin literature in the two following centuries, or indeed any awareness of Apuleius' work before his compatriot Augustine of Hippo. Neither Petronius nor Apuleius can claim to have influenced another major work in Latin literature in the way that the Greek novel influenced Philostratus' *Apollonius*.

Further reading

A number of works offer contextualising introductions to the Greek and Roman novels. Hägg (1983) and Holzberg (1995) are learned, although the hypothesis of 'bourgeois' readership no longer commands wide support. Good multi-authored collections include Morgan and Stoneman (1994), Hofmann (1999b), and especially Schmeling (2003b). Other useful collections include Tatum (1994), Panayotakis *et al.* (2003); Pecere and Stramaglia (1996) explore popular literature in the period. Classic essays on the novels can also be consulted in Swain (1999) and Harrison (1999), who provide helpful literature surveys – for which see also Bowie and Harrison (1994), Morgan (1998). Important older scholarship (in German, English, Italian and Latin) can be accessed in Gärtner (1984). For more general surveys of imperial literature, see Bowersock (1969), Bowie (1970), Reardon (1971), Easterling and Knox (1985) part 4: 82–197, Swain (1996), Lightfoot (2000), Whitmarsh (2001a) and (2005b). Steinmetz (1982) remains a useful study of second-century Latin literature.

75 See now May (2006).
76 It is quite unclear whether another work of Apuleius entitled *Hermagoras* was also a novel.

3

HELEN MORALES

The history of sexuality

Interest in the history of sexuality, perhaps more than any other factor, has defined the genre of the ancient novel as we now know it. As the focus in scholarship gradually shifted, during the last few decades of the twentieth century, from women's studies to the study of gender and sexuality, the ancient novels, with their flamboyant attention to the erotic, appealed to the *Zeitgeist*. This led to their greater exposure, largely through the work of the philosopher and cultural historian Michel Foucault, and subsequent discussions.[1] A less positive outcome has been to privilege the 'erotic' novels over other works of imperial prose fiction, and thus to narrow our conception of the genre. Had biography or travel narrative driven the agenda as hard as the history of sexuality has (and is doing), what we commonly understand as 'the ancient novel' might look rather different.[2]

If an interest in the history of sexuality has directed how the ancient novels have been conceived as a genre, then attitudes towards sexuality have influenced the treatment of individual works on an even more fundamental level. They have determined how the novels are transmitted: how the physical texts of the novels reach their readers. Scribes, editors, and translators through the ages have amended and athetised the texts according to their moral beliefs. A revised version of the earliest English translation of Petronius' *Satyrica* in the Victorian era rewrote the 'Pergamene boy' scene of same-sex seduction as the (reassuringly heterosexual) 'Pergamene girl'.[3] The seventeenth-century French translation of *Leucippe and Clitophon* by A. Rémy is not untypical.[4] Rémy hacks out the 'homosexual' scenes and describes the marriage of hero and heroine in great detail (something Achilles Tatius did not do). In his preface 'To the Reader', he justifies the changes as rectifying a corrupted text

---

1 See especially Konstan (1994); Goldhill (1995); Swain (1996) 118–31; Balot (1998).
2 On travel see Romm, this volume.
3 Wilson *et al.* (1708). The original, published in 1694, had rendered the pederastic scenes with lavish enjoyment.
4 Rémy (1625). On this and many other translations and editions see Plazenet (1997) 31–158.

and as aiming to return to the original state of the novel. Sexual criticism masquerades as textual criticism.

The most important example of this, and the one with the greatest impact on how we read the novel today, is the treatment of one particular sexually explicit description in Apuleius' *Metamorphoses*. This short passage, which relates how the *matrona* washed Lucius the ass's filthy genitalia with perfumes and describes the erection it provokes, is excised from most modern editions, and is referred to as the *spurcum additamentum*, the 'dirty addition', hardly a morally neutral name.[5] The description reads as if designed to follow on from an account of the *matrona* stripping off her clothes and anointing her body and that of the ass with balsam oil, and to lead into a description of the woman engaging the ass in sexual intercourse (the whole episode at 10.20–2). The passage has come down to us in the margin of one of the manuscripts of the *Metamorphoses* and whether or not it should be read as an integral part of the novel, or a fragment of another *Ass*-story, or a mediaeval interpolation, is a matter of debate. There are many considerations to take into account when debating the authenticity of the *spurcum additamentum*, but a prominent one is a concern about decency, from Fraenkel who contends that it must have been the work of an anonymous scribe, who 'pursued his queer sport' with an 'unappetising text', to Finkelpearl who wants to preserve the episode as a romantic one: 'the most touching and tender scene between members of the opposite sex'.[6] The current orthodoxy, with only a couple of detractors, is that it should be relegated to the *apparatus criticus* of an edition. In fact, anyone wishing to read the *Metamorphoses* in translation in English will not be able at the time of writing to find one in print that renders the whole episode intact.[7] This despite the fact that, when considered in the full contexts of the 'matron' scene and novel as whole, and not separately, there are compelling reasons not to omit it.[8] As Winkler observes – in language which fully recognises the inextricability of sexuality and textuality – critics who cut the episode 'supplement the sense of the text to fit an imposed moral pattern . . . and at the same time they castrate the text at its most graphic moment'.[9]

Descriptions of sex generate distinctive reading practices. If there is a history of scrutinising sexual episodes in isolation from their narratives in order to excise them, there is a concomitant tradition of focusing upon sexual

---

5 For text and discussion see Zimmerman (2000) appendix 2, with the reservations of Lytle (2003).
6 Fraenkel (1953) 153; Finkelpearl (1998) 155.
7 It is not even in a note in Hanson's Loeb edition of 1989.
8 Most recently and cogently argued in Lytle (2003). See also Pennisi (1970) and Winkler (1985) 192–3.
9 Winkler (1985) 193.

episodes in isolation from their narratives in order better to enjoy them. Both involve raiding, not reading. Claude Simon's picture, in his novel *Histoire*, of schoolboys sniggering over the dirty bits in Apuleius could serve as an emblem for many a reader's engagement with the novels.[10] A history of sexuality and the ancient novel, especially, but by no means exclusively, with Petronius and Apuleius, intersects with a history of pornography.

This is not, however, as we shall see, the aspect of the novels that interested Michel Foucault in *The Care of the Self*, the third volume of his *History of Sexuality*. Foucault's work has been so influential that it forms a necessary point of engagement for any discussion of the history of sexuality and the ancient novel. He makes two major propositions about the 'romances' of the imperial period. First (arguing chiefly from Chariton, Achilles Tatius and Heliodorus), he suggests that the literature of the period celebrates a ' "heterosexual" relation'[11] that 'organises itself around the symmetrical and reciprocal relationship of a man and a woman, around the high value attributed to virginity, and around the complete union in which it finds perfection',[12] that is, marriage. Second, that the 'reflection on the love of boys' during this time 'manifests its sterility'.[13] Pederasty, while still undoubtedly practised, was not privileged in the way it was in classical Greece, and underwent a 'deproblematization'; an 'obsolescence not of the thing itself, but of the problem'.[14] Together, these amount to a revolution in sexual fashioning, a 'new erotics'.[15] This is part of his larger project to investigate a history of sexuality 'as a genealogy of the discourses that produce and constrain desiring subjects, not a history of "sex" as a transhistorical given'[16] (contrary to psychoanalysis, which views sexuality as an instinct or drive inherent in all humans).

The first section of this chapter focuses on *erōs* and marriage in the Greek novel and suggests that while Foucault (and David Konstan who followed and developed his ideas)[17] are right to observe the novel's emphasis on marriage, it is only by reading teleologically – stressing the ending and downplaying the journey towards it – that we can read the novels simply as celebrating marriage. Indeed, as Simon Goldhill in particular has argued, Foucault fails to appreciate the ancient novels as *narratives* and largely ignores their comic and ludic aspects.[18] The second section takes as its starting point the very singular position of Petronius' *Satyrica* in the history of sexuality and then returns to contest Foucault's comments on the love of boys as

---

10 For the incorporation by *nouveaux romanciers* of sexually explicit episodes from Apuleius see Britton (1993) 91 and 102–3.
11 Foucault (1986) 228.   12 Ibid. 232.   13 Ibid. 228.   14 Ibid. 189.
15 Ibid. 228.   16 Boyarin and Castelli (2001) 365.   17 Konstan (1994).
18 Goldhill (1995).

the discussion broadens to include representations of male same-sex desire in the Greek novels too. The final two sections change focus and take the debate further than Foucault did. Feminist classicists, notably Amy Richlin, Lin Foxhall, and Page duBois, have criticised Foucault's work on antiquity. They note that his history largely erases the female desiring subject, and takes for granted, rather than criticises, the subordination of women.[19] Developing these insights in relation to the novel, the first of my final two sections asks whether there is any place for *female* same-sex desire; the second looks at sexual violence and is alert to a history of oppression as well as of pleasure.

Sexuality and the civic

Erōs, 'desire', in the ancient Greek novel is a disruptive force. The young men and women do not so much choose to fall in love as are zapped into an altered state from on high, either by *Eros* himself (theomorphised in Chariton and Xenophon) or by the visual aspect of the beloved which stimulates desire. It threatens the health, sanity, even the lives of those it afflicts.[20] Let me emphasise from the outset that this conception of *erōs* has profound implications for thinking about the sexual subject in the ancient novel. Sometimes characters are represented as subjects, actively desiring; often they are ciphers, through whom and despite whom, *erōs* acts. In the latter representations, it is not clear that the sexual subject is a *subject*, as such, at all (or, at least, subjectivity here is differently configured).[21] It is particularly interesting that sexual agency is portrayed so erratically in the novels, given that they are narratives much concerned with responsibility, with trials and tests that assume active agents. Often we find contradictory representations of agency juxtaposed with one another.[22] The generalisations that follow always need qualifying with close attention to specific differences and variation.

If the narratives are worried by the threat of *erōs*, they are energised by journeys towards something far less destructive: marriage, or the re-establishment of a marriage. It is unusual for *erōs* to be conceived as the foundation of marriage. Love and marriage, did not, in classical Greek culture, go together like a horse and carriage. Or, at least, not this type of love: the destructive, delinquent *erōs*. In linking *erōs* to marriage the Greek

19 Richlin (1991); Foxhall (1998); duBois (1998).
20 See e.g. Ach. Tat. 2.6 and 34; Hld. 2.15.1–3 on *baskanos erōs* (the 'evil eye')
21 This is a complicated area. The idea of the emotions as quasi-external to the self is not uncommon in ancient Greek culture and has many different configurations.
22 Morales (2004) 159–65.

romance, as David Konstan writes, 'inaugurated a new moment in the representation of eros'.[23] Marriage is depicted as a resolutely social and civic affair. This is especially marked in *Callirhoe*, where the marriage is brought about by the assembly of citizens, who plead with the girl's father for permission for the union: 'The city pleads for the marriage, today, of a couple worthy of each other!' (1.1.11). Hermocrates finally agrees to the marriage, because, we are told, he is a lover of his country (*philopatris*, 1.1.12). When they marry, it is an emphatically civic celebration and 'The Syracusans celebrated this day with even more joy than the day of their victory' (1.1.12). Similarly, in *Anthia and Habrocomes*, 'the merry-making filled the city, there were garlands everywhere' (1.8.1). The couple's erotic relationship is metonymic for social and civic harmony. Leucippe's mother describes her husband fighting for his country as 'fighting for other men's marriages' (2.24.2).

These novels, it has been argued, 'idealise social unity'.[24] Erotic desire was harnessed to promote marriage and the subsequent production of children upon whom the maintenance of the aristocracies and empire depended. A strong version of this reading views the novels as propagandistic: '[t]he romance's celebration of sexual passion, then, should be understood as an encouragement to fertility similar in aim to the Augustan marriage legislation that privileged fertile parents and pressured the divorced and widowed to remarry quickly'.[25] This line of interpretation understands 'other modes of sexual encounter' depicted in the novels, such as Clitophon's tryst with Melite, as challenges which are easily subsumed, and which serve to reaffirm the legitimate.[26] It is broadly speaking true that most of the Greek novels ultimately 'valorise the civic ideal', *if* the reader reads for the happy ending, and not the sexual adventures along the way.[27] However, as Janice Radway has shown with her analysis of readers of the modern romance novel, narratives engage their readers in ways that prompt a whole variety of responses, often 'resisting', and 'renegade' readings.[28] A more phenomenological than functional reading might enjoy the digressions and reject the tyranny of teleology and its 'civic message'.[29] Much of the pleasure in the narratives comes from the *tension* between the destructive, wilful, *erōs*, and the cohesive, social bonds of marriage.

23 Konstan (1994).   24 Perkins (1995) 46. See also Swain (1996); Cooper (1996).
25 Cooper (1996) 43.   26 Cooper (1996) 43; Swain (1996) 118–30.
27 Doody interprets the novels as 'the enemy of the Civic' and is explicit that 'the point of the ancient novel is not in its ending': Doody (1996) 471, 61. See further Balot (1998); Morales (2004) 228–9.
28 Radway (1984).
29 Cooper argues for the novels' 'carrying . . . [a] civic message': Cooper (1996) 24.

Gay classics

Petronius' *Satyrica* is a gay classic. *The Advocate* lists it in its *100 Best Lesbian and Gay Novels*, alongside works like Thomas Mann's *Death in Venice* and James Baldwin's *Giovanni's Room*. The *Satyrica* has a privileged place in the literary history of homosexuality. Two illustrations will have to suffice. The first involves the so-called 'Wilde' translation (in my view one of the best translations of the novel). In 1902 this new English translation – the first not to censor the sexual scenes of the novel for over 150 years – was published in Paris by Charles Carrington (1906). The translation was attributed to 'Sebastian Melmoth', a pseudonym used by Oscar Wilde, who had died two years previously, living in impoverished exile after his imprisonment for 'the love that dare not speak its name'. It is now widely agreed to be a literary hoax, designed to trade on Wilde's notoriety for sexual impropriety.[30] Wilde was a classical scholar, and the attribution also gained some plausibility from a reference to Petronius in *The Picture of Dorian Gray*. The translation brings together two literary geniuses, satirists both infamously associated with homosexuality, at the same time as it writes the *Satyrica* into a very different, late Victorian, sexual discourse. In the preface to one of Carrington's later publications, *The Trial of Oscar Wilde*, Charles Grolleau makes explicit (in a rather baroque fashion) the comparison between Wilde and Petronius, and the persecutions they suffered: 'we are suddenly called upon to witness the heart-rending spectacle of the slow death-agony of a haughty, talented poet, a Petronius self-poisoned through fear of Caesar or a Wilde whom a vicious and over-wrought Public had only half assassinated, raising his poor, glazed eyes towards the marvelous Light of Truth'.[31]

Several decades later – and this the second example – the *Satyrica* was of considerable appeal in the Swinging Sixties, a very different moral climate. Paul Gillette's 1965 translation advertises 'a catalogue of erotic adventures, a carnal circus of bisexual delights'. In 1968 Federico Fellini's *Fellini Satyricon* was released, a film loosely adapted from Petronius.[32] Fellini outdoes the novel's sexual extravagance, adding characters like the hermaphrodite and the nymphomaniac whose sexual anguish must be assuaged every hour. Some of Gillette's 'complete and uncensored' translation was published in *Playboy*, as was Fellini's 'pictorial essay' of the film.[33] The *Satyrica* continued to be read as literary pornography, and has become synonymous with sexual anarchy.[34]

---

30 See Boroughs (1995) for full discussion.   31 Quoted at Boroughs (1995) 21.
32 See further Fusillo, this volume.   33 May issue (1970) 105–11.
34 A modern *Satyrica*, a study of *fin de siècle* North American sexuality, fashions itself as an ancestor of Petronius' work and promises 'a journey across a new sexual frontier': Eurydice (1999).

Of course the designations 'gay', 'bisexual' and 'heterosexual' are inappropriate to use in relation to ancient sexual behaviours.[35] There is no such thing as gay *Classics*. However, despite this, the reception of the *Satyrica* has so firmly inscribed it as queer (in the sense of challenging sexual norms) that the novel, homosexuality and pornography are inevitably culturally implicated.[36] It is impossible for the text now to be free of its stamp as a 'gay classic' – there is too much cultural weight behind this image. Its role in denaturalising heterosexuality, and in giving gay relations the authority of precedents from antiquity can be celebrated, even as we might recognise that, in many ways, the *Satyrica* is much less queer than its reception insists.

In fact, in the context of other contemporary literary representations of sex, the *Satyrica* is a potent cocktail of the queer and the conservative. It is unusual in giving the starring roles to three male characters who have sex with other males more often than with women (though it is far from unusual in its interest in pederasty *per se*). The work and its characters are named for lechery and appetite. The *Satyrica* (from the Greek adjective *satyrikos*, 'about satyrs') takes us to a world of mythical, half-human, half-goat creatures, who are represented on many a vase painting as attempting to rape maenads, huge penises held aloft, and the title evokes a long literary tradition of satyr literature. The adventures of 'In-crotch', (Encolpius), his beloved boy 'Mate' (Giton), and rival 'Un-shagged-out' (Ascyltus) are extraordinary in their sheer sexual excess. They take part in the sexual initiation of the seven-year-old 'All-night-long' (Pannychis). Giton has sex with her while the others watch through a peephole (one of *Satyrica*'s many scenes of voyeurism[37]). They are repeatedly assaulted, and endure sexual betrayals and insults, all under the wrathful eye of Priapus, the Roman 'fertility' god whose enormous erect phallus promises both comedy and sexual aggression.

Petronius' sexual carnival queers the (largely) hetero, (often) chaste universe of the more 'romantic' Greek novels. It stages a plurality of pleasures (and more often pains), but it is far from a celebration of male sexuality. In fact, the phallus in the *Satyrica* is more often flaccid than erect; sex interrupted more frequently than enjoyed. 'She diligently applied herself to my groin, which was now as cold as if it had died a thousand deaths' laments Encolpius of one of his many episodes of impotence (*Sat.* 20). As Margaret

---

35 Halperin (2002) is the most nuanced argument for historicism (though the nastiness of his tone towards Richlin and Brooten makes it unpleasant to read). His discussion of the differences between episodes of sodomy in the so-called 'adultery tale' in Apuleius and Boccaccio is particularly pertinent: Halperin (2002) 38–41, following Walters (1997).
36 'Queer' in the sense of challenge and contest: see Kirsch (2000). Petronius would have had to have been written after the Greek novels *intentionally* to parody them (as Heinze (1899) argues he did), but not to 'queer' them.
37 Analysed from a psychoanalytical perspective by Sullivan (1968).

Anne Doody puts it, the '*Satyrica*'s importance as a literary sexual document resides in its acknowledgement of the weakness of the flesh. It calls the bluff on the masculine ideal, the notion that male sexuality is easy, unspoken, authoritative, and authoritarian.'[38] However, far from (just) revelling in sexual licence, Petronius exposes the deterioration of Neronian society through its excess and indulgence. The sexual disorder of the *Satyrica* is part of a wider social disorder. It is also reflected in the breakdown of language, with puns and riddles enacting on a linguistic level what adulterous liaisons do on a narrative level.[39]

One of the disturbing characters whom Encolpius and Ascyltus encounter in Quartilla's brothel is a well-dressed *cinaedus* (*Sat.* 21). The *cinaedus* is distinguished by his effeminacy and sexual insatiability. *Cinaedi* were 'ideological scare-figures for Roman men'.[40] No one called *himself* a *cinaedus*: it was a term of abuse levelled at another. Indeed Encolpius and Ascyltus accuse each other of behaviour typical of *cinaedi* (*Sat.* 9. and 81). *Cinaedi* were always figures of ridicule; men who had sex with boys were not. Even if the abuse directed at the *cinaedus* has some similarities with anti-gay prejudice now,[41] his crime was primarily against gender, not sexuality (and this is a good illustration of how gender was *not* coterminous with sexuality in the ancient world). It was the femininity of the *cinaedus* that was deviant, not his sleeping with men.

A boy like Giton was supposed to submit to the sexual attentions of older men, but not to enjoy being penetrated so much (if at all) that he showed signs of effeminacy and was at risk of being thought a *cinaedus*. The difficulty in policing this cultural expectation is exposed in the tale of the Pergamene boy (*Sat.* 85–7). Eumolpus relates how he schemed and bribed his way into kissing and fondling the beautiful son of his host at Pergamum, for whom Eumolpus had been acting as carer and tutor. One night, after Eumolpus has failed to deliver an extravagant gift that he had promised, the boy is angry and rejects his advances: 'Go to sleep or I'll tell my father.' Eumolpus will not take no for an answer: '[I] took my pleasure by force in spite of his half-hearted resistance.' The sting in the tale is that the boy, 'after he'd complained for some time that he'd been deceived' not only enjoys the penetration, but mithers his lover for more and more until, exhausted, Eumolpus exclaims, 'Go to sleep or I'll tell your father.' The anecdote is 'a deliberate reversal of the situation in Plato's *Symposium*, in which the youth Alcibiades, enamored of Socrates' love of truth and mastery of his own desires, unsuccessfully attempts to seduce his chaste tutor'.[42] This parodic relationship plays a more

---

38 Doody (1996) 112–13.   39 Tanner (1979) 52–7.
40 Williams (1999) 175.   41 As discussed in Richlin (1993).
42 McGlathery (1998) 209; see further Dimundo (1983); Hunter (1996).

sophisticated role within the narrative than I am able fully to discuss here. The point worth underlining is that, with *Satyrica* and all the ancient novels, the history of sexuality is an emphatically *literary* history. Within this literary history, which draws on a vast repertoire of texts from the Greek and Latin canon, Plato's *Symposium* takes pride of place.[43]

Foucault's discussion of sexuality and the novels is inadequate on several fronts. He suggests that Petronius and Apuleius are unusual in their interest in pederasty, but in doing so fails to appreciate similar preoccupations in other imperial Latin literary and philosophical texts (and some Greek ones).[44] He contends that reflection on homoerotic desire in the first few centuries CE 'lost some of its intensity, its seriousness, its vitality' in comparison to reflection in the classical period, and that it is unimaginative, presented 'in a dull way'. In so doing he underplays the subversive possibilities of parodic textual relations like the tale of the Pergamene boy.

In the Greek novels pederastic relationships are not afforded the centrality of the relationship between hero and heroine, and, as we saw in the previous section, most of the novels project (though not without problems) a valorisation of marriage. However, to call them 'marginal and episodic themes' is to downplay their variety and complexity. When Daphnis rejects the idea of having sex with a man – 'He thought slowly and said it was good for billy-goats to mount nanny-goats, but no-one had ever seen a billy-goat mounting a billy-goat, nor a ram mounting a ram instead of the ewes, nor cocks mounting cocks instead of the hens' (4.11) – he uses an argument about what is 'natural' that goes back as far as Plato's *Laws* and looks forward to modern homophobic theories. However, far from being a straightforward denunciation of same-sex love, the joke is on Daphnis. A recurrent motif of the novel, worked through with some sophistication and play between *phusis* and *tekhnē* (nature and convention), is that 'hetero' sex is not (simply) natural, and Daphnis and Chloe have to be taught how to 'do it' and how to grow into being a man and woman.[45]

Males who desire males are characterised differently in different novels. In *Daphnis and Chloe* Gnathon is a character described as *phusei paiderastēs*, 'by nature a lover of boys'.[46] He is an unattractive character: a townie (an intruder into the pastoral world) and a profligate (an *akolastos*): 'He was

---

43 In the Greek novels, the speech about *erōs* spoken by the character Aristophanes is particularly important: see especially Hunter (1996); with Fusillo (1989); Winkler (1994).

44 See McGlathery (1998), esp. 224–7 on Catullus and Martial, Richlin (1991).

45 Zeitlin (1990) and Goldhill (1995) 6–45.

46 Goldhill cautions, 'one must be very careful indeed before assuming that *phusei* (here) can mean anything like an inherent psychological necessity, rather than a set of attitudes and behavioural patterns': (1995) 49.

nothing but a mouth, a stomach, and the bits below the stomach' (4.10). His pederasty is part of his repulsive (and comic) appetite. However, pederastic lovers in other novels – Hippothous and Hyperanthes, Hippothous and Cleisthenes in *An Ephesian Tale* and Clinias and Charicles, Menelaus and his beloved in *Leucippe and Clitophon* – are not so negatively characterised. These homoerotic relationships may be 'asymmetrical' but it would be a mistake to think that it follows that they are unreciprocal or not in any way mutual. Charicles shows gratitude to his lover for bestowing gifts on him and is appalled at the prospect of marriage to woman. Hippothous decides to settle in Ephesus with Anthia and Habrocomes and he adopts Cleisthenes as his son (5.15.4). As Konstan says, 'The parallel between the two couples at the end of the novel seems . . . to offer a model for an enduring association, comparable to marriage.'[47] He views this relationship as 'arising out of' the couple's pederastic relationship, but marking a clear break from it: 'Hippothous' adoption of Clisthenes marks the termination of their pederastic relationship.'[48] However, it would strange to assume that the relationship moved from an erotic to a chaste one; there is nothing to suggest that this would be the case. 'Adoption' is perhaps the closest that two male lovers could get to a socially recognised legal bond like marriage. This episode highlights the inequality in social provision for same-sex and 'hetero' couples, but at the same time as suggesting significant similarities between those couples' love.

Just as 'asymmetry' in pederasty does not mean that the relations are devoid of reciprocity and mutuality, 'symmetry' in the amorous relations between hero and heroine, 'is not equivalence (and certainly not equality)'.[49] Marriage inscribes *inequality*; sexuality here is the foundation of men's control over women. Daphnis and Clitophon enter marriage with experience of sexual intercourse; Chloe and Leucippe have none. After Callirhoe marries Chaereas and is pregnant with his child, he kicks her in the stomach during a jealous rage so hard that she is knocked unconscious and left for dead. Mutuality and equality might be the fantasy peddled by certain elements in the narrative that suggest a 'symmetry' of sorts, but it is not a fantasy that we should collude with. Moreover, in one of the novels there is an explicit debate about whether it is better for a man to love boys or women.[50] The arguments may be traditional,[51] but this is hardly a 'deproblematisation' of pederasty. In fact, the most striking thing about this debate is that there is no judgement at the end of it. In contrast to similar debates

---

47 Konstan (1994) 56.　　48 Ibid. 62 n. 8.　　49 Goldhill (1995) 160 *contra* Konstan (1994).
50 Ach. Tat. 2.35–8.　　51 See Cantarella (1992) for similar debates.

in Pseudo-Lucian (where pederasty wins) and in Plutarch (where loving women wins), the debate in Achilles Tatius leaves the reader to decide, leaves the issue precisely as a *problem*.

Women desiring (women)

The debate over the superiority of women or boys as sexual partners contains one of the most extraordinary representations of woman's desire in ancient literature; a description of a woman's ecstasy during orgasm, unparalleled in its detail, even in Ovid's *Art of Love*.[52] The ancient novels are full of desiring women. Although some of these, like Tryphaena and Circe in the *Satyrica*, are stereotypes of libidinous women familiar from satire and other literature, others, like Callirhoe, Chloe and Chariacleia in the Greek romance novels, desire their husbands or husbands-to-be without (as, for example, their counterparts in Greek tragedy) being punished for that desire. Sexually predatory women who threaten the couple's union, especially foreign women who abuse their power, like Heliodorus' Egyptian queen Arsace, typically come to a bad end, but Achilles Tatius' lustful Melite provides an exuberant exception even to that rule. The celebration of the female desiring subject is a radical innovation of this genre, even if that desire often romanticises marriage, and serves an imperial and patriarchal agenda. My discussion of the desiring female subject in this section will focus on a novel which is too often dismissed as marginal to the Greek romance novels (and which is ignored by Foucault) but which is of interest to anyone attempting to trace a history of female sexuality in the ancient world.

According to the ninth-century summariser who is our primary source, Iamblichus' *Babylonian Affairs* (originally a long and sophisticated narrative) 'acts out affairs of passion' (73b24), including one between two women, Berenice and Mesopotamia. It dramatises same-sex female relations, and possibly even marriage between the two women. Homoerotic female desire is comparatively rarely represented in ancient literature, despite the iconic status of the poet Sappho.[53] In the ancient novel, there is a marked absence of close female relationships, with the exception of that between Callirhoe and Plangon. Adrienne Rich has argued that rather than making a distinction between women who have genital sexual relations with other women and those who do not (a heterosexual model of sexuality) we should see women

---

52 Ach. Tat. 2.37. On the *Art of Love* and the 'invention of the heterosexual' see Habinek (1997).
53 See the essays in Rabinowitz and Auanger (2002), none of which, however, mention the novel.

on a continuum of closeness (and thus a continuum of resistance against patriarchy, as female bonding constitutes resistance).[54] The ancient novels, which promote female rivalry over female friendship, provide few representations that could be judged part of a 'lesbian continuum'. This makes the amorous relations between Berenice and Mesopotamia all the more extraordinary. The fact that *Babylonian Affairs* only survives in Photius' epitome, and a few fragments, makes it very hard indeed to assess how this relationship was originally represented. We are told there was: 'A digression about Berenice, who was daughter of the king of Egypt, and about her wild and unlawful (or 'unnatural'; *ekthesmon* is an unusual word in this context) passions: and how she has relations with Mesopotamia' (77a 20). Whether 'wild' and 'unlawful' refer to Iamblichus' portrayal of the relationship, or are Photius' judgements, we are unable to tell. He is often censorious about the works he summarises.[55]

Later in the epitome we learn that Mesopotamia is mistaken for Sinonis, the major female protagonist of the novel, who is in love with a youth named Rhodanes, but who has attracted the desire of Garmos, the king of Babylon. Mesopotamia is captured and taken to Garmos, who recognises that she is not Sinonis and gives her to his eunuch, Zobaras, to have her beheaded. We are then told: 'Zobaras, who having drunk from the fountain of desire, and checked by his desire for Mesopotamia, spares her, and takes her away with him to Berenice, who is now queen of Egypt after her father's death, and on account of her war is threatened between Garmos and Berenice' (77b27). There is an ambiguity in the Greek that makes it uncertain whether Berenice marries Mesopotamia or has her marriage performed. Bernadette Brooten, in her important work on female homoeroticism, is too confident when she writes, 'Iamblichos was one of several second-century authors to write about marriage between women.'[56] As Alan Cameron points out, the Greek conflates two different formulae, one for getting married, the other for celebrating someone else's marriage.[57] The *Suda* encyclopaedia mentions two details of Iamblichus' novel: '[It] is about the passion of Rhodanes and Sinonis, in thirty-nine books. He tells of Zobaras the eunuch, lover of the gorgeous Mesopotamia.' It is possible that Berenice oversaw the marriage of Mesopotamia to the eunuch, or that she herself married the girl (both queer liaisons, in different ways).[58]

---

54 Rich (1980). This approach has been criticised by some as being 'lesbianism-lite': see Walby (1990) 121.
55 See Hägg (1975) and N. Wilson (1994).   56 Brooten (1996) 51.
57 Cameron (1998). Cameron shows how the other evidence for female marriage is equally tenuous.
58 Juvenal expresses disgust at eunuchs marrying (1.22).

Cultural stereotyping is present in the portrayal of Berenice's desire. Her love for another woman is not untypical of representations of Egyptians as practising woman–woman love and marriage.[59] The connotations of the title of the novel are also relevant. Babylonia was associated with prostitution, and sexual practices connected with temple service.[60] Mesopotamia's mother is a priestess of Aphrodite. Other stereotypes of Babylonians, such as their interest in sorcery, are a focus of the narrative.[61] It is not clear quite how these cultural stereotypes map onto the sexual behaviours of characters in the novel, but it is likely that they did. Lollianus' *Phoenician Affairs* represents stereotypes of Phoenicians, including sexual ones.[62] A history of sexuality is always also a history of cultural identity.

Brooten, Cameron and other critics who have discussed the sexuality of Berenice and Mesopotamia have viewed the characters realistically, that is to say as literary characters, as representations, however imaginative, of people. Clearly this is one obvious way of reading. However, protagonists in ancient novels are rarely characterised in the same way as they are in, for example, Jane Austen's novels. They often play emblematic and symbolic roles, as well as dramatic ones. An awareness of this will prove crucial for our understanding of the sexual relations between Berenice and Mesopotamia. I want to suggest that this episode of the *Babylonian Affairs* can be read metaphorically, or even allegorically, in the service of a highly politicised narrative. Various factors are worth considering. The *Babylonian Affairs* is highly unusual among the Greek novels in being framed by a specific, and specifically *Roman*, social and political context. Half way through his account, Photius writes:

> The author says that he himself is a Babylonian, and that he was schooled in the magic arts, and also in Greek culture and education, and that he flourished under Sohaemus, the Achaemenid and Arsacid, a king from a line of kings on his father's side, and yet who also became a member of the Senate at Rome and then a consul, and then a king again of Greater Armenia. This was the period in which he says he flourished. He expressly states that Antoninus was ruling the Romans,[63] and that when Antoninus (he says) sent the emperor Verus, his adopted brother and son-in-law, to make war on Vologaeses the Parthian, he himself foretold the war: that it would happen and how it would end. And that Vologaeses fled across the Euphrates and Tigris and that the land of the Parthians became subject to Rome. (75b27)

59 Brooten (1996) 66, 232–3. 60 See e.g. Herodotus' *Histories* 1.199, with Lerner (1986).
61 At 74a17, 75b16, fragment 27 Stephens-Winkler = *Suda* 1.257.23.
62 Henrichs (1972) 11; Winkler (1980); Morales (2004) 48–50.
63 Not Antoninus Pius, but his adopted son Marcus Aurelius (reigned 161–80 CE), who took the additional name Antoninus when he became emperor.

An ancient commentator writing in the margin of the major manuscript of Photius' *Library* tells that Iamblichus learned about the language and culture of Babylon from his tutor, a Babylonian who 'was taken prisoner in the time when Trajan invaded Babylonia' [i.e. 115/16]. We have no idea to what degree this autobiographical information is fabricated. What is important is that it gives the novel an overt concern with contemporary politics and with conquest. The events of the narrative may be set in a legendary Mesopotamian past, but they are framed by an explicit interest in the Mesopotamian present. Mesopotamia in this novel is not just a person, but a *place*, and a place, moreover, under Roman occupation. Her affair and marriage to Berenice have a very different meaning when viewed metaphorically. Sexual metaphors involving rape or marriage are common ways of thinking about conquest,[64] and Mesopotamia (the girl)'s capture (by Garmos' men), escape, and marriage can be read as signifying Mesopotamia (the land)'s colonisation, rebellion, and eventual submission to Roman rule. Colonial concerns are mapped onto the body, as contemporary politics proves one discourse that constructs female sexuality and *viva versa*.[65]

Incest, violence and rape

The anonymous *History of Apollonius, King of Tyre* speaks about a female response to, and resistance towards, male desire. It begins with the rape of an unnamed princess, by her father, king Antiochus:

> whipped on by the frenzy of his lust, he took the knot of his daughter's virginity by force, in spite of her lengthy resistance. When the immoral act was over he left the bedroom. But the girl stood astonished at the immorality of her wicked father. She tried to hide the flow of blood: but drops of blood fell onto the floor. (1.13–14)

This novel should be read as a significant text in any cultural history of incest in the western tradition. It is an exploration of relationships between fathers and daughters, in which the negative paradigm of Antiochus and his daughter does not just contrast with later father–daughter pairings, but haunts them with the disquieting suggestion that they might not be so dissimilar after all.

The novel, written some time in the period 200–600 CE, can be read as part of a *longue durée* of conceptualising incest. As the Oedipus myths also

64 Dougherty (1993) is fundamental.   65 Morales (2006).

showed, incest leads to riddles, and the perversion of sexual relations renders direct communication impossible. Antiochus is depicted as a victim of forces larger than himself: 'driven by immoral passion and inflamed by lust he desired with his own daughter, and he began to love her in a way unsuitable for a father. He struggled with madness, he fought against passion, but he was defeated by desire' (1.6–9). The daughter's response is to be ashamed and seek suicide: 'rather than reveal my parent's crime, I prefer the solution of death. I shudder at the thought that this shame may become known to the people' (2.9–11). Her nurse dissuades her from suicide, but later in the novel we learn that she and her father, while he is raping her, are killed by a lightning-flash. The victim, as well as her abuser, is punished for his crime. A history of sexuality that considers *Apollonius* will be a history of (women's) oppression, as well as (men's) pleasure.

There are many scenes of sexualised violence in the ancient novels. They are often pornographic, both in the sense that they are sexually explicit, and also in the more specific understanding of the term to mean the denigration of women by men.[66] In the Greek romance novels, much of the violence is described within dreams, descriptions of pictures, and mythological tales. This is a process of disavowal (it's just a dream, only a story . . .)[67] but the violence cannot be contained within these inset descriptions, which leave their residue on the characters and events in the main narrative. It has been argued that the violence in the novels exposes, and hence criticises, the abuses of patriarchy, rather than perpetuating them, but this is to 'read against the grain' of the narratives.[68]

One striking aspect of the Greek novels is the sheer relentlessness with which women are threatened with rape. Anthia, in *Anthia and Habrocomes*, faces rape sixteen times. The heroines never are actually raped, but their narratives repeatedly take pleasure in the fantasy of their defilement at the same time as they exhibit them as paragons of chastity.[69] The fantasy of the virgin/whore is a potent one in these novels.[70] At the same time, there is an intense interest in what virginity and chastity *are*. What does it mean when Charicleia says her desire is a 'chaste desire' (*sophron erōs*, 4.18)? Or when Clitophon asserts 'know that I have imitated your virginity, if there be a male equivalent of virginity' and 'If there is such a thing as virginity in a man, I have kept it up to this day, at least in relation to Leucippe'?[71]

---

66 Dworkin and MacKinnon's definition: see Walby (1990) 118–19.
67 Morales (2004) 183–4.
68 Winkler (1990) 126; see the criticisms of Goldhill (1995) 30–45.
69 On virginity and chastity in the imperial period see especially Brown (1988).
70 Morales (2004) 218–20.   71 Ach. Tat. 5.20.5, 8.7.5.

The ancient novels invite an active interrogation of virginity and chastity as much (as Foucault would have it) as a celebration of them. This they share with a genre intimately related to them: hagiography, 'a queer, late version of the ancient novel, emerging at the intersections of romance with biography, historiography, panegyric, martyrology'.[72]

This chapter has alternately nuanced and criticised Foucault's analysis of the ancient novel. It has posed the question of what a feminist history of sexuality and the novel would look like, and has argued that sexuality in the Greek novels typically operates to control women, even as the novels also recognise that and how 'good' as well as 'bad' women desire. In all too brief analyses of the city's investment in sexuality, of (male *and* female) same-sex love, of incest, rape, and resistance, and of sexual relations as metaphor as well as practice, I have traced the complexities of the novelistic discourses of sexuality, insisting both on the historical contingency of their constructions of sexuality, and on important commonalities between then and now. It is fitting that a discussion of 'new erotics' should close with a glimpse in the direction of hagiography. For, as Christianity introduces the idea of sin into *its* novels, it will mark a watershed in the history of sexuality and gives us both a familiar tale – and a whole new story.[73]

Further reading

The most stimulating work on sexuality and the Greek novels is Goldhill (1995). It is a largely literary study; Perkins (1995) and Cooper (1996) are better at considering the Greek novels' representations of sexuality in their social, cultural and philosophical contexts. Doody (1996) and Konstan (1994) are illuminating on the individual Greek and Latin novels (though beware Doody's wacky goddess-worship approach). Foucault's discussion of the novels in the third volume of his *History of Sexuality* has dominated the debate. Sharp critiques of his approach are found in MacKinnon (1992); Boyarin and Castelli (2001); duBois (1998); Foxhall (1998) and Richlin (1998). Konstan (1994) develops Foucault's readings of the novels; Goldhill (1995) is more critical. Foucauldian studies have skewed the agenda; consequently the most striking omission in scholarship on the novels and the history of sexuality is psychoanalysis. There is little good material on psychoanalysis and the novel, although Sullivan (1968) is still fundamental reading

---

72 Burrus (2005) 18.
73 Many thanks indeed for criticism and other help to Richard Fletcher, Simon Goldhill, Richard Hunter and Judith Perkins.

on Petronius. More recently, our understanding of sexuality and the novels has been expanded in two exciting areas: the interrelation between the novels and Christian martyr texts, especially Burrus (2005), and (following the important work of Gleason (1995) and Gunderson (2003) on sexuality and rhetoric) on the impact of declamation on the novels' representations of sexual practices: Richlin (1996) and Morales (2004).

4

SUSAN STEPHENS

Cultural identity

The *Alexander Romance* is a fictionalised account of Alexander's conquests that stands at what many take to be the beginning of the novel writing enterprise in antiquity.[1] The story opens with the last pharaoh of Egypt, Nectanebo II, learning that his country was about to be conquered, fleeing to Macedon, setting up shop as a magician, and seducing Philip's queen Olympias. Nectanebo, not Philip II, fathers Alexander, and as a result Alexander is both Macedonian-Greek and Egyptian, a potent fiction that enables him to lay claim to Egypt. At the same time he remains the pupil of Aristotle and the heir of his apparent father, Philip.

Heliodorus' *Charicleia and Theagenes* is the last of the five Greek novels that have survived intact. One of its main characters, white-skinned Charicleia, was exposed at birth, rescued and brought to Greece where she was raised as an upper-class Greek girl. After adventures that carry her from Greece to Egypt and Ethiopia, she is reunited with her natural parents, who happen to be the black-skinned king and queen of Ethiopia. Charicleia appears Greek, but biologically she is not Greek at all. At the moment of her conception, her mother was gazing at a picture of Andromeda awaiting rescue from the sea monster by Perseus. That image of Greek womanhood was so powerful that it altered the course of nature and the resulting white child was exposed to protect her mother's reputation.[2] In *The Alexander Romance* and *Charicleia and Theagenes* the conventional oppositions of Greek and barbarian are intentionally joined in characters whose behaviour clearly allows them to act Greek, whatever their ethnically distinctive parentage. These extreme fictions adumbrate a Hellenism that was no longer limited by birth or civic identity, but that might be otherwise

---

1 Though much of it dates from the third century CE, it retains a core of material from about the third century BCE (see 'Index of Greek and Roman novelists'). For the *Alexander Romance* as a proto-novel see Stoneman (1994) and Dowden's introduction to his translation at Reardon (1989) 650–4.
2 For Charicleia 'passing' as Greek see Perkins (1999); also Whitmarsh (1998).

acquired. This new Hellenism could be transmitted by education (*paideia*) and expressed itself as an accumulated set of predispositions and practices held in common by the dominant social orders in the cities that encircled the Mediterranean.

The Alexander Romance and *Charicleia and Theagenes* may provide extreme examples, but they are not unique. Most of the ancient novels take place in locations where Greeks (however defined) necessarily encounter non-Greeks and thus explicitly contrast ethnicities and cultural behaviours.[3] That the action of such fictions should take place outside of mainland Greece is in part a reflection of historical circumstance.[4] The rise of ancient prose fiction coincides with the period of late Hellenistic and Roman imperial expansion. The gradual spread of first Greek and then Roman military power over south Italy and Sicily, North Africa, Greece, and the ancient Near East created new political boundaries and administrative hierarchies that altered the patterns of social integration for large numbers of people. This new world gave rise to figures like Josephus, a high-caste Jewish priest living under Roman rule, who wrote an account of his people in Greek; or Lucian, who claimed to be a Syrian native who learned Greek, became a travelling rhetorician, and resided for some time in Gaul teaching Greek to Romans; or Apuleius, a North African devotee of Platonism, who wrote Greek stories in Latin. What these men had in common was a world controlled by Roman military and administrative power, a Greek rhetorical education that provided the avenue for social advancement and a heritage that might be separate from both. These men, and thousands like them, who were Romanised Greeks, or Hellenised Syrians or Egyptians or Jews, occupied a cultural space in which identity, education and language, belief systems and social arrangements were fluid. In fact, most of the authors of ancient fiction who identify themselves live outside mainland Greece, in North Africa, southern Turkey or Syria, where non-Greeks (and non-Romans) must have constituted the majority of the population. The Greek novels seem generically disposed to prefer the marginal parts of the known world. Our earliest self-identified author is Chariton, who claims to be from Aphrodisias, in the south-west of modern Turkey. Chariton's characters travel from Sicily to Babylon, and finally back to Sicily. Xenophon is surnamed 'of Ephesus' because his novel begins and ends in that city (also in south-western Turkey), and the action has roughly the same range as Chariton's novel (without the Persian episode). In Achilles

3 Bowie (1991) 188–95 discusses the Hellene–barbarian opposition in the novels of Chariton, Xenophon of Ephesus, and Achilles Tatius.
4 For Greek identity constructed under Roman rule see e.g. Swain (1996); Whitmarsh (2001a); Saïd (2001); Konstan and Saïd (2006). Thompson (2001) provides an historical example of how 'Greek' functioned as a status category that might be acquired by a subaltern population.

Tatius' novel the main character, Clitophon, claims to be 'Phoenician'. The geographic range is from western Turkey to modern Lebanon, Syria and Egypt. Heliodorus says he is a Phoenician from Emesa (in modern Syria). His main character is an Egyptian priest steeped in Greek learning, and the novel's main characters travel from the centre of old Greece (Delphi) through Egypt to Ethiopia, where they remain.

The same trends are to be found in novels known only from fragments or from the epitomes of Photius.[5] The two main characters in *Metiochus and Parthenope*, like the figures in Chariton's novel, travel over Greece, Sicily and Persia. Antonius Diogenes' *Wonders beyond Thule* was a travel adventure with philosophical leanings, whose characters traversed the known world from the far south to the far north (the mythical Thule). There are even fragmentary novels in which Greek characters are not central, if they appear at all: these tales feature Ninus, the first king of Nineveh (in ancient Assyria), Sesonchosis, a pharaoh of Egypt, and in Iamblichus' *Babylonian Affairs* we meet Garmos, the cruel and violent king of Babylon, and his successor, Rhodanes.[6] Iamblichus explicitly identified himself as a non-Greek: 'a Syrian by birth . . . not a Syrian in the sense of a Greek living in Syria, but a native'.[7] In these fictions Greeks do not always behave better than non-Greeks; sometimes non-Greeks display greater moral authority and self-control; in some Greeks disappear, though the behaviours associated with Greek civilised values (*paideia*) do not.[8]

Only one extant Greek novel resists this trend: Longus' pastoral novel, *Daphis and Chloe*, takes place entirely within a Greek social milieu, juxtaposing the country (the peasantry, enduring values and true love) to the city (aristocrats, social and sexual predators). It too seems to position itself against some norm or readers' expectation for travel adventure: as the tale opens, capture by Phoenician pirates, a cliché that in other novels leads to foreign lands and repeated encounters with non-Greeks, is humorously averted (1.28–30). For Daphnis and Chloe, seemingly the children of peasants who discover their upper-class origins, it is not their Greek identity but class that is at issue. The two early Roman novels similarly address status, but in contexts where status is articulated against a Greek background or behavioural patterns identified as Greek. The surviving sections of Petronius' *Satyrica*

---

5 On Photius (and the various fragmentary novelists discussed below), see the 'Index of Greek and Roman novelists'.
6 Though characters with Greek names (e.g. Trophime) do appear in this novel, Rhodanes and Sinonis, the names of the hero and heroine are not Greek.
7 Photius 75b27; Stephens and Winkler (1995) 181, 194.
8 *Apollonius, King of Tyre*, which seems to be a Latin translation of a Greek romance, also conforms to this pattern as its characters traverse the south-eastern Mediterranean from Lebanon to North Africa. See Schmeling (2003a) 517–51.

are set in the formerly Greek areas of south Italy and Marseilles. Apuleius, who is from Madaurus in Latin-speaking North Africa (about 250 km or 150 miles south of Tunis), locates the action of his *Metamorphoses* in Greece, albeit away from the traditional centres of Hellenism. These two novels by virtue of the language in which they were written (Latin) privilege the Roman elites of the empire and now Greek becomes a marked category, an 'other' against which to measure being Roman.[9]

In what follows I will focus on the interface of 'Greek' and non-Greek behaviours and identities, rather than class or gender (also important identity markers that will be taken up elsewhere in this volume), working from the premise that prose fiction served as a means not only of negotiating conflicting claims about the past and what it meant (how Greeks under Rome might still think of themselves as Greek),[10] it also allowed experiment with paradigms for understanding and acting in a world where 'Greek' covered more than one social, political or ethnic reality. At the formal level of narrative, themes like infant exposure, travel to distant lands, shipwreck, capture by pirates or bandits provided a vocabulary of action through which all too real experiences like loss of status or confrontation with different social mores might be safely imagined and resolved. If in *Daphnis and Chloe* these types of events are confined to a Greek milieu, the fact that most other extant Greek and Roman novels stage similar events outside of locations where ethnic identity could remain unambiguous suggests that self-consciousness about such identities was more central to these fictions than we usually acknowledge.

That said, a striking feature of these texts is that despite their temporal, regional and stylistic differences they construct being Greek in remarkably similar ways. Speaking Greek is the *sine qua non*: Chariton's Callirhoe, for example, divides the world into homeland (Syracuse), Ionia, which is foreign, but still Greek-speaking, and the interior of Persia, which is barbarian because it is not Greek-speaking (5.1). Characters do engage in Greek-specific practices like the gymnasium and symposium, but many social activities come culturally unmarked, or similarly marked in more than one culture. The latter phenomenon tends to create a generic template for certain types

---

9 Romans are non-Greek, but never 'barbarian'. See Saïd (2001) 287, who observes that 'the old Greek/barbarian dichotomy is often transformed by the addition of the Romans as a *tertium quid*'. The erasure of Rome from the idealised Greek novels allows the dichotomy to be maintained. It may also have meant that in some circumstances 'barbarian' served as a covert equivalent for Roman power or behaviour (see Connors's chapter in this volume).

10 The essays in Goldhill (2001a) provide a wealth of examples for constructing and retaining Greek identity. See, in particular, Whitmarsh (2001b) for the intersection of travel on the margins and cultural identity.

of events that undermine cultural specificity. For example, in Achilles Tatius (3.24) the peculiarly Egyptian festival of the phoenix bird returning from Ethiopia to bury his father[11] requires a five-day suspension of military activity. Later when Clitophon is on trial in a Greek milieu (7.12), the advancing procession of Artemis requires a similar suspension of all legal activity. Or in *Anthia and Habrocomes* we find the heroine prays as fervently to the Apis bull (5.4.8) as she does to Artemis (3.5.5).

Though descent was an important means of asserting Greek identity,[12] it is not central in the novels. In two of the earliest novels, Chariton's *Callirhoe* and *Metiochus and Parthenope*, the characters do have fine pedigrees: Callirhoe is the daughter of the Syracusan general Hermocrates and Parthenope the daughter of Polycrates, the tyrant of Samos. Later, in Heliodorus, Theagenes claims descent from Achilles, but the assertion has more to do with the multilayered Homeric allusivity within the text than an ethnic identity that drives the plot.[13] More commonly the Greek characters have no famous relatives, and little or no distinction is drawn between a Greek born in Syria or Egypt and the native Syrian or Egyptian who may speak Greek (even though such distinctions were, in historical practice, vital for those negotiating the social landscape, and are alive in rhetorical and other late Greek writing).[14]

An index of how ethnicity plays out in the novels is how characters are identified in comparison to what we can infer from their historical situation. In Achilles Tatius, for example, we meet four different figures: Clitophon, the protagonist, who claims to be 'Phoenician by birth' (1.31, *Phoinikē genos*). Though the ancestors he claims for himself have thoroughly Greek-sounding names, such nomenclature is not a reliable indication of ethnicity in the second century CE:[15] Clitophon might be an assimilated Phoenician, or from a mixed Greek and Phoenician family (the most likely), or from a purely Greek family settled in Tyre. Clitophon (the narrator) does not say.[16] Menelaus describes himself as Egyptian in birth (2.33.2, *to de genos Aiguptios*), speaks both Greek and Egyptian and behaves 'Greek' in that he mourns

---

11 It is worth noting that the festival of the phoenix is not authentically Egyptian, but seems to have been borrowed from Herodotus (2.73).

12 See discussions in Bowie (1991) and Woolf (1994).

13 Whitmarsh (1998) 103 claims that 'the Ainianians have been transformed, thanks to Theagenes' ingenious genealogy, from Homeric bit-parts to a collective embodiment of Hellenism'. He further cautions that the Ethiopian tale should not be read as a simple reflection of any contemporary historical notion of cultural identity, but as 'a playful negotiation of literary tradition' (p. 124).

14 Saïd (2001) 286–95 and Woolf (1994) 129–31.

15 Roman + Greek names like Antonius Diogenes, however, usually indicated Greeks who held Roman citizenship.

16 So too Heliodorus, who claims to be a 'Phoenician man' (10.41.4, *aner Phoinix*).

his boy lover and has been exiled by his city for three years. Presumably he was from a Greco-Egyptian family who lived up river, not a higher status 'Alexandrian'. Then there is the leader of cavalry troops stationed in Egypt, who also speaks Greek. He has the Greek name of Charmides. The fictional time of the novel is not made clear, but if we make the usual assumption of a second-century CE date, Charmides should have been a Roman citizen.[17] Finally the *boukoloi*,[18] who live in reed huts in the marshes, speak only Egyptian. In the novel Menelaus, Clitophon and Charmides behave as social equals bonding through their common language; and it is language, not only the behaviour of the *boukoloi*, that locates them outside of the parameters of civilised exchange.

If Greek identity is not always fully parsed in the novels, neither is that of non-Greeks. Despite the wide range of ethnicities known from the regions in which novel characters wander, we find a recurring set: Persians, Phoenicians, Egyptians, Ethiopians. Non-Greek peoples may be distinguished from each other in a rudimentary way, but they remain Hellenocentric projections of the other, with behaviours often less subtly delineated than the stereotypes to be found in Herodotus. Persians are powerful kings (like Artaxerxes) and their attendants are eunuchs (like Bagoas) and satraps. Egyptians are good priests or bad (and therefore magicians)[19] or they may be marsh-dwelling bandits (*boukoloi*).[20] When in *Charicleia and Theagenes* the high priest of Memphis joins the *boukoloi* in response to a plot that deprives him of his office, we remain confined to stereotypes (bandits/priests); missing are the political leaders, soldiers, merchants or craftsmen who populated contemporary Egyptian literature.[21] Recent attempts to identify explicitly 'Phoenician' elements in the *Leucippe and Clitophon* of Achilles Tatius and *Phoenician Affairs* of Lollianus[22] can produce nothing more idiosyncratic than that Phoenicians are noted for worshipping Astarte, discovering Tyrian dye, temple prostitution and possibly child sacrifice.[23] Information about foreign religious and social practices is superficial at best, often inaccurate,

---

17 Lewis (1983) 19–20: 'During most of the period of Roman rule the army of occupation consisted of two legions of Roman citizens, plus various auxiliary units of provincials . . . under Roman officers.' For the ethnic composition of the army in Egypt see Alston (1995) 39–52. Nothing in the novel suggests the Ptolemaic period, but if it were located then, Charmides could have been a mercenary in Ptolemy's armies from any number of places in the Mediterranean.

18 On these see Rutherford (2000).

19 See e.g. Morgan at Reardon (1989) 406 n. 69 (on Hld. 2.33).

20 For the apparent exception, *Sesonchosis*, see below.

21 For a brief survey of Egyptian fiction contemporary with the Greek novels see Tait (1994) 203–22.

22 Stephens and Winkler (1995) 314–57.

23 Morales (2004) 48–50. We could add piracy to this distinguished list of cultural achievements.

and tailored to Greek readers: in Heliodorus, for example, the most distinctive feature of Egyptian Memphis, the cult of the Apis bull, is never mentioned, probably because the cult's overt theriomorphism would have undercut the lofty, intellectualising tone of the priest Calasiris, who narrates this section.[24] We learn instead of the Memphite temple of Isis, a goddess long assimilated by Mediterranean Greeks. Meanwhile, the novels give us no contemporary barbarians with the power and stature of the client kings of territories ringing the Roman empire. The only foreign figures who wield power directly or though surrogates are the geographically (and sometimes historically) distant Persians and Ethiopians.

Most Greek novels give no indication of historical time, or they situate their action in a time when Greek military power was at its height. For plots located in the fifth or fourth centuries BCE, Rome is necessarily absent and Greek can be staged as the dominant culture. Barbarian Persia was still a mighty empire whose rulers could be granted a status more or less equal to Greeks, especially since Greece had defeated Persia in the fifth century BCE. In Chariton, for example, when Callirhoe, the daughter of the fifth-century Syracusan general, Hermocrates, is introduced to the Persian king his response is: 'I must take proper care of the daughter of Hermocrates, who defeated my worst enemy, the Athenians' (5.8.8), thus playing out principles of guest-friendship prized throughout Greek culture. Though in the real time of the novels' composition (more or less the first four centuries CE) the political and legal, if not social, hierarchy placed Rome and Roman citizenship on top, Greeks and assimilated Greeks next, and the barbarian peoples lowest of all, fiction can experiment with the notion that all men are brothers under the skin. Also it may have been a deliberate narrative strategy to obscure these potentially divisive status variations within the Roman empire.[25]

Being Greek is seemingly tested when characters leave their native shores, are deprived of their accustomed status through misfortune, and have to negotiate dangerous circumstances and unfamiliar behaviours. Consider this encounter in Xenophon's *Anthia and Habrocomes*: the heroine Anthia has been captured by pirates and handed over for sale in the slave market in Alexandria. Her beauty attracts the attention of an Indian king, Psammis, who happens to be in Alexandria on business.

---

24 In *Anthia and Habrocomes*, however, Greek Anthia not only visits the Apis temple, she prostrates herself before the god (a bull) and asks for an oracle (5.4.8–11).

25 It is very possible that the tendentiously named twin boys, Tigris and Euphrates, and their sister, Mesopotamia, who look exactly like the hero and heroine, and the frequent mistakes in identity that drive Iamblichus' *Babylonian Affairs* are meant to play out the artificial nature of status and/or ethnic inequality; but speculation on the basis of Photius' epitome is a high-risk game.

As soon as he bought her the barbarian immediately tried to force her to intimacy. At first she refused but finally gave the excuse to Psammis (for barbarians are by nature superstitious) that her father had dedicated her at birth to Isis until she reached the age for marriage, and she said that there was still a year to go . . . Psammis believed her.   (3.11.4)

The dynamics are clear. Barbarians are lustful, superstitious and gullible. Greek Anthia, even though a girl, is clever and resourceful, and capable of outwitting the barbarian. But these clichéd behaviours are not restricted to Greek–barbarian interaction. Greeks also enslave Greeks, and Greek characters regularly try to force their attentions on the heroine, who cleverly resists. Achilles Tatius provides a more typical example of characters that cannot be easily classified as Greek/barbarian by their behaviour alone. Menelaus, the Greco-Egyptian mentioned above, rescues Leucippe from the Egyptian bandits planning to sacrifice her to the gods, while the hero of the novel, her lover, can only watch and wring his hands. Pretending to be a new recruit to the outlaw band (and indistinguishable from them), Menelaus uses theatrical props to simulate the human sacrifice. Clitophon's response is to fall at his feet and 'prostrate himself before him as a god' (3.23.1); the language used for this action suggests the prostration (*proskunesis*) that Greeks typically associated with the stereotypical barbarians, the courtiers of the Persian Great King.

Finally, in this passage from Heliodorus, the Egyptian priest Calasiris not only knows his Homer better than his Athenian companion, he is capable of a hermeneutic sophistication far in advance of his auditor. Cnemon asks how the gods had told Calasiris where he should take the young lovers. Calasiris responds:

In the manner, my son, that the wise Homer hints, though the many miss his allusion. Somewhere he says: 'I easily recognised the forms of his feet and legs from behind him as he went away. Gods to be sure are easily recognised'.   (*Iliad* 13.71–2)

[Cnemon replies:]
I am apparently one of the many then, and perhaps in quoting that passage you wanted to make this very point, Calasiris. I know that I was taught the common meaning of the lines with the text, but I am ignorant of the embedded theological implication.   (Hld. 3.12.2)

Calasiris' explanation of Homer's deeper meaning demonstrates the breadth of his learning (*paideia*), since Homer was a lynchpin of the educational system. Also, since his auditor was Athenian, and Athens was generally taken to be the epicentre of Hellenism, Calasiris' more profound understanding can easily be read as an intermediary in the passing of *paideia* from the old centre (Athens), via an Egypt suffused with Neoplatonism, to the Ethiopian periphery – just as the young Greek couple move from Delphi through Egypt to their new home in Meroë (in Ethiopia). However we may choose to nuance this movement, the exchange also reinforces stereotypes, as it confirms the traditional view that Egyptians are more religious than any other people (except the Ethiopians), a view common in Greek writing from at least the time of Herodotus.[26]

While all the novels depend on status reversal to cast characters' cultural values into relief, for the Greek novels, as I said above, the presence of Rome is almost entirely muted, though most (if not all) were written under Roman rule. One of the few indications of Roman presence is to be found in Xenophon's *Anthia and Habrocomes*: here Egypt is governed by a 'prefect' (4.2.1), although nothing is made of it. (In other novels we find it ruled by a Persian satrap, a condition that ended in the fourth century BCE.[27])

For the Roman novels, however, anxieties about status and status reversal are played out against an ever visible backdrop of Roman power. There are no principled or elevated characters like Calasiris, but a variety of behaviours from farcical to disgusting, often illustrated by recourse to Greek anecdotes known as Milesian tales (for example, Petronius' 'widow of Ephesus' story (*Sat.* 111–12), or Apuleius' 'tale of the tub' (*Met.* 9.5–7)) that lend a cynical narrative tone. Apuleius' retelling of a Greek story in Latin automatically makes the Greek characters and locations 'other'. Greeks serve as a source of risqué humour, though Roman power is not exempt from critique. In the *Metamorphoses* we find a world of unresponsive and arbitrary human institutions. Bandits appear to rob or kidnap at will. Soldiers of the imperial army are portrayed not as keeping peace, but as adding to the precariousness of human affairs by brutalising the poor. Note for example the Roman soldier who commandeers the ass from a gardener who legally owns him; when the gardener protests, he finds himself under arrest (9.40).[28] The Greek protagonist, Lucius is a well-to-do young man, but hardly a model of civilised *paideia*. He has a decided taste for magic that accidentally turns him into an ass. As the ass he experiences the life of the underclass, and resumes his

---

26 E.g. Herodotus 2.57–9. Two Egyptians – Nectanebo in the *Alexander Romance* and Paapis in Antonius Diogenes – are 'bad'. But their negative behaviour (magic practice) also falls within standard Greek stereotypes of Egyptians, and can be thought of as the dark side of Egyptian religiosity.

27 Iamblichus may have inserted historical data about Roman Syria into his *Babylonian Affairs*, but it is not at all clear from Photius' summary (75b27) whether they belonged to a frame, an aside, or to the narrative. See Stephens and Winkler (1995) 182–4, 192, and Millar (1993) 489–92.

28 For an excellent discussion of the historical context of the *Metamorphoses* see Millar (1981).

human form only to devote himself to the worship of the Egyptian deities Isis and Osiris. Isis is portrayed in lofty terms as a universal force: 'my divinity is one, worshipped throughout the world, though under different aspects, with various rites, and many names' (11.5), but our last glimpse of Lucius finds him identical to a figure often mocked in Roman writing, a bald-headed 'Egyptian' priest.[29]

Petronius' *Satyrica* is more recognisably Roman than the *Metamorphoses*, but the characters who carry the action (Encolpius, Giton, Ascyltus), the parasitic rhetor (Agamemnon), and the inept poet (Eumolpus) have Greek names, and their picaresque adventures seem to re-enact events from Homer's *Odyssey*. The *Satyrica* also links being Greek with dissolute behaviour. The explicitly homoerotic nature of the novel is cast as Greek (with nods and winks at Plato's *Symposium*), and Greek *paideia* comes under attack in the opening fragments as Encolpius laments the status of contemporary oratory, attributing it to the florid Asian style of speaking that has overwhelmed the pure Atticism of classical writers like Thucydides, Demosthenes and Plato. He accuses those who teach and practise rhetoric of bloated and meaningless sentiments devoid of a moral centre. The idealising Greek novels, in contrast, have a predilection for trials in which rhetorical skills can be displayed, and the writing often betrays a rhetorical training.[30]

The Roman freedmen who populate the *Satyrica* are venal and vulgar, but rather less dissolute than Encolpius and his friends. Consider for example the speech by a fellow freedman at Trimalchio's dinner party, who has taken exception to Ascyltus' snide laughter:

> He's laughing. What does he have to laugh at? Did his father pay money for him as a baby? You are a Roman knight? And I am a king's son. 'Why then are you a slave?' Because I wanted to, I'd rather be a Roman citizen than a tribute-paying kinglet. And now I hope I live in a way that no man laughs at me . . . I paid a thousand denarii for my freedom and I was made a priest of Augustus for free. And I hope to die and not have anything to blush for in my grave . . . You see the lice on another, but not your own vermin. You alone see us as a joke . . . I was a slave for forty years, but no one knew whether I was a slave or a free man . . . I worked hard at pleasing my master . . . And I lived in a house where some tried to trip me up here and there but thanks to my master I managed to swim. These are real victories; to be born free is as easy as saying 'come here'. (57)

29 In contrast, the Greek *Ass* attributed to Lucian lacks a conversion at the end; the main character is simply returned to his former self. On the significance of change, see Winkler (1985) 224–7.
30 See e.g. Reeve (1971); Bartsch (1989).

The speaker claims a preference for Roman mores (and the opportunity for a more secure social advancement), rejecting his supposedly royal barbarian origins even at the price of slavery. He implicitly validates the 'Roman' virtues of hard work, duty, and respect in contrast to the moral shabbiness of Ascyltus, a Roman knight, with his inclination for things Greek. In Apuleius the Greek Lucius is given to first to magic and then to (excessive?) religious devotion; and Apuleius' anecdote in which a town councillor named Barbarus (Barbarian) is cuckolded by his Greek-named wife Arete ('Virtue'), implies a certain contempt for Greek cultural pretensions, since 'Greeks' might well be assimilated barbarians, and *aretē* was a cornerstone of Greek moral philosophy.

For Petronius and Apuleius Greeks had a lower social status (regardless of their previous cultural accomplishments) than their Roman readers and thus furnished an easy (and politically safer) target for satirising. Moreover, the emphasis on Greek decadence is consonant with other Roman writing, in which the status and destiny of Rome as humanitarian bringer of civilisation to all peoples is deliberately set against the failure of Greek cultural achievements.[31] In contrast the extant Greek novels privilege the well-to-do Greek-speaking urban dwellers of the empire and unqualified happy endings, though we might ask why this should be. On one level the emphasis on being Greek found in idealising novels also reflects historical reality. A superficial Greek culture, based on the need for an administrative elite with a common language, was ubiquitous, the glue that held together the eastern Roman empire where Romans were less visible, and texts written in Greek obviously had Greek readers as their target audience. Novels, when working out of simple Greek/non-Greek oppositions, will have consciously or otherwise promoted in readers a sense of common if anodyne Greek identity, regardless of social condition; when novels present Greeks and non-Greeks as indistinguishable in action or moral fibre, they act to undercut notions of ethnic essentialism. Although national literatures continue to flourish among non-Greek peoples during this period, the assimilation of Greek culture by non-Greeks was the quickest road to social advancement. For our Lucians, Iamblichuses, and Josephuses, Greek civilised values (*paideia*) brought enhanced status and perks, and a heightened awareness or double consciousness of the differences (or lack of differences) between Greek and non-Greek.

Kinship under the skin plays out differently for Greeks and non-Greeks, however. For the former to comment on the humanity or culture of the latter often seems to be little more than the condescension of the ruling

---

31 Woolf (1994) 118–23.

classes (whether subconscious or thinly disguised), for the latter it may express a more serious desire for equal status and recognition. *Charicleia and Theagenes*, for example, has the appearance of a novel that articulates the superior ethical and moral values of a non-Greek culture, especially since Ethiopia always remained outside of the Roman empire. But in fact Persinna, the black Ethiopian queen, resorts to the characteristically Greek practice of infant exposure (with birth tokens as in Greek tragedy) to jumpstart the plot. The wise and generous Egyptian high priest, Calasiris, though whose tireless efforts the now seemingly Greek girl with her faithful lover is returned to her home and patrimony, behaves like a thorough Hellene.[32] The Ethiopians throughout the novel have the reputation for surpassing wisdom, but they are not perfect. It is through their encounter with Hellenism that they are induced to abandon their last vestige of barbarism – human sacrifice. Here Greek and barbarian complement and are finally fused, as Hydaspes and Persinna recognise Characleia as their legitimate heir and marry her to her Greek lover. The final image in the novel (rather like the end of the *Magic Flute*) is of the Greek pair, Charicleia and Theagenes, becoming priests of the Sun and Moon, then riding into Meroë together with their black parents/parents-in-law. The succession of the white-skinned children to the Ethiopian throne may easily be read as Greek culture yielding pride of place to barbarian, but even more it is a triumph for Hellenism, since the couple is completely unfamiliar with the culture of its new kingdom. Despite some genuine Egyptian and Ethiopian material in the novel, the narrative mechanics are entirely drawn from the Greek cultural repertoire: Homer, visual representation like Andromeda, infant exposure, and Greek assumptions about barbarians (human sacrifice), and, most of all, whiteness.

In this context I should like to consider a subset of ancient fictions focused on historical figures of non-Greek lands. The majority are known only from fragments or epitomes, but they all have common features: the characters are kings of barbarian lands, Persia, Egypt or Babylon, but their behaviour is indistinguishable from that of the best educated of Greek manhood. The earliest such pseudo-historical fiction is *The Education of Cyrus* (*Cyropaideia* in Greek) by the Athenian Xenophon. It focuses upon the coming of age of the young Cyrus, who grows up to become – from a Greek perspective – a model king of Persia. These works often begin with the proper education of princes and progress to first military expeditions, but then the stories veer off to include increasingly larger components of the erotic – passionate love

---

32 Even Calasiris' claim that Homer was Egyptian has a parallel in Herodotus' assertions about the Egyptian origins of some Greek religious practices (2.57–9).

and its bitter consequences or betrothal and separation – that do not appear in any historical tradition. In the *Education of Cyrus*, for example, we find the interlude of Araspas and Panthea: she is the beautiful and faithful wife of one of Cyrus' enemies, now held captive, whom Araspas, Cyrus' lieutenant, falls in love with and tries to corrupt, first by persuasion and then by threatening force. Cyrus prevents him from acting on his threats, and the moral of the tale seems to be that Love is a force than cannot be withstood and that Cyrus, the wise prince, has the good judgment to avoid temptation.[33] In later fictions, the erotic plays an even more prominent part, for example, in *Ninus*, the erotic and the military adventures seem equally balanced.[34] Finally, disguise and temporary loss of status seem to be standard fare, as the young prince embarks upon a series of complicated adventures ranging over much of the Near East, before the stories eventually comes to a close. We even find this pattern in the *Alexander Romance* when, intrigued by the accounts of her incredible beauty, Alexander, disguised as one of his own guardsmen, sets out to meet the Candace of Meroë. The powerful queen recognizes him, saying: 'What can you do? As important a king as you are, you are in the power of a mere woman' (3.18–23).

Although the characters of these nationalistic dramas may originate in non-Greek traditions, in such novels their behaviour is assimilated to that of the Greek-speaking educated classes within the Roman empire. Figures who were portrayed as great world conquerors in earlier Greek historians are seen behaving as well brought-up Greek youths, respectful of their elders, speaking in polished rhetorical periods, and adapted to Greek cultural norms. For example, Semiramis, who in Diodorus' historical account is a fierce and independent queen leading her own armies and occasionally disposing of unwanted lovers (2.4–20), in *Ninus* becomes a shy and tongue-tied girl confined to the women's quarters, and too embarrassed even to admit to her aunt that she is in love with her cousin (to whom she is betrothed).[35] In a fragment from the *Sesonchosis* novel, the young hero incognito and in exile from his homeland is a guest of a local petty king, when the king's daughter, Meameris, falls in love with him at first sight. The young woman languishes in moonstruck distress:

And at length, Meameris, entered the walk and arrived at the place where Sesonchosis was standing. She stood looking down at the flow of the water. Then she glanced at Sesonchosis and saw that he was [not alone]. Grieving at this in her soul, she went away. After she had been attended, she reclined at the

---

33 Tatum (1989) 165–79.   34 Stephens and Winkler (1995) 23–30.   35 Ibid. 41.

feast and reluctantly took what was placed before her; she kept remembering the youth's handsomeness, and when [she did not] succeed in covering her feelings, one of her fellow banqueteers . . .[36]

This type of scene is a staple of Greek fiction, and if standard Greek names were substituted for Sesonchosis and Meamiris, from the events readers would be hard put to identify the characters as barbarian.

Martin Braun, the first to study this set of quasi-historical fictions, has argued that non-Greek figures like Ninus or Sesonchosis, along with obscure local legends, grew into subjects for Greek history as well as popular fiction in the early Hellenistic period, because such characters and legends served as foci for native resistance to Greek rule.[37] This has proved an enduring thesis because the spread of the power of Alexander's Successors initially met with fierce native resistance. For the later Hellenistic and Roman period, however, Braun's argument becomes less cogent. Not because resistance to imperial authority was absent – it was not. Nor are we lacking a literature of resistance: numerous texts in Greek ranging from the so-called *Acts of the Pagan Martyrs* to Josephus' *Against Apion* testify to powerful anti-Greek and anti-Roman sentiments. However, the extreme degree of assimilation to Greek culture to be found in Greek novels like *Ninus* from the first century BCE/CE or the somewhat later *Sesonchosis* hardly suggests protest. The good-looking boy (in disguise) with his lovesick girl friend that we saw above is a long way from this same king in Herodotus, the fierce world conqueror who insults his opponents by marking their names with signs for female genitalia (2.102.5). Alternative explanations suggest themselves: if Xenophon's *Education of Cyrus* led the way, it was written by an Athenian Greek of the fourth century BCE modelling a young and idealised barbarian king for Greek consumption. To continue recasting barbarian kings as idealised Greek youths in the Roman period is arguably to assert (in the fictional mode) the abiding values of Hellenism at a time when those values were being challenged or overshadowed by Rome.

Equally such historical fictions may be attempts by assimilated non-Greeks to write the histories of their own local heroes not by creating warlords to rival their conquerors and to focus rebellious sentiments, but by casting them in Greek garb. That is, to portray young foreign kings acting out an idealised Hellenism and, in so doing, serving to efface the distinctions in behaviour between Greek and barbarian so prominent in classical Greek self-fashioning. It is easy to spot the barbarian in the *Alexander Romance*. It is Nectanebo, the treacherous oriental, complete with all the clichés: he

36 Ibid. 263.   37 Braun (1938) 1–31.

practises magic, he is sexually uninhibited and he consorts with outlandish gods, like the ram-headed Amon. In contrast, young foreign princes like the Persian Cyrus, the Babylonian Ninus or the Egyptian Sesonchosis, are proper Boy Scouts: loyal, trusty and true. They exercise in the manly skills of war, horsemanship and swordsmanship. They behave in a manner that mimics *paideia*; they heed their elders and either avoid the dangers of erotic involvement entirely, or experience it as a further test of character. *Ninus* and *Sesonchosis*, like the *Alexander Romance* and *Charicleia and Theagenes*, are important for an overall understanding of fiction writing in antiquity because they present characters whose fictional identity depends upon the blending of Greek and non-Greek. The question: 'who is he?' is fundamental to the *Alexander Romance*. To the question 'is Alexander Greek?' or 'is he Egyptian?' we must give the answer: 'he is both'. Who is Sesonchosis? Is he a mighty Egyptian pharaoh or an idealised Greek youth? Who is Charicleia in *Charicleia and Theagenes*? Is she an Ethiopian princess or an idealised Greek heroine? Within the novels they are both.

'Greek' identity however asserted or enacted, I suggest, is central to the fiction-writing enterprise in antiquity. In a world where 'Greek' covered a range of classes, behaviours and even ethnicities,[38] a world in which Syrians or Egyptians or Jews might also claim to be Greek and/or Roman; where bilingualism or trilingualism is the norm for the literate classes; where Greek education provides the means for social advancement for already upper-class non-Greeks (who had their own high culture) 'who you are' might be answered in more than one way. Experiments with or testing of the boundaries of 'Greek' identity may account for the persistent foreign presence in seemingly Greek narratives, for the Hellenising of such seemingly foreign characters, customs and locations, and for the erasure of Rome, which if present reduces the status of Greeks to subalterns. It may also account for the fictionality of fiction. History or oratory or philosophy are modes of discourse that by relying upon or attempting to present what is true in particular instances, can only lead to separation, to a plurality, to alienation. It is the fictional mode of discourse that serves to create an alternative model of reality – like the bicultural fathering of Alexander – that allows both the author and the readers indulge in 'what if', cushioned by the safety of the text.

Further reading

For the construction of Greek identity, see especially Hall (2002), Malkin (2001). There are a number of recent studies of cultural identity for the period

---

38 E.g. Thompson (2001).

in which the novels were being written: Goldhill (2001a) is a good place to start, offering helpful theoretical approaches, breadth and readability. A more literary construction of cultural identity is to be found in Whitmarsh (2001a). Other studies include Bowie (1970) and Swain (1996); Miles (1999) focuses on late antiquity. For studies on the novel see in general Swain's chapter 'The Greek novel and Greek identity', in Swain (1996) 101–31, Kuch (2003); and more narrowly Bowie (1991), Whitmarsh (1998), Perkins (1999). For the intersection of fiction and history see Tatum (1989), Bowersock (1994), Stoneman (1994).

5

TIM WHITMARSH

Class

Novels and the elite

Where do we pitch the novels, in terms of social class? This is a more difficult question than is often admitted. The authors, to begin with them, can rarely be pinpointed demographically. The Latin novelists were no doubt high-powered individuals: Petronius was probably Nero's courtier,[1] and Apuleius' father – a *duumvir* or chief magistrate in his city of Madaurus – was rich enough to leave his sons the hefty sum of 2 million sesterces (*Apology* 23.1). The Greek writers are, however, more shadowy. Chariton describes himself as 'from Aphrodisias, a clerk (*hypographeus*) to the rhetor Athenagoras' (1.1.1): even if this is biographically true – and there is good reason to suspect an erotic novelist who styles himself 'Charming, from the City of Aphrodite' – it is hard to guess except in the broadest terms what kind of echelon such a professional occupied in first-century CE Aphrodisias. Heliodorus' descent 'from the race of the sun' (10.41.4) looks like a claim to hereditary priesthood, but the same uncertainties apply. If Heliodorus, and Achilles Tatius with him, did indeed become Christian bishops (as later tradition maintained), then they can hardly have been socially insignificant, but the chances are that these reports are fictions.[2] Finally, Iamblichus, whose *Babylonian Affairs* survives only in fragments and summary, is reported in a late source to have been born of slaves, although this notice has been suspected, with some justice.[3]

Despite the paucity of hard evidence, particularly in the Greek world, there is now a strong consensus for the view that the novels were composed by and for the elite.[4] There is much to recommend this claim, and indeed little

---

1 Introduction, p. 4.   2 Introduction, p. 13.
3 *Suda* s.v. Iamblichus; Stephens and Winkler (1995) 180–2.
4 The 'hardest' evidence is the high-class papyrus upon which the preserved fragments are composed: see esp. Stephens (1994), and more generally Bowie (1994a), Hunter in this volume. The more recent view contradicts older hypotheses of a 'bourgeois' readership (Hägg (1983) 90–101; cf. Holzberg (1995) 32–3). Cavallo (1996), however, suggests popular readers.

directly to contradict it (although we shall introduce some nuance over the course of this chapter). A more fundamental question, however, remains to be asked: what do we *mean* by class? More often than not, critics have conflated two different aspects of social identity: the phrase 'the educated elite' is used casually, as though education and wealth were coterminous. They are, certainly, intimately related: in general, only wealth could buy education, and education was a sign of social distinction (for reasons that we shall discuss below). But a moment's reflection will remind us of the potential pitfalls of this assumption. In Petronius' *Satyrica*, the central characters are educated, indeed pretentious, Greeks; but they are also on a mission to 'expunge our poverty' (10). The novelist and erstwhile 'clerk' Chariton meanwhile, like Encolpius and his friends, is saturated in the ideology of literary civilisation: he uses the word 'educated' as a compliment, and alludes learnedly throughout (to Homer, Sappho, Euripides, Thucydides, Xenophon and others).[5] We might take these as signs of his elite status, until we recall that the ex-slave Epictetus also uses the language of education, and references, among others, Homer, Aristophanes, Sophocles, Euripides, Plato and Xenophon.

We are on no surer ground when we turn to consider readers. With the exception of Petronius' *Satyrica*, the novels certainly focus upon and embrace the values of upper-class Greeks, but there is no more reason to assume that this directly reflects their ancient readership than there is to conclude that modern readers of Jilly Cooper are uniformly rich, suave and attractive. In fact, the drive to mark the novels' readers as elite is primarily motivated by issues in contemporary academia, and the desire to reclaim the novels as sophisticated literature: bad texts are read by poor people and women, good texts by rich males.[6] For sure, there were indeed elite readers of the novels, such as the wealthy individual in Syrian Antioch who commissioned a mosaic depicting a scene from *Metiochus and Parthenope*.[7] But this does not mean that the novels were exclusively, or even primarily, targeted at such a group. The fact that we know, conversely, of no sub-elite readers of the novels is no surprise, in that elite readers are infinitely more likely to leave traces of their literary tastes.

Literary elitism

Questions of economics and demographics are, in fact, a partial distraction from the real issues. We shall never be able to determine the average income of a reader of a novel – nor indeed what that kind of information would

5 Robiano (2000); Manuwald (2000).   6 For this point see Egger (1994b) 32–3.
7 Hägg and Utas (2003) 57–64. It is possible that the scene depicted derives from a mime (Introduction, n. 49) rather than the novel. On elite readers see further Hunter, this volume.

tell us about her understanding of the text. What we can do, however, is consider how the novels engage their readers' sense of themselves as the educated, the *literary* elite. This is not to downplay the real-life importance of finances, but to insist that literary and economic elitism, while related to each other, operate in fundamentally different ways. Status qualifications based directly upon wealth are, at least in principle, easy to determine: to decide whether an individual has enough cash to qualify as a *zeugitēs* in Solonian Athens, or a knight in Rome, is in effect simply a matter of quantification. To decide whether someone is 'educated' or not is altogether more difficult, particularly in a world without academic qualifications. For all that imperial literature repeatedly speaks of 'the educated' as a distinct class,[8] the boundaries were hazy and ill defined. The status of educated civility, being *doctus* (in Latin) or *pepaideumenos* (in Greek), can only be attained in the eyes of others; and while there were certain recognised standards, there was always the risk that one person's cultured refinement was another person's crass ignorance.

How does education relate to economics? It is helpful here to invoke Pierre Bourdieu's influential concept of 'cultural capital', that is, education and 'civilised' values.[9] According to Bourdieu, monetary capital can be converted to and from cultural capital, which are needed to provide a veneer of legitimacy, in the form of supposedly qualitative differences, to the arbitrary hierarchies of society. Thus far, this is a relatively orthodox Marxist account of 'abstraction', the process whereby domination is disguised and transfigured by ideology. Bourdieu also insists, however, that cultural capital is much more difficult to control than its economic equivalent. It cannot be banked and then drawn upon at will. It is a dangerous, unstable, investment: its value can go down as well as up. For all that societies depend upon ideological myths of universal, unproblematic values – we are all expected to know what a person of 'taste' looks like, for example – an individual's status is only as good as her public perception, which can be suddenly altered by an unfortunate *faux pas*, or indeed a stunning coup. We shall return presently to this idea of the slipperiness of elite literary status.

The idea of educatedness as a strategy of social distinction is inherent in the ancient concept of literature from at least the fourth century BCE, when intellectual life began to shift away from the public sphere into more

---

8 References and discussion at Whitmarsh (2001a) 90–130.
9 See Bourdieu (1977) esp. 159–97; influential upon the accounts of imperial literature by Gleason (1995), Schmitz (1997), Whitmarsh (2005b). In discussing Greece and Rome, I have in fact brought Bourdieu's 'cultural capital' (which he sees as rather static and conservative) closer to the fluidity and dynamism of 'symbolic capital' (i.e. reputation, 'honour'); this is because education in the ancient world was, as we have said, less regulated and 'official' than in the industrial societies on which Bourdieu's studies of pedagogy are based.

rarefied, elitist institutions such as Plato's Academy, Aristotle's Lyceum and the Alexandrian Museum. The consequences of this transformation were pronounced: to claim intellectual status now meant to segregate oneself from the masses. 'I hate everything to do with the people', the third-century BCE poet Callimachus famously opines (*Epigram* 28.4). This trend was unreversed by time. In Neronian Rome, Seneca could be found writing to Lucilius of his pleasure that he will not be disturbed in his study by all the 'bores', who have gone to the boxing-match (*Epistles* 80.1). Lucian, the Greco-Syrian satirist of the second century CE, writes of the 'law' that distinguishes the articulate response of an educated viewer of a wondrous building from the mute gawping of the 'commoner' (*idiotēs* > English 'idiot': *On the Hall* 2).

Roman society, built vertically around competitive ambition, was highly receptive to this concept. Roman notables vied with each other to present themselves as successful but also generous and humane: in this respect, there was a continuum between the culture of public benefaction (putting on games, mass patronage and bread-doles, paying for buildings) and that of intellectual achievement. In either case, the potentate was staging his selflessness and commitment to real values, and hence bolstering his elite credentials. In this environment, literature was much more than just entertainment or edification: defining oneself as 'educated' (*doctus, pepaideumenos*) was a valuable token in the game of social snakes and ladders. Romans did, however, also experience a certain awkwardness here. A Roman nobleman was expected to have a certain amount of education, but too much might look an abrogation of traditional, rugged Roman values.[10] As a result, many confined themselves to second-order sponsorship of intellectual pursuits: creating libraries, hoarding artworks in their atria, engaging Greek orators, historians or poets as clients.

By the imperial period, then, the ideas of literature and elitism were thoroughly spliced. This is the environment for which a large majority of the novels – among which I count the Roman novels of Petronius and Apuleius, and all of the extant major Greek texts, with the possible exception of Xenophon – were composed.[11] Like most written works of Greek and Roman literature, they presume, and engage, a high level of educated competence in their readers. It takes an experienced, knowing reader to be able to spot the allusions in *Daphnis and Chloe* (see below), to savour the exquisite wordplay in Apuleius' *Metamorphoses*, to navigate the complex narratological seas of *Chariclia and Theagenes*. Textual abstruseness is a way of testing

10 In general on Roman reactions to Greek learning see Petrochilos (1974).
11 Sub-elite novels will be discussed presently. For more on the readership of the novels, see Hunter, this volume.

readers' sophistication, of allowing them to define themselves through their reading.

Educating the reader

I want to move now towards an argument that part of the novels' function was precisely to test the reader in this way. From this perspective, the demographic approach to readership is misguided: the reader's social class (defined in literary rather than economic terms) is not an absolute position that he or she possesses before unfurling the papyrus, but a shimmering mirage generated in the act of reading itself.

Of all the novels, Longus' *Daphnis and Chloe* is most explicitly constructed around the theme of education.[12] To understand how it engages with themes of class, we must first consider how this theme plays out. The plot centres on the young lovers' innocence of love ('they wanted something, but they did not know what they wanted', 1.22.4), and their comical attempts to transcend this through instruction and imitation of fauna. These two sources of learning represent, respectively, culture and nature, the two creative forces that are so central to the aesthetics of the entire work.[13] Neither is successful independently of the other. There are two teachers: the old man Philetas, whose description of an epiphany of Eros is styled by the narrator an 'education' (2.8.1, 2.9.1);[14] and Lycaenion, the sexually voracious neighbour who gives Daphnis an 'erotic pedagogy' (3.19.1; similar language at 3.17.3, 3.18.4, 3.19.2). These lessons, however, are not wholly successful. Philetas' allegory goes over the youngsters' heads, and his advice to 'kiss, embrace and lie down together naked' (2.7.7) is too euphemistic for his literalist audience. When Lycaenion tells Daphnis that practising what he has learned upon Chloe will leave her lying in a pool of blood 'as though slain' (3.19.2, retaining the manuscript reading), he interprets this to mean that he will threaten her life, and is put off. If these cultural forms of education do not result in success, then nor does following examples from the natural world. Immediately before his encounter with Lycaenion, Daphnis has failed with a different tactic, 'embracing her from behind in imitation of the billy-goats' (3.14.5).

At one level, the education theme in *Daphnis and Chloe* represents a putting into practice of the pedagogic theory current at the time, which

---

12 See esp. Winkler (1990) 101–26; Zeitlin (1990) 430–44; Goldhill (1995) esp. 20–37; Morgan (1996) 167–72; Whitmarsh (2001a) 80–3, 100–3.
13 In addition to the works cited in the previous note, see Teske (1991).
14 On Philetas as educator see Whitmarsh (2005d), with further literature.

was analogously concerned with the degree to which cultural instruction can modify natural instincts.[15] At another level, however, it engages readers' own self-perceptions as educated. The narrator promises, in the preface, that his work 'will heal the sick, console the grieving, remind him who has loved and <u>educate</u> him who has not' (pr. 1.3). The text is thus presented as an instruction for the innocent reader, paralleling the process undergone by the young lovers themselves.

Yet no reader can really lay claim to the virginal innocence of Daphnis and Chloe. (At the outset, indeed, the rustic pair are so innocent that they do not even realise they are innocent.) Longus' strategy depends on driving a wedge firmly between the impossibly naive perspective of the lovers and the knowing, educated vantage of the reader. Let us take an example. When Chloe finds the sight of Daphnis beautiful, she 'thought it was the bath itself that was causing the beauty' (1.13.2).[16] The very fact that her thought-processes are deemed worthy of mention indicates that she is misguided, as indeed she obviously is: the narrative point of view is thus sharply separated from hers. Such ironical moments consolidate readers' positions as excluded from this impossibly innocent fantasy. This sense of distance is reinforced, in a different register, by the very learnedness of the text, its allusiveness (particularly to Theocritus, Sappho, Thucydides, Homer) and the limpid euphony of its language.[17] The more learned we are, the further we veer from empathy with the young lovers.

Indeed, the very first words of the text reinforce the idea that we are outsiders, urban interlopers in an otherwise sealed rural microcosm: 'When hunting in Lesbos, I saw in a grove of the Nymphs the most beautiful sight I have ever seen . . .' (pr. 1.1). The narrator, through whose eyes we perceive the story, is a hunter, by implication a visitor from the city for leisure purposes. When he happens (so it seems) upon the grove, the two spheres of rural cult and urban pleasure-seeking collide. This event frames the text as a whole: we are encouraged to see it as an alluring but temporary dalliance with the countryside. Even Daphnis and Chloe themselves turn out to be the children of urban nobles.[18]

The obvious conclusion to draw is that these tactics play to a reader's sense of cultural superiority, provoking a satisfied smile (and titillation too, in the case of the bath scene). But the reader's position is more problematic than this

---

15 Whitmarsh (2001a) 71–87.
16 This scene is interestingly discussed at Goldhill (1995) 9–10.
17 Fully discussed in Hunter (1983).
18 On the predominantly urban perspective see Saïd (1987) 97–107 (references to English-language version).

suggests. Urban visitors are presented in this text as dangerous, predatory figures.[19] In book 2, some 'rich young Methymnaean men, wishing to pass the vintaging season having exotic fun' (2.12.1), put in at shore nearby. Their combination of wealth, urban provenance and pleasure-seeking jars with the reference to the 'vintaging season', which implies serious labour for the rustics. The gap is further underlined by the use of the word 'exotic', which is at first sight inappropriate for a short trip down the coastline. The narrative that follows, however, underlines the differences in values. The rope mooring the ship is then stolen by one of the rustics (who needs it precisely for his vintaging). When the Methymnaeans relocate to nearer Daphnis and Chloe – thinking it a good area for hunting (2.13.2), an instinct they clearly share with the narrator himself – they use a withy to tie the ship. While hunting for hares, their dogs disturb Daphnis' goats, one of whom wanders down to the shore and eats the withy, causing the ship to float away. Daphnis is then beaten up by the Methymnaeans, before a rustic court is convened, which acquits him. The Methymnaeans, enraged, grab Daphnis and try to abduct him. The event causes a war between the cities of Methymne and Mitylene, which ultimately leads to the land being ravaged (2.20.1), and Chloe being abducted (2.20.3). Thanks to a dire epiphany of Pan, and weird Panic phenomena such as dolphins leaping and oars breaking, Chloe is finally returned. Taken as a whole, the episode dramatises the divinely protected sanctity of the countryside, and the consequences that can spring from its abuse by unsympathetic intruders.

These themes of predation and exploitation are developed in book 4, where the economic hierarchy that sustains this rural idyll is revealed: the rustic labourers are serfs to a rich 'overlord' (*despotēn*, 4.5.1), Dionysiophanes (who ultimately turns out to be Daphnis' father). The rustics fearfully smarten up the landscape and themselves. Their master's son Astylus ('City-boy') is described in terms that markedly recall the Methymnaean playboys of book 2: 'he set about <u>hunting hares,</u> as you would expect from a <u>rich young man</u>, devoted to luxury, who had come to the countryside to enjoy <u>exotic</u> pleasure' (4.11.1). Atylus' parasite Gnathon ('Jaws') in particular represents the rapacity of the city, in his attempts to rape Daphnis. Tellingly, he is the only (human) figure in the whole of the novel described as 'educated' – but 'having been educated at the parties of the dissolute in every kind of erotic mythology' (4.17.3), he is hardly a role model for the socially aspirant reader.

---

19 There are rustic predators too, in the forms of the wolf (1.11) and the would-be rapists Dorcon (1.20–2) and Lampis (4.7–8).

The threat posed by this particular party to the rustics in fact never really materialises (the 'excellent' Dionysiophanes (4.13.2) and Astylus are harmlessly genial; even Gnathon's rape attempt falls quite literally flat, into the mud), and of course the narrative resolution at the end demands harmonious social relations. Even so, the echoes of the earlier Methymnaean episode remind us that the relationship between the urban elite and rural poor is unequal and can be exploitative. In particular, there is a subterranean narrative connection between the novel's rich young hunters: Astylus, the Methymnaeans and (so it seems) the narrator, himself. Hunting, it seems, symbolises the aggressive but blasé abuse of the countryside on the part of city-folk.

Daphnis and Chloe's emphasis upon education, then, fits into a wider strategy of exploring the relationship between city and country, between rich and poor. The intellectual gap between urban and rural generates a pleasing irony, but readers are not allowed to bask comfortably in the warm glow of intellectual superiority; instead, they are repeatedly reminded that the pleasures they find in the countryside are paid for by the toil of labourers. Of all the novelists, Longus comes closest to exposing the interconnectedness of social hierarchies and education, what Bourdieu would call economic and cultural capital. For urban readers who pride themselves on their civilised values, this is a discomfiting and subtly subversive message.

Satires on literary elitism

A more aggressively satirical approach to literary elitism comes in Petronius' *Satyrica*. For many readers, this is the embodiment of Roman social snobbery. There are no members of the elite in this text: the central figure and narrator is Encolpius, who, along with his friend Ascyltus, are would-be intellectuals in search of money (*Sat.* 10). Although as impoverished Greeks they are some way down the social hierarchy, they have no difficulty in locating people below them: prostitutes, slaves, and particularly (in the best-preserved episode), the famous assemblage of freedmen at the banquet of Trimalchio. That Encolpius looks down upon the boorishness of Trimalchio – as so often in the Roman empire, intellectual ability blurs into social class – is both indubitable and obvious. The host is, indeed, a laughable figure, with his oenological ignorance (34), credulousness, and serial literary errors ('Diomedes and Ganymede were two brothers, and Helen was their sister . . .', 59; 'do you know the story of Ulysses, how he twisted the Cyclops' thumb?', 48). Like Nasidienus in Horace's satirical portrait (*Satires* 2.8), on which this episode is based, Trimalchio devises the feast as a sign of his largesse and power, but ends up demonstrating only his cultural incompetence.[20]

There is, however, another twist: the supercilious perspective of the narrator Encolpius is arguably undermined by the very absurd pretentiousness of this failed intellectual. Conte, who has pressed this case at the greatest length, argues that a 'hidden author' satirises and undermines the perspective of Encolpius – who is, after all, an incompetent, lecherous drunkard as well.[21] On this argument, the text offers a regressive model of social snobbery: we look down on Encolpius looking down on Trimalchio. Schematic models, however, belie the complexity of reading in practice: the *Satyrica* is a more challenging text than this suggests.[22] The very hiddenness of the hidden author, in Conte's model, is problematic: can we really be sure that the narratorial absurdities are Encolpius' and not Petronius'? Also problematic is the fact that our view of Trimalchio as an ignoramus depends upon Encolpius, who is (as we have said) an unreliable narrator. This makes for awkward moments. When Encolpius asks what are the pictures painted on the wall of Trimalchio's atrium, the latter replies 'The *Iliad* and the *Odyssey*' (29). How is it that Encolpius, this self-proclaimed literary expert, has failed to identify the two most canonical works of ancient literature? Are we to assume that Trimalchio is at fault for commissioning an inept painting? Or that our narrator's grasp upon the literary heritage is not as secure as it might be?

As so often with ancient satire – and the *Satyrica* is, as its name suggests, amongst other things a satirical text[23] – readers are disabused, on reflection, of any initial impression that they can comfortably join a community that defines itself by mocking the excluded.[24] These issues are particularly powerful when we deal with issues of superior and inferior education (a transvalued form of class snobbery, as we have observed): any satire of the ignorant runs the risk of exposing its own ignorance. These risks are amply demonstrated by readers who rush in to sneer at Trimalchio: those scholars, for example, who have fixed upon the freedmen's use of language – which is, needless to say, an artful confection on Petronius' part – as a realistic portrayal of the lower end of the sociolinguistic scale. Other scholars have claimed that the freedmen's language cannot, in fact, be neatly boxed as 'vulgar Latin': there is no substantive distinction between their parlance

---

20 For detailed comparison between the two episodes see Bodel (1999) 39. More generally on dining scenes (unfortunately omitting Petronius) see Gowers (1993).
21 Conte (1996); see further Bartsch, this volume.
22 For more along the following lines see Rimell (2007).
23 See Harrison, this volume.
24 See esp. Plaza (2006) on the role of laughter in Roman satire; also (2000) specifically on laughter in Petronius.

and that of the 'educated' characters.²⁵ Who, then, ends up revealing a poor grasp of proper Latin? Trimalchio, or the scholar who misidentifies his diction?

The challenges of reading social-satirical narrative are brought to the fore in Lucian's *True Stories* (probably composed in the 160s CE).²⁶ This brilliant text – not a Greek novel as the term is conventionally understood, but certainly a congregationalist in the broad church of imperial Greek fiction – describes an imaginary voyage into the Atlantic Ocean, thence to the moon, a whale's belly, the underworld, and more. In his other satirical works, Lucian is fond of distinguishing the reactions of the ignorant from those of the educated. For example, the wordsmith Lexiphanes (who may be a figure for Julius Pollux) uses a rare word for 'charcoal': 'the common folk stood agape when their ears were struck by this unusual word, but the educated (*pepaideumenoi*) laughed at both you and your admirers' (*Lexiphanes* 24).²⁷ Similarly, the prologue pitches the *True Stories* as relaxation for 'those who are serious about literature' (1.1) – in other words, the intellectual elite. His audience thus identified, Lucian proceeds to tell us that

> each of the events described contains a not uncomical riddle, aiming at some of the ancient poets, historians and philosophers who have written many ridiculous and mythical things. I would give their names, if it were not that they would be evident to you from your reading. (*True Stories* 1.2)

Most readers have taken this claim at face value, assuming that each of Lucian's episodes has an intertextual undertow; but the very difficulty of agreeing on which models underlie which passages should give us pause.²⁸ Even if we had not lost the vast amounts of Greek literature that we have done (including Antiphanes of Berge and Pytheas of Massilia, two crucial predecessors in the genre of fictional travel-writing), it is unlikely that we would be able to find cast-iron precedents for (for example) the battle between the Sun-men and the Moon-men, or the cork-footed figures who can run on the ocean. At one level, then, Lucian's claim that an intertext underlies all of his episodes is a misrepresentation. He does, after all, proceed to the famous paradox that 'I tell one truth, namely that I tell lies', *True Stories* 1.4: does this also include his intertextual claims? At another level, however, it is also a Petronius-style joke, turning the satire back onto his readership: what does it mean for us if we cannot identify the allusions? Can we ever be sure that

---

25 Petersmann (1985). On stylistic realism see also Laird, this volume.
26 On Lucian's satirical strategy see Whitmarsh (2001a) 247–94, with further literature. For a more sustained reading of the *True Stories* along these lines see Whitmarsh (2006).
27 See further *On the Hall* 2, *Zeuxis* 12.
28 For Georgiadou and Larmour (1998), Lucian's target is philosophers; a different range of texts is identified by Rütten (1997), Camerotto (1998), and Möllendorff (2000).

we have got them all? Are we inside or outside the club of high-status literary *cognoscenti*?

Bottom-up novels

Not all of the novels, however, seem targeted at the literary elite in this way. Of the extant Greek works, Xenophon's *Anthia and Habrocomes* is the least linguistically demanding and stylistically refined, and has no direct allusions to other literature (although there may be echoes here and there).[29] Even those who believe the text to be epitomised do not hold that the 'original' was ambitious in literary terms.[30] Whether *Anthia and Habrocomes* is actually based upon an oral tale, as one scholar has held,[31] or merely a written text with fewer pretensions, it does not engage the reader *qua* possessor of education. The same is perhaps true of the Greek *Ass* narratives. The version preserved in the manuscripts of Lucian is not without its flourishes,[32] but overall the Greek is simple, unelaborated and accessible. The Latin *History of Apollonius, King of Tyre* (perhaps based on a Greek original), again, is written in a simple style, with widescale use of 'vulgar' Latin, although this may represent a mediaeval overlay.[33] In the cases of both the Lucianic *Ass* and the *Apollonius* scholars have suspected that the simplicities are due to epitomisation, but this is to misconstrue the nature of this kind of simple narrative: rather than hypothesise a perfect 'original' from which our imperfect texts are descended, we need to think in terms of a profusion of parallel versions. In the case of the *Ass*, we now have a papyrus fragment (P. Oxy. 4762) showing proving that multiple different versions did exist (this one has an external narrator). The *Apollonius*, meanwhile, survives in a number of different 'recensions', much like the Greek *Alexander Romance*.[34]

Should we be speaking of these as 'popular' romances? At one level, it clearly makes sense to separate them from the 'literary–elitist' texts

---

29 Principally of Chariton, although it is in fact far from certain that Xenophon is the later text (see 'Index of Greek and Roman novelists'). O'Sullivan (1995) 145–70 discusses the relevant passages; his view is that Xenophon is earlier. The opening description of Habrocomes as spurning Eros arrogantly has obvious similarities with Euripides' *Hippolytus*, but whether this counts as an 'allusion' (so Cueva (2004) 36–9) or a fluid sharing of motifs is open to debate.
30 The theory originates with Bürger (1892), who nonetheless maintains that various parts are intact. See the helpful survey of the issues by Kytzler (2003) 348–50.
31 O'Sullivan (1995).
32 In particular, it contains medical language and Herodotean echoes, detailed in Van Thiel (1971).
33 Brief discussion at Schmeling (2003a) 538–40; see more fully Kortekaas (1984).
34 For more on popular narrative, and on the possibility of versions in the form of mimes, see Introduction, n. 49.

considered in the previous two sections: there is none of the rich intertextual depth or linguistic artfulness, and no sign at the thematic level of any engagement of the reader's identity *qua* educated literary expert. Yet it is dangerous to hypothesise for any classical literature a 'popular' status, in the contemporary sense of a mass market.[35] There is no evidence (in the form of, say, papyrology) to suggest that Xenophon or the *Ass* were bestsellers. The best candidate is the *Alexander Romance*, undoubtedly a popular text in the sense that it spread across cultural boundaries, being translated into Syriac, Pahlavi, Arabic, Armenian and so forth. This, however, is not testimony that it was read by the sub-elite. In fact, we are in the same state of general ignorance about the demographic range of the readership as with the more supposedly 'highbrow' novels.

Nevertheless, there are ways in which the novels do seem to leak into popular literature. The first is the use of novel forms as so-called 'national literature', to preserve the memory of great leaders: Alexander is the obvious example – the *Alexander Romance* seems to derive from a tradition that celebrated his continuation of the native Pharaonic line, by making him the son of Nectanebo – but we can also point to now-fragmentary texts that treat the Egyptian pharaoh Sesonchosis (= Senwosret I)[36] and the Assyrian Ninus.[37] These texts (discussed more fully by Susan Stephens in this volume) contain traces of local consciousness that is rare in the more cosmopolitan, elite literature that forms the majority of our ancient literature.

The other socially significant use to which the novels were put is in religion. The novels make widespread use of religious imagery, employ motifs of divine patronage and vengeance, and often owe their narrative structures to liturgical myth (particularly those of rites of passage).[38] Given this saturation in religious language, it is unsurprising to find the novels influencing popular religion. What is surprising, however, is that our primary evidence is not pagan but Jewish and Christian (and even, rather later, Islamic).[39] The Greek romance form in particular, with its focus upon endurance in the face of oppression, readily recommended itself to authors of Christian martyr acts.[40]

Social polyphony

The sense of an association, however loose or distant, between novels and popular literature is actively manipulated even in the 'elite' texts. Storytelling never loses its association with popular discourse. This is most evident

---

35 Hunter, this volume.   36 Stephens and Winkler (1995) 246–66.   37 Ibid. 23–71.
38 See Zeitlin, this volume.   39 Above, p. 000.   40 Perkins (1995); Cooper (1996).

in Apuleius: the elite status of both the author (a rich and celebrated fig-ure in his own lifetime) and Lucius the narrator (educated, and of 'ancient stock': *Met.* 1.1) is offset against the various folksy stories included within the narrative, including the 'old women's tale' (4.28) of the Cupid and Psy-che narrative. The link with popular story-telling, however, is also invited by the form itself. Like epic, the novel is a predominantly narrative form of literature. Unlike forms built around individual expression (such as lyric and drama), it can glide easily between different temporal and spatial set-tings, adopting multiple perspectives upon the way. This facility allows for a larger social canvas, encompassing beggars, bandits, nurses, prostitutes, fishermen, slaves and slavers, pirates, traders, and more. This diversity is not new with the novel. Already in Homer, we have in the *Iliad* the lower-class rabble-rouser Thersites, and in the *Odyssey* the swineherd Eumaeus (noble-born but enslaved), the nurse Eurycleia, and even Odysseus disguised as a beggar. Greek and Roman drama gives a crucial (if ancillary) role to slaves, primarily as plot movers; indeed, slaves, as features of everyday life, make regular appearances throughout ancient literature. It is arguably in the novel, however, that we meet the widest range of social types.[41]

According to Mikhail Bakhtin's theory of polyphony, such class pluralism is a definitive feature of novels in general, which he sees as open-ended spaces where multiple voices are arranged in a non-hierarchical way. For Bakhtin, such prose literature is the product of a historical shift away from the epic world, where the powerful enforce ideology authoritatively, towards a relativistic world where values are no longer absolute.[42] Despite Bakhtin's view that the Greek and (to a lesser extent) Latin novels display polyphony only to a limited extent, his ideas have been influential on scholars in the field.[43]

Social polyphony of the kind that Bakhtin sees in Dostoyevsky is, how-ever, relatively rare in the novels. Perhaps the best example comes early on in Heliodorus' *Charicleia and Theagenes*, where Cnemon, an upper-class Athenian, tells the tragic story of how he ended up serving a bandit in the Egyptian delta (1.9–17);[44] in book 2, however, the corpse of Thisbe, a slave involved in the same narrative, is found, with a letter that gives her side of the story, portraying her in a much more sympathetic light than Cnemon did (2.10). Heliodorus problematises our initial adoption of the upper-class perspective, and reminds us that there are two ways of telling a story.[45] A similar point might be made in relation to the trial scene, mentioned above, between Longus' Methymnaeans and Daphnis over the goats who ate the

---

41 See in general Scarcella (2003).   42 See esp. Bakhtin (1981b) 259–422.
43 Fusillo (1989); Branham (2002). For a critique see Whitmarsh (2005c).
44 On this narrative see Morgan (1989a).   45 See further Hunter (1998b) 42–6.

withy mooring the ship (2.15–16): the Methymnaeans' outraged protesta-
tion at their loss of their property is outflanked by the humble goatherd's
observation that they should have looked after their dogs and their property
better. In both cases, elite and sub-elite perspectives are played off against
each other, and any normative expectation that the former will be dominant is subverted. A slightly different case comes in the Greek *Ass*, where
a Roman soldier whips a Greek peasant who fails to understand his Latin
instructions; the peasant retaliates, killing the soldier, for which he is ultimately arrested (44). This episode is indeed polyphonic in Bakhtin's sense:
readers are free to take it either as a dramatisation of the repressive brutality
of the occupying army, or as a parable of the just punishment meted out to an
insubordinate.[46]

Yet in general the novelists do privilege the top-down perspective of their
protagonists: it is rare to find any challenge to the truisms that bandits and
pirates are bad,[47] slaves are deceitful and manipulative, nurses are untrustworthy.[48] Once again, however, we need to nuance these ideas, for novelistic
plots typically turn upon changes in status: the protagonists in particular lose
their elite status at the beginning, and recover it at the end. This is most evident in Apuleius and the Greek *Ass*-narratives, where Lucius' metamorphosis
into a beast also transforms his perspective from top-down to bottom-up:
as scholars have noted, his bestial status is repeatedly presented in slavish
terms. But the Greek novels too employ the motif: thus Chariton's Chaereas
and Achilles' Leucippe are temporarily enslaved, Xenophon's Anthia and
the protagonist's wife in *Apollonius, King of Tyre* forced into prostitution
(without, however, compromising their virtue). This forces us to reassess our
class definitions of the protagonists. In the previous paragraph I described
Longus' Daphnis as 'sub-elite', but is that the right word to use of someone
who will turn out to be the son of the estate's owner? This questioning of
social roles is not confined to the main characters: is the label 'upper-class'
(used in the previous paragraph) appropriate to Heliodorus' Cnemon, who
is now the servant of Nilotic bandits?

The literary progenitor of this kind of narrative of status-reversal followed
by restitution is, of course, Homer's *Odyssey*, where the king re-enters his
own house disguised as a beggar, enduring the taunts and aggression of the
suitors. The ambiguities of the *Odyssey*'s presentation of its protagonist's
walk on the wild side have been memorably discussed by Peter Rose: through

---

46 Hall (1995) 52.
47 On the representation of such figures see Hopwood (1998). Heliodorus' Thyamis is perhaps
a more positive bandit, but (like Xenophon's Hippothous, as discussed below) he turns out
to be a member of the elite anyhow.
48 On nurses see Alaux and Létoublon (2001).

Odysseus we view the world through a beggar's eyes, alive to the brutality and hardship he experiences; at the same time, however, we are aware that he is playing a role that he will in time cast off, and that the assumption is apparently widespread (even among otherwise sympathetic figures) that beggars are parasites.[49] Similarly, the novels take us on a tour of the social underclass, allowing us to witness suffering and oppression through the eyes of those who, we know, will inevitably reclaim their high-status positions within society. When, for example, we meet Achilles' enslaved Leucippe besmirched and disfigured by shaving and beatings (5.17), we are confronted with the shocking brutality to which slaves are subjected, and simultaneously consoled that her suffering is only temporary. Most spectacular of all is the status-reversal undergone by Lucius in the Greek *Ass* and Apuleius' *Metamorphoses*: he is not merely enslaved but transformed into a pack animal, situated at the very bottom of the hierarchy of socialised beings, condemned to sufferings that if anything even exceed those of slaves.[50]

There are at least two ways of interpreting such scenes. On the one hand, we could take them as socially conservative, marking perversions of the protagonists' 'true' social identities compromised at the outset and reclaimed at the end. Yet it is equally open to us to take them as evidence for the permeability of social boundaries and the fragility of status, a reminder to the novels' readers that they are all only one kidnapping away from social ruin. Elsewhere, Xenophon's bandit Hippothous turns out to be originally of a noble family (3.2.1), Heliodorus' brigand Thyamis himself is shown to be the heir to a priesthood in Memphis. That this is a literary *topos* that can be traced back to Homer (specifically, the nobly born swineherd Eumaeus: *Odyssey* 15.413–14) does not deny it its disruptive force in the context of the novel: the novels describe a world much like the reader's own, in the sense that sudden and total collapses in personal fortune were indeed possible.

It is, on balance, likely that most of the novels were mostly read by people of a certain social standing: this follows logically from the brute truth that in the ancient world literacy, not to mention literary competence, was heavily concentrated at the apex of the social pyramid. Nevertheless, class is not a straightforward concept in these texts. There are two general conclusions to draw. The first is that the culture of literary elitism is not simply conservative and static; rather, the process of testing the reader's education can be

---

49 Rose (1992) 106–12.
50 For the ways in which Lucius' experiences mirror those of slaves see Hall (1995) 52–4 (*Ass*); Bradley (2000), esp. 113–18, W. Fitzgerald (2000) 93–111 (Apuleius). Another prose fiction of the imperial period focusing on the experience of slavery (if not quite a novel) is the *Life of Aesop*: on its value for the study of Roman slavery see Hopkins (1993).

challenging, in the senses either of wicked game-playing (as in Petronius and Lucian) or of social critique (as in *Daphnis and Chloe*, where the reader's knowing, ironical distance from the rustic naifs is implicitly assimilated to modes of exploitation). The second point is that novels cannot be neatly packaged as 'elite literature', in the way that (for example) the display oratory of imperial Greece, the so-called 'second sophistic', can: novels paint on a wide canvas, incorporating a range of social life, and sometimes even questioning the hierarchical relationships that structured ancient society.

Further reading

On demography and the readership of the novel see Hunter, this volume, with further references. On issues of class and slavery in ancient literature generally, see Rose (1992), Whitmarsh (2004a) 213–26, both focusing on Greek works; McCarthy (2000) and W. Fitzgerald (2000) both offer sophisticated readings of the Roman literature of slavery, the latter including a section on Apuleius (87–114). Hopkins (1993) and Hall (1995), in their different ways, emphasise the view from below embodied in the *Life of Aesop* and the Greek *Ass* respectively. Millar (1981), Futre Pinheiro (1989) and Scarcella (2003) discuss the social structures presumed in the novels (Millar focusing exclusively on Apuleius). The congeniality of the 'ideal' Greek novels to eastern elites is emphasised by Swain (1996) 101–31; see also Mason (1983) for Lucius' elite status in Apuleius.

PART II

The world of the novel

6

FROMA ZEITLIN

Religion

Religion plays a central role in the plot of virtually every ancient fictional narrative, influencing the lives, actions, mentality, practices, beliefs and eventual fates of the characters (and narrators); the types, interventions and motives of divinity or other uncanny forces; the use of mythological exemplars, and more broadly, the array of problems that the entire subject poses for interpretation of the genre's conventions. The novels are full of: temples, shrines, altars, priests, rituals and offerings, dreams (or oracles), prophecies, divine epiphanies, aretalogies, mystic language and other metaphors of the sacred (not forgetting, in addition, exotic barbarian rites). Indeed, religious elements, such as these, familiar to virtually any inhabitant of the ancient world, are richly attested, of course, in history and archaeology. The topography of any ancient city, for example, would be unrecognisable without its temples and shrines, its statues and votive offerings, its frequent public festivals and processions, and its generally familiar modes of worship. Such is the case in the novels, for all their differences, in which its characters range far and wide in the course of their wanderings and communicate with the sacred in these habitual ways, whether in the cities of Asia Minor (Ephesus, Miletus, Rhodes, Sidon, Byzantium), Egypt (Memphis, Thebes, Alexandria), Greece (Delphi, Corinth), Italy (Syracuse, Rome) or elsewhere.

In considering the role of the gods in myth, belief and practice, Donald Mastronarde remarks on their inconsistency. 'They can at times be viewed as guarantors of order and justice and as agents who operate in a predictable manner open to straightforward explanation; at other times, however, they provide an explanation of last resort for what is uncanny, unpredictable, unseen, inexplicable, or intractable for humans.' And he continues, 'this flexibility of the supernatural apparatus . . . is also a function of a system of polytheism and the coexistence of individual gods with the notion of fate or destiny: *moira*, *daimōn*, and *tuchē*'.[1] Mastronarde is referring to the gods of

---

1 Mastronarde (2005) 321–2.

the fifth-century genre of Greek tragedy, but what he observes could equally apply to the world of the novel, except for the vaster geographical sweep in the Hellenistic age and beyond, the unrelenting pressure of more dire circumstances at the mercy of fate or fortune, and the genre's guarantee of a propitious ending with divine approval. Religion offered a creative and adaptable means of comprehending and exploring the central problems of existence, throughout the ancient world.

Religion and the erotic

In this polytheistic system that envisioned its gods in anthropomorphic guise, approaches to divinity acknowledged the supposedly unbridgeable gulf between mortals and those immortal powers that ruled the universe, but also believed in significant contacts that brought the two into frequent and intimate relation through a variety of means. Whether or not one was privileged to 'see the gods' or feel their presence in epiphany or dream, from Homer on, the gods have had their favourites, whom they protect, empower, save and sometimes punish. Given the novel's general focus on erotic life and all-consuming passion, it should come as no surprise that the most active divinities are Aphrodite, Artemis, Eros, Pan and the Nymphs, and Dionysus, with the participation at times of Apollo, whether at his mantic seat in Delphi (Heliodorus) or his oracle at Colophon (Xenophon). Helios is invoked briefly in Xenophon in his shrine at Rhodes and, of course, comes to the fore (now identified with Apollo, and alongside Selene) in the final proceedings in Heliodorus, even though these divinities are not primary agents of the plot. *Tuchē* (Fortune) is omnipresent, as are references to the nameless *daimones* who hound the protagonists.

The one innovation is the introduction of Isis, both in Xenophon of Ephesus and in the last book of Apuleius.[2] The presence of this Hellenised Egyptian goddess, whose worship had spread over the Mediterranean in a variety of functions, including her mysteries, has stimulated lively debate, both as regards the so-called exemplary details of her myth (her arduous journeys in search of her beloved consort, Osiris) and her rites of initiation, whose details are known mainly to us from Apuleius. I shall return to this issue later when assessing the general religious climates of the novels and the theory that esoteric meanings were coded behind the texts.

2 On the gods in the Greek novel see Alperowitz (1992). Hera and Athena, and indeed the rest of the Greek pantheon are absent, while Zeus in Achilles Tatius is represented in the opening *ecphrasis* of the abduction of Europa and mentioned with regard to various of his local shrines in Egypt. In Apuleius' tale of Cupid and Psyche, Venus, of course plays the leading role (to say nothing of Cupid himself), but other gods are invoked along the way: Mercury, Ceres, Juno, Pan, and at the end, Proserpina. In Petronius, Priapus is the regnant deity.

Odysseus may have his Athena, Sappho her Aphrodite, Hippolytus his Artemis. But the protagonists of the novel are merely members of a prosperous elite Greek society (even in the Roman novel). We may hear echoes of literary or mythical allusions (e.g. Helen, Iphigenia, Andromeda, Achilles, Odysseus) that lend their stories greater resonance and prestige, but in the end the vicissitudes of fortune give way to the legitimation of a social order, guaranteed by the gods, that endorses as its all-encompassing goal the conduct of sanctioned marriage under the proper auspices of family and community. Reassuring Leucippe's father in Artemis' temple of his daughter's genuine chastity, Clitophon appeals to the other goddess: 'O Lady Aphrodite, do not be angry at us for spurning you! We did not want to wed without her father present. Now that he is here, O come to us too, we pray, and look kindly upon us' (Ach. Tat. 8.5.8.).

More broadly speaking, why should a love story of two young people, however well-placed as they may be, become a matter of greatest urgency, one that enlists the continuing attention of supernatural powers, 'to engineer the final reunion of the lovers, while Fortune and Chance, conceived as deities, will intervene to disrupt and prolong the action?'[3] Why should Eros and its vicissitudes command a position that subsumes all else to its hegemony? Is there, for example, any intrinsic relationship between the erotic and the sacred, the sexual and the spiritual, the carnal and the transcendent, whereby literal and metaphorical levels may change places or interfuse with one another? In describing the first meeting between Theagenes and Charicleia, the narrator priest in Heliodorus can exclaim: 'In that instant it was revealed to us that the soul is something divine and partakes in the nature of heaven. For at the moment when they set eyes on one another, the young pair fell in love, as if the soul recognised its kin at the very first encounter and sped to meet that which was worthily its own' (Hld. 3.5.4). Does Heliodorus articulate an underlying presumption that the genre of romance can overcome Plato's division between celestial and vulgar love and promise more than the final satisfaction of earthly love? Or does it do no such thing, but rather exploit erotic paradigms and conventions under the umbrella of divinity to enhance a sentimental and sensationalist story?

Of all the unsolved (or rather, insoluble) problems facing a study of ancient prose fiction, this is the issue that is perhaps both the most tantalising and the most vexed. It is the alpha and omega of the novel, one that involves a quest for origins (the riddle of the genre's appearance on the literary stage of the empire) and its teleological purpose(s) – what it all 'means'. The power of the erotic, of course, has a long history in Greco-Roman culture, celebrated

---

3 Anderson (1984) 75.

in theogonies, hymns, lyric poetry, drama and iconography. It is also a topic of discussion for philosophers and gains increased attention from the Hellenistic period onwards in accord with a greater emphasis on the individual and private life. But is more at stake in the narrativisation of desire: the journeys, the ordeals, the *Scheintod*s (apparent deaths) and return to life, the constancy of the lovers, the themes of ascent and descent, and hopes of ultimate salvation in an eventual reunion? And if so, does this 'higher truth' redeem prose fiction of this kind from a generally negative appraisal in antiquity as a species of frivolous (and unsavoury) entertainment? The biographical tradition that names both Achilles Tatius and Heliodorus as Christian bishops[4] may be read, after all, in two ways: either each eventually saw the light of conversion after their earlier literary follies or a bishop's prestige is sufficient to sanitise these texts and to pave the way for pietist or allegorical readings (which begin already, in fact, in later antiquity under the influence of Neoplatonism and Neopythagoreanism and continue on into the Byzantine period).[5]

The Apuleian paradigm

The range of interpretative positions in reading the significance of the pervasive presence of religious elements covers an entire spectrum of opinion that can roughly be divided between two poles, the secular and the sacred, with many shadings in between. The most irreverent view regards the divine apparatus as just that and no more, consisting of conventional motifs, intriguing décor, theatrical display, literary legerdemain or even mischievous parody, designed to seduce the reader, as has been claimed, for example, of the canny Egyptian priest, Calasiris in Heliodorus, who controls so much of the action. With the exception perhaps of Chariton, Xenophon of Ephesus and (arguably) Apuleius, the sacred apparatus is not unjustly open to charges of irony, tongue-in-cheek, sophistry, and, at the least, equivocation of serious intentions.[6]

At the other extreme, however, is the notion that these works are, in fact, religious texts, some of which may even serve as propagandistic vehicles for certain cults (e.g. Apuleius and Isis; Heliodorus and Helios). One theory proposes that the plots of novels are secularised versions of the Egyptian sacred tale of the goddess Isis and her devotion to her consort, Osiris, that leads her to wander the earth, suffer ordeals, in a search for him that

---

4 See 'Index of ancient novelists'.
5 See Philip's allegory of Heliodorus, printed as Colonna (1938) T XIII and translated at Lamberton (1986) 306–11. For a recent discussion and bibliography see Hunter (2005); also Hunter, this volume.
6 In general, see Anderson (1982) who examines the novels under the title of 'Erōs sophistēs'.

ends in a happy reunion. 'The myth symbolised man's [*sic*] voyage through life, through dangers and tribulations to final salvation.'[7] The other, that of Reinhold Merkelbach, goes still further to claim that all the novels (with the exception of Chariton) are actually mystery texts, coded doctrines of rites and myths for initiates of their respective cults, but opaque to the ordinary reader. 'The material of the plots corresponds to elements in mystery ceremonies: adventures, shipwreck, *Scheintod* are initiatory trials . . . the lovers' union is the mystic marriage of the soul with god; and the form of each novel follows the myth of god in question.'[8]

One immediate problem, however, rarely mentioned, is that Merkelbach depended heavily upon a reading of a single text, the Latin novel of Apuleius (*Metamorphoses*). This picaresque tale of a man turned into an ass (and back again) combines farce, magic, mayhem and mystery in a series of bawdy and violent adventures that reaches its climax in the eleventh and last book, just when Lucius in bestial form has reached the limit of degradation and prays for salvation. Broadly speaking, the novel is constructed as a progression from magic to religion, each represented by a female figure – the first in the wanton servant girl Photis and the second in the miraculous epiphany of the goddess. The plot leads from an initial (and disastrous) desire through sexual dalliance to learn the secrets of magical power (hence his accidental transformation into an ass) to the ultimate acquisition of a higher knowledge in the deity, Isis, who after all his sufferings, finally redeems him by her gracious intervention and restores him to human form. The price is initiation into her mysteries and a role in her cult as a priest enjoined to permanent celibacy. As Harrison puts it, 'Photis' initiation of Lucius into the false and enslaving mysteries of sex and magic can [in retrospect] be identified as an inferior and negative version of the true and final initiation into the chaste cult of Isis, where the service of the god is . . . true pleasure.'[9] The unusually detailed account of Lucius' initiation and the ceremonies that celebrate the goddess in all her manifestations have led many to take the text as the record of a true conversion experience, even if some doubt the seriousness of Apuleius' intent.[10] The language is certainly explicit: 'I came to death's frontier and trod the threshold of Proserpina; I was borne through all the

---

7 Hägg (1983) 102, with reference to Karl Kerényi (1927). For a convenient summary of the details of the Isis myth, see Reardon (1991) 170–1.

8 Reardon (1969) 305, summarising Merkelbach (1962). The gods of these mystery cults include Isis (Xenophon, Achilles Tatius, Apuleius); Dionysus (Longus); Helios (Heliodorus); Mithras (Iamblichus).

9 Harrison (2003) 512.

10 For a range of opinions on the veracity and seriousness of Lucius' conversion, see Winkler (1985) 204–47; Shumate (1996); Griffiths (1978); Sandy (1978); Mal-Maeder (1997); and Harrison (2000) 238–52.

elements and returned . . . I approached the gods above and the gods below, and worshipped them face to face.' This is as much as he can impart, he says, to the uninitiated (*Met.* 11.23).

Merkelbach's theory of *Metamorphoses* as an esoteric text also relied on an allegorical interpretation of the embedded story of Cupid (= 'love') and Psyche (= 'soul'; 4.28–6.23), which relates the trials and tribulations of the mortal Psyche to reunite with her beloved, the god Cupid, and her eventual elevation to reside with him in marital bliss on Olympus. Told by an old serving woman in the robbers' cave to console a kidnapped bride, the story in its local context forecasts what seems to be a perfect romance ending to Charite's woes (rescue by her bridegroom and subsequent marriage to him). Lucius and Psyche also have much in common: both characters who at first come to grief through weakness and *curiositas*, then wander and undergo a series of labours and sufferings, and who are finally rescued by the action of divine grace (Venus for Psyche, Isis for Lucius). The *Metamorphoses*, however, is not typical of the genre as a whole. The Platonising tale of Cupid and Psyche may indeed follow in part the trajectory of Isis in search of her lost beloved and resonate deeply with romance motifs,[11] but the Greek idealist novel depends on the sufferings and ordeals of *both* hero and heroine, both masculine and feminine players. Even more to the point, Lucius' eventual rejection of sexuality and earthly desire seems rather a case of the *failure* of the erotic quest: a species of anti-romance, quite at odds with the majority of the extant novels.[12] Instead, the story devolves into a matter of two choices: bad knowledge (magic), bad sex (Photis); good knowledge (religion), no sex (Isis).

There are other reasons why the Apuleian focus on initiation should not be allowed to dominate the agenda. Rituals in mystery cults are defined as individual experiences, 'a form of personal religion, depending on a private decision and aiming at some form of salvation through closeness to the divine'.[13] This fits the profile for Apuleius (on one interpretation), but again is not generalisable to all the novels. Nothing suggests that the aim of the novel was to bring about a closer relationship to the divine, despite the sacerdotal roles bestowed upon Charicleia and Theagenes at the end of their story (Heliodorus). Rather, centred in the here and now, its aim is to bring two human beings, a male and female, into the closest erotic contact, one eventually to be sanctioned by society – and the gods – in a relationship of

---

11 For the pertinence of Platonism throughout the work, see Harrison (2000) 252–9.
12 In fact, the tragic end of Charite's story (her husband murdered by a jealous rival, her vengeance upon him and her own death) signifies the end of the earthly romance plot that might have provided a model for Lucius.
13 Burkert (1987) 12–13.

marriage. Artemis is prominent in her initial role as guardian of chastity,[14] but Eros is the guiding force, as is Aphrodite, who are mischievous, even at times malevolent, but ultimately endorse a triumphant finale in the face of ordeals undergone and faithfulness upheld. Theirs are the 'mysteries' that, as rhetorically invoked in Achilles Tatius, lend the proceedings an air of spiritual transcendence (a point to which I will return).

While the theories of Kerényi and Merkelbach have been amply refuted (although on other grounds), they have, as one critic puts it, been 'strangely influential'.[15] It is as if the very idea of the novel as a potentially religious (hence, significant) narrative has raised the status of the genre and opened the way to a far more favourable assessment of its merits. 'Parallels between life, myth, mystery ritual, and novel' can be explained as resonant of human experience in general through scenarios of initiation or rites of passage that bring about change in the individual and affirmation of identity.[16] 'The novel is a metaphor of life and a metaphor of the mysteries', declares another critic, and both share the same psychological validity.[17] As Northrop Frye's aptly titled *Secular Scriptures* suggests in Roger Beck's reading: 'Journeys out and back, descents to suffering and disintegration, ascents to joy and reintegration, these are the stuff of mysteries and of novels too.'[18]

This desire to forge a link, however attenuated, between mystery cults and the novels is based to a certain degree on a claim of historical circumstances. The period that saw the rise of the novel and its flourishing under the Empire coincided with the spread of the so-called 'oriental' mystery cults throughout the Hellenistic world, and similar reasons are adduced to account for both phenomena. In an age of declining political power, so the argument goes, there was a loss of confidence in traditional religion, and a bewildering fragmentation of life. In the vast expansion of territories and mixtures of peoples, the individual felt a sense of psychological isolation and loneliness that led

14 Ephesus, the site of the goddess' most famous cult, is the point of departure and return for Xenophon's characters, whose home town it is; but also the destination in Achilles Tatius where Artemis' temple furnishes the location for the denouement of the plot, while in Heliodorus, Charicleia is already an acolyte of the goddess at Delphi and will ultimately become a priestess of Selene, Artemis' double.

15 Dowden (2005) 3. On the various refutations see Beck (2003), with literature.

16 Hägg (1983) 103.

17 Dowden (2005) 12, and see too (1999). But one might add that the metaphor of the mysteries is just that – a metaphor all too easily adopted.

18 Beck (2003) 150, citing Frye (1976) 97–157. His larger contention that 'each [novel] in a different way answered to the aspirations of individuals in their encounters with divine providence and human fate . . . both were routes for going to meet the gods' is not convincing. Bowersock's (1994) suggestion (also dependent on Frye) of nascent Christianity's influence on the novel is ingenious but has not won adherents. In general, a more appropriate model (oddly overlooked) is that of initiation into adulthood through rites of passage that follow the trajectory of separation–liminality–incorporation, as adumbrated by Van Gennep (1960), although see Dowden (1999), Whitmarsh (1999), Lalanne (2006).

to a yearning for personal fulfilment and a promise of salvation. But is this description wholly accurate? Simon Swain points out that these ideas 'owe much to views first expressed during the early and middle part of the twentieth century about the spiritual health of the ancient world during the early Empire'. It was 'suggested that traditional systems of religion were breaking down . . . and that cults arose to satisfy a feeling of rootlessness, which was eventually assuaged by Christianity'.[19] Yet historians today, including Swain, are far more sceptical of this image of a society in crisis. Quite the contrary. The Greek cities in the East were flourishing, as were civic cults, and all the evidence points to the vitality of paganism that was enriched, not diminished, by syncretistic tendencies to assimilate new religious elements into existing structures.

From mystery cult to religious pluralism

In fact, when we turn to the Greek novels in particular, Judith Perkins reminds us that 'the romances are filled with numerous divinities in various civic manifestations and . . . portrayed their protagonists as being able to find gods to worship wherever they found themselves (e.g. Isis in Egypt, Helios in Rhodes, Artemis in Ephesus). This was one of the ways, she argues, 'through which the romances conveyed a sense of their protagonists' at-homeness in the many Greek cities of empire, rather than depicting, as some have suggested, individuals isolated in a large and fragmented world'.[20] Moreover, the protagonists are all members of the elite, who are fully restored in their status by their communities upon their return home. Instead of celebrating 'the private nature of personal desire rather than as a function of civic identity' in the promotion of marriage and conjugal relations, as David Konstan had influentially argued, Perkins's reading reverses the terms: 'Social identity,' she suggests, 'began to be perceived or imagined through the language of personal attachment and marriage. The romance used the trope of marriage to talk about social identity and social structures' rather than the reverse.[21] Likewise, as Swain remarks, 'the answer to the question of the novel's origin lies not in reading it as reflection of unhappiness, individual or otherwise, but in seeing it as another outlet for cultural ideals and formulas of the elite, as another expression of their cultural hegemony.' These aristocratic, Greek ideals were now focused on a new ethics of conjugality.[22] In these readings,

19 Swain (1996) 106.
20 Perkins (1995) 49. Nevertheless, one should not overlook the foreign and exotic aspects of the couple's adventures.
21 Perkins (1995) 66, refuting Konstan (1994) 266.
22 Swain (1996) 109. The settings of these novels in the past also reinforces these ideas. See also Whitmarsh (2001a) 17–20.

the successful conclusion to the romance plot may be attributed to what 'Max Weber has called the "theodicy of good fortune", the contention that the elite deserved to be exactly where they were in society', entitled to reclaim their wealth and status and assured of the gods' interest in their affairs.[23] At the same time, while the fantasies of dangerous adventures and erotic passion may well 'supply a dimension of experience absent from the daily routine of a materially prosperous and secure readership', they also, if only vicariously, offer unsettling glimpses into a hostile world of mysterious forces beyond one's control.[24]

Hence, we may still ask why such a 'theodicy' takes the form it does in the romance plot, which despite its often anachronistic historical settings, conventional mythological motifs, and amalgam of previous literary genres (or perhaps because of them), results in a new creation that reflects (and promotes) the religious worldview of the era in which they flourished. The evidence, scanty and scattered as it is, generally points to an increased level of religious engagement, one that promoted a desire for closer personal contact with the gods, especially through dreams, oracles and epiphanies, reports of miracles, aretalogies and mystery initiations. We can identify more strenuous efforts to control the workings of the universe and bring about the 'intervention of superhuman powers in material world' through magic, astrology, theurgical operations and other forms of occultism.[25] Theological speculations, the growth of allegory, and philosophical explorations of divinity and spiritual experience (as in Neopythagoreanism and Neoplatonism) also find their place in the conglomeration of beliefs and practices that make up this world under the empire. In this proliferation of possible attitudes and activities, it is also acknowledged that the 'immense variety of religious experience, geographically, socially, and culturally in the Greek-speaking half of the Empire in the first four centuries CE . . . makes it difficult to generalise with any certainty about the experience of later antique paganism or the reasons for its decline'.[26] Despite substantial indications from archaeology, inscriptions, iconography and literary sources, no clear picture emerges of what has been called 'the shapeless profusion of polytheism' in this period, with what Macmullen calls the 'perceptible' occupying far less space than the 'debatable'.[27]

What matters most finally is not the presence of such elements in romance texts. As Jack Winkler notes, 'every narrative from Homer to Nonnos refers

---

23 Perkins (1995) 55, relying on Gordon's discussion (1990) 238 of the 'veil of power'.
24 Morgan (1995) 146.   25 Macmullen (1981) 70.
26 Anderson (2001) 142, and referring to Macmullen (1981) 62–73, 'The vitality of paganism'.
27 Macmullen (1981) 5. 'Debatable' for M. refers to 'the life that lay, not in paganism observed, but in paganism felt and thought out', 49.

at some point to the rites, language, and beliefs of ancient religions. The point of . . . analysis is to assess the interaction of religious information and fictional imagination',[28] as, in this instance, how that interaction serves the purposes of the genre's erotic themes. Accordingly, the remainder of this essay will take up three brief case studies of that fictional imagination at work in exploring how a few select religious elements are absorbed, adapted, and creatively refined within our texts.[29] First, the topos of 'god-like' beauty in Chariton of his heroine, Callirhoe, in its adaptation of mythic and literary antecedents to suit a vastly expanded political world; second, the reworking of philosophical (mainly Platonic) and mystical themes through rhetorical and sophistic practices (Achilles Tatius and Longus), and finally, the novel as sacred aetiology and the question of Hellenic standards (Heliodorus).

Divine beauty

From the earliest times, the Greeks saw something divine in beauty.[30] The epithet 'like to a god' or a simile comparing a mortal to a specific divinity (especially Apollo, Artemis, and Aphrodite) are well-known poetic attributes epithets, from Homer on, used to describe figures endowed with a charismatic radiance. Virtually all the novels allude to this topos, and in some instances even enhance this comparison by designating heroines as acolytes of a goddess (Artemis in both Xenophon and Heliodorus) or, as in the case of Psyche in Apuleius, as rivals of a goddess herself (Venus).[31]

In Chariton's case, however, the degree of rhetorical insistence on the sight of Callirhoe as something 'supernatural, miraculous or divine' far outstrips any of the other extant romances. Everywhere Callirhoe goes, she dazzles all who gaze on her; sailors, country folk, entire cities – in Syracuse, Ionia and Persia. Advance notice of her arrival draws out crowds to see her to strongest effect in Babylon, where the Great King resides. The Persian court is perhaps the most appropriate setting to showcase Callirhoe, for it is here that all three strands of extravagant homage can be combined: to royalty, erotic beauty and divinity. The notion that Callirhoe may be some goddess who has descended from heaven or arisen from the sea is a repetitive motif. The opening lines describe her beauty as 'more than human'; it was divine (*theion*) neither of a Nereid or a mountain Nymph at that, but of Aphrodite herself' (1.1). But it is only when she crosses the sea to Ionia that the comparison

---

28 Winkler (1980) 156.
29 I follow a roughly chronological order, not so much to map shifts of interest and focus (although these are there) but because this is generally routine practice.
30 See especially Jax (1933).   31 See e.g. Létoublon (1993) 122–4.

becomes a reality, when she appears to the onlookers as an actual epiphany of the goddess and an image of her dedicated in Aphrodite's temple is taken as a cult statue. As for herself, she is hardly mystified ('Stop making fun of me! Stop calling me a goddess – I'm not even a happy mortal', 2.3.7). This is a period, it is true, when more credence is given to divine epiphanies, whether in waking or dreaming. But the confusion between the goddess and her devotee lends the work a scopic intensity that fully merges the sacred and the aesthetic under the omnipotent influence of Eros.

In this oscillation between divinity and her incarnation, both Aphrodite and the human embodiment of her beauty are endowed with a universal, even objective value that crosses the boundaries between Greek and barbarian and indeed is a unifying element across the entire Mediterranean, the source of desire that animates political revolutions as well as private affairs. Despite the anachronistic setting and the allusions to mythic and literary antecedents, critics have suggested engagement with contemporary realities, including a boost for Chariton's hometown, Aphrodisias, and perhaps a discreet reference to the Julio-Claudian house and Venus Genetrix, and hence to Rome. While no firm consensus emerges, the erotic fortunes of Callirhoe, the doublet of Aphrodite (but also of Helen, the Homeric hypostasis of the goddess) suggest some formidable new links between religion and politics.[32]

Sophistics of erotic theology

Achilles Tatius and Longus make strange bedfellows; the first is a sprawling tale of racy adventure, the second, a small-scale miniature, set in an idyllic pastoral space. One suggests a cynical and knowing outlook on life; the other revels in an unimaginable innocence. Yet both texts are products of the extravagant rhetorical movement we call the second sophistic, most likely composed about the same time (in the second century CE), and for all their differences, both richly wrought in style and diction. Even more, both are preoccupied with the origins and nature of Eros, both heterosexual and homosexual, both feature an erotic teacher who gives indoctrination into the mechanics and metaphysics of sexual pleasure as a guide to life. Each teases the reader with allusions to mystic initiations – explicit in the case of Achilles Tatius (more of which later), and indirectly in Longus, whose work promotes the air of a sacred tale. Eros, as the text tells us, wants to make a 'myth' (*muthos*) out of Chloe (Long. 2.27.2) and the appearance of the

32 On epiphany, see Hägg (2002) and Zeitlin (2003); on the novelty of Callirhoe's position, see Biraud (1996) and Schmeling (2005); on contemporary realities, see Edwards (1994), Connors (2002), Alvares (2001–2), and Smith (2005).

city proprietor, Dionysophanes in the autumn of the last book slyly suggests the possibility of a divine epiphany.[33] Finally, both are indebted to Platonic treatises on love, notably the *Symposium* and the *Phaedrus*, for play as for profit.[34] The whole of *Daphnis and Chloe* is set in a rural landscape, reminiscent of the pastoral atmosphere of the *Phaedrus*, while the grove with its plane trees and fresh flowing stream that sets the stage for the entire narrative of Achilles Tatius is entirely suitable for listening to 'tales of love' (1.2.3). Even more, in both texts Eros wins the title of 'sophist' (Ach. Tat. 1.101 and 5.27.4; Long. 4.8.1) in echo of Diotima's famous description of Eros in the *Symposium* as a 'sophist', who is always 'doing philosophy' (Plato, *Symposium* 203d). These two dialogues on Eros were much in vogue during this period, not just in relation to the novel, whose erotics would benefit from Plato's prestige and authority (however playfully or ironically deployed). They generated a larger body of literature (e.g. Plutarch, *Tale of Love* and the more playful pseudo-Lucianic *Love Stories*) that drew upon Plato's spiritual elevation of Eros and its role in the education and enlightenment of lovers, but turned them finally, into platforms for current ideas about the sexes and their reciprocal relations that were oriented now towards marriage and its emotional pleasures, rather than pederastic love, as a means to the soul's ascent.[35]

What is most noteworthy, however, are references to 'mysteries of Eros' (or Aphrodite) as an allocution for sexual intercourse, an expression we might take for granted, but which seems to be an innovative usage arising in this period.[36] According to Burkert, 'to speak of these mysteries became routine mainly under the impact of Plato's *Symposium*', where we may recall, the priestess, Diotima, initiated Socrates into these very 'mysteries' (209e5–210a2).[37] In Plato, the model was the Eleusinian mysteries, which would be familiar to any Athenian. But 'in later romances and related literature', Burkert continues, 'many a lover is prone to propose to his partner initiation

---

33 On *Daphnis and Chloe* as a mystical text involving Eros, Dionysus with perhaps Orphic elements, see Chalk (1960) and less persuasively, Merkelbach (1988).

34 See further Morgan, this volume.

35 On Longus and Plato, see Hunter (1997) and MacQueen (1990) 168–74. On Achilles Tatius see Morales (2004) 50–3; Goldhill (1995) 78, 94–6; and more generally, the fine observations of Whitmarsh (2003). On both texts, see Alvares (2006) 16–18. On the *Phaedrus* in this period, see Trapp (1990) and on Plutarch and Pseudo-Lucian, see Foucault (1986) 193–227, who speaks of 'a new erotics'.

36 Reference to the *orgia* or *hiera* of Aphrodite in the same sense seems to have been a jocular use confined to iambic, comedy and mime: e.g. Aristophanes, *Lysistrata* 832, 893; Cratinus 191 K–A, and Herodotus 1.83. Archilochus refers to sex as 'the divine thing', fr. 196a.16 West.

37 On mystery terminology in Plato's *Symposium*, see Riedweg (1987) 1–29. See also Xenophon, *Symposium* 1.11.1.

into the mysteries of this special god'.[38] Closer inspection, however, does not indicate a widespread use of this language in erotic contexts. In fact, we find the greatest frequency by far in none other than Achilles Tatius, as a sophistic turn of phrase deployed in the interests of seduction.[39] Melite, a presumed widow (her husband supposedly drowned at sea), is a mistress of eloquence, who strives to persuade the reluctant Clitophon (still grieving over Leucippe's second apparent death) to consummate their new marriage: 'Let us enter Aphrodite's inner sanctum', she pleads, 'and initiate ourselves into her mystic liturgy' (5.15.6; cf. 5.26.3, 5.26.10). Her pleas to Clitophon couched in mystic language aptly returns his own rhetoric to him, for he too had used the same terms in the first part of the text, but this time addressed to a still chaste Leucippe (2.19.4, 4.1.3). Earlier, he had begged his erotic teacher, his cousin, Clinias for help in approaching Leucippe – 'tell me how to begin: you have been an initiate for longer than me and you are already familiar with the mysteries of Eros before me' (1.9.7), but if the reply was that Eros is 'self-taught' (1.10.1; cf. 5.27.4), Clitophon eventually proved himself an adept, if also an ill-starred, pupil himself. The language of the mysteries should not surprise us, however, since Melite turned out to be the beautiful woman who appeared to him in front of the closed temple of Aphrodite, who promised him that soon the doors would open and he would even become a priest of the goddess. (4.1.3–8). Melite finally succeeds just once through a last bit of erotic philosophising (Eros teaches discourse as well, 5.27.1), turning Plato, his mysteries and theology once again upside down.[40]

Sacred aetiology and the question of Hellenic standards

In Heliodorus' *Charicleia and Theagenes*, the last, longest and most complex of the extant novels (dated at the latest to the mid-fourth century), 'religion' takes centre stage. Sacred liturgies, festivals, rituals and processions are occasions for sumptuous spectacles. The dreams, omens and oracles that thread

---

38 Burkert (1987) 107. He further observes (108) that the language of the mysteries also became available for obscene allusions, as in the parody of Priapus mysteries in the house of Quartilla, in Petronius. Consider too that the very content of mystery cults, that which made them secret and unspeakable, may well have been the display of genital symbols, both male and female, and overt references to sexuality. See Burkert (1983) 270–1.

39 Once in Char. (4.4.9), once in Hld. (1.17.2), and twenty-one occurrences in Achilles Tatius. Other references at Plutarch, *Tale of Love* 762A, 769A; Alciphron 1.4.3, 1.22; and Pseudo-Lucian, *Love Stories* 32.2. Critics who claim the 'mysteries of Eros' for Longus are using their own metaphor.

40 On possible differences in the novel between the 'mysteries' of Eros and those of Aphrodite, see Bouffartigue (2001); for the outrageousness of Melite's propositions, see Anderson (1982) 32.

their way through the text attest to the workings of destiny's mysterious forces. Divine agencies, for good or for ill, are felt to exert their power in a universe, whose riddling nature characters strive to interpret. Theosophical exegeses on the gods and forms of higher and lower wisdom hint at the esoteric and occult, with shadings of Neopythagorean and Neoplatonic elements. Above all, the cast of characters features a host of sacerdotal figures and religious functionaries. The three adoptive 'fathers' of the heroine, Charicleia, are each affiliated with important cult centres that span a broad geographical sweep: Greece, Egypt and Ethiopia. Charicles presides over Apollo's shrine at Delphi; Calasiris is a voluntary exile from the temple of Isis in Memphis, while Sisimithres heads the council of wise gymnosophists in Meroe, where the regnant deity is Helios.[41] Even the bandit chief, Thyamis, whom we meet at the opening of the work, is a priest, son of Calasiris, whose post has been usurped by his wicked brother (1.19.3). More surprising still, Homer's pedigree, we learn, in a learned disquisition, assigns him the role of bastard son to yet another Egyptian priest (3.14.2). Charicleia herself is an acolyte of Artemis in Delphi and once restored to her birthright in Ethiopia is, together with Theagenes, inducted into the priesthoods of Selene (Moon) and Helios (Sun) before they are wed. Her devotion to purity and chastity surpasses that of any of the heroines of romance that preceded her. Before she meets Theagenes, 'virginity is her god', laments Charicles. 'She has elevated to the level of the immortals, pronouncing it without stain, impurity, or corruption' (2.33.4–5). Even afterward, she embodies a piety and purity that, as one critic suggests, 'incarnates the moral and religious ideal of late antiquity'.[42]

Opinions are deeply divided as to the 'meaning of this obsession with the supernatural', more than is the case with any of the other novels, due as much to its remarkable literary qualities as to a mysteriosophic atmosphere that lends itself to allegorical speculation.[43] A 'mixture of religiosity with erotic intrigue' that combines 'an aura of profundity with sensuous exoticism' perhaps best describes the work.[44] Ethiopia, the destined end of the journey for the couple and the setting of the last book, does indeed usher us into an exotic world. The Black Land of the Sun combines mythic aspects of the Golden Age with utopian fantasies. This theocratic state, ruled by a benevolent priest-king, with the support of a college of venerable sages,

---

41 On the gymnosophists, see Robiano (1992).   42 Hani (1978) 268.
43 Futre Pinheiro (1991a) 359, and see n. 1 for a brief but comprehensive summary of critics and their views. In addition to Szepessy (1957), Heiserman (1977), Winkler (1982), Sandy (1982a), and Morgan (1982), (1989b), (2003); see also Whitmarsh (1998), (1999), and Chew (2007).
44 Lamberton (1986) 148.

seems to suggest the end point of a 'hierarchy of religious enlightenment' that leads 'from Greek (good) to Egyptian (better) to Ethiopia (best)'.[45]

But whose enlightenment? For all its virtues, this land is one that practises human sacrifice, a ritual abhorred by the Greeks. It is what barbarians do. Achilles Tatius and Xenophon both contain scenes of such savage rites, as does the tantalising fragment of Lollianus' *Phoenician Affairs*. But these are bizarre rituals of outlaws, in keeping with their marginal social position and criminal ways. In Heliodorus, by contrast, human sacrifice, to celebrate victory in war, is an ancestrally sanctioned custom (10.7.2), demanded by the populace. King Hydaspes' dilemma will be whether to fulfil his royal role as guardian of laws and mindful of his people's demands or to heed the religious authorities in the persons of the Gymnosophists, who are guardians of justice in judicial disputes and also arbiters of the gods' wishes (10.9). The irony of the conflict is between piety towards the gods (in the form of the victory sacrifice) and the real piety, which is to abjure these savage rites. The arrival of Theagenes and Charicleia as the designated victims is the catalyst of this dilemma, and it is the resolution finally of their identity through a complex series of recognitions and brilliant coincidences (birth tokens, chastity tests, sudden arrival of Charicles from Delphi) that puts an end to this cruel practice. Romance is no longer an end in itself.

As Winkler observes, 'the gods, it seems, wanted the otherwise blameless Ethiopians to accept a fundamental change in religious custom and to this end could find no better means than romance, one whose beauty and intricacy would astonish, charm, and successfully persuade them to abolish human sacrifice once and for all'. It is to this end they 'have fashioned the entire plot of Charicleia's life' (10.7.1).[46] Whether or not this aetiological conclusion is 'religiously meant' (Winkler and others think not), is beside the point. Rather what counts is the bold originality that welds romance and religion together into a new and symbiotic relationship. In Ethiopia one can both assume priesthoods and celebrate matrimonies.

In this best of all possible worlds, the periphery has now become the centre. What might this mean? Are we witnessing a new multicultural cosmopolitanism at this late date in a fusion of Helios and Apollo? Or does the decisive role of Sisimithres, leader of the Ethiopian sages, who both saves Charicleia at birth and now pronounces the gods' will, indicate a shift from Hellenic hegemonic standards to endorse an 'alien wisdom'?[47] Or conversely, given Charicleia's upbringing at Delphi, does nurture trump nature, so that it is 'the

45 Beck (2003) 144. On the representation of Ethiopia, see Lonis (1992) and Hägg (1999–2000).
46 Winkler (1982) 152.
47 Cosmopolitanism: Bowersock (1994) 48; 'alien wisdom': Whitmarsh (1999) 31–2.

absorption of rational, civilised Greeks into their community that redeems the culturally ambivalent Ethiopians from the savage excesses of their own religion'[48] or better perhaps, restores them to the traditional image of their famous piety that this ritual aberration had compromised?

The irony lies in the Greek provenance of the sacrificial motif, and this twice over, in a witty and subversive 'intertextual play with the two *Iphigenia*s of Euripides, where are combined the themes of a king who proposes to sacrifice his daughter for the public good and human sacrifice [demanded in a place] at the end of the world'.[49] In the land of the Taurians, Iphigenia, the priestess of Artemis, rescues her goddess from these barbaric practices and transports her to Greece. Charicleia, for her part, an acolyte of Artemis in Delphi and now a priestess of Selene (the moon) has come *from* Greece *to* this distant land, where she will remain, unlike Iphigenia, both a sacred officiant and a lawfully wedded wife. Or finally, is this intricate tale the gift of Heliodorus, a Phoenician from the city of Emesa, himself a descendant of the Sun, who creates a fictional world in which it is the gods and not the mortals who author the plot?

Conclusion

This brief journey through the varieties of religious experience in the novel has missed out, by necessity, a few stops along the way. Xenophon of Ephesus might have been a point of departure, since it offers a plenitude, if not a surfeit, of religious motifs and elements: shrines and gods scattered everywhere across the Mediterranean, a redundancy of divinities, unexpected miracles, bizarre rites of bandits, to name only a few. But the confusion it engenders by the frenetic pace of the action and the deployment of conventions that sometimes defy logic, whether as to motivation or conclusion (the wrath of Eros at the beginning; the odd message of Apollo's oracle, and especially the indecision as to the major divinity: is it Artemis or Isis) only demonstrates by its counterexample the artistry of the other works that have come down to us, for all its probable value as a vivid, if stylized, representation of a lively and varied Hellenistic milieu.

The most serious omission, however, in this essay is the lack of attention to Jewish and Christian works of prose fiction that were written in Greek. Recent trends in criticism have argued for a more multicultural view of the ancient Mediterranean in its diversity of religious beliefs and practices and have suggested a greater fluidity in the assessment of mutual interests and influences. But for all that, Jewish and Christian works differ quite

48 Lowe (2000) 237.
49 Morgan (2005) 311; already observed by Feuillâtre (1966) 120–1.

substantially from their pagan cousins. Indeed, these so-called novels (or novellas) contain elements that belong to the romance genre: for example, erotic motifs, trials and ordeals, the virtues of constancy, the prominence of women characters and emphasis on chastity. But the major difference is that all these motifs and conventions are deployed expressly in the service of religious ideology with none of the irony, ambiguity, authorial sleight of hand and opportunism that may be read in a typical specimen of prose fiction. For Jews, these works (such as *Esther*, *Daniel*, *Tobit*, *Susanna*) offer affirmations not just of personal identity but also of communal support and salvation. While one novel, *Joseph and Aseneth*, presents an erotic tale that entails the conversion of the would-be bride to the worship of the Hebrew God, Christian texts are regularly geared towards this end in stories of wonder-working apostles (e.g. the so-called Apocryphal *Acts*), whose charismatic influence leads not to erotic fulfilment but to renunciation. Apuleius' Isis book may suggest affinities with these non-pagan works, but they deserve extended discussion on their own.[50]

Further reading

For general studies of religion under the empire, see Lane Fox (1987), Macmullen (1981) and Anderson (2001). On mystery religions, see Burkert (1987). There are no specific works dedicated to religion in the ancient novel, but every general treatment of the genre (see the 'Further reading' section of Bowie, this volume) will allot some space to the topic. See Merkelbach (1994) and Beck (2003) for recent discussions of mystery cults, holy men and aretalogies. Frye's treatment of romance as 'sacred scripture' (1976) is the source of comparisons between mysteries, life and romance and still required reading. For more sociological analyses, see Perkins (1995), Morgan (1995) and Swain (1996). On individual authors, I have found the following most useful. For Chariton, I suggest Edwards (1994), Schmeling (2005), and Zeitlin (2003). On Achilles Tatius, see Segal (1984) and Bouffartigue (2001). On Longus, Chalk (1960) on the mysteries and mythology of Eros and the role of Dionysus in the novel is the place to start, but for more nuanced views, see e.g. Hunter (2003). The religious atmosphere of Heliodorus has elicited the most commentary. See, in particular, Heiserman (1977), Winkler (1982), and Sandy (1982a), (1982c). Morgan has written extensively on this novel and is always worth reading: see esp. (1982), (1989b), (2003). For recent innovative readings, see also Whitmarsh (1998), (1999), and Chew (2007).

---

50 On Jewish novels see Wills (1995) and (2002). Other notable specimens of Christian prose fiction are Pseudo-Clement, *Recognitions*, and *Paul and Thecla*. For Christian prose fiction in general, see the convenient summary of Pervo (2003).

As for Apuleius, the role of Isis and the interpretation of Lucius' 'conversion' in the last book is the fullest representation of religion in action of all the ancient novels. One may consult with profit Winkler (1985), Shumate (1996), Griffiths (1978), Sandy (1978), and Mal-Maeder (1997). See also Harrison (2000) 235–59, offering a fine discussion of Platonism and Platonic motifs; also (2003). On the tale of Cupid and Psyche, Kenney's edition (1990a) is valuable as is Walsh's discussion ((1970) 190–223). The most authoritative work on the Jewish novel can be found in Wills (1995) and (2002). For Christian prose fiction, see Pervo (1987) and (2003) as well as the essays in Hock, Chance and Perkins (1998). A recent and sophisticated reading of Christian and Greek fiction is Burrus (2005).

7

JAMES ROMM

Travel

A recent volume which attempts, as this one does, to provide readers with a broad survey of the ancient novel includes in its final chapter a set of maps traversed by bold-faced lines. The maps generally show the eastern Mediterranean and Near East, and the lines represent the routes followed by the heroes and heroines of the extant novels (as well as of several epics and other narratives) as they roam back and forth, tempest-tossed, across that expanse. These maps form a curious supplement to a study of a literary genre, but one which makes sense given the degree to which this genre relies on a sense of place for its aesthetic effects. 'Travel is such a delineating feature of the ancient novels (except for Longus and Apuleius) that we felt obliged to highlight [the routes of their characters]' remarks the editor, Gareth Schmeling, in his preface, adding his hope that such maps will help readers zero in on the places 'which ancient writers considered fascinating, exotic, enchanting or mysterious enough to warrant visits by their heroes and heroines'.[1] The following discussion takes its cue from Schmeling's words and attempts to supplement, in a verbal rather than pictorial medium, the map included with the present volume.

Maps are indeed a great benefit to readers of the Greek and Roman novels, but there is much also these readers need to know about the character, history and atmosphere of the places frequented in those works. Perhaps a mediaeval *mappa mundi*, with pictures and folkloric legends superimposed on the outlines of each region of the globe, would be the ideal resource, for it would represent in graphic terms the kinds of associations between distant places and alien phenomena that the ancient novelist clearly counted on his audience to make. What follows is an attempt to sketch out some of these associations.

---

1 Schmeling (2003b) 7.

The circumscribed novels

Before turning to the authors whose works tour these distant places and different landscapes, let us look briefly at those whom Schmeling excluded from his map collection on the grounds that their characters do not venture far at all from their starting point.

Longus set his *Daphnis and Chloe* entirely on the island of Lesbos, and a fairly small stretch of the island at that. He seems to have conceived the novel as a kind of literary experiment, an ideal romance that dispenses entirely with the element of travel but instead explores the minute changes and day-to-day developments in a single, unremarkable place. He took his inspiration from the pastoral poetry of Theocritus rather than, as the other Greek romancers did, from epic and historiography; his characters dwell in a generalised and ahistorical green world, which Longus might have situated in almost any thinly settled place (though he perhaps chose Lesbos for his love story because it was home to two great love poets of the archaic Greek world, Sappho and Alcaeus). In this rural setting, the rhythms of life are dominated by the seasons with their attendant changes in the routines of farming and herding, and so time rather than space forms the axis along which Longus advances his plot; he moves his characters from early spring in the first book, to summer and harvest season in the second, then winter and a second spring and summer in the third, and finally a second harvest in the fourth. The world beyond the pastoral bubble is not allowed to intrude except briefly in book 1, in an episode of a pirate raid, and then in a more extensive way in book 4, where the arrival of city-dwellers punctures the bubble and ends the childlike innocence of the main characters. Indeed the book 1 episode can be read as a kind of literary jest, based on a frustration of the reader's generic expectations. Since romance pirates are always carrying romance heroes off to far-away places, the kidnapping of Daphnis seems for a moment to promise sea voyages and high adventure; but the gravitational pull of the pastoral world reasserts itself, and Daphnis is soon back in rural Lesbos.

Apuleius, the author of the Roman novel *Metamorphoses*, took a Greek novelette as the basis of his tale, either the work we now call the Greek *Ass*, or, more likely, some lost work on which this surviving Greek version is based: so we cannot say that he deliberately circumscribed the action of his novel in the way that Longus did. His setting, the region of Thessaly in northern Greece, was already selected for him by his predecessor; it was a place notorious as a centre of witchcraft and magic, making it particularly suitable for the odyssey of the man transformed into a donkey. Neither the

Greek story nor Apuleius' expanded version follows the travels of the hero, Lucius, in a way that could be plotted on a map; in most cases these narratives take place in a generalised semi-rural landscape on the fringes of the Hellenic world, far from the more civilised urban centres of central Greece and the Near East. As in the case of Longus' *Daphnis and Chloe*, these works never depart from that landscape, and indeed move their heroes around in it by very small increments of distance (except when Apuleius has Lucius run off to Cenchreae, near Corinth, in book 10). The leaps they make on the socio-economic scale are, however, huge. Like the Spanish picaresque heroes who would follow them, the Greek and Roman ass-men make a comprehensive tour of the entire class spectrum that defines the society around them. They fall variously into the hands of robbers, soldiers, workmen, slaves, religious fanatics and finally or rather penultimately in Apuleius' case, for he has added the mysterious conversion scene as the resolution of *his* story, a rich widow at the apex of the class pyramid. The travel element of these two stories, in other words, is best plotted not horizontally, on the axis of geographic space, but vertically, in terms of moves up and down the ladder of social status. Their authors use the wanderings of Lucius – an upstanding, well-to-do citizen with good credentials who suddenly finds himself thrust into the form of an ignominious beast – as a vehicle for exploring the extreme highs and lows of bourgeois society, and many intermediate points as well.

Much the same might be said of Petronius in the *Satyrica*, whose hero Encolpius, a *demimondain* with upper-class breeding but no money and a taste for the gutter, ranges similarly up and down the social scale, observing different foibles and maladies at various levels. However Petronius' novel also moves more freely in geographic space than those of Longus and Apuleius, with extant episodes situated in various parts of the Italian peninsula and further fragments suggesting a north–south journey beginning in the Greek city of Massilia (modern-day Marseille). It has been speculated that the *Satyrica*'s final book moved the scene of action to Lampsacus on the Sea of Marmora, the birthplace of the god Priapus and a plausible setting for the resolution of Encolpius' struggle with that deity. Even if this speculation is correct, however, the travels of the *Satyrica* would still have more in common with what I have here termed the circumscribed ancient novels than with the outward-moving, margin-seeking Greek fictions we shall explore below, in that they take place wholly within the bounds of the known, mapped, Greco-Roman geographic sphere. Like the novels of Longus and Apuleius, the *Satyrica* seems to have been interested in exploring the full range and complexity of what lies within that sphere, rather than in venturing outside it.

The orientalising novels

By contrast the great majority of the extant ancient novels show a strong orientalising impulse, meaning that they include travels far from home and seek out encounters with the foreign, the exotic and the marvellous (qualities found predominantly, but not exclusively, in the East).[2] Because these works tend to frequent only a few regions of the globe (as the map in this volume makes clear), it will be convenient in what follows to sort them according to the places their characters visit, rather than discussing them one by one as we have done thus far.

The Achaemenid Persian empire

If Aeschylus could say that his genre was merely 'slices from the great banquet of Homer', then the Greek novelists might have similarly claimed theirs to be slices from the great banquet of Herodotus. It was Herodotus who had first attempted the experiment of taking the entire *oikoumenē* (his term for the known world) as his setting, capitalizing on the advent of the Achaemenid Persian empire, a state that had extended its power into nearly every corner of that expanse. Herodotus too had understood that, for certain readers at least, the periphery of the *oikoumenē* was of much greater interest than the centre: 'old' Greece, the mainland city-states in which most of his readers dwelt or travelled, lacked the novelty and exoticism of Babylon, Scythia, India, Ethiopia and, above all, Egypt, and so the *Histories* gives almost no attention to the former spaces while making long excursuses into the latter, including the enormous Egyptian account of book 2 that occupies more than an eighth of the entire text. And he understood the appeal of the wonders to be found in those foreign locales: great monuments and sumptuous buildings, weird animal and plant life, climatic and geologic anomalies, freaks of nature.

Indeed, it is noteworthy that three of the six surviving full-length Greek novels (*Callirhoe*, *Charicleia and Theagenes*, the *Alexander Romance*), all of those with an identifiable historical setting, take place within the old Persian empire, the same realm adopted by Herodotus as the geographic frame for his narrative. The preference shared by Herodotus and the novelists for Achaemenid Persia as a literary landscape attests to a shared interest in the enlargement of the world that had taken place under that empire, the movement toward what is now termed globalisation. It was the advent of the Persian empire, which had connected the coast of Turkey to the hinterlands of Iran with a well-provisioned Royal Road, that had made access to the

---

2 Kuch (2003) 210–11.

Far East freely available to the Greeks, and whetted their appetite for exotic and erotic oriental tales just as keenly as the opening of the Portuguese trade routes to India had given renaissance Europeans a taste for cinammon and cloves. Herodotus began capitalising on the availability of such imports in the *Histories*, whose opening and closing stories of Candaules' over-passionate love for his wife, and Xerxes' similarly excessive ardour for the wife of Masistes and her daughter, read very much like proto-romances in miniature; and Xenophon in the *Cyropaedia* and Ctesias in the *Persian Affairs* quickly followed his lead. Thanks to the groundwork laid by such authors, Achaemenid Persia became enshrined for later Greeks as a literary landscape ideally suited to the particular kind of erotic intrigue in which the ancient novel clearly delights.

An essential element in this brand of erotic intrigue is the intersection of, or collision between, sexual love and political power. The Greek novelists, again following the lines laid down by Herodotus, found the spectacle of great kings or their officers smitten by love to be highly compelling, and the greatest kings – indeed those dubbed by the Greeks 'Great Kings' – were those of the Persians, or their close kin in other Asiatic empires. Thus the two extant ideal romances that have definite historical settings, those of Chariton and Heliodorus, both play upon the theme of royal might humbled by irremediable passion. Chariton moves the scene of his novel to Babylon for an elaborate spousal-custody trial, thus creating an opportunity for Artaxerxes II, who is to judge the dispute between Callirhoe's rival husbands, to fall in love with the girl himself.[3] Heliodorus by contrast creates a kind of surrogate for the Great King in the person of Oroondates, the Persian satrap of Egypt, and then depicts his wife, the royal heiress Arsace, falling hopelessly in love with the novel's male hero, Theagenes. Beyond these two extant examples we also see oriental potentates laid low by Eros in the *Babylonian Affairs* of Iamblichus, preserved in a summary by Photius; in *Apollonius, King of Tyre*, which survives in a Latin version (probably a translation of a Greek original); and in the fragmentary works *Sesonchosis* and *Ninus*. The Hebrew Bible contains other examples of the same motif, including the story of the *Book of Esther*, which is again an import from, and throwback to, Achaemenid Persia in its heyday.

We have already made reference above to the *ur*-text of this kind, Herodotus' story of Xerxes' irresistible passions for two women at his court, a story that follows Herodotus' account of the final defeat of Persia and thus helps bring the *Histories* as a whole to its conclusion. Herodotus here is clearly constructing a parallel between imperial and erotic overreach,

3 On Chariton's Persia see Baslez (1992).

showing us a king who failed to govern his lust for either sexual or territorial conquests. Interestingly enough, both *Callirhoe* and *Charicleia and Theagenes* also conjoin their tales of royal amours with accounts of wars in which Persia struggles to retain control over the outer fringes of its empire. In the former work Artaxerxes, while scheming to possess Callirhoe, very nearly loses control of Egypt, thanks in large part to the naval defeat Chaereas inflicts upon him; while in the latter Oroondates fails to project Persian power into the pure realm of Ethiopia at the same moment that his wife Arsace is assailing the sexual purity of Theagenes. In both texts, the global reach of the Achaemenid state, its ability to project power toward the farthest corners of the earth, is defeated along with the sexual claims made by its high officials on the virtue of pure youth. Persia at its height represents in these works a presumptuous kind of acquisitiveness, of both land and sexual partners, that must be circumscribed before a happy resolution can be achieved.

In contrast to the lustful Persian royals, the Greek heroes of these novels refuse to parley their political sovereignty into sexual conquest. Chareas for example refrains from making any advances on Artaxerxes' wife, Statira, after capturing her in a raid on the island of Aradus, and ultimately restores her to her husband, who seemingly regains his contentment with licit love. The episode is clearly patterned after Alexander the Great's capture of and reverential behaviour toward Darius III's wife and daughters, a historical event that was enlarged to outsized dimensions in the *Alexander Romance* and other Hellenistic/imperial accounts of the Alexander story. The sexual self-restraint of Alexander in the presence of Darius' women, and the reverence he showed by marrying Roxane rather than making her a concubine, are glorified in these quasi-fictional narratives as part of their collective vision of a noble, just form of empire led by Greeks (and Hellenised Macedonians) rather than Persians. The *Alexander Romance* indeed conflates these two chivalrous episodes by recasting Roxane as one of Darius' daughters, betrothed by her dying father to Alexander and bringing the crown of Asia as her dowry (2.20). Alexander, who had earlier in the *Romance* (2.17) rejected the advice of a senior general to insult Darius' honour by sexually violating his women, is in the end rewarded for his virtue by an elevation to legitimate rule through marriage.

Ethiopia and the upper Nile

The *Alexander Romance* lends itself only with difficulty to our geographically arranged analysis, since many of its episodes take place off the world map entirely (as we shall see below), while others are so vaguely situated that neither reader nor (seemingly) author know exactly where they take

place.[4] Nonetheless Alexander's encounter with Queen Candace of Meroe
(3.18–23) plays out against a distinctively Ethiopian backdrop (even though
we come to it abruptly in the midst of other adventures set in India). Here
again the influence of Herodotus' *Histories* on the Greek novel can clearly
be felt. In book 3 (chapters 18–24) of the *Histories* Cambyses sends spies
to reconnoitre the land of the Ethiopians, spies who are quickly unmasked
by the all-knowing, virtuous king of that land and who thereafter become
tourists gawking at the marvels of the Far South. In the *Romance* it is
Alexander himself who comes in disguise and is taken on a tour of marvels, during which he is unmasked by the wise, stately Queen Candace. The
civilization of the Ethiopians is in this later work distinguished not by its
primitivism and purity, as in Herodotus, but by the sumptuousness and elegance of its material culture, in particular the queen's richly wrought palace;
and the excellence of the queen herself lies not so much in physical strength
as in cunning. Still the tendency to idealize the Ethiopians as a powerful
nation whose wealth and prowess derive directly from moral virtue is similar to what one finds in Herodotus. 'We are purer in soul than the whitest
of *your* peoples', Candace writes to Alexander, in a letter that also promises
gifts of fabulous animals, gold and precious objects (3.18). Here is a land
where riches do not corrupt the spirit, but can be freely enjoyed and freely
given away to visitors; here is a ruler whose wealth does not impede her
wisdom.

A more extensive exploration of Ethiopia as the land of virtuous empire
is found in Heliodorus' *Charicleia and Theagenes*.[5] This novel's portrait
of the tall, pious, Sun-and-Moon-worshipping Ethiopians descends in part
from Herodotus, but also owes something to the Cynic traditions regarding
Indian wise men and their kind, in that a college of Gymnosophists serves
as advisers to the Ethiopian crown. (We shall deal in more detail with the
Gymnosophists or 'Naked sages' below in a discussion of fictions concerning India.) The Ethiopian king, Hydaspes, though master over a variety of
peoples in surrounding territories, exemplifies the spirit of moderate rule
when, in response to entreaties, he remits his subjects' tribute payment for a
period of ten years (10.26). These neighbouring peoples, moreover, willingly
join Hydaspes in his war against the Persian satrap Oroondates, and they
make a fascinating coalition: Troglodytae or 'Cave-dwellers', a race of swift-
footed nomads expert at dodging the enemy after discharging their slings;
Blemmyes, a primitive tribe sometimes imagined (though apparently not by

4 Stoneman (1994) analyses some of the contorted geographic notions behind the *Romance*.
5 For all discussion of the geographic and historical setting of *Charicleia and Theagenes* I am
  indebted to Morgan (1982). On the presentation of Ethiopia / Meroe see also Lonis (1992);
  Hägg (1999–2000).

Heliodorus) as headless men with faces in their chests, who duck under the horses of the enemy cavalry to stab their unprotected bellies; the Men from the Land of Cinnamon, that is, the horn of Africa, expert archers who fight naked except for a net-like hat that holds their bone-carved arrows; and the Seres or 'Silk-people', who disconcert the Persian cavalry by bringing forward elephants, a beast that horses will not approach.[6] In this curious array of subjects/allies, each with its own distinctive, non-technologised form of warfare, we see embodied the peculiarly Ethiopian combination of military might and moral superiority. In imitation of Herodotus in the Scythian account of book 4, Heliodorus has ranged a group of light-armed, fast-moving troops who rely on craft and evasion against the over-equipped Persians with their cumbersome body armour and hide-bound strategies. Indeed the turning point in the battle comes when the Persian cavalrymen, unhorsed by the Blemmyes, prove to be so laden with equipment as to be unable to move, forced to lie motionless 'like chunks of wood' while their foes stab them to death (*Charicleia and Theagenes* 9.18).

Hydaspes' virtuous exercise of political sovereignty and military might is intimately connected by Heliodorus with the holiness of Ethiopia itself, a land sanctified by its geographic position at the wellsprings of the Nile. The Nile, we learn in this novel, is regarded by the neighbouring Egyptians as a god and worshipped in a yearly festival called the Neiloa. Heliodorus explores this festival in an important episode at the end of book 9, in which king Hydaspes, having captured Syene from the Persians, enters the city and is taken on a tour by the local priests. He sees the Nilometer, a device used to measure the annual rises and falls of the water level, and hears the river described as an embodiment of the god Horus, as a giver of life, and even as a creator of earth (in that its silt depositions have built up the northern portions of Egypt where there was once only sea). Hydaspes' response to all this is noteworthy: he insists to the priests that since Ethiopia gives rise to the Nile, it, and not the river, is the proper object of their worship – 'for it is the mother of your gods' (9.22). Heliodorus here plays a kind of geographic leapfrog with the notion, adduced by Herodotus in the *Histories*, that Egypt was the source of the gods subsequently worshipped by the Greeks. In *Charicleia and Theagenes* the sacred realm in which divinity originates has simply been pushed one step further outward in space.[7]

6 The presence in Ethiopia of this last nation comes as a distinct surprise, since the name 'Seres' when used by other authors usually means the Chinese. But in the mind of late Greek scientists like Ptolemy, Africa and Asia were closely connected by way of an undiscovered southerly land bridge, and Heliodorus does not in any case seem to have been overly concerned with geographic niceties.

7 Saïd (1994) 229 expresses a similar view: 'Ethiopia is, in many ways, a kind of super-Egypt.'

The springs of the Nile and the anomalous summer floodings of the river were always considered deep mysteries by the Greeks, for whom winter was the rainy season that swelled all other streams. Heliodorus sacralises this mystery when he allows his character Calasiris to learn the secret of the Nile's floods from a set of holy books known only to a caste of Egyptian priests, as if he were being initiated into a mystery cult (2. 28). Though the explanation is entirely rational and scientific, its very arcanity seems to lend numinous power to the whole phenomenon. Later (9.9) Heliodorus again compares the learning of the Nile secrets to initiation into a mystery cult, likening the river's flooding of the land to the mating of Isis and Osiris. Small wonder then that among the Ethiopians, who are privileged to dwell at the river's source, the office of king overlaps with that of head priest, so that when a transition of power takes place at the novel's end, Theagenes and Charicleia don white sacral mitres rather than golden crowns. The resolution of the novel also entails a peculiar kind of civic purification, in that the rite of human sacrifice this otherwise refined race has practised since ancient times (despite the objection of the Gymnosophists) is banished forever (10.39–41)

Egypt

The holy mysteries of the Nile colours not only the portrait of Ethiopian society in *Charicleia and Theagenes*, but also accounts of Egypt in nearly all the ideal Greek novels (*Daphnis and Chloe* is of course the exception, due to its uniquely static setting).[8] Achilles Tatius in particular expatiates on the strange geography and biology of the Nile in his third and fourth books, and also describes a stratagem by which floods in the river can be used as a weapon (4.13). (In a similar ploy described by Heliodorus, the Ethiopian king uses a Nile flood to rout the Persians occupying Syene.) Xenophon too plays on the paradox of the Nile floods, in a different way: Adapting Herodotus' account of the redemption of Croesus, he describes how Habrocomes' life was saved when a sudden inundation of the Nile quenched the flames of his pyre (4.2). In this last instance the Nile seems to act as a sentient being or a god, though less explicitly than in *Charicleia and Theagenes*, where the river is systematically deified.

Unlike the Nile's upper reaches, where the river's rises and falls can be measured with scientific regularity, the marshes of the Nile delta, home to the infamous Herdsmen (*Boukoloi* or *Poimenes*), serve in these novels as a locus of disorder, brigandage and defiance of state authority. Thus Heliodorus

8 Nimis (2004); also Plazenet (1995).

stages his famous opening scene, the aftermath of a battle won by the pirat-
ical Herdsmen, on the beach at one of the Nile's mouths (3.12); Xenophon
crashes his hero Habrocomes on the same strand, making him a prisoner
of the Herdsmen; and Achilles Tatius builds a major episode of his novel,
comprising most of its third and fourth books, against the backdrop of the
Herdsmen's stronghold, which finally falls to the onslaughts of the Egyptian army. There is also the possibility, suggested by Albert Henrichs in his
edition of Lollianus' *Phoenician Affairs*, that fragment B of this largely lost
novel, which describes a gory rite of human sacrifice, comes from an episode
involving the same Herdsmen and set therefore at the delta of the Nile.[9] It
is hardly surprising that the romances should be interested in bandits, who,
along with storms, shipwrecks and wars, provide the mischances that make
up their plots. But the fact that this particular band of 'desperadoes' was
found at the very hub of the Hellenistic Greek world, on the doorstep of
Alexandria itself and astride the main trade routes that converged there,
clearly made them a key point of interest on the Greek novel's itinerary. The
Nile delta represented a kind of proving ground for the stable civic order to
which the novelists were deeply committed; if lawlessness were allowed to
thrive there, within easy reach of half the world's travellers and traders, then
the centre of that order was less likely to hold.[10]

Even beyond the miraculous Nile, Egypt held many wonders to excite
readers of the Greek romances. Calasiris, himself an Egyptian, articulates in
Charicleia and Theagenes a principle that many of the novelists seem to have
understood: 'The Greeks find all the lore of Egypt irresistible' (2.27), citing
as an example the interrogation he underwent, while visiting Delphi, about
subjects like Egyptian religion, the construction of the pyramids, and the
'underground maze', a set of burial chambers near Thebes. He might have
also instanced Egyptian animal life, for this seems to have been uniquely fascinating to Greek readers, to judge by the frequency of biological excursuses
in the surviving novels. Many animals in Egypt were sanctified because of
the role they played in worship of the gods (a topic alluded to by Calasiris
in his catalogue of exotica), or because they behaved in ways that suggested
intelligence or piety, as in the case of the phoenix bird; in the unique account
of Achilles Tatius, this bird (which originates in Ethiopia but then migrates to
Egypt) buries its dead father beside the Nile in a coffin of myrrh, then flies to

---

9 Henrichs (1972), supported by Winkler (1980) 155–6.
10 Saïd (1994) 230 calls additional attention to the paradoxical physical nature of the Nile
    delta, with its swamps made up half of water, half of land. Herodotus, in a critique of the
    Ionian world maps which used the Nile as a continental boundary, observed that in their
    scheme the delta would fall into neither Asia nor Libya and would constitute a continent
    unto itself (*Histories* 2.16).

Heliopolis for a process of confirmation and inauguration as the new 'reigning' phoenix (3.25). Others, like the crocodile, hippo and Egyptian bull, also the subjects of digressions by Achilles Tatius (2.15, 4.2, 4.19), were appealing merely because of their strangeness and their association with a long literary tradition of Egyptian novelties. A cryptic remark by a mysterious stranger encountered by Calasiris suggests that even the herbs of Egypt, like those of Ethiopia and India, were thought to possess occult properties (2.30). Indeed these three lands, with their overlapping yet distinct galleries of wonders, might be said to form the fertile crescent of exoticism for the authors of the Greek novels.

The Far East and beyond

Let us turn then to the Greek fictional[11] treatments of the third member of this triad, India – the vague toponym assigned by the Greeks and Romans to the furthest east. Following the eastern campaign of Alexander in 327–5 BCE, India came to share with the Nile river the peculiar romance of a place part within, part beyond the reach of exploration. Alexander had brought his army, accompanied by Greek scientists and geographers, as far as the river Hyphasis (modern-day Beas), before a mutiny forced him to turn homeward. Thus the realm lying beyond this river, or, according to some, beyond the Ganges,[12] stood as one of the last stretches of *terra incognita* on the Greco-Roman map of the earth. Proximity to this mystery lent all of India an air of the marvellous and sacred, just as we saw above in the case of Ethiopia, home of the Nile's source.

India, as imagined by the Greeks of the empire, had other features as well in common with the Nilotic lands of Ethiopia and Egypt: it was a hot place inhabited by dark-skinned peoples; it was traversed by pious sages, usually known as Brahmans or *Gymnosophistai*, 'Naked wise men'; it was home to huge and marvellous beasts; and it was defined by the central marvel of an enormous river, the Indus (which was thought to fertilize the soil with annual floods, like the Nile, and which was inhabited by crocodiles and other beasts seemingly identical to those in Egypt). Indeed Alexander, upon first

---

11 The term 'fictional' must be used advisedly, since one of the principal strategies of Greek writers on India was to complicate or subvert traditional boundaries between fact and fiction; the Far East made an appealing literary landscape precisely because it lay beyond the reach of *elenkhos*, the testing process a scientist or historian would use to separate the two. See Romm (1992) ch. 3, and, with special focus on Apollonius of Tyana, Francis (1998).

12 Some later legends claimed that Alexander had reached the Ganges; additionally, contact between the Seleucid kingdom and the court of the Maurya emperors made information about the region west of the Ganges readily accessible. Thus the world map of Ptolemy's *Geography* denoted two regions of India, *intra* ('this side of') and *extra Gangem* ('beyond the Ganges').

exploring the Indus and observing its wildlife, reportedly guessed that the river was connected to the Nile by way of some Asian–African land bridge;[13] while his teacher Aristotle sought to demonstrate some ancient trans-Atlantic connection between the two lands by the presence of the elephant – an animal not then differentiated into two species – in both (*On the Heavens* 298a).

The India–Ethiopia and Indus–Nile connection gets developed into a major theme of Philostratus' fictionalized biography *Life of Apollonius of Tyana*, which takes its hero to both places in the two most prominent episodes of his world-wide spiritual pilgrimage.[14] According to the unique spiritual geography of Philostratus' text, the *Gymnosophistai* ('Naked sages') usually thought to dwell in the Far East had in fact become split into two parts, the *Gymnoi* ('Naked men') of Ethiopia and the *Sophoi* ('Sages') of India. The *Gymnoi*, it seems, had originated as an apostate branch of the *Sophoi*, having emigrated from India to Ethiopia after murdering a semi-divine king Ganges and becoming so defiled that the very land of the Indus valley rejected them (3.20, 6.11). The *Gymnoi* had thereafter settled south of Egypt, usurping a land once belonging to Egyptians, and, after making atonement for Ganges' murder, had continued the cult practices of their original sect but in a now debased form. There, in the torrid climate, they live in the open air, without huts or houses, wearing only the bare minimum of clothing. And in this state of ascetic purity, the *Gymnoi* rail against the Indian *Sophoi*, their former colleagues, whom they regard as cheap tricksters and mountebanks addicted to base luxuries.

The *Sophoi* of India by contrast are depicted as wizard-like supermen who live in a cloud-robed castle atop a sheer plateau, dressing in robes of white wool with white turbans wrapped around their heads. Wielding mystic rings and staffs, they bend all nature to their will, even surrounding themselves with a force-field so as not to get wet when it rains. Springs of wine gush out of the earth at their behest just as for the Bacchants dancing for Dionysus, who is in fact among the gods worshipped by the *Sophoi*, along with Athena and Apollo (3.14). Their other supernatural powers include levitation, control of the climate, telekinesis, divination of the future, and the ability to extract from sunlight a kind of ethereal fire that can continue to burn at night. Where the apostate *Gymnoi* represent an idealised kind of primitivism, these *Sophoi* stand at the opposite pole of development: super-civilized and refined, they

---

13 Arrian, *Anabasis* 6.1.2–6, where it is also reported that Alexander soon discovered his error.
14 In discussing the travel element in Philostratus' work I am indebted to Elsner (1997), especially 28–32.

have developed their spiritual power into a kind of technology that provides them with all the comforts and pleasures they might require.

The choice that confronts Apollonius between these competing forms of spirituality, the highly evolved piety of the Far East and the asceticism of the Far South, is a stark one. Thespesion, the *Gymnoi* leader, compares it to the 'Choice of Heracles' made famous in Prodicus' parable, where the high, steep, rugged road leading ultimately to Virtue diverges from the easy but vicious path of comfort, luxury and indolence. The scene in which Apollonius is forced to make this choice, while the *Gymnoi* await his decision, forms the climax of the novel. In a long speech directed at Thespesion, with all the *Gymnoi* in attendance, Apollonius champions the wisdom of the *Sophoi* over that of their Ethiopian cousins and defends their well-endowed lifestyle against the scorn Thespesion has heaped upon it. Ornament and refinement are not in themselves evil, Apollonius maintains, or else the very gods would need to live like beasts; the simple pleasures which the *Sophoi* reap from their environment are in fact more virtuous than the self-righteous abnegation practised by the *Gymnoi*. And what is more, Apollonius says, the *Sophoi* take precedence over the *Gymnoi* in his education because they lie closer to the origins, both temporal and geographical, of the divine inspiration from which the *Gymnoi* have diverged. He tells Thespesion that he had chosen the Indians, rather than the Ethiopians, as the starting point of his spiritual training because 'those men mingle with purer rays of sunlight, and are therefore more subtle-minded; they have truer understandings of nature and of the gods because they dwell near to those gods and near the beginnings of the life-begetting element of heat' (6.11). (Interestingly enough the character Charmides, in a discussion of elephant lore in *Leucippe and Clitophon*, uses similar reasoning to explain the sweet smell of the Indian elephant's breath (4.5)).

The numinous power of India reveals itself not just in the human sphere, moreover, but also in that of animals, and even waters and stones.[15] The eastern landscape drawn by Philostratus in books 2 and 3 of the *Life of Apollonius* is replete with wonders of nature that seem to draw upon the same energies as do the *Sophoi*; indeed in some cases the *Sophoi* tap these wonders as though they were a kind of cosmic fuel. Thus the leader of the *Sophoi*, Iarchas, describes how his sect, alone among humankind, can harvest the *pantarbē* stone, here said to be a fiery, glowing gem which contains a 'spirit' (*pneuma*) with the power to attract its fellow *pantarbai* to itself (3.46); and other fiery stones with mystic properties are harvested from the eyes of

---

15 See Elsner (1997) 28–30.

the local dragons (3.6–8). The reader also encounters Indian animals that exhibit weirdly ethical behaviours, above all the elephant, whose intelligence, compassion and concern for its offspring are explored in a lengthy digression of book 2 (11–16); animals that seem to feel religious impulses, like the tiger which lifts its front paws in a worshipful pose before the rising sun (2.27); and animals that join with humans in collaborative efforts, like the apes who harvest pepper inaccessible to the Indians in exchange for protection from ravaging lions (3.4). All such material derives from the paradoxographical catalogues popular in Philostratus' day, but when deployed so densely and concentrated in one corner of the globe, it contributes something more than mere ornament to the narrative of Apollonius' life. Just as the Indian *Sophoi* surpass other wise men in holiness due to their proximity to the sun and the gods, so the larger world of nature seems to be animated here by a beneficent and all-powerful intelligence.[16] Marvels (*paradoxa*) in this landscape are not therefore random events or freaks, but evidence of the workings of an omnipresent divine mind.

Marvels of a very different kind, however, populate the Indian landscape in another fictionalised biography of the imperial age, the *Alexander Romance*, as well as in the shorter Alexander texts that often became incorporated into various versions of that work (including in particular *Alexander's Letter to Aristotle*, a work originally written in Greek but preserved in a Latin translation). In the *Romance*'s mélange of folkloric and literary traditions surrounding the march of Alexander into the east, we see a world of marvels that are no longer a resource to be reaped by humankind, as in the *Life of Apollonius*, but rather a terrifying enemy barely able to be held at bay. The hero's approach to the far corners of the earth no longer brings him closer to godhead but forces him to face the inevitability of his own mortality – a tragic version of the quest myth, in which the sources of holiness beyond the *oikoumenē* can never be attained, and death stalks the traveller at every step.

The Alexander story lent itself naturally to such a treatment since it dealt with a great warrior who had died young after having failed in his self-proclaimed goal of reaching the eastern edge of Asia. At the river Hyphasis in 325 BCE, Alexander reportedly told his recalcitrant army that Ocean lay only a few days' march in the distance, though historians have doubted whether he actually believed this to be true. Nonetheless in the popular imagination,

---

16 Indeed Iarchas, leader of the *Sophoi*, describes just such an interrelationship between the divine and natural realms when he teaches Apollonius that the cosmos itself is an enormous animal (*zōon*) that has imparted its consciousness to all the lesser living things brought forth from it (3.34).

Alexander had stopped short within a hair's breadth of the earth's edge, and shortly thereafter had returned to Babylon where he suddenly became ill and died. The *Romance*, which freely rearranges the geography and chronology of Alexander's life and warps recorded facts in dream-like fashion, links these two episodes together into a sequence of cause and effect: Because he could not penetrate the furthest east, the origin and home of divinity, he was doomed to die – a fate he is continually reminded of by the oracles, portents and prodigies he meets along his route.

Mortality, indeed, is the overriding preoccupation of the *Romance*, especially in its third and final book, which is largely concerned with India; even the Brahmans or *Gymnosophistai*, the pious wise men Alexander encounters in India, seem to share this preoccupation. When Alexander asks them what they most want from him, they reply with one voice 'Give us immortality', to which the king sadly replies that he is not able: 'For I too am mortal' (3.16). Even the marvels of the *Alexander Romance*, which for the most part are clustered together in the two so-called 'miracle letters' inserted into the narrative in books 2 and 3, tend to organize themselves around the theme of mortality. In one prominent episode of Alexander's sojourn in search of the Land of the Blessed – a site of eternal life, to judge by its name – the king finds a spring the water of which flashes like lightning. When his cook washes a preserved fish in the water, the fish comes back to life, but Alexander narrowly misses his chance to drink from the spring and so become immortal. Elsewhere, a pair of oracular trees called the Trees of the Sun and Moon warn Alexander not only that he will soon die himself, but his wife and mother too; his entire line will be extirpated (3.17). The marvels and wonders for which the East was famous have in this novel taken on a monitory and menacing aspect very different from their associations with enlightenment and divine guidance in the *Life of Apollonius*.

The 'miracle letters' also show Alexander under attack by the monstrous animal life of India, or stymied in his attempts to investigate it or take samples for further study. Whereas a legend arising in the imperial era had imagined Alexander as a biologist-in-arms, collecting odd plants and beasts and sending them to his former teacher Aristotle, the *Letter to Aristotle* is instead a record of how scientific exploration fails to encompass the monsters of the East, just as western military technology fails to stave them off. Alexander is constantly on the defensive as swarms of creatures – known beasts like lions and scorpions, as well as hitherto unknown serpents, giant crabs and bats, shrews with poisonous bites – charge his army again and again during a long night of horrors beside a watering hole. In this bleak, Boschean landscape, the limitless novelty of the East becomes a nightmarish phantasmagoria, bringing

Alexander up against the limits of Aristotelian rationalism and Macedonian military might.

The Far West / Far North / moon / other worlds

This phantasmagoric aspect of the Indian landscape could also serve comic purposes, as seen in Lucian's *True Histories*, a satirical sketch which similarly features a seemingly limitless array of marvels, though in this case mostly harmless or absurd grotesques. The *True Histories* invokes the Indian wonders tradition at several levels, both explicitly in its invocation of Ctesias and Iambulus in the prologue and implicitly in its discovery of phenomena traditionally associated with the East: vestiges (quite literally here, footprints) left behind by Dionysus and Heracles in their travels. Nonetheless the narrator of the piece describes his journey as a *west*ward voyage from the Pillars of Heracles, undertaken in an effort to find the end of Ocean and see what sort of people were living on the other side. After thus exploiting a longstanding scientific curiosity about other worlds in the western hemisphere, Lucian lifts his narrator's ship into the sky to explore another mystery of science, the surface of the moon. The Moonpeople he finds there form a kind of grotesque fantasy of a homosexual male warrior society, engaged in all-out war with the inhabitants of the Sun. The solemn tones of both Thucydidean historiography and Herodotean ethnography are used to describe this science-fiction episode, with both styles only barely masking the comic exuberance Lucian displays in the prologue to the work, where he tells us not to believe anything we are about to read. (In the dialogue *Icaromenippus* Lucian again sends his hero to the moon, though the lunar surface is in this case more a vantage point for observing the earth than a goal of exploration in itself.)

Irony, fantasy and scientific exploration were similarly mixed together in the lost novel *Wonders beyond Thule* by Antonius Diogenes, with an added element of erotic adventure, constructed on the model of the Greek romance, thrown in for good measure. The island of Thule in the North Atlantic had supposedly been glimpsed by explorers like Pytheas of Massilia but no one in antiquity claimed to have set foot there. Antonius Diogenes however made it the setting in which his characters, an idealised pair of lovers named Dercyllis and Deinias and their cohorts, narrate a complex series of interwoven tales about their travels across the globe. Many of these travels take them to northern Europe, interestingly enough – a frontier of the new Roman world, barely known to classical Greece – including the North Sea, the legendary Rhipaean Mountains (not in this case inhabited by Hyperboreans), and even a land of continuous night near the North Pole. The astronomical and geographic data brought back by Pytheas from regions near the arctic circle have here become fodder for Antonius Diogenes' comic invention, just as Lucian, his close contemporary, makes grotesque sport out of lunar astronomy.

The moon seems to have been the final port of call in the *Wonders beyond Thule*, though whether the heroes of the novel actually set foot there, or only came very close to the lunar surface in their travels to the far north, is difficult to ascertain from the wording of Photius' summary. Nor can we tell what they found there, because Photius, seemingly impatient with the implausibility of this plot move, cuts his account of the episode short. But clearly the same impulse which made the source of the Nile and trans-Hyphasis India such appealing landscapes for the Greek novel – the desire to penetrate mysteries beyond the bounds of empirical inquiry – was also at work in the lunar explorations of Antonius Diogenes and Lucian. Plutarch's dialogue *On the Face in the Moon* contains within it a novelistic tale which amply supports this idea: after the dialogue's participants have tried out various speculations regarding the moon's true nature, their hypotheses are rendered moot by a dream vision relayed at second hand by a nameless Carthaginian stranger. That man had voyaged out beyond the Pillars of Heracles a distance of 5,000 stades, to an island located near Homer's Ogygia, where he had found a sect of semi-divine spirits attending the ever-sleeping god Cronus. From the dreams of this god, as reported by his attendants and then by the Carthaginian, we learn the ultimate truth about the moon.

In these imperial fabulous-voyage texts, both comic and pseudo-scientific, we see a return to the other-world explorations that predominated in the earliest days of Greek fiction, in the proto-novelistic traveller's tales of Iambulus and Euhemerus – or, for that matter, of Homer's Odysseus (to follow the same trajectory Lucian traces in the *True Histories* prologue). Indeed, Greek fiction followed an exocentric path all through its development, seeking out landscapes dominated by the exotic, the bizarre and the impenetrable. Lunar landings evolved as a logical extension (or, in Lucian's case, a *reductio ad absurdum*) of this exocentrism, just as the moon itself was reached, in all three of the texts discussed above, by way of a hyperbolic sea voyage into the far west or north. At the edge of the known the Greek fictional traveller did not fall into an abyss but rose up into the sky, where there were further new worlds to explore.

Further reading

The centrality of travel literature and ethnography to the (particularly Greek) novel have been recognised since Rohde (1914). For recent accounts of ethnographic 'otherness' in the novel see Bowie (1991), Bowersock (1994) esp. 29–53, Whitmarsh (1998), (1999), Kuch (2003). Elsner (1997) is a penetrating discussion of the travel theme in Philostratus' *Life of Apollonius of Tyana*. Romm (1994) discusses the travel theme in Antonius Diogenes and later novelistic literature. More generally on travel literature in antiquity see André-Baslez (1992), Romm (1992), Clarke (1999).

8

JASON KÖNIG

Body and text

The bodies of the ancient novels are hard to ignore: beautiful, chaste bodies, god-like bodies, ugly bodies, dead bodies, fragmented bodies, penetrated bodies, animal bodies, bodies that are hard to tell apart from one another. The novels confront us with these forms insistently. Some of them look easy to interpret, as shining examples of chastity and virtue, qualities that manifest themselves inevitably in beauty. But many of them are enigmatic, unstable, hard to fathom. Here I want to emphasise two main issues in the challenge of reading the novels' bodies: first the way in which these texts both proclaim and problematise the status of physical appearance as a guarantor of inner identity; and second, the way in which the bodies they present us with are so often equivalent in form to the texts themselves, metaphors and mirrors for the very experience of reading.

Bodily integrity and elite identity

The elite society of the imperial period was preoccupied with the way in which social status left its marks on the surface of the human body. The way you dressed, the way you carried yourself, the way you exercised your body said a great deal about who you were. This was an age when gymnasium education,[1] rhetorical prowess (with its obsessive attention to the bearing and physical training of the orator),[2] and philosophically informed attention to bodily self-care[3] were more prestigious then they ever had been, and when public violation and mutilation of the body in punishment were used more routinely and extravagantly than before to signify loss of social status or political influence.[4] Additionally, the development of new types of Christian thinking about the body – the valorisation of chastity and the glorification of the martyred body, now recuperated from its degradation to be a sign of

---

1 König (2005) esp. 97–157.   2 Gleason (1995).
3 Foucault (1986).   4 Gleason (2001) esp. 74–85.

Christian victory – was both an integral part of this world and a profound reshaping of it.[5] And yet the relation between physical form and personal identity was never a straightforward one. The link between body and identity was often hard to guarantee, subject to acute anxiety and to varied interpretation, in need of constant reaffirmation through the repeated performances of day-to-day self-presentation.[6] That is not to suggest that the bodies of the ancient world were always viewed as malleable and unstable. No doubt many people in the Roman world would have felt little discrepancy between their own bodily appearance and (say) social status. My point is rather that that kind of certainty always had the *potential* to be undermined, especially for members of the elite for whom the pressures of public self-display were so strong. As modern sociological thought tells us, the body is the most familiar and tangible aspect of our selves. And yet that sense of fixity is always in tension with an awareness of the body's alienness, an awareness of its capacity to elude our control. There are always moments when the uncertainties and inconsistencies that lie behind even the most confident acts of bodily self-presentation have the potential to resurface.[7] The ancient novels both reflect and adapt these assumptions and anxieties.

I turn first of all to the Greek novels, before moving on to Petronius and Apuleius in the second half of this section. The Greek novel texts share many features with early Christian narrative, through their obsession with the chastity and physical inviolability of their heroes and heroines in the face of torture and attempted seduction.[8] Physical perfection is given great emphasis, for one thing, in descriptions of the protagonists' upbringing and background. In Chariton's novel, for example, there is a recurrent association between beauty and Hellenic good breeding, both in the opening and closing scenes and in the intervening books when the protagonists are removed from the safety of their home city. In these opening scenes, the heroine Callirhoe is introduced to us as daughter of the great Sicilian general Hermocrates. Her beauty draws suitors from all over the Greek-speaking world. Her lover Chaereas is an icon of Greek good-birth and athleticism, trained, like all good Greek citizens, in the gymnasium (1.1). Callirhoe's beauty later acts as a marker and guarantee of her nobility (2.3), outdazzling even the most beautiful women of luxurious Persia (5.3). And their glorious return and reunion in book 8, against all the odds, offers a fantasy image of the triumph of noble, Hellenic virtue, restoring Callirhoe's beauty – further enhanced by her suffering, so the Syracusans believe (8.6) – to its natural home.

---

5 Gleason (1999); Perkins (1995).
6 See e.g. Gleason (1995); also Wyke (1998) on the unstable bodies of the ancient world.
7 Turner (1996); Shilling (1993).   8 Perkins (1995) esp. 41–76.

The fantastical perfection and invulnerability of the elite body is also on show in the many scenes in all of the Greek novels where the heroes and heroines escape unscathed from the ravagings of torture, punishment and imprisonment, often because their beauty compels their enemies to pity (examples below). Here, too, the novels have much in common with other Greek and Roman texts contemporary with them, which are so often preoccupied with examining the physical effects of suffering. That kind of preoccupation is displayed in perhaps its most vivid and – to modern eyes – alien form in the *Sacred Tales* of Aelius Aristides, Aristides' day-by-day catalogue of his own chronic illness and of the assistance he received from the god Asclepius. Pain has the capacity to threaten one's sense of self; it requires elaborate coping mechanisms, which may often involve the 'creation of narrative'. Far from seeking out strategies for ignoring his own pain and the flawed physicality it reminds him of, Aristides engages with it: 'The body, susceptible to pain, disease, old age, and death, seems to be a sign of distance from the divine world, but the creation of a story from the minute details of its physicality paradoxically seeks to transcend its materiality and make it into a sign of divine favour.'[9] Many other texts from the imperial period – Christian narrative included – give similarly intricate attention to the lived experience of bodily suffering, and find ways of recuperating pain, making it into a sign of triumph, not degradation, a defining feature of selfhood, rather than a threat to it.

The Greek novels follow that lead, but they also depart from it strikingly in the sense that many of them go out of their way to avoid detailed description of the physicality of suffering, in contrast with the intricate attention to physical pain which we find in Aristides and in much hagiographic Christian narrative.[10] Heliodorus goes furthest in registering awareness of the way in which even the most resolute of bodies can be ground down by torture. In book 8, for example, the suffering inflicted on Theagenes and Chariclea by the servants of Arsace leaves its mark – if only inconspicuously – on their bodies:

> When Bagoas looked at them, even though they were in chains and by now worn out through torture, still he was impressed by their size and their beauty. (8.13)

Here there is a hint that their unparalleled beauty may have faded, although their powers of resistance are all the more remarkable for being so

---

9 King (1999) 282.
10 Perkins (1995) esp. 80; see also 173 on the differences between novelistic visions of suffering and the picture offered by Aristides; 202–4 on differences between the novels and their Christian hagiographic counterparts.

pointedly grounded in the realities of bodily suffering. More often, however, in Heliodorus and elsewhere, physical pain is written out of the picture, as if it is so far outweighed by mental suffering as to be negligible. Chariton takes that technique furthest, returning obsessively to the scene of emotions in turmoil,[11] emotions that affect the body and the mind in far more over-whelming ways than any externally imposed, human violence. That privi-leging of mental disturbance over external disruption is clear from the very beginning, from Chariton's elaborate descriptions of the divinely imposed internal violence of love-sickness in the opening paragraphs of the novel.

Elsewhere suffering is eroticised, made into an object of viewing, for exam-ple when Clitophon watches mesmerised while his lover Leucippe is (so it seems) disembowelled (*Leucippe and Clitophon* 3.15).[12] And in many cases, especially in Xenophon's *Anthia and Habrocomes*, the elision of physical suffering contributes to an atmosphere of release from the restricting real-ities of the material world. Xenophon's novel lurches from one narrative crux to the next, with an exhilarating disregard both for the complications of bodily restrictions and for the snares of narrative involution. For example, Habrocomes' crucifixion is described with no attention to physical pain:

> the prefect ordered them to take him away and crucify him. Habrocomes was stunned by these misfortunes, but he consoled himself in the face of death with the thought that Anthia too seemed to have died.　　　　(4.2)

He prays to the sun god, and rescue comes within moments:

> A gust of wind suddenly blew up and struck the cross, sweeping away the soil on which it had been fixed from the top of the cliff. Habrocomes fell into the river and was carried downstream. The water did not harm him, the chains did not hinder him, no wild beasts attacked him; instead the current escorted him along.　　　　(4.2)

Anthia and Habrocomes are fantastically incorporeal figures, alluringly free from the physical self-obsessions of Aristides and the other suffering selves of the imperial world.[13]

The Greek novels thus regularly offer us fantasy images of Greek physical beauty and inviolability. At the same time, however, they show a constant awareness of the instability of beauty and of the elite virtue and identity it is taken to guarantee. In that sense, any argument that emphasises the way in which the Greek novels showcase the integrity of the elite body risks underplaying the degree to which that integrity is humorously

11 Fusillo (1990b).　　12 See Morales (2004) 166–9.
13 Cf. Keul-Deutscher (1996) on the all-powerful beauty of Theagenes and Charicleia in *Charicleia and Theagenes*, powerful enough to overcome any threat.

undermined.[14] Most obviously, the protagonists' maintenance of chastity is repeatedly placed at risk, both in the recurring scene of heroines leading on their would-be seducers in order to play for time, and also, more concretely, in the examples of heroes and heroines violating the expectation of sexual fidelity: Daphnis' encounter with Lycaenion (3.16–19); Clitophon's pleasuring of Melite, and her comically sophistical justifications that precede it (5.26–7); and Callirhoe's marriage to Dionysius (2.10–3.2). This last event is prefigured by the comparison in the very opening sentence (1.1) between Callirhoe and the oxymoronic 'Virgin Aphrodite', a figure who encapsulates something of the ambiguities which lurk beneath the respectable beauty of many of the novels' heroines.

Less often noted, but equally persistent, is the tension between recognisability and anonymity in the beauty of the Greek novels' protagonists. In Xenophon of Ephesus, for example, the hero and heroine are repeatedly misrecognised by other characters (4.3, 5.10, 5.12), despite what we are told about their distinctive beauty. In Achilles Tatius, Clitophon encounters Leucippe without recognising her, simply because she has been enslaved and her hair shaved (although admittedly this is after what he thinks is her death; and he does notice a certain resemblance – or so he claims in narrating the story retrospectively).[15] In Iamblichus' *Babylonian Affairs*, most nightmarishly, the hero Rhodanes is regularly confused with a pair of twin brothers, called Tigris and Euphrates, who are exact physical doubles both of each other and of him;[16] and the father of the heroine Sinonis mistakes her for the dead girl Trophime, and kills himself from grief, at which point Rhodanes and his companion Soraechus come close to making the same mistake, and are saved from suicide only at the last moment.[17]

That theme of non-recognition is given a comical twist in book 7 of Heliodorus' *Charicleia and Theagenes*.[18] Here Theagenes is running round the walls of Memphis, watching the bizarre single combat of the brothers Thyamis and Petosiris. The brothers' father Calasiris arrives disguised as a beggar, and stops the fight by running after them and revealing his true identity to them, throwing off his rags like Odysseus. Charicleia has arrived with him, also disguised as a beggar, and she too joins in the chase around the walls, having spotted her beloved Theagenes from a great distance:

14 As Goldhill (1995) shows at length (esp. 1–45, 112–32).
15 At 5.17; cf. 5.7 where he fails to recognise that the headless body he mourns over and buries is not Leucippe's but that of a prostitute executed in her place.
16 Photius, *Library* codex 94 75b41–a6 = Stephens and Winkler (1995) 194.
17 Photius, *Library* codex 94 77a29–b9 = Stephens and Winkler (1995) 197.
18 Cf. Cave (1988) 17–21 on the final recognition of Charicleia in book 10, as part of a broader argument for tensions between resolution and uncertainty inherent in literary traditions of the 'recognition scene' from Homer onwards.

For the sight is often sharp in its recognition of those one loves, and often just a movement or a shape, even if it is far away, is enough to bring an image resembling the beloved before one's mind. Charicleia approached him, as if goaded into madness by the sight, and draping herself around his neck tightly she hung on to him and clung to him and greeted him with mournful cries. But Theagenes, as you would expect, on seeing her face, which had grown dirty and ugly, and her worn-out and tattered clothes, tried to push her away and elbow her aside as if she really was a beggar and a tramp. And then finally, when she refused to let go of him, since she was annoying him and blocking his view of what was happening to Calasiris, he slapped her.   (7.7)

They are, of course, soon reconciled, when Charicleia's true identity is revealed, but it is hard to avoid the impression of undignified, comical overtones contaminating their quasi-Odyssean reunion. The point about the power of love to bring recognition even over huge distances works in this passage for Charicleia, but is immediately and humorously contradicted for Theagenes, despite the fact that his view of Charicleia is at very much closer range than her first sight of him. Moreover, Heliodorus seems to be using this detail in order to explore the workings of specifically elite self-perception by the juxtaposition of Charicleia's poverty and Theagenes' dignity. Theagenes fails to recognise Charicleia partly because her beggarly appearance is incompatible with his view of what a properly brought up young lady ought to look like. He quite literally pushes away from himself the threat of contamination with non-elite identity.

The theme of the transparency of the human body is continued in the novels' repeated preoccupation with the way in which emotions leave physical traces on the surface of the human body.[19] The novels are full of passages describing the outer manifestations of jealousy and fear and shame, and, especially, love, often in the language of medical and physiognomical theory,[20] and we frequently see the novels' characters themselves drawing on that kind of specialised language to interpret those symptoms. The effect reaches its most extraordinary levels in Achilles Tatius, where the gaze of the narrator seems capable of seeing through the physical surfaces of the human form, charting the way in which emotions churn up the insides of the body, forcing themselves through the skin; and the way in which beauty slips its way through the eyes of the onlooker and burrows down into the

---

19 Cf. Maehler (1990) on the novels' fascination with the symptoms of love, and on the uniformity with which those symptoms are described.
20 See Toohey (1992) 273–5, and esp. Morales (2004); also Dickie (1991) on Calasiris' discussion of the effects of the evil eye in *Charicleia and Theagenes* book 3 as a pastiche of Plutarch's theories.

soul. In book 5, for example, the narrator Clitophon describes the love of Melite for him:

> She was not able to take in food, but instead looked at me with all her concentration. For nothing seems sweet to those in love, except for the beloved. Love takes over the whole soul, and does not leave any room even for food. The pleasure of this sight flows in through the eyes and occupies the breast; and there it draws the image of the beloved to itself unceasingly, and imprints it on the mirror of the soul, reproducing its shape. The emanation of beauty is drawn down into the loving heart by unseen rays and impresses its shadow there down below. (5.13)

The arrows of Eros are explained, rephrased, modernised through the language of medical and philosophical theories of vision (although we might also be conscious of the fact that this narrator's self-serving, restrospective descriptions of the women he encounters are less than trustworthy, that his claim to be able to map inner emotions by his analysis of outward bodily signs is far from reliable).[21]

The human body is thus regularly portrayed as a window onto the emotions and virtues which lie beneath it. And yet that sense of the openness of the body to medical analysis is often undermined by the way in which characters fabricate symptoms and manufacture their own bodily appearance.[22] That motif is most strikingly presented in the long story told by Calasiris in books 2–4 of Heliodorus' *Charicleia and Theagenes*, where Calasiris' decipherment of the lovesickness in Theagenes and Charicleia – which draws on contemporary medical discussions of the symptoms of love – is juxtaposed with proudly recounted examples of his own deceptive self-presentation.[23] In book 3, for example, Calasiris correctly diagnoses Theagenes' lovesickness, but chooses to conceal it from her father behind a deliberately theatrical means of display:

> I therefore decided that it was the right occasion to do some wonder-working for him, and to pretend to prophesy things which I already knew. So I gazed at him cheerfully and said, 'Even if you yourself hesitate to confess, nevertheless there is nothing which is unknown to my wisdom and to the gods.' Then I

---

21 Cf. Goldhill (2001b) 167–72 on this passage.
22 E.g. Cnemon's faking of diarrhoea at *Charicleia and Theagenes* 2.19; Anthia's fabrication of epilepsy at Xen. Eph. 5.7.
23 Cf. Apul. *Met.* 10.9, where we see a doctor giving a reliable interpretation of the truth lying beneath the surface of the human body; as with Heliodorus, however, that scene of reliable medical vision is juxtaposed with recurrent descriptions of misleading bodily appearance and deceptive medical treatment (e.g. 10.2, 10.12, 10.25), as Gleason (1999) 288–9 has pointed out.

paused momentarily and made some meaningless calculations on my fingers, and shook my hair around, acting like someone in a trance; and then I spoke, 'You are in love, my child.' (3.17)

This scene draws on the common image of the manipulative holy-man.[24] It also draws on the image of medical diagnosis as magic, imagery that the second-century CE doctor Galen exploits but also strives to dissociate himself from in his medical writing.[25] Calasiris' ability to decipher physical symptoms is thus intertwined with reminders of the manipulative deceptiveness of his own bodily self-portrayal, and with connotations of ingenious trickery masquerading as learned medical diagnosis.[26]

There is, then, a recurring fascination within all of the Greek novels with the degree to which physical appearance guarantees internal reality. The link between virtue and bodily beauty is repeatedly asserted, but also – even in the texts of Chariton and Xenophon which have so often been classed as 'idealising' texts – humorously undermined. Threats to the human body and to its chastity are of course very much more prominent in the Latin novels of Petronius and Apuleius, as we shall see in a moment, and in the sex-filled Greek fragments – like Lollianus' *Phoenician Affairs* and *Iolaus* – which have sometimes been categorised as parodic or comic versions of the 'idealising' Greek novels. But the evidence I have outlined here suggests that we should be cautious of drawing any distinction between 'idealising' and 'non-idealising' fictional traditions in the ancient world, at least in terms of their representation of the human body. Even the most noble and upstanding of the novels' heroes and heroines find it conspicuously difficult to guarantee bodily beauty and virtue.

These anxieties about elite physicality are signalled more extravagantly in the theme of fragmentation and physical vulnerability of the human body. This theme is conspicuous within the Greek texts I have discussed – most strikingly in the opening of Heliodorus' novel, which shows us body parts strewn over a beach, mixed with the remains of a banquet, without any immediate explanation for the situation, an image which anticipates the challenge we face as readers to piece together the disjointed threads of the novel's narrative[27] – but it surfaces most insistently in the novels of Petronius and Apuleius. Glenn Most has drawn attention to the prevalence of bodily dismemberment in Neronian Latin poetry, for example within the

24 Anderson (1994) 185–6.   25 Barton (1994) 136–7.
26 Winkler (1982) suggests that the narrative reveals Calasiris to be ultimately trustworthy despite his fabricated appearance, on the grounds that his Odyssean manipulation of both narrative and personal identity is in the service of admirable ends; Baumbach (1997) disagrees, re-emphasising Calasiris' ambiguous identity as both sage and charlatan.
27 See Winkler (1982) 96–100; Bühler (1976).

tragedies of Seneca and within Lucan's epic *Civil War*. He suggests that this obsession may be 'the symptom of an anguished reflection upon the nature of human identity and upon the uneasy border between men and animals';[28] and he relates it to questions asked within Stoic philosophy about the continuity of personal identity, and more specifically about the extent to which mutilation of a body will lead to the 'loss of personal identity of that body's owner'.[29] As Most points out, Petronius' *Satyrica* (which is almost certainly itself a Neronian text) exemplifies that pattern well, through its 'scenes of and allusions to threatened amputation of the *membrum virile* and other forms of mutilation of the body'.[30] It does so also through its repeated visions of failed consumption, eating and drinking which threaten the integrity of the human body, spilling out beyond the body's boundaries (on which more in a moment); and through the fragmentation of the narrator's voice, which lurches between so many different poses at different points in the narrative.[31] It may even be that Neronian Rome, with its obsessive theatricalisation of public life – at least for those who were linked, like Petronius (if the author of the text has been correctly identified as Nero's 'arbiter of taste'), with the imperial court – provoked particularly acute questions about the links between outward appearance and inner reality, questions that Petronius' bodies pose in provocative ways.

These images of dismemberment are taken to their furthest extreme, however, in a text of the second century CE, Apuleius' *Metamorphoses*. Apuleius' obsession with questions of physical form and personal identity has less to do with the theatricality of the imperial court than with his status as a member of the culturally mobile second-century elite, as an African orator and philosopher who flaunted his ability to perform in both Greek and Latin.[32] He shows a fascination with shifting personal identities not only in the *Metamorphoses*, [33] but also in more avowedly 'autobiographical' works like the *Apology*, where he defends himself against charges of magic while at the same time flaunting his own shape-changing abilities in the fields of linguistic and cultural self-fashioning, in contrast with the ignorant parochialism of his accusers. In line with those preoccupations, the *Metamorphoses* is full of fragmented and penetrated bodies. Pamphile's magical ingredients include 'surviving leftovers of inauspicious birds, and a spread of numerous body parts from lamented and even buried corpses: on one side noses and fingers, on another, flesh-covered nails from the victims of crucifixion, elsewhere the

---

28 Most (1992) 405.   29 Ibid. 406.   30 Ibid. 396 and 428 n. 28.   31 Rimell (2002).
32 On Apuleius' relation with sophistic culture, see Sandy (1997) and Harrison (2000).
33 The theme of bodily metamorphosis is present within the Greek novel tradition too: not just in the Greek *Ass*, but also in the inserted narrative of Pan and Syrinx at Long. 2.34, and the same story at Ach. Tat. 8.6.

preserved blood of butchered human bodies and maimed skulls twisted from the teeth of wild animals' (3.17), a treasure-trove which prefigures the frequent risks to bodily integrity which Lucius is destined to undergo once he is changed to a donkey by his own misuse of Pamphile's magical substances. Lucius' owners in book 8 are warned of the dangers of the road they are about to travel along in similar language: 'And then they told us that the whole route we were to follow was covered with half-eaten human bodies, and that the road shone from the whiteness of human bones stripped of their flesh' (8.15). Again, these seemingly gratuitous snippets of gory detail are related to the more profound threat to personal identity and bodily integrity which Lucius himself undergoes as a result of his transformation to a donkey. He is exposed to the threat of physical mutilation and horrible death;[34] he is aware of the danger that his new body may be causing the gradual dissolution of his human identity,[35] and his bodily transformation is described as a kind of fragmentation, a separation from his true self. Shortly before his rehumanisation, for example, he looks forward to eating the roses which he knows will act as an antidote to the ointment which caused his original transformation: 'recently the roses had burst forth, breaking through their spiny covers and breathing odours of cinnamon – roses that would restore me to my former Lucius' (10.29).[36] Here his reunion with his former self is cast as a bizarrely distorted version of the reunions between hero and heroine which end most of the Greek novels, and Lucius' travails are thus represented as an intensified version of the challenges to elite identity and bodily beauty faced by the Greek novel protagonists. Like those Greek protagonists, Lucius' own respectable, elite ancestry is given prominent attention – for example in his claim to be descended from the philosopher Plutarch[37] – and the physical degradation he experiences as a donkey is presented through the language of social degradation, as he charts on his new donkey's body the marks of slavery and human poverty.[38] Apuleius thus draws on the Greek novels' obsession with the vulnerability of human physical beauty and of the identity it purports to guarantee, but transforms it in order to ask his own more blatantly grotesque and humorous questions about the stability or otherwise of human selfhood.

---

34 E.g. *Met.* 4.3, 4.5, 6.31–2, 7.22–4, 8.31–9.1.
35 See Shumate (1996) 65–71; cf. *Met.* 4.20, where the robber Thrasyleon, who has been sewn into a bear-skin to facilitate his companions' plans for burglary, continues to act as a bear even while he is being mauled to death by dogs.
36 Cf. *Met.* 11.2.   37 *Met.* 1.2 and 2.3.
38 See e.g. 9.12–13, where the horrifying physical condition of the slaves in the mill where Lucius is working is equated with the physical condition of his fellow animals; cf. George (2002) 45, and further Whitmarsh, 'Class', this volume.

Body and text

Our experience of reading these fictional bodies – this is my second main point – is often implicitly linked with our experiences of the detailed texture of the novels themselves. Critical analysis of modern fiction has drawn attention to repeated parallels between body and text, and those insights, I suggest, have important and generally underestimated implications for our understanding of the (insistently corporeal) novels of the Greek and Roman world. Peter Brooks has analysed from a psychoanalytic perspective the way in which the allure of the physical bodies of fiction often parallels readerly desire for mastery over the complexities of the text.[39] He argues that

> In modern narrative literature, a protagonist often desires a body . . . and that body comes to represent for the protagonist an ultimate apparent good, since it appears to hold within itself – as itself – the key to satisfaction, power, and meaning. On the plane of reading, desire for knowledge of that body and its secrets becomes the desire to master the text's symbolic system, its key to knowledge, pleasure, and the very creation of significance.[40]

He suggests, further, that the fascination and inscrutability of the female body in particular is often a driving force of narrative. The desire to know the individuals we encounter in reading, to see beneath the surfaces of the body and of the text, is a motivating force for readers and characters alike, although in both cases desire is always necessarily veined with frustration, as we are brought up against the impossibility of ever fully knowing or possessing another's body, or ever fathoming in full the physical surfaces of the texts we look at or listen to.

For Mikhail Bakhtin, meanwhile, the body is a crucial image within his analysis of the workings of novelistic discourse, especially in his writing on Rabelais.[41] All human utterances, by Bakhtin's account, are inescapably ingrained with the many different meanings and connotations imposed on them by previous users of language. In the novel form those intertextual qualities often take on a special intensity. The novel revels in the richness of competing voices and tones woven into it, 'dramatising as complexly as possible the play of voices and contexts enabling speech or writing as social acts'.[42] Novels, in other words, often gain their most distinctive effects by drawing into themselves ideas and speech patterns from across an enormous

---

39 Brooks (1993).   40 Ibid. 8.

41 See Bakhtin (1984a), and discussion by (amongst many others) Dentith (1995) 66–8 and Holquist (1990) 89–90; see however Rimell (2002) 123–39 for criticism of Bakhtin's reading of the story of the widow of Ephesus at *Satyrica* 110–12.

42 See Branham (2002b) xix; see also Branham (2005) for discussion of the applicability of Bakhtin's approaches to the Greek and Roman novels.

range of human experience, setting them into dialogue with each other. In much the same way, the grotesque bodies of Rabelais' world are interwoven with the world around them through repeated scenes of eating and drinking, copulation and defecation, dismemberment and cannibalism. The boundaries of Rabelais' bodies, in other words, like his novels themselves, are not stable; they constantly threaten to spill out into the world around them, and to be permeated by that world: 'the body is, if you will, *intercorporeal* in much the same way as the novel is intertextual. Like the novel, the body cannot be conceived outside a web of interrelations of which it is a living part'.[43]

Associations between body and text are deeply ingrained both in the structure of the Greek and Roman novels and in the detailed texture of the reading experiences they offer. One reason for this is the fact that broad characterisation of any of these texts is necessarily intertwined with our judgement of its protagonists. Thus the mildly titillating air of compromised respectability which is such a central feature of all the surviving Greek novels, and which has been a driving force for so much later interpretation of them – interpretation that has oscillated between praise of the novels' moral exemplarity and of their eroticism, often without sufficient acknowledgement of the way in which these two qualities are inextricably and paradoxically combined with each other – is a direct consequence of the ambiguity between seductiveness and virtuousness in their main characters' beauty. But other links are more enigmatic and more artful. In Iamblichus' *Babylonian Affairs*, for example, the author's presentation of physical doubles for his main characters is paralleled by the structure of the work, which repeatedly replays the same scenes in more than one form.[44] The bewildering experience of mistaken identity is thus something we experience through our own difficulty as readers in telling different scenes apart. In Heliodorus' *Charicleia and Theagenes*, the unfathomability and cultural hybridity of Charicleia – the Ethiopian/Greek heroine, born white from black parents – and of Calasiris – the Greek-Egyptian sage whose mendacity and accompanying physical deceptiveness we have glimpsed already – are images for, and mirrored by, the text itself. Like the bodies of Charicleia and Calasiris, the novel's tricky surface is full of puzzles and riddles; like them it does finally reveal its secrets. Like Charicleia, it also flaunts its own cultural hybridity, its own transgressive literary genealogy, by its relocation and reformation of the *Odyssey* and other founding texts of Greek cultural tradition.[45] In the very opening scene of the novel, to take just one example, Charicleia's body is set up as a text to

43 Holquist (1990) 90.   44 Stephens and Winkler (1995) 184–6.
45 Whitmarsh (1998).

be deciphered, a starting point for the slow and winding move towards narrative resolution in the books which follow. Our only access to the opening scenes of the novel comes through the bewildered perspective of the barbarian bandits who encounter her nursing Theagenes on the body-strewn beach. At several points, their incomprehension of Charicleia is implicitly linked with our own:

> When they had moved a little way from the ship and the corpses around it they were confronted by a sight even more puzzling than the last. A girl was sitting on a rock, a sight of such amazing beauty that she seemed to be a goddess . . . These things terrified them. Ignorance of what had happened terrified them even more so than the sight itself. Some of them said she was a goddess – the goddess Artemis, or the goddess Isis worshipped in that region; others said she was a priestess who had been maddened by the gods and had committed the great slaughter they had seen. That is what these men thought, but they did not yet know the truth. (1.2)

Charicleia's body of course turns out to be marked with the bizarre truth of her origins – and of the origins of the story she inhabits – in more literal ways than the bandits can ever know, especially in 10.15 where the black birthmark on her arm acts as a guarantee of her identity, a sign of her origins written indelibly on her skin. As it turns out, these onlookers of book 1 never will 'know the truth' in the sense that we as readers will come to know it. The 'yet' of that final phrase is not really there for the bandits, but for us, a sign of what is in store for us, and a sign that our deciphering of Charicleia and of the plot will be parallel with each other.

It is, however, the two Latin texts of Petronius and Apuleius that offer us the most visceral intertwining of corporeal and novelistic texture. One of the further points Glenn Most makes in his analysis of the dismembered bodies of Neronian literature is about the fragmented literary style that they mirror:

> There is an obvious correlation between the scenes of amputation of the human bodies in the works of Seneca and his contemporaries on the one hand and the dismemberment of the body of the sentence for which Seneca was celebrated on the other. What happens to the bodies of the characters in Seneca's and Lucan's fictions corresponds to what happens to the bodies of these fictions as well . . .[46]

Those insights, again, are important for Petronius, whose own text revels in its own fragmentariness and disjointedness in such extraordinary ways, and whose cannibalisation of so many different poses and genres[47] parallels

---

46 Most (1992) 408.   47 Connors (1998).

the many scenes of indiscriminate and barely controlled consumption with which the narrative confronts us. Victoria Rimell has recently made the image of text as body the single guiding metaphor for her analysis of Petronius, drawing attention to the ways in which the text offers itself to us for our consumption, but also always threatens to take control over us as readers, just as all food – and especially the food of the *Satyrica* – has the capacity to blend with and even threaten the identity of its consumer: 'literature in the *Satyricon* is no longer just written, static and containable, but is imaged as a live body, a flesh or food ingested in the process of learning and spewed out from bodies in performance: inside the consumer, it is a volatile force transmuted in the process of digestion which may also gnaw away its host from within'.[48]

The text, in other words, repeatedly challenges the distinction between inside and outside. For one thing – like Apuleius' *Metamorphoses* – it shows us bodies whose boundaries are insecure and vulnerable. For example, the orgy at the house of Quartilla (*Satyrica* 16–26) is packed with the language of permeation and penetration. Quartilla pricks Encolpius' cheek with a hair-pin (*Satyrica* 21) in an attempt to stop his resistance; the *cinaedus* ('deviant', 'catamite') who arrives immediately afterwards 'at one moment cut into us, forcing apart our buttocks, the next moment defiled us with his stinking kisses' (*Sat.* 21), violating the integrity of their bodies, and at the same time spreading the vile influence of his own. Those images of penetration are juxtaposed with the vision of Encolpius' erectile dysfunction, a sign of the body's refusal to conform, its alienness to its owner. Once again, in the description of Encolpius' impotence, it is a *cinaedus* who breaks down the distinctions between inside and outside:

> Having got to the end of his poetry, he spattered me with the foulest of kisses. And then he got on to my bed, and ripped off my covers, despite my resistance. He worked for a long time and vigorously on my groin, but in vain. Streams of sweaty gum began to flow down from his forehead, and between the wrinkles of his cheeks there was so much make-up that you would have thought he was an unprotected wall suffering the effects of a rain-storm. (*Sat.* 23)

As before, the image of violated boundaries (the bed cover ripped away) is juxtaposed with the permeability of the *cinaedus'* skin. And the whole episode is fuelled by Quartilla's aphrodisiac potion (*Sat.* 20), another instance of the way in which food and drink in the novel take over their consumer's

48 Rimell (2002) 9.

bodies – although in this case the effects are distorted by Encolpius' impotence: the potion draws him even further into the threateningly nightmarish eroticism of the orgy, but without the empowerment it seems to promise.

When we reach Trimalchio's banquet, the imagery of bodies bursting out beyond their bounds reaches even higher levels of intensity. Early on, for example, Trimalchio gives a commentary on the blockage of his bowels and the medical help he has sought, before announcing that everything is on the mend: 'Besides, my stomach is rumbling; you'd think it was a bull making that noise. So if any of you should wish to satisfy the needs of nature there is no reason to be ashamed of it. None of us was born solid. I don't think there's any torment so great as having to hold oneself in' (*Sat.* 47). This rumbling of Trimalchio's stomach is an omen of what is to come, as the imagery of regurgitation and spillage is actualised in the banquet's dishes: the stuffed pig, who spills out sausages and black puddings when its stomach is slit (*Sat.* 49); and the cakes which spurt out saffron and other unpleasant liquid into the faces of those who touch them (*Sat.* 60). In addition – and crucially – the image of uncontrollable consumption is applied to texts within the novel. In the opening paragraphs of the work as it survives, for example, Agamemnon and Encolpius criticise contemporary conventions of oratorical education for stuffing the heads of boys with hackneyed material, repeatedly using the imagery of gluttony and luxurious cuisine to describe that process (*Sat.* 1–5).

Eumolpus, the bombastic orator and poet, shows himself to be the victim of a similar fate, despite his insistence on his own originality (*Sat.* 118), through his two excruciating long poems, which regurgitate in horrifyingly mangled form the conventional verses and themes with which he has been force-fed (89, 119–24).[49] It is hard to avoid the suspicion that Petronius' text is doing the same to us, taking over our bodies and minds like some monstrous parasite, threatening to burst out from us again in unintended forms at any moment.

The bodies of Apuleius' *Metamorphoses*, however, deserve the most sustained dissection. The significance of that work's title (assuming it is authentic)[50] is not immediately clear, given the relative absence of physical shape-changing within the novel. It is, of course, appropriate to the narrator's own transformation into animal form, but that in itself does not account for the plural – more than one metamorphosis – unless it can be explained by the fact that Lucius himself undergoes a second transformation, back to human form,

---

49 Ibid. 77–97.
50 For summary of debate see Harrison (2000) 210 n. 1; Shumate (1996) 56.

at the end of the book. Admittedly there are other examples of bodily transformations in Apuleius' text,[51] but these are peripheral to the main action. The contrast with Ovid's *Metamorphorses*, which is so packed with physical shape-changing, and where each separate transformation receives such uncompromising attention, is striking. And yet the title's importance becomes clearer, I suggest, if we recognise the prominence of the other types of (non-corporeal) transformation that Apuleius magics into being.[52]

For one thing there are linguistic metamorphoses at the heart of the work. This is a translation and adaptation of a Greek work – the work on which the Greek text of (Pseudo-?) Lucian's *Ass* also seems to have been based[53] – set in mainland Greece, with Greek characters speaking, via Apuleius' pen, in idiosyncratic and highly sophisticated Latin. How far, Apuleius seems to be asking us, does translation bring cultural transformation? Can the Greek *Ass* maintain its identity when it is squeezed into the body of Apuleius' extravagant Latin? Is this the same story, or does its Latinness pull it unavoidably out of shape, just as Lucius' own personality is warped and twisted by its relocation into his new donkey's body? Those questions correspond to Apuleius' fascination with questions of cultural and linguistic transformation in his *Apology*, to which I drew attention earlier.

Even more striking – especially for a reader who knows nothing of Apuleius' Greek model – are the *Metamorphoses*' shifts in tone. The work as a whole is full of non-sequiturs, and abrupt, inadequately motivated changes of direction.[54] This is a text which thematises disjunction both in its imagery and in the recurring rhythms of its paragraph structure and narrative progression. The most prominent of those disjunctions comes, of course, at the beginning of book 11, where Lucius is converted not only (back) into human form, but also into a devoted worshipper of the goddess Isis. We might expect this re-transformation to restore to us the original narrating voice of the opening books, but in many ways Lucius' voice in book 11 sounds unfamiliar. The prologue to the novel famously challenges us to identify the narrator ('who is he . . .?'). That challenge is made more difficult there by the (irresoluble) impression that the speaker of the prologue may not be the same as the teller of the story that immediately follows.[55] In book 11, the challenge

---

51 E.g the witch Meroe's tranformation of three of her enemies into a beaver, a frog and a ram at *Met.* 1.9, and her tranformation of Aristomenes into a tortoise at 1.12; the statue of Actaeon's transformation into a stag at 2.4; the transformation of the witch Pamphile to a bird at 3.21.
52 Cf. Shumate (1996) 56–7 for a similarly broad reading of the text's metamorphoses; also Finkelpearl (1998) for an account of Apuleius' allusive reshaping of earlier genres and texts.
53 For summary of debate, see Harrison (2003) 500–1.   54 Winkler (1985) *passim.*
55 See Kahane and Laird (2001) for a wide range of different approaches to this problem.

is renewed, and it is hard to avoid the impression that we are listening here to a new narrator.

One of the effects of that shift in book 11 is to make it difficult for us to be sure about how far the two parts of the text can be unified with each other. The task of responding to that difficulty has, of course, occupied a great deal of scholarly energy on the work.[56] One approach has been to make the whole novel into an Isiac morality tale. By that standard there is a disjunction here – disjunction which is enhanced by the recurrent imagery of cleanliness, light, wholeness, in contrast with the darkness, squalor and fragmentation of the rest of the novel – and the opening ten books can be explained precisely by their difference from the Isiac ending, as embodiments of the life which can finally be rejected and comprehended with the assumption of Isiac wisdom. Alternatively, as has often been noted, book 11 invites us to consider it as a continuation under a slightly different guise of the comic absurdities which have preceded it, through its repeated hints that the new Lucius shares some of the faults of gullibility and stupidity which characterised his pre-Isiac, pre-asinine predecessor. Ultimately, of course, it is impossible to be confident in any fully unifying interpretation of the novel, just as it is impossible (for the narrator and for us) to be confident that Lucius is the same Lucius once he gets under the skin of his new donkey's body. I do not wish to suggest that the bodily changes of the novel can explain the notorious disjunctions at the end of the novel. My point here is simply that that shift of focus in book 11 is one which the rest of the work has prepared us for. It is a shift which is fully in line with the way in which the world of the novel works. By this stage we have already experienced – through ten books, and in the most grotesque physical detail – the challenge of seeing how far bodily metamorphosis brings underlying changes in identity. In book 11 we are suddenly confronted with a different question, but one which is framed in the same terms, and which is no easier to answer – about how far individuality can survive profound shifts of religious alignment; and how far the body of narrative – as *we* experience it in reading – can maintain its individuality in the face of such profound shifts in tone and generic alignment, of the kind Apuleius flaunts in wrenching us away from the nightmarish novelistic world of the first ten books. In other words, Apuleius uses the bodies of his texts to ask questions about the degree to which changes in outer form can ever co-exist with continuity of identity. The whole text forces us to experience in both comically absurd and morally resonant ways a set of related dilemmas about how far voice and identity change when other things – language, bodily shape, generic form, religious allegiance – are wrenched out of their familiar alignment. In that sense the

56 See Shumate (1996) 7–14 for summary of recent approaches.

Metamorphoses offers perhaps the most powerful example of all of the way in which the bodily texture and narrative texture of the ancient novels are interwoven with each other.

Further reading

There has been a large amount of recent work on the human body in the Greek and Roman culture of the imperial period, much of it emphasising the body's role as a locus for performance of elite identity, but also as a source of anxiety and an object of debate: see e.g. Gleason (1995) and (2001); König (2005), esp. 97–157; see also Wyke (1998b) and Porter (1999) for collections of essays covering all periods of classical antiquity. There has, however, been surprisingly little interest in treating the novels from the same perspective. One exception is Perkins (1995), who engages with Foucault (1986) in discussing the Greek novels' representations of pain and suffering by comparison with philosophical writing and Christian hagiographic texts from the same period. Goldhill (1995) similarly engages with Foucault in exposing the Greek novels' sophisticated and provocative play with the ideals of chastity and equality that these texts have often been taken to recommend. Rimell (2002) goes furthest in analysing relations between body and text in the novels, in using the body as a guiding metaphor for her characterisation of Petronius' *Satyrica*. See also Toohey (1992) and Maehler (1990) on symptoms of lovesickness; Toohey discusses overlaps in that area between the novels and medical writing of the imperial period. On eroticised viewing of the body in Achilles Tatius, see Goldhill (2001b), and further Liviabella Furiani (2000–1). On beauty in Heliodorus, see Keul–Deutscher (1996).

For sociological theorisation of the role of the body in society (focused mainly on modern society), see Turner (1996) and Shilling (1993). For analysis of the role of the body within modern (eighteenth- to twentieth-century) art and literature, from a psychoanalytic perspective, see Brooks (1993).

9

LAWRENCE KIM

Time

Introduction

In his monumental work *Time and Narrative*, Paul Ricoeur distinguishes 'tales about time', like *The Magic Mountain* or *Remembrance of Things Past*, from 'tales of time', which all narratives are by virtue of the fact that they are read and unfold in time.[1] Few would put the ancient novels into the former category; they are not explicitly about time in an abstract sense, that is, they rarely discuss time in a philosophical or reflective fashion. Much scholarship has instead focused on how the novelists manage their 'tales of time' – for example how Heliodorus manipulates the temporal order of events in his narrative or how Apuleius orchestrates a subtle shifting between his narrator Lucius' past and present temporal point of view.[2] We can even speak of the tempo or pace of the novels when we examine the way in which they vary the relationship between narrating time (measured in words and pages) and narrated time (measured in days, hours, years). Such narratological work on the novelists' deployment of time has produced valuable insight into their story-telling technique, and I refer to it throughout this chapter.[3]

But there are other ways of talking about the novels' conception of time. Every novel conveys a certain temporal feeling to its readers – what Ricoeur calls 'the fictive experience of time'[4] – not only through explicit commentary and rendering of narrative time, but also via thematic content, employment of temporal reference and the depiction of its characters' experience of time. One influential attempt to describe novelistic genres on the basis of their represention of such temporal (and spatial) experience, or *chronotope*, was proposed by the literary theorist Mikhail Bakhtin. For Bakhtin, the ancient novel played a crucial role in his articulation of this concept, and I want

---

1 Ricoeur (1985) 101.   2 E.g. Hefti (1950); Winkler (1985) 135–79.
3 See in general Fusillo (1989), 213–19, (2003b) 280–8; Lowe (2000) ch. 10; Hägg (1971) on Xenophon, Chariton and Achilles; Futre Pinheiro (1998) on Heliodorus; Van der Paardt (1978) on Apuleius.
4 Ricoeur (1985) 100.

to use his insights on time and the ancient novel as a framework for this article. But before we turn to Bakhtin directly, I want to spend some time elaborating upon his claim that the ancient novels' 'temporal categories are extremely poorly developed' ((1986) 11).

Historical time

One of Bakhtin's central contentions is that in the ancient novel 'time in and of itself lacks any significance or historical colouring'. The novels, he claims, have little sense of 'historical localisation, that is, significant attachment to a particular historical epoch, a link to particular historical events and conditions' ((1986) 15). On the face of it, this is a somewhat surprising assertion. Traditionally, scholars have seen a close connection between the ancient novel and ancient histories; both, after all, are extended prose works narrating events that have taken place in the past. The titles of some of the novels contain phrases – *Ephesiaca* ('Ephesian affairs'), *Babyloniaca* ('Babylonian affairs'), even *Satyrica* ('Satyric affairs') – that recall those of well-known historical works such as Ctesias' *Persica* ('Persian affairs') and Xenophon's *Hellenica* ('Greek affairs'), and at least seven of the known novels are set in a past quite distant from the Roman present in which they were written.[5] Moreover, the earliest of these – *Ninus* and *Metiochus and Parthenope* – also featured historical figures as their protagonists, and the genre has also been linked with the romantic and sensational content of Hellenistic 'tragic historiography'.[6]

Such connections, however, have perhaps been overemphasised. There are as many 'contemporary' novels as historical ones, and certainly none of the extant novels could be mistaken for a history.[7] Moreover, the primary interest of the novelists is not so much with the subject-matter of historiography as with its literary form. Chariton, as both Carl Müller and Richard Hunter have shown, is not attempting to pass his novel off as history but rather is self-consciously playing with the tension between historiographical form

---

5 The eponymous heroine of Chariton's *Callirhoe* is the daughter of the late fifth-century BCE Syracusan general Hermocrates, and the setting of Heliodorus' *Charicleia and Theagenes* presupposes a time when Egypt was under Persian rule, anywhere from the late sixth to the late fourth century BCE. Antonius Diogenes' *Wonders beyond Thule* takes place around the beginning of the fifth century, *Metiochus and Parthenope* in the late sixth–early fifth century, Iamblichus' *Babylonian Affairs* at a time pre-Persian empire (sixth century), *Ninus* in ancient Assyria, sometime before the seventh century, and finally *Sesonchosis* in an even more ancient Egyptian milieu. On ancient historical novels, see Hägg (1987).
6 Bartsch (1934); Hunter (1994); Ruiz-Montero (2003) 42–8 (with bibliography).
7 Compare the greater concern for historical people and events in ancient epistolary fiction: Holzberg (1994); Rosenmeyer (2001) 193–252.

and erotic content; likewise the affectations of authorial uncertainty and his-toriographical mannerisms that John Morgan has uncovered in Heliodorus are part of the novelist's own negotiation of the conventions proper to truth and fiction.[8] Even this intertextual play with historiography can perhaps better be seen as bound up with an issue common to *all* narrative genres from epic to forensic oratory – how to bestow credibility on one's story. The frequency with which the novels play with framing devices (paintings, buried manuscripts, embedded narratives) that vouch for the authenticity of their stories suggests an awareness of the problems and possibilities involved in writing any narrative, not just history, that purports to speak of events that have actually happened. In fact, one could argue that such devices are more prevalent outside historiography – the *Odyssey*, utopian fiction, Platonic dialogue – than in it.

One important element of historical writing, however, is conspicuously missing from the novels: dating. None of the extant novels specifies a par-ticular year or other chronological reference point situating their narratives in the historical timeline.[9] Although readers can often extrapolate a rough idea of a given novel's temporal situation, the novels essentially float in time, untethered to particular historical events. The classical backdrop of Chariton and Heliodorus' novels remains impressionistic and idealised,[10] and similar-ities of plot and characters often make it difficult to distinguish their worlds from the 'contemporary' ones of Xenophon and Achilles. The historical posi-tioning of these latter is even more vague; while their stories are most likely set in the Roman imperial period, there are very few references to anything that might rule out a Hellenistic backdrop.[11] Longus' *Daphnis and Chloe* similarly evokes a timeless atmosphere completely devoid of any evidence of its date. And although the 'comic-satiric' novels of Petronius, Apuleius and Pseudo-Lucian display a much stronger sense of their Roman milieu, the precise chronological position of their narratives has proved difficult to determine on the basis of internal considerations, and calendrical time is largely ignored; while Petronius and Apuleius are the only novelists to

---

8 Müller (1976); Hunter (1994) (cf. Alvares (1997)); Morgan (1982).

9 Seneca's *Apocolocyntosis* ('Pumpkinification'), which opens by dating the events to follow, and highlights the issue of time throughout is an interesting comparison text: see Robinson (2005).

10 Baslez (1992) on Chariton's depiction of the Persian empire; Morgan (1982) and Futre Pinheiro (1989) on Heliodorus. See also Scarcella (1981).

11 In any case there is no overt indication that would suggest to the reader that the novels are *not* contemporary, and the mention of Alexandria in both texts implies a post-classical setting. For detailed discussion of Achilles see Plepelits (2003, first published in 1996) (cf. the counter-arguments of Swain (1996) III n. 31); on Xenophon, Ruiz-Montero (1994); Rife (2002); and Kytzler (2003).

mention specific days of the month, such dates are never linked to a particular year.[12]

One significant difference, however, between the comic-satiric novels and their ideal counterparts is the former's attention to contemporary *Roman* life (to be discussed in the concluding section). The ideal novels, on the other hand, notoriously avoid mention of Rome, Romans or Roman things whatsoever.[13] Such conscious forgetting of contemporary circumstance has been linked with the archaising tendencies of the second sophistic. In particular the ideal Greek novels' amalgam of Rome-less present and Greek past bears a remarkable resemblance to what Donald Russell has dubbed Sophistopolis, the imaginary composite classical Greek city in which imperial orators set the convoluted speeches of declamation.[14] Simon Swain has read the novels' timeless Greek setting as a fantasy space, beyond Roman control, where the moral and political ideals of their imperial Greek elite audience – urbanisation, Hellenism, fidelity and marriage – were continuously rehearsed and reaffirmed.[15] Although he perhaps underplays the ways in which the novels can problematise these dominant ideologies – for example, Heliodorus' sophisticated exploration of ethnic and national identity, Longus' subtle playing on the opposition between city and country[16] – Swain is surely correct to see some connection between the novels' depiction of the world and the ideological underpinnings of the stories they tell.

The Greek novelists' aversion to mentioning their historical present stands out even more when they are contrasted with other contemporary writers, where we see greater evidence of what Bakhtin calls the ability to 'see time' and view it in dynamic terms.[17] For instance, Chariton and Heliodorus set their stories in the classical past but never call attention to the gap between that past and their present; compare the considerable self-consciousness about this vast divide that runs through Dio Chrysostom's 'novelistic' *Euboean* and *Borysthenitic* orations. Alternatively, the profound way in which Pausanias and others describe the artefacts, buildings, and the landscape of the second century as embodied with a localised connection to the past is nearly absent from the worlds of Achilles' and Xenophon's novels. Such interest is evident among the ideal novels only in *Daphnis and*

---

12 Petronius: 1 July (38), 26 July (53). Apuleius: 12 December (11.26). Note that Petronius' dates are only incidental details on inscriptions or in financial accounts, not indications of narrative time.

13 Connors (2002) and Schwartz (2003) are recent attempts to 'read' Rome into Chariton's *Callirhoe* despite this absence. See also Connors, this volume.

14 Russell (1983); cf. Swain (1996) 110, and Bowie (1970) 9.   15 Swain (1996), at 101.

16 Saïd (1987); Whitmarsh (1998); Perkins (1999).

17 For Bakhtin (1986), the novels of most interest, such as those of Rabelais and Goethe, depict 'man's individual emergence . . . [as] inseparably linked to historical emergence' (23).

Chloe, where the characters inhabit an old world, rich in myths, rites and objects imbued with tradition and linking the children to the past. Yet even here this past is a timeless, literary one associated more with pastoral and the countryside than with a particular historical period.

The organisation and deployment of time in the novel

The novels' attitude toward historical time, however, can be seen as symptomatic of a more basic set of restrictions encompassing the novelists' use of time in general. First of all, we can note the relatively brief period of time encompassed by the novels' plots. No novel covers more than a couple of years in its protagonists' lives (if one discounts occasional and brief accounts of childhood), even though nothing prevents them from spanning decades or centuries in the manner of Herodotus' or Thucydides' *Histories*.[18] A similar conservatism characterises the organisation of time within this limited period. Aside from Heliodorus, the novelists tell their stories with only minor deviations from a chronologically linear pattern and rarely refer to events before or after the temporal boundaries of their stories (e.g. via flashbacks). All structure their narratives with individual episodes that, while often packed with incident, rarely extend beyond several days' duration.[19]

As a result of this limited framework, the dominant temporal units in the novels are the day and the night, and most indications of the time announce daybreak or nightfall.[20] References to months, seasons and years are rare, as are long gaps of time unfilled with action.[21] This is why a narratorial comment such as 'Six months had now passed . . .' (Ach. Tat. 5.8.1), unremarkable in a modern novel, comes over as a bit startling; both length and specificity are unusual.[22] Conversely, the days and nights are rarely broken up into smaller units of time; the hour in its durational usage ('for an hour') appears only in Petronius (e.g. *Sat.* 69, 87, 103, 141) and temporal expressions such as 'at mid-day' (Ach. Tat. 2.7.1) or 'around the first watch of the night' (Apul. *Met.* 3.21, 11.1) are only occasionally employed.[23] In essence,

18 This temporal restriction perhaps reflects the influence on the novel exerted by Homeric epic, on which see Lowe (2000).
19 Hägg (1971) ch. 1, ch. 5.
20 Cf. Hägg (1971) 43–4 on Chariton. To take another example, Apuleius opens many of his books (2, 3, 4, 7, 8, 11) with an indication of the time, usually dawn.
21 Seasons (and festivals) are primarily mentioned when important to the plot (e.g. sailing: Char. 3.5.1; Ach. Tat. 8.19.3) and not as indications of the passing of time (Hägg (1971) 26, 64); *Daphnis and Chloe* (on which see below) is of course an exception, as is Apuleius, where the changing of the seasons allows a rough dating of the length of the novel.
22 This use of the month to mark durational time in the primary narrative is rare. Cf. Chariton 2.8.5, 2.10.5.
23 Hägg (1971) 71–3 on Achilles' temporal expressions.

the novelists' time units remain restricted to the days and nights, dawns and dusks, employed since Homer.

More significant for our purposes, however, is the vagueness and inconsistency with which the novelists mark time's passage, particularly its duration. Xenophon is the extreme case; he rarely specifies how many days are spent in a particular activity or lie between different episodes, leaving temporal vacuums that render it impossible to calculate how much time passes from the opening of the novel to its conclusion. The temporal span of Chariton's narrative is similarly unclear, although he is more scrupulous with his time references.[24] Both authors can incorporate specific durations into their plots when they think it appropriate (the 'seven' months of Callirhoe's pregnancy (3.7.7), the thirty-day delaying tactics of Anthia (2.13)). The point is that such precision is not essential to their project; in general the action that fills the time, not the lapse of time itself, is what matters.[25] As Tomas Hägg observes apropos of *Callirhoe*, 'a huge number of *events* lie between departure and return, not *time* as a concrete substance'.[26] When Chariton's characters recap their adventures to others, for example, they take care to relate accurately the order of the events but fail to reveal the length of time involved, even when this is quite significant. The effects of time are thus rarely remarked upon by narrators or characters, an odd fact given the possibilities that the temporal length of one's troubles or separation offers for rhetorical lamentation.

Not even more detailed authors such as Heliodorus and Apuleius always bother to mark the time. On the one hand the temporal synchronisation on display in *Charicleia and Theagenes* is impressive: it begins in the middle of the story (*in medias res*, as the Latin phrase puts it) and gradually reveals chronologically prior events through a series of retrospective embedded narratives, requiring readers to reconstruct the chronology of events rather than having it presented to them.[27] The first six books, which manage to cover some twenty years of backstory, are concomitantly packed into a carefully marked ten-day span. Once the story 'catches up' to the opening scene, however, and the plot adopts a more standard linear motion, Heliodorus' temporal marking begins to resemble Chariton's, with frequent unspecified gaps of time. A similar pattern occurs in Apuleius' *Metamorphoses*, in which

24 Hägg (1971) 201 considers it 'fruitless' to estimate the duration of *Anthia and Habrocomes*, but estimates two to three years for *Callirhoe* (194); Lowe (2000) guesses eighteen months to three years for each novel.
25 Cf. Reardon (1982) 20 (= (1999) 181): Chariton wanted readers, '[d]eprived . . . of a firm objective "handrail" . . . to turn . . . to . . . the emotional *sequence* of events . . .'
26 Hägg (1971) 196.
27 Hefti (1950); Futre Pinheiro (1998) 3152–6; Lowe (2000) 242–5. The total duration of the novel is around forty days (similar to that of the *Iliad*).

an initial care in marking time becomes more intermittent after book 6.[28] Moreover in Heliodorus the temporality of the embedded narratives (such as those spoken by Cnemon and Calasiris) is much more abstract, fluid and hazy than that of the main action;[29] the temporal relation of Apuleius' inserted tales to the main narrative is even less clear due to their frequently indirect connection with Lucius himself.[30]

The lack of any real need to record the time in the ancient novel is exemplified *a contrario* by Achilles Tatius, who shows a rather idiosyncratic exactitude in marking the time between episodes – 'after ten days' (4.15.1), 'for five days' (5.17.1).[31] But his industry in this regard has no discernible effect on the narrative; often nothing happens in these intervals, and the specification of days seems superfluous. It simply doesn't matter very much how long each episode, or the story as a whole, lasts. Thus while *relative* time is important in the novels – to synchronise meetings, chance encounters or near misses – *absolute* 'clock' time, that is, whether something occurs in a particular month, year or day or takes x amount of time, is of little concern. The use of the word *hōra* in the Greek novels illustrates this tendency; it is never used in its sense of durational 'hour', and only rarely refers to a particular hour of the day (e.g. Hld. 8.14.2), but commonly signifies an undifferentiated 'moment' in time – e.g., 'on that very day and hour' (Hld. 7.6.5).

What are we to make of such observations? On the one hand, the lack of consistent attention to quantitative, or clock, time in the ancient novels is not as conspicuous as it would be in, let's say, a detective story. After all, most readers of these novels (except perhaps those of *Anthia and Habrocomes*) seldom notice these lapses in temporal marking. But when coupled with the novels' restricted temporal parameters and vague historical positioning, such reticence leads one to suspect, along with Bakhtin, that the novels' self-imposed limits in this regard might have something to do with the kind of story they tell and the tradition in which they are working. Let us now turn to exploring such a possibility.

Adventure time

Bakhtin saw the ancient novels' relative lack of interest in time as profoundly related to their status as *adventure* novels, that is, narratives organised

---

28 Heliodorus: Futre Pinheiro (1998) 3153. Apuleius: Van der Paardt (1978).
29 Futre Pinheiro (1992) 285–6.
30 Cf. Zimmerman (2000) 13–15, on the embedded tales in book 10.
31 Hägg (1971) 66–7, 71–2, 75, 207–9. A good example of Achilles' general meticulousness about time is Clinias' retrospective day-by-day explanation at 5.10 of his movements after the shipwreck had separated him from Clitophon. Cf. Anderson (1997) 2282.

around the episodic and extraordinary experiences of their protagonists.[32] The temporality associated with these adventures, or *adventure time*, is best elucidated in his treatment of the ideal Greek romances (apart from *Daphnis and Chloe*). Although these novels are ostensibly about the meeting and (re-)unification of two lovers, Bakhtin points out that the bulk of their stories consists of the adventures that lie between the initial passion and final consummation. By the end of each novel, however, the experience of their adventures has had no effect upon the lovers, who have not significantly aged, developed or matured, and love each other in precisely the same way as before. For Bakhtin, this is the whole point of the romance – the couple's love for each other never changes, despite near-deaths, kidnappings and other suitors. The novels are thus organised around a series of ordeals designed to test the characters' faith in each other and to reaffirm what had already existed from the beginning – their love.

From a narrative perspective, however, the adventures are essentially superfluous; the ending (marriage or union) is exactly what would have occurred had the lovers not been separated in the first place. The episodes of adventure that are framed by the 'normal' events of love and marriage are thus termed by Bakhtin as 'an extratemporal hiatus between two moments of biographical time' that 'leaves no *trace* in the life of the heroes' ((1981) 90). This 'hiatus' is governed by *adventure time*, which 'consists of the most immediate units – moments, hours, days – snatched at random from the temporal process' ((1986) 11). Wars, shipwrecks and bandit attacks strike without warning and are introduced by phrases like 'suddenly' or 'at just that moment', emphasising the abruptness with which the normal flow of time is interrupted ((1981) 92). Here what matters is not duration or points in time but only 'fortuitous encounters (temporal junctures) and fortuitous non-encounters (temporal disjunctions)' (116); 'the days, hours, minutes . . . are not united into a real time series . . . they do not become the days and hours of a human life' (94). The result is a tenuously related series of events governed by the logic of random contingency. Moreover, the episodes are potentially infinite and reversible, that is, they have no necessary conclusion and could be re-ordered without essentially changing anything.

Adventure time has a profound effect on the space in which it unfolds as well as the characters that move to its rhythm. A narrative based on contingency and unpredictability requires an expansive undifferentiated space far from the lovers' homeland (with its normal, biographical rhythms of life).

---

32 What follows is a very selective condensation and amalgamation of Bakhtin (1981) 86–129 and (1986), which offer two overlapping and occasionally contradictory schemes; for more complete summaries, see Morson and Emerson (1990) 375–92, 405–19, and Branham (2002). I discuss *Daphnis and Chloe* and the comic-satiric novels in subsequent sections.

Even though these places, such as Ephesus or Miletus, are real, they are essentially interchangeable and abstract, since their only requirement is to have no organic link with the lovers (99–102). This explains the novels' vague positioning vis-à-vis history and contemporary life that we discussed above; any connection with specific events, practices or places would restrict the power of chance essential to adventure time. In these spaces, outside of the social networks that define and empower them, the lovers are rendered passive and powerless in the face of chance and fortune; 'a purely adventuristic person is a person of chance' (95).

Bakhtin is thus less concerned with issues of marking time or narrative structure than with the novels' temporal worldview; the chronotope is his 'attempt to delineate time as an organising principle of a genre, the ground or field against which the human image is projected'.[33] Bakhtin's concept of adventure time identifies a central reason why the ancient novel seems so different from its more modern varieties: the former's temporal logic is geared toward *lack* of change. One of the primary functions of recording the passage of time in narrative is to register change, whether that be aging, emotional development or the transformation of character. In the Greek romance, focused as it is on the testing of the unchanging, enduring love of the two protagonists, this sort of time does not really matter and hence does not need rigorous recording. The romance's relative lack of interest in quantitative time and history is thus not seen simply as arbitrary, but linked to broader generic imperatives.

We can perhaps get a better idea of the romance's particular configuration of time and characters if we glance briefly at Lucian's *True Story*, a parodic adventure novel similar to the romance but organised around a different theme – travel – and revealing a very different attitude toward time. During his fantastic ocean voyages, Lucian, the narrator, constantly records the time at which events happen and the length of time spent on each of the various islands. He explains how he kept track of time in the belly of the whale by observing the regular (hourly) openings of its mouth, resulting in datings such as 'on the fifth day of the ninth month, around the second opening of the mouth' (1.40). Even on the Island of the Blessed, where it is always spring and the light is always like that of the dawn (2.12), Lucian somehow manages to be aware of how much time has passed. On the one hand, this interest in quantitative time owes something to Lucian's general fascination for numbers, and part of the joke lies in the absurd hyperbolic exactitude with which Lucian records fantastic events.[34] But it is also linked to the fact that Lucian and his companions are constituted as fundamentally

33 Branham (2002) 171.   34 Fusillo (1988a); Scarcella (1985).

different characters from the wandering lovers of the Greek romance. If adventure time is predicated on chance and alien worlds traversed by powerless individuals, travel time, as Bakhtin calls it (without direct reference to Lucian), presupposes a different 'image of man' and world. Lucian actively and willingly embarks on his travels and is fully participant with the people and things he encounters.[35] The world is not constituted as alien, but *exotic*; the traveller's homeland and status provide a stabilising point of view, and the itinerary imparts organisation to temporal sequence.[36] For Lucian time is something to be measured and thus controlled; like Robinson Crusoe, another novelistic traveller, he feels the need rigorously to mark time's passage in order to provide a framework, a system of order, for his otherwise disconnected and uncertain adventures.[37] The use of time and the attitude toward it in the *True Story* are thus intimately connected to an alternative type of narrative and protagonist distinct from that of the Greek romance.

Bakhtin's largely negative characterisation of the Greek novel's adventure time, abstract space and unchanging heroes, has understandably been the target of frequent objections. Critics have argued that characters *do* sometimes change, the particularity of places *does* sometimes matter, chance does *not* always control the narrative.[38] There is no doubt that Bakhtin is sometimes over-schematic in his portrayal of a genre that, after all, represents the inverse of the complex realist novels that he valued. But it is hard to deny that adventure time is a powerful heuristic tool that accounts for a great deal of the genre's peculiarities. Bakhtin himself allows for 'minor chronotopes' that interact with and enrich the major ones (like adventure time) characteristic of each genre, as well as those, like that of the road or the meeting, proper to individual literary motifs.[39] It might then be more productive to analyse further how other temporalities intervene to complicate adventure time than to question its general validity.[40] In the brief space I have here, I want to suggest a few ways of exploring this issue, first by examining a psychological, erotic time that exists in somewhat dialectical fashion with the dominant adventure time of the Greek ideal novels, and then by discussing Bakhtin's

35 Cf. Dinias' description of his travels as 'the seeking of knowledge' in Antonius Diogenes' *Wonders beyond Thule*, a similarly conceived 'travel novel'.
36 Cf. Bakhtin's brief remarks on travel in the Greek novel at (1981) 103–4, not to be confused with the travel novel described in (1986).
37 Cf. Goody (1991) 77–81.
38 Cf. Konstan (1994); Smith (2005) on Chariton. Ballengee (2005) and Whitmarsh (2005c) offer critical elaboration of Bakhtin's ideas.
39 Bakhtin (1981) 252–4; cf. Morson and Emerson (1990) 425–9; MacAlister (1996) 19–23.
40 Branham (2002) 168. Billault (1991) has much of interest along these lines. See Ladin (1999) for a further development of the idea of the chronotope.

treatment of the everyday time of the Roman novels, with an additional glance at book 11 of Apuleius' *Metamorphoses*.

Erotic time: leisure, love and repetition

We begin with *Daphnis and Chloe*, the novel which most clearly defies Bakhtin's claims about the Greek romance. Here change and the meaningful passage of time are integral elements; Longus charts the development of the two children's love, deploys the natural cycle of the seasons to lend it a strict temporal structure, and situates the story in a Lesbos sealed off from the outside world. Nevertheless, as Bakhtin recognised, *Daphnis and Chloe* is 'cut through by shafts of adventure-time' ((1981) 103) – that is, by the standard motifs of the genre (albeit in somewhat pastoralised form) such as the bovine destruction of the pirate boat or Pan's rescue of Chloe from the Methymnean warship. On each such occasion the lovers are traumatically separated and reunited, and the experience leaves little physical or psychological trace upon them. The difference is that these adventures are intermittent irruptions into an otherwise peaceful, pastoral existence, rather than a continuous series of episodes in foreign lands. Bakhtin thus characterises *Daphnis and Chloe* as governed by a hybrid chronotope combining adventure time with *idyllic time*, defined as a blend of natural, cyclic time and the everyday time of the pastoral.[41]

Alain Billault, noting that the mostly passive vigilance required by Daphnis and Chloe's herding duties affords them plenty of time to enjoy the countryside, has perhaps more appropriately described idyllic time as 'leisure time', marked by stability and continuity, and delimited by the cycle of the seasons.[42] In H. H. O. Chalk's classic analysis, Longus' narrative generally adheres to a basic pattern repeated at the advent of each new season; a description of that season, an outline of the children's reactions to it, and finally the notable events occurring within its timeframe.[43] To such a depiction of leisure we might add the importance of repetition. The first two stages of this process usually entail outlining habitual and repeated activities, first of nature (e.g. cicadas singing, apples falling) and then of the two children, employing imperfect verbs and temporal words such as 'sometimes' and 'often': 'Sometimes Daphnis bathed, at other times he hunted fish, and often he drank . . .' (1.23). This *iterative* mode of only narrating a scene or event once, even though we are to understand that it occurred

---

41 Bakhtin (1981) 103. His brief remarks are somewhat opaque and undeveloped, and I freely adapt them here; for more on the idyllic–cyclical chronotope, cf. 224–36 and (1986) 22.

42 Billault (1996).   43 Chalk (1960) 39–44. Cf. Scarcella (1968).

repeatedly, is uncommon in the other novelists, but essential to Longus' style.[44] Such descriptions establish a regular rhythm against which the singular, but temporally unmarked, 'events' of the season occur (e.g. the meeting with Philetas, Daphnis' sex lesson with Lycaenion). Thus while Longus maintains a framework of regularly measured seasonal progression, the episodes within those seasons detailing the education and development of the children usually float free; they happen 'one day', or 'after some time had passed'.

This emphasis on repetition and leisure is not, however, solely the result of the pastoral setting or the cycle of the seasons. It also resonates with the temporal rhythms of the different kind of love foregrounded by Longus, one that has to do with the process of forming a union, and not with its enduring power. This kind of love is built up of little moments, inconsequential in themselves, but indispensable for a gradual erotic development marked by a certain leisure and repetitive quality antithetical to the urgency and singularity of adventure time.

Daphnis and Chloe is often seen as an anomaly because of this focus on process, but other novelists also engage with a similar erotic time. The most direct parallel is in Achilles Tatius' first two books, where Clitophon is trying to seduce his cousin Leucippe in a setting far removed from the alien world of adventure time;[45] the lovers are safely ensconced at home and hence can be (relatively) active agents who develop and change as they fall in love. The use of the iterative mode to describe the stages of this courtship – for example, 'whenever I was before the door, I lifted my eyes up to watch her . . .' (1.6.6) – calls attention to its repetitive nature and the slow pace (often specified) of Clitophon's progress.[46] In fact, Clitophon's cousin Clinias explicitly emphasises the constant effort and iteration required for successful seduction: 'The greatest entry into persuasion is <u>continuous</u> company with the beloved . . . the <u>habit</u> of daily sharing encourages reciprocity' (1.9.5–6).

But if Achilles' treatment of Clitophon's courtship slows down time in this manner, stretching it to the lengths proper for erotic development, it does not directly interfere with the overarching temporality of the novel in the way that Longus' does. Achilles' erotic time occupies the *biographical* time

---

44 An aspect of narrative *frequency* (Futre Pinheiro (1998) 3161). As Hägg (1971) 40, 60–1, observes, Xenophon and Chariton employ the iterative mode primarily as a means of transition between episodes; rather than saying 'four days later' they write 'and she was doing x for the next several days. And then . . .'

45 Cf. Hägg (1971) 76, and Sedelmeier (1959) on the peculiar narrative rhythms of this episode. Calasiris' narrative of Theagenes and Charicleia's falling in love is told in retrospect (*Charicleia and Theagenes* 3–4), but has a similar temporal rhythm.

46 Cf. 2.3.3 and 2.19.2. Brief remarks on Achilles' use of the iterative at Hägg (1971) 74.

mentioned by Bakhtin as framing (here preliminary to) the central adventure time of the novels.[47] But by his extension of an episode – the couples' falling in love – which Chariton and Xenophon dispense with in a few pages, Achilles renders more palpable the juxtaposition of two disparate types of temporal experience fundamental to the novels – one proper to courtship and the process of love, and the other to the endurance of ordeals.

There are certain cases, however, in which erotic time infiltrates the main body of adventure time itself, not because of any change in the lovers' unswerving loyalty to each other, but because the ordeals they face are frequently of an *erotic* nature, when they become the objects of others' desires.[48] In these episodes, the spotlight shifts onto these rival lovers and time becomes perceived through their eyes as that proper to courtship, requiring a certain amount of leisure time as well as a safe, domestic space in which to unfold. Thus in *Callirhoe*, Dionysius' estate and the Great King's palace at Babylon are the appropriate settings for portraying the incremental stages in the development of their masters' love, such as the 'kiss' Callirhoe bestows on Dionysius or Artaxerxes' repeated visits to the women's quarters ('he continually went to . . .', 6.1.7).[49] Time is further stretched out due to lack of reciprocation; the rival lover tries on the one hand to distract himself from the power of Eros through leisure activity (e.g. Dionysius' unwillingness to leave his dinner party, Artaxerxes' decision to go hunting) but also to prolong the presence of his beloved.[50]

It is perhaps no accident that these spurned lovers, along with Daphnis and Chloe, are portrayed with a psychological depth often lacking in the heroes. The erotic time of the Greek novels is the primary arena for the development of a *psychological time* possessing 'a subjective palpability and duration', that Bakhtin considered one of the Greek novels' more original contributions ((1986) 15). Clitophon also seems more psychologically individualised and 'real' in the first two books, while he adheres to the model of the more stereotypical romance hero once adventure time begins. Such an erotic time, marked by leisure, deferral, expansion and iteration opens up the possibility, however, limited, for psychological development, and is just as much a part

---

47 Cf. MacAlister (1996) 20–1. In Apuleius Lucius' affair with Photis, an episode marked by frequent use of the iterative mode, takes place before his transformation into an ass ushers in adventure time.

48 Lowe (2000) 227. Xenophon's novel is almost farcical in this respect; nine different men fall in love with Anthia.

49 On Artaxerxes see Daude (2001) and Toohey (1999) 269–73. When the Egyptian revolt brings Artaxerxes' love to an end, Chariton makes evident the antithesis between erotic and adventure time: 'haste pleased all not to delay even a single day . . .' (6.8.5).

50 Dionysius lingers at his country estate; Artaxerxes postpones making a decision on Callirhoe. MacAlister (1996) 21–2 has seen also in Callirhoe's developing relationship with Dionysius an instance of biographical time re-asserting itself against adventure time.

of the Greek novel as an adventure time marked by haste, urgency and unpredictability.[51]

Everyday time, the Roman novel and time in Apuleius

Bakhtin identified a second novelistic genre in antiquity: the adventure novel of everyday life. These texts, Apuleius' *Metamorphoses*, Petronius' *Satyrica*, and the *Ass*,[52] resemble the novels of ordeal in that they too are dominated by the episodic, fragmentary and rapid pace of adventure time,[53] ushered in by some traumatic event – Lucius' transformation into an ass, Encolpius' angering of Priapus (or exile?). Moreover, just as in the Greek romances, adventure time has no concrete effect; after regaining human form Lucius, in the Greek *Ass*-narrative, remains just the same as before his transformation, and nothing suggests that Encolpius' experiences render him any different at the end of the *Satyrica* (on Apuleius, see below).

What distinguishes these novels, however, is a shift in the *space* where the adventures take place; the protagonists no longer wander at random through abstract 'alien' territory, but on the 'road', along the sides of which they witness a more familiar, *everyday* world, but one focused on private life, particularly its obscene, lower elements.[54] Like the alien lands of the Greek romance, however, the everyday remains an 'other' world that the protagonist passes through and observes, but is never fundamentally affected by. The time associated with these representations of everyday life is therefore 'scattered, fragmented, deprived of essential connections . . . not permeated with a single temporal sequence' (128). Nevertheless, through the use of the everyday, 'space becomes more concrete and saturated with a time that is more substantial: space is filled with real living meaning . . .' (120). By offering glimpses into certain 'hidden' areas of contemporary society – for example, Apuleius' description of slaves in a mill or Petronius' of feasting freedmen – these novels 'reveal *social heterogeneity*' (129). For Bakhtin, everyday time thus functions primarily as a way of incorporating a certain kind of *historical* time into adventure time with a sensibility absent from

---

51 As Futre Pinheiro (1998) 3161–2, notes, one of Heliodorus' only uses of the iterative mode is in the Arsace episode.

52 I include the *Ass* here, even though Bakhtin fails to mention it. As we shall see, Bakhtin's decision to focus on Apuleius results in considerable confusion. What follows is thus my attempt to describe everyday time in a way that applies at a basic level to all three novels, and then to incorporate Bakhtin's comments on Apuleius into my own examination of the use of time in book 11.

53 See Zeitlin (1971a) 652–66.

54 On the chronotope of the road, see (1981) 243–5, and on everyday life ('the underside of real life', 128) 123–9.

the Greek romance.[55] This particularly applies to the *Satyrica*, in which, as Bakhtin remarks, 'traces of historical time (however unstable) turn up in the social heterogeneity of this private-life world', and Trimalchio's feast is 'to some extent a *temporal whole* that encompasses and unifies the separate episodes of everyday life' (129).[56]

This account of everyday time, however, omits (and indeed contradicts) a major part of Bakhtin's argument: his insistence that the everyday adventure novel distinguishes itself from the Greek romance through its focus on *change*. While this is true of the one novel that Bakhtin examines in detail, Apuleius' *Metamorphoses*, where Lucius converts to the Isis-cult, it is clearly unsatisfactory as a general description of an adventure novel of everyday life. The plot of the *Ass*, which Bakhtin ignores, is in outline identical to the *Metamorphoses*, but ends with Lucius' return to human form *sans* epiphany, and there is no indication that Encolpius will become 'other than what he was' (115) in the *Satyrica*.[57] Furthermore, it is unclear what connection this notion of change has with the supposedly distinguishing feature of this type of novel, that is, everyday time. Branham has pointed out that Bakhtin's analysis of Apuleius depends upon a third sequence, defined in moral-religious terms, that proceeds along the series: 'guilt→punishment→redemption→blessedness' (118). By superimposing this sequence onto an otherwise random string of adventures, Apuleius transforms them into a meaningful and temporally irreversible narrative of purification and rebirth while the low, everyday life experienced by Lucius corresponds to the punishment stage. In this way, the moral sequence ends up unifying both adventure and everyday time.[58]

How then does this moral–religious sequence function *temporally* in Apuleius' novel? Bakhtin says little about this, but we can perhaps elaborate. The religious element that Bakhtin speaks of is concentrated in the eleventh book; the priest's speech to Lucius at 11.15 explicitly re-evaluates the entire preceding story in terms of religious redemption.[59] Time too takes on a greater significance in the eleventh book than in the rest of the novel. Suddenly we have datable events like the *Ploiaphesia*, the ritual opening of the sailing season in the Isis-cult known to have occurred on 5 March (11.17),

---

55 Cf. Millar (1981) on the surprising acuity with which Apuleius conveys a sense of socio-economic relations and even 'what it meant to be a subject of the Roman Empire' (63).

56 See Branham's Bakhtinian analysis of the Trimalchio episode, with its frequent references to clocks, death, dates and time: Branham (2002) 178–80, and the very different discussion of Toohey (2004) 197–221.

57 Although see Branham (1995) on the *Satyrica* as the one true ancient 'novel' in Bakhtinian terms, and one that does foreground change.

58 Branham (2002) 175–7.

59 Winkler (1985) 8–10. Bakhtin was well aware of this; see his quote at (1981) 118.

and Lucius himself notes his arrival on 12 December at Rome (11.26). These two dates, implicit and explicit, are unique to the novel, and furthermore have ritual significance. As Anne Witte has observed, these dates, as well as the spring full moon that opens the book draw 'the episode into the cosmological realm', marking a break from the previous books' lack of 'transcendental time'.[60] Within this realm of cosmic-religious time, Lucius now experiences permanence and stability instead of the fragmentation and uncertainty of adventure and everyday time.

Not only does Isis appoint the day of Lucius' salvation (11.21, 22), but the events of that day proceed just as the goddess had ordained. Despite the extraordinary nature of Lucius' return to human form, chance and the unexpected have no place here; adventure time is firmly over. The narrative concentrates on Lucius' slow path from devotee to initiate to priest with its fixed periods of ritual service, abstinence and waiting. If something out of the ordinary occurs, such as a strange dream, we quickly learn that this too has been dictated by the goddess. There is a growing sense throughout this book that human time and life are subordinate to a higher cosmic order; Isis, as the incarnation of the moon and 'the first child of the ages' (*saeculorum progenies initialis*, 11.5) and Osiris, as the sun, symbolise an eternal temporal movement that dwarfs everything else, and by which the phases of Lucius' life are now regulated.[61]

Isis, in her speech to Lucius, makes clear that her control of time not only governs Lucius' present, but also his future – 'the rest of your life's course (*vitae tuae curricula*) is bound to me' – and beyond: 'when you have traversed your life's path and go down to the underworld, there also you will worship me . . .' (11.6). Furthermore, the new sense of time foregrounded in book 11 that now dominates Lucius' present and future life also stretches back to reinterpret the *past*, his sojourn through adventure and everyday time, as the necessary descent into error that leads Lucius to redemption. With the last lines of the novel, Lucius is additionally reintegrated into historical time, as he enters a priesthood with a tradition stretching far back into the past, 'founded in the times of Sulla' (11.30) some 250 years earlier. Under the aegis of Isis, Lucius' life – his past, present and future – is thereby unified into a single meaningful whole. By demanding that what Lucius has experienced must be related to what lies ahead, Apuleius' incorporation of book 11 and its cosmic-religious time onto the basic narrative of the *Ass* transforms the *Metamorphoses* into a hybrid form, rather than the model, of the adventure novel of everyday life: the novel of crisis and rebirth.

60 Witte (1997) 42. See also Beck (2004) on 'cosmic time' (311) in book 11.
61 Cf. 11.26: 'Behold the great Sun, when the zodiacal circle had been run through, had completed a year . . .'

Further reading

For the novel's relation to history see Swain (1996) ch. 4; to historiography, Ruiz-Montero (2003). On historiographical elements in Chariton, see Hägg (1987), Hunter (1994) and Whitmarsh (2005c); in Heliodorus, Morgan (1982). Hägg (1971) is a treasure-trove of information on the use of time in Xenophon, Chariton and Achilles; for similar if less comprehensive narratological treatments of temporality see Futre Pinheiro (1998) on Heliodorus and Van der Paardt (1978) on Apuleius (as well as the Groningen *Commentaries* series on individual books), as well as Lowe (2000) ch. 5 on the Greek novels as a whole. More generally Billault (1991) provides a useful, if somewhat diffuse, overview on time in the Greek novel; see also his (1996) for an excellent treatment of time in *Daphnis and Chloe*. Finally, Bakhtin (1981) 84–258 and (1986) are two overlapping articles on the chronotope; for a good summary and commentary see Morson and Emerson (1990), Ladin (1999), and *apropos* of the ancient novel, Branham (2002), who also expands upon Bakhtin's brief remarks on Petronius.

10

CATHERINE CONNORS

Politics and spectacles

The surviving Greek and Latin novels depict a world of cities, but mostly keep Rome itself out of sight. The racy Latin novels by Petronius and Apuleius (and his Greek source) are set in the imperial present, but make few direct remarks about Rome and its emperors. The (more-or-less) chaste, idealising and nostalgic Greek novels by Chariton, Longus, Achilles Tatius and Heliodorus are mostly set in vaguely classical times, when Greek cities were still free. Nevertheless, just as historians write the story of their own times as they tell the story of the past, so too the escapist fictions of the novelists do not escape their imperial context.

Some critics interpret the nostalgic setting of the Greek novels as a strategy of withdrawal. On this view, when Alexander and his successors and then Rome rule over Greece and Asia Minor, city-state gives way to empire, and the traditional work of citizenship is no longer as consequential as it once was: elite audiences are drawn to the novels' stories of individuals adrift in a chancy world. Others, by contrast, understand the nostalgic and idealistic Greek novels as an affirmation of a specifically Greek cultural identity and a celebration of the continuation of Greek civic practices after the imposition of Roman hegemony.[1]

Although Roman imperial power was a visible presence in the cities where novels were written and read, the novels do not take on politics explicitly. However, they do each use politically inflected metaphors to describe the power that the gods exert over the characters. The political tinge of

---

1 Social context of authors: Morgan (1995). On the position of Greek intellectuals in the Roman empire, Bowie (1970) is a good point of entry; from there, one can proceed to large-scale studies of Greek cities in the Roman empire by Jones (1940) and Millar (1993). On the Greek novels as a nostalgic withdrawal, Bakhtin (1981) 108; Reardon (1991) 28–9; Konstan (1994) 218–31. Bowersock (1994) 33 emphasises the imperial dimensions of the geography of the novels. For the novels as an affirmation of Greek cultural identity see Swain (1996) 101–31; Whitmarsh (2001a) emphasises the dynamic aspects of the construction of cultural identities in novels and other genres produced within in the empire's polyglot world; cf. Goldhill (2001b) esp. 194.

a novel differs depending on whether its controlling god acts like a citizen, a landowner, a playwright, or an emperor. Many of these metaphors are derived from the idea of staging a public spectacle, and the novels also make additional references to spectacle.[2] Across the spectrum of the surviving novels written in Latin and Greek during the Roman empire, political metaphors and literal and metaphorical references to spectacle express ideas about civic and political life in the Roman empire. The differences among the ancient novels' representations of civic spectacles, institutions and practices reveal the range of options available to elite readers as they negotiate the interface between local civic practices and global Roman *imperium* (dominance).[3]

From theatre to amphitheatre: the politics of spectacle

The novels' references to spectacle range from the Athenian theatre to the Roman arena. Spectacle, in the sense of an event enacted before the eyes of the community, displays the power relations of the stager, participants, and audience, and as such it is always a political act. Greek and Roman spectacle were, however, socially and politically distinct. Classical Greeks liked to see freeborn citizens compete against each other in the theatre, the stadium, the chariot racecourse, and, on a more intimate scale, in the athletic matches of the gymnasium or the wrestling school.[4] The practice of spectacle was quite different at Rome. Rather than fellow citizens, Romans preferred to see foreign professionals, slaves, prisoners of war, or condemned criminals in their theatres, racetracks, arenas and amphitheatres.[5] A further contrast lies in the prominence given at Rome to elite patronage. During the Roman Republic, elected officials helped pay for the staging of theatrical spectacles and other attractions at public religious festivals; the presentation of successful spectacles was part of a successful political career. Also during the Republic prominent individuals might stage gladiatorial games. Under the empire such spectacles came to be more and more under the control of the emperor; particularly in the amphitheatre and the circus, subjects beheld the generosity and power of the emperor, and his power to punish

---

2 See Saïd (1994) 221–2, for a brief and perspicuous account of references to theatres in the novels.
3 On the term *imperium* see Richardson (1991).
4 On the connections between politics and drama at Athens, see Cartledge (1997); for full details of the competitions, see Wilson (2000).
5 For a useful overview of spectacle in the Roman world, with comparison to Greek spectacle, see Dodge (1999). Potter (1999) provides a detailed introduction to the social world of Roman performers.

his subjects. At the same time, the people viewing the spectacle could also express their communal will in the presence of the emperor.[6]

These marked differences between Greek and Roman spectacle were keenly felt. The construction of an amphitheatre in a Greek city was a way of imposing a Roman identity upon it. In a number of Greek cities amphitheatrical spectacle invaded the theatre itself: among other modifications new walls or parapets between the seats and the stage were installed at Athens, Corinth and elsewhere to protect spectators from wild animals and other dangers.[7] Some Greek voices protested against the innovations, complaining about the barbarity of Roman spectacle.[8]

Chariton and the spectacle of democracy

The idealising Greek novels are in one sense a nostalgic imagining of a world without such signs of Roman empire; but as in the physical remains of the Greek theatres of the period, the structures of empire remain visible at the edges. Chariton, the earliest of these writers, uses references to public spectacle to contrast the somewhat democratic political organisation of Syracuse with the absolute monarchy exercised by the Persian king. The people (*dēmos*) of Syracuse repeatedly express their views in public assemblies and direct the actions of the plot. Under the urging of Eros as 'demagogue', they convince Hermocrates to allow Chaereas and Callirhoe to marry (1.1.12). After Chaereas kicks Callirhoe and believes he has killed her, the people race to the agora for the trial of Chaereas (1.5.3). After Chaereas' ship meets up with Theron's, Theron is captured and brought to Syracuse. Amid the outcry as he is brought to shore, Hermocrates determines that it would be 'more lawful' for him to be brought to an assembly of the people in the theatre for a trial (3.4.3). The presence of the people is crucial to the determination of Theron's guilt because it is a fisherman in the crowd at the theatre who recognises him. Under torture Theron confesses, though he does not reveal the name of Callirhoe's purchaser. He is duly sentenced to death; though Chaereas pleads that he be spared for a while so that he may come along on

---

6 Political context of dramatic productions in the Roman republic: Gruen (1992) 183–202. Development of arena spectacle: Coleman (1990), (1993); Potter (1999). Wiedemann (1992) 165–83 discusses the interactions of emperor and audience; Gunderson (1996) emphasises the socially coercive aspects of Roman spectacle. Evidence for dramatic performance during the empire: Jones (1993).

7 Dodge (1999) 233–4 briefly surveys theatre adaptation; Welch (1999) provides detailed analyses of changes made to the theatres at Athens and Corinth. On the theatre at Mytilene see Williams (1989) 164.

8 See Philostratus, *Apollonius* 4.22; Dio of Prusa, *Oration* 31.121; Lucian, *Demonax* 57; with Welch (1999) 130–1.

the expedition to show them where Callirhoe was sold, Hermocrates thinks the rule of law is more important, so Theron is executed immediately.

This subordination at Syracuse of the ruler's interests to the rule of law points up the contrast between Greek and Persian political systems. In Babylon, conversely, comparisons between events in the Persian court and actions in a theatre emphasise the contrast between democratic and autocratic political systems. In a scene where the wives of the leading Persians meet with Statira, the Persian king's wife, 'there was a vote, as in a theatre' to select a beautiful rival to Callirhoe (5.3.4). During the trial in the court of the Persian king when Callirhoe sees that Chaereas is alive, the narrator breaks in to compare his work with a staged spectacle: 'What poet ever brought such a surprising story to the stage?' (5.8.2). After Mithridates produces Chaereas to defend himself from the charge of adulterously using a forged letter from Chaereas to approach Callirhoe, the king decides to hold a second trial. In anticipation the whole city is full of reactions to the turn of events: 'one might say that all Babylon was a courtroom' (6.1.5). The joke here lies in the difference between Syracuse, which has dedicated civic spaces for political and judicial assemblies, and Babylon, which (at least in Chariton's rendering) does not.

What began in the streets and assemblies of Syracuse ends there. When Chaereas and Callirhoe return to Syracuse, the people cry out 'let us go to the assembly' (8.7.1) because they want to see the couple and hear about their adventures. The crowd (*dēmos*) asks Chaereas to tell the whole story. As Chaereas stands in the theatre before the people, the classical drama, with its actors and chorus, is replaced by one man's narrative of love and adventure. So too, perhaps Chariton would have it, the corporate, civic enterprise of classical drama is replaced by the solo performance of an imperial novel.

Citizen Eros

Chariton's novel looks back to a world before the Roman empire, but features of Roman political life do also show up in his narrative. The fact that the villain Theron is executed by crucifixion (3.4.18) is a reflection of Roman rather than Greek practice. In Miletus, Dionysius' position as a wealthy landowner and the 'freedmen' with whom he associates (2.3.3) seem to reflect the Roman period more than the classical past.[9] In addition, the Persian empire functions for Chariton as a metaphor for the Roman empire. The description of the trials held in the Persian king's household seems to evoke Roman imperial practices, and the 'freedmen' among the advisors of

9 See further Saïd (1999) 92–3.

the Persian king (5.4.6) are more Roman than Persian.[10] Chariton deploys these details not out of historical ignorance but because for his elite Greek audience the issue of how an individual in a Greek city is to relate to Roman imperial power can be a pressing one.

Similar issues drive Chariton's representation of divine control over the plot. Chariton allots considerable control over events in his plot to the people of Syracuse, but he is clear that a god (sometimes Eros, sometimes Aphrodite) is also directing events. Throughout the novel the language of love is the language of politics, and the divinities directing the plot do so in distinctly political terms. Against the background of political rivalry between Hermocrates and Ariston (Chaereas' father), Eros is described as 'contentious', 'fond of rivalry' (*philoneikos*, 1.1.4). Most strikingly, when the two young people first see each other, Chariton says the god 'took civic action' (*politeusamenou*) to bring about their meeting (1.1.6, cf. 5.1.1). Aphrodite too takes civic action: in Miletus, Aphrodite is said to have 'politicked' (*epoliteueto*, 2.2.8) another marriage for Callirhoe. The metaphor of civic action indicates that Aphrodite's plan for Dionysius to marry Callirhoe is a plan with civic consequences. These are borne out in the clear hints that Callirhoe's son is destined to be raised by Dionysius and return in adulthood to rule Syracuse (2.11.2, 3.8.8, 8.4.6, 8.7.11–12), through which Chariton encourages readers to associate Callirhoe's child with the historical Dionysius I of Syracuse (c. 430–367 BCE).[11]

In Babylon too the language of politics is used as a metaphor to describe passionate feelings, but here the politics of love are those of the king's court rather than the citizens' Syracuse. When the king decides to summon Mithridates, Dionysius and Callirhoe to court, he does so in part because 'in his isolation, wine and darkness had been his advisors (*sumbouloi*) and had reminded him of the part of the letter' which was about Callirhoe (4.6.7). Later, it is Eros who keeps reminding the king of Callirhoe's beauty (6.7.1). Chariton also describes the role of Eros in the unfolding of events at Babylon in terms that fit the Persian king: Eros was 'dispatching' one mission from Caria (Mithridates and Chaereas) and another 'more famous one' from Ionia (Dionysius and Callirhoe, 4.7.5). Here Love undertakes precisely the kind of long-distance messaging in which the Persian king must engage to keep the empire running smoothly. Indeed, Chariton describes such procedures when the king gives the order to mount a military expedition at news of the revolt in Egypt (6.8.7). Other distinctive aspects of the Persian king's power are his status as master of his subjects (who are thought of by Greeks as his

10 See Alvares (2001–2) and Schwartz (2003), each emphasising the subtle yet powerful qualities of Chariton's allusions to contemporary imperial practice.
11 Connors (2002) 15–17.

slaves) and the way that he moves majestically from one imperial residence to another. These aspects of royal power inform the king's own understanding of Eros as a powerful invader and enslaver: 'Great and mighty Eros has taken up residence in my soul. It is difficult to admit, but I have truly been made captive' (6.3.2).

Chariton's Eros wields power within various political registers: a nimble bicultural negotiator, at Syracuse he is a demagogue, but in Babylon he is a trusted adviser, or even a Great King himself. In this, Chariton's Eros is a model of an elite provincial citizen of the Roman empire. This is not surprising: Chariton announces at the very beginning of the story that he is clerk to Athenagoras in Aphrodisias. This city had a tradition of exploiting its connection to Aphrodite (Venus) to enhance its relationship to Rome. Recent archaeological investigations have explored the architecture, artwork and inscriptions which monumentalised these deft negotiations with Rome.[12] In a similar way, Chariton's novel celebrates the ways in which Greek civic ideology can assert itself and protect its interests in its interactions with a distant empire.

City and country on Longus' Lesbos

Ancient readers picking up the Greek novel by Longus would deduce from his name that the author was in all likelihood a Roman citizen.[13] While the politics of Longus' metaphorical language and his references to spectacle are not as explicit as those of Chariton, they still reflect constructions of civic ideology in the imperial period. Most of the novel's action is situated within the pastoral countryside, but its frame and viewpoint are distinctly urban.[14] The narrative proper begins 'There is a great and beautiful city of Lesbos called Mytilene': in the Greek, *polis* ('city') is the first word (1.1). The narrator goes on to explain that the city has many canals and marble bridges: 'you would think you were looking not at a city but at an island' (1.1). So too as readers we may feel as if we are watching Daphnis and Chloe grow up within the rustic landscape of the island of Lesbos, but at the end, when it is revealed that Daphnis and Chloe are in truth citizens of Mytilene (Daphnis is the son of the Mytilenean landowner who owns the estate), it turns out it has been an urban story all along.

As in the other novels, gods control the events of the plot. When Chariton talks about the gods controlling the plot, he uses words such as 'politick' and 'demagogue', which generally refer to the sphere of public life. By contrast,

---

12 Chariton's Aphrodisian perspective: Connors (2002), with further references. On the monuments at Aphrodisias, Smith (1987), (1988), (1990).
13 Morgan (1995) 137.   14 Saïd (1987), (1994).

Longus uses metaphors of nurturing to describe the way that the gods control the plot. Yet, because the reproduction of citizens is understood to be at the centre of Greek civic life, Longus' metaphors of nurturing also have a political dimension.[15] An old man, Philetas, tells Daphnis and Chloe that Eros has appeared in his garden. Figuring himself as a herdsman, Eros tells Philetas that he relaxes in the garden after he 'puts Daphnis and Chloe out to pasture' (2.5). Philetas tells Daphnis and Chloe 'you have been dedicated to Eros, and Eros cares for you' (2.6). While Longus clearly revels in the beautifully detailed and sympathetically described natural setting of his novel, his account of Eros' control of the plot may also be understood in political terms. Philetas makes much of Eros' powers, saying that he rules the whole world and 'the gods that are his peers' (2.7); Eros' power here sounds suspiciously like that of a Roman emperor, *primus inter pares*. As the plot unfolds, though, the actual 'work' of protecting Daphnis and Chloe and making things happen is done by the nymphs and Pan. This *de facto* distribution of labour among the gods replicates that of the 'real' world depicted in the novel: the powerful man visits occasionally, may play at doing rustic work, but his wishes are for the most part carried out by a subordinate rural staff.

The position of a wealthy man in relation to his community also emerges from Longus' references to spectacle. When urban visitors come to the estate for a festival, Daphnis pipes to his goats while they sit 'as at a theatre'. What really impresses the visitors is that 'No one had seen household slaves so obedient to the command of their master' (4.15). The mere notion of comparing a 'chorus' of dancing goats to a troupe of household slaves is a reflection of prosperous urban households full of slaves in Roman imperial times.

The role of spectacle in civic life holds the key to Chloe's origins. When her father Megacles recognizes the tokens he had abandoned with her, he says that he gave her up because he had inadequate funds to raise her in the face of heavy civic obligations of a sort most famous in classical Athens: 'I spent my money on sponsoring triremes and paying for public choruses.' Despairing at the idea of raising her in poverty, he decked her with tokens and exposed her 'knowing that many are glad to become parents even in this way' (4.35). Worry over the tension between paying for triremes and choruses and providing a dowry kept Megacles from bringing up a new citizen: no state can sustain itself under such conditions. The recognition of Daphnis and Chloe is a happy ending for the two of them: with the money now available to them there are no obstacles to their marriage, and their parents are delighted

---

15 Longus' metaphors of nurturing: Bowie (2005).

to rediscover them. But in a larger sense the births of their children will also lead to a happy ending for the city: on the morning after their arrival in Mytilene, the whole city 'felt a pregnant woman's craving for the young man and the young woman' (4.33; there is textual uncertainty here).

Achilles Tatius: Fortune's drama and its skilful citizen actors

Achilles emphasises visual experiences and phenomena throughout the novel.[16] His use of theatrical metaphor is part of this overall obsession with visuality. At the beginning of his narrative, Clitophon says, 'Fortune began the drama' (1.3.3). As we shall see below, Heliodorus, Petronius and Apuleius also use the metaphor of the goddess of chance staging a spectacle, but their spectacles are distinctly gladiatorial. By contrast, Achilles' spectacle is much more that of Athenian drama, with its citizen playwrights, actors, chorus and audience. In a description of the false sacrifice, we are told, 'Fortune worked with us' (3.22.3). Later, Clitophon says that she 'constructed a new drama against me' (6.3.1). Elsewhere, he describes the goddess as a kind of instructor or trainer: 'there still awaited us another *gymnasion* of Fortune' (5.2.3, 'exercise'; cf. Winkler's 'obstacle course'). Both a citizen playwright and a trainer in the gymnasium exert control over the bodies of free men. Thus, the particular ways in which Fortune controls the plot seem to take account of Clitophon's status as a citizen.

In keeping with this notion of Clitophon as a citizen actor, Achilles' references to spectacle repeatedly emphasise the skill of performers. Just after meeting Leucippe, Clitophon has a heart-to-heart talk about love and marriage with his cousin Clinias, who recommends a gentle approach to Leucippe: 'don't use force, even if she resists'. In Clinias' view, a lover must combine the qualities of *chorēgos* (originally the person who trained and led the chorus, subsequently the person who paid the cost of the play) and actor (*hypokritēs*): 'master (*chorēgēson*) your part (*hypokrisin*) (cf. Whitmarsh (2001c), 'assume the directorial role') so that you don't ruin your plot (*drama*)' (1.10.7). Crucial to Clinias' metaphor is the idea that a performer has the potential, through his mastery of the craft of spectacle, to make the play succeed or fail.

Leucippe too plays an actor's role. In the garden scene, Clitophon intends his conversation with Satyrus about the erotic reasons for a peacock's display of its feathers to be overheard by Leucippe. As narrator, Clitophon says that Leucippe happens to be standing 'right opposite' the peacock, and that the peacock was, by chance, at that moment displaying the 'theatre (*theatron*) of

16 Morales (2004).

its feathers' (1.16.2). The word *theatron* brings out not just the curving shape of the peacock's feathers, but also its distinctive 'eye' markings. Leucippe is being watched theatrically. Later, her ability to play the role of a sacrificial victim convincingly will be essential for her survival (3.20–1). And Leucippe tries to make smart decisions about playing the role of a slave girl on Melite's estate as she resists the advances of Thersander (6.16.4–6).[17] In all of these references to spectacle, techniques developed in the Greek city for public performance are appropriated for private use. Achilles' interest in the ability of a performer to succeed through skilful use of the voice and body allows his characters a striking degree of agency: Fortune can stage the drama, but it is up to the actors to turn in a successful performance. Achilles' emphasis on his characters' effective practice of theatrical craft within a drama scripted by Fortune has a striking real-world counterpart in Plutarch's advice for aspiring politicians in Greek cities under Roman rule: 'imitate the actors, who put their own feeling, character and honour into the performance, while they heed the prompter and in rhythms and metres avoid going beyond the authority granted to them by those in power'.[18]

Eros, *hybris*, slavery and tyranny

On one level Achilles' characters see themselves as successful performers who craft effective spectacles in order to solve problems. But at the same time they are also subject to the domination of Eros over their bodies. The body's vulnerability to physical mastery is both a natural phenomenon and a civic construction. That is to say, in the particular cases of Greek and Roman culture, the political institutions of slavery, war and legal procedure determine the circumstances under which a body is vulnerable to attack. Enslaved bodies can be struck by those who claim to be their masters, whereas free men have recourse against their attackers – they can bring their attackers to court and charge them with a crime (*hybris* in Greek, *iniuria* in Latin). When people call a ruler a tyrant, part of what they mean is that he treats free citizens as though they were slaves.

Achilles expresses the domination of Eros over the characters in terms that reflect the politics of Greek cities in the Roman empire. As was the case with Chariton and Longus, it is important to appreciate that Achilles' metaphors allude to a variety of political experiences. So, when the unnamed frame narrator of the novel looks at the painting of Europa and the bull, the narrator says that Eros, who is impudently leading the bull, is ruling 'sky and earth and sea'. This version of the literary topos of the power of love figures

17 On theatricality in Achilles, see Morales (2004) 60–77.   18 *Precepts on Statecraft* 813F.

it in terms that compete with Rome's global *imperium*, which is typically described as mastery on land and sea.[19] Clitophon then interrupts the frame narrator's meditations on Love's global power: 'I have suffered outrageous attacks (*hybreis*) from Love which are just as great' (1.2.1). *Hybris* is a violent, sometimes sexual, attack on a person; offenders could be prosecuted for it under Athenian law. It is of course a very old idea to compare love to a wound, but when Clitophon says here that he has been victim of *hybris* at the hands of Love, Achilles envisions Love's wounds within a legal and civic context.

Hybris is a recurring theme throughout the work.[20] As Clitophon sees it, Eros commits crimes against him and he has no legal remedy against them. Understanding his own experience in this way shapes all of Clitophon's perceptions. In introducing his praises of erotic relations with women, Clitophon deplores Zeus's abduction of Ganymede: 'he was kidnapped and violated (*hubrizetai*) like a tyrant's victim. A most disgraceful spectacle this, a lad hanging from bird's claws' (2.37.3, trans. Whitmarsh (2001c)). This mythical 'spectacle' of a 'tyrant's victim' looks a lot like an allusion to the 'fatal charades' of the Roman arena.[21]

In inflicting *hybris* on people, Eros treats them in the way in which a tyrant treats his subjects. In a related figure, Achilles describes the experience of being in love as analogous to being enslaved.[22] In contrast to elegy's well-known focus on the 'servitude of love' in the context of elite male households in the city of Rome,[23] Achilles associates love with enslavement to and hybristic treatment by a tyrant. In one of the novel's most memorable scenes, Leucippe resists Thersander, who lusts for her and believes her to be his slave. Using the power of her voice to protect her body, she tells him that *his* behaviour is slavish, that he is not acting as a 'free man', nor as a 'wellborn man' (6.18.6). She tells him he is being a tyrant (6.20.3), and says 'I am naked, and alone, and a woman, I have one shield, my freedom' (6.22.4).

Clitophon too manages to use his voice to defend the integrity of his body from *hybris*. At the beginning of book 8, Thersander punches Clitophon

---

19 On descriptions of Roman universal mastery of the earth and sea, see Nicolet (1991) 29–56.
20 Callisthenes' *hybris* is the catalyst for the abduction of Calligone (2.13.1); Panthea, suspecting that Leucippe has been having pre-marital sex, wishes that her daughter had suffered '*hybris* according to the custom of war' (2.24.3, 4). Melite says she is suffering *hybris* in Clitophon's rejection of her (5.25.2, 5.25.7, 5.26.1).
21 See e.g. Martial *On the Spectacles* 6, 8, 9, 10, with Coleman (1990).
22 See ch. 4, this volume.
23 See Lyne (1979); Murgatroyd (1981). The motif appears sporadically in Greek; of special importance for Achilles is Plato, *Symposium* 183a, 184b–c; *Phaedrus* 252a. McCarthy (1998) explores the power dynamics at issue when an elite Roman man claims to be the slave of his mistress.

and draws blood. Clitophon says, 'in response to the tyrannical treatment I received, I gave a tragic performance' (8.1.5). When a crowd has gathered in response to his shouts, he says, 'I am a free man, from a notable city' (8.3.1). The phrase 'from a notable city' is the same one used by Paul (in *Acts* 21:39) when he asserts his status as a Roman citizen to request that he be tried at Rome. Without insisting that Achilles Tatius is making an allusion to the story of Paul, it is still important to observe the parallel. Both Clitophon and Paul are trying to claim civic privileges for their bodies within a Roman imperial framework.[24] What Clitophon and Paul say, I think, is what Achilles' privileged readers would say if they found themselves in a similarly perilous situation. Both the Clitophon scene and the Paul scene show just how far the empire could and could not reach into day-to-day life. A citizen could expect his body to be safe from assault only if he could use his voice effectively to assert his citizen status.

Heliodorus and the spectacle of power

Heliodorus uses the technical vocabulary of the stage to present his novel as a version of theatrical spectacle.[25] His references to theatre emphasise two kinds of absolute power: the power of spectacle to silence and even mystify viewers, and the absolute power of the one who stages the spectacle over those who play the parts. Again and again Heliodorus makes it clear that neither audience nor performer has any chance to resist the power at work in the creation of the theatrical spectacle. The novel opens by describing the scene of carnage on the shores of the Heracleotic mouth of the Nile, as if 'the god' staged a 'spectacle' (*theatron*) for the mystified Egyptian bandits who are looking at it (1.1.6). As readers, we are mystified too: Heliodorus implies that he is the equivalent of the god, with an equal power to exert stunning and mystifying control over his audience. Theagenes identifies with a theatrical character's point of view when he complains bitterly that the *daimōn* is making a theatrical spectacle out of his and Charicleia's misfortunes. He is even afraid that the *daimōn* may be so eager for the glory of staging an impressive spectacle that he will force the lovers to commit suicide (5.6.2–4). Here we are in the world of the Roman arena, far from the classical Athenian stage. Charicleia makes a similar complaint when she is angry and resentful about her separation from Theagenes: alone in her room at Nausicles' house she says: 'let us dance' for the *daimōn* who is controlling her destiny; and 'let us sing mourning songs, and let us perform lamentations like a pantomime actor' (6.8.3).

---

24 On the legal issues involved in Paul's situation, see Garnsey (1970) 75–6.
25 Walden (1894).

There is an especially intense concentration of theatrical imagery when several strands of the plot come together at Memphis in book 7.[26] Here too the focus is not on the impressive nature of the spectacle in itself, but on the powerful divine force which creates spectacle. Thyamis chases his brother and rival Petosiris around the city, while the inhabitants watch 'like those judging in the theatre' when suddenly 'either some god or chance adds to the tragedy' (7.6.4): their father Calasiris arrives just in time to stop their battle. The staging, some time later, of the spectacle of Charicleia's execution (she is to be burned alive) would have been recognisably Roman to Heliodorus' audience (8.9).[27] At the end of the novel, when the audience of Ethiopians realises, even though they do not hear much of what is said, that Charicleia will not be sacrificed by her father, Heliodorus says that this is either because they figured it out from what had happened so far, or that it had happened 'from the same divine force which had staged the whole thing' (10.38.3). The divine power that directs spectacles in Heliodorus is impossible to resist or negotiate with. It is not the power of a citizen competing with his fellow citizens to stage or act the spectacle, which will be voted best, but the power of an emperor who uses spectacle to express his dominance.

These 'escapist' Greek novels, then, do not escape completely from their Roman imperial context. In the Greek novels, Rome is 'both nowhere and everywhere'.[28] From the novels' literal and metaphorical references to spectacle and to politics, key terms emerge as characteristic of each novel's distinctive ideas about the dynamics of civic life in an imperial world. Chariton's Eros is a citizen negotiator, equally adept at getting the local populace and the distant monarch to do his wishes; Longus' Eros is a landowner whose minions do all the real work. Achilles' characters succeed in protecting their privileges as citizens by achieving skilful performances in the roles Fortune composes for them, while Heliodorus' god stages a spectacle over which he wields absolute control. In the Roman world a privileged member of a Greek city might understand his political identity in each or all of these ways: citizen negotiator, powerful landowner, effective advocate in defence of citizen privileges under threat, or an all but powerless subject of a distant tyrant.

Liberty, tyranny and the arena in the *Satyrica* and in Neronian Rome

In the Latin novels by Petronius and Apuleius, Rome has something of the 'nowhere and everywhere' quality that it has in the Greek novels. Again as in the Greek novels, these Latin authors speak literally and metaphorically

---

26 Marino (1990).   27 So Potter (2004) 201–2; cf. Lalanne (2002) 229–30.
28 Schwartz (2003) 391.

about civic spectacles in ways which explore the issue of freedom (in Latin, *libertas*). For Romans, a free man is above all not a slave; he is also not a convicted criminal, not the subject of a tyrant. A free man is entitled to civic prerogatives that allow him to control what he speaks, and what happens to his body and his property and household, and to enforce this control through the use of persuasive speech in the courts if necessary. Rome understands its Republic as characterised by the *libertas* of its free citizens. When institutions of Republican governance are superseded by the emperor's power, *libertas* is talked about differently. Emperors wish to present themselves as benevolent protectors of the people's *libertas*. When tensions arise, particularly between emperors and those who have the most to lose in the obsolescence of Republican political institutions, the traditional aristocratic *libertas* becomes a term of resistance, and a means of describing a wise man's independence from an emperor's tyranny.[29]

Like the Greek novels, Petronius' outrageously funny and bleak *Satyrica* talks about spectacle and chance in ways that invite nostalgic reflection on freedom in an age of imperial dominance. The spectacle is gladiatorial; the imperial power in question is specifically Neronian (Petronius is in all probability to be identified with the Petronius described by Tacitus as Nero's courtier, forced to commit suicide in 66 CE).

The *Satyrica*'s anti-hero, the hapless Encolpius, travels (in the surviving fragments, mainly in southern Italy) on the margins of society, always on the lookout for a free meal and a warm bed, and constantly needing to escape from situations that somehow threaten his free status. He has a companion named Giton, for whose affection he has a rival in Ascyltus. The possibilities, real or illusory, of gaining and losing *libertas* are present in the novel's episodes at Trimalchio's house, on Lichas' ship and in Croton.[30] *Libertas* balances on the point of a sword in literal or metaphorical references to gladiatorial spectacle. One particular feature of the spectacle that seems to interest Petronius is the *missio*, when a gladiator who has surrendered is reprieved from death to fight another day. While in actual practice a gladiator who was granted *missio* from the arena was not in fact 'freed' from further service, Petronius does seem to link *missio* (and the related verb *dimittere*) with escape from gladiatorial and other servitude, thus with *libertas*.[31]

Encolpius himself is not a slave, and he has the trappings of an elite free man's education. Some trouble with the law seems to have resulted in

---

29 On *libertas* during the Republic, see Fantham (2005); on the discourse of *libertas* in the transition from Republic to empire, see Wirszubski (1968) and Gowing (2005), esp. index, s.v. *libertas*; Roller (2001) 213–87, analyses the application of master–slave discourse to the relation of emperor to his aristocratic subjects.
30 See also Rimell (2002) 181–90.   31 See Coleman (2000) 488 on the practice of *missio*.

Encolpius being sentenced to fight in the arena, from which he subsequently escaped because of an earthquake which caused the earth to gape: Ascyltus calls Encolpius a 'filthy gladiator, whom . . . the arena let go' (*dimisit*, 9.8; cf. 81.3). At Trimalchio's, the spectacle of the arena is reduced to a domestic scale. When Encolpius wonders why a boar is served wearing a freedman's cap, he is told that the boar was 'set free' (*dimissus*) from yesterday's dinner and returns now 'like a freedman' (41.4; cf. 66.7). Next, while a slave boy acts the part of the wine god Dionysus (also known in Rome as Liber), Trimalchio says 'Dionysus, be Liber' (*liber esto*). Taking *liber* as 'free' the boy snatches up the boar's cap and plays the part of one being manumitted from slavery. Trimalchio's answer shows he's really still master: 'you will not deny that I possess *liberum patrem*' (41.8) – where *liberum patrem* can mean both a father who is free and the god Liber Pater ('father Liber'). When Trimalchio leaves the room to relieve himself, Encolpius jokes 'when the tyrant was gone we attained liberty' (41.9).

Later, Encolpius is reunited with Giton and meets a poet, Eumolpus, who secures passage for the three of them on a ship. When Encolpius learns that the ship belongs to Lichas, who knows them and has a grudge against them, he reacts to this coincidence like a gladiator surrendering to his opponent: he lays bare his throat and cries out, 'Fortune, at last you have defeated me entirely' (101.1). In effect, since Encolpius survives his gladiatorial surrender, he understands his escape from the ship as a version of *missio*, much like his earlier escape from the arena (9.8, 81.3). After a storm, shipwreck and the death of Lichas the companions make their way toward Croton, where Encolpius and Giton decide to play the part of Eumoplus' slaves as part of a scheme to insinuate him with the legacy hunters of Croton. Since they are giving Eumolpus permission to treat them as slaves, they swear a version of the oath by which free men hire themselves out as gladiators: they agree to be burned, bound, beaten and killed by the sword (117.5). As this quasi-gladiatorial scheme ('like real gladiators', 117.5) gets going on the road to Croton, Eumolpus performs a poem on the civil war between Caesar and Pompey. Although this snatch of historical epic seems wildly out of place in the episodic tale of Encolpius' adventures, it shares with the novel an emphasis on the role of Fortune in directing the action.[32] Fortune is summoned by the god of the underworld and bidden to set the war in motion (*Civil War* 67–121); Caesar advances on Rome, and is happy to ally his cause with chance: 'let the die be cast with Fortune as judge' (*Civil War* 174); Fortune watches as Pompey flees before Caesar's advance (*Civil War* 244).

---

32 See Zeitlin (1971a); Connors (1998) 100–46; Rimell (2002) 77–97, each with further references.

In addition, even though the word *libertas* does not appear in the poem, I think it can be understood as part of the novel's engagement in discourse of *libertas* because in telling the story of the civil war, it also tells of the origins of the Julio-Claudian emperors, and the consequent loss of Republican *libertas*.[33]

Petronius twice elsewhere evokes *libertas* in contexts that contrast Republic with empire. A denunciation of contemporary rhetoric occurs at the beginning of the surviving fragments of the novel. Encolpius criticises orators who play the role of a citizen who shows off the 'scars I have suffered for public *libertas*' (1.1). The Republican topos of displaying actual wounds suffered for the state is here strongly contrasted with the extravagant oratorical fictions enthusiastically perpetrated during the empire. In a subsequent scene, Giton tells Encolpius that when he resisted Ascyltus' advances, Ascyltus drew his sword and said, 'if you are Lucretia you have found Tarquin' (9.5). Ascyltus' threat to Giton refers to the moment from which Republican *libertas* originated on the point of a sword in the overthrow of the Tarquins after the rape of Lucretia and her suicide-by-sword. The joke is, of course, that there is no Lucretia in the *Satyrica*. But people like Seneca and Lucan (and later, Tacitus) would say that there is no (Republican) *libertas* in Nero's Rome either.

In considering the politics of the *Satyrica*, J. P. Sullivan argued that Petronius mocked Seneca and Lucan to win favour with Nero.[34] I wonder, though, if this way of thinking might assimilate Petronius' point of view too closely to Nero's own eventual decision to force the suicides of Seneca and Lucan. Although Petronius is not usually included in discussion of the shifting discourses of *libertas* under the emperors, I think the *Satyrica* should be brought into the conversation. Furious Lucan, enduring Seneca and insouciant Petronius all view Republican *libertas* as something denied them by Nero in particular and emperors in general. The *Satyrica*'s 'quasi-*missio*' narratives of chance-driven escape strike me as Petronius' novelistic version of what possibilities can lie beyond such a loss of *libertas*. In the end, like Seneca and Lucan, Petronius was compelled to commit suicide by Nero but made a point of meeting death on his own terms.[35] In the end too, even Nero himself could not escape the arena: the Flavian Colosseum was built to take the place of the lake which was part of Nero's Golden House: as Martial says,

33 When Eumolpus introduces the poem, he implies that his handling of divine themes shows that it is the work of a 'free spirit' (118.6). In the poem itself, one feature of the corruption at Rome that led to the civil war is the fact that the 'excellence characteristic of free men' (*Civil War* 42) has 'collapsed' (43).

34 Sullivan (1985) 153–79.

35 Tacitus, *Annals* 15.60–4 (Seneca), 15.70 (Lucan), 16.19 (Petronius).

'what had been the tyrant's is now the people's pleasure' (*On the Spectacles* 2.12).

Greek society and Roman spectacle in Apuleius' *Metamorphoses*

Both Apuleius' *Metamorphoses* and the related Greek *Ass* are set in Greece during the period of Roman rule, but Apuleius redraws the geographical and ethnic map of the narrative and adds important elements (principally the conversion to Isis at the end).[36] Even though the *Metamorphoses* is similar in so many details to the *Ass*, the two stories have quite different takes on the politics of Roman Greece.

Edith Hall's political reading of the Greek *Ass* emphasises Lucius' strong connections to Rome. He has a Roman name, and his brother's name is Gaius, another typically Roman name. Since the governor recognises who he is, he is probably a Roman citizen, though this is not stated explicitly. He is from Patras, a city with especially strong links to Rome since it was refounded by Augustus after his victory at Actium and awarded special privileges.[37] Hall argues persuasively that a story of the abusive treatment of a Roman from Patras would have special point for a Greek author and his audience.[38] Rather than use a nostalgic story set in the classical past to make Rome invisible, as the idealising novelists do, the author of the *Ass* uses magic to make the Roman from privileged Patras disappear beneath the skin of an ass. Lucius understands his political and social invisibility when the bandits hit him. He attempts the typical citizen's response to a beating – 'Oh Caesar', in effect an appeal for protection under the law – but can only bray 'O' (*Ass* 16). The thrill for a Greek audience would lie in imagining the Roman's experience of political invisibility and social degradation.

In Apuleius' Latin version of the story, probably written in the 160s CE, the first-person narrator says in the prologue that he is of Greek ancestry and learned Greek as a child. Subsequently he travelled to Rome and learned Latin without a teacher (1.1). We learn later that he lives at Corinth (2.12), and his present trip to Thessaly began from Corinth (1.22). Luca Graverini, in a perceptive reading of the novel as a 'study in the problem of the relationship between Greece and Rome,' has argued that the history of Corinth is crucial for understanding its significance in Apuleius' novel. The city was destroyed in 146 BCE (the same year as the destruction of Carthage); it lay desolate until Julius Caesar established a colony there in 44 BCE.[39]

---

36 On the relationship between the *Ass* and the *Metamorphoses*, see e.g. Harrison (2003a) 500–2.
37 Strabo 8.7.5; Pausanias 7.18.6–9.   38 Hall (1995).
39 Graverini (2002) esp. 66; on other aspects of Lucius' Corinth see Mason (1971) and Harrison (2002).

Corinth and Lucius both have a history of becoming Roman in catastrophic ways: both had Greek identities, became enslaved, emptied out of humanity and Greekness, and then eventually re-established as Roman. The Roman spectacle at Corinth in which Lucius is to perform is a visible symbol of the city's violent transformation into a Roman colony, and it is in fleeing from that spectacle that Lucius escapes from his past.

Even before the climax of events in spectacle at Corinth, references to spectacle have been an important theme in the novel, part of its strategy of contrasting mere physical pleasures with the true pleasures of Greek philosophical knowledge and Isiac religious enlightenment. As the action begins, Lucius encourages Aristomenes to tell his story by citing the example of the sword-swallower he (Lucius) marvelled at in Athens in the Painted Stoa (1.4). This one-man sword show contrasts with the publicly staged gladiatorial sword contests that the novel is full of.[40] Scenes in the novel also evoke or refer to the Rome practice of beast spectacles.[41] In addition, Lucius describes the god directing the action as one treating him like a convicted criminal or an enslaved prisoner of war who has been deprived of *libertas* and sentenced to the arena. As in the *Ass*, Lucius comes to understand his transformation as a loss of freedom on the surface of his skin (now hide) when his reaction to being beaten by the bandits is 'to run to the civil authority and to free (*liberare*) myself from my troubles by the mention of the honored name of the emperor' (3.29). Shortly thereafter he glimpses some roses and he thinks he is getting something like an imperial pardon: 'Jupiter himself at long last offered me unexpected safety' (3.29). Fortune inflicts 'torture' upon Lucius (7.16, 7.17), and he thinks that she saves him from one situation for future troubles (7.20). She expresses her will through nods (4.12.3, 7.20, 9.1), like an absolute ruler. When Lucius regains his human form he is still caught up in the images of enslavement: the priest of Isis says 'when you begin to be the slave of the goddess [Isis], then you will more fully recognize the benefit of your freedom' (11.15). And Isis too expresses her will through nods (11.21, 25).

The story of Psyche and Cupid introduced by Apuleius into the tale also makes much of the interaction between Roman spectacle and Greek society. Apuleius' gods clearly inhabit something that looks very like Rome.

---

40 Socrates sought 'the pleasure of a renowned gladiatorial spectacle' (1.7). Thelyphron was travelling to see 'the Olympic spectacle' (2.21). Romanising the erotic 'wrestling' with Palaestra described at length in the *Ass* (8–10), Lucius calls his evening with Photis 'gladiatorial games of Venus' (2.15); Photis warns him that 'Today's battle will have no dismissal' (*missionem*, 2.17).

41 Scenes of, or evoking, beast spectacle: 3.26, 4.13, 4.20–1, 6.27 (cf. *Ass* 23), 7.13, 8.17, 10.16, 10.18, 10.22, 10.23, 10.29, 10.34.

Recognisably Roman law and customs obtain among the gods.[42] Cupid's lavish country house is described as looking like the sort of 'palace' Jupiter would use if he had business with humans (5.1): the clear implication is that Jupiter would visit humans the way that Roman emperors would visit their provincial subjects. When Venus tells Mercury to announce a reward for the return of Psyche, she promises kisses as a reward; they can be collected 'behind the Murcian turning post' (6.8.2). The spot is the site of a shrine of Venus in the Circus Maximus at Rome.[43] A topographically savvy reader would also know about the Circus' monumental display of Rome's mastery over Egypt, the Egyptian obelisk Augustus had dedicated to the Sun god and erected on the 'spine' (the central section, with the turning posts at each end) of the Circus Maximus.

The gods not only live in a version of Rome, they operate under a version of Roman law. Venus claims that Psyche's unborn child will be born illegitimate because her union with Cupid was a 'marriage between unequals' as defined by Roman law (6.9). Venus is in effect saying that no *conubium* (legal capacity to marry) exists between Cupid and Psyche. When Cupid appeals to Jupiter to ask if he can have Psyche, Jupiter says that he will grant the request, even though Cupid has given him a lot of trouble over the years by making him pursue love-affairs 'against the laws, and even the Julian law itself' (6.22), that is, in violation of the Augustan laws against adultery. Jupiter summons the 'conscript gods' to a *contio* (an assembly called by a priest or magistrate) in the 'heavenly theatre' on pain of fine. On the grounds that Cupid needs to settle down in marriage, Jupiter grants Psyche to him and makes her immortal so that the marriage will no longer be unequal (6.23). In the old-fashioned Roman way, Psyche passes into the hand of her new husband (6.24), and their child, named *Voluptas* (Pleasure), is born legitimate.[44]

The fact that Apuleius' gods have such a characteristically Roman political life is significant as well as amusing. Like Lucius, Psyche is treated as a slave, and undergoes divine transformation. Both Psyche and Lucius are admitted in the end into a recognisably Roman world. In the *Ass*, Lucius' Roman connections are something to be mocked and humiliated for, and in the end, as his same old self, he beats a quick retreat to Patras. By contrast, Apuleius' Lucius and Psyche achieve new Roman connections as a reward

---

42 See Kenney (1990a) index, 'Roman references'.
43 Tertullian, *On the spectacles* 8. Apuleius builds a network of horse-racing images: 1.1, 4.2, 10.35.
44 On the legal issues involved, see *Met.* 6.9.6 with the note of Kenney (1990a) on Venus' suspicions about the union; and more generally Osgood (2006). See further Treggiari (1991) on Roman marriage.

for their suffering. They each move to a version of Rome for a new and better life: Psyche to a heavenly version of Rome as a new immortal, and Lucius to the earthly Rome as an initiate of Isis (11.26) and an increasingly successful practitioner of Roman law (11.28, 30). Whether one reads Lucius' initiation into the cult of Isis as a transcendent religious experience or a pointed mockery of such experiences, Apuleius' picture of Rome as a place which can welcome newcomers affirms the transformational potential of the Roman empire in a positive way which is quite different from the glimpses of empire and its spectacles offered by the Greek novels.

Even so, darker glimpses of the history of Roman intervention in Greece may be visible at the edges of the tale of Charite, the girl who is imprisoned along with Lucius in the bandits' cave, and to whom the old woman tells the tale of Psyche. The cave is presumably relatively near Actium, for when Charite's husband Tlepolemus arrives in disguise, he pretends that he is the leader of a band of bandits who were hunted down by the emperor's command (nod, *nutus*) after they committed a robbery at Actium (7.7); this is 'a second, novelistic battle of Actium',[45] the battle at which the forces of Augustus defeated those of Antony and Cleopatra.

When the slaves on Charite's family's estate hear the news of her death, they fear 'the novelty of a different master' and, taking Lucius, they abandon the property (8.15). This brings Lucius to a new episode in his adventures, but such abandonment of an estate in north-western Greece has a historical resonance too, perhaps already signalled when the slave messenger who tells Charite's tale says that he tells 'such things as more learned men, to whom Fortune has given pens, could justifiably put on paper in the form of history' (8.1). That is, Augustus mandated forced resettlements as part of the establishment of Nicopolis, the city he built to commemorate his victory at Actium. For Pausanias the memory is vivid: 'Calydon with the rest of Aetolia had been laid waste by the Emperor Augustus in order that the Aetolian people might be incorporated into Nikopolis above Actium' (Pausanias 7.18.8, Loeb trans.). Augustan interventions in the landscape around Nikopolis are archaeologically attested.[46] If Psyche's mythical integration into a distinctly Roman divine world and Lucius' move to Rome offer an optimistic view of the possibilities a Roman future could offer a lucky (elite) individual such as Apuleius himself, the quasi-historical tale of the abandonment of Charite's family estate might, at least for some readers, acknowledge the costs and consequences of Roman intervention in Greece.

By now it will be clear that Greek or Latin, nostalgically chaste or decadently contemporary, all the ancient novels are *Roman*. What these novels

---

45 Harrison (2002) 54.   46 Alcock (1993) 132–45.

say about spectacle and civic life reinforces the social construction of the privileges of free elite men in the Roman empire. When novels keep Rome and its imperial spectacles *almost* in sight readers have the space to explore a range of strategies for living and dying in an imperial world.[47]

Further reading

On the civic and cultural context within which the Greek novels were written and read, Bowie (1970) remains a good starting point; Morgan (1995) provides evidence for the social context of the novels' authors and audiences. Cooper (1996) considers the social and political dimensions of the Greek novels' representations of reproduction of citizen households. Whitmarsh (2001a) and the essays collected in Goldhill (2001b) emphasise the variety of ways that Greek identity could be enacted and performed during the Roman empire. Hall (1995) perceptively charts the political context of the Lucianic *Ass* in Roman Greece. Bodel (1994) is an acute guide to Petronius' engagement with and distortion of Roman social codes and practices. Petronius' relation to Nero is discussed by Sullivan (1985) and possible political readings of Eumolpus' *Civil War* poem are considered in Connors (1998). Also useful for coming to grips with the *Satyrica*'s slippery politics is the nuanced overview of Roman aristocratic reactions to imperial power in Roller (2001). Distinctively Roman aspects of Apuleius' *Golden Ass* are brought into sharp focus in articles by Millar (1981), Bradley (2000a–b), Graverini (2002), Rosati (2003), Zimmermann (2005) and Osgood (2006).

---

47 My work on this chapter was supported by a Research Fellowship granted by the Simpson Center for the Humanities at the University of Washington. I am grateful to Luca Graverini, Stephen Hinds and Sandra Joshel for their generous advice, and I am indebted as well to Ashli Baker and to H. J. Mason and others in the audience at the 2005 meeting of the Classical Association of the Pacific Northwest and the Classical Association of the Canadian West at which I presented a portion of this project.

PART III

Form

11

SIMON GOLDHILL

Genre

'What is time?', worried St Augustine. 'I know what it is, provided no-one asks me.'[1] Augustine brilliantly captures the paradoxical truth that 'time' is an essential everyday term which everyone uses comfortably, but which becomes increasingly hard to understand the more one thinks about it – and Augustine thought very hard about time. For literary criticism, 'genre' is a similarly necessary but baffling term. It is an essential element of literary history and of our responses to literature: one of the first engagements with any text by a reader is the recognition of genre, and it would be hard to imagine a literary history that did not depend on genre as an organising category. Yet what is at stake in the term 'genre' or, more specifically, 'the genre of the novel', is less easy to determine. In what ways does calling a text a 'novel', or excluding a text from the 'genre of the novel', matter? How does it affect what writers write and how readers read? Is genre a question of formal qualities, that is, a set of stylistic elements, which any text must have in order to be classed as a novel? Or is there more at issue – politics, sociology, the expectations of readers? The first section of this chapter investigates the issues underlying the term 'genre' and, more specifically, 'the genre of the novel'; the second section looks at how 'genre' has played a crucial role in the critical history of the ancient novel; the third section looks at some specific texts to see how the use of the term 'genre' can open and close avenues of appreciation of ancient fiction. The simple question which underlies these discussions is this: what difference does it make to call a particular work a 'novel'?

Why does genre matter?

'There are no *genreless* texts'.[2] Stephen Heath's lapidary statement emphasises that for every reader who approaches a text, and for every writer who

---

1 *Confessions* 11.14.   2 Heath (2004) 163.

produces a text, there is always a frame of expectation that stems from a cultural knowledge of a society's practices of writing: 'To write or read at a given time in a given society is to engage with current conventions of writing and the expectation of what it can be.'[3] In such general terms, genre forms the ground rules of the business of reading and writing, that is, the knowingness which guarantees that, for all its lists of names and its catalogue format, the telephone directory is not read as a genealogical epic; or the acceptance of convention which makes it evident that it would be a grotesque category error if a member of the audience tried to prevent Othello from killing Desdemona. As such, genre stabilises the production and consumption of texts, and it must be true that however creative and original any particular piece of work is, there are no genreless texts.

Heath's demand of cultural and historical specificity, however – 'at a given time in a given society to engage with current conventions' – also importantly emphasises that there is a socio-politics of genre, which has all too often been forgotten in formalist analyses of particular genres. Genre is a name for how the representative or the typical is encoded. It is thus normative at different levels. 'Current conventions' include not just formal attributes of texts, but also socially defined contexts for an engagement with a text: a play needs a theatre, and a theatre has strongly marked and policed patterns of audience behaviour and actors' practices – the social contract for drama's performance. This is part of the genre of drama. Molly Bloom in James Joyce's *Ulysses* curled up in bed with a box of chocolates, a novel and an active fantasy world of her own, is an iconic image of how novels are consumed in modernity. How novels are read (by women, with sentimental emotion, with dangerous fantasising . . .) has always been seen as part of the genre of the novel, and why the genre of the novel has often been seen as worrying. So the modern genre of 'Romance', a subset of the genre of novel, cannot be separated from the commercialism of its production, the nature of its largely female, lower middle-class audience, and the rapid circulation of its volumes: its generic expectations are laid down with explicit requirements and restrictions by publishers with specific regard to this reading experience.[4] This in turn has a historical relation to the sociology of the development of a reading public for the novel in the eighteenth and nineteenth centuries: what the novel was, what its moral impact was, who its readership should be, were all topics discussed intensely as the novel grew in popularity.[5] Genre cannot be fully accounted for in purely formal literary terms: audience, context of

3 Ibid. 4 See Radway (1984); Radford (1986); Modleski (1982); Thurston (1987).
5 See Raven *et al.* (1996); Gallagher (1994); Chartier (1994); de Jean (1991); Flint (1993); Armstrong (1987); Watt (1957).

performance, circulation of texts, and self-aware critical discussion all play a role.

Genre's force of convention also has a powerful *emotional* effect, however. A genre summons pleasure – 'summons', in the strong sense of appealing for, demanding, calling forth (what Althusser calls 'interpellation').[6] Comedy calls forth laughter, the lyric sublime emotions, the novel the enchantment of narrative . . . To resist such pleasures is to deny the genre. Genres are ways of organising emotional expectations. Genres structure the reader's emotional contract with fiction (and other forms of writing), and so have the reader's emotional complicity. Genre is thus a formative element in the construction of the typical – and thus normative – scene of communication. It is part of how society projects and promotes – regulates – the functioning of communication in and as culture. Starting from Plato's intense worries about tragedy's emotional impact, there is a long tradition of critical concern with each genre's emotional effect – both as a psychological and as a social issue. So, wickedly placing herself in this moralistic tradition, Jane Gallop reflects on how some books made her cry and some made her masturbate (in this she is firmly traditional: both are common reactions to the novel according to concerned critics from the eighteenth century onwards),[7] and she asks: what is it about reading novels that produces bodily fluids?[8]

The typical or normative is also expressed, however, in terms of social values. Epic as a genre, for example, encodes – explores, debates and projects – models of heroism and masculinity, models which have their own history, as even a cursory comparison of Homer, Apollonius, Virgil, Milton, Walcott insists. When Jane Austen begins *Pride and Prejudice* with 'It is a truth universally acknowledged that a man in possession of a good fortune must be in want of a wife', she is knowingly intertwining the social value of the institution of marriage, so essential to the world she depicts and the world she lived in, with the narrative form of the novel with its dedication to the eventual linking of a couple in marriage in its final chapter. The interlocking of narrative form and social value gives a particular power to the normativity of genre.[9] So the private experience of the modern novel – its expected scene of reading – and the novel's typical thematic focus on individual character have been persuasively linked to the post-enlightenment sense of subjectivity.[10] Genre's implication with *social* value is profound and multiform.

The politics of genre are perhaps most strikingly evident, however, when a genre comes into being in response to politics. 'Black fiction', 'the

---

6 Althusser (1971) 160–73.
7 See Laqueur (2003) 320–30, as well as the works cited in n. 4. Rousseau referred to 'books that are read with one hand'.
8 Gallop (1988) 18.   9 See Brooks (1984).   10 See e.g. Tanner (1979); Eagleton (1982).

post-colonial novel', 'women's writing', have each come to be recognised as genres of the novel in reaction to the exclusions and social deprivations of 'current conventions'. The specific attributes of such genres are demarcated ('recognised'), as a claim for status is asserted ('recognised'), in a dynamic that cannot be separated from the politics of society. The politics of genre here are the politics of representation, in all senses. (Should not the genre-defining Roman elegiac poets, Tibullus, Gallus, Propertius, Ovid, for example, be read thus as significantly coming into existence in and against the powerful social norms of the empire?) Genre also defines what can be seen and accepted. Genre brings valorisation.

What is more, such generic recognition can become sharply regulatory. Rules are made, and, above all, enforced in a social setting. French classical drama, for example, is set within a critical matrix which is fundamental to its production and reception: scholars and playwrights such as Racine and Corneille commented explicitly and at length on the theory of drama and criticised particular plays on the basis of those theories.[11] Plays failed because they did not observe the rules of genre. Genre becomes a major factor in the policing of literary culture: the law of genre. In the ancient world, generations of formal training in rhetoric, with the discipline's professionalised handbooks and self-conscious awareness of strategies of persuasion, inevitably altered any audience's appreciation of a particular oratorical performance. From Isocrates to Libanius, a recognition of the 'rules of rhetoric' is an integral element of rhetorical performance and its critical reception. The regulation of genre plays a fundamental role in the impact literature has in society.

Heath's focus on 'contemporary conventions' and the historically specific moment of generic innovation or regulation does not imply, however, that genres do not have histories, or, perhaps most importantly, that genres do not construct continuities over time. Such continuities, however, must be seen as dynamic systems. There is a well-defined and extensive tradition of ancient epic, founded on Homer and stretching at least to Nonnus in the fifth century CE. To write epic is to set oneself in and against a tradition, with all the self-consciousness of such a self-positioning. Writing within the genre of epic is an activity, an activity that constructs tradition as much as it participates in it (and epic, of course, is particularly concerned with the construction of tradition in a self-reflexive way, both with regard to the *klea andrōn*, the 'fame of men', and with regard to the foundation myths of culture). Genre becomes a way of engaging with cultural memory – of instantiating memory.

---

11 See Cave (1988) 83–115.

Genre makes the past present through affiliation of form, and thus anchors literature within history.

I have begun with this emphasis on the broad socio-political force of genre because it is so often undervalued in discussions of genre in the ancient world. There are in particular three common critical strategies, which my focus on socio-politics is designed to mitigate. First, genre is all too often treated solely or primarily as a formalist question, where attributes of a literary genre are listed, and then a particular work is considered as a member of the genre according to whether it has (enough of) those attributes or not. Although such formal questions are in themselves interesting and indeed necessary lines of enquiry, particularly when classical poetry is so aware of its own generic memory, one less satisfactory result of such formalism is that the role of the reader seems to be limited to the acknowledgement of *topoi*, the social scene of reading is unexplored, and the nature of any cultural or political impact of poetry – its performative power – is drastically restricted. The recognition of a *topos* may be a beginning but should never be the end of criticism.[12]

Second, and more worryingly, genre is often treated as an ahistorical system: 'The genres are as old as organised societies; they are also universal',[13] writes Cairns in the most stringent rejection of the relevance of cultural context: 'In a very real sense antiquity was . . . a time-free zone'.[14] A genre is forever.[15] Such a grounding principle makes it necessarily hard to see any culturally or historically specific import of any particular work of literature through the lens of generic analysis at any rate. Third – and this point depends on the first two principles – genre is treated as a rigidly delimited subject. If a genre is defined by its formal characteristics, and exists in a 'time-free zone', it is hard indeed to bring it into contact with the essential frames of politics, desire and cultural change.

The texts that we call the ancient Greek novels and the Roman novels that seem to respond to them come into being only after Greece has been conquered by Rome. These narratives took up elements from earlier literature, but 'the novel' cannot be considered as 'universal' or 'as old as organised societies'. It is part of the flourishing of Greek and Latin prose in the empire, part of the changing world of empire culture. Looking at the novel as a genre involves broaching the question of why it appears when it does, how it relates to the literary culture of the period, and how its formal characteristics speak

---

12 See Conte (1996): 'genres are to be conceived of not as recipes but as strategies; they act in texts not *ante rem* or *post rem* but *in re*' (112).

13 Cairns (1972) 34.   14 Ibid. 32.

15 Bakhtin (1981) distinguishes the novel as 'the sole genre that continues to develop', the only genre 'younger than writing and the book' (1).

to the culture in which it is read. It will not do to look at the generic claims of the novel in purely formal terms, or as ahistorical, or as a bounded system. What makes the genre of the novel such a fascinating issue is trying to answer the overlapping questions of how the novel fits into literary history, and how the formal characteristics of these texts contribute to the cultural impact of this new type of fiction.

Is there a genre of the ancient novel?

It is no straightforward matter, however, to look at the ancient novel as a genre. There are, first of all, some pressing difficulties concerning the fundamental issues of the word 'novel' itself and the very recognition of the genre of the novel as a genre. The term 'novel' is not ancient.[16] There is no word used by ancient writers that links the books we refer to as 'the ancient novel' as an exclusive or defined category. There is an extensive range of generic vocabulary for different types of writing in the ancient world. A formalist critic like Menander Rhetor lists and defines the characteristics of many specific types of production (from wedding songs to *propemptikons*, or 'valedictory performances'); Lucian talks of his shifts between rhetoric and dialogue as generic choices; Quintilian's literary history refers to satire as specifically Roman; Ovid can write in his elegiac poetry about what elegiac poetry is; epic and tragedy are discussed as recognised types of literature. But no critic mentions the novel (or any similar term) as a category, or refers to our novels individually or collectively until many years after their heyday.[17] One of our most important sources for the traditions of Greek fiction is Photius, the ninth-century Byzantine bishop, who gives us summaries of various works: but even he has no term for the novel, and includes many texts in his survey of his library which we would hesitate to include as novels in this volume.

The Greek texts themselves only very rarely refer to their own composition. The terms they use are very general: 'erotic tales' (*erōtikoi muthoi*), is how the narrator of Achilles Tatius' *Leucippe and Clitophon* refers to the story that follows; the narrator of Longus' *Daphnis and Chloe* promises a 'text'

---

16 The term seems to appear first in the renaissance, particularly with regard to the short prose pieces of Boccacio (who is heavily influenced by the Roman novel, of course).

17 Scholars have come up with only three potential references to novels in all our literature of the period. Philostratus (*Lives of the Sophists* 524) in the third century refers to a work called *Araspes and Pantheia* maliciously circulated under the name of a rival by Celer; this is sometimes thought to be a novel (about which we know nothing, however); Philostratus also attacks one Chariton for his *logoi* (*Letter* 66), but we do not know if this is the (first-century) novelist. The emperor Julian sniffily dismisses 'fictions' (*plasmata*) 'in the form of histories, such as love stories and all that sort of stuff' (*Letter* 89b). The lack of any term to denote the novel even in these examples is patent.

(*graphē*) to 'rival (*antigrapsai*) a painting (*graphē*)'; Heliodorus, the latest and longest of the novelists, refers to his 'composition (*suntagma*) of the Aethiopic tales concerning Theagenes and Charicleia'; Chariton announces that his 'last book [or 'chapter', *suggramma*] will be most pleasant for the readers'.[18] *Logoi, muthoi, graphe, suggramma* and even *suntagma* are the most general terms for literary composition and give no sense of any specific generic affiliation. The Latin novels are no more explicitly marked: *fabula* (story), *sermo* (discourse), and the like.[19] In both the texts themselves and in the criticism of the ancient world there appears to be no recognition of a genre of the novel.

There are two different reasons, however, why it is contested how the term 'novel' may or may not be applied to these ancient texts. The first concerns readers' expectations. As we have seen in the first section of this chapter, genre is fundamental to the organisation of a reader's expectations, a reader's pleasures, a reader's engagement: in short, genre is an essential aspect of the reader's contract with a text. To name texts 'novels' is to establish such a contract. So if there is no ancient recognition of a genre of the novel, it can be argued that it will distort our understanding of the expectations of readers and writers to impose such a frame upon these texts. The response to such a criticism, as we will see shortly, is to reject it as excessively nominalist. That is, the non-existence of the *name* 'novel' in ancient Greek does not outweigh the fact that there are so many parallels of structure, form and theme between the different texts, and also that there are so many apparent manipulations of the expectations established by such parallels, that even without the name 'novel' these texts demonstrate all the marks of generic organisation. The first concern with using the term 'novel', then, is not simply whether such a critical concept existed in the ancient world, but what the implications of the presence or absence of such a term are for the ways an ancient reader or writer approached these texts.

The second worry concerns valorisation and status. The re-invention of the novel in the eighteenth century was a scandalous event. The first novels were difficult to classify, morally and intellectually, as were the emotions and reading practices involved. Yet already by the nineteenth century, the novel had become a privileged form of literature, and novelists such as Charles Dickens or George Eliot were – and remain – culture heroes (for all that a novel like *Madame Bovary* could appall and be immensely successful at the same time). The history of the novel has become a history of status as well

18 Ach. Tat. 1.2; Long. *Proem* 1; Hld. 10.41.4; Char. 8.1.4. See Bowie (1985). Whitmarsh (2005a) argues that the Greek novel is generically denoted by titling conventions.
19 On the proem of Apuleius see Kahane and Laird (2001); see also the sensible remarks of the introduction to Harrison (1999).

as of literary form, and it is no surprise that nationalism and other political demands have become integral to this history: French, Spanish and English critics, for example, tell the story of the rise of the novel with quite different national emphases. So too the novel is a crucial factor in the construction of a post-colonial culture and provides an essential part of the literature of feminism, say. Using the term 'novel' for these ancient texts raises a set of questions therefore for literary history, and for the standard accounts of the rise of the novel with their focus on the eighteenth century: are these ancient texts the 'true story' of the origin of the novel – rather than eighteenth-century England, Spain or France? To write a history of the novel that begins seriously with the Greco-Roman novel, one would need to trace, for example, a development through the Christian middle ages, and see how the suffering heroine of the ancient novel travels through Christian novelistic writing (such as the Pseudo-Clementine *Recognitions* along with saints' lives) towards the later moral heroines (with all their comic counterparts too). The politics of the rise of the novel in the eighteenth century would need to look back through the popular rediscovery of the ancient novel in the seventeenth century towards the politics of imperial fiction in antiquity. The forgetting of the ancient novel is itself an important strand of modern literary culture.[20]

Such a genealogy affects how the ancient texts are viewed. The Victorians in general found the novels distasteful: they were post-classical (secondary, derivative, second-rate), and they exhibited a 'foul, hypocritical sophistication',[21] which challenged the idealism of classical value: 'detestable trash', as Macaulay sniffed.[22] It is a contemporary critical commonplace that the modern re-evaluation of the ancient novel specifically rejects both the judgement of the Victorians and the ideology that supported such a judgement. The use of the word of 'novel' can be used to indicate this change of status, especially when set in contrast to the term 'romance'. '"Romance" is most often used in literary studies to allude to forms conveying literary pleasure the critic thinks readers would be better off without.'[23] (The difference between 'Romance' and 'Novel' is a problem especially in English: in French (novel = *le roman*), Italian (*il romanzo*) or German (*der Roman*) the distinction is harder to make.) 'Romance' is therefore commonly used defensively or dismissively with an eye on the all too common negative evaluations of the quality of the ancient Greek texts. It is striking that several of the earlier critical studies that began the re-evaluation of Greek fiction preferred 'romance': Perry's *The Ancient Romances* (1967), for example, or Hägg's *Narrative Technique in Ancient Greek Romances* (1971). Almost all of the very many

20 For one attempt as such a history see Doody (1996).
21 Rohde's phrase for *Daphnis and Chloe* (Rohde (1914) 549).
22 Quoted by Williamson (1986) 23.   23 Doody (1996) 15.

recent books on this subject, however, refer consistently to 'the novel', even when they note that 'romance' is the 'conventional' nomenclature. (Bryan Reardon, however, goes against this trend: he wrote on 'The Greek Novel' in 1969, edited *Collected Ancient Greek Novels* in 1989 (where however he refers to 'romances' in his introduction) and in 1994 published *The Form of Greek Romance*.) To refer to Greek prose fictions as 'the ancient novel' is also a valorisation of these works in the contemporary marketplace.

A similar journey from Victorian dismissiveness to modern approbation can be traced in the construction of the scene of reading. For many Victorian critics it seemed obvious that the readership for these books was largely made up of women or the vulgar (less well-educated, lower class). There is almost no reliable evidence for the readership of these books in our ancient sources, however, and this hypothesis seems to extend assumptions drawn from contemporary ideas about the readership of romance, in order to match ancient readers with the modern critics' judgement of the value of the ancient texts themselves. More recent considerations of a potential readership, however, have emphasized the high level of intellectual sophistication especially in the so-called sophistic novels (Longus, Achilles Tatius and Heliodorus, in particular), as well as the Roman novels of Petronius and Apuleius. These now seem texts fully imbued with the *paideia* (culture, education) of the literary elite.[24] The novels often seem to expect an acquaintance with the great texts of Greek literary tradition: Homer, Virgil, Plato, Thucydides and so on.[25] The discussions of characters in the novels find parallels in the elegant and poised prose of the second-century masters of rhetoric such as Lucian and Dio Chrysostom, as well as more scholarly types such as Plutarch or Aelian. What is more, the scenes of reading *in* the text are witty, knowing, and cultured.[26] Consequently, modern discussions have emphasised that the readership for the novels is likely to be similar to the readership for other texts of the second sophistic: a broadly educated and culturally adept elite. (It need hardly be added that this is likely to mean mainly men.) Recognising the genre of these prose fictions as 'the novel' comes hand in hand with a recognition of the texts' worth and an expectation of a sophisticated male audience.[27]

Nevertheless, despite these difficulties surrounding the recognition of the 'genre of the novel', putting the texts of Greek prose fiction together and

24 See Hunter (1983); Winkler (1985); Bartsch (1989); Zeitlin (1990); Goldhill (1995); Conte (1996); Morales (2004).
25 See Morgan and Harrison in this volume.
26 See Ach. Tat. 1.6.6 with Goldhill (1995) 70–1 on the erotics of books; see also Rosenmeyer (2001) 133–68 on letter-writing and reading.
27 See Bowie (1994a); Stephens (1994). Egger (1999) and Haynes (2003) wish to maintain a positive image of female readership. See also Hunter, this volume.

analysing them as a genre has proved a crucial move in their evaluation. The five extant Greek novels are grouped together usually as the 'ideal novel', so-called because they are all love stories in which an aristocratic young man and young woman of exceptional beauty fall in love, are separated and experience multiform adventures in the pursuit of their perfect love. The result is always a long-delayed but triumphant (re)union. Occasionally a case has been made to exclude one or other of the novels from the set (*Daphnis and Chloe* because it is pastoral, say), but such restrictions do not allow sufficiently for creative variety within the genre.[28] The 'ideal novels' are distinguished from a variety of other Greek prose writing of the same period – travelogues, fantastical or philosophical; collections of tales; biographies and the like. It is these five texts (together with fragments of several other possibly similar works) which are usually taken to instantiate the genre of the Greek novel.[29]

The Greek 'ideal novels' are also to be distinguished from the Roman novels. Petronius' *Satyrica* and Apuleius' *Metamorphoses* have Greek forefathers amid their multiform and multifarious ancestors:[30] Apuleius announces his text is a 'Milesian tale' and a 'Grecian story', which is usually taken to allude to the same book of which the Lucianic *Ass* is a briefer version;[31] Petronius, since Heinze, has been taken as a parody of the Greek 'ideal novel'.[32] But their aggressively vulgar, sexually explicit, and socially varied narrative world, full of inset narratives, satiric extremes, and shifting linguistic registers, seem peculiarly Roman. The two Roman texts were acknowledged in antiquity as having enough features in common to be classed together,[33] but they pose a further problem for the determination of the genre of 'the novel' as a genre. Are the Roman texts to be treated as a different culture's expression of the same turn to extended prose fiction – a national version of the genre of the novel, as it were? Or are they to be seen as a different type of literature, a satiric and carnivalised refraction of the privileged forms of Roman prose, which turn only a leery eye towards the world of Greek romance?

The determination of genre necessarily involves strategies of exclusion, and the boundaries of what is meant by 'the ancient novel' are especially open to contestation in the territory *between* Greek and Roman fiction. The Roman novels with their bawdy, picaresque priapism, coupled with their humiliation, riotous humour and outrageousness, are never known as 'Romances'. Yet the Roman texts' awareness of Greek material, as well as our modern interest in ancient fiction, makes a connection between the

28 See e.g. Fusillo (1989).   29 See Bowie (1985); Reardon (1991).
30 See Barchiesi (1986); Mason (1978) for discussion and bibliography.
31 See Mason (1978).   32 Heinze (1899).   33 Macrobius, *Dream of Scipio* 1.2.8.

Greek and Roman texts inevitable. Furthermore, the long history of the novel intertwines Greek and Roman fiction too. The Roman novel has a powerful impact through Boccacio and Rabelais right up to *Great Gatsby* and beyond, much as Heliodorus and Longus have a similarly instrumental effect on the development of European prose. Alongside the Greek novel, around which most issues of genre have clustered, the Roman novel runs a more disreputable, scurrilous, and parodic course.

There have been three main ways in which the recognition of genre has been essential to modern understanding of the Greek novels (each of which *mutatis mutandis* is also applicable to the Roman novels). The first is narratological. Seeing the novels together has allowed critics to explore with some sophistication the narrative techniques of these texts.[34] Heliodorus' *Charicleia and Theagenes*, for example, with its flashbacks, multiple story lines, and untrustworthy narrators, has itself been the subject of some exceptional analysis, but the very complexity of what is the latest of the five novels illumines and is illumined by the artful *faux* simplicity of *Daphnis and Chloe*, the cultivated élan of Achilles Tatius, and the dramatic surprises of Chariton. Each of these novels is a narration of a journey towards a climax in fulfilled love, and each, with a self-conscious delight in the twists and turns of narrative expectation and surprise, depicts the struggles of a young couple to reach union. The recognition of genre allows us to appreciate the sheer variety, skill and exuberance of these texts' narrative technique.

Second, seeing the novel as a genre requires a re-evaluation of its place in literary history. Every major genre – epic, tragedy, pastoral and so forth – is hard to define by means of a list of necessary and unique elements. The novel is more difficult than most. It seems to have so many ancestors (and friends and relations).[35] It clearly looks back to tales like Xenophon's stories of love and adventure in his *Cyropedia*; its love stories echo the plots of New Comedy; Hellenistic erotic myth like the Acontius and Cydippe story in Callimachus' *Aetia*, and Hellenistic rhetorical and philosophical training also filter through; its debt to second-sophistic rhetorical schools is even more strongly marked. It is only by viewing the texts together as a genre that the full scale of their genealogy and the full impact of their *bricolage* can be appreciated. The novelty of the novel can only be delineated when it is recognised how, as a genre, it is written in and against a long literary and cultural tradition.

---

34 See Hägg (1971); Winkler (1982), (1985); Morgan (1999); Fusillo (1989); Zeitlin (1999); Conte (1996); Rimell (2002); Whitmarsh and Bartsch, this volume – all with further bibliography.
35 See Rohde (1914); Hunter (1983); Goldhill (1995); Whitmarsh (2001a) – all with further bibliography.

Third, the flourishing of the genre of the novel has been taken as a sign and symbol of major ideological shifts in empire culture. On the one hand, none of the ideal novels shows any recognition of Rome, for all that the lovers travel the Mediterranean. The scene of the novels may be historical (Chariton), an idealised pastoral locale (Longus), or a generalised 'Greek World' (Achilles Tatius), but the realities of the Roman empire play no role at all. This is strikingly different from the other prose of the period, and from the Roman novels. Thus the novel as a genre is seen as a space to imagine Greekness without Rome: it is thus a telling source for understanding the construction of the image of Greek cultural identity in the empire.[36] On the other hand, the novel's projection and promotion of an idealised image of lovers of the same age, matched in desire, beauty, class and fortitude in their desire, has been seen to embody a move away from classical ideals of erotic subjectivity and erotic practice – part of the development of the conditions in which Christianity could flourish. Michel Foucault's *History of Sexuality* has been especially influential here: but classicists have responded with more careful and developed analyses.[37] The genre of the ancient novel, like the eighteenth-century novel, has found a significant place thus in the history of subjectivity and sexuality.

Reading the novel through genre

Identifying a 'genre of the novel' has been fundamental to their critical reception, then. In this third section of the chapter, I want to look at how a generic reading is particularly productive, and then, finally, raise a question about the delimitation of the genre of the novel.

Although there are many rhetorical, narrative and thematic resources which have been instrumental in constructing the idea of the genre of the novel as a genre, I want to outline here just one particular thematic nexus which is both basic to the plotting of the novels and essential to the conceptualisation of the genre as contributing to the history of sexuality and the self. This concerns the sexual activity of the hero and heroine and the idea of faithfulness and virginity (terms which will, of course, be central to Christianity's reworking of classical culture for its own new morality – as well as to the modern novel from *Pamela* to Molly Bloom). This brief discussion is designed to show how insightful it is to view the different texts as a generic system.

---

36 See Bowie (1970); Goldhill (2001a); Whitmarsh (2001a); Stephens, this volume and Connors, this volume.
37 See Morales, this volume for discussion and bibliography.

In Chariton's *Callirhoe* one of the many narrative surprises is that the lovers are married by the end of the first chapter. Both beautiful, both noble, both wealthy, their marriage seems blessed. It is only when Chaereas' jealousy, prompted by the disappointed suitors, results in the girl's apparent death (and then her snatching by pirates) that their separation takes place – a separation that, as for many erotic tales, grounds all the adventures to come. Chaereas pursues Callirhoe across the Mediterranean heroically. Callirhoe is not merely the object of desire for increasingly powerful figures (up to the Great King of Persia himself), but also marries a man called Dionysius, in whose house the child of Chaereas and herself is born, and left to grow up, when the lovers are finally re-united and return home to Sicily. It is striking that the heroine, like Helen of Troy, to whom she is compared, has more than one husband, while Chaereas chastely pursues his lost bride. The lovers' faithfulness to each other and their purity are not merely tested: the story also needs to negotiate the facts of Callirhoe's time abroad rather carefully . . .[38] For all that Chariton is an early novelist, perhaps the earliest, he nevertheless expects his readers to grasp the generic rules he flouts.

In Achilles Tatius, the heroine Leucippe would have been quite happy to sleep with the hero Clitophon in book 2, but her mother burst into her bedroom to prevent such a generic problem. She had had a nightmare that her daughter was being murdered by a robber, who had inserted a sword in her vagina and ripped her in two (2.23). (It is typical of Achilles Tatius' knowingness to write such a pointed dream.) When at the end of the novel, Leucippe has survived a time with pirates, and the violent sexual approaches of several men, she triumphantly – if not without irony – passes a virginity test. Clitophon, meanwhile, boasts to Leucippe's father that 'if there is such a thing as virginity in a man, that's what I have preserved for Leucippe up to this moment' (8.5). Clitophon has already described sex with women at length, based on his experience with prostitutes, and, most shockingly, has been successfully seduced in prison by a married woman. His first-person account of chastity and faithfulness underlines the considerable potential for disingenuousness and self-interest in love stories. Achilles Tatius' novel may end with the union of young lovers, but it has played many an ironic game with that model before its fulfilment.

In *Daphnis and Chloe*, the hero and heroine are so innocent that they do not even know the word *erōs*, and need to be taught every aspect of the facts of life. Although Chloe is briefly captured by the requisite pirates, the lovers are kept separate by ignorance more than geography. They wish to consummate their desire, they even lie down naked together, but are frustrated by

---

38 See Goldhill (1995) 127–32.

their own innocence. Daphnis is given sex education finally by an older (and self-interested) teacher, Lycaenion, a married woman who takes him into the woods. If Achilles Tatius delights in the knowingness of his characters, Longus finds ironic delight in his lovers' innocence: both take immense and sophisticated narrative pleasure in the potential ironies of the precarious journey towards the marital union which graces their final chapters.

Both the hero and heroine of Heliodorus' *Charicleia and Theagenes*, however, have to pass a virginity test in the final book, and both pass triumphantly. Charicleia has 'made a god of her virginity' (2.33.5), and, even more strikingly, Theagenes, although when they kiss becomes sexually excited, agrees to be chaste until their marriage and 'held out without difficulty and maintained his self-control (*sōphrosunē*), proving himself the master of his pleasure even when taken by desire' (5.4.5). In Heliodorus, for all the narrative games of this most complex of texts, virginity, faithfulness and self-control are constants.

The nature of this sense of self-control in Heliodorus can only be properly understood against the generic tradition of the ideal novel, and its games with sexual licence and chaste lives; similarly both the innocence of Daphnis and Chloe, and the knowingness of Leucippe and Clitophon make sense within and against such generic potentialities. While it is always incautious to generalise too broadly from our partial evidence, it is worth noting how these novels move from a heroine with two husbands, through novels which playfully maintain the chastity of its heroines while the hero enjoys the licence of double standards, to a more austere world where both hero and heroine are passionately committed to chastity. It is such a narrative of genre that has helped place the novel, as a genre, to the fore in the history of the culture of this formative period for the west.

Generic analysis is productive, then, but a worry remains. In the burgeoning Greek literary culture under the Roman empire, there are many types of prose writing, which also form a context and frame for the prose fictions I have been discussing. The hero of Achilles Tatius, for example, travels around the Mediterranean and comes into contact with – and comments on – strange sites, odd pictures, bizarre animals and perplexing events.[39] This can and must be seen in terms of the travels in Chariton, Heliodorus (and other novels) as well as the refusal of international travel in the pastoral novel of Longus. But it is also relevant that Pausanias produced his great account of travelling around Greece; that Philostratus' *Life of Apollonius of Tyana* is another lengthy prose narrative where a hero travels the world on a voyage of discovery (as in a very different way is Lucian's *True*

---

39 See Romm, this volume.

Stories or Diogenes' *Wonders beyond Thule*). The paradoxes Achilles loves find an echo both in the academic discourse of Plutarch or Aelian, and in the more outrageous work of Ptolemy Chennos ('the Quail'). The Lucianic (or Pseudo-Lucianic) *Ass* and *Love Stories* give a different light on erotic prose tales. Even the discussions of pictures and other sights seem close to the popular ecphrastic literature of the time.

This diffusion of prose, of prose narrative, of prose narrative about love (and travel), of prose narrative about love and travel written by sophisticated Greeks, trained in rhetoric, raises a question about the secure boundaries of the genre of the novel.[40] It may be harder to distinguish a genre of the novel or limit the genre, when each of our texts is put back into the frame of Greek *paideia*. Indeed, the novels seem to suppose – to express and help formulate, to 'summon' – a reading subject who is *pepaideumenos* ('educated', 'cultivated') a key term of value in Greek cultural life, a key way of expressing a privileged Greekness across cultural life in general in the empire.[41] As such, the novel texts are only one voice in the broad project of articulating an educated Greek engagement with the world.

The novel, as Bakhtin knew, is a polyphonic text. It draws other voices into itself, and makes us read other texts differently. The very porousness of its form means that if we are to give the novel a cultural context and understand its social and intellectual force as a genre, then we need to read novels not just as a genre but also as texts in constant and dynamic interaction with the intellectual and social life around them. Considering these texts as prose fictions within the full range of Greek prose writing, rather than as 'the genre of the novel', will give a different image of their social and intellectual impact. A full picture of 'the ancient Greek novel' needs both to see how the different works spark off each other, creating and playing with reader expectations, and yet to recognise how precarious and porous the genre of the novel is.

Further reading

Generic questions have focused particularly on the Greek rather than the Roman novel, because of the perception that the former are generically stereotyped (see e.g. Létoublon (1993)). This formalist approach, emphasising certain generically 'required' features, has in turn led scholars to try to identify which ingredients derive from which other genres (part of the legacy

---

40 Nimis (1994) goes so far as to argue that the 'novel is anti-generic, unable to be specified as a single style of discourse' (398). The novel is indeed a hybrid form, but this does not make it 'anti-generic'.
41 See Bowie (1970); Anderson (1989); Schmitz (1997); Whitmarsh (2001a); Goldhill (2001a).

of Rohde (1914)): see e.g. Kuch (1989), Reardon (1991), Ruiz-Montero (2003). Indeed, some scholars (partly under the influence of Bakhtin (1981), at least on one interpretation) have sometimes argued that the novel is not a genre at all: see Nimis (1994), and – from a different angle – Fusillo (1989, in Italian). Selden (1994) attempts to capture the novel generically under the heading of the rhetorical figure of syllepsis (arguing that the texts are generically disposed towards generating multiple readings). Whitmarsh (2005a) reasserts the claim for generic unity, on the basis of titling conventions. We now have, however, a much expanded view of the range of Greek fiction circulating in antiquity thanks to papyrus discoveries (Stephens and Winkler (1995)): this should caution against any easy generic assumptions based on the fully surviving texts alone.

In line with the general prejudice against the 'derivative' nature of Roman culture, the generic status of Roman novels has been explored predominantly in relation to Greek 'sources': see e.g. Heinze (1899) for Petronius as a parody of a Greek novel, and Jensson (2004) as a version of Odysseus' stories in the *Odyssey*; Mason (1978) on the Greek sources of Apuleius' *Metamorphoses*. The relationship with the genre of the 'Milesian tale' is also significant: see esp. Harrison (1998c).

12

ANDREW LAIRD

Approaching style and rhetoric

> One Day after this as she came into the Room where all we poor children
> were at Work, she sat down just over against me, not in her usual place as
> Mistress, but as if she set herself on purpose to observe me and see me Work:
> I was doing something she had set me do as I remember, it was Marking
> some Shirts which she had taken to Make, and after a while she began to
> Talk to me: Thou foolish Child, says she, thou art always Crying; (for I was
> Crying then) Prithee, What dost Cry for? Because they will take me away,
> *says I*, and put me to Service, and I can't Work House-Work; well Child,
> says she, but tho' you can't Work House-Work, as you call it, you will learn
> it in time, and they won't put you to hard Things at first; yes they will says
> I, and if I can't do it they will Beat me, and the Maids will Beat me and
> make me do great Work, and I am but a little girl, and I can't do it, and
> then I cry'd again till I could not speak any more to her.[1]

Style is an essential characteristic of the modern novel.[2] In the passage above,
from Daniel Defoe's *Moll Flanders*, it is not narrative technique so much as
the *style* – syntax, and the selection, arrangement and use of words – that
is crucial to Moll's portrayal of herself as a child. Verbal repetition ('thou
art always Crying; (for I was Crying then)') and paratactically arranged
sentences or phrases ('and I am but a little girl, and I can't do it, and then I
cry'd again') link the spoken dialogue of Moll's recollection to her present
discourse. The expression of these sentences has a childish quality, even
though it is really the adult Moll Flanders who is telling the story.

That effect in Defoe is related to an identifiable stylistic device that is common to the point of being almost ubiquitous in fiction in German, Russian
and the romance languages, as well as in English. This is the *merging* of the
voices of narrator and character known as 'free indirect discourse' (or 'FID'),
which can be illustrated by the following passage from Dostoyevsky's *The
Idiot*:

---

1 Defoe (1989) 47, discussed in relation to Apuleius at Laird (1990) 150–4. On Defoe's fictional
  style, see Columbus (1963).
2 This perception is shared by critics of varying persuasions including Cohn (1978), Shklovsky
  (1966), Genette (1980), Booth (1965), and practising novelists ranging from Forster (1964)
  and Ricardou (1967) and to Lodge (1992).

And why did he [Prince Mishkin] avoid going straight up to him and turn away as if he didn't notice anything, although their eyes had met. (Yes, their eyes had met! And they had looked at one another.) Didn't he himself, after all, want not long ago to take him by the arm and go with him *there*? Didn't he himself, after all, want to go to him tomorrow and say that he had been to see her? Didn't he himself, after all, renounce his demon on his way there, in mid-course, when suddenly joy flooded his soul? Or was there indeed something or other in Rogozhin, that is in *today's* whole image of the man, in the sum total of his words, gestures, behaviour, looks, that might justify the prince's terrible forebodings and the infuriating insinuations of his demon?[3]

Examples of FID abound in Jane Austen, Gustave Flaubert, D. H. Lawrence, Virginia Woolf, James Joyce . . . It is actually difficult to find novelists, past or present, respected or otherwise, who do *not* write sentences in this mode, and who do not seem to be writing them most of the time.[4] It is a technique that has been been seen to constitute the essence not only of the novel but of literariness itself. Yet classical authors employ FID only rarely.[5] And it is all the more striking – if little remarked upon – that this mainstay of fictional expression in our own epoch is hardly ever found in the 'novels' of antiquity.[6]

Style is just as essential to Greek and Roman fiction, although it works in a very different way. This first section of this chapter will review some practical differences between ancient and modern conceptions of style in this regard. Those differences in turn point to a fundamental categorical distinction between ancient romance and the modern novel – a distinction that recent scholarship has tended to play down. A short account of the properties of ancient fictional style will follow, but emphasis will also be laid on aspects that can be appreciated in translation. The final part will turn to rhetoric, the major determinant of fictional style in antiquity: there is the

---

3 Dostoyevsky quoted at Voloshinov (1973) 156.
4 See further Pasolini's thought-provoking 'Comments on free indirect discourse' in Pasolini (1988) 79–101. For other discussions of Dostoyevsky conceiving FID in ideological terms, see n. 8 below
5 De Jong (1987) 118–22 gives some examples from the *Iliad* which are classed (at 39) as 'implicit embedded focalization'; Perutelli (1979) considers FID in Virgil. Macrobius discussed FID in Virgil under the head of *addubitatio*: Laird (1999) 176–7. The only remotely comparable examples of this mode continuing for more than a couple of lines in classical literature are in Roman imperial epic (Ovid, *Metamorphoses* 8.24–42; Valerius Flaccus, *Argonautica* 7.296–330). The more flexible nature of indirect discourse in Greek makes the clear identification of FID more difficult.
6 No mention of FID is apparent in the thorough survey offered by Hägg (1971). Laird (1999) 106–7 considers stylistic devices that might correspond to FID in the first-person narratives of Petronius and Apuleius.

possibility that rhetoric, far more than being a mere adornment of fiction, may have been responsible for generating it in the first place.

Style, ancient and modern

In our own era, style is hardly ever considered an exclusively linguistic phenomenon.[7] It has been allied to political considerations by some critics who conceive it as reflecting changes in historical or literary-historical conditions of composition and reception: Voloshinov, for instance, regarded the passage of *The Idiot* quoted above 'as bound up with the transposition of the larger prose genres into a silent register, i.e. for silent reading'.[8] But style has been far more frequently linked to conceptions of realism and the very idea of representation itself (although these conceptions are never without political implications either).[9] In spite of occasional assertions to the contrary, the connection between style and representation underlies most narratological, rhetorical and other formalist approaches to modern fiction.[10] Erich Auerbach's *Mimesis: the Representation of Reality in Western Literature*, written more than fifty years ago, has been one of the most influential articulations of the connection between style and realism. It contains a celebrated treatment of Trimalchio's banquet in the *Satyrica*:

> The romance . . . *fabula milesiaca* ['Milesian tale'], the genre which doubtless includes Petronius' work, is – in the other specimens and fragments which have come down to us – so crammed with magic, adventure and mythology, so overburdened with erotic detail, that it cannot possibly be considered an imitation of everyday life as it existed at the time – quite apart from the unrealistic and rhetorical stylisation of its language . . . Now if Petronius marks the ultimate limit to which realism attained in antiquity, his work will accordingly serve to show what realism could not or would not do. The Banquet is a purely comic work. The individual characters, as well as the connecting narrative, are consciously and consistently kept on the lowest level of style in both diction and treatment. And this necessarily implies that everything problematic, everything psychologically or sociologically suggestive of serious, let alone tragic, complications must be excluded, for its excessive weight would break the style . . . In modern literature, the technique of imitation can evolve

7 The applications of stylistic criticism to English literature in Fowler (1981) and (1986) are explicitly socio-linguistic; the linguistic criticism of fictional style in Leech and Short (1981) presupposes a 'realist' (see my following discussion) conception of literature.
8 Voloshinov (1973). Compare the classic study of Dostoyevsky in Bakhtin (1984b).
9 For the twentieth century compare again Pasolini (1988) and the conflict between Brecht and Lukacs about socialist realism as well as n. 15 below.
10 See e.g. Booth (1965); Genette (1980); and the discussion of the 'reality effect' in Barthes (1982).

a serious, problematic, and tragic conception of any character regardless of type or social standing, of any occurence regardless of whether it be legendary, broadly political or narrowly domestic; and in most cases it actually does so. Precisely that is completely impossible in antiquity . . . on the whole the rule of the separation of styles . . . remains inviolate.[11]

Not everyone today will accept that Petronius' work is a straightforward example of the 'Milesian tale', or necessarily agree with the way that genre is characterised here.[12] Nor will it be conceded that *Dinner at Trimalchio's* is a 'purely' comical piece – leaving aside the rest of the *Satyrica*, this episode has its darker sides.[13] And it can also be countered that the separation of high, middle, and low styles *was* disregarded and challenged in ancient rhetorical and poetic theory as well as in practice, from the fifth century BCE onwards.[14] Nonetheless, Auerbach's study succeeded in showing that modern literary realism – the excerpts I have given from *Moll Flanders* and *The Idiot* may serve as examples – had no proper equivalent in classical literature. Even the parody of Trimalchio's Banquet is ultimately static and 'two-dimensional', according to Auerbach, because of Petronius' incapacity to probe or clarify the social historical forces that led to the forms of the Latin language apparently lampooned in the *Satyrica*.[15] And as a general rule, literary style is not an instrument of verisimilitude in ancient fiction. Richness, sophistication and variety there may be, but these attributes do not serve the end of realism; indeed they often run counter to it.

Any kind of story-telling will guarantee a minimum distinction between the style of a narrator's discourse and that of his characters (the latter are obviously more prone to speak in the first person or to make use of present and future tenses). But classical narrative adds very little to that minimum: it is quite normal for the words spoken or thought by characters in epic, historiography and fiction to conform to the stylistic tenor predominant in the narrative of the particular work to which they belong. Exceptions may occur in dialogues or in prose fiction when the context or function of a character's utterance happens to converge with the 'inclusion' of registers from another identifiable genre of writing.[16] A speech by Clitophon in Achilles Tatius' *Leucippe and Clitophon* provides an instance of this:

11 Auerbach (1953) 30–1.   12 On the 'Milesian tale' see n. 32 below.
13 Conte (1996) 182; Bodel (1994).
14 See e.g. Aristotle, *Rhetoric* 3.7 and Horace, *Art of Poetry* 89–98 (with the comments of Brink (1971) 174–97).
15 Auerbach (1953) 31–3. Anderson (1991) 23, 25 n. 37 is a response to Auerbach's reflections, in the realm of political and cultural theory. The study of political representation in Pitkin (1972) also has consequences yet to be developed for literary studies. Laird (1999) 247–58 considers the contemporary ideological significance of treatments of 'vulgar Latin' in the *Satyrica*.
16 See Morgan and Harrison in this volume, and n. 33 below.

At any rate it is love which the magnet feels for iron: and if the magnet may only see and touch the iron, it attracts it to itself, as if, within itself, it possesses a kind of erotic force. Is this not a show of affection of a loving magnet for the iron which is beloved? And about plants the pupils of philosophers say this – and I would call this argument a myth if the children of country folk did not say the same thing. The argument is as follows: that one plant can fall in love with another – and that a palm is more likely to be subject to desire – and they say that there are male and female palms . . .   (1.17–18)

Clitophon's adduction of various *exempla* to support his thesis here (he goes on to describe the 'marriage' between different running waters and the 'mystery of love' between reptiles) recalls the style sometimes employed by Plato's Socrates. Clitophon is using this cod-philosophising as a strategy to seduce Leucippe.[17] So the adoption of this artificial form of communication is really for the development of the story: it does *not* actually signal an effort on the part of Achilles Tatius to represent naturalistically the individual quality of Clitophon's typical manner of speaking. The fact that comparable intrusions of philosophical expression into characters' speeches in other Greek and Latin romances function in similar ways lends support to this conclusion.[18]

In sum, the routine attribution of distinctive lexical registers to specific personages *purely as a function of characterisation* is virtually absent from ancient fiction (the *Satyrica* included).[19] Also more or less absent, as we saw earlier, is the idiom of FID. These features are the very fabric of psychological portraiture which has been the *raison d'être* of the conventional novel for more than three centuries. Thus, irrespective of the interest and appeal that the ancient romances may have for many contemporary readers, the now widespread designation of these productions as *novels* is in a sense misleading, and it could rightly antagonise purist devotees of the modern form.[20] Of course calling works of Greek and Latin fiction 'novels' reflects a desire to commend and promote them – and this desire may provide one explanation for the current degree of reticence about style *per se* in recent critical

---

17 Compare Morales (1995) 41–3.
18 As well as the evocation of the *Symposium* by Philetas in Longus, *Daphnis and Chloe* 2.7 (discussed in the next section of this chapter), compare too Eumolpus in *Satyrica* 83, and *Apollonius, King of Tyre* 4–5, discussed at Laird (2005) 228–9. The inheritance of the stock character from drama (e.g. the nurse, the erotic instructor or *praeceptor amoris*), is indirectly aligned to questions of style, and could represent another impediment to naturalism in ancient fiction.
19 A distinction between the quality of Encolpius' diction and that of the freedmen affirmed in Smith (1975) xxi, 220, and elsewhere has little empirical basis: Laird (1999) 249–55.
20 Modern and early modern fiction can resemble ancient fiction; sometimes even specifically emulating it: cf. Lucian's influence on More's *Utopia* and Swift's *Gulliver's Travels* as well as the likely influence of Heliodorus on Johnson's *Rasselas* – but none of these works are 'novels' in the stricter sense.

discussions: style is the one quality which highlights, all too embarassingly, the formal gulf between ancient prose fiction and the modern novel.[21]

Aspects of ancient fictional style

There is another reason why style in ancient fiction has not received as much discussion as thematic and historical aspects of the genre. Study of ancient fiction, particularly the Greek novel, has been intensifying at a time when classical literature is being studied in translation more than ever before, and a wider range of it than ever before. This is a good thing but there is a consequent risk that recognition of all that is involved in assessing ancient fictional style in its own terms may be obscured. Many of the discursive features of modern style *can* be conveyed in translation – FID is common to most European languages – but the stylistic hallmarks of ancient fiction are not so easily rendered: registers of diction (use of poetic words, archaisms, neologisms, vulgarisms etc.) and particular forms of syntax and sentence arrangement cannot be directly or easily converted from one language to another. And particularly where Greek and Latin writing is concerned, rhythm, rhyme and other kinds of acoustic patterning are common features of *prose* literature – features that, though they may have originally been considered indispensable, will not be apparent to readers of Greek and Latin texts in translation.[22]

Longus, for instance, is a widely acknowledged master of verbal artistry: 'the ornate style of D[*aphnis*] & C[*hloe*] with its balanced phrases, rhymes, and assonances must at least in part, be an attempt to reproduce the characteristics of Greek bucolic poetry in which balance and antithesis are major organising principles'.[23] Longus' style also seems to have been heavily influenced by the forms of expression employed by the fifth-century rhetorician Gorgias of Leontini.[24] Some impression of the balances, parallels and antitheses can be given from an exemplary passage – the celebrated description of Love given to Daphnis and Chloe by the sagely cowherd Philetas (*Daphnis and Chloe* 2.7) – by breaking up the translated text into smaller verbal

---

21 The comparison of Heliodorus' penchant for neologism to that of James Joyce at Sandy (1982c) 79 may be legitimate, but it is symptomatic of the 'desire' referred to here. It must be significant that influential essay collections in English on Greek and Roman fiction, such as Tatum (1994), Morgan and Stoneman (1994), Hofmann (1999b), Swain (1999), Harrison (1999), do not contain specific discussions of style (if style is conceived as distinct from narrative technique).

22 Work on euphony and sound is important in this regard: Porter (1989), (2001).

23 Hunter (1983) 90. On balance and antithesis in Theocritus, see Dover (1971) xlv–xlviii, cited by Hunter. For a full study of Longus' style (in German) see Valley (1926).

24 Hunter (1983) 90.

units.[25] The resulting 'prose poem' gives something of the effect of the Greek, even though the rhymes and the numbers of syllables in the original cannot be retained:

> Love is a god, my children;
>> he is young,
>> beautiful,
>> and winged;
> and so he enjoys youth,
>> pursues beauty,
> and makes souls take wing.
>
> Zeus has not so much power as he has:
>> he rules the elements
>> he rules the stars,
>> he rules his fellow gods –
> more completely than you rule
>> your goats and sheep.

Thus presented, even this short excerpt obviously recalls the kind of antithesis and pairing of parallel expressions employed by Gorgias in his *Encomium of Helen* (8–9):

> Speech is a great prince,
>> who, with his most tiny
>> and most invisible body,
> accomplishes the most godlike works:
> for he has the capacity
>> to stop fear
>> to remove sorrow
>> to create joy
>> and to increase pity –
> I shall prove how this is so.[26]

There are also more general echoes of Plato – particularly the affirmation of the god's power and his association with youth in *Symposium* 195a.[27] And it is very possible that a sentence from later in Philetas' speech recounting how he suffered from Love as a young man:

25 This passage is from the translation of Longus by Christopher Gill in Reardon (1989) 306. The configuration of the text to convey its acoustic patterning is adopted from Hägg (1983) 37. McCail (2002) also adopts this technique.
26 The English version here is my own. See MacDowell (1982) 17–19 for discussion of Gorgianic prose style.
27 Morgan (2004a) 182–4 on this passage.

My soul was in pain;
my heart pounded;
my body was frozen

recalls Sappho fr. 31.5–6, a poem which seems to be echoed elsewhere in *Daphnis and Chloe*.[28]

Poetic qualities of this kind may be seen to enhance appreciation of the text under scrutiny even if they are not considered essential to its theme. However sometimes the particular choice and arrangement of words even in a short passage can bear directly on broader questions of interpretation.

An enumeration of the stylistic attributes of every ancient fictional author is beyond the scope of this short discussion, which, as its heading indicates, is only an approach to the subject. However it remains to point out that some features of style – on a more 'macro' level than diction or sound effects – can be detected in translation. Generic inclusiveness is one of the most frequently noted qualities of style in ancient prose fiction. For instance, the interweaving of prose and verse in the language of Petronius' *Satyrica* and the fragmentary Greek *Iolaus* explicitly signals that a process of generic absorption is going on.[29] 'Where there is style, there is genre.'[30] While genre is often the first recourse for modern scholars who seek to make sense of classical texts, in antiquity there was evidently far more abundant and explicit critical reflection on *style*, and study of genre seems to have resided primarily in the realm of stylistics.[31] Thus Apuleius, in the Prologue to his *Metamorphoses* (1.1), signals his work's membership of a generic community precisely in terms of style:

> But let me join together different stories in *that Milesian discourse* (*sermone isto Milesio*) . . . indeed this very change of voice (*vocis*) corresponds to the style (*stilo*) of switchback lore (*desultoriae scientiae*) that I have approached: I begin a story of Greek origin.

28 *Daphnis and Chloe* 1.17.4, 1.18.1. Hunter (1983) 73–6 offers a detailed discussion of the relation between Longus and Sappho.

29 The disjunction between the main text and the elements it incorporates becomes a palpable feature of the style of such fictional works (cf. Connors (1998); Courtney (2001) 20). This disjunction was possibly a feature of the Milesian tale; perhaps of Menippean satire too (Relihan (1993)). Compare too Bakhtin (1981) 5: 'The novel parodies other genres (precisely in their role as genres); it exposed the conventionality of their forms and language; it squeezes out some genres and incorporates others into its own peculiar structure, reformulating and re-accentuating them.'

30 Bakhtin (1986) 66.

31 Rosenmeyer (1985) and Farrell (2003) point to the relatively limited role of genre in ancient conceptions of discourse. Reassessments of the role of metre in Morgan (2000) and Cavarzere, Aloni and Barchiesi (2001) are also pertinent.

The text is linked to Milesian tales.[32] The Greek connection points to a general feature of ancient prose fiction which is *stylistic* as much as it is cultural: even if such fiction is in Latin, it involves Greek characters who inhabit a world that is predominantly Greek.

Allusion, as the passages excerpted above from Achilles Tatius and Longus have also shown, is a stylistic trait – and this becomes all the more evident if allusion is conceived in terms of intertextuality.[33] Verbal or phrasal echoes of other texts can sometimes be detected in translation. For example, the opening sentence of of Chariton's romance *Callirhoe*:

> Chariton of Aphrodisias, a clerk of the lawyer Athenagoras, will relate a love story that took place in Syracuse (1.1)

is well known for recalling the first sentence of Thucydides' *History*:

> Thucydides, of Athens, wrote the history of the war that the Peloponnesians and the Athenians waged against each other (1.1)

This is of more than passing significance: the echo helps draws attention to a sustained but subtle appropriation of the historian's 'omniscient' style that are to be found in *Callirhoe*.[34] The objects, modes and functions of such allusions vary from one text to another – an evocation of Livy in Petronius also bears on the style of the part of the *Satyrica* in which it occurs, with a different effect.[35]

Allusions like this alert us to another fundamental dimension of literary style: narrative technique. Narrative, though it is widely understood as the form of a story and thus amounts to the language or expression of a story, is conventionally conceived as a category distinct from style. This is probably because the salient features of *narrative* style in ancient fiction which are discussed elsewhere in this volume – the use of first or third person, embedded narrative, the presentation of characters' thoughts, and especially the rapid exchange of dialogue – can all be discerned in translation.

---

32 Courtney (2001) 20–1; Bitel (2001); Moreschini (1990); and Harrison (1998c) 61 all consider Milesian tales in relation to Roman fiction.

33 Intertextuality is, above all, a poetic feature of *language* and thus of style, as Kristeva who first coined 'intertextuality' makes clear: Kristeva (1981) 66. Laird (1999) 36–40 and Fowler (2000) 115–17 both distinguish intertextuality from allusion. See also Morgan and Harrison in this volume.

34 Traces of historiographical style in Chariton's language are discussed in Hägg (1971), 315–16, 329. See also Hunter (1994).

35 The rape recounted by Lucretia at Livy, *History* 1.58.2 is recalled in *Satyrica* 9.2–5: as in Livy, the victim's objections are not given in direct speech; as in Livy, Petronius has the victim's account ascribe direct discourse to the assailant instead.

Rhetoric and style

Rhetoric is sometimes implicitly and misleadingly identified with style.[36] However, while literary production, ancient and modern, could be seen (from a formalist perspective) as *consisting* in the aspects of style outlined above, the relationship of rhetoric to literature is complex and varied. Rhetoric is both part of ordinary linguistic behaviour (as it involves the innate abilities of anyone who speaks or writes) and is an attempt to control and manipulate language itself in order to influence addressees, audiences or readers (as an 'art' of speaking).[37]

The potency and centrality of rhetoric in Greek and Roman literature risks being underrated because of a routine conception of rhetoric as something which has a subservient or ancillary role. Rhetoric is mistakenly regarded as a supplementary tool an ancient author uses once he has worked out his general purpose: thus it is generally considered as a non-essential attribute of a text, rather than as something which invigorates, informs or even causes that text to come about in the first place. Some light can be thrown on the relation between rhetoric and ancient fiction by consideration of the seventh or 'Euboean' oration by Dio of Prusa, a Greek orator and historian who was born in the middle of the first century CE. The oration begins as follows:

1. I shall now relate something I saw myself, not something I heard from others. Perhaps garrulousness is natural for an old man and he does not easily reject any subject that comes his way – something just as true of a wanderer as it is of an old man. The reason for this is that both have experienced many things which they take pleasure in remembering. Anyhow I shall tell of the kind of people I came upon in practically the centre of Greece and the kind of life they lead.

2. I happened to be sailing across from Chios with some fishermen in a very small craft at the end of the summer season. A storm broke and we barely got over to the Hollows of Euboea in safety. The crew ran their boat up on a rough beach under the cliffs and scuppered it. They then went off to some purple fishers who had anchored at a nearby breakwater, as they intended to stay there and work with them.

3. Left alone, not knowing in what town I could seek safety, I wandered about along the seashore in case I might see any ships sailing past or riding at anchor. Having gone on for some distance without seeing any person at all,

36 The index entry for 'style' ('*See* **rhetoric**'!) in Reardon (1991) 193, a study devoted to the 'form' of Greek romance, illustrates this well enough.
37 This dual significance is something Aristotle sets out very clearly at the beginning of his *Rhetoric*: Solmsen (1941); Rorty (1996).

I came upon a deer which had just fallen from the cliff edge to beach where it was lapped by the waves but still breathing. And after a moment I thought I could hear the barking of dogs from above – but only just, on account of the noise from the sea.

4. After I went on and with some difficulty got up to a high place, I saw the dogs running around and confused: I realised the animal had been forced by them to jump down from the cliff. Then a moment later I saw a man, a hunter by his dress and appearance . . .

5. He then asked me 'Stranger have you seen a deer running away here?' I replied to him 'There he is – in the surf'. And I led him and pointed it out. Then he dragged it from the sea and cut off its hide with a knife . . .

(Dio of Prusa, Oration 7.1–5.)

The slow pace and considerable detail of this narration are unusual for the beginning of a speech, but these elements would be conventional at the opening of a fictional work. The speaker's claim to present an account of something he experienced is no less conventional – and it helps to frame and introduce the actual narrative, which begins at 7.2. The mention of a sea voyage and shipwreck so early in the action will further incline modern readers who know the Greek romances to feel that they are in a familiar realm. There are two echoes of the *Odyssey*: the speaker's promise here at the end of 7.1, 'to tell of the kind of people I came upon' recalls 'He saw the cities and knew the minds of many men' (*Odyssey* 1.3); and 7.4, 'After I went on and with some difficulty got up to a high place' recalls a routine formula (e.g. *Od.* 10.97). The excerpt here also shows that this first-person narrative contains short pieces of dialogue as well as records of the narrator's impressions and thoughts.

The hunter invites the speaker to his home and during their journey he explains the circumstances of his family (7.10). He goes on to tell an embedded story (7.22–63) which turns out to be longer than the first-person narrative that encloses it. The hunter describes the only time he journeyed to the nearby city: his lowly existence became the subject of debate in the assembly about his alleged failure to pay rent for living on common land. The original narrator then takes the floor – to describe the hospitality he receives from the hunter and the love between a young boy and girl in the household whose marriage he is invited to attend (7.80). This section of the text has often been directly compared with Longus' *Daphnis and Chloe*.[38] The entire narrative amounts to twenty-five or thirty pages – but then there is an abrupt change:

---

38 Hunter (1983) 66–7 and Russell (1992) 9 cite specific convergences.

Now I have not told this long story idly, or, as it may seem to some, merely to spin a yarn, but to present an illustration of the manner of life that I propounded at the beginning and of the life of the poor – an illustration drawn from my own experience for anyone who wishes to consider whether in words and deeds and in interactions with each other the poor are less well off than the rich because of their poverty, where living a harmonious and natural life is concerned, or whether they are better off in every respect.   (Dio of Prusa, *Oration* 7.81)

It is revealed that the preceding narrative has served as a parable or *exemplum* to illustrate the speaker's forthcoming arguments.[39] The subsequent part of the oration is almost as long as the story that has gone before: it thus stands in virtual equivalence to it. But there is no apparent tension between the exemplary tale and the argumentation it heralds. The facility of the transition engineered here indicates the interdependence of the two parts of this text: neither the narrative nor the sermon which follows it has evident priority. Such a paradigm suggests the extent to which rhetoric and argument might have been 'built into' the conception of the romances which this oration so clearly resembles.

The works of second sophistic orators and savants have many elements in common with the works of fiction produced in the same period: descriptive ecphrases, sustained disquisitions on specific themes or dilemmas were all as much elements of oratory as they were of romance. The tendency to ask who imitated whom – did writers of romance follow orators or was it the other way round? – may itself be symptomatic of a modern enthusiasm for essentialising the 'ancient novel' as a firm generic category. In any case, it is easy to see how text-book problems set for students of public speaking could have mutated into plots for romances and vice versa.[40] A two-way traffic on these lines may have obtained in imperial Rome. This short theme for declamation from the *Controversies* of the Elder Seneca could easily pass as an epitome of an ancient romance:[41]

PROSTITUTE PRIESTESS
A virgin was captured by pirates. She was bought by a pimp and became a prostitute. She asked for an allowance from those who came to her. When she could not get anything from a soldier who came to her, she killed him when he struggled with her and used force. She was accused, acquitted, and returned to her kinsfolk. She seeks a priesthood.   (Seneca, *Controversies* 1.2)

---

39 Anderson (2000) and Said (2000) consider Dio's use of narrative.
40 This idea goes back to Rohde (1914).
41 For an introduction to the *Controversies*, see Winterbottom (1974). Bonner (1949) is still an indispensable introduction to the whole subject of declamation.

Arguments for and against the girl's suit are then rehearsed by different speakers – allowing the narrative to be developed and embellished as the case is discussed. Unfortunately no contemporaneous discussions of the *Greek* romances survive to let us know whether they had an educational function in the Hellenic world which might have been comparable to that of the declamatory scenarios in Seneca's *Controversies*. However, Roman literature has bequeathed us Encolpius' criticism of the detrimental effect declamatory illustrations like Seneca's can have on public speaking in Petronius' *Satyrica*:

> When they come into the courtroom, [students] think that they have been trans-ported into another world. And so I think that the poor young men are turned into complete idiots by the schools, because they do not hear or see anything in those places which bears on practical life. Instead they are confronted with pirates standing in chains on the beach, tyrants writing edicts which order sons to cut off their fathers' heads, oracles given in response to a plague urging that three or more virgins be sacrificed. *(Satyrica* 1.1)

Encolpius is against the use of such scenarios in a rhetorical education because, he says, they are unrealistic. But there is a further irony here, which many readers of Petronius seem to miss: Encolpius' speech is taking *us* out of our own world into a fictional realm where the sorts of circumstance he enumerates here will turn out not be so far-fetched after all: Encolpius him-self will be declaiming alone on a beach abandoned by his companions; his best friend is soon to rape and kidnap his lover; and he will be submitting himself to a variety of humiliations to cure the impotence he attributes to Priapus. Thus Petronius offers what turns out to be a reflexive comment on the mutation of such quandaries into novelistic plots – a comment that is borne out as the *Satyrica* proceeds.

First-person fiction is closer to oratory than any other kind of writing although the connections between the two have yet to be explored in depth. It is no coincidence that the only other major work of Latin prose fiction – Apuleius' *Metamorphoses* – was written by an author who was celebrated as an orator in his own lifetime.[42] Rhetoric pervades the *Metamorphoses*. A specific episode can serve to highlight the complexity of its influence. At the end of book 2, the narrator, Lucius, relates how he and a manservant ran into some trouble, as they returned drunkenly to his lodgings:

> The light on which we were relying was put out by a sudden gust of wind, so that we could hardly free ourselves from the darkness of improvident night. Stubbing our toes on the pavement we returned to our lodgings in exhaustion.

---

42 Harrison (2000) has highlighted the *Metamorphoses* as the work of a Latin sophist. See also Tatum (1979) 136.

Just as we approached, supporting each other – behold – three stocky, sizeable figures were breaking down our doors with all their strength and they did not seem in any way deterred by our presence, but in a contest of strength which was all the greater they carried on the beating all the more intensively. They looked to both of us – and to me especially – like robbers of the most ruthless sort. So I immediately drew the sword that I had concealed in my cloak for occasions just like this. Without hesitating I flew into the midst of the thieves and I ran each of them through, as I struggled with them in turn, until, finally, they gasped out their breath at my feet, pierced with several gaping wounds.   (*Metamorphoses* 2.32)

The next day Lucius finds himself on trial for the murder of three men. This is exactly the sort of dilemma with which the rhetorical schools would test a student's expertise. In Apuleius' story, though, the predicament seems to be for real. Lucius' defence speech will be considerably longer than the original narrative and his presentation to the court of the events he has already related opens with a *captatio benevolentiae*, an appeal to his listeners' goodwill:

But if your kindness will grant me a public hearing for a little while, I shall easily inform you of the fact that I am not on this capital trial through any fault of my own.   (*Metamorphoses* 3.4)

In its resemblance to the appeal to the reader at the opening of the *Metamorphoses* itself, this instance of declamation is paralleled to the very work of fiction we are now reading:

But let me join together different stories in that Milesian discourse, and caress your kindly ears with a charming whisper.   (*Metamorphoses* 1.1)

Hyperbole, vivid detail, and embellishment (including direct discourse) which are as much the stuff of fictional invention as they are of oratorical narrative find their way into Lucius' declamatory version of the previous night's events:

I saw some extremely ruthless robbers trying the entrance and endeavouring to tear away the doors of the house by wrenching out the hinges. Once they had violently torn off all the bolts which had been precisely set in place, the robbers directly began to deliberate with each other about the elimination of the inhabitants. The one whose hand was readier and bulk larger was egging on the others like this:

'Come on boys, let's attack with our manly courage and vigorous strength while they're sleeping. Drive all hesitation and all cowardice from your hearts. Let murder stroll through the house with sword drawn. Anyone who lies asleep should be slaughtered and whoever may try to fight back should be struck down. That way we'll come out safely, if we leave no one safe in the house.'

Citizens, considering it the duty of a good citizen, and at the same time fearing greatly for my hosts and myself, I confess, I charged on those desperate thieves to rout them and frighten them off with the little sword which accompanies me for dangers of this sort. (*Metamorphoses* 3.5)

In this new narrative offered to the court, Lucius' servant has been airbrushed away. Now that he is on trial, Lucius has spun the story in such a way as to elicit commendation as well as sympathy from his audience:

I thought that I would not only be free of guilt, but also truly worthy of public praise. (*Metamorphoses* 3.6)

The reader has been shown how a model declamation (this defence speech) can be developed from the dilemma posed by a 'controversy' (here represented by Lucius' awkward situation in the wake of the previous night's events).

However, the speech does nothing to convince the judges who propose the defendant be tortured, since it is unlikely that he could have killed three able-bodied men alone. But first Lucius is compelled to uncover the bodies of those he murdered. This leads straight to the astonishing *dénouement*: the 'victims' are three inflated wineskins, which were slit in the places where he thought he had stabbed the robbers. Lucius has become the laughing-stock of the crowd assembled in the theatre. For the reader this is unsettling: Lucius' earlier account of events and the speech he gave in his defence are simultaneously exposed as fabrication. The past few hours presented in the story prove to be nothing more than the construction of a controversy that has turned out – even in the realm of this story – to be purely imaginary. Within the frame of the very text we are reading, rhetoric, like the empty inflated wineskins, has generated something out of nothing.[43] Indeed the *Metamorphoses* itself can be read as a protracted speech by an accomplished rhetorician who applies persuasion to his audience – possibly even to the extent of convincing them of the truth of his story.[44] Pragmatically, fiction and rhetoric can virtually be equated: both work on the levels of content and form; both of them can trick us in a disquietingly similar way.

The overt reference to declamation in the *Satyrica* and the marked applications of its techniques in the *Metamorphoses* show that an increase of

---

43 The image of the 'inflated wineskins' may have a bearing on the excesses of declamatory rhetoric. At *Satyrica* 1, declamation is characterised as 'swollen in subject matter and the emptiest clatter of phrases'.

44 See n. 42 above.

self-consciousness about the role of rhetoric in fiction accompanied the adoption and customisation of the form of the Greek romance by Petronius and Apuleius. In that respect alone, the work of these two Latin writers could provide us with a valuable foothold when it comes to interpreting the productions of their Greek predecessors and contemporaries. Perhaps the authors who developed prose fiction in Greece should be regarded primarily as rhetoricians – especially given that so many of its conventions are also conventions of second sophistic rhetoric, which follow the prescriptions of rhetors such as Hermogenes and of the authors who set out rules for rhetorical composition.[45]

Descriptions of nature, places, artworks, objects, and individuals, the pathologies of love and other emotions, para-philosophical disquistions, set-piece speeches – all these elements that we tend to regard as the essential *content* of the novel are capable of evaporating into the forms and topics of conventional post-Aristotelian rhetoric. The very conception of fiction, after all, depends on a form of persuasion: 'recounting imaginary events, which yet could have occurred'.[46] On this basis, apprehension of rhetorical style proves central to an understanding of the nature of ancient fiction. While style is essential to modern fiction in one way (because it facilitates naturalistic representation), it is no less essential, in other ways, to the fiction of antiquity. Moreover, through the mediation of rhetoric, style might help to account for the very genesis of what is now known as the ancient novel.

Further reading

Walter Pater's 1889 essay, 'Style' (reprinted in Pater (1973)), and Lucas (1955) are classic discussions. The influential theory of the 'autonomy of styles' developed in Wolfflin (1917) is also important for literary theory and criticism. In the wake of Russian formalism and French structuralism respectively, Sebeok (1960) and Chatman (1971) – which contains Roland Barthes' essay 'Style and its image' – are valuable collections. An important new philosophical exploration of language as the embodiment of an individual voice by Kenaan (2005) has further theoretical implications for conceptions of literary style as a kind of autograph. Auerbach (1953) is still the best panoramic

---

45 See Kennedy (2003).
46 *Rhetoric to Herennius* 1.13: 'The kind of narrative based on the exposition of events has three forms: legendary *(fabula)*, historical *(historia)*, and realistic *(argumentum)*. The legendary tale comprises events neither true nor probable, like those transmitted by tragedies. The historical narrative is an account of exploits actually performed but removed in time from the recollection of our age. Realistic narrative recounts imaginary events, which yet could have occurred, like the plots of comedies.' Compare Cicero, *On Invention* 1.27, *In Defence of Sextus Roscius Amerinus* 47, and Quintilian, *The Education of the Orator* 2.4.2.

account of style and representation in literary history; Cohn (1978) is illuminating on the modern novel; Leech and Short (1981) has a more explicitly linguistic perspective. Many studies of fictional style have been heavily influenced by narratological method: especially Rimmon–Kenan (1983), Genette (1993) and Cohn (1999).

On the Greek novel: Bakhtin (1981) is a literary-historical overview of novelistic style; Perry (1967) is more empirical; Reardon (1991) and Hägg (1971) are detailed discussions. Hägg (1983) contains many observations on individual authors. For style in Longus, see Hunter (1983) 84–98. On Heliodorus, the chapter entitled 'Embellishing the story' at Sandy (1982c) 75–89 is helpful; see too Feuillatre (1966).

For the Roman novel: von Albrecht (1989) treats Petronius (125–35) and Apuleius (167–76). Specifically on Petronius, Petersmann (1999) and Connors (1998) are wide-ranging discussions. On Apuleius: Finkelpearl (1998) is a thought-provoking study of literary expression; Callebat (1968) and (1978) are linguistic and historical in approach; Tatum (1975) 135–59 is a very accessible survey. Essays in Kahane and Laird (2001) offer closer insights on style in Apuleius and other ancient fictional authors. O'Hara (1997) is a paradigmatic treatment of ancient literary style.

13

JOHN MORGAN AND STEPHEN HARRISON

Intertextuality

1. THE GREEK NOVEL

John Morgan

Texts are not written or read in a cultural vacuum. Their ability to signify derives from and is defined by their relations to the whole corpus of pre-existing literature. Texts therefore cannot be straightforward, self-contained vehicles of their authors' intended meanings, but must be read through and within a complex cultural matrix. These are truths universally acknowledged, and the cluster of ideas that they represent is conveniently termed *intertextuality*.[1] Intertextual relations can, of course, be relatively simple or complex; authors can use them knowingly or unawares, actively or inertly. Although classicists have started to use the word *intertextuality* only recently, they have long been aware of the notion it denotes. Classical literature is congenitally and compulsively allusive; commentaries on classical texts traditionally make a practice of accumulating parallels, albeit often without much explicit sense of their allusive weight or interpretation of its function. *Allusion*, however, is included in but not coterminous with *intertextuality*: an allusion is something an author makes, deliberately, perhaps decoratively, perhaps with profound meaning; intertextuality is a property of texts when actuated by their readers, and not necessarily consciously deployed by their authors; it may relate to a specific intertext, but equally to a more general literary praxis.

It is obvious that the Greek novels are, in certain respects, similar to each other, and also to other literary forms. Earlier scholarship tended to interpret these shared features in one of two ways. Either they were indices of the novel's poverty of invention and its parasitic relation to the 'great authors' of the classical period. Or else they were evidence for the novel's origins

---

1 The term was coined by Julia Kristeva, whose ideas, developed by Barthes and other theorists, have a much wider field of vision than that pursued in this essay; for introduction to intertextual theory, see Allen (2000).

in a particular preceding genre, from which various scholarly narratives of emergence and evolution might be constructed. Such ideas now seem rather quaint: to us it is clear that this last-born in the litter of classical genres was forever self-consciously labouring to legitimise itself, and that its appropriation of other authors and forms is better understood as the negotiation of a respectable position within a self-validating literary tradition. And, far from being mere borrowed plumage, many of the allusions in the novels are in sophisticated and intelligent dialogue with important intertexts. It should come as no surprise that the new meanings so generated are as often commentaries on literature as visions of 'life': intertextuality is a defining feature of literariness, and we no longer disesteem the novels for not offering a naive mimesis of reality. In this inevitably cursory survey, it will be impossible to catalogue the intertextualities of the novels, or even fully to map the terrain. Instead, I shall first briefly examine how the genre as a whole locates itself in relation to genres such as epic, drama or historiography. Second, I shall glance at two of the novels, those by Longus and Heliodorus, in more detail by way of illustration. Finally, I shall consider ways in which these writers were in dialogue with their own genre.

The bulk of the surviving novels were composed in the second century CE, the period of the so-called second sophistic, when the Greek elite was re-forming a cultural identity for itself by re-enacting the glorious past. The novels play to this agenda, both in terms of their dramatic date and settings, but also in their annexation of classical forms and themes. As texts of extended narration, their obvious points of contact with the forms of the classical tradition were epic and historiography, while their plots of love and intrigue find their point of reference in Athenian New Comedy.

The earliest novel to survive complete, Chariton's *Callirhoe*, tells the story of a beautiful woman with two husbands, the first of whom goes east in search of her; the story climaxes in a war in which west confronts east, and eventually the heroine is recovered by her first husband. The broad analogy with the story of Helen, abducted by Paris and reclaimed by Menelaus in the Trojan War, is obvious. The narrator underlines the Homeric resonances by frequently quoting *verbatim* from the *Iliad* and the *Odyssey*.[2] At one level these quotations serve as meta-literary markers of generic affiliation, applicable not just to Chariton's own text but to the whole genre of which it is a member. At another they activate meanings specific to Chariton. A series of quotations, for instance, assimilates the love of Chaereas and Callirhoe to the Iliadic relationship between Achilles and Patroclus. This not

---

2 Müller (1976); Laplace (1980); Biraud (1986); Fusillo (1990); Manuwald (2000); Hirschberger (2001).

only elevates the general tone of Chariton's narrative, but casts Chaereas as a new Achilles, so that his anger and jealousy, which power the early stages of the plot, become a re-writing of the wrath of Achilles, and his apparently uncharacteristic emergence as a strategic genius and leader of men a counterpart of Achilles' martial supremacy. At the same time, the quotations draw attention to the distances between novel and epic: the values of heterosexual bourgeois romance and its players gain specificity and identity through being compared to, and thus differentiated from, those of epic homosexual passion and heroism.

Similarly, Callirhoe is distinguished by comparison from the Homeric Helen. But simultaneously she is assimilated to Penelope, the archetypal faithful wife, reunited with her husband after a protracted chain of adventures.[3] The *Odyssey*, with its combination of travel adventures and marital reunion validated as a correct narrative destination, is the principal foundation-text of romance. To greater or lesser degree, and with varying degrees of specificity, all the novels are descants on the second Homeric epic.[4]

Epics, of course, are written in verse, and the transposition of verse genres into prose is characteristic of Greek literature of the imperial period. But novels from their inception also related to the primary classical prose narrative form: historiography. All novels maintain the pretence that their story is true, though the knowingness with which they play with this pretence is a good index of their levels of sophistication. The *Ninus Romance* takes its principal characters from what was perceived as oriental history. Chariton's story is written in the interstices of real history, using Thucydides as background, while the fragmentary *Metiochus and Parthenope* fills in the gaps in Herodotus, its protagonists being the son of Miltiades and the daughter of Polycrates, tyrant of Samos.[5] More importantly the narrators of the earliest novels represent themselves in the manner of historians: Chariton's novel opens with a statement of identity and theme closely modelled on the openings of Hecataeus, Herodotus and Thucydides, and his narrative stance and mannerisms are based on those of the historian Xenophon.[6] It is no coincidence that apart from Xenophon of Ephesus we know of at least two other novelists named Xenophon, presumably pseudonymously.[7] Even

---

3 At 5.5.9 Callirhoe's appearance in the courtroom at Babylon summons quotations from the Trojan elders' reaction to Helen (*Iliad* 3.146) and the suitors' response to the appearance of Penelope (*Odyssey* 18.213).
4 The most explicitly Odyssean is Heliodorus, discussed in more detail below.
5 Hunter (1994); Maehler (1976); Hägg (1985).   6 Morgan (2004b).
7 Xenophon of Cyprus and Xenophon of Antioch, both listed in the Byzantine lexicon known as the *Suda*.

more emancipated novelists such as Longus and Heliodorus never entirely jettisoned this historiographical pose.[8]

While introducing himself historiographically Chariton's narrator nevertheless identifies his subject-matter as a love story. From the opening sentence there is a pervading tension between form and content, each intertextually aligned with a different genre. The erotic intrigues of the typical novel-plot correspond more closely to the plot of Menandrian comedy than to anything else, and if we had more of Menander's plays we would doubtless recognise allusions to specific plays that now elude us.[9] Even so, we can identify several almost-quotes in Chariton, particularly in the form of erotic maxims, functioning, as do the Homeric references, as signs of generic proximity and shared values. Other novels employ New Comic character-types, such as the clever slave (Satyrus in Achilles Tatius), or the parasite (Gnathon in Longus, his very name echoing comic models).[10] The sub-plot at the beginning of *Charicleia and Theagenes* is set in Athens and deliberately engineered on comic lines, forming a significant moral antithesis to the main plot.[11] But, as with epic, the transposition of material from one form to another draws attention to important differences. Although the novels make copious use of dramatic scenes, and even make frequent allusions to their own theatricality, their narrative form liberates the action from the physical restrictions of the dramatic stage. Novel-plots range across the whole known world, and include incidents too spectacular ever to be staged. So, whereas in the case of epic the novels renegotiate the ethics of the earlier genre within a formal similarity, with comedy there is a sense of re-inventing and improving on the comic form while retaining much of its generic value-system.

It is hardly a surprise that the relative sophistication of the novels is reflected in the use each makes of intertextuality. In this respect, as in most others, Xenophon's *Anthia and Habrocomes* seems the most primitive of the five. On the other hand, the novels of Achilles Tatius, Longus and Heliodorus, as well as being narratologically the most complex, are also those that most reward intertextual exploration. I am going to concentrate on the latter two, simply because between them they cover the broadest spectrum of intertexts and use them in a number of interesting ways.

Longus' *Daphnis and Chloe* is unique in being a 'pastoral romance'. This means in effect that Longus has produced a hybrid between the conventional plot-shape of the novel (albeit eccentrically modified) and a setting derived substantially from Theocritean pastoral. Scholars have not been slow to

---

8 Longus' narrator terms his work 'a history of love' (1.1.1); for Heliodorus see Morgan (1982).
9 Crismani (1997) pushes the evidence to its limits.   10 Morgan (2004a) 229 for details.
11 Paulsen (1992); Bowie (1995).

identify the many and often subtle allusions to Theocritus, and to interpret the ways that Longus exploits them.[12] It is common enough for Longus to take a motif from Theocritean pastoral and recast it in narrative form. So for example, the amoebean songs of Theocritus' shepherds are transposed as a contest in which Daphnis and the cowherd Dorcon each extols himself (in prose naturally), but this contest becomes an important plot-engine when Chloe awards Daphnis the prize of a kiss, so awakening his first feelings of love. The key symbol of Theocritean pastoral, the 'ivy-cup' (*kissybion*) which forms the basis of a vivid description (*ekphrasis*) in the first *Idyll*, reappears as a gift from Dorcon to Chloe (1.15.3), and one of its scenes – a boy weaving a cricket-cage, itself a programmatic representation of Alexandrian poetry's artful intricacy, musical sweetness, and retreat from unpleasant reality – is literally enacted when Daphnis himself makes a cricket-cage (1.10.2); the narrative even repeats the Theocritean neologism *akridothēra* for this cage.[13]

Longus' use of Theocritus is not passive or unreflective, however. The most important single reference to the pastoral poet consists in the name of the hero, Daphnis. But whereas in Theocritus' programmatic first poem Daphnis is dying of mysteriously unhappy love, Longus' novel traces how he and Chloe discover the joys of requited love and, through it, of marriage, family and social continuity. This is a radical contradiction of a central Theocritean theme, and in a sense the story of Daphnis and Chloe is a didactic one of movement from the idea that love is a sickness in need of cure to recognition of it as the supreme good in human life. Longus, in other words, engages with an intertext to communicate his own vision. This dialogue is focused by one of the closest allusions to be found in any of the Greek novels. At the beginning of his eleventh *Idyll*, Theocritus writes:

> There is no other medicine for love, it seems to me, Nicias, neither ointment nor powder, than the Muses. (11.1–3)

In Longus, the shepherd Philetas, having given Daphnis and Chloe their first lesson on the 'name of love', tells them:

> There is no medicine for love, nothing that can be drunk or eaten or uttered in song, except a kiss and an embrace and lying down together with naked bodies. (2.7.7)

Longus here replaces the pessimistic belief that a lover's only recourse is to pour his heart out in song with an optimistic suggestion that all love requires is acceptance and consummation. The point gains intertextual force by being

---

12 Valley (1926); Rohde (1937); Mittelstadt (1970); Cresci (1981); Effe (1982); Hunter (1983); Cozzoli (2000); di Marco (2000); Czapla (2002).
13 With the same textual variant *akridothēkē*.

placed in the mouth of a character who bears the same name as another Hellenistic poet, acknowledged by Theocritus himself. Only fragments of the work of Philetas of Cos survive, but the character's role in the novel is such that it difficult to believe that Longus did not have the poet in mind: in particular Philetas' sermon on the nature and beneficent power of love (2.7) is full of elevated poeticisms. One can only guess, however, exactly what Longus has done with Philetas. It seems unlikely, given his handling of Theocritus, that the intertextuality is merely decorative: perhaps Longus 'corrects' Philetas as he 'corrects' Theocritus. However that may be, another important intertextual moment occurs later in the novel when Philetas, the master piper of the rustic community, donates his pipes to Daphnis as reward for a premium performance, and prays that he will in turn pass them to a worthy successor (2.37.3). This inscribes Longus' view of his place in a literary tradition: Philetas was succeeded by Theocritus, here represented by his principal character, Daphnis, whose 'worthy successor' can be none other than Longus himself.

Daphnis and Chloe is set on the island of Lesbos, and thus another of Longus' primary intertexts is the poetry of the Lesbian poetess Sappho.[14] The symptomology of love experienced by the protagonists in book 1 – pallor, sleeplessness, loss of appetite and so on – derives from her poetry, but the recurrent joke is that these signs are taken from an artificial literary system and 'naturally re-invented' by naive and ill-educated rustics. The most explicit Sapphic reference comes when Daphnis climbs a tree to fetch Chloe a beautiful apple.

> One apple tree had been picked, and had neither fruit nor leaf. All its branches were bare. But at the topmost point of its topmost bough was a single apple, big and beautiful, and the fragrance of this one fruit was stronger than all the others together. The apple-picker had been afraid to climb up and had not bothered to fetch it down. (3.33.4)

This reworks lines from a famous epithalamium or wedding-song by Sappho, in which (we are told by the late orator Himerius) the apple represents the bride's virginity, which has been left for her husband to pick:

> As the sweet-apple blushes on the bough-top, on the top of the topmost bough, and the apple-pickers have forgotten it – no, they have not completely forgotten it, but they could not reach it. (fr. 105 L–P)

Knowledge of the intertext is essential for full understanding of Longus' episode. Daphnis has just been initiated into sex by a kindly neighbour, who

14 Hunter (1983) 73–6; Pattoni (2004).

has warned him of the pain that the loss of her virginity will cause Chloe. Deterred from taking his beloved's virginity physically he does so in a way whose figurative sense depends on intertextuality. Immediately before the apple-episode, the couple's foster-parents have agreed to their marriage and Daphnis has for the first time spoken of Chloe as his wife: the reader is thus cued to read the episode as foreshadowing the projected wedding-night, and as such it establishes the modalities of married masculinity, as Daphnis overrides the wishes of his cautious bride-to-be.

If the first three books of *Daphnis and Chloe* are dominated by pastoral intertexts, the final section of the novel is much closer to New Comedy. This shift of intertextual genre coincides with the plot's shift to urban and social concerns, particularly respectable and financially secure marriage. Longus abandons his usual pattern of seasonal division and characteristic episodes, and instead produces a continuous and unified drama of intrigue and recognition. The cast-list of the last book includes such New Comic staples as the parasite, the feckless young man-about-town, and the potentially obstructive parents, and there is a high proportion of speaking-names, drawn from the comic stage: Lycaenion ('little wolf'), Gnathon ('Jaws'), Astylus ('City boy'), Eudromus ('Good at running'). Although the homosexual parasite Gnathon poses a temporary threat, the newly re-oriented intertextuality is a proleptic guarantee of a happy ending, as in any other comedy.

Heliodorus' *Charicleia and Theagenes*, in contrast, connects itself to the elevated genres of epic and tragedy. The narrative begins in the middle of the story, whose beginnings are filled in by a retrospective narration, which ends at almost exactly the mid-point of the text. This structure immediately recalls that of the *Odyssey*, and Heliodorus plays with this intertext throughout the novel. The role of Odysseus, for instance, is divided between the three main characters. First, the retrospective narrator, the Egyptian priest Calasiris, is a notoriously slippery and duplicitous creation, who has proven endlessly interesting to commentators. He begins his lengthy narrative with a quotation from the beginning of Odysseus' (2.21.5), and has an emblematic encounter with Odysseus himself, who appears to him in a dream (5.22.2–3). In the course of his narrative Calasiris expounds the doctrine that Homer, like him, was an Egyptian exile living in Greece. Not only is Calasiris' narration marked by Odyssean ambiguity, but the Odyssean intertext provides the key to his character throughout the novel. Even his experiences reflect those of Odysseus, notably in an encounter with an Egyptian necromancer that closely echoes the Homeric encounter with the dead (6.12).

Second, the heroine Charicleia is also assimilated to Odysseus by the nature of her story, which is a *nostos* or a journey home to the land of her birth. Her ten-year sojourn in exile at Delphi, as the foster-daughter of the high-priest Charicles, corresponds to Odysseus' ten-year detention by the nymph Calypso, whose sexual enslavement of the hero is mirrored by Charicles' desire for his foster-daughter to marry against her will. Like Odysseus she escapes by sea and is shipwrecked. She too is a cunning piece of work, ever ready with a plan to fend off unwanted attentions. She shares the underworld-invoking scene with Calasiris, and arguably plays the more Odyssean role by being the recipient of a prophecy from the realm of the dead. Heliodorus, however, does not like things to be too straightforward. Her militant chastity aligns her with Penelope, a connection made explicit in Odysseus' message to Calasiris, just in case any reader missed the point (5.22.3). Like Odysseus' story, Charicleia's concludes with a reunion with her father and the re-assumption of due regal position.

Third, the hero Theagenes is also aligned with Odysseus by having a scar on his leg by which he may be recognised when disguised (5.5.2). At the end of the novel he has to perform two athletic feats of strength, corresponding to Odysseus' contest of the bow and likewise leading to his recognition. However, Theagenes is more frequently assimilated to Achilles, his ancestor. He distinguishes himself by being 'swift-footed' in a race at the Pythian Games, and on her bed of love-sickness Charicleia can only repeat a line from the *Iliad* naming Achilles (4.7.4). However, the role of Achilles is also divided: Thyamis' pursuit of his brother Petosiris three times around the walls of Memphis unmistakably recalls Achilles chasing Hector around the walls of Troy (7.6).

This is far from exhausting Heliodorus' exploitation of Homeric epic, but at least gives an idea of the complexity with which Homeric roles are exchanged. Alongside these allusions is a series of further mythic analogues drawn predominantly from tragedy. The *Hippolytus*, for instance, is doubly evoked: first in Cnemon's sub-narrative about his lustful stepmother,[15] and second in the episode where Theagenes is assailed by the nymphomaniac Persian princess Arsace and her pandering nurse Cybele.[16] This double reference compels the reader to compare Cnemon to Theagenes, and thus explains why the former is disqualified from ever reaching Ethiopia. The combat between Thyamis and Petosiris mentioned above also evokes the fight between Eteocles and Polynices before the walls of Thebes, with Calasiris now recast in the role of Oedipus. And the action of the last book, set at the ends of the earth, where a father confronts the necessity to sacrifice his own daughter for the public good, seems to combine the action of Euripides' two Iphigenia plays.

---

15 Hippolytos is named at 1.10.2.   16 Pletcher (1998).

However, Heliodorus' use of the dramatic stage extends beyond such specific examples. His novel is shot through with metaphors relating to stage action,[17] but the tragic references seem to cling only to certain characters, particularly Theagenes and Charicleia, elevating them to tragic stature. Cnemon, on the other hand, is cast as a character in a typical comic intrigue, complete with scheming slave. Although he sees himself as a tragic Hippolytus-like figure, and tries to shape his narrative accordingly, he is continually undercut by comic reminiscences.[18] The intertextuality here, in other words, functions as a device of characterisation, and reinforces and illuminates the moral lines of the novel.

Lastly, all of the novels may be read as being, in some sense, in dialogue with each other and their genre. In fact it is not easy to discover precise allusions in one novel to another, though it would undoubtedly have been easier had the surviving population pool been larger. Some episodes in Xenophon seem to have been 'inspired' by Chariton (for example the burial alive of the heroine), and one's impression is that Xenophon is trying to outdo his predecessor in the extravagance of his invention. There may be some contact between Achilles Tatius and Longus as regards their use of *ekphrasis* (description) of a painting as an introductory device.[19] And it has been suggested that Heliodorus alludes to Longus.[20] However, the more important point is that even the very earliest novels seem to be subjecting to some sort of critical scrutiny a degree-zero novel-plot (which may indeed never have existed as an individuated written text). So Chariton cuts through the idealisation of romantic love and gives us a heroine who, uniquely in the genre, becomes pregnant by the hero and is forced to accept a bigamous second marriage for the sake of her foetus. This second husband, again uniquely among the 'rivals' in the novels, is a sympathetic and decent man, subject to inner crises of conscience and dignity. All this looks like a reaction against prior stereotypes. Xenophon, in his less sophisticated way, is concerned to pack as much action as densely as he can into the shortest text, competing not just with Chariton but with a putative 'typical' novel. In confining his action to the island of Lesbos, Longus was able to miniaturise many of the conventional adventures and so subject them to a sort of critical parody. His plot also probes the commonplace of love at first sight by presenting a story of erotic education: this affective movement replaces the travel-element of the typical novel. Achilles Tatius destabilises the whole genre by employing an unreliable first-person narrator whose sentimental pretensions mirror

---

17 Walden (1894); Marino (1990); Montes Cala (1992). See further Connors, this volume.
18 This summarises the detailed arguments of Paulsen (1992).
19 Nakatani (2004).   20 Bowie (1995).

those of the genre itself; here too stereotypical material is stretched to comic breaking point. Finally Heliodorus recasts a fairly conventional plot into a radically fragmented and anachronic narrative structure, and in so doing spotlights the hermeneutic processes of reading fiction. None of the novels, this is to say, would be the way it is if it were not in intertextual dialogue with at least some conception of what novels normally were.

2. THE ROMAN NOVEL

Stephen Harrison

The two Roman novels, Petronius' *Satyrica* and Apuleius' *Metamorphoses*, are just as fundamentally intertextual. Scholarship has drawn much from, and can clearly be associated with, what might be called the 'intertextual turn' in the study of Latin poetry in the 1980s;[21] this has been one of the factors in the reorientation of the Roman novels in the last generation from a specialist and marginal interest to a central area of Latin literature.[22] Their allusive range is extensive (see below), but most obviously they present plots that parody both the grand epic narratives and the sentimental boy–girl story-lines of some Greek novels.[23] Epic poetry provided a key predecessor of the novel as a long fictional narrative, with many episodes and structures that could be suitably and recognisably reworked to lower literary effect; while the unrealistically romantic Greek plots offered ready targets for comic sub-version, an opportunity taken with gusto by both Petronius, with his tales of homosexual infidelity and impotence, and Apuleius, with his episodes of adultery and bestiality. But the *Metamorphoses* is also linked to the tradition of the low-life and sexually explicit Greek *Ass*-novel, represented for us by the extant *Ass* attributed to Lucian, to which it is evidently closely related.[24] The *Ass*, the fragments of the Iolaus papyrus (see below) and Lollianus' *Phoenician Affairs* show that sexually explicit low-life realism was not limited to Roman fiction;[25] thus the two major Roman novels preserve an earthy Greek tradition as well as parodying the idealistic plot-lines of the more decorous Greek novels.

---

21 Hinds (1998); and for explicit application of such ideas to Apuleius see Finkelpearl (1998).
22 Walsh (1970) is an important milestone here.   23 Walsh (1970) 7–31.
24 See also *P. Oxy.* 4762. I would agree with most modern scholars (see Mason (1999)) in viewing both the *Ass* and the longer Apuleian *Metamorphoses* as derived independently from the lost Greek *Metamorphoses* of Lucius of Patras which was still available in the Byzantine period to be summarised by Photius, *Library* codex 129.
25 Barchiesi (1986). Texts and translations of the Greek fragments in Stephens and Winkler (1995).

Literary texture – Petronius

The literary affinities of the *Satyrica*, though only partially recoverable owing to its fragmentary preservation, have naturally been a key aspect of its interpretation. Until the publication of the Iolaus papyrus in 1971, most scholars were happy to acknowledge that the prosimetric form (i.e. combining prose and verse) of the *Satyrica*, its most striking formal feature, was derived from the Roman prosimetric tradition of Varro's Menippean satires, fantastic and moralising narratives that remain only in fragments. But the discovery of the Iolaus-papyrus, evidently part of a low-life prosimetric narrative in Greek that has no apparent Menippean connections and looks very like a Greek *Satyrica*[26] has caused some rethinking.[27] The remains of Varronian Menippean satire suggest a surreal whimsicality and a strong ethical and moralising content, which Petronius conspicuously lacks; and though the *Apocolocyntosis* ('Pumpkinification') of Seneca, the only fully surviving Latin Menippean satire, suggests that this literary form was revived in Petronius' own Neronian period, its explicit function as a topical pamphlet sets it apart from the *Satyrica*, which contains observations on contemporary culture rather than specific attacks on named individual contemporaries.

Yet the connection with other types of Latin satire, implicit in the title *Satyrica*, is strong. The theme of *captatio*, legacy-hunting, which dominates the final extant episode set in Croton (*Sat.* 124–41) is the topic of Horace, *Satires* 2.5, while the central episode of Trimalchio's banquet looks back to Horace, *Satires* 2.8, where the self-important host Nasidienus gives a dinner that is so unpleasant that the more discriminating guests (including Horace and Maecenas) finally run away, just as Encolpius and his friends eventually flee from Trimalchio's grossness (*Sat.* 78). Characteristically, this satiric basis of the banquet is leavened with other allusions. The literary discussions, the tales told in turn by the freedmen, and the late entrance of Habinnas all recall elements of Plato's *Symposium*, another text parodied here;[28] likewise, Trimalchio as host with a lavish house and a shrewish wife relates parodically to a famous epic episode, the entertainment of Odysseus by Alcinous in the *Odyssey* (books 7–12), recalling in several respects the rich and luxurious king with a splendid palace and dignified queen who elicits tales from his guests in an episode that forms several books and a substantial section of its work.

Most reconstructions of the *Satyrica* suggest that it was on an epic scale in terms of its number of books: twenty or twenty-four are most likely, given

26 Parsons (1971); see also Stephens and Winkler (1995).
27 Astbury (1977); Barchiesi (1986); Conte (1996) 140–70. See also *P.Oxy.* 4762.
28 Cameron (1969); Bessone (1993).

that the banquet seems to contain parts of books 14–16.[29] In terms of the overall framing of the plot, there is an especially close parodic connection with the *Odyssey*,[30] as indeed there is in Apuleius (see below). Encolpius' apparent subjection to a curse from the god Priapus which afflicts him with impotence is evidently a low-life version of the curse of Poseidon on Odysseus, and Encolpius' picaresque wanderings (including a sea voyage) reflect Odyssean travels, especially in the typically unsuccessful and humiliating sexual encounter in Croton with a beautiful woman named Circe (*Sat.* 126–32) in which Encolpius adopts 'Polyaenus', a Homeric epithet of Odysseus (*Iliad* 9.763), as a *nom de guerre*. The *Aeneid* is also clearly alluded to; this is especially noticeable not only in the subject-matter of Eumolpus' poem on the fall of Troy (see below), but also in the episode of the Widow of Ephesus (*Sat.* 111–12), which apart from suggesting connections with the Milesian Tales (see below), evidently provides a comic version of Virgil's narrative of Aeneas and Dido in the story of the soldier who seduces the apparently inconsolable widow through the offer of food and then sex, a story that even includes ironic citations from the Dido episode (111.12 = *Aeneid* 4.34, 112.2 = *Aeneid* 4.38).

A further generic strand in the *Satyrica* is the mime;[31] this is clear in the comically histrionic behaviour of the homosexual love triangle, and especially in the banquet.[32] Trimalchio himself is a highly theatrical character: the dinner that he puts on as a demonstration of his wealth and status in fact has more to do with the subcultural world of popular shows, especially the mime, than with the higher cultural levels at which Trimalchio unsuccessfully aims. In the terms of the mime, Trimalchio is a sort of *archimimus* (star and director), and the drama of the banquet is partly the drama of his progressively revealed life-story, accompanied in mime fashion with continuous music from his house orchestra.

Another major element of literary intertextuality in the *Satyrica* resides in the two long poems recited by the poetaster Eumolpus.[33] The first of these, already noted, consists (*Sat.* 89) of sixty-five iambic trimeters, which draw their plot from the first third of *Aeneid* 2, and their metre, style and rhetorical treatment from the tragedies of the younger Seneca. The much longer poem on the civil war between Caesar and Pompey in 295 hexameters (*Sat.* 119–24) plainly recalls Lucan's *Civil War* in its metre and subject-matter; it is introduced by a preface (*Sat.* 118) in which Eumolpus' criticism of young poets who graduate from the rhetorical schools to write epic poems without the traditional divine apparatus (an innovation 'corrected' by Eumolpus in

29 Harrison (1998a).   30 E.g. Sullivan (1968) 92–3.   31 Panayotakis (1995).
32 Rosati (1983).   33 Connors (1998); Courtney (2001) 140–3, 181–9.

his poem) is clearly aimed at Lucan's rhetorical style and striking removal of the Olympian gods. A similar effect is achieved in the episode that opens the remains of the novel as we have it, in which Encolpius launches a fierce attack on the vices of contemporary declamation (*Sat.* 1–2), in a scene set within a rhetorical school.[34] These elements place the *Satyrica* in a context of contemporary Neronian literary polemic,[35] as well as characterising Eumolpus as a mediocre poet (though he criticises Lucan and emulates Seneca, he comes across as inferior to both); they also stress the multigeneric texture of the Roman novel (see below).

The literary texture of the *Satyrica* thus derives some of its chief effects from the incongruous collision between high culture and low life, between intellectual concerns and a sensationalist and scatological plot. Conte (1996) sees Encolpius as a 'mythomaniac narrator', a naive young intellectual reading the low-life events of a sordid story in terms of elevated literary models such as epic and tragedy, while placed by the 'hidden author' (the Petronius of the text) in low-life melodramatic situations from novelistic and pantomimic contexts, with irony resulting from the evident gap between the two. This presents a key model for negotiating the gap that the narrative technique of the novel plainly opens up, and also makes for a sophisticated narrative effect (see Bartsch in this volume).

Literary texture – Apuleius

Though the main shape of the plot of the *Metamorphoses* is derived directly from the Greek *Ass*-tradition, to which the extant *Ass* (together with a brief papyrus fragment) is our primary witness,[36] this material is also framed by allusions to other literary traditions.[37] Chief among these genres is the epic: Apuleius, writing at least partly for a learned audience that knew both Latin and Greek literature, was able to draw upon the epic tradition in both literatures. As in the *Satyrica*, the relationship is partly parodic: the eleven books of the *Metamorphoses* clearly recall but fall short of the twelve books of the *Aeneid*, and the sensational storyline of books 1–10 involving (e.g.) sex, black magic, varieties of crime and bestiality presents material of a much lower register, using Virgilian allusion for comic and contrastive effect.[38] Even Psyche's descent into the Underworld, the dramatic climax of her search for her lover Cupid in the famed central tale of the novel (*Metamorphoses* 6.16–21), is an entertaining rerun of Aeneas' similar descent (in *Aeneid* 6: note the coincidence of book numbers),[39] and is part of an

34 Kennedy (1978).   35 Sullivan (1985).   36 Above, n. 24.
37 The best general survey is Finkelpearl (1998).
38 E.g. Harrison (1997); Graverini (1998).   39 For details see Finkelpearl (1990).

especially wide spectrum of literary allusion in this more ambitious part of the novel.[40]

Once again, the *Odyssey* is a prominent intertext.[41] The initial educative travels of the young Lucius *en route* to Hypata in *Metamorphoses* 1–3 recall the travels of Telemachus in the opening books of the *Odyssey* (1–4), but suitably transformed for its new generic context: Lucius is characteristically rash, ignorant and ill-behaved (e.g. in seducing his host's slave), where Telemachus showed prudence and diplomacy, and Lucius' transformation into an ass seems just reward for his stupidity and concerns with fleshly satisfactions. The disguised infiltration of the heroic Tlepolemus into the cave of the robbers in book 7, his defeat of them and his rescue of his *fiancée* plainly reflect the return of Odysseus to Ithaca, his destruction of the suitors and his reunion with Penelope. Lucius himself, looking back to his time as an ass, recalls the opening lines of the *Odyssey* in describing how he benefited from his bestial shape in getting to know more about the world (9.14), but Lucius' continued gullibility in the cult of book 11 shows that he has in fact learnt little from his experiences.[42]

A further epic text of importance is Ovid's homonymous *Metamorphoses*. Apuleius' treatment of human/bestial metamorphosis,[43] and perhaps his treatment of sexual passion[44] both owe much to Ovid, and the programmatic highlighting of metamorphosis as a theme in the famous prologue of the *Metamorphoses* is also an Ovidian note,[45] as is the commonly exploited tension between the ending of plot-segments and books.[46] The erotic works of Ovid, together with those of the other love-elegists, are also laid under contribution in the love-story of Cupid and Psyche.[47] Other literary genres used include Greek tragedy, to amusing effect: Aristomenes' sentimental address to his hotel bed (*Met.* 1.16) is clearly a parody of the doomed Alcestis' apostrophe to her marriage-couch in Euripides,[48] while the career of the murderess of *Metamorphoses* 10.2 is a lurid sensationalisation of the Phaedra/Hippolytus story, which has even been used to attempt to reconstruct the lost *Phaedra* of Sophocles.[49]

Prose texts (outside the Greek *Ass*-tale tradition) are also significant. As in the *Satyrica*, formal rhetoric (a key Roman taste) plays an important part in the novel's literary texture. Where Petronius had included rhetors as characters and introduced comments on contemporary declamation (see above),

---

40 See the studies in Zimmerman *et al.* (1998).
41 Harrison (1990b); Frangoulidis (1992a), (1992b), (1992c).
42 For my views on this disputed part of the novel see Harrison (2000) 238–52.
43 Bandini (1986); Krabbe (1989).   44 Müller-Reineke (2000).   45 Scotti (1982).
46 Harrison (2003b).   47 Mattiacci (1998).
48 Mattiacci (1993).   49 Zwierlein (1987).

Apuleius adds a whole episode to the Greek *Ass*-tale, in which Lucius is falsely arraigned for a triple murder, as part of the city of Hypata's honouring of the god of Laughter on his festival day (*Metamorphoses* 3.1–12). Though this may recall the prominence of trial-scenes in some of the Greek novels, and may also allude to Apuleius' own trial (attested by the extant *Apology*, delivered in 157–8 CE), the main feature of the style is a brilliantly constructed (and entirely fictional) Ciceronian defence speech by Lucius, pulling out all the oratorical stops and showing that Lucius is a true child of his sophistic and rhetorical age. Declamatory rhetoric is not neglected either: *Metamorphoses* 9.35–8, which narrates a dispute between a rich and a poor man, presents a classic declamatory case, and there are a number of other elements from the same tradition.[50] Historiography also plays a role: the dramatic but comically unsuccessful feats narrated by the robbers who steal Lucius-ass and kidnap the girl Charite clearly relate parodically to events in Herodotus and Thucydides, as well as to the tradition of robbertales in the Greek novels,[51] and the novel contains other traces from Sallust and Livy.[52]

The use of Platonic dialogues in the *Metamorphoses* is unsurprising, given Apuleius' likely authorship of an extant arid doxographical work on the doctrines of Plato (*On Plato*),[53] his claims to be a 'Platonic philosopher' (*Apology* 10), and his otherwise gratuitous introduction at the novel's beginning (*Metamorphoses* 1.2) of the claim that his protagonist is descended from Plutarch, the most important literary figure in Middle Platonism, whose work certainly influenced Apuleius.[54] The symposium of the robbers in *Metamorphoses* 4, where various tales of brigandage are told, like the tales of the freedmen in Petronius' banquet of Trimalchio (see above), recognisably parodies the speeches about Love in Plato's *Symposium*; indeed, the long tale of Cupid and Psyche later told by the drunken old housekeeper of the robbers can be seen as a comic version of the climactic speech on Love of the priestess Diotima narrated by Socrates in Plato's work.[55] The scene of the death of the character Socrates (very unSocratic in his carnal appetites) is appropriately set in idyllic topography that recalls that of Plato's *Phaedrus* (*Metamorphoses* 1.18 ~ *Phaedrus* 229a), an entertaining literary joke. Scholars have, however, been divided on the significance of the further allusion to the *Phaedrus* (248c) at *Metamorphoses* 5.24: does it suggest that the tale of Cupid and Psyche is to be read as a full Platonic philosophical allegory about Love and the Soul,[56] or is it simply more literary entertainment?[57] Similar

---

50 Van Mal-Maeder (2003).   51 Loporcaro (1992); Harrison (2002).
52 Graverini (1997).   53 Harrison (2000) 195–209.   54 Walsh (1981).
55 Harrison (1998b).   56 E.g. Kenney (1990b); O'Brien (2002) 77–90.
57 Harrison (2000) 252–9.

issues cluster around about the clear link between the emphasis on 'curiosity' (*curiositas*) and its negative consequences in the *Metamorphoses* and Platonic doctrine on psychic disorder:[58] is this a full enlistment of Plato's ideas about the soul as part of the novel's supposed allegorical function, or merely learned intertextual play on a par with the use of other literary texts? Thus issues of intertextuality are necessarily wrapped up with the key issues of interpretation in Apuleius' novel: the playful treatment in the novel of often elevated literary texts provides important evidence that its overall purpose is literary–comic entertainment rather than philosophical–religious enlightenment.

Common features

Thus the two central Roman novels can be seen to have a number of elements in common. It is perhaps surprising that so few echoes of the *Satyrica* can be detected in the *Metamorphoses* perhaps a century later[59] (although here we must recall how little of Petronius is preserved): amongst the most notable are the melodramatic attempted suicide in the inn (*Satyrica* 94.8 ~ *Metamorphoses* 1.16), the humble hospitality motif, in each case involving a comparison with Callimachus' *Hecale* (*Satyrica* 135.15 ~ *Metamorphoses* 1.23), and the ghost-story at the feast told at the host's insistence (*Satyrica* 61.1 ~ *Metamorphoses* 2.20.5). These between them bring out the key features which the two works share: sensational tone and other low-life interests, sophisticated narrative technique including the manipulation of the first-person voice and the use of inserted tales, and an overall purpose of comic entertainment set in a culturally ambitious literary framework. I have argued elsewhere[60] that at least the first two of these three elements derive from the tradition of the Milesian Tales, to which I shall now turn.

Scholars have reconstructed the Milesian Tales as witty and salacious brief narratives, originally associated with the name of Aristides in the Hellenistic period and then translated into Latin by Sisenna in the first century BCE. It can be argued that such tales were strung together through a tale-telling narrative frame, perhaps a collection of accounts of sensational goings-on in the Ionian fleshpots of Miletus.[61] It is commonly assumed that Petronius' stories of the Boy of Pergamum (*Sat.* 85) and the Widow of Ephesus (*Sat.* 111) are drawn directly from this tradition (note how both are located in Ionian cities near Miletus) and that a number of the inserted tales in Apuleius also come from this source (e.g. that of Thelyphron in *Metamorphoses* 2; note

58 DeFilippo (1990).   59 Walsh (1978).   60 Harrison (1998c).
61 See again Harrison (1998c); also Jensson (2004).

how Thelyphron describes himself as 'coming from Miletus' (2.21), perhaps a statement of literary as well as geographical origin). Apuleius, indeed, alludes more openly to the Milesian tradition as a source in his programmatic prologue (*Metamorphoses* 1.1 describes his work as being 'in that Milesian style'), and suggests later on towards the beginning of the central Cupid and Psyche tale that his novel falls into the literary category of 'Milesian [*sc.* tale]' (4.32). Given the almost complete lack of fragments from the Milesian tales, we can say nothing of their own literary texture, but since they were translated by Sisenna, a major historian described by Cicero as an 'educated man' (*Brutus* 228), it may be that the combination of low content and sophisticated literary texture so characteristic of both Roman novels was found there too.

The wide range of literary parody in both Petronius and Apuleius and its conjunction with low-life and amusing content intersects in a number of interesting ways with the writings on the novel of the Russian critic Mikhail Bakhtin. Bakhtin's influential theory of the novel as an 'open' literary form, a generic and polyphonic mixture, which he himself noted in Petronius and Apuleius,[62] clearly matches the mixture of levels and genres we have seen in these authors; it is difficult to deny that the Roman novel at least depends heavily on the identities of other genres to achieve its own characteristic effects. Bakhtin also argued that the novel developed as a more comic/realistic form of the epic in antiquity,[63] and again we can see close connections with the Roman novel as discussed above:

> Alongside direct representation – laughing at living reality – there flourish parody and travesty of all high genres and of all lofty models embodied in national myth. The 'absolute past' of gods, demigods and heroes is here, in parodies and even more so in travesties, 'contemporised'; it is brought low, represented on a plane equal with contemporary life, in an everyday environment, in the low language of contemporaneity.[64]

We might add that the Roman novel as examined here also lays much stress on the mixture of low and high elements that Bakhtin identified elsewhere (in his work on Rabelais and Dostoevsky) as characteristic of the carnivalesque.

This combination of intertextual learning, high and low culture and experimental generic polyphony can be appropriately contextualised in the contemporary culture of the Roman empire of the first and second centuries CE. Both novels are written in learned periods, the *Satyrica* amid the revival of literary culture under Nero, the *Metamorphoses* in the second sophistic, and both consequently presume a learned readership with an extensive

---

62 Bakhtin (1981) 111–29; Fusillo (2003b) 279–80.
63 Bakhtin (1981) 3–40.   64 Ibid. 39.

repertoire in Greek and Latin literature. The combination of high literary and low sensationalist culture clearly appeals strongly to Roman taste, not unlike the 'fatal charades' of the arena, where criminals were horribly executed in detailed parodies of mythological stories.[65] And the search for generic diversity and mixture fits a period in Roman culture where the great exemplars of the key genres, especially poetic genres, already occupied the centre ground of literary space, necessitating circuitous and inventive routes of experimental literary enterprise such as we find in the artistic and allusive prose of the Roman novels.

Further reading

The Greek novel

Scholars have long been aware of the similarities between the Greek novels and other literary genres, but until comparatively recently tended to interpret them as evidence of the novel's origin. Although its broad hypothesis of an evolutionary development is no longer tenable, Rohde (1914, in German) remains a fundamental repository of material. The first chapter of Fusillo (1989, in Italian) provides a methodologically important overview. Reardon (1991) discusses and defines the novel genre in relation to other literary forms. On specific novels, Morgan (2004a) offers a largely intertextual reading of *Daphnis and Chloe*, and Paulsen (1992) works out a powerful reading of Heliodorus as exploiting the resources of epic, tragedy and comedy to invest his text with dignity and meaning. Virtually all of the standard works on the novel have something to say about intertextuality, though they do not always use the word. Otherwise, there is a great quantity of informative work on the subject, but mostly in the form of articles dealing with specific authors and themes, some of which are referenced in the chapter, but a synoptic interpretive study of intertextuality in the Greek novel remains to be produced.

The Roman novel

Walsh (1970) is an important milestone in the appreciation of the subtle literary texture of Apuleius and Petronius, as is Sullivan (1968) for the latter; how far they moved things along can be judged by a glance at the view of the Roman novels in Perry (1967). For an up-to-date (if somewhat austere) view of the density of reference in Petronius see Courtney (2001); for the same on Apuleius (with more nuance) see Finkelpearl (1998). Conte (1996) provides

---

65 Coleman (1990); see further Connors, this volume.

a balanced view on the affinities of Petronius with epic and the Greek novel and is a sympathetic guide; Winkler (1985) was the catalyst for a much more subtle and rewarding approach to almost every aspect of Apuleius' novel. For works covering contact with single literary kinds, Panayotakis (1995) is important on Petronius and mime; on Apuleius and comic drama, see May (2006). For collections containing important articles on these topics see Zimmerman et al. (1998) and Harrison (1999); the latter's introduction (xi–xxxix) also has a useful survey of scholarship.

14

TIM WHITMARSH AND SHADI BARTSCH

Narrative

1. THE GREEK NOVEL

Tim Whitmarsh

Narrative is now a permanent fixture in modern criticism on the Greek novel.[1] Under the pervasive influence of narratology, popularised particularly by Gérard Genette and Mieke Bal,[2] concepts such as 'embedded narrative', 'narratees' and 'focalisation' (these terms will be glossed in the course of my discussion) have become a familiar part of the armoury of literary theory.[3] This chapter has no pretensions towards recapitulation of the standard formal analysis of the narrative structure of the novels, for which the reader can consult works that are readily available.[4] Instead, it seeks to show how a grasp of narrative and narrative theory can offer a sharply defined critical vocabulary permitting a subtler grasp of wider issues of literary and cultural interpretation.

Novels, after all, specifically challenge their readers to decode a variety of types of speech, assembled more or less loosely into a single framework. At one level, the issue is one of genres: the Greek novels allude to a staggering range of different literary forms, from epic, lyric and drama through historiography and philosophy to oral narrative.[5] More than this, however, they also incorporate a variety of different perspectives upon the world, and strategies for understanding it. Slaves and lower-class persons figure prominently in all the novels; indeed, social roles are fully mobile, to the extent that

1 Hägg (1971); Winkler (1982); Bartsch (1989); Morales (2004); Morgan (2004b–f).
2 See especially Genette (1980); Bal (1993).
3 For a convenient summary of critical terms, see de Jong (2004) xv–xviii.
4 Hägg (1971) offers a detailed formal analysis of Chariton, Xenophon and Achilles. The best comprehensive analysis along these lines is Morgan (2004b–f), dealing with narrators and narratees; later projected volumes in the same series will deal with other narratological phenomena.
5 See Morgan and Harrison and Goldhill, this volume.

the protagonists themselves are often required to play the roles of slaves.[6] Even in such an elevated example of the form as Heliodorus' *Charicleia and Theagenes* – suffused as it is with literary allusion and Neoplatonism – the opportunity to speak is granted to an Athenian courtesan, a commercially minded merchant, a deaf Zacynthian fisherman and a Greek nurse working in the Persian court.[7]

The novels cast themselves as repositories for multiple narrative voices, often partisan and competing. As Mikhail Bakhtin (one of the most influential critics in studies of the novel, both ancient and modern) would have it, they embody 'the socially heteroglot multiplicity of [the world's] names, definitions and value judgements'.[8] Ultimately, for sure, the voice of elite, patriarchal, heterosexual Greek society always wins out at the end, as the narratives conclude in joyous marriage (or its restitution) within a major civic centre. And yet there are invariably, for the reader, residual memories of alternative narrative positions. Chariton's *Callirhoe* concludes with Chaereas narrating the story to the Syracusan public in the theatre, while Callirhoe has been sent back inside the house (8.7.3). This might look like a reassertion of the public role of the aristocratic young male, and his right to monopolise narrative presentation; but Chaereas does not and cannot tell the whole story, which only Callirhoe knows. The woman may be in effect silenced by social convention, but we know how much she knows. At the end of Longus' novel, Daphnis and Chloe are recognised as the children of urban grandees, and marry; but despite this normative-seeming return to the city, they are said to have henceforth 'lived most of their life in the pastoral way', and to have given their own children rustic names (4.39). Even Xenophon, no doubt the least complicated of the novelists, culminates not with Anthia and Habrocomes, but with the pederastic bandit Hippothous (5.15.4). Although it is surely right to see these texts as *predominantly* normative, in cultural terms, a careful analysis of the narrative texture can allow us to locate the numerous 'further voices'[9] audible within them. Narratology is an invaluable tool, allowing us both to map these out and (as we shall see) to identify those significant points where the process of mapping fails.

---

6 See Whitmarsh, 'Class', this volume.
7 Hld. 1.11–17, 2.8–11, 5.1–4 (etc.), 2.23–4, 5.1–6.11, 5.18–22, 7.9–28. For the proposal that Thisbe's letter offers an alternative, lower-class perspective on matters, see Hunter (1998b) 42–4.
8 Bakhtin (1981) 278. On the influence of and resistance to Bakhtin among classicists, see Branham (2002), (2005).
9 I take this phrase from Lyne (1987).

Narration and focalisation

A narrative is a representation in words of a series of events; or, in Aristotle's terms tragedy, an 'imitation (*mimēsis*) of action' (*Poet.* 1450a2–3). Narratologists lay great store by this process of representation. In particular, they distinguish firmly between the sequence of events, whether real or imagined, in their totality – which they call the 'fabula' – and the 'story', the sequence as represented in a written or verbal text, which is necessarily the product of the narrator's idiosyncratic process of selection and ordering. If I write my autobiography, the sum of events that have really happened to me constitutes the fabula; the censored and self-serving confection that appears in the book will be the story. By comparing the story to the fabula (in so far as we can reconstruct the latter), we can identify the idiosyncrasies of the narrator. Any narrative will have to be 'focalised': it will be presented from a certain more or less identifiable point of view, or series of points of view (much as a movie is composed of a series of sequences taken from different angles).

Sometimes, literature draws explicit attention to this phenomenon of focalisation, particularly in the case of embedded narratives (i.e. narratives recounted within the larger narrative). In Achilles Tatius' *Leucippe and Clitophon*, Clitophon, the protagonist and major narrator recaps his adventures to Leucippe's father. When he comes to the part of the story which involves him having sex with a married woman, Melite, in full knowledge both that her husband and his girlfriend are in fact alive, 'I omitted my performance of the act, reshaping the story into one of chaste self-control, although I told no actual lies . . . one of my actions in the plot alone I overlooked, namely the "respect" I subsequently paid to Melite' (8.5.2–3). This scene of narration within the novel – Clitophon the narrator, presenting to Leucippe's father and the other 'narratees' (i.e. internal recipients of narrative) – clearly invites a self-reflexive, metaliterary comparison with the process that we readers are undertaking. Unlike the narrative that *we* are reading, this one is narrowly circumscribed, the focaliser explicitly marked as a somewhat embarassed would-be son-in-law.[10]

Clitophon's use of this technique implicitly alludes to Odysseus' apparent omission of his relationship with Circe in the narrative he presents to Penelope in Homer's *Odyssey*.[11] Yet it also resonates strongly with the central themes specific to the erotic novel, which cluster around the kind of

---

10 Cf. Sostratus' reassurance, 'don't be shy' (8.4.3; Chaereas is similarly said to be initially 'shy' at *Callirhoe* 8.7.4). A full account of the phenomenon of internal narratees can be found at Morgan (2004b–f); see also Morgan (1991) on Heliodorus.
11 Hom. *Od.* 23.321; cf. Whitmarsh (2003) 199–200.

dangerous sexual intrigue that must not be spoken of. Chariton's Callirhoe, for example, writes a secret letter to her second husband, Dionysius, explaining events as she sees them and entrusting her son to him to raise. 'This was the one thing she did without the knowledge of Chaereas' (husband number 1), we are told (8.4.4). Nor is her explanation to Dionysius entirely truthful, eliding as it does the fact that the father of the child is Chaereas (nor does the latter know this).[12] In Heliodorus' *Charicleia and Theagenes*, again, Queen Persinna exposes her daughter for fear of accusations of adultery, presenting her narrative of events in a hieroglyphic tapestry on Charicleia's swaddling band (4.8). There is no suggestion that her story is in any way deceptive (like Callirhoe's), but it is certainly focalised from a very different vantage to that of any other narrative found in the novel. Addressed by mother to daughter, this tearful lament is 'your pitiful story and mine too' (4.8.6).

Such embedded narratives certainly serve to vary the texture of the entire novel, and to increase the sense of multiple perspectives upon the complex ethical knots that lie at the heart of the texts. In particular, they permit women's voices to be heard, voices that would otherwise be smothered by the patriarchal environment within which the novels are set. These episodes also serve to position the reader carefully, as the recipient of particularly privileged information. On the one hand, we get access to embedded private narratives – intimate oral conversations, letters – that other literary genres might ignore. On the other hand, we are repeatedly made aware of the limited perspectives embodied in these narratives. The full narrative that constitutes the novel as a whole, by implicit contrast, provides a fuller insight into the 'truth' of the erotic intrigue. In the examples from Achilles and Chariton cited above, for example, the minor (?) deceptions practised by the protagonist-narrators in question are set against the reader's command of the true story of events. The macro-narrative of the novel zooms in and out of these private mini-narratives, celebrating its own ability both to reveal and to transcend their risqué contents.

Who focalises?

As we have seen, embedded narratives can offer us alternative, repressed perspectives to the text's dominant voice. But what is this dominant voice? Can we always be sure with what ideologies the primary narrator of a novel is aligned? At one level, assuredly, we often can be. Let us take a brief example

---

12 The critical importance of this lies in the dynastic motif: Chariton's narrative leaves open the possibility that Callirhoe's son will become the historical Dionysius I, tyrant of Syracuse. See Naber (1901); Perry (1967) 130, 138.

from *Daphnis and Chloe*. After Lycaenion has initiated Daphnis into the ways of sex, she forewarns him that Chloe will bleed. The primary narrator describes Daphnis' response: 'As a new learner (*artimathēs*), he was fearful of the blood and believed that blood could only come from a wound' (3.20.2). Here, as so often in this text, the focaliser is one who is anything but a 'new learner': the narrative voice encourages the reader to take shared pleasure in comic irony, as poor Daphnis struggles to assimilate the information provided by Lycaenion, beginning from the hopelessly naive premise that blood only appears when there is a wound.

Identifying focalisation, however, is not always a straightforward process. Can we imagine alternative readings of the passage discussed above? Heterosexual sex is associated with violence throughout *Daphnis and Chloe*:[13] Dorcon attempts to rape Chloe (1.11); the story of Pan shows him attempting to rape Syrinx, and subsequently cutting down the reeds into which she has metamorphosed (2.34, a story that the two children subsequently mime out). The Greek word for 'rape' is *bia*, literally 'violence'. When Daphnis finally does deflower Chloe, we are told, the wedding guests outside the door sing 'with a harsh and ungentle voice, as though breaking up the earth with tridents' (4.40.2). In the context of this general association of deflowering with sexual aggression, can we be confident in our initial reading of Daphnis' interpretation of Chloe's anticipated bleeding? Is not Daphnis right, at one level, that the loss of a girl's virginity is indeed a kind of wounding? From this vantage, we might conclude that Daphnis' status as 'new learner' marks him not so much as a naif, as one with a raw, privileged insight into the practice and politics of sex. The clumsy certainty implied by the narrator is, perhaps, misguided.[14]

Related to this kind of sceptical reading of the narrative voice is the phenomenon of 'deviant focalisation',[15] embodied in those moments where the text pulls us up short, demanding that we think hard about whose perspective is being adopted. At 3.14.5, for example, Daphnis emerges frustrated from his and Chloe's attempt to copy the sexual practice of sheep and goats: 'he sat down and cried because he was less learned (*amathesteros*) than rams in relation to erotic deeds' (3.14.5). Whose perspective is embodied in the word *amathesteros* ('less learned') – that of the naive Daphnis, or that of the knowing narrator? Both interpretations make sense. Daphnis might be taken comically to understand animals anthropomorphically, that is in terms

13 Winkler (1990) 118–26.
14 For other instances of subversion of the narratorial voice in *Daphnis and Chloe*, see n. 18 below.
15 See esp. Fowler (1990).

of learning and study;[16] as the episode as a whole shows, his grasp on fundamental distinctions between human and animal forms of social relationship is weak. The narrator, on the other hand, might be emphasising the complicity between himself and the learned readership, for whom Daphnis' rustic naivety might well be evaluated in terms of his lack of education. In cases like this, pondering the question of the identity of the focaliser – and it must remain, precisely, a *question* – forces us to confront the genuine slipperiness of this text.

True stories?

It remains to be considered how trustworthy the voice of the novels' primary narrators is. In a famous analysis of Petronius' *Satyricon*, Gian Biagio Conte coined the phrase 'the hidden author'.[17] Petronius' text is (at least in the portions that we have) wholly narrated by its protagonist, Encolpius; according to Conte's reading, however, the 'hidden author' Petronius intervenes repeatedly to frame Encolpius as a comically pretentious ('mythomaniac') narrator. Do the Greek texts encourage readers to question the primary narrators in a similar way?

This kind of question attaches itself particularly to 'homodiegetic' narrators, that is, those who are also agents within the text.[18] The most celebrated case in a Greek novel is the narrative of Calasiris in books 2–5 of Heliodorus' *Charicleia and Theagenes*. This tricky Egyptian priest, as Winkler's famous analysis shows, is characteristically elusive as a narrator too.[19] In particular, his narrative contains an apparent contradiction: he claims on separate occasions *both* that he chanced upon Charicleia accidentally in Delphi *and* that he had been specifically mandated to look for her by her mother, queen Persinna.[20] Calasiris is not, of course, the primary narrator of the novel as a whole, but the secondary narrator of an embedded narrative such as we discussed in the previous section. Even so, his story occupies such a significant portion of the text, and indeed fills in so much of the missing plot that it practically substitutes for primary narrative for long stretches. And what kind of message does this give to the reader? We are left with, at best,

---

16 So Bowie (2005) 77.
17 Conte (1996); for a critique see Rimell (forthcoming). See further Bartsch, this volume.
18 See however Morgan (2003b), (2004e) 510–16 for an analysis of Longus' narrator (who is wholly external to the action) as an insensitive urbanite.
19 Winkler (1982); for other narratological analyses, cf. Futre Pinheiro (1991); Hunter (1998b) 51–6. Baumbach (1997) argues that Calasiris' account of his trip to Ethiopia was an expedient lie to persuade Charicleia – which if true would hardly increase his credibility as a narrator!
20 This clash was first identified by Hefti (1950); see the works cited in the previous n. for various attempts to reconcile the two versions.

uncertainty as to how Calasiris' troublesome narratorial authority relates to that of the primary narrator.[21]

The best example, however, comes in Achilles Tatius' *Leucippe and Clitophon*. Here, an unnamed narrator describes his arrival in Sidon, where he meets Clitophon as he gazes at a picture of Europa; Clitophon then proceeds to present his narrative in his own voice, which becomes the remainder of the text.[22] This is the same Clitophon who (as we have seen) later proves himself an adept manipulator of narrative in his account of events to Leucippe's father. That this is the only Greek novel almost entirely narrated by a character within the narrative[23] raises all sorts of tricky questions, particularly as to the extent to which we can trust the judgement of Clitophon (who indeed proves himself sexist, heterosexist and bigoted throughout).[24]

There are a number of indications that his approach to literary narrative is fickle and unreliable. Early in book 1, we find him wandering around with a book; but his pretence at reading it is in fact only a mask for his ogling of Leucippe (1.6.6). Elsewhere, we find him astonishingly insensitive to the narrative of his cousin Clinias, when the latter's boyfriend has died in a bizarre horse-crash: he reports the laments, but glozes the aftermath. 'After the funeral, I immediately hurried off to find Leucippe', he tells us (1.15.1). So apparently indecent is Clitophon's desire to switch from narrative codes from pederastic tragedy to heterosexual pursuit that one commentator has argued that a portion of the text must have dropped out.[25] Is this a man to whom we can entrust the accurate reporting of the fabula?

A further complexity lies in the complex chain of transmission. Even before we reach the example of Clitophon's recapitulation, the narrative is already doubly embedded (Achilles the author presents the unnamed narrator presenting Clitophon's words). A number of scholars have noted that the framing structure looks to Plato's *Symposium*, where Plato scripts Apollodorus reporting Aristodemus' account of the dialogue (and as in Achilles there

---

21 The least convincing part of Winkler's analysis is his over-simple extrapolation from Calasiris' unreliable narrative to that of the primary narrator.

22 There is, then, no return to the initial frame at the end; what is more, there is no explanation of how Clitophon passes from Byzantium (where the text finishes) to Sidon (where it begins). Modern scholars have preferred the explanation of strategic open-endedness: see Fusillo (1997a); Morales (2004) 144–5; Repath (2005). For a different interpretation, see Most (1989).

23 On this phenomenon see Hägg (1971) 124–36, 318–22; Reardon (1994); Whitmarsh (2003). Antonius Diogenes' *Wonders beyond Thule*, Lucian's *True Stories* and the Lucianic version of the Greek *Ass*-narrative are also presented (wholly or mainly) homodiegetically; for the parallel Roman tradition, see Bartsch's section of this chapter, with n. 33.

24 For Clitophon's 'blindness to himself' see Morgan (1996b) 180–6; for his sexism, Morales (2004) *passim*; also Whitmarsh (2003).

25 Pearcy (1978); for more along these lines, see Whitmarsh (2003) 201–3.

is no return to the outer frame at the conclusion).[26] In the Platonic text, problems of transmission are foregrounded: we are told not only that the event occurred a long time ago (172b–c), but also that Aristodemus passed out before the evening was done (223b), and his memory is hazy of the final speeches (223c–d).[27] Given this famous precedent, can we be sure that Achilles' narrators, Clitophon and his unnamed interlocutor, are transmitting the story accurately?

Ancient literature did not have a strong conceptualisation of what we would call 'fiction'.[28] What it did have is a well-developed sense of pleasure in unreliable narrative, a tradition that can be traced from Homer's Odysseus through to Lucian's *True Stories* (where the narrator proudly boasts that 'the one true thing I shall say is that I am a liar', 1.4).[29] As we have seen, the novels position themselves well within this arc: despite all the now well-understood realistic motifs borrowed from historiography,[30] they also exploit multiple focalisation to engender a strong sense of the relativising of narrative truth. This phenomenon is, to be sure, more pronounced in some places than others: there is little sense, for example, that the primary narrators of Xenophon's or Heliodorus' novels are presenting their own narrative in an ironic manner. Even so, as we have seen, large tracts of Heliodorus' text (at any rate) are dominated by the self-ironising narrative of Calasiris. If the primary narrator is unwilling to compromise the authority of his own narrative, he nevertheless supplies his readers with an alternative narrator who is worthy of all our most probing scepticism.

According to Bakhtin, novels are born of a period of desacralisation, when authority is no longer held to be invested in any particular individuals. I hope to have shown that narratology can show us how the Greek novels (of which Bakhtin himself was, it must be said, no great champion) take pleasure in the multiplication of perspectives upon their central action. It would certainly be misleading to claim that their relativism is thorough-going and all-embracing, since – as we have seen – their central narrative trajectory is pulled towards the elite, patriarchal Greek community. Even so, such conservative

---

26 Winkler (1989) 284 n. 72; Morales (2004) 145. The exchange of stories in book 8 of Achilles occurs precisely at a symposium (cf. 8.4.1–2).

27 See esp. Halperin (1992).

28 See Gill and Wiseman (1993), and specifically on the novels Morgan (1993). Rösler (1980) argues that the concept of 'fictionality' arose in the classical period as a result of the distancing effect of the widespread use of writing – but this is at best a different phenomenon to fiction in the modern sense.

29 On the narrative shenanigans of the *Odyssey* see esp. Goldhill (1991); on those of the *True Histories*, see esp. Fusillo (1988a); Rütten (1997); von Möllendorff (2000).

30 Morgan (1982), (1993); Fusillo (1988a) 57–68 argues for a more parodic relationship to historiography.

forces claim no monopoly on these texts: we are constantly being asked to check our readings against the alternative viewpoints that are played out in these opulent narratives.

2. THE ROMAN NOVEL

Shadi Bartsch

The history of autobiography in the west often takes as its origin Augustine's *Confessions*: it is our first extended prose narrative to describe a true personal history, in this case one of error and redemption. The prose texts in the first person that precede this work in antiquity all stand at one remove from autobiography by reason of genre, scope, purpose, or truth value: Greek and Roman oratory, Cicero's letters and Caesar's commentaries, Achilles Tatius' romance *Leucippe and Clitophon*, and, of course, the Roman novels of Petronius and Apuleius.[31] If, however, we were to look for a turn towards interest in the narrator *per se* – who is speaking, what is his relationship to his story, how does he filter the events he describes, and how does the author reveal him to us through and despite his voice – the strange and debased voices of Petronius' Encolpius and Apuleius' Lucius would demand our attention first of all. The former a runaway slave or freedman,[32] the latter all too much an ass, these two narrators present us not only with an unusual relationship of speaker to self,[33] but also with the first instances of a first-person prose narrative from antiquity in which the protagonist in his normal life would usually be denied a public voice: one the emasculated figure of a runaway criminal with no citizenship rights, the other the lowly figure of the ass, most undignified of the domestic animals. These two voices let the reader into a world no elite narrator would supply. They also manage to leave the nature of their own identity, in the end, curiously unresolved.

The *Satyrica*

Encolpius as narrator

Both Encolpius and Lucius are (in Genette's terminology) 'homodiegetic' narrators: they tell a story about themselves, and as such they figure as characters in the narratives they author (a 'heterodiegetic' narrator, by contrast,

---

31 Laird (1990) 136 characterises the Roman novel as perhaps the first instantiation of 'continuous fictional narrative presented through the first person form'.
32 On the status of Petronius' characters, see Whitmarsh, 'Class' (this volume).
33 Neither Antonius Diogenes' *The Wonders beyond Thule* nor the (pseudo?-) Lucianic *Ass* shows the same degree of interest in the narrator's identity.

would tell a story in which he or she did not appear).[34] The two are also 'extradiegetic', which is to say that as homodiegetic narrators, they also relate stories within their narrations in which they do not participate. In Apuleius' *Metamorphoses*, the play between between inclusion in one's own story and the telling of a story about another is, as Winkler (1985) clearly demonstrates, one of the thematic concerns of the work. In Petronius' *Satyrica*, the question of the narrator's relationship to the stories in which he is extradiegetic emerges less sharply as a central issue. On the other hand, here the relationship of the homodiegetic narrator to his own story raises highlights the issue of 'focalisation': how the description of events is influenced or warped by the particular perspective of their narrator.[35]

Encolpius' focalisation of the story he tells is noteworthy on several counts. A homodiegetic voice usually provides the reader with an interpretive framework within which to judge the speaker's relationship to the events he is recounting: they are related either as they occur or in retrospect; the speaker either takes a critical distance from his former self or remains in harmony with the judgments and perspectives of that self; any such distance may be implied or explicit, and the narrating voice may seem to be identical to or divergent from the stance of the implied author of the work. In addition, the use of the first-person voice gives rise to the expectation that the speaker knows himself: his emotions, his reactions, his thoughts are on record for us to hear.[36] In Encolpius' case, however, these expectations are not met. Not only is the relationship of the focalising narrator is to that of his focalising protagonist self elusive, but neither of these two representations of the ego-voice appears troubled by the line dividing role-playing or the imitation of literary models from lived experience. We do not come to know Encolpius; the lack of a consistent focalisation of his own behaviour leaves an empty hole in our attempts at interpretation.[37]

That the *Satyrica* represents the one-time adventures of the narrator as recalled by him at a later date is clear, since Encolpius explicitly refers to remembering, or retelling, on several occasions (e.g. *Sat.* 30.3, 56.10, 65.1, 136.4).[38] Similarly, the narrator sometimes knows details which the protagonist could not know – for example, that Oenothea's killer geese are 'sacred' (126.4), or that the man who seizes Encolpius' cloak used to plead in the law courts (15.4), or that the Syrian thieves were Syrian (22.3). And

---

34 See Genette (1980).
35 For the notion of focalisation, see Bal (1997). I am not concerned in this chapter with a strict narratological analysis of the two novels.
36 Horace's Davus (*Satires* 2.7) and the comic slave offer earlier examples of first-person non-elite characters.
37 Slater (1990) 50–85 and *passim*.
38 For many of these references, see Beck (1975) and Plaza (2000) 21–2.

Encolpius repeatedly tells us stories in which we are made to share his limited perspective at the moment of the event he describes: for example, he falls over in a fright when he sees a fierce dog, but then realises it was a painted *trompe-l'oeil* creature (29.1).[39] Since such failures in perception can be presented as failures in sophistication (cf. 'I damned my stupidity', *Sat.* 41.5), Beck (1973 and 1975) has argued that we should read the narrator of the story as an older, wiser Encolpius looking back at his youthful naivety, and thus speaking to us in a voice that colludes with our judgement as readers.[40]

Not everyone would agree. Veyne (1964) suggests that the rift occurs not in the distance between a present narrator and the antics of his former self, but in a manipulation of the narrating voice by the historical author, *Petronius*, in order to show up the gaucheries of the world around the narrator. Following Auerbach ((1953) 24–49), he argues that Petronius' use of the first person in the *Dinner* represents perfectly neither Encolpius nor Petronius himself, but sets into play instead 'a constant game between the twin figures of his own identity and the perspective of the author' ((1964) 302–3). That is, although modern autobiography is predicated upon the unity of this voice at any given temporal point, here the protagonist veils his actions with a false naivety, and the first-person perspective works tongue-in-cheek to mock Trimalchio's taste. Those who are duped by tasteless freedmen are precisely tasteful people, and their error condemns the idiots.[41]

Veyne is thus compelled to draw a distinction between the *Dinner* and the rest of the novel (such as we have it). On his view, it is 'auto-irony' (*self*-mockery) that informs the rest of the *Satyrica*, and that Encolpius now loses all the sense of privileged vision and taste which we association with Petronius.[42] On the other hand, Beck's depiction of a naive protagonist and

---

39 A few further examples can be found at *Sat.* 33.7, 49.7, 60.2; for more comprehensive lists, see Beck (1973) and (1975).

40 Rimell (2002) ch. 2 has a good discussion of this theme in *Dinner at Trimalchio's*, as does Slater (1990). As Beck himself acknowledges, however, it is not always clear that the text does provide us with a later, wiser judgement upon the actions of the narrative; often it is left to us to react with scorn or hilarity at the protagonist's behaviour via the narrator's indirect depiction of the limitation and bias of the protagonist's reaction (as in the Daedalus episode). When it comes to the material outside the *Dinner*, Beck (1973) focuses on verse passages, which he argues represent the older narrator's reproduction of the protagonist Encolpius' musings at the time. But it is difficult to find support for his claims in the prose, while the voice behind the poetry is still the object of scholarly disagreement.

41 Goga (1998) agrees with and builds upon this analysis. Beck (1975), who disagrees with it and claims that the irony due to age change, not *fausse naïveté*, points out with good cause that Encolpius' internal self-criticism in the boar passage makes no sense otherwise. As Walsh (1970) 81 points out, Encolpius is 'faithful to the convention of self-mockery with which the Milesian story-teller leads the laughter against himself'.

42 Yet just because Encolpius makes more fun of others in the *Dinner* does not mean that he is a different narrator (as Veyne would have it), just that his own play-acting is eclipsed by that of the others, especially Trimalchio and the servers. Knight (1988–9) reviews the views

a wiser, later narrator allows for a more consistent narrator. But here too there are problems, precisely because the narrator's actual relationship to the protagonist is not cleanly drawn. When the narrator seems to know things that the protagonist could not, signs of temporal switch or distance may be absent, leading to a confusing omniscience in the character of the present-tense using protagonist. Sometimes it is not clear how even the narrator came to know these details – such as what the matron and Eumolpus talked about before the protagonist watched the latter's sexual antics with the children of the former through a keyhole (140).[43] Here homodiegetic and extradiegetic narrators run into each other without explanation, the latter speaks as if he were the former, and, as elsewhere, the question of past protagonist/present narrator seems to lose its point.

The 'mythomaniac self'

A more recent interpretive tack is represented by the work of Conte (1996) on Encolpius as a 'mythomaniac' narrator. Conte points out that one of the central traits of Encolpius' self-representation in the *Satyrica* is his tendency to mythologise or dramatise his immediate circumstances, to model his circumstances or his speech after some epic hero, or cast himself as a recognisable speaker borrowed from declamatory rhetoric: the spurned lover, the survivor of shipwreck.[44] In *Sat.* 81, for example, Encolpius rents a place near the shore and secludes himself there for days, beating his breast at the fact that his lover has been torn from him. His model is, of course, *Iliad* 1.348–50: his seaside hut is Achilles' tent, his Briseis the boy Giton. But it is not a model he shows himself *consciously* adopting; nor, as Conte points out ((1996) 4), is it a model that Petronius takes pains to mark for us: 'In his mind reality itself will inevitably be interpreted within parameters laid down by the famous models . . . But Petronius plays a subtle game: he does not force the models upon the reader's attention, but simply hints at them faintly through generic features.'[45]

Inevitably, reality soon intrudes. As he sails out from his lodging to seek vengeance, Encolpius' rage is undercut by a chance encounter with a soldier who notices that our hero is wearing effeminate Greek slippers, and the illusion is shattered (*Sat.* 82.1–3). We can never take the melodrama seriously: although Encolpius rarely misses an opportunity to sound epic or tragic or

---

of Walsh, Veyne and Beck, and concludes that Encolpius may at points reflect the ideas and personality of Petronius without representing him.

43 See the examples in Courtney (2001) 35–39. Similar attention to these passages may be found in Jones (1987).

44 On Encolpius' Homeric models, see Conte (1996) 1–18. On Encolpius' declamatory models, see 45–66 and *passim*.

45 Klebs (1889) first suggested the model of the *Odyssey*. See also Rimell (2002) ch. 6.

somehow grandiose (*megalopsychos*),[46] he (or others) subvert the occasion, often by recourse to the interchangeable semantic field of sex/food/money to undercut any noble pretensions or epic references in a given episode ((1996) 109–16). Or simply the semantic field of the non-heroic: 'Thank fate that that soldier's intervention saved me', Encolpius muses upon his return from the slipper episode. Thus Petronius pulls the strings and mocks his protagonist, and we laugh with him. The main difference from the arguments of Beck and others, then, is that when we privilege the novel's theatrical scenarios instead of the temporal gap between narrator and protagonist, we lose our wiser, older Encolpius, who seems to have been traded in for the older, wiser hidden author.

Questions still remain. It is striking that there is no point at which our narrator himself acknowledges the theatricality of his behaviour. There seems to be only one point in the prose narrative of the *Satyrica* in which the narrator (or protagonist – again, a distinction is hard to make here) points to play-acting: Giton has slashed his throat with a razor to dissuade Encolpius from trying to hang himself, and has fallen to the floor. When Encolpius in turn snatches up the razor, determined to live no longer, he finds with astonishment that he saws at his throat with no success: the razor was a prop for stage-deaths, and its blade retractable. (*Sat.* 94.8–15). All of which our narrator characterises as 'a play was being staged between lovers' (*Sat.* 95.1). But this is precisely at a point where Encolpius' melodrama has been, as it were, authentic: he did not know Giton's razor was a fake. Elsewhere, we are given no evidence to suppose that Encolpius' self-interpretation is not always authentic, or that he does not believe in the noble sentiments he spouts – even when these consist of a declamation-school lament over the hated Lichas, drowned unexpectedly in a storm, his body flotsam on the shore.[47]

At the same time, the gulf between how Encolpius interprets his behaviour (or the grandiose rhetoric in which he indulges) and what he actually does is so large as to demand interpretation. He hated Lichas in life, but when the man washes up on a seashore, Encolpius launches into a tragic soliloquy on the uncertainties of life. He is sulking over Giton, but he depicts himself as an Achilles. He finds himself impotent, and his genitalia become Virgil's fallen Euryalus. The lack of information we are granted into the mindset of this performative stance renders us, perhaps like him, confused between

---

46 On Encolpius' longing for the sublime, see Conte (1996) 37–72.

47 This chapter does not cover the question of the verse insets into the *Satyrica*, several of which explicitly confront the issue of theatricality (e.g. 80.9). Who is speaking here? There is nothing in the prose to suggest that it should be the wised-up narrator (see further n. 40).

'authenticity' (for want of a better word) and theatricality.[48] We are on the outside of his performance, never on the inside, and bridging this gap is not a privilege afforded us by the narrator's representation of self.[49] This confusion is not unlike the effect of the *Metamorphoses*' elusive narrator as well.

The *Metamorphoses*

The preface

The most famous question of Apuleius' *Metamorphoses* may well be *Quis ille?* – 'Who is that fellow?' – which appears within several sentences of the opening of the prologue to the novel. Although the source of the interjection remains unspecified, the question itself is posed of the prologue's narrator, the very man who has just promised to soothe our ears with a charming murmur.[50] As many scholars have pointed out, his abrupt opening 'But I shall tell you . . .' places the reader in the position of a 'you' and already plunges us into a dialogic stance with this voice,[51] and into a readerly contract as well: in return for being charmed, we will listen to his string of Milesian tales about 'the shapes and fortunes of men switched into other appearances and then switched back via a shared bond' (*Met.* 1.1).[52] A problematic geographic and familial genealogy follows: 'he' (*ille*) has spent his childhood in Athens, Corinth, and Sparta; he has studied at Rome, and he was travelling to Thessaly (whence his family hailed) when . . . . And the story starts.

Notoriously, these details and the nature of the introductory promise make it difficult for us to assign *ille* to any known voice. Can we attribute it to an isolated prologue speaker, who is not to be identified with any character in the novel but rather as a separate Master of Ceremonies, perhaps like the prologue-speakers of Plautine plays? Is it the ass, telling his story at the end of his adventures, but prior to his conversion to human form (and to

---

48 For this reason, I would disagree that the *Satyrica* could be recast into the third person with no loss (thus Laird (1990) 144), because the relationship to theatricality would no longer be confusing.

49 At *Sat.* 117.4, of course, Eumolpus plans out a mime for the others to act in. For a discussion of all Petronius' theatrical elements, including mime-like scenarios and settings in the novel, see Panayotakis (1995).

50 Some critics have seen the *quis ille* as the interruption of a third voice still, neither narrator nor reader: see esp. de Jong (2001). It is however quite reasonable to suppose that the narrator himself is asking this question: having told us the kind of story that he proposes to tell us, he pauses to say: '*Quis ille?* you might ask.' Well, here's who I am: etc.

51 On *at ego tibi* see e.g. Scobie (1975) *ad loc.*; Winkler (1985) 25–37; 50–6; Laird (1990) 137; de Jong (2001); Fowler (2001); Tatum (1979) 26. For a list of oral markers, see Kahane (2001) 232–3. Zimmerman (2001) and Laird (1990) both discuss the occasions on which the narrator turns to address his reading audience in this novel.

52 On this contract and its similarity to Plautine prologues, see Smith (1972) 513–20; Tatum (1979) 25–7; Dowden (1982), (2001); Winkler (1985) 183–203; and James (2001).

priestly status)?[53] Is it the first-person voice of the book itself, as Harrison (1990a) has suggested?[54] Is it Apuleius himself, our author (despite the fact that his native tongue was probably Latin), as suggested much later by the narrator's use of 'from Madaurus' (*Madaurensem*) to describe himself at *Met.* 11.27? Is it the character Lucius, which would explain the lack of any distinct break between the prologue and what ensues?[55] What to make of the fact that the prologue speaker calls the novel a fictional and libidinous string of stories, while Lucius presents the story as a true biographical account, and, moreover, is presumably writing as a priest of Isis?[56] Could the point to the confusion be simply to set into motion these very questions about the narrating voice, to suggest to us that we *can't* pin the author down?[57]

These questions matter because they set into motion a search for identity that proves to be, at the end, one of the major interpretive problems of the *Metamorphoses*, and that pivots on the relationship of (a) who tells the story (here, the homodiegetic narrator Lucius) to (b) whom the story is told (to our surprise, at the end of book 11, it turns out that we are not reading a string of Milesian tales so much as an autobiography of – Lucius, but now as priest of Isis). These two figures – *auctor* ('author') and *actor* ('agent'), in the terminology of Winkler (1985) – coalesce at the novel's end, but in a way that leaves a gap between them rather than affirming their shared bond. For the last book of the *Metamorphoses* does not so much leave us with an assertion of the narrator's actual identity as illuminate the contents of books 1–10 as a puzzling and self-blind backdrop that undermines our final answer: that the narrator is a priest of Isis.

Book 11: the Isis-book

As almost every scholar of the *Metamorphoses* has remarked, Apuleius' addition of an eleventh book, in which we learn of the new and present identity

53 For this view, see Smith (1972); Laird (1990).
54 As Harrison points out, the motif of the speaking book is well known in classical literature, especially in prefatory contexts. Other arguments in favour: the book asks tolerance for the 'Egyptian papyrus' of which it is made; Sparta, Athens and Corinth are neither Apuleius' origin nor Lucius', but refer to the fact that the book originally appeared in Greek; the migration to Rome represents the translation of this version into Latin by Apuleius. For the scholarship on the *Madaurensem* passage in book 11, see Harrison (2000) 1–2. Penwill (1990) 223–6 suggests that when Osiris said that Asinius would meet a Madauran he meant Apuleius, not Lucius, that is, he would meet the novel and be incorporated into it, but Asinius misinterpreted the prophecy and thought he must have meant Lucius.
55 So Van der Paardt (1981) and de Jong (2001), with additional bibliographical support at n. 52. For difficulties in accepting this thesis, see Harrison (1990) 508. For verbal and thematic connections between the prologue and the last chapter of book 11, see James (2001).
56 These are the objections of Harrison (1990a) 508; they are contradicted in turn by de Jong (2001) 206–7.
57 Winkler (1985) and Henderson (2001) both suggest that our confusion about the narratorial voice is the point of the novel.

of the narrator telling the story, drives a disorienting wedge between the first ten books and what follows. After a vision in which Isis instructs Lucius on the procedure for his metamorphosis back to human form, our narrator eventually undergoes three consecutive and expensive initiations into the cults of Isis and Osiris, a sequence that causes him some temporary anxiety about fraud and thoroughly drains his resources. Nonetheless, at the end of the narrative, in keeping with his role as a *pastophoros* ('icon-bearer') of Osiris, he is going about his business at Rome happily and with shaved head. But his readers are left in some confusion, for here the story abruptly stops with the verb 'I was going' (*obibam*). There is no link back to the beginning, to our charming whisper, to the pre-transformed narrator, or to the production of the very narrative we are reading. And while we hear twice that Lucius will be the subject for a book (1.12, 6.29), we never hear that he will *write* this book himself, nor that he will do so as a priest of Isis and Osiris. [58]

Our puzzlement, then, is generated by the lack of a backwards-and-forwards looking nexus between books 1–10 and book 11. And our options are several. We can either surmise that (a) the *narrator* has all along concealed his identity because he did not want us to read with foreknowledge of who he really is; or (b) the *author* has concealed the narrator's identity all along because the rift between the asinine narrative and the priestly narrative is part of the point of the author's point in writing the *Metamorphoses*; or (c) that book 11 is meant to let us meld author and narrator into each other and read the ending as yet another (series of) metamorphoses. These possibilities overlap with each other and are not exclusive, but they do provide some idea of what the stakes might be in the writing of book 11 – which, of course, like the prologue and the inset stories, was *not* part of the narrative of Apuleius' model, the *Metamorphoses* of Lucius of Patrae, and so *was* part of Apuleius' conscious purpose for his work.

Suggestion (a) is useful if we want to take the Isis book as a narratorial rebuke. As with the pre-converted Lucius, our curiosity and our enjoyment of Milesian tales is a weakness; at the end, we are meant to reflect retroactively on our own not-very-Isiac enjoyment of tales of adultery and deceit. In other words, the priestly narrator has cooked up an elaborate subterfuge to render us, too, ass-like in our interests and in our eagerness to hear and suspend disbelief (cf. Lucius at *Met.* 1.2). Indeed, Gowers ((2001) 78) has suggested that the theme of our potential asinity is already raised by the prologue; ears

---

58 This does not mean that the narrator never looks back at the protagonist while the story is in progress: cf. 6.25.1–4, 1.1.10–12. See Smith (1972). Yet when the narrator's voice is not suppressed, it is still not that of a priest of Isis; e.g. 8.31, 9.13, 9.32, 10.2, 10.7.

that are stroked into receptivity focus attention 'on the reader's most *asinine* characteristics'.[59] Are we, most un-Platonically, lured into emotive responses to a story that turns around to rebuke us at the end?

On the view of (b), the most interesting question with which to respond to the question of *Quis ille?* would be: 'What would a narrative look like in which the narrator concealed his own, his very own, reality?'[60] The most striking example of this phenomenon already present in the *Metamorphoses* is the tale told by Thelyphron (beginning at *Met.* 2.21).[61] A guest at Byrrhena's banquet, he responds reluctantly to the company's request to retell a 'tale' about a victim of mutilation. With the gestures of a professional story-teller, he launches into the story of a corpse that he, Thelyphron, was paid to guard overnight to protect from witches fond of stealing facial parts from dead men. The narrator ('Mr Weak-Wit') relates that he fell into a deep sleep from which he awoke the next morning with a start – was his ward alright? Everything on the corpse's face seemed to be in place, and Thelyphron happily accepted his pay, when the grieving widow was accused of adultery and murder. The corpse was revivified to reveal the truth, and to prove the validity of his testimony he reveals details that no one else could know: because the dead man's name is Thelyphron as well, the poor guard mistakenly heeded the witches' call to the corpse and it is consequently he – our narrator – who has suffered mutilation. Thelyphron puts his hand, in horror, to his nose and ears – they come off his face, simply wax. This is the end of the story, and the narrator – who *now* tells us he is wearing linen bandages where his nose should be – is revealed not as the heterodiegetic narrator he seemed, but as the subject of his own story. But no one – neither intradiegetic nor extradiegetic narrator – has bothered to reveal to us up front this detail that would make all the difference in the telling.

It is not until we get to the end of Lucius' story that we realise just how symptomatic this tale is of the larger narrative of the novel itself.[62] A heterodiegetic narrator promises to weave together various tales for our enjoyment and delectation, giving no hint that the narrative will finally be about his own transformation; at the end, we discover that we have been

---

59 The narrator may not be immune to charges of asinity either, he of the *rudis* ('uncultivated') Latin usage; there may be a pun here on *rudio* ('I bray').

60 Winkler (1985) 110. Too (2001) 177 suggests that Apuleius' narrative 'invites the reader to detach the text from authorial presence and identification' altogether.

61 For an extensive discussion, see Winkler (1985) 110–16.

62 Stories and audiences can be just as disjointed as stories and narrators in this novel. In *Met.* 2.1 Lucius thinks the tales he hears might have an implication for his own life. But where the story might actually have an implication, he draws no conclusions.

dealing in reality with a tale whose narratorial focus is first extradiegetic, then (in book II) homodiegetic. The outcome of his transformation (that Lucius is a priest of Isis) is strictly concealed for the first ten books, nor does Lucius' newly asexual and priestly bent emerge in the selection of stories told.[63] As Winkler asks: 'What kind of narrator can efface the end of the tale that literally marks him for life, so that he not only recounts events as they seemed to him before the awful revelation but in no way avoids the almost unbearable irony of that time between his mutilation and its discovery?'[64] Reflection upon self is utterly absent from this tale; there is 'no integration of present narrator with the past character'.[65] The fact that neither narrator (asinine or priestly) provides a helpful perspective on the part of the story in which he does not participate leads Winkler to suggest that neither books I–10 nor book II can be privileged as the authorised version; it is our effort to do so that provides the most interesting problem.[66]

Finally, if we follow (c) in reading Lucius' transformation first into a man, then into an initiate of Isis, and then into an icon-bearer of Osiris as a continuing play on the theme of metamorphosis (and a progression that makes Lucius look rather asinine, or at least overly credulous), we move out of interpretive stasis into some sort of stable perspective. For one, we can now read the reference to the narrator as 'from Madaura' (11.27) as a metamorphosis as well: of Lucius into a figure that has to be identified with the extradiegetic narrator – that is, Apuleius.[67] For as we know, Lucius himself was a Greek, probably born in Corinth, while Apuleius was from Madaura. This theory found surprising early support from Erwin Rohde,[68] who argued that everything after *Met.* 11.27 refers to Apuleius: it is he who wins 'glory for his studies', who pleads cases in the Roman forum, who

---

63 Contrast the post-pagan Augustine's constant and oppressive presence in the *Confessions*.

64 Winkler (1985) 112.   65 Ibid. 115.

66 One might think book II is privileged as a source of truth because of Lucius' reports of the simultaneous matching dream shared by him and the priest of Isis (cf.11.13; the priest addresses him as Lucius at 11.15). And indeed, if not for this detail it would be very easy to dismiss Lucius' initiation in book II as a sure hoax.

67 Van der Paardt (1981) points out three possible answers to this 'crux': Apuleius has slipped; the manuscripts are corrupt; or the blending of author and alter ego is intentional. Options one and two, and their proponents, are discussed (and dismissed) in Van der Paardt (1981) 98–102. Walsh (1970) 184 suggests that the adjective acts as a *sphragis*, a closing 'seal' that indicates the author's identity. Some scholars have also argued for either Lucius or Apuleius rather than a combination; see discussion of these options in Harrison (1990a), who points out (a) that Apuleius, son of a *duumvir* of a town that was a Roman colony from the Flavian period onward, could hardly be the object of the triple geographical origin spoken by the narrator (Corinth, Sparta, Athens); and (b) that the autobiographer Lucius would not present his life story as a collection of Milesian tales.

68 Rohde (1885) 77.

was initiated into a cult in Greece, and who has suffered from a loss of his patrimony (compare *Met.* 11.28 with Apuleius' account of his own life at *Apology* 23 and 55).[69] So, as Van der Paardt concludes, at 11.27 'a fictitious person [the priest of Osiris] . . . learns by way of a divine encounter or message that the protagonist is no one else but the author':[70] a final example of the novel's theme of metamorphosis.

There is, of course, no right answer to these questions. It is tempting, though, to read Lucius as a figure who in the end (like Aristomenes' Socrates) provides yet another Milesian tale, that of himself; here is another upside-down tale of humiliation by women with supernatural powers (in Lucius' case, both Fotis and Isis). In a way, this lets us have our interpretive cake and eat it too: the lack of narrative circularity lets us see one after all, a figure that is transformed and then returned into its original shape: Lucius, the human ass, who will believe anything he hears.

The voice from *la boue*

Encolpius and Lucius are, in a manner of speaking, both slavish, one as a human, the other as an ass. Their lowly position in society has the advantage of letting us experience scenarios and situations that would not come from the mouth of a Roman elite: not only do the ass's status and large ears let Lucius satisfy his 'curiosity',[71] but also, as Fitzgerald has pointed out, 'the very mobility and omniscience of the narrator derives from the powerlessness and inconsequentiality of the hero as chattel'.[72] Both Encolpius and Lucius are variously subject to beatings, use as a sexual tool, humiliation and paralysis. Encolpius is surely the first buggered man to voice a personal narrative in a text for the elite, and the ass too has his moment of gigolodom in his service of his wealthy lady-friend (*Met.* 10.19–22). Both lack the ability to look after their own best interests, for want of money, sexual potency, a human voice or due to self-delusive beliefs. As stand-ins for a Roman elite male, they are piteous: lacking in agency over others and in mastery over their own bodies.

---

69 Another apparent reference to an author who cannot be Lucius occurs at 4.32, when Apollo speaks in Latin rather than Greek because of the book's 'author': Lucius seems to have been a native Greek-speaker.

70 Van der Paardt (1981) 105–6.

71 Cf. *Met.* 9.13: 'There was no solace anywhere for my torturous existence except that provided by my innate curiosity, for everyone freely said and did whatever they wished, since they counted my presence for little.'

72 W. Fitzgerald (2000) 97.

The theme of slavery is particularly interesting here. Lucius, of course, is well-known for his uncontrollable curiosity and his slavish enjoyment of sex (his 'servile pleasures', *Met.* 11.15; our narrator waxes newly negative on curiosity at 11.23, as does the priest of Isis at 11.15). In Stoic terms, and perhaps in simple Roman terms as well, he is enslaved from the start, and in his transformation into an ass, he embodies in bestial form the state of mind formerly belied by his aristocratic appearance (Fitzgerald (2000) 99 cites a graffito comparing slave labour to ass labour; compare *Met.* 7.3, where Lucius calls himself a slave along with his horse). Encolpius only pretends to be the slave of Eumolpus (starting at *Sat.* 103), of course, but he may actually have a slavish past as well.

It is striking that *these* characters provide our first speakers of extended prose narratives in the ancient world. The interpretive polyphony behind the voices of these first-person narrators, the humiliations they suffer, the confusion about their identity and intentions, and, in Petronius, the dissolution of boundaries between the theatrical self and the lived one: all of these characteristics point to a genre that not only aimed at laughter but also at transgressive play with voice, gender and class. It is one of the strange quirks in the history of the novel that Augustine, of all people – that master of self-exploration and self-transformation – should have taken the *Metamorphoses* as Apuleius' own effort towards an autobiography (*City of God* 18.18).

Further reading

The Greek novel is relatively well-served for narratological analyses. Hägg (1971) explores the techniques used in Chariton, Xenophon and Achilles. Morgan (2004b–f) discusses narrators, narratives and narratees in each of the five extant texts; see also Fusillo (1991), and Futre Pinheiro (1998) on Heliodorus. On the significance of Calasiris' narrative in Heliodorus, see esp. Winkler (1982); also Futre Pinheiro (1991b). On the presentation of the narrators in Longus and Achilles, see (respectively) Morgan (2003b), Whitmarsh (2003). On internal scenes of narration, see Morgan (1991).

For Petronius, attention has focused primarily on the ironies generated by the first-person narration of Encolpius. Beck (1973), (1975) argues that readers detect an older Encolpius comically but genially looking back over the naive pretensions of his youth. Conte (1996), by contrast, reads the fantastical constructions of Encolpius the narrator as undermined by the 'hidden author' Petronius. Jensson (2004) argues that the *Satyrica* is a Romanised version of Odysseus' yarns to the Phaeacians in books 9–12 of the *Odyssey*.

Similar questions have haunted Apuleius' *Metamorphoses*, particular since Winkler (1985) brilliantly analysed tensions between Lucius the *auctor* (narrator) and *actor* (agent in the story). As discussed above, critics have also explored the apparent slippage between Lucius and Apuleius himself: see especially Van der Paardt (1981). For more formalist observations on Apuleius' narrative technique see Van der Paardt (1978).

PART IV

Reception

15

RICHARD HUNTER

Ancient readers

Readers of novels

POET O anxieties of mankind! O how great is the emptiness in matter!
BYSTANDER Who will read this?
POET Are you talking to me? No one, by Hercules.
BYSTANDER No one?
POET One or two people, or no one.
BYSTANDER A shameful and wretched outcome.

(Persius, *Satires* 1.1–3)[1]

'Who read this?' is a question which scholars of the ancient novel, perhaps more than those engaged with any other Greek or Roman literary form, have persistently and anxiously posed. The opening of Persius' first *Satire*, a poem that may close with one of the very few references in literature of the high classical period to one of the extant Greek novels,[2] ought to make us ask 'Does it matter?' We might, however, first consider why the Greek (in particular) novel has attracted this special anxiety about readership – and why it does indeed matter.[3]

The ancient novel – in all its manifestations – first arose in a period of increased levels of and use of literacy and an ever-widening availability of books;[4] it was, despite the major contributions that epic, drama, and historiography (to go no further) made to it, essentially a new form, and such

---

1 I print the most commonly accepted speaker distribution; for other possibilities and the doxography see Kissel (1990) on this passage.
2 *Callirhoe* is offered as afternoon entertainment for those who appreciate only vulgar and unsubtle buffoonery. The possibility that this refers to Chariton's novel seems to have fallen out of favour with commentators on Persius; a mime or a play (based on the novel?) or the name of a prostitute are the now commonly accepted explanations.
3 Both Tatum (1994) and Schmeling (2003b) have chapters on the readership of the Greek novel, but not a parallel chapter for Petronius and Apuleius (though note Dowden's contribution to Tatum (1994)).
4 This is incontestable, whatever qualifications are necessary to notions of very widespread reading skills (Harris (1989)).

'novelty' naturally brings with it questions of readership and the cultural context of those readers. Moreover, the fact that the novels, partly because they were not blessed with a 'classical' heritage, did not enter educational curricula before the Byzantine period makes that context both problematic and interesting. The patterns of circulation and reception of the ancient literature about which we know most were largely determined by the partly complementary phenomena of elite taste and scholarly choice, the inherent conservatism of school curricula, and the market-forces of the book-trade; a literary form that, to some extent at least, flourished independently of these factors assumes potentially great significance for what it might tell us of ancient society. Moreover, certain novels clearly did have a long and rich influence on various traditions, most notably the *Alexander Romance* and (in the east) *Metiochus and Parthenope*,[5] and the study of classical narrative here has important ramifications for the wider spread of fiction; although the study of the diffusion of the novel and the question of the ancient readership are different matters, there is a clear overlap between them, and this too lends urgency to the present subject.

Some of the scholarly concern with questions of readership, particularly in the earlier stages of the modern revival of interest in the novel, arose from a sense of embarrassment at the perceived low stylistic quality, or at least intellectual sterility, of the surviving works. 'Who *could* read this?' was the (usually) unspoken question. The answer, of course, was 'people not like us', and the range of glosses given to that answer is a familiar litany which needs no rehearsing: Perry's 'children and the poor-in-spirit' and 'young or naïve people of little education' are the most frequently quoted examples.[6] Richard Heinze's persuasive argument that Petronius' *Satyrica* is (among other things) a mocking parody of the Greek 'ideal novel' did nothing for the modern reputation of those novels, but (more importantly) reinforced the feeling that serious people in antiquity did not take those novels seriously (and certainly did not devote much time to reading them).[7] Two obvious caveats may be entered. First, parody of this type does not necessarily mean that the parodied form is held in low esteem by the apparently elite audience for the parody; and, second, the writing and appreciation of such parody exploits a particular rhetorical construction of what the parodied texts are like, and does not necessarily either depend upon on detailed knowledge of the originals or offer trustworthy evidence as to their nature.

A now very familiar handful of ancient texts is standardly adduced in support of the view that the educated elite was dismissive of the quality of the ancient novel: Persius on 'Callirhoe' (cf. above), an abusive 'epistle' by

5 See 'Introduction', p. 13.   6 Perry (1967) 5, 56.   7 Heinze (1899).

Philostratus to one 'Chariton' (*Letter* 66), and even a letter of Julian from 363 CE forbidding the priests of Asia Minor from reading 'fictions from previous generations in the form of history, stories of *erōs* and all such things' (*Letter* 89, p. 169 Bidez), a testimony that one might have thought pointed to the potential attraction of such texts for educated men.[8]

Not even Petronius and Apuleius are spared. Macrobius adduces the Latin pair as examples of 'stories stuffed with the fictional happenings of lovers', which 'aim only at delighting the ear', and expresses his amazement that a philosopher such as Apuleius 'wasted his time' on such things, which he then banishes to the nursery.[9] Macrobius has the opening of the proem of Apuleius' *Metamorphoses* in mind,[10] whereas it is the echo of that opening by the old woman who narrates 'Cupid and Psyche' ('I shall forthwith distract you with witty stories and old wives' tales', *Met.* 4.27) that is picked up in an alleged letter of the emperor Septimius Severus abusing Clodius Albinus:[11] 'I am more upset that some of you considered Clodius worthy of praise as a cultured man, when he busies himself with old wives' tales and grows old amidst the Punic Milesian tales of his countryman Apuleius and other literary trivia' (*Augustan History*, *Clodius Albinus* 12.12). Such observations are, of course, part of the self-representation of the truly serious man; Apuleius' singularly elusive and ironic self-deprecation is taken at face value and reinforced by the imposition of the familiar hierarchies of education and 'culture'.

Recent years have, however, seen an increasing appreciation of the sophistication and wit of Longus, Achilles Tatius and Heliodorus; scholars have, despite the silence of the ancient sources, found a place for these works within accepted ideas about the literary culture of the Roman empire. Achilles at least is now represented by six papyri of the second and third centuries,[12] and some measure of his secure place in elite culture would seem to be offered by the clear imitations of *Leucippe and Clitophon* in the Greek literature of the fifth century CE, namely the erotic epistles of Aristaenetus, the *Dionysiaca* of Nonnus, and Musaeus' *Hero and Leander*.[13] That Aristaenetus also

---

8 Julian also proscribes iambic poets such as Archilochus and Hipponax, Old Comedy (or at least the 'iambic' part of it), and the writings of Epicureans and Sceptics. Whitmarsh (2005a) 607–8 gives reasons for doubting that Julian is here actually referring to 'novels'.

9 *Commentary on 'The Dream of Scipio'* 1.2.8–9. For the parallel with the later remarks of 'Philip the Philosopher' cf. Hunter (2005) 129.

10 Cf. also *Commentary* 1.2.7 'Stories (*fabulae*), whose very name professes their falsehood, are designed merely to give pleasure to the ear or as a protreptic to proper behaviour', which also looks to the opening of Apuleius' preface.

11 Cf. Winkler (1985) 53–4.

12 Cf. Garnaud (1991) xxiii–xxv; Laplace (1993); Cavallo (1996).

13 For Aristaenetus cf. Mazal (1971), *Index Auctorum* under 'Achilles Tatius'; for Nonnus cf. Keydell, *RE* 17.907, 915; for Musaeus cf. Kost (1971) 29–30.

clearly borrows from Xenophon of Ephesus[14] ought, however, to make us reflect upon the purposes of the now habitual modern division of the extant Greek novels into 'pre-sophistic' (Chariton, Xenophon) and 'sophistic' (Achilles, Longus, Heliodorus). Another work of considerable literary ambition, though one very different from *Leucippe*, the *Wonders beyond Thule* of Antonius Diogenes[15] is also cited often enough to suggest that it had a significant readership among the educated (*pepaideumenoi*); to judge by Photius' summary, the narrative complexity of tales within tales in this work made the Odyssean structures of Heliodorus' novel seem by comparison entirely straightforward.[16] *Daphnis and Chloe*, however, remains one of antiquity's mysteries: there are no papyri and no certain allusion to this remarkable text before the Byzantine period.[17] Heliodorus has so far appeared on only one 'ancient' text (a parchment codex of the sixth or seventh century),[18] though he was apparently known to fifth-century Christians.[19]

As for the allegedly 'pre-sophistic' novels of Chariton and Xenophon of Ephesus, and the many fragments of similar texts such as the *Ninus Romance*, 'there was no such thing as "popular literature" in the Roman Empire, if that means literature which became known to tens or hundreds of thousands of people by means of personal reading'.[20] The principal arguments for this position are general considerations of literacy and book-production and, specifically, the relatively few papyrus fragments of both known and lost novels.[21] This latter criterion cannot be pushed too hard, simply because of the elements of chance in survival and because, despite the important place that Egypt occupies in most novels, it may be that the form enjoyed its greatest flourishing in western Asia Minor, from where papyri do not survive. Be that as it may, there is, as Susan Stephens pointed out, no obvious difference in the physical quality and scribal carefulness of the 'pre-sophistic' and 'sophistic' papyrus fragments and also no consistent difference between 'novel' papyri and ancient texts of 'mainstream' authors. Neither papyrology nor the sociology of antiquity, in other words, offers support to the idea of a

---

14 Cf. Gärtner, *RE* 9A.2087. It is, however, a curious phenomenon that all apparently certain borrowings are from book 1 of *Anthia and Habrocomes*.

15 Cf. Stephens and Winkler (1995) 101, 'far and away the most cited of the ancient novels (which is not the same as being the most read)'; Bowie (2002a) 58–60.

16 Cf. Stephens and Winkler (1995) 116.

17 Various pre-Byzantine echoes of Longus have been suggested: cf. e.g. Bernsdorff (1993) for Lucian and Bowie (1995) for Heliodorus. For Longus and Alciphron cf. Hunter (1983) 6–13.

18 Cf. Gronewald (1979). Both Heliodorus and, above all, Achilles are well represented in Byzantine lexica; for Heliodorus cf. Colonna (1938) 361–72, and for Achilles, Vilborg (1955) xxxii–xxxiv (cf. also Plepelits (1980) 48–9).

19 Cf. Socrates, *Church History* 5.22 (= Heliodorus, T 1 Colonna). For a possible echo of Heliodorus in another fifth-century text, cf. Morgan (1998a) 75–6.

20 Harris (1989) 227.   21 Cf. Stephens (1994); Stephens and Winkler (1995).

'trashy' literature for the modestly educated, an idea that itself derives in part from modern situations and elite constructions of the past. Just as, moreover, Petronian parody does not necessarily tell us anything about the parodied texts, the fact that the 'old wives' tale' of 'Cupid and Psyche' clearly imitates (particularly in its earlier parts) the manner and motifs of a novel such as Xenophon's *Anthia and Habrocomes*[22] tells us little about the resonances of such a fiction.

There are clear differences within the five extant 'ideal' novels in terms of literary and stylistic elaboration (Atticism, admittance of hiatus etc.),[23] sententiousness and moralising,[24] and so forth. Thus, for example, Xenophon's description of the Ephesian festival at which Habrocomes and Anthia meet (1.2–3) and Heliodorus' parallel account (in the mouth of Cnemon) of the meeting of Theagenes and Charicleia at Delphi (3.1–5) have many similarities and motifs in common (both heroines, for example, play the rôle of Artemis); Heliodorus has, in fact, often been thought to build directly upon Xenophon's narrative.[25] Heliodorus is, however, clearly far richer, more elaborately detailed ('local colour'),[26] makes use of Homeric echo and allusion, and is explicitly self-conscious about the use of the rhetorical, ecphrastic tradition (3.4.8–9); can one move in any simple way from the demands which a text makes upon its readers to the identity of those readers? In general, Heliodorus' whole novel may be seen as an attempt to incorporate and surpass the novel tradition that has preceded him,[27] and a novel such as Xenophon's, if not the *Anthia and Habrocomes* itself, is clearly in his sights. Charicleia's false tale to Thyamis at 1.22, 'Our story is this: by race we are Ionians; we belong to the nobility of Ephesus', seems indeed to play with the place of Ephesus in 'simple fictions' which are to be shown (by Heliodorus) to be inferior to Heliodorus' extraordinary conception. The novelists are in fact the ancient novel readers about whom we know most:[28] Apuleius' elaborate hermeneutic strategies for the 'reading' of the Greek *Ass* are a cardinal

---

22 Cf. e.g. Kenney (1990a) on 4.28.
23 Reeve (1971); O'Sullivan (1995) 135–9.   24 Morales (2000).
25 Gärtner, *RE* 9A.2080–2; I have not seen M. Schnepf, *De imitationis ratione quae intercedit inter Heliodorum et Xenophontem Ephesium commentatio* (1887).
26 Cf. Nilsson (1957) 243–5. Xenophon's claim that at the Ephesian festival 'it was the custom for the girls to find husbands and the young men wives' (1.2.3) looks like a regularising gloss upon the idea of the festival as the site for 'falling in love at first sight', an idea presumably as familiar in ancient life as in literature. We ought, however, to remember that the *Suda* credits Xenophon with a work *On the City of the Ephesians*; O'Sullivan (1995) 2 is very sceptical about this claim.
27 Cf. Winkler (1982); Hunter (1998b) 47–8; such an interpretation does not depend upon the dating of Heliodorus (for which see the 'Index of Greek and Roman novelists').
28 The interpretative essay on Heliodorus by 'Philip the Philosopher' is normally dated to the Byzantine period, though some have argued for a date in late antiquity, cf. Hunter (2005) 125–6.

text in the history of interpretation, and Xenophon's novel very probably reworks Chariton,[29] just as *Anthia and Habrocomes* itself may have found imitators.[30]

Recent scholarship has also explored extensively the possibility of a female audience for the novel. Brigitte Egger adduced the 'emotional gynocentrism' of the novels as an argument for a significant female readership,[31] but expressions and descriptions of, on the one hand, female sexual desire (cf. esp. Xen. Eph. 1.9–10) and, on the other, empowerment as the objects of male desire seem as likely to fuel male fantasies as to offer women a way of voicing that which social convention restricts them from themselves voicing too openly. It must be admitted that there is little positive evidence in favour of the 'female readership' hypothesis, and at best the question remains open.[32]

If attempts to generalise about 'the readership of the ancient novel' inevitably fall foul of the very variety of texts with which we are confronted, then similar dangers face any attempt to draw conclusions from the world that the novels create. There is great variation in, for example, the 'social realism' of the world they portray,[33] but certain patterns recur. Consider the opening of Xenophon's *Anthia and Habrocomes*: 'In Ephesus, there was a man, one of the very leading citizens, called Lycomedes.' As has often been observed,[34] western Asia Minor is very prominent in the extant Greek novels: in addition to the 'Ephesian story of Anthia and Habrocomes', Chariton claims to come from Aphrodisias, and an important part of the action takes place on the coast of Asia Minor; *Daphnis and Chloe* is set on Lesbos; important elements of *Leucippe and Clitophon* are set in Byzantium and Ephesus, and similar geographical inferences may be drawn from what we know of some of the fragmentary novels. With all due caution, we may say that the eastern Aegean and the western Asiatic coast have as good a claim as any to be central to the development of the novel. Second, we may note Xenophon's stress upon Habrocomes' father's status, 'one of the very leading men there' (1.1.1.), a phrase that recurs repeatedly through the work (cf. 2.13.3, 3.2.1, 3.9.5, 5.1.4); Habrocomes himself is the very model of the educated, elite citizen: 'He combined physical beauty and intellectual accomplishments. He engaged in the full range of cultural and educational activities, and his

---

29 Cf. Gärtner, *RE* 9A.2082–6; Papanikolaou (1973a) 153–9; many have, inevitably, held that the relationship is the other way round, cf. O'Sullivan (1995) 145–70.

30 Cf. Stephens and Winkler (1995) 278 on the 'Antheia' fragment.   31 Egger (1994a).

32 Cf. the summary in Haynes (2003) 2–10. West (2003) has suggested that at least the early novels were recited to women while they spun and wove, as a way of beguiling the time.

33 Apuleius' *Metamorphoses* hold a special place here: cf. Millar (1981); Fitzgerald (2000) 87–114. For an illuminating study of the mixture of archaising and 'realistic' material in the socio-legal position of women in the 'ideal novel' cf. Egger (1994a).

34 See esp. Bowie (1994) 450–1, (2002a) 57–8.

customary pursuits were hunting, riding, and fighting under arms' (1.1.2). This novel, then, allows us to read about the eventful lives of *important*, elite people, who have, as their aristocratic names proclaim, a grand status in the present day similar to that of historical and quasi-historical figures such as Sesonchosis, Ninus and Semiramis, Polycrates of Samos, and Hermocrates of Syracuse, who appear in the novels set in the distant past. Does that mean that we ourselves, the audience, are not such important people? Or (rather) that we in fact move in similar social circles, or that novels appealed to both 'ordinary' people and the elite? In favour of the second alternative, it has been been argued that the privileging of an ideal of married, heterosexual love, based on mutual fidelity and partnership (*homonoia*, 'like-mindedness': cf. Chariton 1.3.7) and offering both emotional and physical satisfaction, is most easily understood precisely within elite circles of the Hellenised empire during the second and third centuries CE.[35]

Here, as often, it is Achilles' novel which stands somewhat apart: the characters are indeed from the well-to-do elite classes, but Leucippe's beauty, however striking, is not of the superhuman kind that causes everyone who beholds her to imagine her a goddess (contrast Chariton's Callirhoe), and the fate of the characters does not affect whole societies. It is tempting to connect this to the first-person form of Achilles' narrative, which is also clearly crucial for the amusing weakness of the central male character, Clitophon. There is indeed a relationship between the characters of a fiction and its audience; the first-person invites readers to assimilate the experiences of the characters to their own lives, whereas the third-person of Chariton and Xenophon creates a wondering admiration and emotional sympathy for characters far removed from the readers' experience.

Readers in novels

Scenes in which characters tell each other their life story (their *diēgēmata*, 'narratives') are prominent in the ancient novels; such scenes may amount, with more or less explicit self-referentiality, to an oral telling of the novel we are reading.[36] The novels, however, also make important use of scenes in which texts of various kinds (letters, inscriptions etc.) are actually read. This inscribed doubleness may have significance for the reception of works which may have been both read and read out to listening groups, but it is also important to their generic sense.[37] The novels are written texts, which – to

---

35 Cf. Swain (1996) 118–31.
36 Cf. Hunter (1994) 1066–7. There is a particularly good example at Xen. Eph. 5.9.6–8, where Anthia must confess that 'the narrative of Hippothoos' is a closed book to her.
37 For the generic status of the novels see Goldhill, this volume.

greater or lesser degrees – lay claim to the methods and purposes of oral story-telling and – to greater or lesser degrees – advertise and exploit this constructed in-betweenness for various literary purposes. For example, the old lady's introduction to the 'Cupid and Psyche' episode advertises the coming tale as an oral performance, by echoing the prologue without the prologue's pointed references to writing ('if only you will not disdain to look upon an Egyptian papyrus inscribed with the sharpness of a reed from the Nile'). By contrast, the obvious self-referentiality of a later passage glories in the writtenness of the *Metamorphoses* as a whole: 'I shall tell you what happened from the beginning. It is a sequence of events which persons more learned than I, writers whom Fortune has invested with fluency of the pen, can appropriately commit to paper as an example of historical narrative (*in historiae specimen*). In a nearby town . . .' (8.1.3, trans. P. G. Walsh).[38]

This constructed dichotomy between modes of reception is used in many different ways. Thus Longus, at the heart of whose subject lie themes of natural art and artificial nature,[39] presents his narrative as a response to a pre-existing story preserved on a painting (a *graphē*), but which requires another kind of *graphē* ('writing') in order to reach an audience. Chariton frames his novel between two assertions of authorship ('I, Chariton of Aphrodisias, shall relate . . . This is my history of Callirhoe'), but closes the narrative proper with a speech – an address to Aphrodite – of his heroine (and, presumably, title-figure); this is the only novel of which we know to end in such character-speech, if the first-person narrative of Achilles is excluded, and here the voice of 'Callirhoe' is set in pointed tension with a claim of ownership over *Callirhoe*.

At the conclusion of Xenophon's novel, Anthia and Habrocomes dedicate in the temple of Artemis at Ephesus 'dedications and, particularly, a [or 'the': the text is uncertain] *graphē* of all that they had suffered and done'. *graphē* here is likely to be a 'written record' (presumably an inscription), rather than a painting;[40] it cannot quite be, as some have taken it,[41] 'the novel which we have just read', as the story pointedly continues for another couple of sentences, thus making clear that inscription and novel are not co-terminous. There is clearly here, however, some kind of gesture towards the written text's sense of its own future (a very familiar aspect of, in particular,

---

38 Cf. e.g. Finkelpearl (1998) 116–17.   39 Cf. e.g. Hunter (1983) 38–52; Teske (1991).

40 For 'painting' cf. e.g. Bowie (1978) 1164. That the word used is *graphē*, rather than *epigramma* (cf. Wouters (1990) 473), does not seem to me decisive; a fairly extensive record is clearly envisaged.

41 Cf. e.g. Winkler (1985) 240–1, arguing for a reading of Apuleius' *Metamorphoses* as a 'temple dedication'.

Apuleius' novel, e.g. 2.12, 6.29, 8.1). So too, in the B and C redactions of *Apollonius, King of Tyre*, king Apollonius writes an account of 'his own fortunes, and those of his family' and deposits one copy in his library and one in the temple of Diana at Ephesus (where his wife has served as priestess during the long years of their separation). The written record serves as a kind of counterpoint to the oral account of his story which Apollonius, ordered to do so by a dream, gives at the temple and which leads to the mutual recognition. The author thus creates – and foreshadows – both oral and written versions of the same narrative within his text.

Leucippe and Clitophon offers an interesting variant on this pattern. The last three and a half books take place at Ephesus, and at their heart lies a virginity test under the aegis of Ephesian Artemis. In the course of the last book the leading characters recount their stories at a series of dinner parties: here, then, an oral account is 'deposited' at Ephesus, and indeed a thank-offering at the temple is the goal (*telos*) to which both the story and the generic expectations of the audience have been directed. On the other hand, Artemis may not have been too pleased with the way in which this novel had preserved the letter but not the spirit of her chastity-ordinances; an eternal written record of such behaviour, preserved in her own temple, might have been an irony too far for her, or even for Achilles. Instead, we get the next best thing: an oral record deposited, not with Artemis, but with her priest who hosts the dinner parties, and whose own lubricious character (8.9.1) makes him a very appropriate 'ideal reader' for, and hence guardian of, this novel.[42] This interpretation is reinforced by the way in which Achilles plays in this scene with notions of authorship and the possibilities of intervention in narrative. Clitophon's richly allusive (Homer, Plato etc.) re-telling allows Leucippe to tell her story in her own words (8.16), but his own account of what happened to him (8.5) is in indirect speech, that form which – in Gérard Genette's familiar analysis – imposes and emphasises the mediation of a composing 'author', as also do the verbs, 'remove' (8.5.2, 8.5.5) and 'alter' (8.5.2), with which he tells of his 'telling'.[43]

If such techniques dramatise the notion of authorship, novel 'readers' are also not hard to find, and not merely in the individuals and crowds who listen and react to – and thus guide audience response to – the tales they hear.[44] Achilles' hero himself notes, with respect to the story of Apollo and Daphne, that 'erotic stories fuel the flames of desire' (1.5.6),[45] and the famous story in (?) Lucian's *Love Stories* – a young man shut himself up all night (like a reader?) in the temple at Cnidos and, to judge by a stain upon the

42 Cf. Fusillo (1996) 59.   43 Cf. Whitmarsh (2003) 199–200.
44 Cf. e.g. Morgan (1991).
45 Discussed by e.g. Goldhill (1995) 67–8; for the statue itself cf. Stewart (1997) 97–106.

marble, ejaculated upon the statue of Aphrodite – may be paradigmatic for a real or imagined response to the impossibly beautiful and statue-like heroines of the novel.[46] A version of this construction of the reading experience is perhaps in fact dramatised in *Apollonius, King of Tyre*. The king's daughter, Tarsia, preserves her virginity while 'working' in a brothel and earns large sums of money by telling her story ('the story of the novel') to every potential customer.[47] The men come in wanting sex and leave in floods of piteous tears; Tarsia's telling, moreover, removes her clients' lust (34), so they leave not only poorer, but also somehow 'satisfied'. That these clients are one kind of potential reader of *Apollonius* is an idea that is written into the text. Athenagora and his friend, Tarsia's first two clients, subsequently conceal themselves to watch Tarsia 'perform' with others; such spying would normally have sexual activity as its object (cf. Petronius, *Sat.* 28.4–5), but here the two men, like we ourselves, are spying on an adventure narrative.

What is it indeed that male readers want from the novel: to admire the suffering and virtue of chaste heroines, or to fantasise about having sex with them, or are these activities inseparable? Chariton's explicit reference to his readers at 8.1.4 is perhaps not to be taken without a touch of irony:

> And I think that this last book will prove very pleasurable (*hēdiston*) to its readers: it cleanses away the grim events of the earlier ones. There will be no more pirates or slavery or lawsuits or fighting or suicide or wars or conquests; now there will be lawful love and sanctioned marriage.
>
> (trans. Reardon, adapted)

What kind of pleasure (*hēdonē*) do readers actually seek in the novel? Any answer must of course take account of the very variety of the ancient texts that we classify as novels, but we should remember too that both authors and readers were aware of that variety. We are not to imagine that no one who read, say, Chariton's *Callirhoe* was not also familiar with novels of the earthier type represented by, say, Lollianus' *Phoenician Affairs*. The very variety of 'the ancient novel' allowed novelists to exploit the expectation of a diverse and complex audience response, and that in turn might suggest a diverse and complex audience for the novels themselves.

---

46 Fuller discussion in Hunter (1994) 1073–6.
47 For another version of this motif cf. Xen. Eph. 2.9.4: even a goatherd is moved by Anthia's story. For the parallel scenario of Seneca, *Controversies* 1.2 cf. Panayotakis (2002); Hunter (2005) 128–9.

Further reading

The surveys in Bowie (1994) and (2003) and Stephens (1994) offer the best introduction to the subject and presentation of relevant evidence; Egger (1988), (1994a–b) and Haynes (2003) consider the question of a female readership. On ancient literacy in general see Harris (1989). Hägg (1983) ch. 3 offers a readable general introduction to the issues.

16

JOAN B. BURTON

Byzantine readers

After an interval of some eight centuries, the genre of the novel was resurrected in twelfth-century Byzantium by four writers: Theodore Prodromos, Niketas Eugenianos, Eustathios Makrembolites and Constantine Manasses. They modelled their four novels after the novels of the second sophistic period, particularly those of Achilles Tatius and Heliodorus. Points of similarity include plot elements, characterisations and stylistics, as well as lavish use of allusion and rhetorical display. Like the novels of the second sophistic, the Byzantine novels were written in Atticising Greek and addressed principally a learned audience. In an intensely Christian world, these new novels also resurrected the ancient novels' pagan gods and rituals. Yet in reviving the novel, these writers were also striving to create something different and new. Evidence from such varied sources as collections of sayings, poems and critical writings shows a continued readership of the ancient novel during the mediaeval Greek period. The best evidence of a sophisticated and attentive readership of the ancient novels is found in the twelfth-century revivalist novels.

Many factors can be associated with the genre's revival. With the rise of Christianity the appeal of the novel had transferred to other types of narrative, for example, to apocryphal stories and saints' lives, with their novelistic themes of chastity, trials, separations, reunions and salvation in the end. The decline of the writing of saints' lives by the twelfth century in Byzantium left an opening for the revival of the novel.[1] Also, the crusades might have prompted a desire to reinforce Greek identity against the Latin west by setting a heightened value on the Greek past. Anna Komnene, the emperor Alexios I Komnenos' daughter, promoted the use of Atticising Greek.

A long tradition of anxiety about the moral tone of the ancient novels offers a backdrop for the revival. Defensive and apologetic interpretive approaches

---

1 Beck (1977) 63.

are well attested. For example, the supposed conversions of Heliodorus and Achilles Tatius into Christian bishops, along with a general Byzantine taste for allegorisation, helped justify continued readership of the ancient novels.[2] Even so, the ninth-century scholar and churchman Photius in his reader's guide, the *Library*, tempers a recommendation to read Achilles Tatius (for his style) with the warning that 'obscenity and impurity of sentiment impair his judgment, are prejudicial to seriousness, and make the story disgusting to read or something to be avoided altogether' (codex 87.66a21–4). Heliodorus, in contrast, is praised by Photius for 'show[ing] a desire for the strict observance of propriety' (codex 73.50a17–18) and Iamblichus for 'mak[ing] less show of indecencies than Achilles Tatius' (codex 94.73b25–6, trans. Freese (1920)). Yet Achilles Tatius' novel garners praise for moral content also, as in a ninth-century epigram ascribed to Photius or Leo the Philosopher (*Palatine Anthology* 9.203.10).[3] In the eleventh century, Michael Psellus defends Heliodorus against criticism of 'unseemly elements of the plot' (44) and expresses disapproval of Achilles Tatius' moral tone: 'in order to give rhetorical pleasure, he is prepared to make his meaning indecent' (91–2, trans. Dyck). In the mid-twelfth century, George Tornikios' funeral oration for Anna Komnene sums up longstanding anxieties regarding the reading of pagan literature – with its 'polytheism', 'violations of virgins', and 'abductions of youths': 'this study they rightly thought dangerous even for men, and for women and girls excessively insidious' (2, trans. Browning (1990)).

The twelfth-century novels are reflective of contemporary moral ideals: for example, they set a high premium on chastity and introduce the motif of a wedding held inside a temple (reflecting the Christian custom of church weddings). But the Byzantine novels also include motifs and themes that undermine this idealism. Rather than mitigate the theme of abduction, Prodromos has the hero himself engage in a violent, non-consensual abduction.[4] Rather than include an overt infusion of Christianity, the novels resurrect pagan gods, rituals and beliefs. Fictive discussions regarding the possibility of resurrection and the function of religious offerings also reflect controversies of Christian practices and beliefs.[5] The use of allusions to the Biblical *Song of Songs* in an explicitly erotic passage in Eugenianos seems on the surface to run counter to the mystical, allegorical readings favoured by the church.[6] If pre-marital sex between hero and heroine never takes place in Makrembolites, it is not for want of trying, and erotic dreams are prominently featured.

---

2 MacAlister (1996) 108–12.   3 See Dyck (1986) 82.
4 Burton (2000); cf. Jouanno (2001) 335–6.   5 Burton (1998).
6 Burton (1998) 201–3; cf. Roilos (2005) 205–7, 211–14.

The twelfth-century revival of the novel is notable for its brevity and intensity, with all four novels written within a relatively short period mid-century.[7] At least three of the four writers are known to have been closely associated with the court at Constantinople. After this brief period, learned novels in Atticising Greek apparently ceased to be written. When the genre reappears, perhaps in the mid-thirteenth century, it is in a significantly different form: the vernacular romance. Links can, of course, be drawn between the vernacular romances and the twelfth-century novels,[8] but foreign influences were also in play, and the romances moved in new thematic directions, with royal protagonists, castles, ogres, jousting and pre-marital sex.

In recent years scholars have focused on such areas as Christian symbolism, social issues and intertextuality.[9] I concentrate here on how the novels themselves, in suggesting modes of genre and readership, show that they conceive of themselves as not merely imitative of the ancient novels but rather creative and original. The novel of Manasses exists only in fragments and because of space limitations is not considered here; the other three novels are complete and include self-reflexive moments that highlight engagement with past texts, underscore innovation and suggest authorial concerns about reception.

Prodromos and the recreation of the ancient novel

Prodromos signals his debt to Heliodorus by starting his novel *in medias res* (in the middle of things), with a pirate attack on a city. Other Heliodoran features include retrospective, embedded tales and a philosophical discussion of human sacrifice. Prodromos' novel might be summarised thus: after misadventures abroad – including a king's near sacrifice of the hero and his friend, an incident involving a she-bear, and several notable feasts – the hero and heroine are brought home by their fathers and wed in a temple. In overall tone, the novel is heavily rhetorical and philosophical.

An emblematic episode in the middle of the novel, Gobryas' feast, includes elements strongly suggestive of self-reflection on what it means to revive and recreate the genre of the novel. The feast takes place in the context of a dispute between the pirate king Mistylos and Bryaxes, king of Pissa [*sic*], over a city. While Mistylos frames his reply to a threatening letter of Bryaxes, he has his

---

7 Dating: MacAlister (1991); Magdalino (1992); Beaton (1996) 80–1, 211–12; Jeffreys (1998) 192, (2000); Agapitos (1998) 144–8, (2000a) 181–5; Roilos (2005) 7–11.
8 Agapitos (1991) 95, 213–22; Beaton (1996) 147–54.
9 E.g. Jouanno (1989), (1992), (1994), (2000), (2001); Garland (1990); Beaton (1996); MacAlister (1996); Burton (1998), (2000), (2003), (2006); papers in Agapitos and Reinsch (2000); Nilsson (2001); Labarthe-Postel (2001). Roilos (2005) offers a more general analysis of the poetics of the novels.

chief satrap, Gobryas, entertain the letter-bearer, Artaxanes. The description of the feast – including roast lamb stuffed with live birds, an entertainer and an elaborately decorated drinking cup – extends this interlude for over 300 lines (4.114–417).

The first element of Gobryas' feast is a hybrid dish of roast lamb (4.124–9):

> A roast lamb was set in the middle,
> and when Artaxanes seized it
> and started to cut it open, tear it apart to eat,
> there emerged from its belly
> baby sparrows, which rose up with wings
> and flew over the satrap's head.

An obvious classical antecedent for this hybrid dish is the elaborate wild boar served during Trimalchio's feast in Petronius' *Satyrica* (40.3–8). Meat dishes stuffed with other creatures are not otherwise unattested in the ancient world, of course, but elsewhere the stuffing, so far as we have evidence of it, is cooked.[10] The shared details of the carving of the dish and the live birds that fly forth suggest possible allusion. Strengthening this impression is the fact that in both dishes, the animal is male but presented as if giving birth.[11] In both Petronius and Prodromos, the meat dish is interpreted to a guest who recoils from the interpretation, and in both texts, an entertainer follows, who sings lyrics connected with the host.

Descriptions of hybrid dishes often function in texts in metaliterary ways.[12] As in the case of Petronius' stuffed boar, so too in Prodromos' text, in the suspended moment of a feast, the appearance of a hybrid dish seems representative of the innovation, mixture of genres and fledgling quality of a new literary project. Gobryas' subsequent assertion that the hybrid dish illustrates his master's powers to alter nature, bring forth monstrous new beings (even make soldiers give birth to puppies), seems also reflective of authorial power; confusions of gender and species within fictions are often linked with issues of literary legitimacy.[13] For Prodromos' Christian readers, such representations of a creator-being would have further disturbing over-tones, as would the descriptions of male conception, and the entertainer's fake death and resurrection.[14]

The shared emphasis in Gobryas' and Trimalchio's feasts on manipulating nature and confusing life and death, human and animal may bolster the

10 E.g. Macrobius, *Saturnalia* 3.13.13; Athenaeus, *Sophists at Supper* 4.129b.
11 Cf. Baldwin (1990); Beaton (1996) 75.　　12 Gowers (1993) 40–6.
13 Branham (1989) 41–4; Whitmarsh (2001a) 76–8, 87. Compare Lucian, *You Are a Prometheus in Words* 7.
14 Burton (1998) 190–5.

case for Petronius' influence.[15] Other parallels include the host's rhetorical manipulation of the feast. There is evidence of continued knowledge of the Latin novels in the west early on,[16] but not in the east, where knowledge of Latin was rare among learned Byzantines before the thirteenth century. Yet Manuel I's court, characterised by contact with the Latin west, could have provided a context for discovery of this famous passage of Petronius' novel.[17] By centrally focusing on a Pissan–pirate conflict, complete with 'Byzantine' ceremonial and a satirical pirate feast (4.9 to 6.146), Prodromos expands his novel's genealogy beyond the 'idealistic' Greek novels and includes Petronian parody and satire as well.

The breaking of a drinking cup at the feast is another emblem of the creativity of Prodromos' engagement with past literature.[18] The last two elements of Gobryas' feast – the entertainer's lengthy song (4.243–308) and an extended description of a cup decorated with narrative scenes (4.331–411) – recall the balancing of song and cup in Theocritus, *Idyll* 1. The entertainer's song links Mistylos with Helios and includes Theocritean refrains; the cup is covered with scenes related to Dionysus – men harvesting and processing grapes, dancers, and Dionysus interacting variously with bacchantes and satyrs.[19] Theocritus' cup contrasts with Achilles' shield in Homer's *Iliad*; both these classical antecedents are notable for their programmatic qualities, and Prodromos clearly places his cup within that tradition. Prodromos' gemstone cup also specifically recalls Achilles Tatius' rock-crystal wine bowl, with its Dionysiac imagery (Ach. Tat. 2.3).[20]

But before describing the wine cup, Prodromos has it slip from the drunken Artaxanes' hands and break into pieces (4.324–6). The destruction of an elaborately described work of art is in itself a radical moment, almost unprecedented in ancient literature.[21] Why break such a magnificent cup? The breaking of an emblematic cup, we might conclude, itself represents innovation; breaking the cup can also stand as a meta-literary symbol for breaking a literary mould.[22]

A drinking cup is often opposed to the martial world.[23] At the centre of Prodromos' romance novel, a battle intrudes with all its martial horror and

---

15 Confusions of life and death at Gobryas' feast: the burnt womb giving birth; Satyrion's fake death, with lamentation (4.230–1, 233); Artaxanes' corpse-like stupor (4.414–15, 417). Trimalchio's dinner as funeral feast: Rimell (2002) 185–8.
16 E.g. Macrobius, *Dream of Scipio* 1.2.8. John of Salisbury and Trimalchio's dinner: Martin (1979).
17 Angold (1997) 226–40; Magdalino (1993) 221–6. Cf. Roilos (2000) 115–16.
18 Further, Burton (2006) 552–7. 19 On this ecphrasis cf. Labarthe-Postel (2001) 361–2.
20 Since *kratēr* could also refer to a chalice, I translate Prodromos' wine vessel as 'cup' rather than 'bowl'.
21 Cf. Ovid, *Metamorphoses* 6.103–33. 22 Cf. Lucian, *You Are a Prometheus in Words* 2.
23 E.g. *Palatine Anthology* 11.48; *Anacreontea* 4 West.

epic overtones; the feast is a suspended moment within that martial activity, a delay while a letter is crafted in reply to a military challenge. Thus the wine cup's peaceful Dionysiac scenes contrast with the onslaught of war. The fact that the victorious king's representative breaks the cup and the vanquished king's representative mourns its loss suggests an element of foreshadowing here as well.

Yet why describe the cup after it is broken rather than before? It is not King Mistylos here but the author who has the power to bring the cup back together, resurrect the dead, make the past live again. The establishment of a sense of continuity with the past is an aim of much of Byzantine literature. But insofar as this cup specifically recalls (and elaborates upon) Achilles Tatius' precious Dionysiac bowl (2.3), by shattering the cup first and then describing it the author shows that the project of reviving the novel also involves breaking with the past in order to recreate it, give it new life.[24]

Does Prodromos live up to the promise represented by the breaking of the cup? Innovations of his novel include the motif of a forcible, non-consensual abduction by the hero (unprecedented in the ancient novel), satiric parallels between pirate ceremonies and contemporary court rituals,[25] troubling uses of Christian allusion (including expressions of scepticism regarding resurrection),[26] and similarly bold experiments.

Eugenianos and the erudite reader

Eugenianos also opens his novel *in medias res* with an attack on a city; his novel too is nine books long and written in twelve-syllable verse. In brief, captured successively by Parthians and Arabs, then separated by the heroine's fall from a cliff into the sea, the hero and heroine eventually reunite in a provincial town, from which they return home to be wed. The twelfth-century novels in general are characterised by a minimalist approach to plot, with less action and fewer characters than the ancient novels. Eugenianos innovates by making his novel lyrical and pastoral: he fills it with meadows and gardens that recall those of Longus and Achilles Tatius (among others) and includes a multiplicity of erotic songs, letters and laments.[27]

Eugenianos sets his novel apart from Prodromos' by recasting the god Dionysus as a major player. As we have seen, in the middle of Prodromos' novel a cup with Dionysus' image is broken, and the god is not mentioned again. Eugenianos picks up this discarded god and makes him central to his novel: Dionysus becomes the principal god, the patron and guarantor of

24 Cf. Beaton (1996) 67.   25 Harder (1997) 144–7.
26 Burton (1998) 183–95.   27 Further, Burton (2006) 557–71.

the hero and heroine – they meet at his festival and are wed in his temple. Dionysus' magnified role in Eugenianos recalls his central importance in Longus. Eugenianos also highlights links between Dionysus and Christ, and between Zeus and the Christian Father-God.[28]

The novel's self-conscious engagement with the ancient novels is made explicit in book 6 when, for the first time in the tradition of the Greek novel, a fictive character refers directly to past novels. An innkeeper's son tries to court the heroine by citing a series of examples of lovers from past literature, including Heliodorus' Arsace and Theagenes, and Achaemenes and Charicleia, and Longus' Daphnis and Chloe. Kallidemos' citations reveal him to be a startlingly inept reader (for example, he cites these Heliodoran 'couples' as examples of reciprocated love), and his seduction fails.[29]

The figure of Kallidemos also offers a test of the importance of appearing cultivated to win the girl (a novelist's fantasy but also perhaps a social reality among the elite of the time).[30] Kallidemos' characterisation underscores the ideal of the erudite man even as it dismantles it by transposing it to a pretentious fool. An issue for the Byzantine novelists was how to position self against past; in reclaiming past literature, they offered ways to reinforce Hellenic identity. What did this mean for a contemporary reader's sense of his or her own Hellenism? Did the revivalist novel offer readers an attractive way to reinforce their 'Attic' Greek and thereby define themselves as elite? Kallidemos' difficulties in interpreting past texts underscore the gap between past worlds and contemporary readers, a gap widened by the distance between pagan and Christian beliefs and gods.

Eugenianos' novel seems to delight in taking standard motifs from the ancient novels and recasting them with meta-literary implications. For example, near the novel's end, Eugenianos introduces the radical innovation of having a character, Kleandros (a friend of the hero and heroine), successfully die for love (8.311–14).[31] The plot, already fairly minimal, almost halts now, with the funeral of Kleandros (9.1–14) and the heroine's extended lamentations (9.15–107). Although a reunion with their fathers intervenes, the heroine continues her lamentations, extending them now to her friend's dead girlfriend (whom she never met) and wailing at length at her tomb (9.216–56). Lamentation by parents and friends was a standard motif in the ancient novels, as elsewhere; yet at the close of Eugenianos' novel, a kind of anti-novel intrudes, with the heroine's lamentations taking over.[32] This

28 Burton (1998) 205–8.   29 Jouanno (1989) 350–1; Burton (2003) 255–62.
30 See Magdalino (1984) 66; Mullett (1984).   31 Discussion at Burton (2003) 266–7.
32 Cf. Homer, Iliad 24.722–75.

innovation shows Eugenianos exploring the limits of the genre, with grief and despair overshadowing the standard happy ending.[33]

Makrembolites and audience response

Makrembolites' chronological position among the twelfth-century novelists is uncertain, but he is generally associated closely with Prodromos and Eugenianos.[34] His novel distinguishes itself in important ways: his is the only twelfth-century novel written in prose and the only one to present the whole story from a first-person perspective (following Achilles Tatius).[35]

In some ways Makrembolites' novel is the most distilled of the twelfth-century novels. The novel focuses on a more muted world of heralds of religious festivals and symbolical art works. The plot, closely tied with the hero's inner, subjective life, progresses mostly through art works, dreams and dinner parties; sub-plots are greatly reduced; pirates play negligible roles. When confronted with a sexually aggressive female, Makrembolites' hero (a herald for a religious festival) at first misunderstands, and then has erotic dreams and struggles with the issue of deserting his sacred vows. As in Achilles Tatius, a relative gives the hero much-needed counsel on how to pursue the relationship. The slow pacing of the novel delays the elopement to book 7; later, after a series of misadventures (including a ship captain's supposed sacrifice of the heroine and several pivotal dinner parties), the lovers return to be wed in the garden of the heroine's family home.

An innovation in Makrembolites' novel is the lavish development of the motifs of ecphrasis (a description of a work of art) and allegorisation.[36] The long tradition of ecphrasis in ancient literature begins with Achilles' shield; from the Hellenistic period on, ecphraseis were also used to explore the subjectivity of the fictive characters doing the viewing.[37] There are also strong traditions in the ancient novel of characters helping heroes interpret works of art (e.g. Ach. Tat. 5.4) and of characters tutoring heroes in the art of love (e.g. Ach. Tat. 1.9–11). Makrembolites innovates by bringing these traditions together and extending the experience: showing the hero learning about love through viewing and interpreting a series of paintings over time (spanning three books).

Although ecphraseis are plentiful in the ancient novel,[38] they do not take over the text as in Makrembolites. Books 2 and 4 are filled with close examination of a multitude of paintings (young girls, a naked Eros, men

33 Burton (2003) 262–7.　　34 References in n. 7.　　35 Alexiou (1977); Nilsson (2001).
36 Further, Burton (2006) 571–7.　　37 Goldhill (1994) 216–23; Burton (1995) 95–107.
38 Bartsch (1989).

of various races, ages and occupations); the hero and his companion study their inscriptions and assign allegorical meanings. By providing allegorical readings within the text, an author might seem to restrict the reader's engagement with the text. But by placing these interpretations in the mouths of self-interested characters (a fledgling lover and his enabling companion), Makrembolites' text raises allegorisation itself to a level of thematic interest, with the various interpretations inviting agreement or disagreement.[39]

A brief example underscores Makrembolites' interest in the link between subjectivity of aesthetic experience and allegorical interpretation. The last painting the hero and companion see in the garden is of an old man, clearly cold (4.16). In interpreting this painting, they compare the old man with a soft-skinned young girl (4.18), a comparison that reflects their erotic preoccupations. In the context of paintings of the twelve months, this old man personifies winter and old age; yet the hero's addition of the young girl gives the interpretation a subjective spin, with the months' implied lesson of 'seize the day' becoming also 'make love to the heroine'.[40] Thus the eroticism of the viewer's gaze reinforces an understanding of the meaning of the whole.[41]

By linking the hero's initiation into erotic love with the process of allegorically interpreting paintings, Makrembolites' novel situates itself obliquely within a culture that values serious, religious allegorisation. Philip's essay on Heliodorus illustrates the desire to allegorise ancient novels to offset their erotic subject-matter: 'Charicleia is a symbol of the soul and the mind which orders it; for mind linked to soul is glory and grace'.[42] Makrembolites' novel (with its direct linkage of ecphraseis with erotic dreams; see esp. 3.1) complicates that desire by eroticising the very process of allegorisation itself.

Evidence shows continued readership of the ancient novels during the mediaeval Greek period. Anxiety regarding moral content dominated much of the critical discourse, although ancient novels were also admired for their rhetorical style. The twelfth-century Byzantine novels, with their intertextuality, crossing of genres, and transformations of the tradition, show their authors reading and responding to the ancient novels at a high level. They seem to have expected an audience familiar with the ancient novels and able to appreciate their allusions. These novels are self-reflexive about the project of reviving a genre and also self-aware of issues regarding attracting

---

39 Cf. Roilos (2005) 145–9.   40 Cf. Hesiod, *Works and Days* 518–19; Beaton (1996) 85.
41 For viewers separating subjective (erotic) responses from larger designs of works of art, cf. Herodas 4 (Burton (1995) 97–102).
42 T XIII in Colonna (1938); translation from Wilson (1983) 217 (see also Lamberton (1986) 306–11). Attribution: Conca (1994) 13–15 (eleventh/twelfth century); Agapitos (1998) 128 n. 21 (fifth-century Constantinople). See further Hunter, this volume.

a readership for learned, 'pagan' novels. They were reviving not a canonical past literature but rather a past literature decidedly not approved by traditional canons of taste, a controversial genre requiring justification and allegorisation. Self-conscious of what was expected in an ancient novel, they were also working against expectation, experimenting with its limitations. They did not respond to the anxiety of reception by taking an easy road but rather challenged readers with ironical transformations of Christian themes and satirical vantages on Byzantine customs. In doing so, these new novels also brought the ancient novels back to life, to be re-read, re-evaluated, and creatively rewritten.[43]

Further reading

Recent editions and translations have now made these novels more accessible. Editions include Marcovich (1992), (2001), Conca (1990), and Mazal (1967); translations include German (Plepelits (1989), (1996)), French (Meunier (1991)), Italian (Conca (1994)), Spanish (Moreno Jurado (1996)), and English (Burton (2004)). From the rich store of publications that have appeared in recent years, there is room here to mention only a few. Kazhdan (1967) and Hunger (1968), (1978), (1980) provided important impetus toward the now general reassessment of these novels. Alexiou (1977) offers a seminal literary reading of a single novel (Makrembolites). Book-length treatments are few. Beaton (1996), gives a fundamental, broad survey of mediaeval Greek romance. MacAlister (1996) addresses dreams and suicides in the novels. Nilsson (2001) provides a narratological study of Makrembolites' novel. Roilos (2005) offers a wide-ranging study of the poetics of the novels.

Essays with special interest in the reception of ancient literature include Jouanno (1989), (1992), (1994), (2000), (2001), Garland (1990), Agapitos (1998), Burton (2000), (2003), (2006), and papers in Agapitos and Reinsch (2000); Labarthe-Postel (2001) treats ecphrasis. Jeffreys (1980), (1998), Mullett (1984), and Magdalino (1992), (1993) discuss the context of the Comnenian court; Cupane (1974) explores Western influences. Beck (1984), Burton (1998), and Harder (2000) treat Christianity. For a useful survey of scholarship to 1998, see Agapitos (2000b). Jouanno has published an annual bibliographical review, since 2000, of publications on the Byzantine novel (in *The Petronian Society Newsletter*, http://www.ancientnarrative.com/PSN).

---

43 Thanks to T. Jenkins for valuable comments on this essay.

17

MICHAEL REEVE

The re-emergence of ancient novels in western Europe, 1300–1810*

Foretastes of the Greek novel on the eve of print

In 1453, Francesco Griffolini, already known for Latin translations of Greek works, borrowed from the new Vatican Library four Greek manuscripts: of Thucydides, Demosthenes, Heliodorus, and Lucian. The official who recorded the loan entered the third as 'Eliodorus' history of matters in Ethiopia'.[1] Whether Griffolini would have expected a Thucydidean history or just a story, he did not translate Heliodorus, and no other reader is known before Politian, who read far enough into *Charicleia and Theagenes* to meet the giraffe (10.27). Few scholars of the day would have been capable of shedding light from so recondite a quarter, and in so timely a translation, on the creature that had crowds agape when the sultan of Egypt sent Lorenzo de' Medici one as a present in 1487.[2]

Politian's reading also took in Longus and Xenophon of Ephesus, but from Longus' '*Story of shepherds* in four very stylish books' he cites only the garb of Philetas, particularly his sandals (2.3.1), and from Xenophon, 'no less appealing' than his Athenian namesake, he translates a passage early in the work, the procession to the temple of Artemis (1.2.2–5). He brings the passages to bear on problems in Catullus and Martial.[3] The manuscript in which he read them is immediately identifiable, because no other of Xenophon has survived from his day and it had been in Florence, to which it owes its symbol F in modern editions, since at least 1425. In a sequence interrupted only by a snippet opportunistically fitted into a blank space at the end of Achilles Tatius, it includes Longus, Achilles Tatius up to 4.4, Chariton and Xenophon. Some manuscripts of Greek novels had been in Italy longer, and indeed some of these may have been written in Greek-speaking Calabria.

---

* I dispense with references easily found in modern editions. Before long I intend to publish a version that deals more fully with the history and editorial use of the manuscripts, with vernacular translations, with Huet's *Essai*, and with points of controversy.

1 Devreesse (1965) 41 (cf. 31 no. 265), 49 no. 109.
2 Politianus (1489) chapter 3.   3 Politianus (1489) chapters 2 and 51.

Into print: Heliodorus, the Lucianic *Ass*, Apuleius' *Metamorphoses*

Before the world received further news in print about any of the four novels preserved in F, Heliodorus was published in his entirety, at Basel in 1534. For several reasons, the publication was an unusual event. After Chrysoloras answered a call to Florence and arrived there in 1397 from Constantinople to teach Greek, his pupils immediately turned their hand to translating works of Greek prose, some of which were translated more than once before print came into use. Consequently, much was available for printing in Latin a generation before the printing of Greek gathered pace in the 1490s. Heliodorus, however, first appeared in Greek. Furthermore, there is no sign that the editor, Vincentius Obsopoeus, knew any of the other Greek novels. His manuscript, rescued by a soldier, he says, from the library of Matthaeus Corvinus when the Turks in 1526 ransacked Budapest, survives in Munich, and it contains no other novel. When he ventures a context for *Charicleia and Theagenes*, it is historiography, 'to which Greek writers adopt a bolder approach than Latin, allowing themselves many a liberty: take Herodotus'. Nevertheless, a eulogy of history follows, and the dedicatees, namely the senators and patricians of Nuremberg, where Obsopoeus had once passed an agreeable part of his life, will also find in the work the full range of human emotions, a model of conjugal loyalty, a style second to none, and ample instruction in ethnography and natural history. One grateful reader was Conrad Gesner, who under 'Heliodorus' in his 1262-page encyclopaedia of literature quotes Obsopoeus' preface and adds this: 'some years ago, the spirit moved me to look at the work, and I liked it so much that I did nothing else until I had reached the end; and were the Greek text not marred in numerous places by corruptions, I should have enjoyed it far more'.[4]

A long work like *Charicleia and Theagenes* might seem destined to circulate on its own, but in fact one of the oldest manuscripts combines it with Achilles, and another with the Byzantine novelist Eustathios Makrembolites. Various combinations occur in later manuscripts. That amounts, if not to contextualisation, at least to an acknowledgement of similarity. The most striking example is the presence of four novels in F. The antiquity of such combinations, however, is hard to determine.[5]

---

4 Gesner (1545) f. 301r. The simultaneous labours of Dörrie, Colonna and Rattenbury left several discrepancies and loose ends, but almost no work has since been done on the transmission of Heliodorus, even by Colonna (1987), who gives bibliography up to 1982. Note, however, Mazal (1966); Gronewald (1979); Sandy (1984–5); Antoniou (1995).

5 The only work on transmission that covers more than one novel is Dörrie (1935), but it is inaccurate and in many other respects has been superseded. The most recent study that impinges on several novels actually concerns Eustathios: Cataldi Palau (1980). Totals of manuscripts (apart from excerpts and copies of printed editions): Eustathios 43 (a chastening fact); Heliodorus 24; Achilles 22; Longus 11.

Absent from any of these manuscripts is a Greek novel that did indeed circulate in combination, but with other works attributed to the same author: the Lucianic *Ass*. Many of Lucian's dialogues were read in Byzantine schools both for their content and for their style, and pupils happily transplanted them to Italy.[6] Poggio, author of his own *Amusing Stories*, translated the *Ass* into Latin about 1450 and equipped it with an introduction addressed to Cosimo de' Medici.[7] When he read Apuleius' *Metamorphoses*, he thought the author had experienced the story or else made it up, and he found these alternatives confirmed by Augustine in the *City of God* (18.18). Then, in a volume of works by Lucian, he encountered one called *Ass*, and curious about its contents he read it, only to find that the same story had befallen Lucian too. Obviously Lucian or another Greek had made it up. As an exercise Poggio set about translating it, not to repeat what Apuleius had done but to show that this old 'comedy', which passed for an Apuleian innovation, was on no account to be taken as true but had been produced by Lucian as a satire on magical practices, in keeping with his habit of poking fun even at gods, to say nothing of the human race. The translation was first printed not in Italy but at Augsburg about 1477, simultaneously, though separately, in Latin and a German translation, each illustrated. Despite his ass's head, Lucius cuts a dapper figure as he takes the potion from Palaestra.[8] Not illustrated, however, is the tender scene at Thessalonica where a rich and attractive lady makes love to the ass (50–1); on the contrary, the German translator explains that he could not bring himself to corrupt his readers by including anything so unchaste. Neither translator betrays any doubt that the author was Lucian, but their printers had other ideas: in Poggio's preface Lucian becomes Lucius, and the printer of the German version not only breaks up the work with headings, of which the first is 'How Lucius Apuleius was changed into the form of an ass', but rounds it off with a colophon that makes Lucius Apuleius the author of the Greek original. Accordingly, the edition has been described as the first edition of Apuleius' *Golden Ass* (i.e. *Metamorphoses*).[9]

The first edition of the *Metamorphoses*, however, had appeared in 1469 from a German press at Rome – a very different volume, which contains

6 Robinson (1979) 81–95; De Faveri (2002). 7 Walser (1914) 231.
8 See *ISTC*. Both versions are rare, but a facsimile has been published of the German version (Munich 1922) with an epilogue by E. Weil. At much the same time as the *Ass*, Poggio also translated Lucian's *True History*, but that translation remains unprinted, doubtless because another, by Lilius Castellanus (Lilio Tifernate), has been in print since 1475/6 (with spaces for illustrations); see Dapelo and Zoppelli (1998); Jaitner-Hahner (2002). Doody (1996) reproduces pages of various novels: from manuscripts plates 3, 14–15, 26, and from printed books, mostly for their illustrations, plates 18–25, 27–31, 38.
9 Rosenthal (1912).

Apuleius' whole output and presents him in Bussi's preface, addressed to pope Paul II, first and foremost as a Platonist and Plato as second only to God.[10] The *Metamorphoses* escaped from this elevated company only to find itself in a forest of learned commentary (Bologna 1500), put together by Filippo Beroaldo at a time when Apuleius' exuberant language had begun to win admirers and imitators.[11] An illustrator let in some light (Venice 1510), but rescue did not come until Boiardo's Italian version appeared in a slimmer and smaller volume illustrated with more woodcuts (Venice 1518); still more were added to later editions, and one that shows the two witches urinating on a prostrate Aristomenes (1.13.8) leaves nothing to the imagination. The Queen of Heaven, though, played no part in the rescue, because Boiardo replaced book 11 with the sardonic conclusion of the Lucianic *Ass*.[12] Finer and more elaborate illustrations than those in the Italian translation, to the number of seventy-nine and done in two stages by different artists, accompany the first German translation (Augsburg 1538), which on its title page announces that the story not only shows how God saves mankind from bestiality, a lesson supported with a quotation from Psalm 31, but is also fun to read.[13]

Presentation: Heliodorus, *Apollonius*, and vernacular romances

We left the senators and patricians of Nuremberg four years before (1534) taking time off from affairs of state and about to read the historian Heliodorus. They would have to read him in Greek, though, and in a volume of 242 pages each at first sight like every other except where a new book starts. Even when they went unillustrated, long stories were not always presented in this uninviting way. *Apollonius, King of Tyre*, so popular already in Latin that several versions survive,[14] was soon printed in German translation (Augsburg 1471),[15] and wherever it falls open the reader's eye will almost certainly be caught by a heading such as 'How a poor fisherman tells

---

10 The preface has been reprinted by Botfield (1861) 68–78 and Miglio (1978) 11–19. The standard edition of the *Metamorphoses* is Robertson (1972).

11 See D'Amico (1984). Bussi already comments on Apuleius' rich and varied language, and words are picked out in the margin of a later edition (Venice 1493).

12 Fumagalli (1988).

13 The work of the second artist is reproduced by Schreyl (1990) II nos. 1174–1214, together with the first artist's frontispiece, I p. 177; for discussion see I pp. 176–80. On the translation see now Häfner (2003); Plank (2004); I owe these references to Julia Gaisser, who will shortly publish a book on the early reception of the *Metamorphoses*. Other translations: Castilian (Seville c. 1513–16), French (Paris 1518), Italian in full (Venice 1550), English (London 1566).

14 Kortekaas (1984) prints two versions on facing pages, Schmeling (1988) three in sequence. On the diffusion and influence of the work see Archibald (1991).

15 Schmitt and Noll-Wiemann (1975); *Appolonius* (so printed in the incunable) has an epilogue by H. Melzer.

King Apollonius of his poverty and gives him directions to the city of Pentapolis', 'How the queen gave birth to a daughter at sea and how she died in childbirth and was thrown into the sea in a coffin etc.' The attractive suggestion has been made that such aids were thought appropriate to romances and other vernacular works, not least because instalments might be read out in company, but not to works in the ancient languages; and the evidence offered includes Obsopoeus' Heliodorus.[16]

The only mediaeval manuscript of an ancient Greek novel that has much articulation beyond the division into books is the manuscript of Heliodorus borrowed by Griffolini, where the marginal notes added by the same hand include summaries of episodes or topics.[17] No more than Obsopoeus, however, did Jacques Amyot articulate his French translation of Heliodorus, published anonymously at Paris in 1547 and again with revision in 1559,[18] or Warschewiczki his Latin translation of 1552, commended to the printer by Melanchthon. All three of these books are handsome folios, but Amyot's printer issued pocket versions of both his editions, and in the Lyon reprints there follows a 'Table of noteworthy things contained in the Ethiopian history', not in an alphabetical index like Warschewicki's, which has over 400 entries mostly keyed to names, but as they come up, book by book; in book 10, for instance, the giraffe is there, even if only as 'Gift of the Axiomites'. When Thomas Underdowne translated Warschewicki's version (1569?), he advertised on his title page that he was assisting the reader from the outset with summaries of each book, and the title page of W. B.'s Achilles (1597) repeats the wording of Underdowne's second edition (1577). Furthermore, 'the notes in the margene' of Underdowne's translation 'wil wel supplie the want of a table', for instance 'Two reasons why the cockes crowe', 'Age beside other discommodities maketh menne hard of hearing.'

Amyot: moral and literary standards

Convergence in presentation, however, masked a distinction important to Amyot and some of his successors. In the preface to his Heliodorus, Amyot grants that a work of fiction such as this will be read above all for relaxation, but he argues that it has merits absent from stories that people have been used to reading in French, which provide no intellectual matter and shed no light on the past but seem more like the fantasies of someone in the hot flush of a fever than the creations of anyone intelligent and discerning.

16 Dionisotti (1997).   17 Conca (1989) 225–7, 235–41.
18 From a calligraphic manuscript owned by Francis I, Paris, B. N., Fr. 2143, Bonnefon (1883) printed a translation of book 1 made by Lancelot de Carle from Obsopoeus' edition possibly before Amyot made his.

Fiction requires verisimilitude, which Heliodorus observes; furthermore, he brings all forbidden and dangerous passions to an unhappy end, and he constructs his plot in an unusual way, like heroic poets. Altogether, Amyot's thoughtful preface takes four lines of approach: moral, intellectual, generic and narratological. Underdowne, who in the fuller preface to his second edition concentrates on the moral and generic, puts Amyot's contrast more explicitly: 'Mort Darthure, Arthur of litle Britaine, yea, and Amadis of Gaule, etc., accompt violente murder, or murder for no cause, manhoode: and fornication and unlawfull luste, friendely love. This booke punisheth the faultes of evill doers, and rewardeth the well livers.'[19]

The morality of the extant novels has been debated since their earliest mention, and the debate has been sharpened not just by transmission in a Christian culture but by what purport to be biographical facts about two of the authors: Heliodorus and Achilles have each had a bishopric conferred on them.[20] *Daphnis and Chloe*, absent from the Byzantine debate, flirts with pornography as it explores awakening love. Unless it is for moral reasons, however, that some Greek novels have failed to survive at all, there is no evidence of censorship in the manuscripts before the fifteenth century, when a recension of the Lucianic *Ass* cuts down the narrator's gymnastics with Palaestra (6–10) and omits the episode at Thessalonica mentioned above (50–3).[21] We have met censorship in the German *Ass*, and the corresponding passage is drastically cut in the German *Metamorphoses* of 1538; similarly, the printer of Amyot's Longus suppressed the details of Daphnis' initiation into sex by Lycaenion, the young wife of an old husband (3.18.3–4), with the clumsy result that the translation jumps from 'as follows' to 'After this lesson'.[22] For either Longus or Achilles the calendar of editions lends itself to being used as a measure of social attitudes or more narrowly of the control imposed by church or court.[23]

Whatever pretensions ancient novelists may have had, in the titles of their novels and beyond, to following in the footsteps of historians, the generic context in which Amyot sets Heliodorus looks like a response to Obsopoeus, whose Greek text he was translating. Be that as it may, his simultaneous comparison and contrast with mediaeval romances are still playing themselves out in discussions of the novel as a genre.

---

19 The influence of Heliodorus has been studied by Oeftering (1901); Prosch (1956); Sandy (1982c) and (1982a); Berger (1984).
20 Introduction, p. 13.　　21 Van Thiel (1972) xix–xxiii.
22 A reprint (1718) supplies the missing details from the Greek.
23 Barber (1989) 9–10, 27–9. In n. 4 on p. 53 he reproduces from Pia (1971), though without saying how 'œuvres érotiques' are defined, the number published in every decade from the 1540s to the 1790s.

Print runs, readers and the last manuscripts

Vernacular translations give rise to another question about habits of reading, because many of them are extremely rare. Were few copies printed, or did all the copies fall apart through use, or have snobbish collectors and librarians not thought them worth keeping on the market or the shelves? Sweynheym and Pannartz printed 275 copies of Bussi's Apuleius,[24] and in 1500, when Beroaldus published the *Metamorphoses* at Bologna with dense commentary in the margins, he was expecting the printer to run off about 2,000. Neither Bussi's Apuleius nor Beroaldus' is rare today, but of the twenty incunables that have been recorded of *Apollonius, King of Tyre*, nineteen of them vernacular, the British Library has only one.[25]

For someone who set greater store by his work on Plutarch, Amyot took impressive trouble over Heliodorus. Shortly after his translation appeared, he joined the French ambassador in Venice, and there or at Rome, between 1548 and 1552, he collated manuscripts on his copy of Obsopoeus' edition. Three times between 1547 and 1555, Henricus Stephanus also visited Italy, and he too examined manuscripts of Greek novels, among them F: besides making or commissioning a collation of Achilles, he read enough of Longus to publish in 1555 renderings in Latin pastoral of two episodes from book 1, both preserved only in F.[26]

The speed with which printed editions could put a stop to the production of manuscripts is seen in Munich Gr. 96, where the scribe copied books 1–3 of Heliodorus and then wrote 'the rest have not been copied because they can be found in print; copying even these was a mistake'. For the novels, much of the evidence for the continued production of manuscripts can be associated with two figures at Rome: Giovanni Onorio, who in 1535 became a copyist and restorer of Greek manuscripts at the Vatican, and the antiquarian and collector Fulvio Orsini, librarian to the Farnese family and then himself a corrector at the Vatican.[27]

Already by 1538 a manuscript of Longus had been made available to Annibale Caro, who set about translating him into Italian; but though he promised someone a copy of the translation in 1554 and lived until 1566, by which time he too, like Orsini, had become an artistic adviser of Alessandro Farnese, it remained unpublished until 1786.[28] What did appear in Caro's

---

24 *BMC* IV (1916) 15.
25 See *ISTC*. The one Latin incunable (Utrecht c. 1474) is also rare. On print runs and rates of survival see Neddermeyer (1998) 74–9, 110–56, 752–70; for some astonishing scales of loss, Trovato (2004) 27–9.　　26 Dalmeyda (1934a).
27 Agati (2001), who indexes the novelists collectively as 'romanzieri greci'; Nolhac (1887).
28 *DBI* 20 (1977) 497–508 (C. Mutini); on Alessandro Farnese as a patron of the arts, *DBI* 45 (1995) 65–70 (C. Robertson).

lifetime was Amyot's once again anonymous translation of 1559, made from a manuscript taken to Paris for Francis I in 1539;[29] but the first version to appear from an Italian press, at Naples in 1574, was a free adaptation in over 2,000 Latin hexameters, under the title *Foundlings*, by an acquaintance of Orsini's in the circle of Alessandro Farnese, Lorenzo Gambara.[30]

Achilles was first printed, though without his name and books 1–4, in a Latin version of 1544 by A. Cruceius, made from a manuscript that a pilgrim later took somewhat incongruously to the monastery of St Catherine on Sinai.[31] Anyone who considered the work not serious enough for its illustrious dedicatee should remember, said Cruceius, that Cicero tells how Scipio and Laelius relived their boyhood by gathering seashells (*On the Orator* 2.22); and he picked out Achilles' aphorisms with capitals and inverted commas. An Italian version by L. Dolce followed in 1546,[32] but in the meantime Conrad Gesner had revealed that all eight books were in the Vatican, and a complete Italian version by F. A. Coccio appeared in 1550/51, a complete Latin version in 1554.

Orsini himself wrote a manuscript of Longus and Achilles in 1553 and in 1569 was planning an edition of Achilles,[33] but in the event his only service to the printing of the novels came towards the end of his life, when he supplied Raphael Columbanius with collations of Longus made on an extant proof of the first edition (Florence 1598), Bodl., Auct. K 4 18. At his death in 1600 Orsini's collection included not only his own manuscript but several others valued by modern editors. In 1593, Friedrich Sylburg, Palatine librarian at Heidelberg, encouraged Orsini to supply him with manuscripts of the novels for printing by Commelinus;[34] but when Commelinus' press issued in 1596 Heliodorus and in 1601 the first Greek edition of Achilles, together with Longus and the thirty-six love stories sketched for Virgil's friend Gallus by Parthenius,[35] the editors owed most to Palatine manuscripts.[36] Besides adding an account of variants, they divided the page into two columns and equipped all three novels with a facing Latin version: Heliodorus with Warschewiczki's, Achilles with Cruceius', and Longus with Gambara's *Foundlings*, a stopgap that strained the layout

---

29 Lestringant (1986).   30 *DBI* 52 (1999) 53–4 (Angela Asor Rosa).
31 Hagedorn and Koenen (1982) viii n. 7.
32 On Dolce, a prolific writer, adapter and translator, with a strong interest in Dante, Boccaccio and Ariosto, see *DBI* 40 (1991) 399–405 (G. Romei).
33 Nolhac (1887) 151 n. 5, 163–4, 164 n. 1, 186, 190.   34 Ibid. (1887) 443–4.
35 These were first published by the doctor Ianus Cornarius (Basel 1531), who maintained in his preface that love was a disease and love stories an undervalued remedy.
36 The latest editor of Achilles, Garnaud (1991), draws selectively on the material assembled and analysed in Vilborg (1955). As Vilborg was charged by Russo (1958) with misreporting manuscripts, it has to be hoped that Garnaud worked more carefully.

but had the unintended advantage of showing what Gambara had done.[37] A new facing Latin translation of Longus was supplied in 1605 by Gothofredus Jungermanus. Commelinus and his friend Hoeschel also planned an edition of Eustathios 'and similar works', but none appeared until Gilbert Gaulmin followed suit at Paris with bilingual editions of Eustathis (1617, 1618 with notes) and another Byzantine novelist, Theodoros Prodromos (1625). 'Dear reader,' he says in the former 'my rather full Prolegomena could not be printed. They dealt with all the erotic writings of the ancient Greeks. They will be published shortly, I hope, with another volume of the same material'; but they were not. Gaulmin used a manuscript of Theodoros put at his disposal by Salmasius, and Salmasius in turn, when he came to edit Achilles (Leiden 1640) after abandoning his plan for a corpus of Greek love stories, cut off his brief remarks about novels with an unfulfilled promise: 'but more about this elsewhere'. In his remarks, however, he ranks Achilles with Heliodorus above the froth (*nugae*) of Eustathios and Theodoros and suggests that the novel reached Asia Minor from the Persians, who also passed it by way of the Arabs to Spain and France.

Huet and the formation of a canon

The gap that Gaulmin and Salmasius left was filled in 1670 when Pierre Daniel Huet contributed to the first edition of the novel *Zayde* a letter to the ostensible author entitled *De l'origine des romans* ('On the origin of novels').[38] Like many seventeenth-century polymaths, Huet had command of numerous languages, and the work is a multicultural and broadly chronological survey of story-telling shaped into a set of generic, moral and historical arguments. Huet concentrated on prose and even built it into his definition of the novel: 'novels properly called are works of fiction about the adventures of lovers, artistically written in prose, for the pleasure and instruction of readers'. Against a multifarious background of oriental fiction, he demarcated a corpus by setting out three phases in the history of the novel: the ancient novel, taken over from the east; the mediaeval novel, a degenerate form of historiography to which benighted northerners had sunk in the dark ages; and the modern novel, at its best, for instance here in *Zayde*, a paragon of disciplined standards.

One of the most striking things about Huet's survey is that he nowhere mentions *Apollonius*. Did he know only mediaeval versions and therefore regard it as mediaeval? If he saw Welser's edition (Augsburg 1595), made

37 Angell Daye's adaptation of Longus (London 1587) was compared with its source, Amyot's version, by Wolff (1912) Appendix A, pp. 465–9.
38 Huet (1670).

from an old manuscript at Augsburg that had 'grecising but very clumsy illustrations', he would have read in the preface the editor's reasons for supposing that the author was Greek and the Latin translator a Christian of late antiquity.[39]

Also very striking is something apparently simple that Huet did for the first time. From Greek novels he proceeds to Latin, and despite citing Petronius as a literary critic (by mistaking his character Eumolpus for the author) he takes it almost for granted that the *Satyrica* in its full form was a novel. The work had previously been regarded as a *satira* (or *satyricum opus*), whether in the sense of satire or of *prosimetrum* (a medley of prose and verse). Had anyone before Huet demarcated a corpus of ancient novels in both languages?

More Greek novels, new episodes and some assessments

The corpus available to Huet had recently been augmented by a missing episode of Petronius' novel, though he nowhere mentions the discovery, and would be further augmented from a single manuscript, first in the eighteenth century by two more novels and then in 1810 by a missing episode of another. Since then, only papyri have yielded new material, none of it more than scraps but some of these disproportionately eye-opening.

How much of Petronius' novel reached the Carolingian revival is not known, but the disjointed excerpts made at that time, in which verse and discussion of literature bulk large, constitute most of what survives in mediaeval manuscripts and all that Italian humanists could find to print (Milan c. 1482). The text of this first edition goes back to a copy that Poggio had sent Niccoli from Britain, the only copy of any ancient novel except *Apollonius* known to have been in Britain before the sixteenth century. In this version Trimalchio appears out of the blue and merely quotes the incomparable verses of 'Publilius' (55.4–6). About a century later, however, French scholars spliced these excerpts with a larger set taken from at least two mediaeval manuscripts now lost and a smaller set taken from a mediaeval anthology still extant. The sexual explicitness of the printed material had already raised eyebrows,[40] and the possessors of the new material affected coyness about divulging it. The text that nevertheless resulted, which first appeared in 1575, sets Trimalchio in the context of his dinner party, but the thread of the story breaks after the verses of 'Publilius' (55.6), and the narrator and his friends are next seen after making their escape (79.1). About 1650, however,

---

39 On illustrated manuscripts and editions of *Apollonius* see Archibald (1991) 94–6.
40 Gyraldus (1545) 561–3.

a corrupt but continuous account of the dinner party, in fact the longest continuous section of the novel to have survived, came to light in Dalmatia, surprisingly in a manuscript written in 1423 and apparently at Florence, where one would have expected it to attract attention; but evidently someone whisked it off uncopied to Dalmatia.⁴¹ When *Dinner at Trimalchio's* was published (Padua 1664), the speeches of the freedmen were almost entirely new, and their linguistic peculiarities sparked allegations of forgery.⁴² That debate quickly subsided when it was realised that the peculiarities were an element of Petronius' characterisation, not of his own language; but the relationship between what survives of the novel and what survived in the middle ages, and between that and what Petronius wrote, still poses one of the most tantalising problems in the study of the ancient novel. The elder Burman, who assembled in two huge volumes (Utrecht 1709; 2nd edn, Amsterdam 1743) published and unpublished contributions from the previous 150 years, expressed the paradoxical view that the excerpts had been made by prurient monks. Should people object to his labours on so improper a work, well, they were doubtless pricked by a guilty conscience because they recognised themselves as Petronius' target.

The manuscript that yielded the next discoveries was F, which so far as anyone knows had been lying unconsulted for 150 years at the Badia in Florence when Montfaucon's systematic exploration of libraries brought it back to light in 1700.⁴³ The time that it still took for Xenophon of Ephesus to be published in Italian by A. M. Salvini (1723) and in Greek and Latin by A. Cocchi (London 1726), and Chariton in Greek by J. P. d'Orville with a Latin translation by J. J. Reiske (Amsterdam 1750), is less easy to blame on the difficulty of reading the manuscript or obtaining a transcript, though the story of the various transcripts is tangled enough, than on a fear of disappointing readers familiar with the more sophisticated work of Longus, Achilles and Heliodorus.⁴⁴

Cocchi expressed amazement, when there were so many useful things to write about, that people for centuries had made up unlikely stories about besotted lovers, and Xenophon received his first accolade from a French translator (1748). An English translator, Mr Rooke (London 1727), had encountered a difficulty:

---

41 Müller (1995) gives the latest account of the transmission, but not much has changed since I summarised it: (1983) 295–300.
42 Grafton (1990).
43 Montfaucon (1702) 354, 365–6, 394–5.
44 The latest edition of Xenophon is O'Sullivan (2005). Papanikolaou (1973b) reports the manuscript inadequately and has a very inaccurate introduction; see my review (1976). Editions of Chariton include Molinié (1979); Goold (1995); and Reardon (2004).

I must not however omit acquainting my readers, that I have given a different turn to one passage, towards the beginning of the third book, because it would not have sounded well in an English ear; and whatever toleration the ancient Greeks might plead, it is entirely repugnant to the genius and customs of our country. Whosoever understands the original may easily find out the deviation, and to those who do not, the knowledge thereof is no ways material: this I only add, lest any should pretend to accuse me for want of skill in the language, and take this passage for a handle.

Fair Hyperanthes, that is, has surrendered his last letter (3.2). The French translator spared him but added a footnote: 'one must remember that these are Greeks or actually a Thracian, still worse'.

D'Orville introduced his large and undisciplined commentary with the lukewarm testimonial that any planks from the shipwreck of ancient literature deserved attention; furthermore, it was easier to say that Chariton 'lacks notable faults than that he has great virtues to commend him'. Once again a translator offered a more inviting assessment (1752):

> As regards the other things rightly held against novels, this one is completely free of them. Nothing improbable, nothing off the point; great variety of incident, not arresting perhaps but certainly plausible and all of it well orchestrated; no prolixity in the narrative, but everything is recounted with suitable economy, and also with a stylistic dignity more to be expected of a historian than a novelist.

If one can trust what he says in a reprint (1756), the translation rapidly sold out on the strength both of Chariton's merits and of his own.

In this Italian translator's praise of Chariton the wheel has turned full circle: Chariton joins Obsopoeus' Heliodorus among the ranks of historians. Far from opening up new debates on any broader front, the publication of Xenophon and Chariton merely complicated the question of priority, which like most of his predecessors d'Orville resolved in favour of Heliodorus.

As no other novels were known to remain unpublished, the time might have seemed ripe for P. M. Paciaudi's mainly bibliographical *Introduction to Ancient Love Stories*, included shortly after his death in an elegantly printed Longus (Parma 1786),[45] and for the corpus of Greek novels planned by Salmasius and also mooted, d'Orville says, by Montfaucon. In 1792–8 C. W. Mitscherlich carried out the plan, but without Chariton; and in 1797 a *Bibliothèque des romans grecs traduits en français* ('Collection of

---

45 Another edition for bibliophiles (Paris 1802), with nine plates by Prudhon and Gérard captioned in Greek, Latin and French, measures 485 x 330 mm, of which an unaccented Greek text in a new font occupies only 220 x 140. Would anyone ever have sullied the margins?

Greek novels translated into French') sandwiched ten volumes of ancient and Byzantine novels between one volume of Parthenius and the *Love Stories* transmitted as Plutarch's and one of Lucian's *True History* and *Ass*. All this rounding up, however, came too soon. In 1810, once more from F (now at the Laurenziana after the suppression of the Badia), Paul-Louis Courier published a passage of several pages always known to be missing in the rest of the tradition from book 1 of *Daphnis and Chloe* – the passage where Chloe unsettles first herself by bathing Daphnis and then Daphnis by awarding him, in a competition with his rival Dorcon, the prize of a kiss (13.1–17.4). Courier achieved the further distinction of editing the whole novel from the only manuscripts that have turned out to matter.[46] That he nearly caused an international incident by leaving an inky slip of paper in F at the crucial place may well be the best-known fact about the transmission of any ancient novel,[47] but it probably did his sales no harm.

When a new French translation of *Daphnis and Chloe* was published in 1757 face to face with Amyot's, the translator gave this justification:

> Very few people read the Greek text of Longus; few have the capacity to read either Moll's or Jungermann's Latin version; and those who read Amyot's translation number less than is commonly thought, because all the ladies are put off from the start by an outdated and obsolete style.

These ladies go back beyond George Thornley, who announced his *Daphnis and Chloe* (London 1657) as 'a most sweet and pleasant pastorall romance for young ladies' and dedicated it to 'young beauties' before addressing 'the criticall reader', to Angelo Decembrio's *Politia litteraria*, dedicated to Pius II (pope 1458–64), where two speakers treat stories written in the vernacular as suitable for their wives and children on winter evenings.[48] Of the Greek novels, however, *Daphnis and Chloe* has proved the most durable on more than one level. In 1718 a reviser of Amyot's version had said that love and pastoral simplicity were depicted in the novel with such grace and naturalness as to have won for it the esteem of connoisseurs. In the same vein, Villoison introduced his edition of 1778 with a protest against the label 'Sophist', first given to Longus in the edition of 1601; but he then painted a less ingenuous author on a broad canvas of literary history by embedding his eulogy of him in an elaborate argument about good and bad kinds of imitation. How could

---

46 That the rest derive from them was established by Van Thiel (1961), and it remained only to report them fully and accurately, as I hope to have done (1982). Vieillefond has also published an edition (1987) with a very discursive though not always accurate introduction, not least on the editorial history of the novel and on its influence.

47 Vieillefond (1987) xli–xliv.   48 Witten (2002) 1.6, pp. 163–4.

Huet not have seen that he must be ancient and not Byzantine? Goethe was already an admirer of the novel when he hailed Courier's new passage as 'really its summit'.[49]

Apuleius and 'folk tales'

Petronius' novel and the *Metamorphoses* have fared even better. Inconspicuously, the *Metamorphoses* has woven itself into the fabric of western culture, and one section of the *Metamorphoses* in particular – the story of Cupid and Psyche (4.28–6.24), related by a 'deranged and drunken old crone' to lift the spirits of the kidnapped Charite.

As the *Metamorphoses* and *Charicleia and Theagenes* are the longest and most complex of the ancient novels, it is no surprise that episodes were picked out and printed either on their own or in thematic collections. When book 1 of *Charicleia and Theagenes* appeared in 1551–2 with a Latin translation, it was not an excerpt but a trailer for a larger project;[50] but when an English translation of the Delphic episode appeared in 1567, before Underdowne's full translation, it accompanied other love stories.[51] Boccaccio, *Lineages of the Pagan Gods* 5.22, retold Apuleius' story of Cupid and Psyche, which he met not just in context but also in the partial summary that Fulgentius in late antiquity allegorised in his *Mythologies* (3.6). In W. Adlington's English translation of the whole novel (London 1566) *Cupid and Psyche* is the only part singled out on the title page, and La Fontaine followed up the first edition of his *Fables* (Paris 1668) with a much expanded and altered prose version, *Les amours de Psiché et de Cupidon* (Paris 1669).

In its outlines and many of its details, *Cupid and Psyche* closely resembles a Greek novel: boy meets girl, separation and hazardous journeys follow, but they are finally reunited. Already in their identity, however, since the boy is the god Desire and the girl Soul, lie strong hints of deeper meaning, reinforced in the story itself by divine bans on curiosity and disobedience and by the birth of Pleasure. Here in *Cupid and Psyche* if anywhere in the *Metamorphoses*, it might seem, is the Platonic philosopher Apuleius; but the rich texture of the story more often evokes the poets banned from Plato's state, and its varied episodes and colourful dialogue create an imaginative world unparalleled in Plato's myths, to say nothing of Greek novels. 'In a city that shall be nameless there were a king and queen'; they had three beautiful daughters, two just ordinarily beautiful but the third, Psyche, quite out of

---

49 Schönberger (1980) 33–5.   50 Mazal (1966) 182, 184–5.
51 *Amorous Tales* (London 1567) ff. 10r.–27v., 'The historie of Chariclia and Theagenes gathered for the most part out of Heliodorus a Greeke authour'.

this world. Already in the opening sentence and the contrast between one beautiful and two plainer daughters one feels transported to the world of Cinderella, and as the story unfolds in its unembarrassed mixture of everyday reality and magical fantasy, bringing Psyche to a palace staffed by invisible servants, exposing her to her sisters' jealous spite, and setting her a succession of apparently impossible tasks, it fills one's mind with echoes of other things that one heard on one's grandmother's knee. In short, it is a fairy tale.

When the Brothers Grimm published in 1812 the first edition of their *Kinder- und Hausmärchen* ('Tales for children and the family'), collecting folk tales became a large industry, and the motifs and patterns that recur in them have been indexed. One can therefore see very quickly that many stories resemble *Cupid and Psyche* in varying degrees.[52] How does that come about? Broadly, two explanations can be entertained: that the motifs used by Apuleius are those of oral story-telling, which has the same characteristics in places and periods far apart; or that later occurrences go back in some way to Apuleius. The prevailing view is the former, but the latter has a great deal on its side, above all the transmission of the *Metamorphoses*.

A number of rare classical texts were copied at Montecassino from old and often damaged exemplars between about 1020 and 1140. One of these was the *Metamorphoses*, of which the three oldest manuscripts are all in Beneventan, the script of the region;[53] but from then until after 1300 no knowledge is shown of the *Metamorphoses* or the other works of Apuleius' preserved with it. Petrarch, however, annotated a copy no later than the early 1340s. More important, a letter that Boccaccio wrote in 1339 bristles with phrases from the *Metamorphoses*, especially book 1; *Decameron* 5.10 and 7.2, composed by 1351, rework stories of adultery from book 9; and probably in the later 1350s he wrote out a copy of his own.[54] Up to the 1350s, few of the motifs in *Cupid and Psyche* recur anywhere in western literature, and those that do belong to the earlier stages of the story, as far as Psyche's dismissal by Cupid. Precisely that much of the story had been

52 See Aarne and Thompson (1961), the latest edition of Aarne (1910); Thompson (1955–8). On *Cupid and Psyche* see Aarne and Thompson (1961) 140–5 nos. 425, 428; and Swahn (1955).
53 On the character of Laur. 68.2 (s. xi), which editors regard as the archetype, see Pecere (1984), (1986) 30–4, (1987). The most controversial question that Pecere raises is whether something is missing from the end of the *Metamorphoses*.
54 Fiorilla (1999), with plates. I repeat or summarise here what I set out in (1991) 145–7; for documentation see nn. 53–7 there; Baglio *et al.* (1999) 192–5, 224–38. Garfagnini (1976) 311–20 published from the margins of a fourteenth-century manuscript in Florence a 'metaphorical' and spiritual interpretation of the *Metamorphoses* read as a sequel to *On Magic* (the transmitted title of Apuleius' *Apology*).

retold, and the rest summed up in one brief sentence, by Fulgentius, whose *Mythologies*, unlike the *Metamorphoses*, had a fairly wide circulation in the middle ages; and Fulgentius' version readily accounts for all the occurrences that antedate the 1350s. When, therefore, motifs from *Cupid and Psyche* appear in such works as Basile's *Pentamerone* (1634–6) or the French original (1740) of *Beauty and the Beast*, written when the *Metamorphoses* had long been available in several languages, or appear again in oral stories of the nineteenth century closer to these works than to *Cupid and Psyche*, for instance in giving the girl a lover who is not just maliciously alleged to look nasty but really does look nasty, it is highly improbable that they came from an oral tradition old enough to have inspired Apuleius.[55] On the contrary, the very notion of folk tales – 'orally transmitted *Märchen*, polished and perfected over centuries by generations of peasant storytellers'[56] – is a romantic fiction, and its acceptance has done Apuleius the same injustice as two other great story-tellers of classical antiquity, Homer and Herodotus.[57]

However, 1810 has become 1812, and 1812, as I have just shown, was the overture to a new phase in the history of story-telling.

Further reading

The works of broadest scope devoted to the reception of the novels have been written by students of English literature: Wolff (1912), Doody (1996). On *Apollonius* see Archibald (1991), Pittaluga (1999); on Apuleius, Haight (1927), Fehling (1977), D'Amico (1984), Rollo (1994), von Albrecht (1997) II 1460–63, and a forthcoming book by Julia Gaisser; on Heliodorus, Oefter-ing (1901), Prosch (1956), Sandy (1982a), (1982c): 95–124, Berger (1984); on Longus, Barber (1989), Vieillefond (1987); on Lucian, Robinson (1979); on Petronius, Grafton (1990), von Albrecht (1997) II 1232–6. On the rediscovery of the Latin novels see Carver (1999). Conca (1989) has cast a discerning eye on some manuscripts of Greek novels. Editors of single novels usually list their predecessors and give some account of the manuscript tradition, but on the manuscripts few are up to date, and they tend not to say much about

---

55 I follow here Fehling's brilliant monograph (1977), especially pp. 29–44. Nothing more important has been written about the reception of ancient fiction. Rollo (1994) challenges not Fehling, whose literary approach he shares, but the view that no one in northern Europe read the *Metamorphoses* before the fourteenth century.
56 Griffin (1996).
57 Since Fehling wrote, powerful support for his case against folk tales has come from scholars not concerned with antiquity: Ellis (1983); Grätz (1988), esp. pp. 270–71. On the Cyclops in the *Odyssey* and the pyramid-robber in Herodotus see Fehling (1977) 89–97.

presentation or translations, on which bibliographies of printing, many of them still in progress, are a fuller and more reliable guide: for the fifteenth century, *ISTC*; for the sixteenth, various compilations with a national or even local focus such as Martín Abad (2001), essential supplements to the sketchy *Index Aureliensis* of sixteenth-century books, which at the time of writing has not yet reached the end of E; for English books of the sixteenth century see *Early English Books Online*.

18

GERALD SANDY AND STEPHEN HARRISON

Novels ancient and modern

Many people brought up in English-language educational systems are under the impression that the modern novel is a mid-eighteenth-century development. In fact, a rich tradition of novels and attendant literary theory originated in continental Europe as early as the end of the sixteenth century and continued into the seventeenth century. Part 1 of this chapter focuses on the impact of the ancient Greek novels on the development of extended prose fiction, that is, the novel, in parts of early modern western Europe. During that period continental European novelists, especially in France, were learning from ancient Greek novelists how to construct extended, complex, plot-driven stories in prose, and literary theorists were explaining how to achieve 'heroic' tone and fashion 'heroic' prose narratives in the mould of epic poetry.[1] By the end of the seventeenth century the lessons of narrative manipulation and the creation of appropriate tone had been learnt fully in much of western Europe. Beyond that point these features had become so thoroughly naturalised in the novels of western Europe that it becomes impossible to distinguish between direct imitations and adaptations on the one hand and imitations of imitations on the other hand. Part 2 carries the story from the middle ages into the twentieth century, focusing on the complex reception of the Latin realistic novels in Europe and beyond.

1. GREEK NOVELS AND THEIR INFLUENCE

Gerald Sandy

The ancient novels have had a practically immeasurable impact on the development of prose fiction in Europe and North America. The story is even more complex in that the reception of ancient texts involves not simply 'echoing' or acknowledging influence, but fundamentally reworking and appropriating

---

1 Fusillo, this volume, addresses the issue of nineteenth-century contempt for 'unheroic' fiction.

for multiple ideological and cultural purposes.[2] A complete account would require a substantial book; in the limited confines of a single chapter-section I have opted to focus upon the qualities of the ancient Greek novels such as narrative technique and moral purpose that early French novelists and European literary theorists promoted. My aim is to explain how those qualities came to be selected and transmitted to early modern western Europe. I have also put the emphasis on extended prose imitations and adaptations of ancient Greek novels. Thus, very little account will be taken of passing references to ancient Greek novels such as the allusion to the pirate Thyamis ('th' Egyptian thief') in Heliodorus' *Charicleia and Theagenes* in Shakespeare's *Twelfth Night*,[3] or even of incidental episodes derived from ancient Greek novels, many of which occur, for example, in Sir Philip Sidney's *Arcadia*; or of eighteenth-century novels written in the style of the ancient Greek novels.[4]

The discovery of the ancient Greek novel

The most important event in the discovery of the ancient Greek novel in early modern western Europe occurred in central Europe, specifically, in Hungary in 1526. The chapter by Michael Reeve in this volume traces in detail that event and other events that helped to bring the literary form now known as the novel and its potential for local adaptation within the range of literary theorists and practitioners in sixteenth- and seventeenth-century western Europe. I shall mention here only that the recovery of a manuscript containing Heliodorus from the smouldering ruins of king Matthias' Bibliotheca Corviniana in Budapest, Hungary, led ultimately to the first edition in 1536 of the Greek text, and in turn to Jacques Amyot's translation of it into French in 1547 or 1548. Until this time, which coincides with the beginnings of the institutionalised teaching of ancient Greek in France, the ancient Greek novels were scarcely known in western Europe. The rediscovery of the ancient Greek novel in France was part of the humanistic enterprise of 'unlocking and exposing all the sealed tombs of classical antiquity . . . and of dispersing and offering . . . their wealth . . . to the public', in the words of Guillaume Budé.[5] After the publication of Amyot's translation French and other western European novelists were to use it and other ancient Greek novels as guides, as writers moved away from the phantasmagoria and tales

---

2 For this point see esp. Hardwick (2003).   3 Act V, lines 120–3.
4 Hamilton (1972). See Doody (1994) for an especially engaging study of eighteenth-century English novels written 'in the style of'. The 'Further reading' section addresses some other gaps, such as the impact upon Italian and Iberian literature.
5 Budé writing to Erasmus. The letter is available in Allen *et al.* (1906–58) II.397.

of chivalry of the late middle ages.[6] His translation of Longus set the pattern for pastoral romances during the renaissance throughout western Europe and in combination with Sir Philip Sidney's *Arcadia* steered many of the earliest English-language attempts at fictional prose narrative in the direction of pastoral romance. From the middle of the sixteenth century to the end of the eighteenth century hundreds if not thousands of novels in western Europe were based directly and indirectly on translations of ancient Greek novels.

Literary theorists and historians

A far wider range of Greek novels existed in antiquity than was transmitted to early modern western Europe. Readers of Greek in Egypt during the Roman imperial period, for instance, could have read in the ancient Greek novels available to them of catamites, cannibalism, cross-dressing and ritualistic murder of children.[7] Near the middle of the ninth century, Photius, the patriarch of Constantinople, summarises the plot of an ancient Greek novel that has not otherwise survived: Antonius Diogenes' *The Wonders beyond Thule*. At the end of his summary he states of Antonius Diogenes, whom he labels 'the father of fictional stories':

> In this story in particular, as in [other] fictional works of its kind, there are two especially useful things to observe: first, that he [viz. Antonius Diogenes] presents a wrong-doer, even if he appears to escape countless times, paying the penalty just the same; second, that he shows many guiltless people, though on the brink of great danger, being saved many times in defiance of expectations.

This is the putative paradigm – wanderings, love affairs, dangers, last-minute escapes, punishment of the wicked and so on – and these are the models used by Photius to establish the norms that were transmitted to early modern western Europe. Amyot (in the preface of his translation) and literary theorists of the period focus on Heliodorus' masterful manipulation of a complex plot, which they compare with that of Homer, especially in the *Odyssey*. Amyot's manifesto for extended prose fictional narrative recommends the epic-style opening in the middle of the story (*in medias res*), the consequent flashbacks and delayed dénouement:

---

6 See Balard (1986); Plazenet (2002); Sandy (1982b), (1984–5); (1996); and Stone (1979) for details of Amyot's translation and its influence.
7 Sandy (2003) 737. See also Stephens and Winkler (1995) and Sandy (1994).

(Heliodorus), like epic poets, begins his story in the middle. This causes readers at the outset to be amazed and creates in them a passionate desire to understand the beginning (of the story).[8]

This conflation of the 'rules' for composing epic poems and novels *à la grecque* continued until well into the seventeenth century, as evinced in the first systematic history of prose fiction, P.-D. Huet's *Treatise in Letter Form on the Origin of the Novels* (*Lettre-traité sur l'origine des romans*, 1670), which categorises 'conforming novels' as those that follow 'the rules of the epic poem'.[9] In his analysis of the fragmentary novel known as the *Babylonian Affairs* of Iamblichus, Huet observes, 'He has inelegantly followed the chronological order [of events] and has not in the manner of Homer hurled the reader at the outset into the middle of the story', adding that 'Heliodorus has surpassed him [*viz.* Iamblichus] in the arrangement of the story'.[10]

In the preface of his translation Amyot concedes that *Charicleia and Theagenes* has certain shortcomings. It is, when all is said and done, only a fictional story and, consequently, lacks grandeur. Amyot is here engaging in a sixteenth-century literary debate that centred on the harmful effects of reading fiction such as *Amadis de Gaule*.[11] He does not define 'grandeur', but it is clear from what follows that the missing 'perfection' is the failure of the central male character Theagenes 'to perform any memorable feats of arms' in the manner of an epic hero ('executer nulz memorables exploitz d'armes'). It is against this backdrop of the discrediting of romances of chivalry, of what Amyot calls 'ecritz mensongers' and 'livres fabuleux' ('deceitful writings' and 'fabulous books') and the promotion of classical norms that the twenty-year grip of *Amadis de Gaule* on French readers was to be broken. In place of such novels, in which there is 'no erudition, no knowledge of antiquity, in a word, nothing from which anyone can derive anything of use', Heliodorus provides 'beautiful discourses drawn from natural and moral philosophy' and 'lifelike human passions . . . with such propriety that one would not derive from it a cause or example of wrong-doing. For all illicit and wicked

---

8 Quoted from the 'Le Proesme du translateur' of the second edition of 1559. For additional details and bibliography see Berger (1984); Plazenet (2002); Sandy (1982b); and Stone (1979).

9 Huet (1670) 182. See Sandy (2003) 745–50; Selden (1994); and Reeve in this volume for additional details.

10 Huet (1670) 156–57.

11 See Fumaroli (1985); Hardee (1968) 26–30; Plazenet (2002) 264–5; Sandy (1982b) 170–4; and Reeve in this volume.

passions come to a bad end and, conversely, those that are good and proper come to a desirable and happy end.'[12]

The qualities that Amyot, like Photius, singles out – epic deeds, epic-poem structure, moral purpose – were to prevail until the publication in 1678 of Madame de La Fayette's (or Lafayette's) *The Princess of Clèves* (*La princesse de Clèves*). It initiated a literary debate that eventually undermined the privileged position of 'les Poëtes Heroïques' ('epic poets') promoted in Amyot's preface. Henceforth equally sentimental novels tended to be set in a recognizably contemporary world populated by realistic characters, ironically in the case of *The Princess of Clèves*, which is set in the court of King Henri II of France whose two sons Amyot tutored.

French adaptations

The earliest known attempt to base a post-mediaeval extended prose narrative on an ancient Greek novel is represented by Nicolas de Montreux's (or Montreulx's) *Collection on Chastity* (*Oeuvre de la chasteté*). It appeared in three parts, each separated by two years, starting in 1595.[13] Of the three volumes, the second, *The Love of Cléandre and Domiphille* (*Les amours de Cléandre et Domiphille*, 1597), is modelled most extensively on *Charicleia and Theagenes*; the third volume, *The Collection on chastity continued by the chaste and faithful love of Criniton and Lydie* (*L'oeuvre de la chasteté continué par les chastes et fideles amours de Criniton et Lydie*, 1599), incorporates substantial material from Achilles Tatius' novel *Leucippe and Clitophon*.[14] In spite of his modest skills as a writer, Montreaux's pioneering efforts deserve our attention for a number of reasons.

First and most basically, Montreux's position at the forefront of the enterprise of assimilating ancient Greek novels to the literary sensibilities of early modern western Europe confirms the subtitle of Daele's book: *Arbiter of European Literary Vogues of the Late Renaissance*.[15] Second, in spite of the claim on the title page that 'the entire [work is] the creation of Ollenix of Mont-Sacré' (the anagram used by Montreux), the dedication in the first volume of the series, *The Love of Criniton et Lydie* (1595), accurately represents the lineage of the second volume:

12 Quoted from Amyot's preface.
13 The limited information about de Montreux is available in Daele (1946). See also Miotti (1996) and Sandy (2003) 750–4.
14 I have not been able to consult the third part, which is available only at the Bibliothèque du Mans. My knowledge of it is based on the summary provided by Daele (1946) 158–61.
15 Daele (1946).

Therefore, accept this work . . . which follows in form and subject the leadership of several learned writers, some of the most famous and knowledgeable writers on Earth. Such as the very highly esteemed Christian philosopher Achilles Tatius in his *Leucippe and Clitophon*, the learned bishop Heliodorus in his *Ethiopian Story* and the knowledgeable Boccaccio in his *Filocopo*.[16]

Third, the emphasis that Montreux in the passage quoted above puts on his sources' knowledge and philosophical and religious credentials underscores the moral purpose that Amyot argued should be inherent in a novel. Fourth, Montreux himself is a bridge between mediaeval romances of chivalry and the type of sentimental novel rooted in the distant past that was to dominate the literary scene in early modern western Europe during most of the seventeenth century. He contributed one volume, *The Sixteenth Book of Amadis de Gaulle* (*Le seiziesme livre d'Amadis de Gaulle*, 1577), to the twenty-one-volume French version of the saga of Amadis de Gaule, the origins of which belong to the Iberian peninsula and date back to as early as the thirteenth or fourteenth century. Montreux's contribution does not owe anything to any of the ancient Greek novels, but an Italian contribution that eventually became the twentieth volume in the French series is modelled extensively on *Charicleia and Theagenes*, and may have alerted Montreux to the possibility of adapting ancient Greek novels.[17] Fifth, Montreux appears to have taken to heart Amyot's regret that *Charicleia and Theagenes* suffers from a lack of epic grandeur. The first page of part 1 pronounces:

For there is no more praiseworthy form of bravery than that which is constant in the face of its enemies, which holds fast when under attack and does not dishonour its name by falling deeply into the vices by which it has been attacked.[18]

Also of interest is the role of the Greek masters in providing lessons for the deployment of complex narrative. Here the focus is on Heliodorus, cited by Amyot and early literary theorists as the best model for 'the heroic poets'. Montreux has adopted the epic 'beginning in the middle' structure also employed by Heliodorus. Part 1 (1595) of the three-volume ensemble opens with the narrative already in progress. Criniton has just killed a rival for the hand of his beloved Lydie. The circumstances that led to the quarrel between the two rivals are not explained until part 3 (1599). Still in

16 'follows . . . the leadership': for this and other metaphors used during the renaissance of imitation/adaptation see Pigman (1980).
17 The volume in the *Amadis de Gaule* series that Gabriel Chappuys translated from Italian into French in 1581 incorporates elements of Heliodorus' *Charicleia and Theagenes* (O'Connor (1970) 242–5).
18 See also Miotti (1996) 55.

part 1, because of a misunderstanding, Lydie and Criniton part ways, the latter of whom in his disheartened wanderings encounters a hermit named Cléandre, whose account of the circumstances that led to his becoming a hermit occupy the rest of part 1 and all of part 2 (1597). Like the priest Calasiris in Heliodorus' novel, Cléandre was motivated by a combination of star-crossed love and religious conviction to seek refuge in the solitary circumstances in which Criniton found him near the beginning of part 1. Thus the opening *in medias res* ('in the midst of the plot') of the ensemble has set the stage for two 'flashbacks' that are reminiscent of the accounts of their past lives as refugees of unrequited love provided at their fortuitous meeting by Calasiris and Cnemon in Heliodorus' novel.

Montreux's rudimentary attempt to implement the lessons provided by Heliodorus is evident in the static intrusion of the script of the play *Cléopâtre* that Cléandre gives to Criniton to read. This episode occupies 116 pages, some 15 per cent of the volume of 1595.[19] The impulse to include the script probably derives from Heliodorus' frequent use of extended dramatic metaphors.[20] Montreux appears to have attempted to combine this Heliodorean practice with the Greek novelist's equally frequent tendency to generate suspense by deferring essential information.[21] The reader, like Scheherazade in *1001 Nights*, wants to know, 'What happens next?' Both features – drama and delayed dénouement – are associated in Heliodorus' novel with, among others, a character named Cnemon.[22] Like Cléandre in Montreux's novel, he is a vagabond victim of unrequited love. In Heliodorus all the seemingly unrelated and superfluous characters, events and delays prove ultimately to have a direct bearing on the progression of the plot.[23] Montreux's 116-page dramatic script, however, does not advance the narrative.[24]

It would probably be a mistake to suppose that advances in narrative ability are directly attributable to chronological progression rather than to the innate skill of individual authors. Nonetheless, one can readily discern a great improvement in narrative art in Jean Baudoin's *The Story of Negreponte* (*Histoire Negre-Pontique*, 1631).[25] To provide only one example, Baudoin concentrates the Heliodorean texture by consolidating four of the characters in the Greek novel into two. Charicleia's two priestly benefactors, Calasiris

---

19 Montreux staged a play of the same title in 1595.   20 Walden (1894).
21 In general see Cave (1990) and, with specific reference to Heliodorus, Sandy (1982c) 33–7.
22 See Morgan (1989a).
23 Sandy (1982c) 37–9.
24 Miotti (1996) 57 n. 32 observes that the pagination of the framed drama is separate from that of the rest of the volume.
25 This neglected minor masterpiece is now available in a modern edition, edited and with a scholarly introduction by Plazenet (1998). See also Sandy (1982c) 116–18, (1982b) 179–85 and (2003) 754–8.

and her foster father Charicles, are combined by Baudoin in the person of Hierosme. Moreover, one of the three people reported in flight at the beginning of the story and who is now among the listeners to Hierosme's embedded narrative turns out to be his brother Baptiste (alias Palemon). He has 'been reduced to a life of piracy, attempting with the aid of one ship to punish to the best of my ability that cruel enemy of the name of Jesus Christ', that is, the Ottoman ruler Mahomet II, who had taken Negreponte (ancient Euboea, modern Evvia) from the Venetians in 1470. As listener he corresponds to Cnemon, the patient auditor of Calasiris' tale; as unwilling pirate he corresponds to Calasiris' son, the brigand Thyamis. In place of the inorganic set-pieces that disrupt the narrative flow in Montreux, Baudoin has successfully integrated seemingly unrelated characters and events that resonate with the past and provide impetus for future developments in the story.

I shall conclude this section by reviewing two French adaptations that have especially notable features. F. Gerzan's *The African Story of Cléomede and Sophonisbe* (*L'Histoire afrikaine de Cleomede et de Sophonisbe*, 1627–8), a sprawling work of two volumes and some 2,000 pages, is linked to Baudoin's more refined novel by a dedicatory 'Ode' composed by Baudoin, the pose that 'an aged Greek', like Baudoin's 'Greek monk', has provided the author with the authentic details that comprise 'the true history' of what follows and precise imitation of the opening sentence of Heliodorus' novel (or of Baudoin's imitation of it). What makes Gerzan's novel notable is its unparalleled combination of imitations of Heliodorus, Apuleius' Latin *Metamorphoses*, Achilles Tatius and Iamblichus' fragmentary novel, the *Babylonian Affairs*.[26] Gerzan's novel also provides an opportunity to include Italy, where narrative verse prevailed as the mode of adaptation, and Germany in this survey of the heritage of ancient Greek novels in early modern western Europe. The only other work known to me that combines imitation of Apuleius and Iamblichus is canto 14 of Giambattista Marino's *L'Adone*. Marino was in Paris at the time of Gerzan's literary activity, and his *L'Adone* was published there in 1623. The translation of Gerzan's novel by Phillip von Zesen helped to set the stage in Germany for the popularity of novels 'in the Greek style' in the second half of the seventeenth century.[27] J. Hérembert's *The Amatory Adventures and Fortunes of Pandion and Yonice* (*Les aventureuses et fortunées amours de Pandion et d'Yonice*) deserves mention because of its early date (1599) and overt adherence to the ancient Greek novels: 'taken from ancient Greek authors', as the title goes on to declare. It is also notable

---

26 Details in Sandy (1982b) 185–9 and (2003) 762–3.   27 Oeftering (1901) 82.

for its rigorous adherence to the ancient Greek novel of Achilles Tatius and consequent defiance of the moral standards of the time.[28]

English-language adaptations

The work of rediscovering, translating and adapting ancient Greek novels had already been accomplished in France and elsewhere in western Europe before the process was duplicated in the English-speaking world.[29] The word 'duplicated' is appropriate in the case of early English-language adaptations of ancient Greek novels. Because the advanced study of ancient Greek took root in England later than in France and elsewhere in western Europe, the process was dependent on earlier French and other European initiatives. James Sandford's *The Amorous and Tragicall Tales of Plutarche. Whereonto is annexed the Hystorie of Chariclia and Theagenes* (1597) highlights this dependence. The limited Heliodorean material (book 4) is derived from Warszewicki's Latin translation of the Greek novel and Politian's Latin translation of Plutarch;[30] and it seems likely that the notion of combining Heliodorus and Plutarch was inspired by Amyot's celebrated translations of the two authors. In the same year William Burton's translation of Achilles Tatius was based on della Croce's Latin translation of the Greek novel. Similarly, Thomas Underdowne's translation in 1577 of the entirety of *Charicleia and Theagenes* was derived from Warszewicki's Latin translation. Angel Day's English version of Longus' *Daphnis and Chloe* (1587) was based on Amyot's pioneering efforts in French. Even the adaptations were sometimes dependent on adaptations rather than on original sources. This is evident in the prefatory 'An Apologie for **ROMANCES**' in Sir George Mackenzie's *Aretina; Or, the Serious Romance* (1660):

> Who should blush to trace in these paths, which the famous Sidney, Scuderie, Barkeley, and Braghill hath beaten for them, besides thousands of Ancients . . . ? I shall speak nothing of that noble Romance written by a Bishop [i.e. Heliodorus], which the entreaty of all the Eastern Churches could never prevail with him to disown.[31]

---

28 Details in Sandy (1982b) 176–9 and (2003) 760–2. Daele (1946) 161 mistakenly states that Hérembert's novel is based on that of Heliodorus.
29 I.e. not just in England: Sir George Mackenzie, for instance, whose *Aretina* is mentioned below, was a Scot. See Spiller (1977).
30 Lathrop (1933) 164–5.
31 Sidney, of course is Sir Philip Sidney, author of *Arcadia*; Scuderie either or both of Georges and Madeleine de Scudéry; Barkeley presumably John Barclay, the French-born Scot who wrote the novels *Euphormionis Satyricon* (1603–7) and *Argenis* (1621); see further Harrison, below. I know nothing of Braghill.

Less than two decades later *Evagoras* (1677), by L. L., Gent., (i.e. Gentle-man) highlights the difficulty of distinguishing between direct and indirect imitations of ancient Greek novels by writers of English-language novels. In the preface the author seems to suggest that English-language novels derived from French intermediaries are out of favour:

> Booksellers are grown men of mode too, they scorn any thing of this kind below an **Originally in F[rench]** in the Title Page, with a **Made English,**

and the prefatory tribute by N. Brady underscores the apparent French derivation:

> Thy Maiden Muse sores [sic] not to bombast strains,
> Nor with her flagging Wings does sweep the Plains;
> But in the middle way does even fly,
> Follows the Dedalean Scudery.

The anonymous author of *Triana* (1654) 'scorn[s] any thing . . . below an **Originally in**' Spanish or Italian:

> I present not a Translation out of the Spanish, or from the Italian Originall; this is common Pander to mens fancy, hoping to vent them under that title with the more applause.

Even before the period to which the prefatory material quoted above belongs English prose that displays any traces of ancient Greek novels is marked by an eclectic range of influences: Italianate novelle, Greek and Roman myths, legends and history and English translations of translations of Achilles Tatius, Heliodorus and Longus. This diverse material is character-istically used as incidental rather than as integral components of plot-driven action.

Two partial exceptions to the last statement are Sir Philip Sidney's *Arcadia* and some of Robert Greene's many works. One of Sidney's contemporaries, Gervase Markham, states in the prefatory 'To The Reader' of his *The English Arcadia* (1607), 'The onely to be admired Sir Philip Sidney [drew] . . . both from *Heliodorus* and [Montemayor's] *Diana*.'[32] This statement captures per-fectly Sidney's blending of the previously distinct genres of chivalric romance and pastoral. It does not, however, specify that Heliodorus contributed more to Sidney's narrative technique than to the content of his *Arcadia*.[33]

---

32 Quoted from Hamilton (1972) 30.
33 What Wolff (1912) 307–28 calls the 'grandiose framework from Heliodorus'. 'Incidents from Greek Romance' are indexed in Wolff under 'Sidney, Sir Philip'. See also Salzman (1985) 55.

Robert Greene seems to have imitated every earlier literary work that had proved to be popular.[34] In his two best-known works, *Pandosto* (1588) and *Menaphon* (1589), 'at last the story is the thing', in the words of C. S. Lewis; and substantial parts of the stories are demonstrably derived from Achilles Tatius, Heliodorus and Longus.[35] However, Greene's eclectic plundering of sources as diverse as Lyly's *Euphues*, Sidney's *Arcadia*, mediaeval romances of chivalry, Italian novelle and ancient Greek novels is symptomatic of many of the early English attempts to write prose fiction. The diffused results often make it impossible to isolate material derived directly from ancient Greek novels.

One way to distinguish between the early English and French authors of prose fiction is to think of the former as professional writers, the latter as scholarly writers. Greene 'would, as [Thomas] Nash[e] tells us, 'yark up' a pamphlet 'in a night and a day' to meet a publisher's demand of a 'best seller'.[36] In contrast, the process of producing prose fiction in France was a scholarly enterprise from the start. For his translations of Heliodorus' and Longus' novels Jacques Amyot searched for and collated Greek manuscripts.[37] Baudoin's and Gerzan's claims to have published the contents of the manuscripts that had happened to have come into their possession may be untrue, but their fictional stories reflect the sprit of the French quest for accurate knowledge of classical antiquity.

2. ROMAN NOVELS AND THEIR INFLUENCE

Stephen Harrison

Though the more romantic *Apollonius, King of Tyre* had a considerable influence on a wide range of literary works in both the mediaeval and Renaissance periods,[38] the realistic comic novels of Petronius and Apuleius were the Latin texts that definitively shaped the beginnings of western prose fiction. There was only sketchy mediaeval awareness of these authors before their renaissance rediscovery and printing:[39] in the case of the *Satyrica* in particular, though it stimulated an extant prosimetric (mixed prose and verse) narrative in England in the thirteenth or fourteenth century,[40] and some of its stories such as the 'Widow of Ephesus' achieved a wide currency,[41] its very fragmentary preserved state until the seventeenth century (see below) limited its influence in the renaissance. Apuleius may have been known to

---

34 Wolff (1912) 367–76; Salzman (1985) 58.
35 Lewis (1954) 422. For the 'borrowings' see Wolff (1912) 376 and as indexed under 'Greene, Robert': 'Borrowings from Achilles Tatius', 'Relations to Heliodorus' and 'Relations to Longus'.
36 Quoted from Wolff (1912) 367.   37 Sandy (1984–5).   38 Cf. e.g. Archibald (1991).
39 Carver (1999).   40 See Connors (1999).   41 Huber (1990a).

Chrétien de Troyes in the twelfth century[42] and was certainly used in some of the tales of Boccaccio's *Decameron* of 1353;[43] the tale of Cupid and Psyche with its romantic and quasi-allegorical tone, always the most popular part of the novel, was much employed in fifteenth and sixteenth century neo-Latin and Italian literature.[44] The *Metamorphoses* also provided some material for the great Italian verse romances from outside the Cupid and Psyche tale: Ariosto's *Orlando Furioso* (1532) includes a scene (12.88ff.) clearly drawn from *Metamorphoses* 4, in which Orlando hears the tale of a young lady captured by robbers and liberates her from their cave.

But it is in the Spanish Golden Age that we see the clearest influence of Apuleius on the emerging tradition of European prose fiction.[45] Indisputable traces of the *Metamorphoses* can be found in the first picaresque romance, a comic tale of the miscellaneous and wandering adventures of a low-life (anti-) hero, the anonymous *Lazarillo de Tormes* (1545),[46] and in the work of Cervantes. Quite apart from the work's generally Apuleian framework of anti-heroic comedy, parody of higher literature, complex narrative voice and inserted tales, the episode in *Don Quixote* (Part 1 (1605), ch. 35) in which the Don attacks a set of wine-skins believing them to be a hostile giant, clearly owes something to Lucius' 'slaughtering' of the enchanted wine-skins at the end of book 2 of the *Metamorphoses*. Likewise, the tale of Cupid and Psyche is evidently laid under contribution in *Persiles and Sigismunda* (1617), where in one of the inserted tales a Scottish countess is about to stab the son of her husband's supposed murderer but stops and drops her lantern on him when she is taken aback by his Cupid-like beauty.[47] Thus both the parodic and the more romantic aspects of Apuleius' work were appreciated by his earliest novelistic imitators.

Apuleius, Petronius and the early modern novel

Apuleius was broadly known in England in the Elizabethan period through the translation of Adlington (1566), which is likely to have been read by Shakespeare.[48] The comparison of Apuleius' elaborate diction in the *Metamorphoses* with the more traditional classical lexicon of Ciceronianism had been a key element in the Latin prose style wars amongst humanists,[49] and in John Lyly's *Euphues: or the Anatomy of Wit* (1578), stylistic Apuleianism is a prime factor in one of the early works of English prose fiction. *Euphues*

---

42 Rollo (1994).
43 *Dec.* 5.10 and 8.8 ~ *Metamorphoses* 9.22–8; *Dec.*7.2 and 8.8 ~ *Metamorphoses* 9.5–7
44 Cf. Scobie (1978); Moreschini (1994).
45 See Scobie (1978) and Martos (2003) lxxxv–ix.
46 Carver (2000–1) 341–2.   47 D. Wilson (1994).
48 Tobin (1984).   49 D'Amico (1984); Prete (1988).

is short on plot and long on moralising speeches, conversations and letters about love which owe more to the Greek romance tradition than the Roman novels, but its extraordinarily abundant and musical verbal texture, with rhyme, alliteration, assonance and isocolon, parodied by Shakespeare (*1 Henry IV* II.iv.393ff.), strongly recalls the style of the *Metamorphoses*. Take, for example, a typically elaborate speech by the hero: 'If nature bear no sway, why use you this adulation? If nature work the effect, what booteth any education? If nature be of strength or force, what availeth discipline or nurture? If of none, what helpeth nature?.'[50] Similar Apuleian influence on emerging English prose fiction can be seen for example in Sidney's *Old Arcadia* (c. 1581), which alludes to the story of Cupid and Psyche, picks up Lyly's stylistic euphuism, and adopts some Apuleian structural and narrative techniques.[51] These courtly romance adaptations of Apuleius provide an interesting sanitisation of the earthy tradition of the Roman novel.

Though the then extant remains of Petronius had been printed in 1482, it was only in 1669 that the full text of the *Satyrica* as we know it today was published,[52] followed by the first English translation (Burnaby 1694). The *Satyrica* had already excited novelistic imitation a century previously, in Thomas Nashe's colourful *The Unfortunate Traveller* (1594), which provides a Petronian parallel to the contemporary Apuleian *Euphues*. In this work the hero Jack Wilton has various adventures set in the time of Henry VIII, including sensational narratives of violence, rape and torture; it is a picaresque tale with a prosimetric frame and a wide range of literary pastiche and parody, which certainly shows the influence of Petronius, and perhaps that of Apuleius as well.[53]

More ambitious were the much longer neo-Latin prose fictions of the French-born Scot John Barclay. He published in 1603 the first part of a satirical prosimetric novel with the title *Euphormionis Lusinini Satyricon* ('the *Satyricon* of Euphormio of Lusinia'), parodying the utopian form of the neo-Latin novel begun by More's *Utopia* (1516): Euphormio is a stranger who visits and wonders at the bizarre political and religious institutions of contemporary Europe, and there are a number of elements drawn from Petronius, as the work's title might suggest.[54] Barclay's other neo-Latin novel was the *Argenis* (1621), very popular with contemporary readers (two English translations appeared in its first decade of publication). This has been described as a 'baroque combination of political treatise, historical allegory and

---

50 Cited from Salzman (1987) 97.   51 Carver (1997).
52 For the history of the text of Petronius see Reeve, this volume.
53 Cf. Walsh (1970) 241–2; Kinney (1986) 341–3, 357–8. I am grateful to Helen Moore for help here.
54 Cf. Walsh (1970) 238–9.

romance of chivalry',[55] and has an idealising romantic plot in the Heliodoran tradition: the heroine Argenis is a princess who has four suitors and marries the worthiest one after many adventures which reflect contemporary history and politics.[56] Further neo-Latin novels influenced by the Roman tradition followed in continental Europe, especially after the publication of the complete text of the *Satyrica*;[57] in 1659 Walter Charleton published his *Matrona Ephesia* ('The matron of Ephesus'), an elegant retelling of *Satyrica* 111–12 with learned expansions reflecting on love, which was rapidly translated into English;[58] and in 1685 came the *Psyche Cretica* ('Cretan Psyche') of Johann Ludwig Prasch (1685), which combines imitation of Barclay's *Argenis*, Virgil's *Aeneid* and Apuleius.[59]

In the eighteenth century, the realistic, bawdy and low-life tradition seen in the great English picaresque novelists could be plausibly argued to reassert the earthy character of the Roman novel. Though the most important acknowledged sources of these writers are the French tradition of Rabelais and Lesage's much later *Gil Blas* (1715–35; translated by Smollett in 1749; see further below) and the Spanish tradition of Cervantes, some general resemblances with the Roman novel tradition are clear. This is especially so when these works are contrasted with the more sentimental Greek-style romances of Richardson's *Clarissa* (1740) and *Pamela* (1748).[60] In the plots of travel, low-life adventures, and inserted tales of Smollett's *Roderick Random* (1748) and *Peregrine Pickle* (1751) we find clear Petronian imitation. In *Roderick Random* the hero is actually urged to read Petronius by the corrupt aristocrat Earl Struttwell as an author 'who will always be held in esteem by every person of wit and learning', and priggishly answers that Petronius 'wrote with great ease and vivacity' but was too 'lewd and indecent' (ch. 52), while the character of the unsuccessful poet Melopoyn (chs. 61–3) echoes Eumolpus in more than his name. In *Peregrine Pickle* the hero, in the course of his Grand Tour, is treated by the pretentiously gastronomic Doctor to a gross dinner in Paris, which plainly recalls *Dinner at Trimalchio's* (in ch. 48, entitled 'The Doctor prepares an Entertainment in the Manner of the Ancients, which is attended with divers ridiculous circumstances').

The most extraordinary work of eighteenth-century British fiction, Sterne's *Tristram Shandy* (1759–67), proclaims Cervantes and Rabelais as its models,[61] and though its remarkable narrative somersaults recall aspects of

---

55 Hofmann (1999) 11; see Ijsewijn (1983a); Salzman (1985) 149–55.
56 See Connors (2005), and the recent edition of the *Argenis* by Riley and Huber (2004).
57 Grafton (1990).   58 Huber (1990b).   59 Ijsewijn (1983b).
60 For this aspect of Richardson's work see Doody (1994).
61 E.g. Volume 3 Chapter 19: 'by the ashes of my dear Rabelais, and dearer Cervantes' (for Cervantes see also Volume 1 Chapter 10, for Rabelais Volume 3 Chapter 22).

Apuleian technique, specific influence from the Roman novels is hard to find despite its broad range of literary allusion, though it has been interestingly suggested that its occasional pseudo-fragmentary appearance may reflect the lacunose transmission of Petronius.[62] In Fielding's *Tom Jones* (1749), on the other hand, there seems to be a clear harnessing of the general literary thrust of the Roman novel. This work is proclaimed as a 'heroic, historical, prosaic poem' (book 4 ch.1) or as 'prosai-comi-epic writing' (book 5 ch.1), and repeatedly parodies ancient epic narrative to describe its low-life plot. Especially notable are the 'Homeric' cat-fight of the churchyard where Molly Seagrim defends herself against the violent envy of other local women (book 4 ch. 8, entitled 'A battle sung by the muse in the Homerican style, and which none but the classical reader can taste'), which can be compared with the comic battle on shipboard at Petronius, *Satyrica* 107, and the parody of epic dawn-formulas at book 11 ch. 9, which reprises a recognisable Apuleian technique.[63] This para-epic stance, though this link is never openly stated, is difficult to disassociate from the Roman novelistic tradition, where it is similarly central (see Harrison in Morgan and Harrison, this volume).

Elsewhere in eighteenth-century Europe, in France the influence of Apuleius can be clearly seen in Le Sage's French Gil Blas (1731–5), already noted above as an important stimulus for the English picaresque novel. The episode in which *Gil Blas* is captured by robbers and taken to a cave with an old housekeeper (1.4–10) plainly owes much to the experiences of Lucius and Charite in *Metamorphoses* 4.[64] In Germany, Wieland's *Die Geschichte von Agathon* ('The story of Agathon', 1773–94), the work of an author of considerable classical learning, combines idealistic Greek romance with some elements from Apuleius: the chaste and moral hero Agathon is kidnapped by pirates, falls in love with an ex-prostitute who renames herself Chariclea after the heroine of Heliodorus, and is ultimately revealed to have a sister named Psyche.[65] Any Roman influence is here sanitised through literary and philosophical idealism.

Victorian views: Lytton, Pater, Sienkiewicz

The perennially popular story of Cupid and Psyche makes a brief appearance in two ironic comments on romantic episodes in Thackeray,[66] but in general the leading writers of the English Victorian novel (Dickens, Eliot and Trollope as well as Thackeray) show little detectable influence from Roman prose fiction. Though all except Dickens have some concern to demonstrate

---

62 See Doody (1996) 254.   63 See Harrison (2003b).
64 See Hijmans *et al.* (1977) 214–15.   65 Cf. Doody (1996) 256.
66 *Pendennis* (1848–50) ch. 64; *The Virginians* (1857–9) ch. 22.

more conventional classical learning, the dubious reputation of Petronius in an age of professed decency and the religious complexities of Apuleius in a strongly Christian era may have made it less desirable to show knowledge of the ancient novel, and such relatively recondite allusions ill fitted the new mass readership of the Victorian novel in an age of rapid cultural change.

Not unnaturally, it is historical novels on the Roman empire which show most interest in Petronius and Apuleius. The first of these is perhaps the most popular historical novel of the whole nineteenth century, Lytton's *The Last Days of Pompeii* (1834, hereafter *LDP*). Its final pages and footnotes present the work as the supposed history of bodies and buildings discovered at Pompeii in the previous century, and there is a clear interest in archaeological realism and reconstruction. But more interesting is the fact that this book, which seems with J. G. Lockhart's *Valerius* (1821) to be the first historical novel in English set in the Roman empire, is suitably conscious of its novelistic predecessors in Roman literature. The prosimetric structure of the novel, with a number of casually inserted songs and poems, matches Petronius, but is also paralleled in the novels of Walter Scott, which Lytton explicitly praises in his preface; likewise, its location in Campania close to the main scenario of the *Satyrica*, and the proximity of its dramatic date to Petronius' own lifetime may be accidents of history but encourage a general comparison.

Several episodes in *LDP* are more specifically drawn from Petronius.[67] In book 1 ch. 3, the hero Glaucus holds a sumptuous dinner party at his house, of which the entrance is described in great detail; this, especially the mosaic decorations and the famous *trompe-l'oeil* guard dog (cf. *Satyrica* 29.2), recall the elaborate description of the entrance of the house of Trimalchio (*Satyrica* 28–9). The banquet which follows with its select fare and musical accompaniment has some links with *Dinner at Trimalchio's*, but the true descendant of that famous fictional meal is that described in book 4 ch. 3, 'A fashionable party and a dinner à la mode in Pompeii'. There another dinner is given by the hedonistic Diomed. Like Trimalchio, Diomed is a rich merchant who 'affected greatly the man of letters', and though unlike Trimalchio he does not dominate the conversation at his own dinner by suggesting literary topics or by making comic errors of learning and mythology, the two guests whose more cultured perspective we see (as in Encolpius and Ascyltus' comments on Trimalchio) condemn him as 'a vulgar old fellow'. The diners are entertained by acrobats, are given punning presents, and a precious ornament is dropped by a slave, all elements which recall the 'Banquet'. But it is not just *Dinner at Trimalchio's* which is laid

---

67 See in more detail Harrison (2004).

under contribution: in book 1 ch. 7 we find a recitation by the bad poet Fulvius in the baths at Pompeii which plainly recalls the recitation of the bad poet Eumolpus in the baths at *Satyrica* 89, with the same audience reaction of stone-throwing (note too that 'Eumolpus' also turns up as a gladiator-name at book 5 ch. 3). Equally strong traces of Apuleius are also to be found.[68] An authorial footnote suggests that Lytton had read the *Metamorphoses* in Latin and expects some of his readers to have done so.[69] There are four allusions to the ever-popular story of Cupid and Psyche, including a symbolic account of its significance in Christian terms (book 5, 'Chapter the Last'),[70] which reflects a larger pattern in the novel by which the pagan philosophical and religious elements in Apuleius' work are systematically Christianised by Lytton. The prominence of Isis in *LDP* surely reflects the prominence of that goddess in Apuleius' novel; in *LDP* her mysterious eastern cult, presided over by the arch-villain Arbaces, is seen as an inferior and devilish competitor to early Christianity as traditional Olympian paganism breaks down, an inversion of Isis's role as saving deity in the *Metamorphoses*. Such 'correction' can also be seen in the overall trajectory of the novel: the eventual conversion of the hero and heroine to Christianity mirrors the eventual conversion of Apuleius' hero to Isiac religion. Likewise, the climactic saving of the hero from the perils of the arena just before the eruption of Vesuvius (book 5 ch. 9) could reflect the equally climactic escape of Lucius from the arena at Corinth in *Metamorphoses* 10.

Lytton's novel thus shows considerable awareness of his generic predecessors and some effort to resemble two surviving Roman novels and to recall their most famous episodes, but also a strong concern to reprocess the literature of Roman paganism to Victorian Christian ends.

I turn now to two historical novels where the two ancient novelists actually appear as minor characters. Pater's *Marius The Epicurean* (1885), in its account of the philosophical and spiritual education of the young Marius as he moves from pagan religion through philosophy to Christianity, narrates Marius' boyhood reading of the *Metamorphoses* and his appreciation of its elaborate 'jewelled' style and potential for allegory despite many coarse elements, and includes an elaborate retelling of the Cupid and Psyche story in more than twenty pages (chs. 5 and 6). Soon after, Marius and his friend Flavian attend the festival of the Ship of Isis at Pisa, surely an allusion to

---

68 Harrison (2004).
69 The footnote is the sole note to book 2, which concludes: 'A witch of a lighter character, and manners less ascetic, the learned reader will remember with delight in the "Golden Ass" of Apuleius; and the reader who is *not* learned, is recommended to the spirited translation of that enchanting romance by Taylor.'
70 For the other three cf. book 1 ch. 8 (*bis*), book 5 ch. 9.

the description of the same festival in *Metamorphoses* 11. Rather later in the novel, Marius meets Apuleius at dinner at the house of a friend (ch. 20), hears some of his rhetorical performances later to emerge in the *Florida*, and converses with him about Platonic demonology in a conversation which condenses parts of *On the God of Socrates*. Here the stress is on trying to recreate the personality of Apuleius rather than using his novel, though the performance over dinner of an entertainment called the *Death of Paris* surely recalls the performance of the pantomime of the Judgement of Paris described in detail in *Metamorphoses* 10.30–1.

The appearance of Apuleius in *Marius* is part of Marius' on-going education, exposing him to Platonist ideas, which he finds inadequate. But the long summary of his most famous episode and allusions to several other scenes in the *Metamorphoses* suggest (as in Lytton) a recognition in a Victorian novelist of generic predecessors at Rome. The elaborate style of Apuleius also clearly appeals to Pater, another high stylist, and ultimately the influence of the *Metamorphoses* on *Marius* has more to do with a striving after a precious and decorative 'decadent' style than with real engagement with Apuleian themes and ideas. Here, once again, the more earthy aspects of the Roman novel are edited out.[71]

Quo Vadis? (1896, English translation 1941), by the Polish writer Henryk Sienkiewicz (Nobel Laureate for Literature 1905), is now best known for its adaptation in the 1951 film version of the same title.[72] The (fictional) hero of the book, Vinicius, is Petronius' nephew, and this allows Petronius to play a considerable role in the plot, largely as the hedonistic and cynical 'arbiter of taste' at the court of Nero. Early in the novel Petronius gives Vinicius a copy of what he calls the '*Satyricon*', presenting it as a *samizdat* work (part 1 ch. 2); Vinicius immediately comments on its unusual prosimetric texture, and is told by the author to concentrate on *Dinner at Trimalchio's* when he reads it.[73] This is presumably because Sienkiewicz held that this part of the work is meant to satirise Nero, as interpreters have sometimes argued; Petronius' contempt for the emperor whom he is forced to serve is evident throughout the novel. But there is little further attempt to say much about the book or to use its material; the novel has luxurious feasts but none especially close to the *Dinner*, and Petronius' death-scene when he is forced to suicide by Nero (part 2 ch. 33) resists the temptation to include the novel amongst Petronius' last dispositions. Indeed, the only overt use of Roman novelistic material in *Quo Vadis?* is a brief allusion to the beauty of Psyche as a parallel for that

---

71 On *Marius* and Apuleius see further Brzenk (1978) and Harrison (2004).
72 On the film see Wyke (1997) 138–46; Solomon (2001a) 217–21; below, p. 337.
73 Later, in a scene which seems slightly inconsistent, we see Petronius working on the *Dinner* (part 1 ch. 12).

of the heroine, the Sarmatian (Polish) girl Lygia.[74] But once again we find a novelist writing about the Roman empire showing at least some awareness of Roman generic predecessors.

Roman novels in the twentieth century and beyond

The novels of the twentieth century have been more interested in Petronius than in Apuleius; the sexual, satirical and comic content of the *Satyrica* has been more to modern taste than the *Metamorphoses* and its apparently problematic religious and symbolic element, though Apuleian narratological complexities are interestingly echoed in some self-conscious fictional types such as the *nouveau roman*. The creative reprocessing of the *Odyssey* in James Joyce's *Ulysses* (1922) is of course a central topic of Joyce commentary and criticism, but it has not been much noted that the general concept of applying a recognisably Homeric framework to low-life, urban, bodily and bawdy material which involves prosimetric texture and a good deal of literary allusion and parody strongly recalls the *Satyrica* (see Harrison in Morgan and Harrison, this volume). *Ulysses* makes only one clear allusion to Petronius,[75] but it resembles the *Satyrica* considerably in general terms. Another famous novel from the 1920s influenced by Petronius is *The Great Gatsby* (1925), treated by Massimo Fusillo in his chapter in this volume.[76]

This appropriation of the Petronian satiric tradition to criticise empty materialism emerges again in more recent US fiction: Edwin 'Bud' Shrake's *Peter Arbiter* (1973) adapts the *Satyrica* in some detail to attack the oil-rich Texas of the 1970s, but much better known is Tom Wolfe's *The Bonfire of the Vanities* (1986). In this brilliantly excoriating account of New York socialites in the 1980s era of telephone-number Wall Street salaries, chapter 15 ('The Masque of the Red Death', a comic-horror reference to Poe) narrates a hyper-luxurious dinner party at the Fifth Avenue apartment of 'some over-bearingly vulgar people named Bavardage, a glorified travelling salesman and his wife' in which over-elaborate décor and food, pretentious guests and fashionable lip-service to the arts (the guest of honour is Lord Aubrey Buffing, an ageing gay English poet of conservative views who echoes Petronius' Eumolpus) combine to recall *Dinner at Trimalchio's*.

In English literature, it has been plausibly argued that Antony Powell's *Dance to the Music of Time* sequence (1951–75) has some similar Petronian

---

74 Part 2 ch. 13: 'Do you recollect Psyche, that incomparably beautiful of virgins and goddesses?' (cited from Sienkiewicz (1941) 227).
75 In the 'Oxen of the Sun' section, Joyce (1969) 405: 'unless she were another Ephesian matron'.
76 Orignally entitled *Trimalchio* (see F. S. Fitzgerald (2000)). For the Petronian connections see also Mackendrick (1950); Briggs (2000); Fusillo, pp. 330–1 below.

elements in its social satire,[77] and in modern Italian literature much appropriation of Petronius is to be found.[78] Most recently, Robert Harris' *Pompeii* (2003) has used the destruction of Pompeii as the framework for an accomplished thriller, and presents an extravagant dinner given by the tasteless millionaire freedman Ampliatus at which sneering comparisons of the host with the Petronian character Trimalchio are openly made by aristocratic guests, thus suggesting not only the *Satyrica*'s early readership but also the specific satire of *Dinner at Trimalchio's*.[79]

It is harder to find important modern fictions for which Apuleius is similarly significant. The major Dutch novelist Louis Couperus, having produced a version of the Cupid and Psyche story in *Psyche* (1898, English translation 1908), went on to write *De Verliefde Ezel* ('The ass in love', 1918, no English translation), which retells the rest of the *Metamorphoses*. Though in *Psyche*, in which the main characters are fittingly homonymous descendants of the Cupid and Psyche story in Apuleius, he provides some interesting perspectives and variations on the original in a jewelled and sentimental style which strongly recalls the fairy tales of Oscar Wilde, neither novella has achieved as high a status in Dutch or world literature as some of Couperus' other work.[80] C. S. Lewis' *Till We Have Faces* (1956), another re-telling of the story of Cupid and Psyche, develops and expands Apuleius' episode considerably, for example casting a single sister of Psyche (here named as Orval; contrast the anonymous pair of the *Metamorphoses*) as the main, sympathetic character genuinely motivated to help her sister: but its heavy-handed apparatus of sub-Tolkien mythical plot has meant that this novel has not enjoyed the success of the author's other quasi-allegorical fictions. Quite different is Marie Darrieussecq's best-selling *Pig Tales* (1997; first published in French as *Truismes*, 1996): in this entertaining satire on the corruption of modern society, a 'masseuse' acquires the capacity to metamorphose into a pig, and the novel's salacious exploration of a low-life world, its comic deployment of the issue of human/animal metamorphosis and its ironic use of quasi-religious salvation through an exotic African figure clearly owes much to Apuleius as well as to Kafka.

Modern fictions about the Roman world continue to be written; indeed, there has been a recent increase in their number and popularity.[81] These novels clothe familiar modern genres in Roman colour (e.g. the detective stories

---

77 Wiseman (1992) 62.   78 See Fusillo, this volume.
79 Harris (2003) 142–54, esp. 144.
80 On Couperus and Apuleius see Visser (1978) and van der Paardt (1989); *Psyche* was recently republished in English translation (Couperus (1999)). I am grateful to Maaike Zimmerman for advice here.
81 For this recent fashion see interestingly Davis (2000). For a database of novels on the Roman world see http://loki.stockton.edu/roman/fiction/

of Lindsey Davis or Steven Saylor), provide quasi-biographical accounts of intriguing major figures or events (e.g. significant emperors or (following Lytton) the destruction of Pompeii),[82] or explore ancient works outside the novel genre (e.g. Virgil's *Aeneid* or Ovid's *Metamorphoses*)[83] but have not yet probed the works of the Roman novelists themselves. The twenty-first century awaits perhaps a refashioning and creative exploration of the Roman tradition of prose fiction.

Further Reading

Doody (1996) provides the broadest overview of the influence of ancient fiction on the modern novel, though many of her generalised arguments and formulations are controversial. The reception of the ancient novels is a key topic in the niche journal on ancient fiction, *Ancient Narrative* (www.ancientnarrative.com), and in its predecessor the *Groningen Colloquia on the Novel* (for the nine volumes in this series see details at www.forsten.nl). In spite of its advanced age (first published in 1814), Dunlop (1888) lives up to its original copious title: *A history of fiction: being a critical account of the most celebrated prose works of fiction, from the earliest Greek romances to the novels of the present day* (revised by H. Wilson and published in 1896 as *History of Prose Fiction*) and is still a useful global survey for such basic matters as plot (volume 2 of the 1842 edition, which begins with Boccaccio, has been digitised by Google and can be consulted online at http://books.google.com).

For the Greek novels, Lestringant (1986) traces the influence of Amyot's translation on the development of pastoral romance in western Europe. Plazenet (1997) compares sixteenth- and seventeenth-century French imitations and adaptations of ancient Greek novels with their English-language equivalents. Home to *Amadis de Gaule*, picaresque novels and Cervantes, the Iberian Peninsula has a rich history of prose fiction as well as drama, narrative verse and literary theory linked to ancient Greek novels. Much of this material is surveyed by Futre Pinheiro (2003) and Billault (1992). Narrative verse such as Lodovico Ariosto's *Orlando furioso* and Torquato Tasso's *Gerusalemme liberata* that incorporates snippets of incidental details from the ancient Greek novels prevailed in Italy during the sixteenth and seventeenth centuries. Bertoni and Fusillo (1998) provide a detailed account of the more fully integrated Heliodorean texture of Giambattista Basile's

---

82 For classic novels on emperors see e.g. Graves (1934a) and (1934b); Wilder (1948); Yourcenar (1955); Vidal (1962); for Pompeii see recently Lawrence (2001) [mystery, for children], Harris (2003) [adult thriller, see above].

83 See Bloch (1977); Ransmayr (1990).

narrative poem *Teagine*. The familiar pattern of influences from the Middle East contributing to the development Greek artistic forms appears to have been reversed at times in the case of the ancient Greek novel, as explained by Davis (2002) and Hägg and Utas (2003). Details of the contribution of the ancient Greek novels to non-literary artistic representations are provided by Lossky (1986), Quet (1992) and Stechow (1953).

On the reception of Petronius and Apuleius in European literature, Walsh (1970) has a helpful final chapter; more recent and especially useful are the essays in Hofmann (1999b). On the reception of Petronius, Gagliardi (1993) provides a stimulating if often rapid account; on that of Apuleius, see Haight (1927, now out of date), Carver (2008) and Gaisser (2008). Texts of the *Argenis* of John Barclay and the *Psyche Cretica* of Johann Ludwig Prasch (together with further material on these novels and their authors) are conveniently available online on the home page of Professor Mark Riley, http://www.csus.edu/indiv/r/rileymt/

19

MASSIMO FUSILLO

Modernity and post-modernity

The contemporary reception of the ancient novel

Although this is the last chapter in this volume, the modern reception of ancient texts should not be considered a mere learned appendix. We inevitably read any kind of text from the perspective of our culture; a creative rewriting by a modern artist is an extension of the process of cultural dialogue that underlies all interpretation. The specific case of the novel is quite complex, because modern attitudes towards this genre have slowly changed from hostility to acceptance, finally achieving the dominant position they have now. This process has influenced not only our understanding but even our conceptualisation of the ancient novel. The analysis of contemporary rewritings, as we shall discover, can shed new light on these issues.

Let us begin with a significant date: 1876. In this year Erwin Rohde – a prominent figure in the worlds of classical philology and the history of religion, a supporter of Friedrich Nietzsche in his polemic against the German academy – published a huge work on the Greek novel, still considered a critical masterpiece.[1] In the same year Leo Tolstoy was completing the publication of *Anna Karenina*, which he had begun in 1873. This synchronism can be a good starting point for getting to grips with the meaning of the ancient novel in contemporary culture. At the end of the nineteenth century, a new philological approach to the ancient novel began just at the time when the modern novel definitively reached a hegemonic position in the system of literary genres, and enjoyed its most flourishing era. The extraordinary success of this modern literary genre inspired philologists to seek out equivalent texts in antiquity, and therefore to construct so thorny and controversial a field of study as the ancient novel. Thorny and controversial first of all because it is clearly a modern term for a genre that ancient rhetoric and literary theory never codified;[2] second, because in ancient literature borders

---

1 Rohde (1876); reference in this volume is to the third edition (1914).
2 Above, pp. 190–2.

between fiction and non-fiction, as, in general, those between literature and other forms of discourse, were more vague and unstable.[3]

Choosing a significant date as a point of departure is, at one level, an arbitrary segmentation of fluid and gradual processes. On the one hand, there were critical approaches to the ancient novel before 1876, even if they were not philological in the same way.[4] On the other hand – and this is much more important to stress – in Rohde's book we still find the various factors that inhibited a profound critical evaluation of the ancient novel in the ninenteenth century, and its circulation among a larger public: the typical Victorian censorship of sexuality; the classicist's prejudice against late antiquity and post-classical literatures; the academic bias against any kind of 'popular' literature. Rohde's devaluation of Greek novels is absolutely clear even if one confines oneself to reading the index: the part devoted to textual analysis fills more or less only one-fifth of the entire book. The author focuses his interest much more on the genealogy of the novel (which genre gave birth to this new literary form?), and on the analysis (a masterly one, for sure) of literary *topoi* and their persistence in the novel. Following an extremely widespread interpretative pattern, deeply rooted in ninenteenth century idealism and historicism (but powerful even now), the novel was considered by Rohde a degraded form of more authentic and original genres, particularly epic[5] but also historiography, tragedy, rhetoric. This is one of the reasons why ancient novels were excluded form the educational curricula, and generally from the canon of western classics. Many of the factors conspiring against the ancient novel mentioned above still exerted influence in the twentieth century: in 1948 another German scholar, Rudolf Helm, could label in a handbook Longus' *Daphnis and Chloe* a 'pornographic' novel.[6]

If we turn to the other side of the synchronism which was our starting point, we find a similarly fluid situation. When Tolstoy published his first masterpiece, *War and Piece* (1863–9), he advised his publisher not to use the term 'novel'; from Gorky's memoirs we learn that Tolstoy considered it as a kind of *Iliad*.[7] There are several reasons behind the choice of such a canonical ancient antecedent: his dissatisfaction with the European bourgeois novel, the search for a less conventional and more open form, the need to construct in Russia a modern epic tradition.[8] But at the same time there is still a trace in

3 Goldhill, this volume.   4 See Reeve, this volume.
5 This is notably the position of Hegel (1993); and Lukács (1971); I discuss this critical polarity in Fusillo (2002).
6 Helm (1956) 51.
7 Letter to M. N. Katkov (the editor of the journal publishing the first instalments), 3 January 1865; Gorky (1948) 57.
8 Christian (1962) 112–17; Griffiths and Rabinowitz (1990).

this attitude of a long-lasting (if sporadic) cultural paradigm that undervalues the novel as a secondary, morally dangerous, entertaining genre, too inclined to arouse pathological identification in its (mostly female) public, and too focused on private life, love and sexuality. The history of real (from Flaubert to Salman Rushdie) and metaphorical trials against the novel has lasted in fact for several centuries and involved intellectual groups and institutions in numerous contexts.[9]

Now, at the beginning of the twenty-first century, this situation has completely changed. On the one hand, the hegemony of the novel in our cultural life is stronger than ever: it has few academic enemies, and is identified almost *tout court* with literature by the larger public. On the other hand, the critical almost conceptualisation of the ancient novel has reached an extremely high level of sophistication. Two different and autonomous processes, of course; and it goes without saying that the second is much more circumscribed and of less cultural significance. But they are linked by an interesting parallelism. Modernist experimentation at the beginning of the twentieth century, the development in the 1960s of a general theory of narrative (narratology), the return to grander, more traditional plots in post-modernism, the philosophical, anthropological, historiographical and psychoanalytical reflections on the centrality of narrative in human experience, the increasing development of fiction in post-colonial and non-western cultures, the breaking down of any rigid hierarchy between high and low culture: all these are elements that have contributed to making the novel a pivotal and crucial genre in contemporary culture. And this process must be considered the basic assumption for the development of a new critical and creative approach to the ancient novel.

Moreover, ancient novels show, from a thematic point of view, a remarkable convergence on some central issues of recent critical theory, particularly sexual and ethnic identity. Coming from the eastern regions of the Roman empire, and being repeatedly focused on travels and love, the Greek novel in particular offers valuable cues. It is not by chance that Michel Foucault, a leading light in the development of post-structuralist literary criticism, gave a prominent position to the Greek erotic novel in his *History of Sexuality*,[10] a gesture that has been considered in detail by among others Simon Goldhill, in his *Foucault's Virginity*.[11] On the other hand, Heliodorus' *Charicleia and Theagenes* evokes a complex polyphony of cultures, expressing at the same time a hybrid and fluid idea of ethnicity, far from the classic idea of separation between Greek and barbarian, and with considerable contemporary relevance. It is a quite unique example among ancient constructions of the

---

9 Siti (2001).   10 Foucault (1986) 228–34 (the culminating chapter).
11 Goldhill (1995).

other.[12] Ancient novels have become more and more documents of crucial cultural transformations.

The creative reception of Longus' *Daphnis and Chloe*

How did the long and gradual legitimisation of the ancient novel in the twentieth century affect its creative reception? Before answering this question, we should narrow down the complex concept of creative reception. In its first and immediate sense, the expression implies a direct and substantial relationship between two texts. In our case, a modern text – another novel, a drama, a movie, a painting, a piece of music, a performance – rewrites and reinvents an ancient novel, or generally the ancient novel as a genre (in this case the relationship is less direct). But we can still speak in terms of reception if we identify a broader dialogue between ancient novels and modern texts: if we focus on the persistence of themes and narrative strategies that have their origin in the ancient novel, but at the same time have a quite larger diffusion. This second category must be treated with extreme caution: there is always the risk of lacking specificity, and lapsing into overly broad and universalising Jungian archetypes. Still, the comparison between two different and autonomous cultural systems can be extremely stimulating and show the incredible vitality of long-standing constants.

Regarding the first, more direct, kind of reception, we should note that what is immediately clear is the distinct difference between the Greek and Roman novel, the latter having in fact a much wider circulation. After its remarkable success in the baroque period[13] the Greek novel never regained such a prominent status. The inexorable progress of the psychological novel over the last two centuries has minimised the public taste for Greek novels: they have often been labelled as naive, and criticised as devoid of psychological introspection (which is, in fact, present but with a different form and meaning in ancient, and generally in pre-romantic literatures). Moreover, their exaltation of conjugal love, chastity and fidelity reads as quaint. Even recent re-evaluations of their sophistication have not yet spread out of academic circles. Writers and artists who aim at establishing a dialogue with ancient literatures still prefer the more canonical genres of epic and tragedy (from Christa Wolf to Derek Walcott, from Wolfgang Rihm to Lars von Trier), or address themselves to the more flexible category of myth. Novelists who look for a direct ancient model inevitably find more consonance with Petronius' loose structure, and with his polymorphic treatment of sexuality.

---

12 See Selden (1998); Perkins (1999); Whitmarsh (1998), (1999).
13 See Sandy in Sandy and Harrison, this volume.

This is a general trend, but there are some interesting exceptions. They all regard Longus' *Daphnis and Chloe*. His relative success is due primarily to the bucolic mode and its long-lasting appeal, and, to a lesser extent, to Goethe's enthusiastic approval of this novel.[14] The polarity between nature and culture, the central role played by landscape, the gradual discovery of sexuality, the fascination for simple rural life clearly combined with a latent urban voyeurism, are all factors exploited by twentieth-century reception (and indeed by contemporary criticism).

Longus' novel is associated with a pivotal episode in the history of music and dance: the ballet *Daphnis and Chloe*, based on the splendid score by Maurice Ravel. Its history is rather complex. In 1904 the Russian chore-ographer Michel Fokine, who played a crucial role in the history of dance because of his development of a new kind of theatrical harmony, wrote a libretto inspired by Longus' novel, which remained unperformed. It is inter-esting, however, that he first conceived of his reformist programme of ballet (later exposed in a letter to the *Times* in July 1914) by working on just this project; a programme that implied an artistic exploitation of the entire body and a co-operation between arts.[15] When in 1909 Fokine was engaged by the genial impresario Serge Diaghilev as chief choreographer and dancer of the company 'Les Ballets Russes', he returned to his *Daphnis and Chloe* project; Diaghilev commissioned Maurice Ravel to compose the music, which was delayed until 1912 because of some misunderstandings between composer and artist.

In fact, 1912 was a momentous date for *Les Ballets Russes*: the com-pany abandoned productions drawn from the Russian tradition, and concen-trated on experimentation with new expressive forms, based on international music. *Daphnis and Chloe* had its première on 8 June, with Vaslav Nijinsky as Daphnis, Tamara Karsavina as Chloe, and Adolph Bolm as Dorcon; the décor was designed by Léon Bakst, who recovered the material used for the ballet *Narcisse* of the previous year. The Fokine–Ravel ballet was eclipsed by the major scandal of the *Prélude à l'après-midi d'un faune* ('Prelude to the afternoon of a faun'), Nijinsky's debut as choreographer for the famous score by Debussy. The two productions have in common inspiration drawn from the dancing figures of Attic vases, and therefore an unusual empha-sis upon profile movements. The postponement of *Daphnis and Chloe*, and Diaghilev's clandestine installation of his lover Nijinsky as the new choreog-rapher, forced Fokine to break with the *Ballets Russes*; there were, moreover, violent accusations, in both directions, of choreographic plagiarism. Despite

14 This can be deduced from his diary (1807 and 1808), and especially from the *Conversations with Eckermann*; see Hägg (1983) 211–13.
15 See Beaumont (1935); Horwitz (1985).

the quarrels, *Daphnis and Chloe* became part of the standard repertoire, and has often been revived:[16] the 1958 performance in Paris is particularly noteworthy, because of the set designed by Marc Chagall. The encounter between the famous painter and Longus' novel, inspired by two travels in Greece, produced also a series of gouaches for a Tériade edition (1961), that illustrate the novel with a purely Chagallian dream-like style and with his characteristic intense colours (particularly evident in *Dorcon's Death* and in *The Winter*).

Ravel's music follows the outline of Longus' story, concentrating on five themes: a dissonant overture, a choral hymn to nature, a brilliant Daphnis theme, a delicate Chloe theme conceived as a waltz, and a bombastic pirates theme, which marks a *topos* of Greek fiction, the opposition of rivals to the main couple. In the novel, the urban and voyeuristic element is embodied by Lycaenion, the girl coming from the city who teaches Daphnis how to have sex (as well as by Gnathon, a male sexual predator of Daphnis' beauty). It is an episode that at once counters the novelistic preference for fidelity (although in a way that leads towards the final triumphant marriage of the couple), and confirms a latent message of this novel, that sexuality is always a cultural, not a natural experience.[17] Ravel's choreographic symphony highlights this point: after a series of dances (among them a sacred one, a grotesque one by Dorcon, and a light *barcarola* by Daphnis), the episode culminates with the evocation of Lycaenion as a kind of Greek Salome, through a seductive arrangement reminiscent of Ravel's *Quartet* and Rimsky Korsakov's *Schéhérazade* (another famous ballet by Fokine).

Longus' tale-within–a-tale on the invention of a musical instrument, Pan's *syrinx*, plays (unsurprisingly) a central role: it is represented, after a lyric evocation of water and birds, in the third picture by the flute – the same symbol of *spleen* beloved by Debussy – with a *habanera* rhythm. The symphony culminates in a bacchanal full of rutilant rhythms (a real *tour de force* for the dancers), reminiscent of Stravinsky's *Firebird*, a 1910 ballet commissioned by Diaghilev, and the first expression of a rhythmic neo-primitivism.[18] This barbaric, Dionysiac vision of Greece had a revolutionary impact at the beginning of the twentieth century on European cultural identity: in the field of music theatre the most significant example is Hofmannsthal and Strauss's *Elektra*, which transforms the Sophoclean model by adding a final triumph of dance and death.[19] Ravel's love for classical symmetry, which strongly differentiates him from Debussy, found an interesting consonance with Longus' style

16 Spencer (1974) ch. 4.
17 Levin (1977); Winkler (1990) 122–6.   18 Jankélevitch (1962).
19 See Goldhill (2002) 108–77 on the scandal of Strauss's 'degenerate *Elektra*' in England in 1910.

and narrative structure, characterised by a marked balancing of elements. The closure, however, amplifies the Dionysiac element of the novel, transforming the triumph of conjugal love into an explosion of primitive violent forces.

Longus' emphasis on landscape, meanwhile, explains his success in cinema. For one of the earliest Greek films, Orestis Laskatos shot a *Daphnis and Chloe* (1931) on the island of Mytilene, the setting for Longus' original. In this silent movie, landscapes and seascapes play a central role, together with a strong fascination with adolescent bodies and their nudity. The urban character of Lycaenion is given the same prominent position as in Fokine and Ravel's ballet: here she is depicted as a vamp with a supple gait. At the same time a sort of choir, heavily active in the central part of the movie, gives expression to the bucolic element and to the celebration of an archaic national past.

Longus' cinematic reception proceeds with *Young Aphrodites* (*Mikres Aphrodites*, 1963), a film by the Cretan director Nikos Kondouros, who more recently made *Byron: Ballad for a Daemon* (1992), on Byron's experiences in Greece. Here too the pivotal element is landscape: an island with a fishermen village on the sea, visited by some shepherds in search of water. The meeting between the two worlds is the occasion for archetypal polarities between natural elements (earth, sea, wind, fire). Freely contaminating Longus with Theocritus, Kondouros makes an impressively original movie, full of archaic force, chiefly based on non verbal communication and visual details, and focused on the discovery of sexuality as a long, arduous and contradictory process, characterised by a profound sense of non-satisfaction; a movie devoid of any consolatory character (the ending is unresolved and sour, rather than the novels' usual happy resolution).

Finally, there is a third, more recent (and more conventional) filmic version of Longus' novel, coming this time not from Greece, but from Russia: Yuri Kuzmenkov's *Dafnis i Khloya* (1993). The film is actually based on a novel by Iurii M. Nagibin, *A Daphnis and Chloe of the Era of the Cult of Personality, Voluntarism and Stagnation* (1992), a prominent Soviet writer, famous for his short stories on the tension between rural and urban Russia, on hunting and fishing (following the trace of Turgenev's *Hunter's Sketches*), on village life and landscape, and on adolescence; and for his film scripts, among which is Kurosawa's masterpiece *Dersu Uzala* (1975) about friendship, isolation and profound communion with nature. *Daphnis and Chloe* is his only novel and his last work, written after the fall of the Soviet Union.[20] Kuzmenkov's

---

20 Terras (1991) 594; Pursglove (1998).

movie follows Longus' narrative of child abandonment and final recognition, including some minor figures such as Dorcon and Gnathon, and amplifies the theme of violent discovery of sexuality – here too we find a very exotic Lycaenion – in a somehow kitschy ancient setting.

In 1954 Yukio Mishima, the most famous and most controversial figure of modern Japanese literature, published *The Sound of Waves* (*Shikosai*), a direct rewriting of *Daphnis and Chloe*. After his dark masterpiece *Confessions of a Mask*, the writer aimed here at controlling Dionysiac passions through a severe classicism, born of a moving voyage to Greece and some consequent reflections on the ancient equilibrium between body and mind.[21] As happens with most successful rewritings, intertextuality works both ways. Reading this quite fluent and agreeable novel (superior to its model, according to Marguerite Yourcenar,[22] and well received by a large, international audience), we rediscover Longus' thematic and narrative kernels: the falling in love as sudden and rationally unrestrainable process; insomnia and monologues as reaction to the sense of self-alienation; the discovery of sexuality as a beastlike element; the consequent sense of estrangement; the psychic correspondence with nature, both in euphoric and in dysphoric contexts; the nudity episode as a culminating point; the aggressiveness of an unreciprocated love and of rivals, and finally dreams as foreshadowing of a happy ending. Some of them are obviously developed according to Mishima's poetics: especially the stress on a pure physical life, on the aesthetic perfection of the masculine body, on adolescent strength and intensity of feelings, as ways to reach the Absolute.[23]

The protagonist, the young fisherman Shinji of a small Japanese island, overcomes at the end the social obstacle to his marriage not through a generically typical final recognition, as in Longus' *Daphnis and Chloe*, but through a heroic action of incredible force and courage. In the last scene Shinji shows to his beloved Hatsue her picture; the narrator adds that she proudly believes that this is what is responsible for Shinji's salvation and triumph, while 'he knew it had been his own strength that had tided him through that perilous night'. This last sentence breaks the conventional symmetry of couples in the Greek novel couples, thus lessening its sentimentalism; and expresses, in an allusive and controlled way, Mishima's love of action that culminated in his theatrical activity as both actor and director, and indeed in the performance of his own ritual suicide.

---

21 Scott and Stokes (1974) 134–8.
22 Yourcenar (1986) 40: 'The melodic line of *The Sound of Waves* is infinitely purer.'
23 Napier (1991) 20–6 (though note the strange sentence on pp. 20–1: 'most versions of the myth [?] end tragically').

The Greek novel and popular literature

We leave now the area of specific intertextual relationship, and focus more broadly on the Greek novel as a set of generic traits. This means that we shall have to deal with the modern category of popular literature, sometimes referred to as 'paraliterature', and generally with other non-literary aspects of cultural industry, such as soap operas and TV series. The Greek novel can be certainly compared, as it has often been,[24] with those modern phenomena, especially because of several common *topoi* and narrative devices (for example the apparent death). It is best to begin by recapitulating the main categories outlined by scholars of paraliterature:[25]

(1) repetitiousness of *topoi* and conventions;
(2) referential illusion. That is a tendency to abolish borders between reality and fiction, and to assimilate cultural and natural, hero and reader, sign and referent, through a transparent narration;
(3) the pansemic dominance of narrative. That is, the finalisation of every single detail in the development of the plot (typical of every traditional form of plot, but strongly emphasised in paraliterature, which refuses any parallel connotative texture), and the consequent pragmatic reception requested of the reader;
(4) the fixed state of characterisation.

Generally speaking, these can be considered structural features common to ancient novels and modern paraliterature (although one should be cautious in applying those categories to ancient texts, especially because originality and psychological characterisation are elements that are not fully developed and privileged until Romanticism). Moreover, in the Greek novel it is easy to recognise, in my opinion, two different phases: a first one, more ingenuous and popular, which could be defined as paraliterary (Chariton, Xenophon); and a second one, much more complex and refined, linked to the second sophistic's neo-rhetoric, which basically does not correspond to the above mentioned categories (Achilles Tatius, Longus, Heliodorus: uncoincidentally, the three authors who enjoyed a rich renaissance and baroque reception). In any case, we might consider this parallelism a mediated form of reception, that can be illuminating from both points of view. It compels us to recognise in antiquity a different use for literature, far from classicists' idealised view of ancient texts as it is from the modern one, because it shows ancient roots in narrative paradigms and strategies exploited by the contemporary cultural industry.

24 For example by Holzberg (1995) 1.   25 Couégnas (1991).

Besides Greek erotic novels, there are various narrative forms that are increasingly read as novelistic. For example *The Life of Aesop*, previously considered a biography and a loose collection of popular traditions, has been recently interpreted as a novel with a coherent structural design: a forerunner of the picaresque genre.[26] From our perspective it is important to point out that this ancient text on slavery and story-telling was the direct model for a 1954 novel (*Aisopos, Sieben Berichte aus Hellas* = 'Aesop, Seven reports from Greece') by Arnolt Bronnen, a pupil of Bertolt Brecht, who rewrote it in terms of class struggle.[27]

The success of the *Satyrica*

Petronius' 'splendid evasiveness'[28] is the main reason given for his splendid success in contemporary culture. Much of this elusive character comes from the text's fragmentary condition, but a careful literary analysis shows that the *Satyrica* was always deliberately episodic: it is a subversive text that plays with reader's expectations, genre categories, narrative roles, linguistic registers. These features were influential upon the novel's multifold transformations at the beginning of the twentieth century, when it became the experimental text *par excellence*. If Petronius' 'realism' – an admittedly thorny critical category[29] – could correspond to novelistic frescos of the nineteenth century (especially those by Balzac and Zola), his open form vividly corresponds to modernist (and post-modernist) expressive revolutions: especially to Joyce's epic of body and language.[30]

A more direct (albeit still distant) intertextual relationship can be found in F. Scott Fitzgerald's *The Great Gatsby* (1925). An earlier version of this widely read novel, first published in 2000 by James L. W. West, was entitled *Trimalchio*: a clear paratextual signal of allusion to Petronius' most famous episode. In this case the relationship is founded on neither narrative open structure nor linguistic contamination; the allusion is rather to Gatsby's staggering enrichment, his vulgar ostentation of money, and his parties as occasions of multifarious, kaleidoscopic social encounters. As in Petronius' *Dinner at Trimalchio's*, a banquet becomes a narrative situation that allows the insertion of long and digressive speeches, transforming the text into a form of conversation novel.

There are, additionally, other less evident points of connection. First the narrator's attitude, which is clearly defined at the very beginning of the novel: 'I am inclined to reserve all judgements, a habit that has opened up many

---

26 See Holzberg (1992a).   27 See Beschorner (1992).   28 Slater (1990) 2.
29 See the brilliant account of Auerbach (1953) 24–49.   30 Kileen (1957).

curious natures to me', declares the first-person narrator Nick Carraway, who will speak, in the eighth chapter, of a 'universal skepticism'. Petronius' first-person narrator, Encolpius, shows a similar habit of observing reality without any moral judgement and with a marked sceptical distance. On the other hand, Gatsby's 'platonic conception of himself' (p. 117), the 'colossal vitality of his illusion' (p. 77),[31] his refusal of reality and his refuge in fantasy, can recall Petronius' characters, not only Trimalchio, but also Encolpius, recently defined as a 'mythomaniacal narrator' because of his reading reality in terms of literary fantasies.[32] In sum, the ancient novel has left only a few traces in Fitgerald's *The Great Gatsby*: we are confronted with a parallelism between two different, autonomous works.

Less direct but more profound is Petronius' relationship with one of the most innovative and significant twentieth-century writers, Céline, especially regarding linguistic contamination, picaresque narration, and some thematic kernels, such as nomadism, sexuality and theatricality.[33] Generally speaking, the twentieth-century novel sees a revival of the picaresque:[34] a genre born in Renaissance Spain (but with extremely large ramifications) and based on autobiographic narration by an anti-hero, social degradation and seriality of travels and adventures. At the same time it sees also a revival of the Menippean trend, that is 'carnivalesque' literature – to use Mikhail Bakhtin's term[35] – which privileges grotesque, bodily and obscene themes, and uses a plurality of voices, languages and styles. Petronius and Apuleius are often considered progenitors of these literary phenomena, the picaresque and the Menippean. Together with (among numerous examples) Kafka's *Amerika*, Thomas Mann's *Felix Krull*, Saul Bellow's first works, Steinbeck's *Tortilla Flat*, Céline's novels – especially his masterpiece, the *Voyage au bout de la nuit* ('Journey to the end of the night', 1931) – embody contemporary picaresque narrative. There are of course significant differences of poetics and culture: in renaissance picaresque novels, as well as in their ancient forerunners, characters are driven by primary needs such as food and money. In his travels from France to Africa and to the States, the *Voyage*'s autobiographical main character, Bardamu, is driven by a cosmic dissatisfaction, a metaphysical disgust and a strong spleen, typical of narrative in the last century. Nevertheless, there are many Célinian features that do evoke Petronius: the artistic re-use of colloquial language; the absolute prominence of sexuality and physical compulsion as the only true forms of authenticity; a poetics

---

31 Both expressions come back in *The Great Gatsby*, the first one in an earlier chapter (6); in *Trimalchio* Gatsby is in fact a more elusive character: we hear his 'true' story first at the end of the novel.

32 Conte (1996).   33 On this category in Petronius see Panayotakis (1995).

34 Haan (1995).   35 See Bakhtin (1981).

of dirt, degradation and corruption; the exploitation of encounters as the main device to produce narration, and as a way of representing multifarious social typologies; theatricality and performativity as most human reactions to the menace of disease and death. Although we never catch Petronius' *Weltanschauung*, in reading the *Voyage* we feel a strong consonance between distant cultural contexts; a feeling that comes back in Celine's other masterpiece, *Mort à credit* ('Death on the instalment plan'), and in some of his later, more controversial novels: for example, *Le pont de Londres* ('London bridge').[36]

In the second half of the twentieth century, Petronius' novel was rewritten and reinvented by avant-garde movements. The leading figure of Italian 'Gruppo 63', Edoardo Sanguineti, published in 1969 a free translation of the ancient novel, entitled *The Play of the Satyricon: an Imitation from Petronius*, written in a low, colloquial north Italian and inspired by a sense of 'antinovelistic shattering'.[37] The same poetics of destructuring and free assemblage characterises the opera *Satyricon* (1973) by Bruno Maderna, a protagonist of European electronic avant-garde music, active in the famous Darmstadt school together with Boulez and Stockhausen, whose productions alternate between ludic and sublime works.[38] Written by Maderna himself and concentrating on *Dinner at Trimalchio's*, the libretto amplifies Petronius' variety of linguistic registers through a clear polyglottism: the basic language is English, but with frequent insertions in French, German, and in the original Latin. The music shows a similar plurality of styles: neoclassicism, expressionistic atonality, aleatory music, concrete music (that is a music which uses noise) on magnetic tape, jazz. In its use of (parodic) quotation, this music is highly Petronian; sometimes totally transformed, sometimes left in their rough materiality, we hear passages from Gluck, Verdi, Bizet, Wagner, Tchaikovsky, Strauss, Puccini, Weill. Very striking is the opening of the opera: a magnetic tape reproduces magmatic fragments of conversations without a recognizable sense, giving that effect of communicative chaos so typical of contemporary art and music. Other remarkable moments are: Fortunata's cabaret aria; Habinnas' praise of money and his telling of the Matron of Ephesus novella (transposed here into the *Dinner*); Trimalchio's flatulence and the chaotic enumeration of his fortune; Eumolpus' duet with Fortunata and his poetic recitation of the *Fall of Troy*; and finally Trimalchio's testament, the culmination of this frenetic series of quotations, suddenly interrupted by a diminuendo alluding to the novel's unfinished character. The

---

36 See Guerrini (1973) and Martin (1990), more focused on *Mort à credit*.
37 'Frantumazione antiromanzesca': so the author in the 'Note' to the 1993 edition.
38 Mila (1999).

entire short opera reads Petronius as a paradigm of a playful and humorous experimentation with sound and language.[39]

Pier Paolo Pasolini's approach to classical antiquity was clearly inspired by psychoanalysis and anthropology, rather than avant-garde approaches, against which he militated forcefully. Nevertheless, in the last years of his life he had been working on a huge novel, *Petrolio*, with a strong experimental character. In an author's note from the spring of 1973, published as preface, Pasolini introduced this unfinished novel as follows:

> *Petrolio* as a whole (from the second draft) should be read as a critical edition of an unpublished text (considered as a monumental work, a modern-day *Satyricon*). Four or five manuscripts of this text, both consistent and inconsistent – some reporting facts while others not – survive. The reconstruction is thus based on a comparison of the various manuscripts preserved (of which, e.g., two apocrypha with bizarre, grotesque, naive, stylised variants). It is also drawn from other materials such as letters by the author (whose identity is still under debate from a philological point of view), letters from the author's friends who know of the manuscript (diverging one from the other), oral transcripts as reported in newspapers, other miscellany, songs, etc. There are also illustrations of the book (probably the work of the author himself). These illustrations are of great help in reconstructing the missing scenes and passages. Their description should be accurate, and the literary reconstruction will be complemented by a figurative, critical reconstruction, as the book's graphics are done at a very high, albeit manneristic, level.

As we can see from this, it was the author's intention for the novel to have an unfinished character by simulating a continuous reconstruction undertaken by the editor-narrator 'using a flat, objective and drab style', a sort of philological metanovel. Pasolini was murdered two years later. By a tragic paradox, a planned incompleteness was to become an actual incompleteness. The novel we read, published posthumously (twenty years after his death) in a critical edition, brings together fragments, hand-written and typed notes, as well as finished and drafted excerpts in some 600 pages out of the roughly 2,000 planned by the author. *Petrolio*, however, is an intrinsically unending work, which denies any structure or literary convention: perhaps it could not have ended other than with the author's death. The reference to the *Satyrica* is, at a more immediate level, a reference to an ancient text, of which only fragments have survived, whose elusive plot we have to reconstruct continuously in its entirety, and whose author has been the subject of some controversy. More generally, this is applicable since usually the *Satyrica* serves as the paradigm for any experimental, open form, which is difficult to

---

39 CD Release by Salabert, Paris. See Fusillo (1997b).

label with a single definition of literary genre and is based on the relentless contamination of languages.

There are, however, more concrete points of connection between Petronius and *Petrolio*. First of all, the narration is characterised by picaresque progression, or 'swarming' (as Pasolini put it himself, citing an essay by Shklovsky on Sterne). Hence, there is a continuous succession of episodes in free association, often produced by the chronotope of fortuitous encounters, beyond the typical organic and centripetal structure of the ancient Greek novel, or the great modern realistic novel. This open form allows for the use of a rich, versatile material, which brings us to the second point: both of the novels are encyclopaedic. Indeed, the *Satyrica* contains digressions on the art of rhetoric, painting and various aspects of the world of the time. In the same way, *Petrolio*'s narration is often broken by metanarrative and metaliterary comments, or by long political, journalistic, or essayistic insets.

This thematic polyphony corresponds closely to a polyphony of expression. Pasolini had always been fascinated by the multilingualism and multistylisation that is perfectly embodied in Petronius. A particularly salient example of multistylisation appears in the form of prosimetrum.[40] Petronius' variegated use of this trope, from brief, parodical quotations to long, autonomous epic insets (e.g. *Iliupersis*), is well known.[41] We can also find a series of brief poetic quotations in *Petrolio*, which range from Aeschylus' *Agamemnon* to Villon and Shakespeare and function fundamentally as a lyrical counterpoint which breaks up the flow of the story. Furthermore, Pasolini had also planned to include a long adaptation of Apollonius of Rhodes' *Argonautica*, set in modern times and with the Golden Fleece replaced by that precious element *par excellence* of fully developed neocapitalism, Black Gold, that is, petroleum, which gives the novel its title. Pasolini had intended to write this partly in Greek, specifically in Kavafis' neo-Greek, thereby producing, instead of a translation, a telegraphic summary in the paragraph titles. This was to be a 'stylistic eccentricity' (see his note 37), a sort of graphic estrangement, which recalls some of the devices of the neo-avant-garde. We should recall finally another meaning, in this case thematic, inherent in the definition of a 'modern-day *Satyrica*': the centrality of sexual promiscuity and homoeroticism, which clearly set Petronius apart from the Greek novel and constitute one of its most distinctive features. In any case, these two themes are essentially Pasolinian, and in *Petrolio* they are expressed through the main character's split between a demonic sexuality and his search for power.[42]

---

40 See Harris and Reichl (1997).
41 See Connors (1998), esp. 1–6 on the technique of incorporating the epic past into the present.
42 For a more detailed analysis see Fusillo (2003a).

These structural and thematic features can be reused in a completely different register. Such is the case of Alberto Arbasino, an Italian writer who shared a long friendship with Pasolini, although not always without its disagreements. In his essay *Certi romanzi* ('Certain romances'), Arbasino proposed a new theory of Menippean satire and considered *Satyrica* as a model for a novel based on continuous digressions and free conversations, particularly on the ironical and cynical observation of contemporary customs. This is a long way from the dark and desperate tones of *Petrolio*, which persist even at moments of grotesque, comic effect. From his masterpiece *Fratelli d'Italia* ('Brothers of Italy', 1963), where the *Satyrica* is often quoted as a model for the travels and the sexual adventures of a gay couple, interwoven with long discussions on novels, paintings, music and theatre,[43] to the more recent *Le Muse a Los Angeles* ('The Muses in Los Angeles', 2000), an excursion through the paintings of the museums of the West Coast, Arbasino chooses an ironical and light-hearted tone, particularly when dealing with homosexual eroticism.

Arbasino's aesthetic leads us to a conspicuous category in contemporary Anglo-Saxon culture: *camp*. First defined by Susan Sontag in 1967, *camp* indicates a mixture of irony, theatricality, aestheticism, and juxtaposition of incongruous elements; a playful re-use of consumer culture; a refined contamination of kitsch with cultivated, high-brow elements.[44] It is a mode characteristic of post-modern culture, and in particular of gay communities, which often have strong relationships with manifold icons. Petronius' ambivalent incorporation of consumer genres (mime, pantomime, sentimental novel) can be read through the lens of contemporary camp.[45] Moreover, one of the reasons why the *Satyrica* arouses more and more interest now is the development first of gay and lesbian studies, and then of queer theory, which affirms the performative nature (that is discursive, mimetic and even parodic) of any sexual identity.[46]

The most famous and significant Petronian re-elaboration is *Fellini Satyricon*, a 1969 movie. Fellini's cinema has a marked picaresque component, privileging an episodic and fragmentary mode of narration, and grotesque, excessive, dream-like imagery. It is not by chance that Kafka's *Amerika*, the masterpiece of twentieth-century neo-picaresque novel, has been an obsessive and never realised project of his career; and that even before *Fellini Satyricon* Petronius' novel was often suggested to him or promised by him to producers, together with other classics such as Dante, Boccaccio and Ariosto,

43 E.g. ch. 8, p. 74.   44 See Sontag (1964); Meyer (1994); Cleto (1999).
45 Wooten (1984), which is however too schematic.
46 Especially in the third, expanded version of 1993. On queer performativity see Butler (1993); Meyer (1994).

although he strongly supported original screenplays and did not like literary adaptations, so beloved by other Italian directors of the same period, such as Pasolini and especially Visconti. When Fellini reread the *Satyrica* in 1967, he was struck by the fragmentary state of the text, and by gaps and blanks between the episodes. This fact gave him the idea of realising the movie as a dream to be reconstructed by the audience, with all the ambivalence between 'puzzling transparency' and 'unreadable clarity',[47] uncanny unfamiliarity and close familiarity.

The oneiric quality is created especially by complex stagings (almost entirely shot in the studios of Cinecittà), by characteristic Fellinian faces staring towards nothing, by hallucinatory and haunting make-up, set and costumes, by strikingly artificial colours (from the dominant blue of the initial theatre scene to the red of the *Dinner*, from the spectral, unreal white of the Hermaphrodite sequence to the earth brown of the Oenothea episode). The sense of cold detachment, the 'reconstruction', is created by camera work and lighting, by an estranged, non-synchronised dubbing, by an electronic, atonal Afro-Asiatic music,[48] and by a more objective tracking technique. It has been claimed that the most typical Fellinian shot is 'a pan that simulates the turning of a character's gaze from right to left (or the reverse), and therefore forces the spectator to share the protagonist's perspective and to identify with him or her'.[49] In the *Satyricon*, however, the large-scale use of a subjective point of view is almost eliminated, and replaced by a shifting perspective, particularly evident in the brothel scene (sequence 2 scene 5), where a spectacular vision of human sexuality (freaks, fat and grotesque old women, sadomasochist rites, bizarre scenes) is offered to our view. This flexuous and sinuous camera is an impressive filmic equivalent[50] of Petronian narrative strategy, of his play with voices and points of view, of his 'hidden author' that sets traps for his characters and his readers. Similarly, the use of various Italian dialects and of some foreign languages recalls Petronian plurality of styles.

From the point of view of literary adaptation, Fellini shows a remarkable creative freedom: supported by the writer Bernardino Zapponi, he created a narrative made of eight long sequences.[51] From Petronius he retained the triangle between Encolpius, Giton and Asciltus; Trimalchio's dinner; the novella of the Matron of Ephesus, told by an effeminate man during

---

47 Fellini (1988) 172–3. See also Wyke (1997) 189: 'The film defamiliarises antiquity and self-reflexively draws attention to the artifice of the world it has created by constantly blurring distinction between the "real" and the "illusory".'
48 Solomon (2001) 332.   49 Bondanella (1991) 245.
50 On this notable technique see Sullivan (2001) 263–4; also Wyke (1997) 188–92.
51 For a structural analysis see Sütterlin (1997).

the *Dinner*, and not in Lichas' ship as in Petronius' novel; and finally the Lichas episode. He also, however, added some original episodes: the theatre sequence with the actor Vernacchio, the brothel scene in the Suburra, the collapse of the Suburra, the assassination of the emperor and the civil war, the villa of the suicides (an allusion to the historical figures of Thrasea Paetus and Petronius himself), the stealing and the death in the desert of the hermaphrodite, and the Festival of Laughter in the magic city, inspired by the second book of Apuleius' *Metamorphoses*. On the one hand, the movie's abrupt ending (a sentence narrated by the voice-over, and interrupted partway through) alludes to the novel's unfinished character, and to Petronius' probable avoidance of narrative closure in his own work.[52] On the other hand, the fact that in the last episode Encolpius plays the role of Theseus in the Labyrinth, and his impotence is cured by the Earth Mother figure Oenothea, adds to the text a new symbolic meaning, which is at the same time Apuleian and Jungian. The movie-dream appears in fact at the end as a voyage into the labyrinth of unconscious, in order to acquire a new force and a new identity. *Fellini Satyricon* seems to suggest a parallelism between viewing a movie conceived as transcription and reconstruction of a dream, and reading a puzzling and challenging text such as Petronius' elusive novel.

Contemporary post-modern culture tends to re-use classical and canonical genres, such as the historical novel. Particularly noteworthy is the renewed fascination with the Roman empire as a metaphor for dehumanistion and chaotic disintegration of our age (the metaphor used by Fellini in his historical insets on the civil war). Following his appearance in the world famous *Quo vadis?* by Sienkiewicz, we find again Petronius as a fictional character in Montheilet's *Neropolis* (1984), where he is a sceptical, refined and powerful figure; in Robert Graves' short story *Epics are out of Fashion* (1965), which sees in Trimalchio's characterisation an allusion to Nero, according to a widespread critical tradition; and in Anthony Burgess' *The Kingdom of the Wicked* (1985), in which Petronius embodies a Nietzschean aestheticism.[53]

In tracing the complex history of Petronian reception, we have already encountered Apuleius' novel, both as a second ancient paradigm of picaresque narration, and as a supplementary source, as in *Fellini Satyricon*. Direct intertextual rewritings of *The Metamorphoses* are more rare in the twentieth century, compared to the renaissance and baroque ages, when the tale of Cupid and Psyche in particular had a rich reception, mostly figurative (see Harrison, this volume). In contemporary culture, the real Apuleian reception can be traced in the largescale revival of the metamorphosis theme,

52 On the anticlosure see Schmeling (1991); on Fellini's ending as 'farewell to antiquity' see Wyke (1998a) 191–2.
53 See Gagliardi (1993) 196–206; Gagliardi's book is however unfocused and unhelpful.

from Kafka to *Pinocchio*, from Salman Rushdie's *The Satanic Verses* to David Cronenberg's famous movie *The Fly*: that is, in completely autonomous works, which nevertheless sometimes evoke some Apuleian themes (the loss of language, the relationship with food and sex, the juxtaposition of euphoric and dysphoric feelings).

The last decades of critical theory have abandoned any abstract definition of literature, and focused more and more on its pragmatic, ever-changing conditions: 'When is art?' has replaced 'What is art?' as the most urgent question.[54] The anti-sublime and anti-literary component of the genre of the novel found a strong consonance with this ideological shift of perspective. Ancient novels in particular thus became part of new critical approaches, and of a new anthropology of literature. In the twentieth century, creative reception clearly privileged the two works to which current aesthetic evaluation has repeatedly given preference: *Daphnis and Chloe* and the *Satyrica*. There are now good reasons to hope for a more various and broader pattern in the twenty-first century, incorporating, for example, Heliodorus' splendid narrative architecture and his impressively cinematographic use of point of view.

Further reading

A transcript of *Fellini Satyricon* is available, edited by Dario Zanelli (1977; original edition 1969). This contains the scenario and the shooting script, quite different from the completed film. For editions of the other texts discussed in this chapter see: Yukio Mishima, *The Sound of Waves*, trans. Meredith Weatherby (1956); Pier Paolo Pasolini, *Petrolio* (1997; Italian edition in *Romanzi e racconti*, ed. W. Siti and S. De Laude, 1998); Edoardo Sanguineti, *Il gioco del Satyricon* (1970; reprinted in 1993, with a 'Nota del traduttore'); Francis Scott Fitzgerald, *Trimalchio: an Early Version of 'The Great Gatsby'*, ed. J. L. W. West III (2000). The latter is a valuable edition, with a record of variants, explanatory notes, illustrations, letters with the publisher and an Appendix on Petronius' Trimalchio.

Critical works on this material are relatively rare. Chapter 5 of Bondanella (1991) offers a rich thematic and stylistic analysis of *Fellini Satyricon*. For a discussion of of Pasolini's relationship with Petronius, see Fusillo (2003b). Sullivan (2001) is a discussion of Fellini's techniques and inventions, and of Petronius' and Fellini's artistic attitudes, devoid of any moralism; a valuable study, mercifully free from the usual prejudices of classicists. Solomon

---

54 See Goodman (1969).

(2001) 274–81 is an analysis of Kondouros' *Young Aphrodites* and *Fellini Satyricon*, focusing on its surrealistic picture of Roman empire and its daily life. Wyke (1997) 188–92 also offers a sensitive reading of *Fellini Satyricon*. Non-anglophone accounts include Beschorner (1992), the first critical study of an interesting Marxistic rewriting, by Arnolt Bronnens, of the *Life of Aesop*; Guerrini (1973) 380–92, on Céline and Petronius: a comparison of form and thematics, based on the concepts of realism; Martin (1990), also on Céline and Petronius (a comparison of genre and narrative techniques); and Sütterlin (1997), an overly formalistic comparison of the narrative structures of Petronius and Fellini *Satyricon*.

REFERENCES

Aarne, A. (1910) *Verzeichnis der Märchentypen*, F. F. Communications 3. Helsinki

Aarne, A., and Thompson, S. (1961) *The Types of the Folktale: a Classification and Bibliography*, F. F. Communications 184. Helsinki

Agapitos, P. A. (1991) *Narrative Structure in the Byzantine Vernacular Romances: a Textual and Literary Study of 'Kallimachos', 'Belthandros', and 'Libistros'*. Munich

   (1998) 'Narrative, rhetoric, and "drama" rediscovered: scholars and poets in Byzantium interpret Heliodorus', in Hunter (1998a): 125–56

   (2000a) 'Poets and painters: Theodoros Prodromos' dedicatory verses of his novel to an anonymous Caesar', *JÖByz* 50: 173–85

   (2000b) 'Der Roman der Komnenenzeit: Stand der Forschung und weitere Perspektiven', in Agapitos and Reinsch (2000): 1–18

Agapitos, P. A. and Reinsch, D. R., eds. (2000) *Der Roman im Byzanz der Komnenenzeit: Referate des Internationalen Symposiums an der Freien Universität Berlin, 3. bis 6. April 1998* (Meletemata 8). Frankfurt am Main

Agati, M. L. (2001) *Giovanni Onorio da Maglie copista greco (1535–1563)*, Boll-Class Suppl. 20. Rome

Ahl, F. M. (1976) *Lucan: an Introduction*. Ithaca

Aitken, E. B. and Maclean, J. K. B., eds. (2004) *Philostratus' Heroikos: Religion and Cultural Identity in the Third Century C.E.* Atlanta

Alaux, J. and Létoublon, F. (2001) 'La nourrice et le pédagogue', in Pouderon (2001): 73–86

Alcock, S. E. (1993) *Graecia capta: the Landscapes of Roman Greece*. Cambridge

Alexiou, M. (1977) 'A critical reappraisal of Eustathios Makrembolites' *Hysmine and Hysminias*', *BMGS* 3: 23–43

Allen, G. (2000) *Intertextuality*. London and New York

Allen, P. S., Allen, H. and Garrod, H., eds. (1906–58) *Opus Epistolarum Des. Erasmi Roterodami*, 12 vols. Oxford

Alperowitz, M. (1992) *Das Wirken und Walten der Götter im griechischen Roman*. Heidelberg

Alston, R. (1995) *Soldier and Society in Roman Egypt*. New York

Althusser, L. (1971) *Lenin and Philosophy and Other Essays*. London

Alvares, J. (1997) 'Chariton's erotic history', *AJPh* 118: 613–29

   (2001–2) 'Some political and ideological dimensions of Chariton's *Chaireas and Callirhoe*', *CJ* 97: 113–44

(2006) 'Reading Longus' *Daphnis and Chloe* and Achilles Tatius' *Leucippe and Clitophon* in counterpoint', in S. Byrne, E. Cueva and J. Alvares, eds., *Authors, Authority, and Interpreters in the Ancient Novel: Essays in Honor of Gareth L. Schmeling.* Groningen (= AN Suppl. 5: 1–33)

Anderson, B. (1991) *Imagined Communities: Reflections on the Origins and Spread of Nationalism*, rev. edn. London and New York

Anderson, G. (1982) *Eros sophistes: Ancient Novelists at Play.* Chico

(1984) *Ancient Fiction: the Novel in the Graeco-Roman World.* London and Sydney

(1989) 'The *pepaideumenos* in action: sophists and their outlook in the early empire', *ANRW* II.33.1: 80–208

(1994) *Sage, Saint and Sophist: Holy Men and their Associates in the Early Roman Empire.* London

(1997) 'Perspectives on Achilles Tatius', *ANRW* II.34.3: 2278–99

(2000) 'Some uses of storytelling in Dio', in Swain (2000): 143–60

(2001) 'Greek religion in the Roman empire: diversities, convergences, uncertainties', in Cohn-Sherbok and Court (2001): 142–63

André, J.-M. and Baslez, M.-F. (1993) *Voyager dans l'antiquité.* Paris

Angold, M., ed. (1984) *The Byzantine Aristocracy, IXth to XIIIth Centuries.* Oxford 22: 115–36

(1997) 'Manuel Comnenus and the Latins', in *The Byzantine Empire, 1025–1204: a Political History*, 2nd edn. London: 226–40

Antoniou, P. (1995) 'Les florilèges sacro-profanes et la tradition indirecte des romanciers Achille Tatius et Héliodore', *RHT* 25: 81–90

Archibald, E. (1991) *Apollonius of Tyre: Medieval and Renaissance Themes and Variations.* Cambridge

Armstrong, N. (1987) *Desire and Domestic Fiction: a Political History of the Novel.* Oxford

Astbury, R. (1977) 'Petronius, *P.Oxy.* 3010, and Menippean Satire', *CPh* 72: 22–31 (repr. in Harrison (1999): 74–84)

Auerbach, E. (1953) *Mimesis: the Representation of Reality in Western Literature*, trans. W. R. Trask. Princeton

Baglio, M., Ferrari, M. and Petoletti, M. (1999) 'Montecassino e gli umanisti', in G. Avarucci, R. M. Borraccini Verducci and G. Borri, eds., *Libro, scrittura, documento della civiltà monastica e conventuale nel basso Medioevo (secoli XIII–XV).* Spoleto: 183–238

Bakhtin, M. M. (1981) *The Dialogic Imagination*, trans. C. Emerson and M. Holquist. Austin

(1984a) *Rabelais and his World*, trans. H. Iswolsky. Bloomington

(1984b) *Problems of Dostoyevsky's Poetics*, trans. C. Emerson. Manchester

(1986) 'The *Bildungsroman* and its significance in the history of realism (toward a historical typology of the novel)', in *Speech Genres and Other Late Essays*, trans. V. W. McGee. Austin: 10–59

Bal, M. (1997) *Narratology: Introduction to the Theory of Narrative*, 2nd edn. Toronto

Balard M., ed. (1986) *Fortunes de Jacques Amyot, Actes du colloque international (Melun 18–20 avril 1985).* Paris

Baldwin, B. (1990) 'Petronius in Byzantium?', *PSN* 20: 9–10

Balinski J. (1992) 'Heliodorus Latinus: Die humanistischen Studien über die *Aithiopika*. Politianus – Warszewicki – Guillonius – Laubanus', *Eos* 80: 273–89

Ballengee, J. (2005) 'Below the belt: looking into the matter of adventure-time', in Branham (2005): 130–63

Balot, R. K. (1998) 'Foucault, Chariton, and the masculine self', *Helios* 25: 139–62

Bandini, M. (1986) 'Il modello della metamorfosi ovidiana nel romanzo di Apuleio', *Maia* 38: 33–9

Barber, G. (1989) *Daphnis & Chloe: the Markets and Metamorphoses of an Unknown Bestseller*. London

Barchiesi, A. (1986) 'Tracce di narrative greca e romanzo latino: una rassegna', in *Semiotica della novella Latina: Atti del seminario interdisciplinario 'La novela Latina', Perugia 11–13 April 1985*. Rome: 219–36 (trans. B. Graziosi as 'Traces of Greek narrative and the Roman novel: a survey', in Harrison (1999): 124–41)

Barns, J. W. B. (1956) 'Egypt and the Greek romance', *Mitteilungen aus der Papyrussammlung der Nationalbibliothek in Wien* 5: 29–34

Barthes, R. (1982) 'The reality effect', in T. Todorov, ed., *French Literary Theory Today*. Cambridge: 11–17

Barton, C. A. (1992) *The Sorrows of the Ancient Romans: the Gladiator and the Monster*. Princeton

Barton, T. S. (1994) *Power and Knowledge: Astrology, Physiognomics, and Medicine under the Roman Empire*. Ann Arbor

Bartsch, S. (1989) *Decoding the Ancient Novel: the Reader and the Role of Description in Heliodorus and Achilles Tatius*. Princeton

Bartsch, W. (1934) *Der Charitonroman und die Historiographie*, Diss. Leipzig

Baslez, M.-F., Hoffmann, P. and Trédé, M., eds. (1992) *Le monde du roman grec: Actes du colloque international tenu à l'Ecole normale supérieure (Paris 17–19 décembre 1987)*, Etudes de littérature ancienne 4. Paris

Baslez, M.-F. (1992) 'De l'histoire au roman: la Perse de Chariton', in Baslez *et al.* (1992): 199–212

Baumbach, M. (1997) 'Die Meroe-Episode in Heliodors *Aithiopika*', *RhM* 140: 333–41

Beaton, R. (1996) *The Medieval Greek Romance*, 2nd edn. London

Beaumont, C. W. (1935) *Michel Fokine and his Ballets*. London

Beck, H.-G. (1977) 'Marginalia on the Byzantine novel', in B. P. Reardon, ed., *Erotica antiqua: Acta of the International Conference on the Ancient Novel, 1976*. Bangor: 59–65

(1984) *Byzantinisches Erotikon: Orthodoxie–Literatur–Gesellschaft*. Munich

Beck, R. (1973) 'Some observations on the narrative technique of Petronius', *Phoenix* 27: 42–61 (repr. in Harrison (1999): 50–73)

(1975) 'Encolpius at the *Cena*', *Phoenix* 29: 271–83

(1982) 'The *Satyricon*: satire, narrator, and antecedents', *MH* 39: 206–14

(2003) 'Mystery religions, aretalogy and the ancient novel', in Schmeling (2003b): 131–50

(2004) 'Lucius and the sundial: a hidden chronotopic template in *Metamorphoses* 11', in Zimmerman and Van der Paardt (2004): 309–18

Berger G. (1984) 'Legitimation und Modell: Die *Aithiopika* als Prototyp des französischen heroisch-galanten Romans', *A&A* 30: 177–89

Bernsdorff, H. (1993) 'Longos und Lukian (Zu *Verae Historiae* 2, 5)', *WS* 106: 35–44

Berti, M. (1967) 'Sulla interpretazione mistica del romanzo di Longo', *SCO* 16: 343–58

Bertoni, C. and Fusillo, M. (1998) 'Heliodorus Parthenopaeus: the *Aithiopika* in baroque Naples', in Hunter (1998a): 157–81

Beschorner, A. (1992) 'Zu Arnolt Bronnens *Aisopos*', in Holzberg (1992a): 155–62
  (1999) *Helden und Heroen, Homer und Caracalla: Übersetzung, Kommentar und Interpretationen zum Heroikos des Flavios Philostratos*. Bari

Bessone, F. (1993) 'Discorsi dei liberti e parodia del *Simposio* platonico nella *Cena Trimalchionis*', *MD* 30: 63–86

Billault, A. (1991) *La création romanesque dans la littérature grecque à l'époque impériale*. Paris
  (1992) 'Cervantès et Héliodore', in Baslez *et al.* (1992): 307–14
  (1996) 'Le temps du loisir dans *Daphnis et Chloé*', in J.-M. André, J. Dangel and P. Demont, eds., *Les loisirs et l'héritage de la culture classique*. Brussels: 162–9
  ed. (2001) *ΟΠΩΡΑ: la belle saison de l'hellénisme. Etudes de littérature antique offertes au Recteur, Jacques Bompaire*. Paris

Binns J. (1978) 'Latin translations from Greek in the English renaissance', *Humanistica Lovaniensa* 27: 128–59

Biraud, M. (1986) 'L'hypotexte homérique et les rôles amoureux de Callirhoé dans le roman de Chariton', in A. Goursonnet, ed., *Sémiologie de l'amour dans les civilisations mediterranéennes*, Paris: 21–7
  (1996) 'La dévotion à Aphrodite dans le roman de Chariton', in M. Dubrocard and C. Kircher, eds., *Hommage au doyen Weiss*. Nice: 137–43

Bitel, A. (2001) 'Fiction and history in Apuleius' Milesian prologue', in Kahane and Laird (2001): 137–51

Bloch, H. (1977) *The death of Virgil*, trans. J. S. Untermeyer. London (German original 1945)

Bodel, J. (1994) 'Trimalchio's underworld', in Tatum (1994): 237–59
  (1999) 'The *Cena Trimalchionis*', in Hofmann (1999b): 38–51

Bondanella, P. (1991) *The Cinema of Federico Fellini*. Princeton

Bonnefon, P. (1883) 'Une traduction inédite du premier livre de *Théagène et Chariclée*', *Annuaire de l'Association pour l'encouragement des études grecques en France* 17: 327–64

Bonner, S. F. (1949) *Roman Declamation*. Liverpool

Booth, W. C. (1965) *The Rhetoric of Fiction*. Chicago and London

Borg, B. E., ed. (2004) *Paideia: the World of the Second Sophistic*. Berlin and New York: 359–76

Boroughs, R. (1995) 'Oscar Wilde's translation of Petronius: the story of a literary hoax', *English Literature in Transition: 1880–1920* 38: 9–49

Botfield, B. (1861) *Prefaces to the First Editions of the Greek and Roman Classics and of the Sacred Scriptures*. London

Bouffartigue, J. (2001) 'Un triangle symbolique: Eros, Aphrodite et Artémis dans le roman de *Leucippé et Clitophon*', in Billault (2001): 125–38

Bourdieu, P. (1977) *Outline of a Theory of Practice*, trans. R. Nice. Cambridge

Bowersock, G. W. (1969) *Greek Sophists in the Roman Empire*. Oxford
  (1994) *Fiction as History: Nero to Julian*. Berkeley, Los Angeles and London

Bowie, E. L. (1970) 'Greeks and their past in the second sophistic', *P&P* 46: 3–41
  (repr. in M. I. Finley, ed., *Studies in Ancient Society*. London: 166–209)

(1978) 'Apollonius of Tyana: tradition and reality', *ANRW* II.16.2: 1652–99

(1985) 'The Greek novel', in Easterling and Knox (1985): 683–99 (repr. in Swain (1999): 39–59)

(1989a) 'Greek sophists and Greek poetry in the second sophistic', *ANRW* II.33.1: 209–58

(1989b) 'Poetry and poets in Asia and Achaea', in Walker and Cameron (1989): 198–205

(1990) 'Greek poetry in the Antonine Age', in Russell (1990): 53–90

(1991) 'Hellenes and Hellenism in writers of the early second sophistic', in S. Saïd, ed., *ΕΛΛΗΝΙΣΜΟΣ: quelques jalons pour une histoire de l'identité grecque.* Leiden: 183–204

(1994a) 'The readership of Greek novels in the ancient world', in Tatum (1994): 435–59

(1994b) 'Philostratus: writer of fiction', in Morgan and Stoneman (1994): 181–99

(1995) 'Names and a gem: aspects of allusion in Heliodorus' *Aethiopica*', in D. Innes, *et al.*, eds., *Ethics and Rhetoric: Classical Essays for Donald Russell on his Seventy-Fifth Birthday.* Oxford: 269–80

(2001a) 'Inspiration and aspiration: date, genre and readership', in S. Alcock, J. Cherry and J. Elsner, eds., *Pausanias: Travel and Memory in Roman Greece.* New York and Oxford: 21–32

(2001b) 'Hadrian and Greek poetry', in Ostenfeld (2001): 172–97

(2002) 'The chronology of the earlier Greek novels since B. E. Perry: revisions and precisions', *AN* 2: 47–63

(2003) 'The ancient readers of the Greek novels', in Schmeling (2003b): 87–106

(2005) 'Metaphor in Daphnis and Chloe', in Harrison *et al.* (2005): 68–86

(2007) 'Links between Antonius Diogenes and Petronius', in M. Paschalis, S. Frangoulides and S. Harrison, eds., *The Greek and the Roman Novel: Parallel Readings.* Groningen: 121–32

Boyarin, D. and Castelli, E. A. (2001) 'Introduction. Foucault's *The history of sexuality*: the fourth volume, or, A field left fallow for others to till', *Journal of the History of Sexuality* 10.3/4: 357–75

Bradley, K. (1994) *Slavery and Society at Rome.* Cambridge

(2000a) 'Animalizing the slave: the truth of fiction', *JRS* 90: 110–25

(2000b) 'Fictive families: family and household in the *Metamorphoses* of Apuleius', *Phoenix* 54: 282–308.

Branham, R. B. (1989) *Unruly Eloquence: Lucian and the Comedy of Traditions.* Cambridge MA

(1995) 'Inventing the novel', in A. Mandelker, ed., *Bakhtin in Contexts.* Evanston IL: 79–87

(2002a) 'A truer story of the novel?', in Branham (2002b): 161–86

ed. (2002b) *Bakhtin and the Classics.* Evanston IL

ed. (2005) *The Bakhtin Circle And Ancient narrative.* Groningen (= AN Suppl. 3)

Braun, M. (1938) *History and Romance in Graeco-Oriental Literature.* Oxford

Briggs, W. W. (2000) 'The Ur-*Gatsby*', *IJCT* 6: 577–84

Brink, C. O. (1971) *Horace on Poetry: the Ars poetica.* Cambridge

Britton, C. (1993) *Claude Simon.* London and New York

Brooks, P. (1984) *Reading for the Plot: Design and Intention in Narrative.* New York and Oxford

(1993) *Body Work: Objects of Desire in Modern Narrative.* Cambridge MA

Brooten, B. (1996) *Love between Women: Early Christian Responses to Female Eroticism.* Chicago

Brown, M. K. (2002) *The* Narratives *of Konon.* Munich

Brown, P. (1988) *The Body and Society: Men, Women and Sexual Renunciation in Early Christianity.* New York.

Browning, R. (1990) 'An unpublished funeral oration on Anna Comnena', in R. Sorabji, ed., *Aristotle Transformed: the Ancient Commentators and their Influence.* Ithaca: 404–5

Brzenk, E. J. (1978) 'Apuleius, Pater and the Bildungsroman', in Hijmans and Van der Paardt (1978): 231–8

Bühler, W. (1976) 'Das Element des Visuellen in der Eingangsszene von Heliodors Aithiopika', *WS* 10: 177–85.

Bürger, K. (1892) 'Zu Xenophon von Ephesus', *Hermes* 27: 36–67

Burkert, W. (1983) *Homo Necans: the Anthropology of Ancient Greek Sacrificial Ritual and Myth*, trans. P. Bing. Berkeley, Los Angeles and London

(1987) *Ancient Mystery Cults.* Cambridge MA

Burnaby, W. (1694) *The Satyr of Titus Petronius Arbiter.* London

Burrus, V. (2005) *The Sex Lives of Saints: an Erotics of Ancient Hagiography.* Philadelphia

Burton, J. B. (1995) *Theocritus's Urban Mimes: Mobility, Gender, and Patronage.* Berkeley, Los Angeles and London

(1998) 'Reviving the pagan Greek novel in a Christian world', *GRBS* 39: 179–216

(2000) 'Abduction and elopement in the Byzantine novel', *GRBS* 41: 377–409

(2003) 'A reemergence of Theocritean poetry in the Byzantine novel', *CPh* 98: 251–73

(2004) *A Byzantine Novel: Drosilla and Charikles by Niketas Eugenianos.* Wauconda IL

(2006) 'The pastoral in Byzantium', in M. Fantuzzi and T. Papanghelis eds., *Brill's Companion to Greek and Latin Pastoral.* Leiden: 549–79

Butler, J. (1993) *Bodies that Matter: on the Discursive Limits of 'Sex'.* New York and London

Cairns, F. (1972) *Generic Composition in Greek and Latin Poetry.* Edinburgh

Callebat, L. (1968) *Sermo cotidianus dans les Métamorphoses.* Paris

(1978) 'La prose des *Métamorphoses*: génèse et spécificité', in Hijmans and Van der Paardt (1978): 167–83

Cameron, Alan (1982) 'Strato and Rufinus', *CQ* 32: 162–73

(1998) 'Love (and marriage) between women', *GRBS* 39: 137–56.

Cameron, Averil (1969) 'Petronius and Plato', *CQ* 19: 367–70

Camerotto, A. (1998) *Le metamorfosi della parola: studi sulla parodia in Luciano di Samosata.* Pisa and Rome

Cantarella, E. (1992) *Bisexuality in the Ancient World*, trans. C. O'Cuileanain. New Haven and London

Capps, E. jr (1949) 'Observations on the painted *venatio* of the theater at Corinth and on the arrangements of the arena', *Hesperia* Suppl. 8, *Commemorative Studies in Honor of Theodore Leslie Shear*: 64–70, 444–5

Carrington, C. (1906) *The Trial of Oscar Wilde*. Paris

Cartledge P. (1997) ' "Deep plays": theatre as process in Greek civic life', in P. E. Easterling, ed., *The Cambridge Companion to Greek Tragedy*. Cambridge: 3–35

Carver, R. H. F. (1997) ' "Sugared invention" or "mongrel tragi-comedy": Sir Philip Sidney and the ancient novel', in *Groningen Colloquia on the Novel* 8: 197–226

(1999) 'The rediscovery of the Latin novels', in Hofmann (1999b): 253–68

(2000–1) ' "True histories" and "old wives' tales": renaissance humanism and the rise of the novel', *AN* 1: 322–49

(2008) *The Protean Ass: the* Metamorphoses *of Apuleius From Antiquity to the Renaissance*. Oxford

Cataldi Palau, A. (1980) 'La tradition manuscrite d'Eustathe Makrembolitès', *RHT* 10: 75–113

Cavallo, G. (1996) 'Veicoli materiali della letteratura di consume: maniere di scrivere e maniere di leggere', in O. Pecere and A. Stramaglia, eds., *La letteratura di consumo nel mondo Greco-Latino*. Cassino: 13–46

Cavarzere, A., Aloni, A. and Barchiesi, A., eds. (2001) *Iambic Ideas: Essays on a Poetic Tradition, from Archaic Greece to the Late Roman Empire*. Lanham MD

Cave, T. (1988) *Recognitions: a Study in Poetics*. Oxford

(1990) '*Suspendere animos*: pour une histoire de la notion de suspens', in G. Mathieu-Castellani and M. Plaisance, eds., *Les commentaires et la naissance de la critique littéraire*. Paris: 211–18

Chalk, H. H. O. (1960) 'Eros and the Lesbian pastorals of Longus', *JHS* 80: 32–51 (repr. in Gärtner (1984): 388–407)

Chartier, R. (1994) *The Order of Books: Readers, Authors and Libraries in Europe between the Fourteenth and the Eighteenth Centuries*, trans. L. G. Cochrane. Cambridge

Chatman, S., ed. (1971) *Literary Style: a Symposium*. Oxford

Chew, K. S. (2000) 'Achilles Tatius and parody', *CJ* 96: 57–70

(2007) 'Divine epistemology: the relation between speech and writing in the *Aithiopika*', in V. Rimell, ed., *Seeing Tongues, Hearing Scripts: Representation and the Modernity of the Ancient Novel*. Groningen (= *AN* Suppl. 7: 279–98)

Christian, R. F. (1962) *Tolstoy's* War and Peace: *a Study*. Oxford

Cichorius, C. (1922) *Römische Studien*. Leipzig

Clarke, K. J. (1999) *Between Geography and History: Hellenistic Constructions of the Roman World*. Oxford

Cleto, F., ed. (1999) *Camp: Queer Aesthetics and the Performing Subject*. Edinburgh

Cohen, D. and Saller, R. (1994) 'Foucault on sexuality in Greco-Roman antiquity', in J. Goldstein, ed., (1994) *Foucault and the Writing of History*. Oxford: 35–59

Cohn, D. (1978) *Transparent Minds: Narrative Modes for Presenting Consciousness in Fiction*. Baltimore

(1999) *The Distinction of Fiction*. Baltimore

Cohn-Sherbok, D. and Court, J. M. (2001) *Religious Diversity in the Graeco-Roman World*. Sheffield

Cole, S. (2004) *Landscape, Gender and Ritual Space: the Ancient Greek Experience*. Berkeley, Los Angeles and London

Coleman, K. M. (1990) 'Fatal charades: Roman executions staged as mythological enactments', *JRS* 80: 44–73

(1993) 'Launching into history: aquatic displays in the early empire', *JRS* 83: 48–74

(2000) '*Missio* at Halicarnassus', *HSCPh* 100: 487–500

Colonna, A., ed. (1938) *Heliodori Aethiopica*. Rome (text repr. as Colonna (1987))

(1987) *Le Etiopiche di Eliodoro*. Turin

Columbus, R. R. (1963) 'Conscious artistry in *Moll Flanders*', *Studies in English Literature* 3: 415–32

Conca, F. (1989) 'Scribi e lettori dei romanzi tardo antichi e bizantini', in A. Garzya, ed., *Metodologie della ricerca sulla tarda antichità*. Naples: 223–46

ed. (1990) *Nicetas Eugenianus:* De Drosillae et Chariclis amoribus. Amsterdam

(1994) *Il romanzo bizantino del XII secolo*. Turin

Connors, C. (1998) *Petronius the Poet: Verse and Literary Tradition in the Satyricon*. Cambridge

(1999) 'Rereading the Arbiter: *arbitrium* and verse in the *Satyrica* and in "*Petronius redivivus*"', in Hofmann (1999b): 64–78

(2002) 'Chariton's Syracuse and its histories of empire', in Paschalis and Frangoulidis (2002): 12–26

(2005) 'Metaphor and politics in John Barclay's *Argenis* (1621)', in Harrison *et al.* (2005): 245–74

Conte, G. B. (1986) *The Rhetoric of Imitation*, trans. C. Segal. Ithaca

(1996) *The Hidden Author: an Interpretation of Petronius'* Satyricon, trans. E. Fantham. Berkeley, Los Angeles and London

Cooper, K. (1996) *The Virgin and the Bride: Idealized Womanhood in Late Antiquity*. Cambridge MA

Couégnas, D. (1991) *Introduction à la paralittérature*. Paris

Couperus, L. (1999) *Psyche*, trans. C. S. Berrington. London (original edn 1908; Dutch edn 1898)

Courtney, E. (2001) *A Companion to Petronius*. Oxford and New York

Cozzoli, A.-T. (2000) 'Dalla poesia al romanzo: motivi poetici nella rielaborazione narrativa di Longo Sofista', *SemRom* 3: 295–312

Cresci, L. R. (1981) 'Il romanzo di Longo Sofista e la tradizione bucolica', *A&R* 26: 1–25; trans. as 'The novel of Longus the sophist and the pastoral tradition', in Swain (1999): 210–42

Cribiore, R. (1996) *Writers, Teachers and Students in Graeco-Roman Egypt*. Atlanta

(2001) *Gymnastics of the Mind: Greek Education in Hellenistic and Roman Egypt*. Princeton

Crismani, D. (1997) *Il teatro nel romanzo ellenistico d'amore e di avventure*. Turin

Cueva, E. P. (2004) *The Myths of Fiction: Studies in the Canonical Greek Novels*. Ann Arbor

Cupane, C. (1974) 'Un caso di giudizio di Dio nel romanzo di Teodoro Prodromo (I 372–404)', *RSBN* 10–11: 147–68

Czapla, B. (2002) 'Literarische Lese-, Kunst- und Liebesmodelle: eine intertextuelle Interpretation von Longos' Hirtenroman', *A&A* 48: 18–42

D'Amico, J. F. (1984) 'The progress of Renaissance Latin prose: the case of Apuleianism', *Renaissance Quarterly* 37: 351–92

D'Arms, J. (1981) *Commerce and Social Standing in Ancient Rome*. Cambridge MA

Daele R.-M. (1946) *Nicolas de Montreulx: Arbiter of European Literary Vogues of the Late Renaissance*. New York

Dalmeyda, G., ed. (1926) *Xénophon d'Ephèse*, Les Ephésiaques. Paris
  (1934a) 'Henri Estienne et Longus', *RPh* 60: 169–81
  ed. (1934b) *Longus*, Pastorales. Paris
Dapelo, G., and Zoppelli, B. (1998) *Lilio Tifernate, Luciani* De veris narrationibus: *introduzione, note e testo critico*. Genoa
Daude, C. (2001) 'Le personnage d'Artaxerxès dans le roman de Chariton, *Chairéas et Callirhoé*: fiction et histoire', in Pouderon (2001): 137–48
Davis, D. (2002) *Panthea's Children: Hellenistic Novels and Medieval Persian Romances*, Yarshater Lectures Series 3. New York
Davis, L. (2000) *The Silver Pigs*. London
De Faveri, L. (2002) *Le traduzioni di Luciano in Italia nel XV e XVI secolo*. Amsterdam
de Jean, J. (1991) *Tender Geographies: Women and the Origin of the Novel in France*. New York
de Jong, I. (1987) *Narrators and Focalizers: the Presentation of the Story in the Iliad*. Amsterdam
  (2001) 'The prologue as pseudo-dialogue and the identity of its (main) speaker', in Kahane and Laird (2001): 201–12
de Jong, I., Nünlist, R. and Bowie, A., eds. (2004) *Narrators, Narratees, and Narratives in Ancient Greek Literature*. Leiden
de Lannoy, L., ed. (1977) *Flavii Philostrati Heroicus*. Leipzig
DeFilippo, J. G. (1990) '*Curiositas* and the Platonism of Apuleius' *Golden Ass*', *AJPh* 111: 471–92 (repr. in Harrison (1999): 269–89)
Defoe, D. (1989) *Moll Flanders*. Harmondsworth
Dentith, S. (1995) *Bakhtinian Thought: an Introductory Reader*. London
Devreesse, R. (1965) *Le fonds grec de la Bibliothèque Vaticane des origines à Paul V*, Studi e Testi 244. Vatican
di Marco, M (2000) 'Fileta praeceptor amoris: Longo Sofista e la correzione del modello bucolico', *SCO* 47: 9–35
Dickie, M. (1991) 'Heliodorus and Plutarch on the evil eye', *CPh* 86: 17–29
Dimundo, R. (1983) 'Da Socrate a Eumolpo: degradazione dei personaggi e delle funzioni nella novella del fanciullo di Pergamo', *MD* 10–11: 255–65
Dionisotti, A. C. (1997) 'Les chapitres entre l'historiographie et le roman', in J.-C. Fredouille *et al*., eds., *Titres et articulations du texte dans les œuvres antiques*. Paris: 529–44
Dodge, H. (1999) 'Amusing the masses: buildings for entertainment and leisure in the Roman world', in Potter and Mattingly (1999): 205–55
Doody M. A. (1994) 'Heliodorus rewritten: Samuel Richardson's *Clarissa* and Frances Burney's *Wanderer*', in Tatum (1994): 117–31
  (1996) *The True Story of the Novel*. New Brunswick
Dörrie, H. (1935) *De Longi Achillis Tatii Heliodori memoria*. Göttingen
Dougherty, C. (1993) *The Poetics of Colonization: from City to Text in Archaic Greece*. New York and Oxford
Dover, K., ed. (1971) *Theocritus: a Selection*. London
Dowden, K. (1982) 'Apuleius and the art of narration', *CQ* 32: 419–35
  (1994) 'The Roman audience of the *Golden Ass*', in Tatum (1994): 419–34
  (1996) 'Heliodoros: serious intentions', *CQ* 46: 267–85

(1999) 'Fluctuating meanings: passage rites', in M. Padilla, ed., *Rites of Passage in Ancient Greece: Literature, Religion, Society*. Lewisburg PA: 221–43

(2001) 'Prologic, predecessors, and prohibitions', in Kahane and Laird (2001): 123–36

(2005) 'The Greek novel and the ritual of life', in Harrison *et al.* (2005): 23–35

DuBois, P. (1998) 'The subject in antiquity after Foucault', in Larmour *et al.* (1998): 85–103

Duff, T. (1999) *Plutarch's* Lives: *Exploring Virtue and Vice*. Oxford

Dunlop, J. (1888) *History of Prose Fiction*, 4th edn, rev. H. Wilson, 2 vols. (repr. New York (1970))

Dupont, F. (1999) *The Invention of Literature: from Greek Intoxication to the Latin Book*, trans. J. Lloyd. Baltimore

Durham, D. B. (1938) 'Parody in Achilles Tatius', *CPh* 33: 1–19

Dyck, A. R., ed. (1986) *Michael Psellus: the Essays on Euripides and George of Pisidia and on Heliodorus and Achilles Tatius*. Vienna

Eagleton, T. (1982) *The Rape of Clarissa: Writing, Sexuality, and Class Struggle in Samuel Richardson*. Oxford

Easterling, P. E. and Knox, B. M. W., eds., *The Cambridge History of Classical Literature*, vol. I: *Greek Literature*. Cambridge

Edmonds, J. M. (1916) Daphnis and Chloe *by Longus, with the English translation of George Thornley;* The *Love romances of Parthenius and other fragments, with an English translation by S. Gaselee*. London and New York

Edwards, D. R. (1994) 'Defining the web of power in Asia Minor: the novelist Chariton and his city Aphrodisias', *Journal of the American Academy of Religion* 62: 699–718

Effe, B. (1982) 'Longos: Zur Funktionsgeschichte der Bukolik in der römischen Kaiserzeit', *Hermes* 110: 65–84 (trans. as 'Longus: towards a history of bucolic and its function in the Roman empire', in Swain (1999): 189–209)

(1987) 'Der griechische Liebesroman und die Homoerotik', *Philologus* 131 (1987): 95–108

Egger, B. (1988) 'Zu den Frauenrollen im griechischen Roman: die Frau als Heldin und Leserin', *Groningen Colloquia on the Novel* 1: 33–66 (repr. as 'The role of women in the Greek novel: woman as heroine and reader', in Swain (1999): 108–36)

Egger, B. (1994a) 'Women and marriage in the Greek novels: the boundaries of romance', in Tatum (1994): 260–80

(1994b) 'Looking at Chariton's Callirhoe', in Morgan and Stoneman (1994): 31–48

Ellis, J. M. (1983) *One Fairy Story too many: the Brothers Grimm and their Tales*. Chicago

Elsner, J. (1997) 'Hagiographic geography: travel and allegory in the *Life of Apollonius of Tyana*', *JHS* 117: 22–37

Endres, N. (2005) 'Roman fever: Petronius' *Satyricon* and Gore Vidal's *The city and the pillar*', *Ancient Narrative* 4: 99–141

Eurydice (1999) *Satyricon USA: a Journey across a New Sexual Frontier*. New York

Fantham, E. (2005) 'Liberty and the people in republican Rome', *TAPhA* 135: 209–29

Farrell, J. (2003) 'Classical genre in theory and practice', *New Literary History* 34: 383–408

Favro, D. (1999) 'The city is a living thing. The performative role of an urban site in ancient Rome: The *Vallis Murcia*', in B. Bergmann and C. Kondoleon, eds., *The Art of Ancient Spectacle*. New Haven and London: 205–19

Fehling, D. (1977) *Amor und Psyche: die Schöpfung des Apuleius und ihre Einwirkung auf das Märchen, eine Kritik der romantischen Märchentheorie*. Mainz

Fellini, F. (1988) *Comments on Film*, ed. G. Grazzini. Fresno

Feuillâtre, E. (1966) *Etudes sur les* Ethiopiques *d'Héliodore*. Paris

Finkelpearl, E. D. (1990) 'Psyche, Aeneas and an ass: Apuleius *Met.* 6.10–6.21', *TAPhA* 120: 333–48 (repr. in Harrison (1999): 290–306)

    (1998) *Metamorphosis of Language in Apuleius: a Study of Allusion in the Novel*. Ann Arbor

Finley, M., ed. (1974) *Studies in Ancient Society*. London

Fiorilla, M. (1999) 'La lettura apuleiana del Boccaccio e le note ai manoscritti laurenziani 29, 2 e 54, 32', *Aevum* 73: 635–68

Fitzgerald, F. S. (2000) *Trimalchio: an Early Version of The Great Gatsby*, ed. J. L. W. West, III. Cambridge

Fitzgerald, W. (2000) *Slavery and the Roman Literary Imagination*. Cambridge

Flint, K. (1993) *The Woman Reader, 1837–1914*. Oxford

Floridi, L. ed. (2007) *Stratone di Sardi*: Epigrammi. Alessandria

Forster, E. M. (1964) *Aspects of the Novel*. Harmondsworth

Foucault, M. (1986) *The History of Sexuality*, vol. III: *The Care of the Self*, trans. R. Hurley. New York

Fowler, D. P. (1990) 'Deviant focalization in Vergil's *Aeneid*', *PCPhS* 216: 42–63 (repr. in Fowler (2000): 40–63)

    (2000) *Roman Constructions: Postmodern Readings in Latin*. Oxford

    (2001) 'Writing with style: the prologue to Apuleius' *Metamorphoses* between *fingierte Mündlichkeit* and textuality', in Kahane and Laird (2001): 225–30

Fowler, R. (1981) *Literature as Discourse: the Practice of Linguistic Criticism*. London

    (1986) *Linguistic Criticism*. Oxford

Foxhall, L. (1998) 'Pandora unbound: a feminist critique of Foucault's *History of sexuality*', in Larmour, Miller and Platter (1998): 122–37.

Fraenkel, E. (1953) 'A Sham Sisenna', *Eranos* 51: 151–4

Francis, J. A. (1998) 'Truthful fiction: new questions to old answers on Philostratus' *Life of Apollonius*', *AJPh* 119: 419–41

Frangoulidis, S. A. (1992a) 'Epic inversion in Apuleius' tale of Tlepolemus/Haemus', *Mnemosyne* 45: 60–74

    (1992b), 'Charite's literary models: Vergil's Dido and Homer's Odysseus', in C. Deroux, ed., *Studies in Latin Literature and Roman History* VI, Collection Latomus 217. Brussels: 445–50

    (1992c) 'Homeric allusions to the Cyclopeia in Apuleius' description of the robbers' cave', *PP* 47: 50–8

Freese, J. H. (1920) *The Library of Photius*, vol. I. London

Frye, N. (1976) *Secular Scripture: a Study in the Structure of Romance*. Cambridge MA

Fumagalli, E. (1988) *Matteo Maria Boiardo volgarizzatore dell' 'Asino d'oro': contributo allo studio della fortuna di Apuleio nell'umanesimo*. Padua

Fumaroli, M. (1985) 'Jacques Amyot and the clerical polemic against the chivalric novel', *Renaissance Quarterly* 38: 22–40

Fusillo, M. (1988a) 'Le miroir de la lune: L'*Histoire vraie* de Lucien, de la satire à l'utopie', *Poétique* 73: 109–35 (trans. as 'The mirror of the moon: Lucian's *A true story* – from satire to utopia', in Swain (1999): 351–81)

(1988b) 'Textual patterns and narrative situations in the Greek novel', *Gronignen Colloquia on the Novel* 1: 17–31

(1989) *Il romanzo greco: polifonia ed eros*. Venice

(1990a) 'Il testo nel testo: la citazione nel romanzo greco', *MD* 25: 27–48

(1990b) 'Les conflits des émotions: un topos du roman grec érotique', *MH* 47: 201–21 (trans. as 'The conflict of emotions: a *topos* in the Greek erotic novel', in Swain (1999): 60–82)

(1994) *Antonio Diogene*, Le incredibili avventure al di là di Tule. Palermo

(1996) 'Il romanzo antico come paraletteratura? Il *topos* del racconto di ricapitolazione', in O. Pecere and A. Stramaglia, eds., *La letteratura di consumo nel mondo Greco-Latino*. Cassino: 47–67

(1997a) 'How novels end: some patterns of closure in ancient narrative', in D. H. Roberts, F. M. Dunn, and D. Fowler, eds., *Classical Closure: Reading the End in Greek and Latin Literature*. Princeton: 209–27

(1997b) 'Il "Satyricon" di Bruno Maderna: un'opera poliglotta', *KLEOS* 2: 231–4

(2002) 'Fra epica e romanzo', in F. Moretti, ed., *Il romanzo 2: Le forme*. Turin: 5–35

(2003a) 'From Petronius to *Petrolio*: *Satyricon* as a model-experimental novel', in Panayotakis *et al.* (2003): 413–23

(2003b) 'Modern critical theories and the ancient novel', in Schmeling (2003b): 277–305

Futre Pinheiro, M. (1989) 'Aspects de la problématique sociale et économique dans le roman d'Héliodore', in P. Liviaballa Furiani and A. M. Scarcella, eds., *Piccolo mondo antico: le donne, gli amori, i costumi, il mondo reale nel romanzo antico*. Naples: 15–42

(1991a) 'Fonctions du surnaturel dans les *Ethiopiques* d'Héliodore', *BAGB* 1991: 359–81

(1991b) 'Calasiris' story and its narrative significance in Heliodorus' *Aethiopica*', *Groningen Colloquia on the Novel* 4: 69–83

(1992) 'Pour une lecture critique des *Ethiopiques* d'Héliodore', *Euphrosyne* 20: 283–94

(1998) 'Time and narrative technique in Heliodorus' *Aethiopica*', *ANRW* II. 34.4: 3148–73

(2003) 'The *Nachleben* of the ancient novel in Iberian literature in the sixteenth century', in Schmeling (2003b): 776–99

Gabba, E. (1991) *Dionysius and the History of Archaic Rome*. Berkeley, Los Angeles and London

Gagliardi, D. (1993) *Petronio e il romanzo moderno: la fortuna del 'Satyricon' attraverso i secoli*. Florence

Gaisser, J. H. (2008) *The Fortunes of Apuleius and the* Golden Ass: *a Study in Transmission and Reception*. Princeton

Gallagher, C. (1994) *Nobody's Story: the Vanishing Act of Women Writers in the Marketplace, 1670–1820*. Berkeley

Gallop, J. (1988) *Thinking through the Body*. New York

Garfagnini, G. C. (1976) 'Un "accessus" ad Apuleio e un nuovo codice del Terzo Mitografo Vaticano', *Studi Medievali* 17: 307–62

Garland, Lynda (1990) ' "Be amorous, but be chaste . . . ": sexual morality in Byzantine learned and vernacular romance', *BMGS* 14: 62–120

Garnaud, J.-P., ed. (1991) *Achille Tatius d'Alexandrie, Le Roman de Leucippé et Clitophon*. Paris

Garnsey, P. (1970) *Social Status and Legal Privilege in the Roman Empire*. Oxford

Gärtner, H., ed. (1984) *Beiträge zum griechischen Liebesroman*. Hildesheim

Gaselee, S., ed. (1969) *Achilles Tatius*, rev. edn. Cambridge MA and London

Genette, G. (1980) *Narrative Discourse*, trans. J. Lewin. Ithaca

    (1982) 'Frontiers of narrative', in *Figures of Literary Discourse*, trans. A. Sheridan. Oxford: 127–44

    (1988) *Narrative Discourse Revisited*, trans. J. Lewin. Ithaca

    (1993) *Fiction and Diction*, trans. C. Porter. Ithaca

George, M. (2002) 'Slave disguise in ancient Rome', in T. Wiedemann and J. Gardner, eds., *Representing the Body of the Slave*. London: 41–54.

George, P. A. (1966) 'Style and character in the *Satyricon*', *Arion* 5: 336–58

Georgiadou, A. and Larmour, D. (1998) *Lucian's Science Fiction Novel True histories: Interpretation and Commentary*. Leiden

Gesner, C. (1545) *Bibliotheca Universalis*. Zürich

Geyer A. (1977) 'Roman und Mysterienritual: Zum Problem eines Bezugs zum dionysischen Mysterienritual im Roman des Longos', *WJA* 3: 179–96

Giangrande, G. (1962) 'On the origins of the Greek romance: the birth of a literary form', *Eranos* 60: 132–59 (repr. in Gärtner (1984): 125–52)

Giannini, A., ed. (1966) *Paradoxographorum Graecorum reliquiae*. Milan

Gilbert, S. M. and Gubar, S. (1979) *The Madwoman in the Attic: the Woman Writer and the Nineteenth-century Literary Imagination*. New Haven

Gill, C. and Wiseman, T. P., eds. (1993) *Lies and Fiction in the Ancient World*. Exeter

Gleason, M. W. (1995) *Making Men: Sophists and Self-presentation in Ancient Rome*. Princeton

    (1999) 'Truth contests and talking corpses', in Porter (1999): 287–313

    (2001) 'Mutilated messengers: body language in Josephus', in Goldhill (2001a): 50–85

Goga, S. (1998) 'Encolpius dans la *Cena*: une aventure de l'ego', *Latomus* 57: 375–9

Goldhill, S. (1991) *The Poet's Voice: Essays on Poetics and Greek Literature*. Cambridge

Goldhill, S. (1994) 'The naive and knowing eye: ecphrasis and the culture of viewing in the Hellenistic world', in S. Goldhill and R. Osborne, eds., *Art and Text in Ancient Greek Culture*. Cambridge: 197–223

    (1995) *Foucault's Virginity: Ancient Erotic Fiction and the History of Sexuality*. Cambridge

    (1999) 'Literary history without literature: reading practices in the ancient world', *SubStance (Review of Theory and Literary Criticism)* 88: 57–89

(2001a) *Being Greek under Rome: Cultural Identity, the Second Sophistic and the Development of Empire.* Cambridge

(2001b) 'The erotic eye: visual stimulation and cultural conflict', in Goldhill (2001a): 154–94

(2002) *Who needs Greek? Contests in the Cultural History of Hellenism.* Cambridge

Goodman, N. (1969) *The Languages of Art.* London

Goody, J. (1991) 'The time of telling and the telling of time in written and oral cultures', in J. Bender and D. E. Wellbery, eds., *Chronotypes: the Construction of Time.* Stanford: 77–96

Goold, G. P., ed. (1995) *Chariton* Callirhoe. Cambridge MA and London

Gordon, R. (1990) 'The Roman empire', in M. Beard and J. North, eds., *Pagan Priests: Religion and Power in the Ancient World.* London: 177–225

Gorky, M. (1948) *Reminiscences of Tolstoy, Chekov and Andreev,* London

Gow, A. S. F. and Page, D. L. (1968) *The* Garland *of Philip,* Cambridge

Gowers, E. (1993) *The Loaded Table: Representations of Food in Roman Literature.* Oxford

(2001) 'Apuleius and Persius', in Kahane and Laird (2001): 77–87

Gowing, A. M. (2005) *Empire and Memory: the Representation of the Roman Republic in Imperial Culture.* Cambridge

Grafton, A. T. (1990) 'Petronius and neo-Latin satire: the reception of the *Cena Trimalchionis*', *JWI* 53: 237–49

Grätz, M. (1988) *Das Märchen in der deutschen Aufklärung.* Stuttgart

Graverini, L. (1997) '*In historiae specimen* (Apul. *Met.* 8.1.4)', *Prometheus* 23: 247–78

(1998) 'Memorie virgiliane nelle *Metamorfosi* di Apuleio', *Maia* 50: 123–45

(2002) 'Corinth, Rome, and Africa: a cultural background for the tale of the ass', in Paschalis and Frangoulidis (2002): 58–77

Graves, R. (1934a) *I Claudius.* London

(1934b) *Claudius the God.* London

Griffin, A. H. (1996) 'Folk-tale', in S. Hornblower and A. Spawforth, eds., *The Oxford Classical Dictionary,* rev. 3rd edn. Oxford: 602–3

Griffiths, F. T. and Rabinowitz, S. J. (1990) *Novel Epics: Gogol, Dostoevsky, and National Narrative.* Evanston IL

Griffiths, J. G. (1975) *Apuleius of Madauros: the Isis Book (*Metamorphoses *Book XI).* Leiden

(1978) 'Isis in the *Metamorphoses* of Apuleius', in Hijmans and Van der Paardt (1978): 141–61

Gronewald, M. (1979) 'Ein Fragment aus den *Aithiopica* des Heliodor (*P. Amh.* 160 = Pack² 2797)', *ZPE* 34: 19–21

Grossardt, P. (2006) *Übersetzung und Kommentar zum* Heroikos *von Flavius Philostrat,* 2 vols., Basel

Gruen, E. S. (1992) *Culture and National Identity in Republican Rome.* Ithaca

Guerrini, R. (1973) 'Petronio e Céline (ovvero la denigrazione del reale)', *Rendiconti Istituto Lombardo* 107: 380–392

Gunderson, E. (1996) 'The ideology of the arena', *ClAnt* 15: 113–51

(2003) *Declamation, Paternity, and Roman Identity: Authority and the Rhetorical self.* Cambridge

Gyraldus, L. G. (1545) *Historiae poetarum tam graecorum quam latinorum dialogi decem.* Basel

Haan, T. (1995) *Posterité du picaresque au Xxème siècle: sa réécriture par quelques écrivains de la crise du sens (Kafka, Céline, Beckett, Gombrowicz, Nabokov).* Assen

Habinek, T. (1997) 'The invention of sexuality in the world-city of Rome', in T. Habinek and A. Schiesaro, eds., *The Roman Cultural Revolution.* Cambridge: 23–43

Habrich, E., ed. (1960) *Iamblichi* Babyloniacorum *reliquiae.* Leipzig

Häfner, R. (2003) '*Ein schönes Confitemini.* Johann Sieders Übersetzung von Apuleius' *Goldenem Esel*: Die Berliner Handschrift Germ. Fol. 1239 aus dem Jahr 1500 und der erste Druck von 1538', *Beiträge zur Geschichte der deutschen Sprache und Literatur* 125: 94–136

Hagedorn, D. and Koenen, L. (1970) 'Eine Handschrift des Achilleus Tatios', *MH* 27: 49–57

Hägg, T. (1971) *Narrative Technique in Ancient Greek Romances: Studies of Chariton, Xenophon Ephesius, and Achilles Tatius,* Acta Instituti Atheniensis Regni Sueciae 8. Stockholm

(1975) *Photius als Vermittler antiker Literatur: Untersuchungen zur Technik des Referierens und Exzerptierens in der* Bibliotheke. Uppsala

(1983) *The Novel in Antiquity.* Oxford, Berkeley and Los Angeles

(1985) 'Metiochus at Polycrates' court', *Eranos* 83: 92–102 (repr. in Hägg (2004): 263–76)

(1986) 'The oriental reception of Greek novels: a survey with some preliminary considerations,' *Symbolae Osloenses* 61: 99–131 (repr. in Hägg (2004) 277–307)

(1987) '*Callirhoe* and *Parthenope*: the beginnings of the historical novel', *CA* 6: 184–204 (repr. in Swain (1999): 137–60; also in Hägg (2004): 73–98)

(1994) 'Orality, literacy and the "readership" of the early Greek novel', in R. Eriksen, ed., *Contexts of Pre-novel Narrative: the European Tradition.* Berlin: 47–81

(1999–2000) 'The black land of the sun: Meroe in Heliodoros' romantic fiction', *Graeco-Arabica* 7–8: 195–219 (repr. in Hägg (2004): 345–75)

(2002) 'Epiphany in the Greek novels: the emplotment of a metaphor', *Eranos* 100: 51–61 (repr. in Hägg (2004): 141–61)

(2004) *Parthenope: Selected Studies in Ancient Greek Fiction (1969–2004),* ed. L. B Mortensen and T. Eide. Copenhagen

Hägg, T. and Utas, B., eds. (2003) *The Virgin and Her lover: Fragments of an Ancient Greek Novel and a Persian Epic Poem.* Leiden

Haight, E. H. (1927) *Apuleius and his Influence.* London

Hall, E. (1995) 'The ass with double vision: politicizing an ancient Greek novel', in D. Margolies and M. Joannou, eds., *Heart of the Heartless World: Essays in Cultural Resistance in Memory of Margot Heinemann.* London: 47–59

Hall, J. (2002) *Hellenicity: Between Ethnicity and Culture.* Chicago

Hallett, J. P. (1997) 'Female homoeroticism and the denial of Roman reality in Latin literature', in Hallett and Skinner (1997): 255–73

Hallett, J. P. and Skinner, M. B., eds. (1997) *Roman Sexualities.* Princeton

Halperin, D. M. (1992) 'Plato and the erotics of narrativity', in Hexter and Selden (1992): 95–126

(2002) *How to do the History of Homosexuality*. Chicago

Halperin, D. M., Winkler, J. J. and Zeitlin, F. I., eds. (1990) *Before Sexuality: the Construction of Erotic Experience in the Ancient Greek World*. Princeton

Hamilton, A. (1972) 'Sidney's *Arcadia* as prose fiction: its relation to its sources', *English Literary Renaissance* 2: 29–60

Hani, J. (1978) 'Le personnage de Charicleia dans les Ethiopiques: incarnation de l'idéal moral et religieux d'une époque', *BAGB* 1978: 268–73

Hanson, J. A., ed. (1989) *Apuleius*, Metamorphoses, 2 vols. Cambridge MA and London

Hardee, A. (1968) 'Toward a definition of the French Renaissance novel', *Studies in the Renaissance* 15: 25–38

Harder, R. E. (1997) 'Diskurse über die Gastlichkeit im Roman des Theodoros Prodromos', *Groningen Colloquia on the Novel* 8: 131–49

(2000) 'Religion und Glaube in den Romanen der Komnenenzeit', in Agapitos and Reinsch (2000): 55–80

Hardwick, L. (2003) *Reception Studies, Greece and Rome*. New Surveys in the Classics 33. Oxford

Harris, J. and Reichl, K., eds. (1997) *Prosimetrum: Crosscultural Perspectives on Narrative in Prose and Verse*. Woodbridge

Harris, R. (2003) *Pompeii*. London

Harris, W. V. (1989) *Ancient Literacy*. Cambridge MA

Harrison, S. J. (1990a) 'The speaking book: the prologue to Apuleius' *Metamorphoses*', *CQ* 40: 507–13

(1990b) 'Some Odyssean scenes in Apuleius' *Metamorphoses*', *MD* 25: 193–201

(1997) 'From epic to novel: Apuleius as reader of Vergil', *MD* 39: 53–73

(1998a) 'Dividing the dinner: book-divisions in Petronius' *Cena Trimalchionis*', *CQ* 48: 580–5

(1998b) 'Some epic structures in *Cupid and Psyche*', in Zimmerman *et al.* (1998): 51–68

(1998c) 'The Milesian tales and the Roman novel', in *Groningen Colloquia on the Novel* 9: 61–73

ed. (1999) *Oxford Readings in the Roman Novel*. Oxford

(2000) *Apuleius: a Latin Sophist*. Oxford.

(2002) 'Literary topography in Apuleius' *Metamorphoses*', in Paschalis and Frangoulidis (2002): 40–57

(2003a) 'Apuleius' *Metamorphoses*', in Schmeling (2003b): 491–516

(2003b) 'Epic extremities: the openings and closures of books in Apuleius' *Metamorphoses*', in Panayotakis *et al.* (2003): 239–54

(2004) 'Two Victorian versions of the Roman novel', in Zimmerman and Van der Paardt (2004): 265–78

Harrison, S. J., Paschalis, M. and Frangoulidis, S., eds. (2005) *Metaphor and the Ancient Novel*. Groningen (= AN Suppl. 4)

Haynes, K. (2003) *Fashioning the Feminine in the Greek Novel*. London

Heath, S. (2004) 'The politics of genre', in C. Prendergast, ed., *Debating World Literature*. London and New York: 163–74

Hefti, V. (1950) *Zur Erzählungstechnik in Heliodors* Aithiopika. Vienna

Hegel, G. W. (1993) *Introductory Lectures on Aesthetics*, trans. B. Bosanquet. Harmondsworth

Heinze, R. (1899) 'Petron und der griechische Roman', *Hermes* 34: 494–519 (repr. in Gärtner (1984): 15–40)

Heiserman, A. (1977) *The Novel before the Novel: Essays and Discussions about the Beginnings of Prose Fiction in the West*. Chicago

Helm, R., ed. (1907) *Apulei opera quae supersunt, vol. 1*: Metamorphoseon *libri XI*. Leipzig

(1956) *Der antike Roman*. Göttingen

Henderson, J. (2001) 'In ya (pre)face . . .', in Kahane and Laird (2001): 188–97

(2002) 'A doo-dah-doo-dah-dey at the races: Ovid *Amores* 3.2 and the personal politics of the *Circus Maximus*', *ClAnt* 21: 41–65

Henrichs, A. (1972) *Die 'Phoinikika' des Lollianos*. Papyrologische Texte und Abhandlungen 14. Bonn

Henry, R., ed. (1959–91) *Photius*, Bibliothèque, 3 vols. Paris

Hexter, R. and Selden, D., eds. (1992) *Innovations of Antiquity*. New York and London

Hidber, T. (1996) *Das klassische Manifest des Dionys von Halikarnass: die praefatio zu* De oratoribus veteribus. Stuttgart and Leipzig

Hijmans B. L. jr *et al.*, eds. (1977) *Apuleius Madaurensis* Metamorphoses Book IV *1–27: Text, Introduction and Commentary*. Groningen

Hijmans, B. L. jr and Van der Paardt, R., eds. (1978) *Aspects of Apuleius' Golden Ass*, vol. 1. Groningen

Hinds, S. (1998) *Allusion and Intertext: Dynamics of Appropriation in Roman Poetry*. Cambridge

Hirschberger, M. (2001) 'Epos und Tragödie in Charitons *Kallirhoe*: ein Beitrag zur Intertextualität des griechischen Romans', *WJA* 25: 157–86

Hock, R. F., Chance, J. B. and Perkins, J., eds. (1998) *Ancient Fiction and Early Christian Narrative*, Society of Biblical Literature Symposium Series 6. Atlanta

Hofmann, H. (1999a) 'Introduction', in Hofmann (1999b): 1–19

ed. (1999b) *Latin Fiction: the Latin Novel in Context*. London

Holquist, M. (1990) *Dialogism: Bakhtin and his World*. London

Holzberg, N., ed. (1992a), *Der Äsop-Roman: Motivgeschichte und Erzählstruktur*. Tübingen

(1992b) 'Ktesias von Knidos und der griechische Roman', *WJA* 19: 79–84

(1994) 'Der griechische Briefroman: Versuch einer Gattungstypologie', in N. Holzberg, ed., *Der griechische Briefroman: Gattungstypologie und Textanalyse*. Tübingen: 1–52

(1995) *The Ancient Novel: an Introduction*, trans. C. Jackson-Holzberg. London

(2003a) 'The genre: novels proper and the fringe', in Schmeling (2003b): 11–28

(2003b) 'Utopias and fantastic travel', in Schmeling (2003b): 621–32

Hopkins, K. (1993) 'Novel evidence for Roman slavery', *P&P* 138: 3–27

Hopwood, K. (1999) 'All that may become a man: the bandit in the ancient novel', in L. Foxhall and J. Salmon, eds., *When Men were Men: Masculinity, Power and Identity in Classical Antiquity*. London: 195–204

Horwitz, D. L. (1985) *Michel Fokine*. Boston

Höschele, R. (2006) *Verrückt nach Frauen: der epigrammatiker Rufin*, Tübingen

Huber, G. (1990a) *Das Motiv der 'Witwe von Ephesus' in lateinischen Texten der Antike und des Mittelalters*. Mannheim

(1990b) 'Walter Charleton's 'Ephesian Matron': Ein Zeugnis der Petron-Rezeption im England der Restauration', *Gronignen Colloquia on the Novel* 3: 139–57

Huet, P.-D. (1670) *Lettre-traité de l'origine des romans*. Paris (*see* 'Bibliographical appendix', below)

Hunger, H. (1968) *Die byzantinische Literatur der Komnenenzeit: Versuch einer Neubewertung*. Vienna

(1978) *Die hochsprachliche profane Literatur der Byzantiner*, vol. II. Munich

(1980) *Antiker und byzantinischer Roman*. Heidelberg

Hunter, R. (1983) *A Study of Daphnis and Chloe*. Cambridge

(1994) 'History and historicity in the romance of Chariton', *ANRW* II.34.2: 1055–86

(1996) 'Education at the margins: response to J. R. Morgan, "*Erotika Mathemata*: Greek romance as sentimental education"', in Sommerstein and Atherton (1996): 191–205

(1997) 'Longus and Plato', in Picone and Zimmermann (1997): 15–28

ed. (1998a) *Studies in Heliodorus, PCPhS* Suppl. 21. Cambridge

(1998b) 'The *Aithiopika* of Heliodoros: beyond interpretation?', in Hunter (1998a): 40–59

(2005) '"Philip the philosopher" on the *Aithiopika* of Heliodorus', in Harrison *et al.* (2005): 123–38

Ijsewijn, J. (1983a) 'John Barclay and his *Argenis*: a Scottish neo-Latin novelist', *HumLov* 32: 1–27

(1983b) 'Amour et Psyché dans un roman latin de 1685: la *Psyche Cretica*', in Zehnacker and Hentz (1983): 337–45

Jaitner-Hahner, U. (2002) 'La traduzione latina delle *Storie vere* di Luciano e le sue vicende attraverso i secoli', in R. Maisano and A. Rollo, eds., *Manuele Crisolora e il ritorno del greco in Occidente*. Naples: 283–312

James, P. (2001) 'From prologue to story: metaphor and narrative construction in the opening of the *Metamorphoses*', in Kahane and Laird (2001): 256–266

Jankélévitch, W. (1962) *Ravel*. Paris

Jax, K. (1933) *Die weibliche Schönheit in der griechischen Dichtung*. Innsbruck

Jeffreys, E. (1980) 'The Comnenian background to the *romans d'antiquité*', *Byzantion* 50: 455–86

(1998) 'The novels of mid-twelfth century Constantinople: the literary and social context', in I. Sevcenko and I. Hutter, eds., *AETOS: Studies in Honour of Cyril Mango, Presented to him on April 14, 1998*. Stuttgart: 191–9

(2000) 'A date for *Rhodanthe and Dosikles*?', in Agapitos and Reinsch (2000): 127–36

Jensson, G. (2004) *The Recollections of Encolpius: the Satyrica of Petronius as Milesian Fiction*. Groningen (= *AN* Suppl. 2)

Jones, A. H. M. (1940) *The Greek City from Alexander to Justinian*. Oxford

Jones, C. P. (1993) 'Greek drama in the Roman empire', in R. Scodel, ed., *Theater and Society in the Classical World*. Ann Arbor: 39–52

(2001) 'Time and place in Philostratus' *Heroicus*', *JHS* 121: 141–9

(2005) *Philostratus*, Apollonius of Tyana, 2 vols. Cambridge MA and London

Jones, F. (1987) 'The narrator and narrative of the *Satyricon*', *Latomus* 46: 810–19

Jouanno, C. (1989) 'Nicétas Eugénianos, un héritier du roman grec', *REG* 102: 346–60

(1992) 'Les barbares dans le roman byzantin du XIIe siècle: fonction d'un topos', *Byzantion* 62: 264–300

(1994) 'L'oeil fatal: reflexions sur le rôle du regard dans le roman grec et byzantin', *Pris-ma* 10: 149–64

(2000) 'Discourse of the body in Prodromos, Eugenianos and Macrembolites', in Agapitos and Reinsch (2000): 81–93

(2001) 'Les jeunes filles dans le roman byzantin du XIIe siècle', in Pouderon (2001): 329–46

Joyce, J. (1969) *Ulysses*. Harmondsworth

Kahane, A. (2001) 'Antiquity's future: writing, speech, and representation in the prologue to Apuleius' *Metamorphoses*', in Kahane and Laird (2001): 231–41

Kahane, A. and Laird, A., eds. (2001) *A companion to the Prologue of Apuleius' Metamorphoses*. Oxford

Kalkmann, A. (1886) *Pausanias der Perieget*. Berlin.

Kazhdan, A. P. (1967) 'Bemerkungen zu Niketas Eugenianos', *Jahrbuch der österreichischen byzantinischen Gesellschaft* 16: 101–17

Kenaan, H. (2005) *The Present Personal: Philosophy and the Hidden Face of Language*. New York

Kennedy, G. A. (1978) 'Encolpius and Agamemnon in Petronius', *AJPh* 99: 171–8

(2003) *Progymnasmata: Greek Textbooks of Prose Composition and Rhetoric Translated with Introductions and Notes*. Leiden and Boston

Kenney, E. J. (1990a) *Apuleius, Cupid and Psyche*. Cambridge

(1990b) 'Psyche and her mysterious husband', in Russell (1990): 175–98

Kerényi, K. (1927) *Die griechisch-orientalische Romanliteratur in religionsgeschichtlicher Beleuchtung*. Darmstadt (repr. 1964)

Keul-Deutscher, M. (1996) 'Heliodorstudien 1: Die Schönheit in den *Aethiopica*', *RhM* 139: 319–33

Kileen, J. J. (1957) 'James Joyce's Roman prototype', *Comparative Literature* 4: 193–203

King, H. (1999) 'Chronic pain and the creation of narrative', in Porter (1999): 269–86

Kinney, A. F. (1986) *Humanist Poetics: Thought, Rhetoric and Fiction in Sixteenth-century England*. Amherst

Kinney, D. and Branham, R. B. (1996) *Petronius, Satyrica*. Berkeley and Los Angeles

Kirsch, M. H. (2000) *Queer Theory and Social Change*. New York

Kissel, W., ed. (1990) *Aules Persius Flaccus, Satiren, herausgegeben, übersetzt und kommentiert*. Heidelberg

Klebs, E. (1889) 'Zur Composition von Petronius *Satirae*', *Philologus* 47: 623–35

Knight, C. A. (1988–9) 'Listening to Encolpius: modes of confusion in the *Satyricon*', *University of Toronto Quarterly* 58: 335–54

König, J. (2005) *Athletics and Literature in the Roman Empire*. Cambridge

Konstan, D. (1994) *Sexual Symmetry: Love in the Ancient Novel and Related Genres*. Princeton

Konstan, D. and Saïd, S., eds. (2006) *Greeks on Greekness: Viewing the Greek Past under the Roman Empire*. PCPhS Suppl. 29. Cambridge

Kortekaas, G. A. A., ed. (1984) *Historia Apollonii Regis Tyri*. Groningen

Kost, K. (1971) *Musaios, Hero und Leander: Einleitung, Text, Übersetzung und Kommentar*. Bonn

Krabbe, J. K. (1989) *The* Metamorphoses *of Apuleius*. New York and Bern

Kraemer, R. S. (1998) *When Aseneth met Joseph: a Late Antique Tale of the Biblical Patriarch and his Egyptian Wife, Reconsidered*. Oxford

Kristeva, J. (1981) *Desire in Language: a Semiotic Approach to Literature and Art*, ed. L. S. Roudiez, trans. T. Gora, A. Jardine and L. S. Roudiez. Oxford

Kuch, H. ed. (1989a) *Der antike Roman: Untersuchungen zur literarischen Kommunkation und Gattungsgeschichte*. Berlin

 (1989b) 'Die Herausbildung des antiken Romans als Litteraturgattung', in Kuch (1989a): 11–51

 (2003) 'A study on the margin of the ancient novel: "barbarians" and others', in Schmeling (2003b): 209–20

Kytzler, B. (2003) 'Xenophon of Ephesus', in Schmeling (2003b): 336–59

Labarthe-Postel, J. (2001) 'Hommes et dieux dans les *ekphraseis* des romans byzantins du temps des Comnène', in Pouderon (2001): 347–71

Ladin, J. (1999) 'Fleshing out the chronotope', in C. Emerson, ed., *Critical Essays on Bakhtin*. New York: 212–36

Laird, A. (1990) 'Person, persona and representation in Apuleius' Metamorphoses', *MD* 25: 129–64

 (1999) *Powers of Expression, Expressions of Power: Speech Presentation and Latin Literature*. Oxford

 (2001) 'Ringing the changes on Gyges: philosophy and the formation of fiction in Plato's *Republic*', *JHS* 121: 12–29

 (2005) 'Metaphor and the riddle of representation in the *Historia Apollonii regis Tyri*', in Harrison *et al.* (2005): 225–45

Lalanne, S. (2002) 'Hellenism and Romanisation: a comparison between the Greek novels and the tale of Psyche in Apuleius' *Metamorphoses*', in Ostenfeld (2002): 225–32

 (2006) *Une éducation grecque: rites de passage et construction des genres dans le roman grec ancient*. Oxford

Lamberton, R. (1986) *Homer the Theologian: Neoplatonist Allegorical Reading and the Growth of the Epic Tradition*. Berkeley, Los Angeles and London

Lane Fox, R. (1987) *Pagans and Christians*. New York

Lape, S. (2004) *Reproducing Athens: Menander's Comedy, Democratic Culture, and the Hellenistic City*. Princeton.

Laplace, M. (1980) 'Les légendes troyennes dans le "roman" de Chariton: *Chairéas et Callirhoé*', *REG* 93: 83–125

 (1993) 'A propos du P. Robinson-Coloniensis d'Achille Tatius, *Leucippe et Clitophon*', *ZPE* 98: 43–56

Laqueur, T. (2003) *Solitary Sex: a Cultural History of Masturbation*. New York

Larmour, D. H. J., Miller, P. A. and Platter, C., eds. (1998) *Rethinking Sexuality: Foucault and Classical Antiquity*. Princeton

Lathrop, H. (1933) *Translations from the Classics into English from Caxton to Chapman, 1477–1620*, University of Wisconsin Studies in Language and Literature 35. Madison

Lavagnini, B. (1922) 'Le origini del romanzo greco', *ASNP* 28: 9–104 (repr. in Gärtner (1984): 41–101)

Lawrence, C. (2001) *The Secrets of Vesuvius*. London

Leech, G. N. and Short, M. H. (1981) *Style in Fiction: a Linguistic Introduction to English Fictional Prose*. London and New York

Lerner, G. (1986) 'The origin of prostitution in ancient Mesopotamia', *Signs: Journal of Women in Culture and Society* 11: 236–54

Lestringant, F. (1986) 'Les amours pastorales de Daphnis et Chloé: fortunes d'une traduction de Jacques Amyot', in Balard (1986): 237–57

Létoublon, F. (1993) *Les lieux communs du roman: stéréotypes grecs d'aventure et d'amour*. Leiden

Levin, D. N. (1977) 'The pivotal role of Lycaenion in Longus' *Pastorals*', *RSC* 25: 5–17

Lewis, C. (1954) *English Literature in the Sixteenth Century*. Oxford

Lewis, N. (1983) *Life in Egypt under Roman Rule*, Classics in Papyrology 1. Oxford

Lightfoot, J. L. (1999) *Parthenius of Nicaea: the Poetical Fragments and the Ἐρωτικά παθήματα*. Oxford

(2000) 'Romanized Greeks and Hellenized Romans: later Greek literaure', in O. Taplin, ed. *Literature in the Greek World*, Oxford: 239–66

(2003) *Lucian: On the Syrian Goddess*. Oxford

Liviabella Furiani, P. (2000–1) 'Il corpo nel romanzo di Achille Tazio', *AN* 1: 134–51

Lodge, D. (1992) *The Art of Fiction: Illustrated from Classic and Modern Texts*. London

Lonis, R. (1992) 'Les Ethiopiens sous le regard d'Héliodore', in Baslez *et al.* (1992): 233–41

Loporcaro, M. (1992) 'Eroi screditati dal testo: strutture della parodia nelle storie di briganti in Apuleio *Met.* IV.9–21', *Maia* 44: 65–78

Lossky, B. (1986) 'Présence de Jacques Amyot dans le décor du château de Fontainebleau', in Balard (1986): 343–55

Lowe, N. J. (2000) *The Classical Plot and the Invention of Western Narrative*. Cambridge

Lucas, F. L. (1955) *Style*. London

Lukács, G. (1971) *The Theory of the Novel: a Historico-philosophical Essay on the Forms of Great Epic Literature*, trans. A. Bostock. London

Lyne, R. O. A. M. (1979) '*Servitium amoris*', *CQ* 29: 117–30

(1987) *Further Voices in Virgil's* Aeneid. Oxford

Lytle, E. (2003) 'Apuleius' *Metamorphoses* and the *spurcum additamentum* (10.21)', *CPh* 98 (2003): 349–65

Maas, E., ed. (1898) *Commentariorum in Aratum reliquiae*. Berlin

MacAlister, S. (1991) 'Byzantine twelfth-century romances: a relative chronology', *BMGS* 15: 175–210

(1996) *Dreams and Suicides: the Greek Novel from Antiquity to the Byzantine Empire*. New York and London

McDermott, M. H. (1983) 'The *Satyricon* as a parody of the *Odyssey* and Greek Romance', *LCM* 8: 82–5

MacDowell, D. M., ed. (1982) Gorgias, Encomium of Helen, *edited with Introduction, Notes and Translation*. Bristol

Mackay, P. A. (1963) '*KLEPHTIKA*: the tradition of the tales of banditry in Apuleius', *G&R* 10: 147–52

MacKendrick, P. (1950) '*The Great Gatsby* and Trimalchio', *CJ* 45: 307–14

MacKinnon, C. (1992) 'Does sexuality have a history?', in D. C. Stanton, ed., *Discourses of Sexuality: From Aristotle to AIDS*. Ann Arbor: 117–36

Maclean, J. K.B and Aitken, E. B. (2001) *Flavius Philostratus: Heroikos*. Atlanta

Macmullen, R. (1981) *Paganism in the Roman Empire*. New Haven

MacQueen, B. D. (1990) *Myth, Rhetoric and Fiction: a Reading of Longus's* Daphnis and Chloe. Lincoln and London

Maehler, H. (1976) 'Der Metiochos-Parthenope Roman', *ZPE* 23: 1–20

    (1990) 'Symptome der Liebe im Roman und in der griechischen Anthologie', in *Groningen Colloquium on the Novel* 3: 1–12

Magdalino, P. (1984) 'Byzantine snobbery', in Angold (1984): 58–78

    (1992) 'Eros the king and the king of *amours*: some observations on *Hysmine and Hysminias*', *DOP* 46: 197–204

    (1993) *The Empire of Manuel I Komnenos, 1143–1180*. Cambridge

Mal Maeder, D. Van (1997) '*Lector intende laetaberis*: the enigma of the last book of Apuleius' *Metamorphoses*', *Groningen Colloquia on the Novel* 8: 87–118

Malkin, I., ed. (2001) *Ancient Perceptions of Greek Ethnicity*. Washington DC

Manuwald, G. (2000) 'Zitate als Mittel des Erzählens – zur Darstellungstechnik Charitons in seinem Roman *Kallirhoe*', *WJA* 24: 97–122

Marcovich, M., ed. (1992) *Theodori Prodromi De Rhodanthes* et Dosiclis amoribus *libri IX*. Stuttgart

    ed. (2001) *Eustathius Macrembolites: De Hysmines et Hysminiae amoribus libri XI*. Munich

Marino, E. (1990) 'Il teatro nel Romanzo: Eliodoro e il Codice Spettacolare', *MD* 25: 203–18

Martín Abad, J. (2001) *Post-incunables ibéricos*. Madrid

Martin, J. (1979) 'Uses of tradition: Gellius, Petronius, and John of Salisbury', *Viator* 10: 57–76

Martin, R. (1990) 'Céline et Pétrone: un "Satyricon" moderne', *BAGB* 3: 253–61

Martos, J. (2003) *Apuleyo: Las* Metamorfosis o El Asno de Oro. Madrid

Mason, H. J. (1971) 'Lucius at Corinth', *Phoenix* 25: 160–5

    (1978) '*Fabula graecanica*: Apuleius and his Greek sources', in Hijmans and Van der Paardt (1978): 1–15 (repr. in Harrison (1999): 217–36)

    (1983) 'The distinction of Lucius in Apuleius' *Metamorphoses*', *Phoenix* 37: 135–43

    (1999) 'The *Metamorphoses* of Apuleius and its Greek sources', in Hofmann (1999): 103–112

Mastronarde, D. (2005) 'The gods', in J. Gregory, ed., *A Companion to Greek Tragedy*. Oxford: 321–33

Mattiacci, S. (1993) 'La *lecti invocatio* di Aristomene: pluralità di modelli e parodia in Apul. *Met*.1.16', *Maia* 45: 257–67

    (1998) 'Neoteric and elegiac echoes in the tale of Cupid and Psyche by Apuleius', in Zimmerman *et al.* (1998): 127–50

May, R. (2006) *Apuleius and Drama: the Ass on Stage*. Oxford

Mazal, O. (1966) 'Die Textausgaben der Aithiopika Heliodors von Emesa', *Gutenberg-Jahrbuch* 1966: 182–91

    ed. (1967) *Der Roman des Konstantinos Manasses*. Vienna

    ed. (1971) *Aristaeneti Epistularum Libri II*. Stuttgart

McCail, R. (2002) *Longus, Daphnis and Chloe, Translated with Introduction and Notes*. Oxford

McCarthy, K. (1998) '*Servitium amoris; amor servitii*', in S. Joshel and S. Murnaghan, eds., *Women and Slaves in Greco-Roman Culture: Differential Equations*. London: 174–92

(2000) *Slaves, Masters, and the Art of Authority in Plautine Comedy*. Princeton

McGlathery, D. B. (1998) 'Reversals of Platonic love in Petronius' *Satyricon*', in Larmour, Miller and Platter (1998): 204–28

Mendilow, A. (1952) *Time and the Novel*. New York

Merkelbach, R. (1962) *Roman und Mysterium in der Antike*. Munich

(1988) *Die Hirten des Dionysos: Die Dionysos-Mysterien der romischen Kaiserzeit und der bukolische Roman des Longus*. Stuttgart

(1994) 'The novel and aretalogy', in Tatum (1994): 283–95

Meunier, F. (1991) *Eumathios: les amours homonyms*. Paris

Meyer, M., ed. (1994) *The Politics and Poetics of Camp*. New York and London

Miglio, M. (1978) *Giovanni Andrea Bussi: prefazioni alle edizioni di Sweynheym e Pannartz prototipografi romani*. Rome

Mignogna, E. (1996) 'Narrativa greca e mimo', *SIFC* 14: 232–42

Mila, M. (1999) *Maderna musicista europeo*, rev. edn. Turin

Miles, R., ed. (1999) *Constructing Identities in Late Antiquity*. London and New York

Millar, F. (1969) 'P. Herennius Dexippus: the Greek world and the third-century invasions', *JRS* 59: 12–29

(1981) 'The world of the *Golden Ass*', *JRS* 71: 63–75 (repr. in Harrison ed. (1999): 247–68)

(1993) *The Roman Near East, 31 BC–AD 337*. Cambridge MA

Miotti, M. (1996) 'Nicolas de Montreux e il romanzo di Eliodoro', in M. Barsi et al., eds., *Il romanzo nella Francia del Rinascimento: dall'eredità medievale all' "Astrea"*, Gruppo di studio sul cinquecento francese 6. Fasano: 51–9

Mittelstadt, M. C. (1970) 'Bucolic-lyric motifs and dramatic narrative in Longus' *Daphnis and Chloe*', *RhM* 10: 211–27

Modleski, T. (1982) *Loving with a Vengeance: Mass-produced Fantasies for Women*. London

Molinié, G., ed. (1979) *Chariton, Chairéas et Callirhoé*. Paris

Möllendorff, P. von (2000) *Auf der Suche nach der verlogenen Wahrheit: Lukians Wahre Geschichten*. Tübingen

Montes Cala, J. G. (1992) 'En torno a la "imposta dramática" en la novela griega: comentario a una écfrasis de espectáculo en Heliodoro', *Habis* 23: 217–35

Montfaucon, B. (1702) *Diarium Italicum*. Paris

Morales, H. (1995) 'The taming of the view: natural curiosities in *Leukippe and Kleitophon*', *Groningen Colloquia on the Novel* 6: 39–50

(2000) 'Sense and sententiousness in the ancient Greek novels', in A. Sharrock and H. Morales, eds., *Intratextuality: Greek and Roman Textual Relations*. Oxford: 67–88

(2004) *Vision and Narrative in Achilles Tatius' Leucippe and Clitophon*. Cambridge

(2006) 'Marrying Mesopotamia: female sexuality and cultural resistance in Iamblichus' *Babylonian Tales*', *Ramus* 35: 78–101

Moreno Jurado, J. A. (1996) Rodante y Dosicles: *Teodoro Pródromos*. Madrid

Moreschini, C. (1990) 'Le *Metamorfosi* di Apuleio, la "fabula Milesia" e il romanzo', *MD* 25: 115–27

(1994) *Il mito di Amore e Psiche in Apuleio*. Naples

Morgan, J. R. (1982) 'History, romance, and realism in the *Aithiopika* of Heliodoros', *ClAnt* 1: 221–65

(1985) 'Lucian's *True histories* and the *Wonders beyond Thule* of Antonios Diogenes', *CQ* 35: 475–90

(1989a) 'The story of Knemon in Heliodorus' *Aethiopika*', *JHS* 109: 99–113 (repr. in Swain (1999): 259–85)

(1989b) 'A sense of an ending: the conclusion of Heliodorus' *Aethiopica*', *TAPhA* 119: 299–320

(1991) 'Reader and audiences in the *Aithiopika* of Heliodoros', *Groningen Colloquia on the Novel* 4: 85–103

(1993) 'Make-believe and make believe: the fictionality of the Greek novels', in Gill and Wiseman (1993): 175–229

(1994) 'The *Aithiopika* of Heliodorus: narrative as riddle', in Morgan and Stoneman (1994): 97–113

(1995) 'The Greek novel: towards a sociology of production and reception', in A. Powell, ed., *The Greek World*. London: 130–52

(1996a) 'The ancient novel at the end of the century: scholarship since the Dartmouth conference', *CPh* 91: 63–73

(1996b) '*Erotika mathemata*: Greek romance as sentimental education', in Sommerstein and Atherton (1996): 163–89

(1998a) 'Narrative doublets in Heliodorus' *Aithiopika*', in Hunter (1998a): 60–78

(1998b) 'On the fringes of the canon: work on the fragments of ancient Greek fiction', *ANRW* II.34.4: 3293–390

(2003a) 'Heliodorus', in Schmeling (2003a): 417–56

(2003b) 'Nymphs, neighbours and narrators: a narratological approach to Longus', in Panayotakis, Zimmerman and Keulen (2003): 171–89

(2004a) *Longus, Daphnis and Chloe*. Oxford

(2004b) 'Chariton', in de Jong *et al.* (2004): 479–87

(2004c) 'Xenophon of Ephesus', in de Jong *et al.* (2004): 489–92

(2004d) 'Achilles Tatius', in de Jong *et al.* (2004): 493–506

(2004e) 'Longus', in de Jong *et al.* (2004): 507–22

(2004f) 'Heliodorus', in de Jong *et al.* (2004): 523–43

(2005) 'Le blanc et le noir: perspectives païennes et chrétiennes sur l'Ethiopie d'Héliodore', in Pouderon (2005): 309–18

Morgan, J. R. and Stoneman, R., eds. (1994) *Greek Fiction: the Greek Novel in Context*. London and New York

Morgan, L. (2000) 'Metre matters: some higher level metrical play in Latin poetry', *PCPhS* 46: 99–120

Morgan, T. (1998) *Literate Education in the Hellenistic and Roman Worlds*. Cambridge

Morson, G. S. and Emerson, C. (1990) *Mikhail Bakhtin: Creation of a Prosaics*. Stanford

Most, G. W. (1989) 'The stranger's stratagem: self-disclosure and self-sufficiency in Greek culture', *JHS* 109: 114–33

(1992) 'Disiecti membra poetae: the rhetoric of dismemberment in Neronian poetry', in Hexter and Selden (1992): 391–419

Müller, C. W. (1976) 'Chariton von Aphrodisias und die Theorie des Romans in der Antike', A&A 22: 115–36

Müller, K., ed. (1995) Petronius Satyricon Reliquiae. Stuttgart and Leipzig.

Müller-Reineke, H. (2000) Liebesbeziehungen in Ovids Metamorphosen und ihr Einfluss auf den Roman des Apuleius. Göttingen.

Mullett, M. (1984) 'Aristocracy and patronage in the literary circles of Comnenian Constantinople', in Angold (1984): 173–201

Murgatroyd, P. (1981) 'Servitium amoris and the Roman elegists', Latomus 49: 589–606

Naber, S. A. (1901) 'Ad Charitonem', Mnemosyne 29: 92–9

Nakatani, S. (2004) 'A re-examination of some structural problems in Achilles Tatius' Leucippe and Clitophon', AN 3: 63–81

Napier, S. J. (1991) Escape from Wasteland: Romanticism and Realism in the Fiction of Mishima Yukio and Oe Kenzaburo. Cambridge MA and London

Neddermeyer, U. (1998) Von der Handschrift zum gedruckten Buch. Schriftlichkeit und Leseinteresse im Mittelalter und in der frühen Neuzeit: Quantitative und qualitative Aspekte. Wiesbaden

Ní Mheallaigh, K. (2005) Lucian's Self-conscious Fiction: Theory in Practice. Diss. Trinity College, Dublin

Nicolet, C. (1991) Space, Geography and Politics in the Early Roman Empire. Ann Arbor

Nilsson, I. (2001) Erotic Pathos, Rhetorical Pleasure: Narrative Technique and Mimesis in Eumathios Makrembolites' Hysmine and Hysminias. Uppsala

Nilsson, M. P. (1957) Griechische Feste von religiöser Bedeutung. Leipzig

Nimis, S. (1994) 'The prosaics of the ancient novels', Arethusa 27: 387–411.

(2004) 'Egypt in Greco-Roman history and fiction', Alif 24: 34–67

Nisbet, G. (2004) Greek Epigram in the Roman Empire: Martial's Forgotten Rivals. Oxford

Nolhac, P. de (1887) La bibliothèque de Fulvio Orsini. Paris

O'Brien, M. (2002) Apuleius' Debt to Plato in the Metamorphoses. Lewiston

O'Connor, J. (1970) Amadis de Gaule and its Influence on Elizabethan literature. New Brunswick

O'Hara, J. (1997) 'Virgil's style', in C. Martindale, ed., The Cambridge Companion to Virgil. Cambridge: 241–58

O'Sullivan, J. N. (1995) Xenophon of Ephesus: his Compositional Technique and the Birth of the Novel. Berlin and New York

ed. (2005) Xenophon Ephesius, De Anthia et Habrocome Ephesiacorum libri V. Munich and Leipzig

Oeftering, M. (1901) Heliodor und seine Bedeutung für die Litteratur, Litterarhistorische Forschungen 18. Berlin

Osgood, J. (2006) 'Nuptiae iure civili congruae: Apuleius' Story of Cupid and Psyche and the Roman law of marriage', TAPhA 136: 415–41

Ostenfeld, E. N., ed. (2002) Greek Romans and Roman Greeks: Studies in Cultural Interaction, Aarhus Studies in Mediterranean Antiquity 3. Aarhus

Oudot, E. (1992) 'Images d'Athènes dans les romans grecs', in Baslez et al. (1992): 101–11

Page, D. L. (1978) *The Epigrams of Rufinus*. Cambridge

Panayotakis, C. (1995) *Theatrum Arbitri: Theatrical Elements in the Satyrica of Petronius*. Leiden

Panayotakis, S. (2002) 'The temple and the brothel: mothers and daughters in *Apollonius of Tyre*', in Paschalis and Frangoulidis (2002): 98–117

Panayotakis, S., Zimmerman, M. and Keulen, W., eds. (2003) *The Ancient Novel and Beyond*. Leiden

Pandiri, T. (1985) '*Daphnis and Chloe*: the art of pastoral play', *Ramus* 14: 116–41

Papanikolaou, A. D. (1973a) *Chariton-Studien*. Göttingen

ed. (1973b) *Xenophon Ephesius*, Ephesiacorum *libri V*. Leipzig

Parker, H. N. (1997) 'The teratogenic grid', in Hallett and Skinner (1997): 47–65

Parsons, P. J. (1971) 'A Greek *Satyricon*?', *BICS* 18: 53–68

Paschalis, M. and Frangoulidis, S., eds. (2002) *Space in the Ancient Novel*. Groningen (= *AN* Suppl. 1)

Pasolini, P. P. (1988) *Heretical Empiricism*, trans. B. Lawton and L. K. Barnett. New York

Pater, W. (1973) *Essays on Literature and Art*. London

Paton, W. R. (1968) *The Greek Anthology*, vol. III. Cambridge MA and London

Pattoni, M. P. (2004) 'Innamorarsi nella Lesbo di Longo: topoi romanzeschi, reminiscenze epiche e saffiche memorie', *Eikasmos* 15: 273–303

Paulsen, T. (1992) *Inszenierung des Schicksals. Tragödie und Komödie im roman des Heliodor*. Trier

Pearcy, L. T. (1978) 'Achilles Tatius, *Leucippe and Clitophon* 1.14–15: an unnoticed lacuna?', *CPh* 73: 233–5

Pecere, O. (1984) 'Esemplari con *subscriptiones* e tradizione dei testi latini: l'Apuleio Laur. 68,2', in C. Questa and R. Raffaelli, eds., *Il libro e il testo*. Urbino: 111–37

(1986) 'La tradizione dei testi latini tra IV e V secolo attraverso i libri sottoscritti', in A. Giardina, ed., *Tradizione dei classici, trasformazioni della cultura*. Bari: 19–81

(1987) 'Qualche riflessione sulla tradizione di Apuleio a Montecassino', in G. Cavallo, ed., *Le strade del testo*. Bari: 97–124

Pecere, O. and Stramaglia, A., eds. (1996) *La letteratura di consumo nel mondo greco-latino: Atti del convegno intemazionale, Cassino, 14–17 September 1994*. Cassino

Pennisi, G. (1970) *Apuleio e l'Additamentum a Metamorphoses X, 21*. Messina.

Penwill, J. L. (1990) '*Ambages reciprocae*: reviewing Apuleius' *Metamorphoses*', in A. J. Boyle, ed., *The Imperial Muse, vol. II: Flavian Epicists to Claudian*. Berwick: 211–35

Perkins, J. (1995) *The Suffering Self: Pain and Narrative Representation in the Early Christian Era*. London

(1999) 'An ancient "passing" novel: Heliodorus' *Aithiopika*', *Arethusa* 32: 197–214

Perry, B. E. (1967) *The Ancient Romances: a Literary-Historical Account of their Origins*. Berkeley and Los Angeles

Perutelli, A. (1979) 'Registri narrativi e il stile indiretto libero in Virgilio' *MD* 3: 69–83

(1991) 'Il narratore nel *Satyricon*', *MD* 25: 9–25

Pervo, R. (1987) *Profit with Delight: the Literary Genre of the Acts of the Apostles*. Philadelphia

(2003) 'The ancient novel becomes Christian', in Schmeling (2003b): 685–709

Petersmann, H. (1985) 'Umwelt, Sprachsituation und Stilschichten in Petrons *Satyrica*', ANRW II.32.3: 1687–705 (trans. M. Revermann as 'Environment, linguistic situation, and levels of style in Petronius' *Satyrica*', in Harrison (1999): 105–23)

Petri, R. (1963) *Über den Roman des Chariton*. Meisenheim-am-Glan

Petrochilos, N. K. (1974) *Roman Attitudes to the Greeks*. Athens

Philonenko, M. (1968) *Joseph et Aséneth*. Leiden

Pia, P. (1971) *Dictionnaire des œuvres érotiques: domaine français*. Paris

Picone, M. and Zimmermann, B., eds. (1997) *Der antike Roman und seine mittelalterliche Rezeption*. Basel

Pigman, G. III (1980) 'Versions of imitation in the Renaissance', *Renaissance Quarterly* 33: 1–32

Pitkin, H. (1972) *The Concept of Representation*. Berkeley, Los Angeles and London

Pittaluga, S. (1999) 'La fortuna di Apollonio', *Studi Umanistici Piceni* 19: 165–75

Plank, B. (2004) *Johann Sieders Übersetzung des* Goldenen Esels *und die frühe deutschsprachige* Metamorphosen-*Rezeption*. Tübingen

Plaza, M. (2000) *Laugher and Derision in Petronius'* Satyrica: *a Literary Study*. Stockholm

(2006) *The Function of Humour in Roman Verse Satire: Laughing and Lying*. Oxford

Plazenet, L. (1995) 'Le Nil et son delta dans les romance grecs', *Phoenix* 49: 5–22

(1997) *L'ébahissement et la délectation: reception comparée et poétiques du roman grec en France et en Angleterre aux XVI et XVII siècles*. Paris

ed. (1998) *Jean Baudoin: l'histoire nègrepontique*. Paris

(2002) 'Jacques Amyot and the Greek novel: the invention of the French novel', in G. Sandy, ed., *The Classical Heritage in France*. Leiden: 237–80

Plepelits, K. (1980) *Achilleus Tatios*, Leukippe und Kleitophon. Stuttgart

(1989) *Eustathios Makrembolites*, Hysmine und Hysminias. Stuttgart

(1996) *Theodoros Prodromos*, Rhodanthe und Dosikles. Stuttgart

(2003) 'Achilles Tatius', in Schmeling (2003b): 387–416

Pletcher, J. A. (1998) 'Euripides in Heliodoros' *Aithiopika* 7–8', *Groningen Colloquia on the Novel* 9: 17–27

Politianus, A. (1489) *Miscellaneorum Centuria Prima*. Florence

Porter, J. I. (1989) 'Philodemus on material difference', *CErc* 19: 149–78

ed. (1999) *Constructions of the Classical Body*. Ann Arbor

(2001) 'Des sons qu'on ne peut pas entendre: Cicéron, les κριτικοί et la tradition du sublime dans la critique littéraire', in C. Auvray-Assayas and D. Delattre, eds., *Cicéron et Philodème: la polémique en philosophie*. Paris: 315–41

Potter, D. S. (1999) 'Entertainers in the Roman empire', in D. S. Potter and D. J. Mattingly, eds., *Life, Death, and Entertainment in the Roman Empire*. Michigan: 256–325

(2004) *The Roman Empire at Bay: AD 180–395*. London

Pouderon, B. and Crismani, D., eds. (2005) *Lieux, décors et paysages de l'ancien roman dés origines à Byzance: Actes du 2e colloque de Tours, 24–26 Oct. 2002*. Lyon

Pouderon, B., ed. with Hunzinger, C. and Kasprzyk, D. (2001) *Les personnages du roman grec: Actes du colloque de Tours, 18–20 novembre 1999*. Lyon

Prete, S. (1988) 'La questione della lingua latina nel Quattrocento e l'importanza dell'opera di Apuleio', *Groningen Colloquia on the Novel* 1: 123–40

Prosch, C. (1956) *Heliodors* Aithiopika *als Quelle für das deutsche Drama des Barockzeitalters*. Diss. Vienna

Puech, B. (2002) *Orateurs et sophistes grecs dans les inscriptions de l'époque impériale*. Paris

Pursglove, M. (1998) 'Iurii Markovich Nagibin', in N. Cornwell, ed., *A Reference Guide to Russian Literature*. London and Chicago: 570–2

Quet, M.-H. (1992) 'Romans grecs, mosaïques romaines', in Baslez *et al.* (1992): 125–60

Rabinowitz, N. S. and Auanger, L., eds. (2002) *Among Women: From the Homosocial to the Homoerotic in the Ancient World*. Austin

Radford, J., ed. (1986) *The Progress of Romance: the Politics of Popular Fiction*. London

Radway, J. (1984) *Reading the Romance: Women, Patriarchy, and Popular Literature*. Duke

Ramelli, I. (2001) *I romanzi antichi e il Cristianesimo: contesto e contatti*, GREC 6. Madrid

Ransmayr, C. (1990) *The Last World: a Novel with an Ovidian Repertory*, trans. J. E. Wood. London (German original 1988)

Rattenbury, R. M. and Lumb, T. W., eds. (1960) *Héliodore, Les Ethiopiques*, 2nd edn. Paris

Raven, J., Small, H. and Tadmor, N., eds. (1996) *The Practice and Representation of Reading in England*. Cambridge

Reardon, B. P. (1969) 'The Greek novel', *Phoenix* 23: 291–309 (repr. in Gärtner (1984): 218–36)

(1971) *Courants littéraires grecs des IIe et IIIe siècles après J-C*. Paris

(1982) 'Theme, structure and narrative in Chariton', *YClS* 27: 1–27 (repr. in Swain (1999): 163–88)

ed. (1989) *Collected Ancient Greek Novels*. Berkeley, Los Angeles and London

(1991) *The Form of Greek Romance*, Princeton

Reardon, B. P. (1994) 'Achilles Tatius and ego-narrative', in Morgan and Stoneman (1994): 80–96

(1994) 'Achilles Tatius and ego-narrative', in Morgan and Stoneman (1994): 80–96 (repr. in Swain (1999): 243–58)

ed. (2004) *De Callirhoe narrationes amatoriae*. Munich and Leipzig

Reeve, M. D. (1971) 'Hiatus in the Greek novelists', *CQ* 21: 514–39

(1976) review of Papanikolaou (1973), *JHS* 96: 192–3

ed. (1982) *Longus, Daphnis et Chloe*. Leipzig (repr. with corrections 1986, 1994)

(1983) 'Petronius', in L. D. Reynolds, ed., *Texts and Transmission: a Survey of the Latin Classics*. Oxford: 295–300

(1991) 'The rediscovery of classical texts in the Renaissance', in O. Pecere, ed., *Itinerari dei testi antichi*. Rome: 115–57

Reinach, S. (1925) 'Un mythe de sacrifice', *RHR* 91: 137–52

Relihan, J. C. (1993) *Ancient Menippean Satire*. Baltimore

Rémy, A. (1625) *Les amours de Clitophon et de Leucippe, tirées du grec d'Achille Statius, Alexandrin*. Paris

Repath, I. (2005) 'Achilles Tatius' *Leucippe and Clitophon*: What happened next?', *CQ* 55: 250–65

Ricardou, J. (1967) *Problèmes du nouveau roman*. Paris

Rich, A. (1980) 'Compulsory heterosexuality and Lesbian existence', *Signs: Journal of Women in Culture and Society* 5: 631–60

Richardson, J. S. (1991) '*Imperium romanum*: empire and the language of power', *JRS* 81: 1–9

Richlin, A. (1992) *The Garden of Priapus: Sexuality and Aggression in Roman Humor*, rev. edn. Oxford

  (1991) 'Zeus and Metis: Foucault, feminism, classics', *Helios* 18: 160–80

  (1993) 'Not before homosexuality: the materiality of the *cinaedus* and the Roman law against love between men', *Journal of the History of Sexuality* 3: 523–73

  (1996) 'How putting the man in Roman put the Roman in romance', in N. Hewitt, J. O' Barr and N. Rosebaugh, eds. *Talking Gender: Public Images, Personal Journeys and Political Critiques*. Chapel Hill: 14–35.

  (1997) 'Towards a history of body history', in M. Golden and P. Toohey, eds., *Inventing Ancient Culture: Historicism, Periodization, and the Ancient World*. London and New York: 16–35

  (1998) 'Foucault's *History of sexuality*: a useful theory for women?', in Larmour, Miller, and Platter (1998): 138–70

Ricoeur, P. (1985) *Time and Narrative, vol.* II, trans. K. Maclaughlin and D. Pellauer. Chicago (French original 1984)

Riedweg, C. (1987) *Mysterienterminologie bei Plato, Philon und Klemens von Alexandria*. Berlin

Riess, W. (2000–1) 'Between fiction and reality: robbers in Apuleius' *Golden Ass*', *Ancient Narrative* 1: 260–82

Rife, J. L. (2002) 'Officials of the Roman provinces in Xenophon's *Ephesiaca*', *ZPE* 138: 93–108

Riley, M. T. and Huber, D. P., eds. (2004) *John Barclay, Argenis*, 2 vols. Assen

Rimell, V. (2002) *Petronius and the Anatomy of Fiction*. Cambridge

  (2007) 'Petronius' lessons in learning – the hard way', in J. König and T. Whitmarsh, eds., *Ordering Knowledge in the Roman Empire*. Cambridge: 108–32

Rimmon-Kenan, S. (1983) *Narrative Fiction: a Contemporary Poetics*. London

Robert, L. (1968) 'Les épigrammes satiriques de Lucilius sur les athlètes', in A. E. Raubitschek, ed., *L'épigramme grec: sept exposés suivis de discussions*, Geneva (= *Fondation Hardt, Entretiens* 14): 179–295

  (1980) *A travers l'Asie Mineure: poètes et prosateurs, monnaies grecques, voyageurs et géographie*. Paris

  (1982) 'La date de l'épigrammatiste Rufinus: Philologie et réalité', *CRAI* 1982: 50–63

Robertson, D. S. ed. (1972) *Apulée: les* Métamorphoses, 3 vols, 4th ed. Paris

Robiano, P. (1992) 'Les Gymnosophistes éthiopiens chez Philostrate et chez Heliodore', *REA* 94: 413–28

  (2000) 'La citation poétique dans le roman érotique grec', *REA* 102: 509–29

Robins, W. (1995) 'Latin literature's Greek romance', *MD* 35: 207–15

Robinson, C. (1979) *Lucian and his Influence in Europe*. London

Robinson, T. (2005) 'In the court of time: the reckoning of a monster in the *Apocolocyntosis* of Seneca', *Arethusa* 38: 109–40

Rohde, E. (1885) 'Zu Apuleius', *RhM* 40: 66–95

  (1914) *Der griechische Roman und seine Vorläufer*, 3rd edn. Leipzig (1st edn. 1876; repr. Hildesheim 1960)

Rohde, G. (1937) 'Longus und die Bukolik', *RhM* 86: 23–49 (repr. in Gärtner (1984): 361–87)

Roilos, P. (2000) 'Amphoteroglossia: the role of rhetoric in the medieval Greek learned novel', in Agapitos and Reinsch (2000): 109–26

  (2005) *Aphoteroglossia: a Poetics of the Twelfth-century Mediaeval Greek Novel.* Cambridge MA

Roller, M. B. (2001) *Constructing Autocracy: Aristocrats and Emperors in Julio-Claudian Rome.* Princeton

Rollo, D. (1994) 'From Apuleius' Psyche to Chrétien's *Erec and Enide*', in Tatum (1992): 347–69

Romm J. (1992) 'Novels beyond Thule: Antonius Diogenes, Rabelais, Cervantes', in Tatum (1994): 101–16

Rorty, A. O., ed. (1996) *Essays on Aristotle's* Rhetoric. Berkeley, Los Angeles and London

Rosati, G. (1983) 'Trimalchio in scena', *Maia* 35: 213–27 (trans. B. Graziosi as 'Trimalchio on stage', in Harrison (1999): 85–104)

  (1997) 'Racconto e interpretazione: forme e funzioni dell' ironia drammatica nelle *Metamorfosi* di Apuleio', in Picone and Zimmermann (1997): 107–28

  (2003) '*Quis ille?*: identità e metamorfosi nel romanzo di Apuleio', in M. Citroni, ed., *Memoria e identità: la cultura romana costruisce la sua immagine.* Florence: 267–96

Rose, K. (1971) *The Date and Author of the* Satyricon. Leiden

Rose, P. W. (1992) *Sons of the Gods, Children of Earth: Ideology and Literary Form in Ancient Greece.* Ithaca and London

Rosenmeyer, P. (2001) *Ancient Epistolary Fiction: the Letter in Greek Literature.* Cambridge

Rosenmeyer, T. G. (1985) 'Ancient literary genres – a mirage?', *Yearbook of Comparative and General Literature* 34: 74–84 (repr. in A. Laird, ed., *Ancient Literary Criticism.* Oxford (2006): 421–39)

Rosenthal, E. (1912) 'Die Erstausgabe von Apulejus' *goldenem Esel*, gedruckt durch Ludwig Hohenwang', *Zentralblatt für Bibliothekswesen* 29: 273–8

Rösler, W. (1980) 'Die Entdeckung der Fiktionalität in der Antike', *Poetica* 12: 283–319

Rossi, V. (1997) *Filostrato:* Eroico, Venice

Rouché, C. (1993) *Performers and Partisans at Aphrodisias in the Roman and Late Roman Periods, JRS* monograph 6. London

Ruiz-Montero, C. (1994) 'Xenophon von Ephesos: ein Überblick', *ANRW* II 34.2: 1088–1138

  (2003) 'The rise of the Greek novel', in Schmeling (2003b): 29–85

Russell, D. A. (1983) *Greek Declamation.* Oxford

  ed. (1990) *Antonine Literature.* Oxford

  (1992) *Dio Chrysostom: Orations VII, XII and XXXVI.* Cambridge

Russo, C. F. (1958), review of Vilborg (1955), *Gnomon* 30: 585–90

Rusten, J. S. (1992) *Dionysius Scytobrachion*. Opladen

Rutherford, I. (2000) 'The genealogy of the *boukoloi*: how Greek literature appropriated an Egyptian narrative motif', *JHS* 120: 106–21

Rütten, U. (1997) *Phantasie und Lachkultur: Lukians* Wahre Geschichten. Tübingen

Saïd, S. (1987) 'La société rurale dans le roman grec ou la campagne vue de la ville', in E. Frézouls, ed., *Sociétés urbaines, sociétés rurales dans l'Asie Mineure et la Syrie hellénistiques et romaines*. Strasburg: 149–71 (trans. as 'Rural society in the Greek novel, or the country seen from the town', in Swain (1999) 81–107)

    (1994) 'The city in the Greek novel', in Tatum (1994): 216–36

    (1999) *see* (1987)

    (2000) 'Dio's use of mythology', in Swain (2000): 161–86

    (2001) 'The discourse of identity in Greek rhetoric from Isocrates to Aristides', in Malkin (2001): 275–300

Salzman, P. (1985) *English Prose Fiction 1558–1700: a Critical History*. Oxford

    (1987) *An Anthology of Elizabethan Prose Fiction*. Oxford

Sandy, G. (1978) 'Book 11: ballast or anchor?', in Hijmans and van der Paardt (1978): 123–40

    (1979) 'Ancient prose fiction and minor early English novels', *A&A* 25: 41–55

    (1982a) 'Characterization and philosophical decor in Heliodorus' *Aethiopica*', *TAPhA* 112: 141–67

    (1982b) 'Classical forerunners of the theory and practice of prose romance in France: studies in the narrative form of minor French romances of the sixteenth and seventeenth centuries', *A&A* 28: 169–91

    (1982c) *Heliodorus*. Boston

    (1984–5) 'Jacques Amyot and the manuscript tradition of Heliodorus' *Aethiopica*', *Revue d'histoire des textes* 14–15: 1–22

    (1994) 'New pages of Greek fiction', in Morgan and Stoneman (1994): 130–45

    (1997) *The Greek World of Apuleius*. Leiden.

    (2003) 'The heritage of the ancient Greek novel in France and Great Britain', in Schmeling (2003b): 735–73

Scarcella, A. M. (1968) *Struttura e tecnica narrativa in Longo Sofista*. Palermo (repr. in Scarcella (1993): 221–40)

    (1981) 'Metastasi narratologica del dato storico nel romanzo erotico greco', *Atti del convegno internazionale 'Letterature classiche e narratologia'*: 341–67 (repr. in Scarcella (1993): 77–102)

    (1985) 'Luciano, Le *Storie Vere* e il *Furor Mathematicus*', *GIF* 37: 249–57

    (1993) *Romanzo e romanzieri: note di narratologia greca*. Perugia

    (2003) 'The social and economic structures of the ancient novels', in Schmeling (2003b): 221–76

Schmeling, G. (1988) *Historia Apollonii regis Tyrii*. Leipzig

    (1991) 'The *Satyricon*: the sense of an ending', *RhM* 34: 352–77

    (1999) 'The *History of Apollonius King of Tyre*', in Hofmann (1999b): 141–52

    (2003a) '*Historia Apollonii Regis Tyri*', in Schmeling (2003b): 517–51

    ed. (2003b) *The Novel in the Ancient World*, 2nd edn. Leiden

    (2005) 'Callirhoe: god-like beauty and the making of a celebrity', in Harrison *et al.* (2005): 36–49

Schmitt, L. E. and Noll-Wiemann, R. (1975) *Deutsche Volksbücher in Faksimiledrucken*, vol. A2: *Appollonius von Tyrus Griseldis Lucidarius*. Darmstadt

Schmitz, T. (1997) *Bildung und Macht: zur sozialen und politischen Funktion der zweiten Sophistik in der griechischen Welt der Kaizerzeit*. Munich

Schönberger, O. (1980) *Longos,* Hirtengeschichten von Daphnis und Chloe, 3rd edn. Berlin

Schreyl, K. H. (1990) *Hans Schäufelein: Das druckgraphische Werk*. Nördlingen

Schwartz, S. (2000–1) 'Clitophon the *moichos*: Achilles Tatius and the trial scene in the Greek novel', *AN* 1: 93–113

(2003) 'Rome in the Greek novel? Images and ideas of empire in Chariton's Persia', *Arethusa* 36: 375–94

Scobie, A. (1969) *Aspects of the Ancient Romance and its Heritage, Beiträgen zur klassischen Philologie* 30. Meisenheim-am-Glan

(1975) *Apuleius*, Metamorphoses (Asinus Aureus) *I: a Commentary, Beiträgen zur klassischen Philologie* 54. Meisenheim-am-Glan

(1978) 'The influence of Apuleius' *Metamorphoses* in renaissance Italy and Spain', in Hijmans and Van der Paardt (1978): 211–30.

Scotti, M. T. (1982) 'Il proemio delle *Metamorfosi* tra Ovidio ed Apuleio', *GIF* 34: 43–65

Scott-Stokes, H. (1974) *The Life and Death of Yukio Mishima*. New York

Sebeok, T. A., ed. (1960) *Style in Language*. Cambridge MA

Sedelmeier, D. (1959) 'Studien zu Achilleus Tatios', *WS* 72: 113–43 (repr. in Gärtner (1984): 330–60)

Segal, C. (1984) 'The trials at the end of Achilles Tatius' *Clitophon and Leucippe*: doublets and complementaries', *SIFC* 77: 83–91

Selden, D. L. (1994) 'Genre of genre', in Tatum (1994): 39–64

'*Aithiopika* and Ethiopianism', in Hunter (1998a): 182–218

Shear, T. L. (1925) 'Excavations at Corinth in 1925', *AJA* 29: 381–97

Shilling, C. (1993) *The Body and Social Theory*. London

Shklovsky, V. (1966) 'La construction de la nouvelle et du roman', trans T. Todorov, in *Théorie de la littérature*. Paris: 170–96

Shumate, N. (1996) *Crisis and Conversion in Apuleius'* Metamorphoses. Ann Arbor

Sienkiewicz, H. (1941) *Quo vadis?*, trans. C. L. Hogarth. London (Polish original 1896)

Siti, W. (2001) 'Il romanzo sotto accusa', in F. Moretti ed., *Il romanzo, vol. 1: La cultura del romanzo*. Turin: 129–92

Skinner, M. (1996) 'Zeus and Leda: the sexuality wars in contemporary classical scholarship', *Thamyris* 3: 103–23

Slater, N. W. (1990) *Reading Petronius*. Baltimore and London

(2001) 'The horizons of reading', in Kahane and Laird (2001): 213–21

Smith, M. S. (1975) *Petronius*: Cena Trimalchionis. Oxford

Smith R. R. R. (1987) 'The imperial reliefs from the Sebasteion at Aphrodisias', *JRS* 77: 88–138

(1988) '*Simulacra gentium*: the *ethne* from the Sebasteion at Aphrodisias', *JRS* 78: 50–77

(1990) 'Myth and allegory in the Sebasteion', in C. Roueché and K. T. Erim, eds., *Aphrodisias Papers*, vol. 1: *Recent work on Architecture and Sculpture, JRA* Supplementary Series 1: 89–100

Smith, S. (2005) 'Bakhtin and Chariton: a revisionist reading', in Branham (2005): 164–92

Smith, W. S. (1972) 'The narrative voice in Apuleius' *Metamorphoses*', *TAPhA* 103: 513–34 (repr. in Harrison (1999): 195–216)

Solmsen, F. (1941) 'The Aristotelian tradition in ancient rhetoric', *AJPh* 62: 35–50, 169–90

Solomon, J. (2001a) *The Ancient World in the Cinema*. New Haven

(2001b) 'The sounds of cinematic antiquity', in M. M. Winkler, ed., *Classical Myth and Culture in the Cinema*. Oxford and New York: 319–37 (org. edn, 1991)

Sommerstein, A. H. and Atherton, C., eds. (1996) *Education in Greek Fiction*, Nottingham Classical Literature Studies 4. Bari

Sontag, S. (1964) 'Notes on "camp"', *Partisan Review* 31: 515–30 (repr. in *Against Interpretation and Other Essays*. New York: 263–74)

Spencer, C. (1974) 'The world of Serge Diaghilev'. New York

Spiller, M. (1977) 'The first Scots novel: Sir George Mackenzie's *Aretina* (1660)', *Scottish Literary Journal* 11: 1–20

Stadter, P. A. (1965) *Plutarch's Historical Methods: an Analysis of the* De mulierum virtutibus. Cambridge MA

(1980) *Arrian of Nicomedia*. Chapel Hill

Stark, I. (1989) 'Religiöse Elemente im antiken Roman', in Kuch (1989a): 135–49

Stechow, W. (1953) 'Heliodorus' *Aethiopica* in Art', *JWI* 16: 144–52

Steinmetz, P. (1982) *Untersuchungen zur römischen Literatur des zweiten Jahrhunderts nach Christi Geburt*. Wiesbaden

Stephens, S. A. (1994) 'Who read ancient novels?', in Tatum (1994): 405–18

Stephens, S. A. and Winkler, J. J., eds. (1995) *Ancient Greek Novels: the Fragments*. Princeton

Stewart, A. (1997) *Art, Desire, and the Body in Ancient Greece*. Princeton

Stone, D. jr (1979) 'Amyot, the classical tradition, and early French fiction', *Res Publica Litterarum* 2: 319–25

Stoneman, R. (1994) 'The *Alexander romance*: from history to fiction', in Morgan and Stoneman (1994): 117–29

(2003) 'The metamorphoses of the *Alexander romance*', in Schmeling (2003b): 601–12

Stramaglia, A. (1999) *Res inauditae, incredulae: storie di fantasmi nel mondo greco-latino*. Bari

ed. (2000) *Ἔρως: antiche trame greche d'amore*. Bari

Strubbe, J. (1984–86) 'Gründer kleinasiatischer Städte', *AncSoc* 15–17: 253–34

Sullivan, J. P. (1968) *The Satyricon of Petronius: a Literary Study*. Bloomington and London

(1985) *Literature and Politics in the Age of Nero*. Ithaca

(2001) 'The social ambience of Petronius' *Satyricon* and Fellini-*Satyricon*', in Winkler (2001): 258–71

Sütterlin, A. (1997) *Petronius Arbiter und Federico Fellini: Ein strukturanalytischer Vergleich*. Frankfurt-am-Main

Swahn, J. . (1955) *The Tale of Cupid and Psyche*. Lund

Swain, S. (1996) *Hellenism and Empire: Language, Classicism, and Power in the Greek Word, AD 50–250*. Oxford

ed. (1999) *Oxford Readings in the Greek Novel*. Oxford

ed. (2000) *Dio Chrysostom: Politics, Letters, and Philosophy*. Oxford

Szepessy, T. (1957) 'Die Aithiopika des Heliodoros und der griechische sophistische Liebesroman', *AAntHung* 5: 241–59 (repr. in Gärtner (1984): 432–50)

(1978) 'Zur Interpretation einer neu entdeckten Liebesroman', *AAntHung* 26: 29–36

Tait, J. (1994) 'Egyptian fiction in demotic and Greek', in Morgan and Stoneman (1994): 203–22

Tanner, T. (1979) *Adultery in the Novel: Contract and Transgression*. Baltimore and London

Tatum, J. (1979) *Apuleius and the* Golden Ass. Ithaca and London.

(1989) *Xenophon's Imperial Fiction, or* The Education of Cyrus. Princeton

ed. (1994) *The Search for the Ancient Novel*. Baltimore

Terras, V. (1991) *A History of Russian Literature*. New Haven and London

Teske, D. (1991) *Der Roman des Longos als Werk der Kunst*. Münster

Thompson, D. (2001) 'Hellenistic Hellenes: the case of Ptolemaic Egypt', in Malkin (2001): 301–22

Thompson, S. (1955–8) *Motif-index of Folk-literature*. Copenhagen

Thurston, C. (1987) *The Romance Revolution: Erotic Novels for Women and the Quest for a New Sexual Identity*. Urbana and Chicago

Tobin, J. J. (1984) *Shakespeare's Favorite Novel: a Study of* The Golden Asse *as Prime Source*. Lanham MD

(1997) *Herodes Attikos and the City of Athens*. Amsterdam

Too, Y. L. (2001) 'Losing the author's voice: cultural and personal identities in the *Metamorphoses* prologue', in Kahane and Laird (2001): 177–87

Toohey, P. (1992) 'Love, lovesickness, and melancholia', *ICS* 17: 265–86

(1999) 'Dangerous ways to fall in love: Chariton I 1.5–10 and VI 9.4', *Maia* 51: 259–76

(2004) *Melancholy, Love, and Time: Boundaries of the Self in Ancient Literature*. Ann Arbor

Trapp, M. B. (1990) 'Plato's *Phaedrus* in second-century Greek literature', in Russell (1990): 141–73

Treggiari, S. (1991) *Roman Marriage*: Iusti Coniuges *from the Time of Cicero to the Time of Ulpian*. Oxford

Trenkner, S. (1958) *The Greek Novella in the Classical Period*. Cambridge

Trovato, P. (2004) 'Dagli alberi reali agli stemmi', *Filologia Italiana* 1: 9–34

Turcan, R. (1963) 'Le roman initiatique: à propos d'un livre récent', *RHR* 163: 149–99

Turner, B. S. (1996) *The Body and Society: Explorations in Social Theory*, 2nd edn. London

Ure, P. (1956) 'The widow of Ephesus: some reflections on an international comic theme', *Durham University Journal* 18: 1–9

Valley, G. (1926) *Über den Sprachgebrauch des Longus*. Uppsala

Van der Paardt, R. (1978) 'Various aspects of narrative technique in Apuleius' *Metamorphoses*', in Hijmans and Van der Paardt (1978): 75–94

(1981) 'The unmasked 'I': Apuleius *Met.* XI.27', *Mnemosyne* 9: 96–106 (repr. in Harrison (1999): 237–46)

(1989) 'Three Dutch asses', *Groningen Colloquia on the Novel* 2: 133–44

Van Gennep, A. L. (1960) *The Rites of Passage*, trans. M. B. Vizedom and G. L. Caffee. Chicago

Van Mal-Maeder, D. (2003) 'La mise en scène déclamatoire chez les romanciers latins', in Panayotakis et al. (2003): 345–56

Van Thiel, H. (1961) 'Über die Textüberlieferung des Longus', RhM 104: 356–62

(1971) Der Eselsroman I: Untersuchungen. Munich

(1972) Der Eselsroman II: Synoptische Ausgabe. Munich

(1974) Leben und Taten Alexanders von Makedonien: der griechische Alexanderroman nach der Handschrift L. Darmstadt

Veyne, P. (1961) 'Vie de Trimalcion', Annales (ESC) 16: 213–47

(1964) 'Le "je" dans le Satiricon', REL 42: 301–24

(1978) 'La famille et l'amour sous le Haut-Empire romain', Annales (ESC) 33: 35–63 (repr. as La société romaine. Paris, 1991: 88–130)

Vidal, G. (1948) The City and the Pillar. New York (rev. edn, 1965)

Vieillefond, J.-R., ed. (1987) Longus, Pastorales (Daphnis et Chloé). Paris

Vilborg, E., ed. (1955) Achilles Tatius, Leucippe and Clitophon. Stockholm

(1962) Achilles Tatius, Leucippe and Clitophon: a Commentary. Stockholm

Visser, E. (1978) 'Louis Couperus and Apuleius', in Hijmans and van der Paardt (1978): 239–46

Voloshinov, V. (1973) Marxism and the Philosophy of Language, trans. L. Matejka and I. R. Titunik. Cambridge MA

von Albrecht, M. (1989) Masters of Roman Prose. Leeds

(1997) A History of Roman Literature: From Livius Andronicus to Boethius, 2 vols. Leiden

Walby, S. (1990) Theorizing Patriarchy. Oxford

Walden, J. W. H. (1894) 'Stage terms in Heliodorus' Aethiopica', HSCPh 5: 1–43

Walker, S. and Cameron, A., eds. (1989) The Greek Renaissance in the Roman Empire: Papers from the Tenth British Museum Classical Colloquium, BICS Suppl. 55. London

Walser, E. (1914) Poggius Florentinus: Leben und Werke. Berlin

Walsh, P. G. (1970) The Roman Novel: the Satyricon of Petronius and the Metamorphoses of Apuleius. Cambridge

(1978) 'Petronius and Apuleius', in Hijmans and van der Paardt (1978): 17–24

(1981) 'Apuleius and Plutarch', in H. J. Blumenthal and R. A. Markus, eds., Neoplatonism and Early Christian Thought. London: 20–32

(1994) Apuleius, The Golden Ass. Oxford

(1996) Petronius, The Satyricon. Oxford

Walters, J. (1997) 'Invading the Roman body: manliness and impenetrability in Roman thought', in Hallett and Skinner (1997): 29–43

Watt, I. (1957) The Rise of the Novel: Studies in Defoe, Richardson and Fielding. Berkeley CA

Welch, K. (1999) 'Negotiating Roman spectacle architecture in the Greek world: Athens and Corinth', in B. Bergmann and C. Kondoleon, eds., The Art of Ancient Spectacle. New Haven and London: 125–45

West, S. (1974) 'Joseph and Asenath: a neglected Greek romance', CQ 24: 70–81

(2003) 'κερκίδος παραμυθία? For whom did Chariton write?', ZPE 143: 63–9

Whitmarsh, T. (1998) 'The birth of a prodigy: Heliodorus and the genealogy of Hellenism', in Hunter (1998a): 93–124

(1999) 'The writes of passage: cultural initiation in Heliodorus' Aethiopica', in Miles (1999): 16–40

(2001a) *Greek Literature and the Roman Empire: the Politics of Imitation.* Oxford

(2001b) '"Greece is the world": exile and identity in the Second Sophistic', in Goldhill (2001a): 269–305

(2001c) *Achilles Tatius, Leucippe and Clitophon: Translated with Notes.* Oxford

(2003) 'Reading for pleasure: narrative, irony and erotics in Achilles Tatius', in Panayotakis *et al.* (2003): 191–205

(2004a) *Ancient Greek literature.* Cambridge

(2004b) 'The Cretan lyre paradox: Mesomedes, Hadrian and the poetics of patronage', in Borg (2004): 377–402

(2005a) 'The Greek novel: titles and genre', *AJPh* 126: 587–611

(2005b) *The Second Sophistic, Greece and Rome* New Surveys in the Classics 35. Oxford

(2005c) 'Dialogues in love: Bakhtin and his critics on the Greek novel', in Branham (2005): 107–28

(2005d) 'The lexicon of love: Longus and Philetas *grammatikos*', *JHS* 125: 145–8

(2006) 'True Histories: Lucian, Bakhtin, and the pragmatics of reception', in C. Martindale and R. Thomas, eds., *Rethinking Reception.* Oxford: 104–15

(forthcoming) 'Hellenistic prose fiction', in M. Cuypers and J. Strauss, eds., *The Blackwell Companion to Hellenistic Literature.* Oxford

Wiedemann, T. (1992) *Emperors and Gladiators.* London

Wilder, T. (1948) *The Ides of March.* London

Williams, C. A. (1999) *Roman Homosexuality: Ideologies of Masculinity in Classical Antiquity.* Oxford

Williams, E. H. (1989) 'Notes on Roman Mytilene', in Walker and Cameron (1989): 163–68

Williamson, M. (1986) 'The Greek romance', in Radford (1986): 23–45

Wills, L. M. (1995) *The Jewish Novel in the Ancient World.* Ithaca

   (2002) *Ancient Jewish Novels: an Anthology.* New York and Oxford

Wilson, B. *et al.* (1708) *The Satyrical Works of Titus Petronius Arbiter, in Prose and Verse.* London

Wilson, D. (1994) 'Homage to Apuleius: Cervantes' *Avenging Psyche*', in Tatum (1994): 88–100

Wilson, N. G. (1983) *Scholars of Byzantium.* Baltimore

   (1994) *Photius, the* Bibliotheca. London

Wilson, P. (2000) *The Athenian Institution of the khoregia: the Chorus, the City and the Stage.* Cambridge.

Winiarczyk, M. (2002) *Euhemeros von Messene: Leben, Werk und Nachwirkung.* Munich

Winkler, J. J. (1980) 'Lollianos and the desperadoes', *JHS* 100: 155–81

   (1982) 'The mendacity of Kalasiris and the narrative strategy of Heliodoros' *Aethiopica*', *YClS* 27: 93–158 (repr. in Swain (1999): 286–350)

   (1985) *Auctor and Actor: a Narratological Reading of Apuleius's* The Golden Ass. Berkeley, Los Angeles and London

   (1989) *Achilles Tatius, Leucippe and Clitophon,* in Reardon (1989): 170–284

   (1990) *The Constraints of Desire: the Anthropology of Sex and Gender in Ancient Greece.* New York and London

   (1994) 'The invention of romance', in Tatum (1994): 23–38

Winkler, M. M., ed. (2001) *Classical Myth and Culture in the Cinema*, rev. edn. Oxford.

Winterbottom, M. (1974) *The Elder Seneca I:* Controversiae *1–6*. Cambridge MA

Wirszubski, C. (1968) *Libertas as a Political Idea at Rome during the Late Republic and Early Principate*. Cambridge

Wiseman, T. P. (1992) *Talking to Virgil: a Miscellany*. Exeter

Witte, A. E. (1997) 'Calendar and calendar motifs in Apuleius' *Metamorphoses* Book 11', *Groningen Colloquia on the Novel* 8: 41–58

Witten, N. (2002) *Angelo Camillo Decembrio, De politia litteraria, kritisch herausgegeben, sowie mit einer Einführung, mit Quellennachweisen und einem Registerteil versehen*. Munich

Wolff, S. L. (1912) *Greek Romances in Elizabethan Prose Fiction*. New York

Wolfflin, H. (1917) *Principles of Art History*. New York (repr. 1986)

Woolf, G. (1994) 'Becoming Roman, staying Greek: culture, identity, and the civilizing process in the Roman east', *PCPhS* 40: 116–43

Wooten, C. (1984) 'Petronius and camp', *Helios* 11: 133–9

Wouters, A. (1990) 'The EIKONES in Longus' Daphnis and Chloe IV 39, 2: "Beglaubigungsapparat"?', *SEJG* 31: 465–79

Wyke, M. (1997) *Projecting the Past: Ancient Rome, Cinema and History*. New York and London

(1998a) 'Introduction', in Wyke (1998b): 1–11

(1998b) *Parchments of Gender: Deciphering the Bodies of Antiquity*. Oxford

Yildirim, B. (2004) 'Identities and empire: local mythology and the self-representation of Aphrodisias', in Borg (2004): 23–52

Yourcenar, M. (1955) *Memoirs of Hadrian*, trans. G. Frick. London

(1986) *Mishima: a Vision of the Void*, trans. A. Manguel. New York

Zanker, P. (1995) *The Mask of Socrates: the Image of the Intellectual in Antiquity*, trans. A. Shapiro. Berkeley, Los Angeles and London

Zecchini, G. (1989) *La cultura storica di Ateneo*. Milan

Zehnacker, H. and Hentz, G., eds. (1983) *Hommages à Robert Schilling*. Paris

Zeitlin, F. I. (1971a) 'Petronius as paradox: anarchy and artistic integrity', *TAPhA* 102: 631–84 (repr. in Harrison (1999): 1–49)

(1971b) '*Romanus Petronius*: a study of the *Troiae Halosis* and the *Bellum Civile*', *Latomus* 30: 56–82

(1990) 'The poetics of eros: nature, art and imitation in Longus' *Daphnis and Chloe*', in Halperin *et al.* (1990): 417–64

(2003) 'Living bodies and sculpted portraits in Chariton's theater of romance', in Panayotakis *et al.* (2003): 71–84

Zimmerman, M. (2000) *Apuleius Madaurensis Metamorphoses Book X: Text, Introduction, and Commentary*. Groningen

(2001) '*Quis ille . . . lector*: addressee(s) in the prologue and throughout the *Metamorphoses*', in Kahane and Laird (2001): 245–55

(2005) 'Les grandes villes dans les *Métamorphoses* d'Apulée,' in Pouderon and Crismani (2005): 29–41

Zimmerman, M. and Van der Paardt, R., eds. (2004) *Metamorphic Reflections: Essays presented to Ben Hijmans at his 75th Birthday*. Leuven and Paris.

Zimmerman, M. *et al.*, eds. (1998) *Aspects of Apuleius' Golden Ass II: Cupid and Psyche*. Groningen

Zwierlein, O. (1987) *Senecas* Phaedra *und ihre Vorbilder*. Stuttgart

Bibliographical appendix on Pierre Huet

Huet, P. D. (1670–71) *Zayde historie espagnole, par Monsieur de Segrais. Avec un traitté de l'origine des romans, par Monsieur Huet*, 2 vols., Paris. A facsimile (Stuttgart 1966) has an epilogue by H. Hinterhäuser. Huet soon published a revised version (Paris 1678), and there is a critical edition by A. Kok (Amsterdam 1942) based on the eighth edition (Paris 1711), probably the last to receive authorial corrections. English translations: *A Treatise of Romances and their Original* (London 1672), *The History of Romances* (London 1715), the latter by Stephen Lewis. The modernised version of Fabienne Gégou (Paris 1971) includes a section on 'Etudes antérieures à Huet sur le roman', pp. 39–42, and an edition of Jean Chapelain's essay of 1647 *La lecture des vieux romans*, pp. 151–200.

INDEX OF GREEK AND ROMAN NOVELISTS

This index offers a brief guide to the surviving Greek and Roman novelists, the major fragmentary Greek works, and certain other central texts that are crucial for the study of the novel. Many issues are uncertain: questions of dating are usually vexed, particularly with the Greek material;[1] titles are also uncertain in many cases;[2] and biographical testimony is largely untrustworthy. For fuller critical discussions see the Introduction to this volume, and also the various essays on individual works in Schmeling (2003b). Lists of editions, commentaries and translations are not intended to be complete; they concentrate rather upon modern, accurate, accessible versions (English-language, where possible). In the case of Greek and Latin texts, as a rule the most recent is the best.

Achilles Tatius, *Leucippe and Clitophon* One of the five Greek 'ideal' novels, although the most scurrilous and racy; it is also the only one of the five to be (almost) entirely narrated by a character (Clitophon). The narrative begins with an unnamed narrator telling how he met Clitophon in the temple of Astarte in Sidon. Thereafter, over eight books, the latter recounts his elopement from Phoenicia to Egypt with his girlfriend Leucippe, their subsequent separation and final reunion at Ephesus. Papyri of the late second century CE are likely to have been written soon after its composition.[3] The *Suda* (entry under 'Achilles Statius' (*sic*)) records that the author also composed an astronomical work, which is probably the work that survives today among the commentaries on Aratus.[4] The *Suda* also claims that Achilles became a Christian bishop in later life, but this testimony is widely (although not universally) suspected. More credence has been given to the *Suda*'s claim (corroborated by the manuscript traditions) that Achilles was Alexandrian, partly on the grounds of his seemingly accurate description of Egyptian fauna; but it is possible that this springs from extrapolation on the basis of the encomiastic description of the city at the beginning of book 5. TEXT: Vilborg (1955); Gaselee (1969); Garnaud (1991). COMMENTARY: Vilborg (1962). TRANSLATION: Gaselee (1969); J. J. Winkler in Reardon (1989) 170–284; Whitmarsh (2001c).

---

1 On the earlier Greek novels see Bowie (2002). For Heliodorus see Morgan (2003) 417–21.
2 For the titles of the Greek novels, see Whitmarsh (2005a).
3 *Pap. Mil. Vogl.* 124; *P. Oxy.* 3836.
4 Scholia on Aratus: Maass (1898). All biographical testimonia (in Greek) at Vilborg (1962) 163–8.

Alexander Romance Numerous stories about Alexander the Great survive from antiquity; the work that modern scholars call the *Alexander Romance* presents the most flamboyantly fantastical, centring on a heroic central character whose (entirely fictitious) acts include descending to the bottom of the sea in a diving bell and a 'romance' with queen Candauce of Ethiopia. The text has an Egyptian-nationalist feel: Alexander is presented as the son of Nectanebo, the last pharaoh. The *Romance* survives in numerous different Greek versions ('recensions'), all different; it was also translated into at least twenty-four languages, generating in total eighty versions. It is composed of numerous strata, some probably dating back to the second century BCE; but the text as a whole probably achieved its current form in the third century CE. TEXT: Van Thiel (1974); Merkelbach (1977). An up-to-date edition by Richard Stoneman is in preparation. TRANSLATION: Dowden in Reardon (1989) 650–735.

Anthia and Habrocomes see Xenophon of Ephesus, *Anthia and Habrocomes.*

Antonius Diogenes, *Wonders beyond Thule.* A Greek work in twenty-four books, preserved in fragments and summary form in **Photius,** *The Library* codex 166. The focus is upon the marvellous features, and stories, encountered by one Dinias during his travels in the Arctic regions (Thule being a mythical island north-west of Britain). The erotic aspect is not as prominent as in the 'ideal' Greek novels, although Dinias (who is already a father when the narrative begins) does take a mistress, Dercyllis. It was clearly a narratological extravaganza, containing at least seven levels of embedded narration. The dating is uncertain, although the author's Roman first name suggests an imperial date. The latest possible date for the work is the middle of the third century CE, when the philosopher Porphyry cites it. TEXT, COMMENTARY AND TRANSLATION: Fusillo (1990a, in Greek and Italian); Stephens and Winkler (1995) 101–72. TRANSLATION of Photius' summary: G. N. Sandy in Reardon (1989) 775–82.

Apollonius, King of Tyre A story composed in simple Latin, probably in the fifth or sixth century CE, but often thought to be a translation of an earlier Greek original (probably of imperial date). The narrative is composed of two phases. In the first, Apollonius seeks the hand of the daughter of King Antiochus of Antioch; he discovers the solution to a riddle posed him by the king, namely that the latter has raped his daughter. Fleeing Antiochus' rage, he is shipwrecked. In phase two, he marries the daughter of the king of Cyrene. Believing her dead, he leaves his daughter in safe-keeping and travels abroad. Upon his return he rescues the latter from a brothel and discovers his wife was not dead. TEXT: Kortekaas (1984); Schmeling (1989). TRANSLATION: G. N. Sandy in Reardon (1989) 736–72.

Apuleius, *Metamorphoses* A Latin novel in eleven books narrated by one Lucius, transformed into an ass thanks to his inquisitive prying into magic in Thessaly. In the eleventh book he returns to human form after eating roses in a procession in honour of Isis, and converts to the goddess' cult. A number of other stories are embedded in the narrative, most notably the central fable of *Cupid and Psyche* (books 4–6). The title of the whole work is transmitted as *Metamorphoses* in the manuscript tradition, but St Augustine calls it *The Golden Ass*.[5] Biographically speaking, Apuleius is the best known of the novelists, thanks in no small part to his own writings (particularly the *Apology*, a stylised defence of his supposed trial for witchcraft). Born to a wealthy family in second-century Madaurus, Apuleius became one of the prominent intellectuals of north Africa, with a reputation as a philosopher and orator (works transmitted under his name included a version of the Aristotelian *On the Cosmos*, *On Plato*, *On Interpretation*, *On Socrates' God*, and the *Florida*, selections from his orations). Philosophical elements can arguably be glimpsed through the scurrility throughout the *Metamorphoses*, particularly in the **Cupid and Psyche** episode. TEXT: Helm (1907); Robertson (1972); Hanson (1989). COMMENTARY: The first ten books, at the time of writing, are covered individually by the series *Groningen Commentaries on Apuleius*; for book 11 see Griffiths (1975). Also Kenney (1990a), on *Cupid and Psyche*. TRANSLATION: Hanson (1989); Walsh (1994).

Ass see Apuleius, *Metamorphoses*, Lucius, *Metamorphoses* and Greek *Ass*.

Callirhoe see Chariton, *Callirhoe*.

Charicleia and Theagenes see Heliodorus, *Charicleia and Theagenes*.

Chariton, *Callirhoe*   One of the five Greek 'ideal' novels, focusing on the adventures of a young Sicilian woman, set in the aftermath of the Athenian campaigns of 416 BCE. Having been attacked by her husband Chaereas in a jealous pique, presumed dead, and buried, she is abducted by tomb-robbers, then pursued by Chaereas ultimately to Babylon; they are finally reunited, and return together to Sicily. It is widely assumed to be the earliest of the extant Greek novels, primarily on the grounds that it avoids the Attic dialect current from the early to mid-second century CE. A reference in the *Satires* of the Neronian poet Persius to a literary work called *Calliroe* (1.134) is often claimed to refer to our text, but discussion remains open. Four papyri dated to the end of the second century CE mark the latest possible date.[6] TEXT: Molinié (1979); Goold (1994); Reardon (2004). TRANSLATION: Reardon in Reardon (1989) 17–124; Goold (1994).

Cupid and Psyche   A love story embedded in **Apuleius, Metamorphoses**, told by an old woman to console a young girl Charite who has been captured by robbers. In the story, the god Cupid ('Desire' ~ the Greek Eros) prevails upon his wife Psyche not to look at him, but she is provoked by her jealous sisters into doing so; after a period of wandering and suffering in penance, she is finally reunited with him. The narrative has been variously read as a Platonic allegory (Greek *psykhē* = 'soul'), a parable about curiosity (one of the central themes of the novel as a whole), and an allusion to the Greek 'ideal' romance.

Daphnis and Chloe see **Longus.**

Dinner at Trimalchio's   The largest surviving complete episode of **Petronius,** *Satyrica*. Trimalchio is a freedman (i.e. a manumitted slave) who has acquired a

---

5 Augustine, *City of God* 18.18.   6 *P. Fay.* 1; *P. Oxy* 1019; *P. Mich.*1; *P. Oxy.* 2948.

massive fortune. As presented by the narrator Encolpius, Trimalchio is pretentious but ignorant, and the dinner party he throws ostentatious and vulgar.

Greek *Ass* The Greek *Ass*-narrative is substantially the same as the central plot of **Apuleius,** ***Metamorphoses***, without the Isiac conversion at the end. Following **Photius**, most critics believe these versions all derive from **Lucius of Patrae,** ***Metamorphoses***. An apparently complete version, presented as first-person narrative, is transmitted among the works of Lucian, although his authorship has been debated. TEXT: Macleod (1967); Van Thiel (1972); Macleod (1974); TRANSLATION: Macleod (1967); Sullivan in Reardon (1989) 589–618. A fragmentary papyrus from Oxyrhynchus gives a different version, a third-person account, featuring a mixture of prose and verse: see *P. Oxy.* 4762, where D. Obbink gives a translation and commentary.

Heliodorus, ***Charicleia and Theagenes*** More fully *The Ethiopian Affairs concerning Charicleia and Theagenes*: the longest (ten books), latest and most intellectually ambitious of the surviving Greek ideal novels. Blending neo-Platonic, Homeric and Herodotean elements, Heliodorus narrates the journey of the eponymous lovers up the Nile from Alexandria to Meroe. Scholars usually place this text in the third or fourth centuries CE (occasionally as early as the second). According to certain ancient sources,[7] Heliodorus became a Christian bishop, but (as with **Achilles Tatius**) this is not widely accepted. Heliodorus was among the most widely read of the novelists in the renaissance and early modern period. TEXT: Colonna (1938); Rattenbury and Lumb (1960). TRANSLATION: J. R. Morgan in Reardon (1989) 349–588.

Iamblichus, ***Babylonian Affairs*** A Greek novel, surviving only in fragments and the summary in **Photius,** ***The Library*** codex 94. Photius implies that the complete work had sixteen books, the *Suda* (entry under the first 'Iamblichus') less plausibly that it had thirty-nine. Set in the Middle East (and apparently containing no ethnic Greeks), it tells of the travels of two young lovers, Rhodanes and Sinonis. Photius tells us that he was a Babylonian, but an ancient marginal note[8] (apparently working from Iamblichus' own account in the text) reports that he was a Syrian, who learned Babylonian and later Greek. TEXT: Habrich (1960). TEXT, COMMENTARY AND TRANSLATION: Stephens and Winkler (1995) 179–245. TRANSLATION of Photius' summary and select fragments by G. N. Sandy at Reardon (1989) 783–97.

Leucippe and Clitophon see **Achilles Tatius.**

Lollianus, ***Phoenician Affairs*** A Greek novel surviving in papyrus fragments (where, exceptionally, the title and author are identified). It appears to have been at the salacious end of the scale, beyond even Achilles Tatius: one of the surviving episodes details a gory human sacrifice, and there seems also to be graphic sexual content (perhaps including pederasty). To judge from the 'Attic' style, it would seem to have been composed in the second or third century CE; it is possible that the author was one of the three sophists by this name who flourished in the period.[9] TEXT AND

---

7 Testimonia I, III in Colonna (1938).
8 Cited at Habrich (1960) 2, and translated at Stephens and Winkler (1995) 181.
9 For whom see Puech (2002) 327–37.

COMMENTARY: Henrichs (1972, in German). TEXT, TRANSLATION AND COMMENTARY: Stephens and Winkler (1995) 314–57. TRANSLATION: G. N. Sandy at Reardon (1989) 809–12.

Longus, *Daphnis and Chloe* A hybrid between the Greek 'ideal' novel and Theocritean pastoral, this four-book narrative tells of a girl and a boy born in the city but exposed and reared in the countryside of Lesbos. The plot is built around their naive attempts to recognise and satisfy their feelings for each other; they are finally reunited with their parents, and married to each other. Nothing is known of the author; even 'Longus' may be a corruption of *logos* ('story'), although it is a *bona fide* name, attested on Lesbos (among other places). The text is composed in stylised and sophisticated Greek, and usually dated to the second or third centuries CE. There are no certain allusions to the text in antiquity.[10] TEXT: Edmonds (1916); Vieillefond (1987); Reeve (1994); Morgan (2004, based on Reeve). COMMENTARY: Morgan (2004). TRANSLATION: Edmonds (1916); C. J. Gill in Reardon (1989) 285–348; McCail (2002); Morgan (2004).

Lucius of Patrae, *Metamorphoses* The lost original Greek text that apparently lies behind **Apuleius, *Metamorphoses*** and the **Greek *Ass*** stories (see also **Lucian**). This work is only known from the summary in **Photius, *The Library*** codex 129. Photius takes it as straight-faced and credulous.

Metamorphoses see **Apuleius, *Metamorphoses*** and **Lucius of Patrae, *Metamorphoses*.**

Metiochus and Parthenope A Greek novel of great popularity in antiquity, but surviving now only in fragments. Its wide circulation is attested to by five papyrus fragments, two depictions on mosaic floors in Syrian households, influence upon other literary forms (notably the Christian martyrdom of St Parthenope), and the ultimate transformation of the story, in the eleventh century CE, into the Persian *Vāmiq u 'Adhrā* (perhaps via Arabic).[11] The story is based in the court of the historical tyrant Polycrates of Samos, whose daughter is mentioned in Herodotus (3.124), and is based upon a standard 'ideal' paradigm of separation of two lovers followed by reunion; it may, however, have had an unhappy ending. The date is uncertain, but stylistic analysis suggests the first century CE. TEXT, TRANSLATION AND COMMENTARY: Stephens and Winkler (1995) 72–100; Hägg and Utas (2003, also containing *Vāmiq u 'Adhrā*). TRANSLATION: of the two substantial Greek fragments, G. N. Sandy at Reardon (1989) 813–15.

Ninus The romance between Ninus (the mythical founder of Nineveh) and Semiramis (a historical Syrian queen) was, apparently, first introduced to the Greek tradition from Persia by the bilingual historian Ctesias, writing at the turn of the fifth and fourth centuries; the story subsequently became widely disseminated, with versions transmitted by e.g. Cornelius Alexander 'Polyhistor'[12] and Plutarch.[13] The novelistic version, representing the dashing national heroes as young lovers, survives in three

---

10 Bowie (1995) however argues for allusion in Heliodorus.
11 These themes are fully discussed by Hägg and Utas (2003).
12 *FGr H* 273 F 81.   13 *Tale of Love* 753d–e.

substantial papyrus fragments; the text was, probably, originally composed in the first century BCE or CE. TEXT, TRANSLATION AND COMMENTARY: Stephens and Winkler (1995) 23–71. TRANSLATION: G. N. Sandy at Reardon (1989) 803–8.

Petronius, *Satyrica* A Latin comic story narrated by one Encolpius, telling of his sexual and other adventures alongside his accomplice Ascyltus and their boyfriend Giton. It survives in disconnected fragments, the longest of which is ***Dinner at Trimalchio's***. The author is usually assumed to be Petronius Arbiter, the courtier of Nero who killed himself in 66 CE.[14] The transmitted title is *Satyricon*, which most scholars believe to be a transliteration of the Greek genitive *-ikōn* often found in book-titles; hence the use in this volume of the nominative form form *Satyrica* (∼ Greek *Saturika*). TEXT: Heseltine (1951, accessible but outdated now); Müller (1995). COMMENTARY: Courtney (2001) offers a concise running commentary; Smith (1975) focuses on *Dinner at Trimalchio's*. TRANSLATION: Heseltine (1951); and especially Walsh (1996), Kinney and Branham (1996).

Philostratus, *Apollonius of Tyana* An account in eight books of Greek of the life, travels and teachings of the first-century CE Cappadocian sage and miracle-worker. Flavius Philostratus, the author, is the well-attested polymath of the early to mid-third century CE. According to his own account, Philostratus was commissioned by Julia Domna (the wife of the emperor Septimius Severus) to polish up an original account written by Damis, Apollonius' companion. Although the text has also been taken extremely seriously as a religious work (the Christian Eusebius vigorously attacked Hierocles for drawing comparisons with the Gospels; Apollonius also resurfaces in the early Islamic tradition as Bālīnās), a number of modern scholars have detected novelistic elements in it. TEXT AND TRANSLATION: Jones (2005).

Phoenician Affairs, see **Lollianus, *Phoenician Affairs*.**

Photius, *The Library* Photius, the ninth-century bishop of Constantinople, was, as well as an important theologian, an avid consumer of Greek literature, pagan as well as Christian. His record of his voracious reading, the *Library*, contains summaries of **Achilles Tatius** and **Heliodorus**, as well as of the novels (now largely lost) of **Antonius Diogenes** and **Iamblichus**. TEXT: Henry (1959–91). TRANSLATION: selections in Wilson (1994).

Satyrica see **Petronius, *Satyrica*.**

Suda A massive, alphabetical, Greek encyclopaedia compiled in the tenth century CE. It contains entries on **Achilles Tatius, Iamblichus** and **Xenophon of Ephesus** – much of it historically unreliable, vague or inaccurate, but nevertheless interesting evidence for the traditions clustering around the novelists.

Xenophon of Ephesus, *Anthia and Habrocomes* More fully *The Ephesian Affairs concerning Anthia and Habrocomes*. One of the five surviving 'ideal' Greek romances: a young man and woman of Ephesus meet and marry; are commanded to

---

14 Tacitus, *Annals* 16.17–20.

travel abroad by an oracle; undergo trials and sufferings; and are finally reunited in Ephesus. The five-book novel is written in strikingly simple Greek; arguments have been advanced that it is epitomised, partly at least,[15] or an originally oral text.[16] The *Suda* (under 'Xenophon of Ephesus') reports that, in addition to *Anthia and Habrocomes*, Xenophon also composed a work 'On the city of Ephesus' (unless that is a descriptive gloss on the title of the novel), and other works. Xenophon was probably writing in the late first or early second century CE, although it is impossible to be absolutely confident. TEXT: Dalmeyda (1926); O'Sullivan (2005). TRANSLATION: D. Konstan in Reardon (1989) 125–69.

15 Bürger (1892); see the discussion at Kytzler (2003) 348–50.   16 O'Sullivan (1995).

GENERAL INDEX

Cambridge Companions to ...

AUTHORS

Edward Albee *edited by Stephen J. Bottoms*

Margaret Atwood *edited by Coral Ann Howells*

W. H. Auden *edited by Stan Smith*

Jane Austen *edited by Edward Copeland and Juliet McMaster*

Beckett *edited by John Pilling*

Aphra Behn *edited by Derek Hughes and Janet Todd*

Walter Benjamin *edited by David S. Ferris*

William Blake *edited by Morris Eaves*

Brecht *edited by Peter Thomson and Glendyr Sacks* (second edition)

The Brontës *edited by Heather Glen*

Frances Burney *edited by Peter Sabor*

Byron *edited by Drummond Bone*

Albert Camus *edited by Edward J. Hughes*

Willa Cather *edited by Marilee Lindemann*

Cervantes *edited by Anthony J. Cascardi*

Chaucer, *second edition edited by Piero Boitani and Jill Mann*

Chekhov *edited by Vera Gottlieb and Paul Allain*

Coleridge *edited by Lucy Newlyn*

Wilkie Collins *edited by Jenny Bourne Taylor*

Joseph Conrad *edited by J. H. Stape*

Dante *edited by Rachel Jacoff* (second edition)

Charles Dickens *edited by John O. Jordan*

Emily Dickinson *edited by Wendy Martin*

John Donne *edited by Achsah Guibbory*

Dostoevskii *edited by W. J. Leatherbarrow*

Theodore Dreiser *edited by Leonard Cassuto and Claire Virginia Eby*

John Dryden *edited by Steven N. Zwicker*

George Eliot *edited by George Levine*

T. S. Eliot *edited by A. David Moody*

Ralph Ellison *edited by Ross Posnock*

Ralph Waldo Emerson *edited by Joel Porte and Saundra Morris*

William Faulkner *edited by Philip M. Weinstein*

Henry Fielding *edited by Claude Rawson*

F. Scott Fitzgerald *edited by Ruth Prigozy*

Flaubert *edited by Timothy Unwin*

E. M. Forster *edited by David Bradshaw*

Brian Friel *edited by Anthony Roche*

Robert Frost *edited by Robert Faggen*

Elizabeth Gaskell *edited by Jill L. Matus*

Goethe *edited by Lesley Sharpe*

Thomas Hardy *edited by Dale Kramer*

Nathaniel Hawthorne *edited by Richard Millington*

Ernest Hemingway *edited by Scott Donaldson*

Homer *edited by Robert Fowler*

Ibsen *edited by James McFarlane*

Henry James *edited by Jonathan Freedman*

Samuel Johnson *edited by Greg Clingham*

Ben Jonson *edited by Richard Harp and Stanley Stewart*

James Joyce *edited by Derek Attridge* (second edition)

Kafka *edited by Julian Preece*

Keats *edited by Susan J. Wolfson*

Lacan *edited by Jean-Michel Rabaté*

D. H. Lawrence *edited by Anne Fernihough*

Primo Levi *edited by Robert Gordon*

Lucretius *edited by Stuart Gillespie and Philip Hardie*

David Mamet *edited by Christopher Bigsby*

Thomas Mann *edited by Ritchie Robertson*

Christopher Marlowe *edited by Patrick Cheney*

Herman Melville *edited by Robert S. Levine*

Arthur Miller *edited by Christopher Bigsby*

Milton *edited by Dennis Danielson* (second edition)

Molière *edited by David Bradby and Andrew Calder*

Toni Morrison *edited by Justine Tally*

Nabokov *edited by Julian W. Connolly*

Eugene O'Neill *edited by Michael Manheim*

George Orwell *edited by John Rodden*

Ovid *edited by Philip Hardie*

Harold Pinter *edited by Peter Raby*

Sylvia Plath *edited by Jo Gill*

Edgar Allan Poe *edited by Kevin J. Hayes*

Alexander Pope *edited by Pat Rogers*

Ezra Pound *edited by Ira B. Nadel*

Proust *edited by Richard Bales*

Pushkin *edited by Andrew Kahn*

Philip Roth *edited by Timothy Parrish*

Salman Rushdie *edited by Abdulrazak Gurnah*

TOPICS